Holiday Tales of Sholom Aleichem

HOLIDAY TALES *of* SHOLOM ALEICHEM

Selected and translated by Aliza Shevrin

Illustrated by Thomas di Grazia

ALADDIN BOOKS
Macmillan Publishing Company
New York

Collier Macmillan Publishers
London

Aladdin Books
Macmillan Publishing Company
866 Third Avenue, New York, NY 10022
Collier Macmillan Canada, Inc.

First Aladdin Books edition 1985

Printed in the United States of America

10 9 8 7 6 5 4 3 2

Library of Congress Cataloging in Publication Data
Rabinowitz, Sholom, 1859-1916.
Holiday tales of Sholom Aleichem.
CONTENTS: Really a Sukkah! – Benny's luck. – A
ruined Passover. [etc.]
1. Fasts and feasts – Judaism – Juvenile fiction.
[1. Fasts and feasts – Judaism – Fiction.   2. Jews in
the Ukraine – Fiction.   3. Short stroies]   I. Shevrin,
Aliza.   II. Di Grazia, Thomas.   III. Title.
PZ7.R110Ho   1979   839'.09'33 [Fic]   79-753
ISBN 0-689-71034-8

Translator's Note

ABOUT ONCE A MONTH a group of us meet to enjoy an evening of Yiddish. We are college professors, townspeople, housewives, some from the old country and others born in America. We share a love for a language fashioned over the centuries to express the longings, passions, delights, and humor of a people who once lived in the small villages, or *shtetls*, of Eastern Europe. At our meetings, we take turns reading stories. When a Jewish holiday approaches, our favorite author becomes Sholom Aleichem, the humorist, satirist, and most beloved of Yiddish writers. It was on his "Tevye" stories that the play and film "Fiddler on the Roof" was based.

Sholom Aleichem, the pen-name of Solomon Rabinowitz, was born in Russia in 1859 and died in New York in 1916. He wrote hundreds of stories which have been read and enjoyed for generations by young and old. It was fitting that he should choose as a pen-name the commonplace, traditional Hebrew greeting, "Peace be with you."

As I was listening to one of his stories for children ("The Esrog"), it occurred to me that although we were adults, we were all responding with the fresh delight of youngsters: chuckling, sighing, laughing, nodding sadly as the story unfolded. I thought, "What a shame that my children and other young people can't enjoy these marvelous tales." True, some are to be found in collections for adults, but I had not seen a book of stories for young readers. This volume is intended to meet that need.

I have selected and translated seven stories with holiday themes. Five have been previously translated and published; two ("The First Commune" and "The Goldspinners") have not been previously published in English. In choosing stories for this collection, I was drawn to the holiday tales, first, because I believe they are among the best stories Sholom Aleichem wrote. Moreover, in telling these stories, Sholom Aleichem accurately showed how Jews celebrated the holidays—not simply as religious observances but as festivals involving the entire family. In these stories we can see and appreciate how all the special customs (the seder at Passover, the sukkah during Sukkos, etc.) were woven into the fabric of family life. Even more important, the stories tell us how individual people experienced these special times of the year, for special they were. They were times to put aside quarrels, worries about poverty, persecution, and hardship. They were times to clean the house from top to bottom, times to get new holiday clothes, times to prepare the holiday dishes, times of togetherness with family and friends, times to commemorate the illustrious past of the Jewish people, and times to thank God for whatever one did have, however little that might be. No one was too poor to celebrate a holiday, even if it meant lighting candles in scooped-out potato shells instead of in silver candlesticks. Whether in one's own house or in an overcrowded apartment, whether in a shed or in an elegant parlor, every person could observe the holidays with equal spiritual merit and emotional fervor.

Not only was Sholom Aleichem a master of Yiddish literature and a great storyteller, he had an intuitive grasp of human nature. He knew exactly how children and their parents would behave. If a mother told her son *not* to do something, as in "The Esrog," that would be the very thing he would be tempted to do. Sholom Aleichem knew that when a youngster gambled away his widowed mother's hard-earned money, he would suffer from acute shame and guilt and have dreams in which he was being punished, as in "Benny's Luck." He knew that when three housewives tried to share the cooking and preparation for a holiday in one kitchen, there would be spite and competitiveness as well as communal spirit, as in "The First Commune."

Although six of the stories are written in the first person from the point of view of a young boy, it is obvious that the boy differs from story to story. In some he has both mother and father, in others only a widowed mother. In some, he is very poor; in others, his family is rather well-off. Sometimes he is an only child and sometimes he has a brother or sister.

I have taken pains to be as faithful to the original language as possible and to render truly every nuance and "untranslatable" idiom or word. In a very few cases extraneous material not considered to be of interest to the young reader has been deleted or condensed. It should be noted that, in the interest of providing variety of setting, the stories in this collection are not placed in the order in which the holidays they describe occur in the calendar year.

However well a translator may do his or her job, a translation is no substitute for the original. I am lucky to have been able to read these stories in Yiddish. I was educated in schools where I was taught to read the Yiddish literary masters in the language in which they wrote. It is my hope that enjoyment of these stories may motivate readers of this book to study Yiddish so that they can read for themselves the truly wonderful works of Sholom Aleichem and other writers as they were written—and aloud, if possible.

The reader's attention is called to the glossary at the back of the book.

I am grateful to my parents, Rabbi Eliezer and Rivkah Goldberger, for a lifetime of living *Yiddishkeit*, encouraged in an environment of scholarliness and love, and for their help in translating archaic and obscure terms. I also wish to thank my editor at Scribners, Clare Costello, for her help and encouragement. My friend Joan Blos provided invaluable support at every stage of the project. Her practical suggestions and knowledge of children's literature were always helpful. In addition, I must thank my friends Louise Kaplan, Shoni and Susie Guiora, Ruth

Kirk, and Joseph Blotner for their careful readings and suggestions. To my children, Dan, Amy, David, and Matt, go my deep regret for failing to teach them Yiddish in childhood, my hope that this collection will help make up for that omission, and my thanks for their encouragement and editorial comments. No words in any language can adequately express the debt of gratitude I owe my husband, Howie, for his loving collaboration in every aspect of this book as in my life.

Aliza Shevrin
Ann Arbor, Michigan
October 10, 1978

Holiday Tales of Sholom Aleichem

Really *a Sukkah!*

During the fall harvest festival of Sukkos, meals are eaten in a home-made shed or lean-to which is covered with leafy branches and is built behind the family dwelling.

THERE ARE PEOPLE WHO have never learned anything but who can do everything, who have never been anywhere but who know everything, who have never given a thought to anything yet understand everything.

"Golden hands!" That's the name given these people, and the world envies and respects them. Such a man lived in our town of Kasrilevka, and he was called "*Really* Moishe."

We called him "*Really* Moishe" because whenever he saw or heard or made something, he was fond of saying, "That's *really* something!"

Supposing we had a good cantor in our shul. "*Really* a cantor!"

Supposing we bought a big turkey for Passover. "*Really* a turkey!"

3

Supposing a frost was expected. "*Really* a frost!"

"My friends, you see before you a poor man—*really* poor!" And so for everything.

Moishe was—I can't quite tell you exactly what he was or how he lived. He was a Jew. But how he earned a living would be hard to say. He survived as thousands, shall I say tens of thousands, of Jews survived in Kasrilevka. He hung around the big landowner in town; well, not exactly around the big landowner himself but around those Jews who hung around the *small* landowners who hung around the big landowner. Whether or not he actually made a living was another story because "*Really* Moishe" was a person who hated to boast about his successes or to complain about his failures. He was always happy, his cheeks were always rosy. His moustache was lopsided, his hat tilted to the side, and his eyes were kind and smiling. Although he was always busy, he could be counted on to walk ten miles to help someone.

That's the kind of man our "*Really* Moishe" was.

There was not a single thing in the world that "*Really* Moishe" couldn't fix—a house, a clock, a machine, a lamp, a top, a spigot, a mirror, a bucket, a cage—you name it.

True, no one could point to the houses or the clocks or the machines that he had repaired, but we were all convinced that Moishe *could* have done it. Everyone used to say that if only he had tools, he could have turned the world upside down. Unfortunately, he had no tools. (Actually, I mean the opposite: it was really lucky he had no tools and the world was not turned upside down.)

It was a wonder that Moishe wasn't pulled apart by all the people who demanded his services. A lock jammed? To whom did one go? To Moishe. A clock stopped? To Moishe. A plugged-up samovar? To Moishe. Cockroaches, beetles, and other nuisances crawling around the house? Whom did one ask? Moishe. A fox stole into the chicken coop and was killing the hens? To whom did one turn for advice? To Moishe. Again Moishe, always Moishe.

True, the jammed lock was eventually tossed aside and forgotten in a closet somewhere, the clock had to be taken to the clockmaker and the samovar to the coppersmith. The cockroaches, beetles, and other nuisances apparently were not terribly frightened of Moishe, and the fox went on doing whatever foxes must do. But "*Really* Moishe" remained the one and only "*Really* Moishe" as before—still "golden hands." I suppose there was some truth in it; the whole world can't be wrong. Here's proof. How come people don't go to you or to me with jammed locks, broken clocks, spigots, cockroaches, beetles, other nuisances, or foxes? Not everyone is alike and talent is, apparently, rare.

It was with this same "*Really* Moishe" that we became very close neighbors, living in the same building under the very same roof. I say "became" because before then, we lived in our own house. But our luck suddenly changed and we came upon hard times. Not wishing to impose on anyone, we sold our house, settled our debts, and moved (it was the night before Rosh Hashanah) into Hershke Mamtzes's house. It was an old ruin of a house, without a garden, without a courtyard, without a porch, without life or soul.

"Let's face it, it's a shack," my mother said with a bitter laugh, and I could see the tears in her eyes.

"Be careful," my father said to her, his face drawn and dark. "Thank God for this."

Why for "this" I don't know. Because we weren't living out in the street? I would rather have been living out in the street than here in Hershke Mamtzes's house. I considered it a great injustice on God's part that He took our house away from us. But even more than the house, I missed the sukkah we had there, a permanent sukkah, one that stood from year to year. It had a flap at the entrance that could be raised and lowered and a beautiful ceiling made of green and yellow branches laid out like Stars of David. Of course, our friends tried to comfort us, telling us that one day we would be able to buy our house back or that, God willing, we would build another one, bigger, better, and handsomer than the old house. But they were no more than words of consolation, cold comfort, just like the words of consolation I heard when I broke (accidentally, of course) my tin watch to bits. My mother had honored me with a spanking and my father dried my eyes, promising to buy me a new watch, bigger, better, and handsomer than the old one. But the more my father extolled the new watch he would buy for me, the more I wept for the old one. Unobtrusively, so my father wouldn't notice, my mother pined after our old home while my father sighed. A black cloud settled over his face and deep creases were etched in his broad white brow. I considered it a great injustice on God's part that He took our house away from us.

"Tell me, if you don't mind, what are we going to do with a sukkah?" my mother remarked to my father a few days before Sukkos.

"I suppose you really mean to say, 'What are we going to do *without* a sukkah?'" my father answered, trying to make a joke of it, but I could see that it was painful for him. He turned away so we couldn't see his face, which had become dark and gloomy. My mother blew her nose in her apron, hiding her tears, and I stood there looking at them both. Suddenly my father turned his face directly toward us and said animatedly, "Wait! Don't we have a neighbor, Moishe?"

"You mean *'Really* Moishe'?" my mother added, and I couldn't tell whether she was joking or serious. Apparently she was serious because within half an hour the three of them—my father, Moishe, and Hershke Mamtzes, our landlord—were outside the house looking for a spot on which to put up the sukkah.

Hershke Mamtzes's house was not too bad a house as houses go, but it did have one fault: it stood too close to the road and had no yard at all. It looked as if someone had misplaced it. Someone had been walking along and lost a house, without a yard, without a real roof, the door on the wrong side, like a coat with the vent in the front and the buttons in the back. If you gave Hershke a chance, he could talk forever on the subject of his house—how they tried to condemn it, how he went to court over the house, how he won his case, and how the house finally remained in his hands.

"Where, Reb Moishe, do you figure on putting the sukkah?" my father asked "*Really* Moishe," and Moishe, hat tilted to the side, was concentrating like a great architect deliberating over an important project and making measurements with his hands from here to there and from there to here. He let it be known that had the house not been placed so badly and had it had a yard, a sukkah with two walls could be built in one day. Did I say one day? In one hour! But since the house had no yard, and four walls would be required, it would take a little longer, but as a result, it would be a *sukkah—really* a sukkah! But most important, the proper material would be needed.

"Material we'll get, but do you have tools?" Hershke asked him.

"Tools can be found, but do you have lumber?" Moishe asked.

"Lumber can be obtained, but do you have nails?" Hershke asked.

"Nails are available, but do you have green fir branches?" Moishe wanted to know.

"Somehow you're very organized today," remarked Hershke.

"Me, organized?" responded Moishe.

They looked at one another and burst out laughing.

When Hershke Mamtzes delivered the first few boards and a pair of wooden posts, Moishe predicted that, God willing, it would be *really* a sukkah. I was very curious to know how he would make a sukkah from these few assorted boards and a pair of wooden posts. I begged my mother for permission to watch Moishe build the sukkah. She agreed and so did Moishe. Not only did he allow me to watch but in fact said that I could be his assistant, which meant I could hand him whatever he needed and hold things for him.

I was in seventh heaven. Imagine, I was helping build a sukkah! And I helped quite a lot. I helped by puckering my lips while Moishe hammered. I helped by joining him for lunch. I helped by shouting at the other children who were underfoot. I helped by bringing him his hammer when he needed a chisel and bringing him his pliers when he needed a nail. Another person in his place would have thrown the hammer or the pliers at my head for that kind of help, but Moishe was a person without malice. No one had ever had the opportunity of seeing him angry.

"Anger," he would say, "is as useful as idol worship. Just as idol worship helps, so does anger help."

Deeply engrossed as I was in the work, I never noticed how and by what miracles our sukkah came to be finished.

"Come, see the sukkah we've built!" I said to my father, pulling him outside by the coattails. My father beamed at our work. Looking at Moishe with a little smile, he said to him, pointing to me, "Reb Moishe, was he any kind of helper at all?"

"He was *really* a helper!" Moishe said, looking up at the roof worriedly. "If only Hershke would hurry up and bring the fir branches, it would *really* be a sukkah!"

Hershke Mamtzes was giving us trouble over the fir branches. He put off bringing them from one day to the next till finally, with God's help, the night before Sukkos he rolled up with a wagonload of thin twigs of fir branches mixed with some reeds that grew in the mud on the other side of our pond, and we got to work covering the sukkah. What I really mean to say is that Moishe himself covered the sukkah and I helped drive off the goats which were attracted to the twigs and branches as if they were rare delicacies. I'll never know what they saw in those bitter green stalks.

Since Hershke Mamtzes's house stood all by itself, the goats came from all directions. No sooner did I get rid of one goat than another turned up. I would chase that one away and aha! here was the first one all over again! I drove them away with a stick: "Off with you! Silly goat, are you here again? Off with you!"

The devil knows how they found out we had fir branches. They must have notified one another. How else would all the town goats know to assemble around our house? And I, all alone, had to wage war against them.

With God's help, all the branches were finally on the sukkah roof. Like idiots, the goats stood still, looking up with bewildered eyes, stupidly chewing their cuds. I had triumphed and called out to them, "Why don't you eat the branches now, you silly goats?"

It appeared they understood me because one by one they went off, searching for some new tidbit to eat. Now we got to work decorating the inside of the sukkah. First of all, we spread yellow sand over the ground, then we draped the walls with blankets belonging to the three families who would share the sukkah. When we ran out of blankets, we used shawls, and when we ran out of shawls, we draped a tablecloth or a sheet. Only then did we bring out the tables and benches, the candlesticks and candles, the dishes and silverware. Each of the three women lit her candles and made the blessing on moving into the sukkah.

My mother, blessed be her memory, was a woman who loved to weep. The Holy Days of Mourning were for her a favorite time. From the time we were forced to give up our house, her eyes were never dry. My father, who himself went around in a daze, would not tolerate her tears and told her she should not sin before God because things could be worse, thank God for that. But there in the sukkah, while blessing the candles, she could cover her eyes with both hands and cry quietly so that no one would see that she was crying. But I wasn't someone you could fool. I saw perfectly well how her shoulders were trembling and how the tears trickled through her slender

white fingers, falling on the tablecloth. I even knew why
she was crying. Luckily for her, my father was preparing
to go to shul and was putting on his threadbare Sabbath
silk coat and wrapping his woven belt around his waist.
He thrust both hands into the belt and with a deep sigh
said to me, "Come, let's go. It's time to go to shul to
pray." I gathered the daily and High Holiday prayer
books, and we went off to shul leaving my mother to pray
at home. I knew exactly what she would do first: She
would cry. She would have a chance for a good cry! And
so it was.

On returning from shul, we entered the sukkah with a
big "Happy holiday!" greeting. As my father chanted the
blessing over the wine and then sang the kiddush with its
beautiful holiday tune, I noticed my mother's eyes, which
were plainly red and puffy. Her nose was shiny too. Nevertheless, to me she looked as beautiful as the Matriarch
Rachel, or Abigail, or the Queen of Sheba, or Queen
Esther. Looking at her, I was reminded of all the beautiful daughters of Zion I had studied about that morning
in cheder. As I looked at my fine mother with her pale,
pure face, set off by her pretty silk holiday kerchief, with
her lovely, large, worried eyes, my heart grieved that
such lovely eyes needed to cry so much, that such lovely
white hands needed to do the cooking and cleaning. I was
disappointed with the Lord above for not giving us
enough money. I prayed to God to bring me good luck so
that I would find a treasure trove of gold and precious
gems. Or let the Messiah come and then we could all go
to Israel where it would be wonderful for everyone.

My thoughts carried me far, far away to the place of my dearest dreams which I wouldn't trade for all the wealth in the world. My father's beautiful holiday tune poured into my ears:

> *Ki vanu vacharta*
> *V'otanu kedashta*
> *Michal ha'amin*

I understood the meaning of these words:

> Because You have chosen us
> And You have blessed us
> Above all the nations

That's no small thing—to be a people chosen by God, to be special like an only child. My heart became light and happy because we were the blessed chosen people. I imagined that I was a prince, yes, a prince, and the sukkah was a palace where the Divine Presence resided. Here sat my mother, the great beauty, the Queen of Sheba, and tomorrow, God willing, we would recite the stirring benediction over the best of all fruit, the esrog. Oh, who could compare himself to me? Who could compare himself to me?

After my father's kiddush, *"Really* Moishe" had his turn. It wasn't my father's kiddush but it was all right. And after him the landlord himself, Hershke Mamtzes—an ordinary Jew, an ordinary kiddush. We went to wash our hands and then recited the blessing over the bread. The three women started carrying in the food—the tasty, warm, fresh, seasoned, wonderful-smelling fish—and everyone sat with his family at his own table. There were many loaves of twisted fresh white bread, there were many hands dunking the soft bread in the hot fish broth, there were many mouths eating. A breeze was blowing through the thin, frail walls of the sukkah and through the sparse fir branches. The candles flickered as we all ate, thoroughly enjoying the holiday feast. In my imagination it was still a palace, a stately, brightly lit palace, and we, Jewish princes, aristocrats, the chosen people, were feasting and living in luxury. Blessed be Israel. May you always prosper, O Jews! I imagined myself saying. No people are as fortunate as you. How lucky you are to have the rare honor of sitting in such a fine sukkah, bedecked with green branches and strewn with golden sand and draped with the costliest tapestries in the world. On the table, the holiday loaves and delicious holiday fish were fit for a king.

Suddenly—*Cr-ra-aash!!* The entire roof of green fir boughs dropped right on our heads, followed by the walls one after the other. A goat came flying through the air, landing right on top of us. Suddenly it was dark, the candles blown out, the tables overturned, and all of us, together with the dishes and goat, sprawled in the sand. The moon shone and the stars twinkled above us. The frightened goat sprang up on its spindly legs, looked around with its guilty eyes like a culprit, and scampered off, leaping impertinently over tables, over benches, and over our heads, bleating "Me-e-eh!" All the candles were out, the dishes shattered, the loaves covered with sand,

and all of us frightened to death. The women shrieked, the children cried. A shambles! *Really* a shambles!

"That's some sukkah you put up," said Hershke Mamtzes, the landlord, to us afterward, his voice sounding as if we had made him pay for the sukkah, "that one goat could wreck it. Some sukkah!"

"That was *really* a sukkah!" said "*Really* Moishe," looking dumbfounded, trying to figure out just how this all could have happened, "*really* a sukkah!"

"Yes, *really* a sukkah!" mimicked the landlord, and everyone joined in, "That was *really* a sukkah!"

Benny's Luck

Chanukah commemorates the triumphant victory of the small army of the Maccabees over the Syrians many centuries ago. Candles are lit for eight days, potato latkes are eaten, Chanukah money is given, and children play games with the spinning top, or dreydl.

MORE THAN ALL MY friends in cheder and more than anyone in the whole town and more than anyone in the world, I loved my friend, Benny Polkovoi. My love was a mixture of real affection, a deep attachment, and more than a touch of fear. I loved him because he was finer, brighter, and craftier than all the other boys. He was devoted and loyal, willing to stand up and fight for me.

I was afraid of him because he was big and quick with his fists. He could beat up anyone at will because Benny was the oldest, the biggest, and the richest boy in cheder. His father, Meyer Polkovoi, even though a tailor with a talent only for sewing army uniforms, was a rich man, a man of means. He had a fine house and a seat at the eastern wall in the synagogue (the third from the Holy Ark).

At Passover he could buy the first-blessed matzo, at Sukkos he could afford the finest esrog, on Sabbath he could invite a poor guest to dinner. He gave sizable donations, offered loans without interest, and sent his children to the best teachers. In short, Meyer Polkovoi did everything he could to rise above his station, to become a man to be reckoned with, one of the accepted and respected elders of the congregation—but it was a lost cause! In our Kasrilevka, you didn't just buy your way to the top. In our Kasrilevka, one's status and origins were not so easily forgotten. In our Kasrilevka, a tailor might try to climb the social ladder twenty years in a row, act and dress and live like a rich man, but to us he would always remain a tailor. There was no soap in the world, so to speak, that could wash *that* stain away. But let's get back to my friend, Benny.

Benny was a fine lad, a chubby fellow with freckles, coarse blond hair, pale pudgy cheeks, widely spaced teeth, and remarkable fishlike, bulging eyes. These bulging eyes were always smiling and mischievous. A snub nose accentuated a taunting, impertinent expression. But somehow that face appealed to me. Benny and I became close friends from the moment we met.

Our friendship was really sealed under the table, right in front of the rebbi, while we were studying the Bible. I first met the rebbi when my mother brought me to cheder. We found him sitting with the students as they were studying the Book of Genesis. He was a Jew with thick eyebrows who wore a pointy yarmulke. No time was wasted on entrance examinations or birth certificates. The rebbi just said to me, "Climb around there on that bench between those two boys."

I climbed onto the bench and squeezed between two boys and was considered "enrolled." A conference between my mother and the rebbi was not necessary either; they had made all the arrangements after the holidays.

"Just remember to study hard, like you're supposed to," my mother admonished me as she lingered in the doorway. She turned her head to give me one last look, a look in which I could detect a blend of love, pride, and pity. I understood that look well; she was pleased that I was sitting with studious children, but it also saddened her that we were to be separated.

I must admit that I was much happier than my mother. I was sitting among so many new friends. They were sizing me up and I was sizing them up. But the rebbi didn't let us sit idle for long. He got right down to the business at hand and sang out loud, chanting, motioning for us to repeat after him, and we complied, one louder than the next at the top of our lungs.

> *V'hanachash*—And the snake!
> *haya*—was!
> *arum*—cleverer!
> *michal*—than all!
> *chayos*—the beasts!
> *hasadeh*—of the field!
> *asher*—that!
> *asah*—He created!

Boys sitting so close together, even though they are swaying and chanting, cannot help getting to know each other by slipping in a few words of conversation between the text of the Book of Genesis. And that's the way it was with us.

Benny Polkovoi, who sat right up close to me, tested me first by pinching my leg, then by staring straight into my eyes. Swaying fervently while singing in unison with the rebbi and the rest of the class, Benny began interjecting his own words into the Bible translation without missing so much as a beat,

V'ha-adam—And Adam!
yadah—knew!   (Here, take these buttons!)
et chavah—Eve!
ishta—his wife!   (Give me some carob and I'll let you
                        take a puff of my cigarette!)

I felt someone's warm hand placing several smooth, small, flat trouser buttons in mine. I must confess that I didn't need buttons, I didn't have any carob, and I didn't smoke, but the notion so appealed to me that I answered him in the same chanting rhythm, swaying along with everyone,

V'taher—and she was with child!
v'taled—and she bore a child!   (Who told you I had
                                      carob?)

That was the way we carried on a conversation until the rebbi sensed that despite my pious chanting and swaying, my mind really wasn't on the Book of Genesis. Suddenly he "put me to the wall," by which was meant he was going to test me.

"You there! What did you say your name was? Surely you can tell me whose son Cain was and who Cain's brother was." Since my mind was somewhere else—who knows where?—under the table with the buttons, I suppose, this ridiculous question struck me as crazy, as if someone had suddenly asked, "When will there be a circus in the sky?" or "How do you make cheese out of snow so it won't melt?"

"Why are you looking at me like that?" the rebbi asked me. "Don't you know what I'm asking? I'm asking you and I want an answer. What was the name of the father of Cain, and what happened between him and his brother, Eve's son, Abel?"

I could see all the boys smirking as they tried to keep from laughing out loud. I didn't think there was anything to laugh at.

"You dope, say that you don't know because we haven't studied it yet," whispered Benny in my ear and jabbed me with his elbow. I did exactly as he said and repeated it word for word like a parrot. The cheder boys burst out laughing. "Why are they laughing?" I thought, looking bewildered at them and at the rebbi. They were doubled over with laughter. All the while I was transferring the buttons from one hand to the other; I counted exactly half a dozen.

"Aha! Let's see what you have there in your hands, my young man! What are you doing down there?" demanded the rebbi and bent down to look under the table.

And you can guess what I got from the rebbi because of the buttons on my first day in cheder.

Whippings heal, shame is forgotten. Benny and I became good friends in the best sense of the word *friend*—one soul rather than two. This is how it happened. When I arrived in cheder the following morning with my Bible in one hand and my lunch in the other, I found the boys in a lively, excited mood. How come? Great news! The rebbi was away! Where to? Off somewhere to a circumcision together with his wife, the rebbitzin. Not *together* with her, mind you. A rebbi never goes anywhere *together* with the rebbitzin. The rebbi always goes first, and behind him the rebbitzin follows.

"Let's make a bet!" cried one of the boys with a notable blue nose, Yehoshua-Heshel was his name.

"How much do you want to bet?" replied another, Koppel-Bunim, a lad with a torn sleeve out of which peeked a dirty elbow.

"A quarter of a pound of carob."

"Let it be a quarter of a pound of carob. What are we betting on?"

"I bet he won't be able to stand more than twenty-five."

"And I say thirty-six!"

"Thirty-six? We'll soon see! Grab him, fellows!"

So commanded Yehoshua-Heshel, he of the blue nose, and before I knew what was happening, several boys had grabbed me and laid me down on a bench, face upward. Two of them straddled my legs, two held my arms, one held my head so I couldn't squirm free, and another stuck two fingers of his left hand (he was most likely left-handed) in front of my nose. He made an O with his index finger and thumb, squinted one eye as if taking aim, half-opened his mouth, and started flicking his fingers at my nose. And what painful flicks they were! With each one I saw stars. Fiends! Murderers! What did they have against my poor nose? Whom had it ever bothered? What about it didn't they like? It was a nose like any other nose!

"Start counting, guys!" ordered Yehoshua-Heshel, "One, two, three!" But suddenly—

Ever since the world was created, miracles have happened suddenly. For example, a person is attacked by bandits. They tie his hands up, sharpen their knives, and tell him to say his prayers. Just then, when they are about to do him in, a hunter appears out of nowhere. The bandits take off and the victim is rescued, raises his hands to God in gratitude, and says a blessing of thanks.

That's the way it was with me and my nose. I don't remember all the details, whether it was at the fifth or sixth flick of the nose that the door opened and in came Benny Polkovoi. The gang immediately let me go and each stood rooted to the spot while Benny took care of them one at a time. He gave each boy's ear a good twist as he warned each of them in turn, "Well, *now* you'll know what happens when you pick on the widow's boy!"

From that time on the boys never touched me or my nose. They were afraid of starting up with the widow's boy who had Benny Polkovoi as his friend, savior, and protector.

"The widow's boy"—that was the only name I was ever known by in cheder. Why "the widow's boy"? I suppose it was because my mother was a widow. She struggled to support herself by running a small shop, mostly selling, as I recall, chalk and carob, two fast-selling items in our Kasrilevka. Chalk was needed for whitewashing houses and carob was a favorite snack because it was sweet, long-lasting, and inexpensive. Schoolboys would spend all their lunch money on these snacks, and the shopkeepers made a good profit from it. I could never understand why my mother was always complaining, claiming she could barely earn enough to pay the shop rent and my tuition. Why was tuition so important to her? How about all the other things a person needs, like food, clothing, shoes, and so on? All she ever thought about was my tuition.

"Since God has punished me," she would say sadly, "and taken from me my husband, and what a husband he was, leaving me alone, a widow with a child, the least I can do is see to it that he has a good education."

How can you argue with that? Don't think that she didn't visit the cheder periodically to check up on how I was progressing. I'm not even talking about saying my daily prayers—she made quite sure that I said them. Her fondest hope was that I would grow up to be the man my father was, may he rest in peace. Whenever she would look at me, she would say that I was altogether "him."

Her eyes would become misty, her face worried-looking and full of sorrow.

May my dear father forgive me, I could never understand what kind of a man he was. As my mother told it, he divided all his time between praying and studying. Was there never a time when, like me, he would long to go outdoors on a summer morning when the sun was not yet too hot and just beginning to rise rapidly in the vast sky like a fiery angel in a fiery chariot drawn by fiery horses, so golden bright that it was impossible to look directly at it? What appeal, I ask you, could the daily prayers have, compared to such a magnificent morning?

Who could prefer sitting and studying in a dark, cramped schoolroom while the brightly glowing sun kept on sizzling and blistering the earth like a giant frying pan? That's when more than anything in the world, you yearn to run down the hill to the pond, that lovely little pond sheltered by green branches from which rises a mist that from a distance looks like the vapors rising from the steam bath. That's when you want to throw off your clothes and jump in up to your waist in the sun-warmed pond whose bottom is miraculously cool with slippery soft mud and where a variety of creatures, some half fish, half frogs, glide and float constantly before your eyes. Strange thin-legged insects and familiar dragonflies skate and skitter over the pond's surface. You feel like swimming across to the other side where the broad, round lily pads show off their white and yellow blooms sparkling in the sun. And there above you is a young green willow tree with soft fresh boughs, and you let yourself drop with your hands into the muddy water, kicking your legs up and down behind you, making believe you're swimming.

And what appeal has sitting at home or in cheder in the evening when the bright red ball is descending to earth on the other side of town, igniting the tip of the church steeple and illuminating the shingled roof of the bathhouse as well as the big old windows of the big cold synagogue? On the outskirts of town, herds of goats are scampering, lambs are bleating, the dust is rising higher and higher, frogs are croaking—all creating a busy, tumultuous din. Who can keep praying at such a time? Who could even think of wanting to study at such a time?

But go talk to my mother. She would tell you that he, my father, was never distracted from prayer; he, my father, was a different kind of person altogether. The sort of a man he really was, may he forgive me, is hard for me to say. I only know that my mother pestered me a lot, reminding me constantly that I once had a father like that. She threw up to me at least ten times a day about the tuition she was paying out for me in return for which she was requiring only two things—that I study diligently and pray fervently.

There was no reason to believe that "the widow's boy" was a poor student; he was no better nor worse than any other boy. But as for praying fervently—*that* I couldn't guarantee. All children are alike in some ways, and he was as much a prankster as any of his classmates. Like them, he enjoyed a bit of mischief; like them, he relished acting up at times. Oh, the tricks we thought of: dressing up the town goat in the rebbi's discarded fur hat with which the rebbitzin cleaned house, and letting it run loose in the streets; tying a paper snake to the cat's tail and tormenting her with it until she ran wild, shattering pots or anything else in her way; locking the women's section of the shul from the outside on Friday evening so the women had to be rescued before they fainted; nailing the rebbi's slippers to the floor or sticking his beard with wax to the table as he slept and then just let him stand up! Oh, the smacks we received afterward when it was discovered who had done it—don't ask! Naturally, you can assume that behind every activity there was a ringleader, a guiding spirit, a chief.

Our ringleader, our guiding spirit, our chief was Benny Polkovoi. It was from his head that the ideas originated, but it was on our heads that the blame fell. Benny—the chubby, red-faced Benny with the bulging fish-eyes—somehow managed to squeeze out of every scrape free as a bird, clean as a whistle, innocent as a newborn lamb, even though he was every bit as guilty as any one of us. Every gesture of his, every grimace, witticism, or mannerism was quickly imitated and adopted by us. Who taught us how to sneak a puff on a cigarette, exhaling through our nostrils? Benny. Who talked us into skating on the ice with the peasant boys in town in the winter? Benny. Who taught us how to gamble with buttons, playing cards and checkers till we lost all our lunch money? Benny. When it came to gambling, Benny was a champion. He could beat us all, winning every cent we had, but when it came to trying to win some of it back—*whoosh!* Benny had vanished! Gambling was one of our greatest pleasures and for gambling we earned the worst tongue lashing from the rebbi. He strongly disapproved of gambling and vowed to break us of the habit once and for all.

"Gambling in *my* cheder? I'll have you gambling with the devil!" the rebbi would shout while shaking out our pockets till they were empty, confiscating their contents while meting out blows on all sides.

But there was one week of the year when we were allowed to gamble. Did I say "allowed"? It was considered a good deed to gamble, a regular commandment! That was the week of Chanukah and we played with the dreydl, the spinning top.

Today's card games and other forms of gambling—poker, roulette, pinochle, and so forth—certainly make more sense than our old dreydl game, but what does it matter as long as money is at stake? Gambling at dreydl can get heated, exciting, and upsetting. It can drive you mad to the point at which you are prepared to sell your soul. It's not so much the money as the keen disappointment: Why did someone else win? Why did the dreydl fall on the winning letter *G* for him and on the losing letters *N*, *H*, or *Sh* for you? You know what I'm talking about, don't you? The dreydl is a four-sided spinning top with a Hebrew letter on each side. You spin it, and depending on which side it falls when it stops, it tells you whether and how much you've won or lost. *N* means none, *H* means half, *Sh* means shoot again, and *G* means

get. The dreydl is really a game of chance. Whoever is lucky, wins. Take Benny Polkovoi, for instance. No matter how many times he spun the dreydl, it always fell on *G*.

"That Benny has all the luck," we boys would say as we put up more money. Benny's response always was "What do you mean, luck? I'm a rich man's son!"

"*G*! Again *G*! What luck!" we screamed all at once as we searched our pockets for more money while Benny, as was his style, spun the dreydl upside down on its thin handle. The dreydl spun around, wobbled back and forth like a drunkard, and fell over.

"*G*!" cried Benny.

"*G*? *G*? Again *G*? I can't believe it!" the boys yelled, scratching their heads and reaching into their pockets again.

The game grew more intense. The participants became more inflamed as they staked their money, shoved one another to get closer to the table, poked each other in the ribs, argued and hurled insulting names back and forth,

"Snotnose!"

"Stutterer!"

"Beanpole!"

"Rag-picker's son!"

With all these compliments flying, we failed to notice that the rebbi had returned and was standing to the side, wearing his warm cap and coat and carrying his prayer shawl under his arm. He was on his way to shul but, hearing all the uproar, had stopped by for a while to look

on as we played dreydl. That day the rebbi didn't inter-
fere; it was Chanukah and we were free to play dreydl
for eight days in a row, as much as we wanted so long as
we didn't fight or pull each other's noses. A sympathetic
man, our rebbi. The rebbitzin lifted their small, sickly
child, Reuvele, into her arms as she stood behind the
rebbi's shoulder looking wide-eyed, taking in our avid
gambling. Benny took on all comers, winning everything
from everyone. Benny was raring to go, Benny was ferocious, Benny was unstoppable. He spun the dreydl again
and again. It turned, wobbled, and finally came to rest.

"Again *G*? Did you ever see such a winning streak?"

Benny demonstrated his great mastery of the game
over and over until he cleaned out all our pockets to the
last penny and then thrust his hands in his pockets as if to
say, "Well, who's next?"

Slowly, we all drifted home, carrying away with us not
only the heartache and shame of losing but the necessity
of having to concoct lies to explain where our Chanukah
money had gone. Each of us invented a different story.
One blurted out that he had spent it all on sweets and
carob. Another made up the alibi that someone had
robbed him during the night. A third came home crying.

"What is it? Why are you crying?"

"I bought a penknife with my Chanukah money."

"So why are you crying?"

"I lost it on the way home."

I too had to come up with a good story, telling my
mother a tale right out of the "Thousand and One
Nights." I did succeed in getting her to give me more

Chanukah money, which I immediately took over to Benny's, where, within five minutes, I was cleaned out again. Back I went to my mother with still another tall tale. In short, brains were busy, minds were working overtime turning out lies and more lies that flew like woodchips. All our Chanukah money wound up in Benny's pocket, gone forever!

But only one of us became so caught up in the dreydl game that he didn't stop at just losing his Chanukah money. He gambled and played dreydl with Benny every day until the last day of Chanukah. That person was none other than myself, "the widow's boy."

Where did "the widow's boy" get money with which to gamble? Don't ask. The greatest gamblers in the world, those who have won and lost great fortunes and rich estates, they would know, they would understand. Ah, me! When the desire to gamble takes hold of him, there is no obstacle that a gambler cannot overcome. He will break through brick walls and iron gates, commit unimaginable crimes. That's what the evil gambling habit will make him do.

First of all, I obtained money by selling everything I owned, one article after another, to my eternal shame. First my penknife, then my wallet, and finally, all my buttons. I had a little box which could open and shut and several gears from an old clock made of fine brass which, when polished, shone like real gold. Everything I owned was practically given away at half-price or for whatever I could get, and off I would run with the money to Benny's place to lose it all. I would leave him, my heart wounded, bitterly disappointed, and very angry. But God forbid, not at Benny! Why should I blame Benny? How was Benny responsible for his good luck? He would console me by saying that if I spun the dreydl and it fell on the G for me, then I would be the winner; but he was spinning it and it fell on the G for him, so naturally, *he* was the winner. That's what Benny said and who could deny it? No, my only disappointment was with myself because I had squandered so much money, my poor mother's hard-earned money as well as my prize possessions, leaving me naked, so to speak, as the day I was born. Even my little Siddur, my daily prayer book, was sold. Oh, that Siddur, that lovely little prayer book! Whenever I remind myself of that little Siddur, my heart aches and my face burns with shame. It was really a treasure, a gem, not a prayer book. It was bought for me by my mother on my father's yahrtzeit, the anniversary of his death, from Petchaya the peddler.

It was a prayer book above and beyond all other prayer books, more like an encyclopedia than a prayer book. It was thick and packed full of information about anything you could ever dream of wanting to know: the Song of Songs, commentaries, Sayings of the Fathers, the Haggadah, all the prayers, laws, and customs for every day of the year and all the holidays, plus a Book of Psalms at the back. Not to mention the binding, the gold lettering, and the bold, clear print. An enchantment, I tell you, a spirit, not a prayer book!

Petchaya the peddler was a man who suffered from

cataracts. His moustache somehow seemed to make his sad face appear smiling. Whenever Petchaya came around and displayed his wares at the door of the synagogue, I could not take my eyes off that little "encyclopedia."

"What are you looking at, young man?" Petchaya would ask innocently, pretending he didn't know of my desire for the Siddur even though I had leafed through it seventeen times, each time asking how much it cost.

"Nothing," I said, "just looking," and I turned away and left quickly so as not to reveal my passion for it.

"Oh, Momma, you should see what a beautiful little Siddur Petchaya has!"

"What kind of a Siddur?" asked my mother.

"Such a Siddur! If I had such a Siddur, I would—I would—"

"Don't you have a Siddur already? What about your father's Siddur?"

"How can you compare them, Momma? That one is just a Siddur, but *this* one is a regular encyclopedia!"

"An encyclopedia!" my mother exclaimed. "Are there more prayers in it? Do the prayers sound better?"

Go explain to a mother what an encyclopedia is, a *real* encyclopedia with red covers, with blue print, and with a green binding.

"Come," my mother said to me one evening, taking me by the hand. "Come with me to shul. Tomorrow is your father's yahrtzeit, so we'll light a candle and on the way home, we'll go past Petchaya's and see what's so great about that little Siddur."

I knew beforehand that on my father's yahrtzeit I could get whatever I wanted from my mother, and my heart was already thumping with anticipation.

Outside the synagogue we found Petchaya with his sack of merchandise still unpacked. Petchaya, you understand, was a man who could not be rushed. He knew full well he had no competition. No one would take any of his business away. It took forever till he untied his pack. I trembled, I shook, I shivered, barely able to stand on my feet while he took his time, as if my nervousness had nothing whatsoever to do with him.

"Show us already," my mother urged him impatiently. "Let's see what kind of a prayer book you have there."

Petchaya had all the time in the world. Where was the fire? Slowly, without hurrying, he untied the sack and spread out his entire merchandise: large and small Bibles, prayer books for men and women, large and small psalm books, holiday prayer books without end, story books, Chassidic tales, and on and on. It seemed to me his supply of books would never end. His sack was bottomless. Finally the smaller items emerged, and among them, my special little Siddur shone forth!

"This is it?" my mother wondered out loud. "Such a little thing?"

"That little thing," said Petchaya, "is more expensive than a big thing."

"How much are you asking—may God forgive my language—for that little pipsqueak?"

"You're calling a prayer book a pipsqueak?" Petchaya

was shocked. He slowly removed the book from her hands and my heart sank.

"Well, tell me already, how much does it cost?" my mother relented. But Petchaya had plenty of time and answered in a singsong, "How much does it cost? It costs, it costs! I'm afraid it's out of your range."

My mother cursed her enemies with nightmares and demanded a price. Petchaya quoted a price and my mother remained silent. She turned her face to the door, grabbed my hand, and said to me, "Come, let's go. We have no more business here. Don't you know Reb Petchaya carries only overpriced merchandise?"

With a heavy heart, I followed my mother to the door, hoping against hope that God would have pity on me and Petchaya would call us back. But that's not the kind of man Petchaya was. He knew we would turn back of our own accord; and that's what happened. We did turn back and my mother pleaded with him to be more reasonable. Petchaya didn't move a muscle, looked up at the ceiling, the white cataract of his left eye glistening, and we walked away and turned back still another time.

"A strange man, that Petchaya!" my mother said to me afterward. "I would rather die of the plague than buy a prayer book from him! It's overpriced. It's shameful. The money could well be used for your tuition, but never mind. In honor of your dear, dead father's yahrtzeit, may he rest in peace, and because tomorrow you will say Kaddish for him, I gave in and bought it for you as a special favor. So you too must do me a favor, my son, and promise me that you'll pray every day faithfully."

Whether or not I actually did pray every day faithfully—well, let's not talk about it. But I adored that little Siddur more than life itself. You can appreciate just how much when I say that I even slept with it, although that's forbidden. The whole cheder envied me my little Siddur, and I guarded it as one would the pupil of an eye. And then, that Chanukah—may God forgive me—with my own hands I delivered it to Moishe, the carpenter's son. He had been dying to get hold of it for some time, but it was I who had to beg *him*, on bended knee, to buy it from me. I gave that little Siddur away for almost nothing! Oh, that little treasure, my very own favorite prayer book! When I think of that little book, I want to cry my heart out and bury my face in my hands with shame. Sold! Traded away, and for what? For whom? For Benny. So that Benny could win a few more pennies from me. But how was it Benny's fault if he had all the luck with the dreydl?

"That's the way dreydls are," Benny said, trying to comfort me as he put away my last few pennies in his pocket. "If you had been the lucky one, you would have won, but I was the lucky one, so I won."

Benny's cheeks were fiery red. His house was bright and cheery. They had a silver Chanukah menorah full of the finest oil with a large shamesh ready to kindle the other wicks. Nothing but the best. From the kitchen one could smell the heavenly aroma of freshly rendered goose fat.

"We're having latkes tonight," Benny told me as we stood at the door, and my stomach rumbled with hunger.

I ran home in my torn coat to find my mother just returning from work, her nose and hands red and swollen, frozen through and through, standing at the oven trying to warm herself. Seeing me, her face lit up.

"Coming from shul?" she asked.

"From shul," I lied.

"Said your evening prayers?"

"Said them," I lied again.

"Warm yourself, my son, and you'll say the blessing on the Chanukah candles. Tonight, thank God, we light the last candle."

If a person experienced only suffering, without a moment's pleasure, without a bit of joy, he would be unable to bear it and would surely take his own life. I'm thinking of my mother, that poor widow, who struggled day and night, worked, froze, starved, and went without sleep and for my sake alone, only for me. So why wasn't she entitled to some happiness once in a while? Each person understands the word *happiness* in his own way. For my mother there was no greater happiness than my chanting the kiddush for her on Sabbath and holidays, my conducting the seder for her at Passover, or my blessing the candles for her at Chanukah. What did it matter whether we used real wine or not on the Sabbath, what did it matter whether we enjoyed special Passover pastries or just stale matzos softened with water for Passover, what did it matter whether we had a silver menorah or used scooped-out potato halves filled with oil for Chanukah? Believe me, neither the wine nor the pastries nor the silver were what really counted. What really counted was something else. It was the actual performance of the kiddush, the celebration of the seder, and the blessing of the Chanukah candles. She didn't have to tell me how she was feeling or explain to me why; her face, smiling and glowing with pride as I chanted the blessing, said it all. Then one could appreciate that *this* was real happiness, *this* was true good fortune.

I bowed my head over the scooped-out potato halves and chanted the blessing and she chanted after me under her breath, word for word with the same melody. I prayed and she looked directly into my eyes as she moved her lips and I knew what was going on in her heart. She was thinking, "Altogether 'him,' his very image. May his years be many." I felt that all I deserved was to be cut up like those scooped-out potatoes. After all, I had deceived my mother and in such an ugly way! I sold my little Siddur and lost the money gambling with the dreydl! I sold it, I gave away my very soul!

The wicks in the potatoes, our Chanukah candles, smoked and sputtered and were finally extinguished. My mother said to me, "Go wash up and we'll eat potatoes with goose fat. In honor of Chanukah, I splurged and bought a jar of goose fat—fresh, delicious goose fat." I washed up happily and we sat down at the table to eat.

"Those who are well off can afford to have latkes the last day of Chanukah," my mother said with a deep sigh, and I thought of Benny's latkes and Benny's dreydl which had cost me such a fortune and my heart felt as if it had been pierced with a needle.

Even during the night my thoughts would not let me alone. I could hear my mother's constant moaning and the creaking of her bed as she tossed and turned. I imagined that the bed too was moaning, not creaking. Outside, the wind howled, rattled the windows, tore at the roof, and whistled in the chimney with a long, drawn-out *pheeeww!* A cricket, nesting in the walls since summer, chirped from its hiding place, "Chireree-chireree!" and my mother didn't stop moaning. Every moan and every sigh reverberated in my heart until I could barely control myself. I was on the verge of leaping from my bed and running to my mother's side, falling on my knees, kissing her hands, and confessing all my terrible sins. But I didn't do it. Instead I drew my blankets over my head so as not to hear my mother's bed creaking and her moaning and sighing.

I shut my eyes tight, the wind whistled and howled—*pheeeww!*—and the cricket chirped, "Chireree-chireree! Chireree-chireree!" and suddenly there seemed to be something spinning before my eyes, something like a dreydl shaped like a person, a familiar person. I could have sworn it was the rebbi with his pointy yarmulke. The rebbi was standing on one leg, Bible in hand, spinning, spinning, spinning like a dreydl, his pointy yarmulke shimmering on his head, his earlocks swirling in the air. No, it wasn't the rebbi but really a dreydl! A strange dreydl, a live dreydl with a pointy yarmulke and flying earlocks. Gradually, gradually, the rebbi-like dreydl or the dreydl-like rebbi stopped spinning and in its place there materialized Pharaoh, the King of Egypt, about whom we had just studied in cheder the week before Chanukah. Pharaoh, the King of Egypt, stood before my eyes stark naked, having just emerged from the pond, and in his hand was my little Siddur, my little encyclopedia, and I couldn't figure out how it had fallen into the hands of this wicked monster who had bathed in Jewish blood.

Then I saw seven cows—thin, haggard, emaciated, nothing but skin and bone with enormous horns and long ears, coming at me all at the same time, their mouths wide open, about to swallow me. Suddenly, there was Benny, my friend Benny. He grabbed the cattle by their long ears and gave them each a good twist while someone wept softly, sighed and sobbed, moaned and whistled and chirped. A figure was standing beside my bed, speaking quietly, gently, "Tell me, my son, when is my yahrtzeit? When will you say Kaddish for me?"

I saw that it was my father from the beyond, my father about whom my mother had told me all those wonderful things. I wanted to tell him when his yahrtzeit was, when I would say Kaddish for him—but I forgot! Just then I forgot! I struggled to remember, rubbed my forehead, tried to remind myself—but I couldn't! Have you ever heard anything like it? I forgot when my own father's yahrtzeit was! Help! Help! Help!

"God be with you! Why are you screaming? What's this yelling about? Does anything hurt you, God forbid?"

My mother was bending over me, holding my head, and I could feel her body trembling and shaking. The dim little bedside lamp was smoking, shedding little light, and I could see my mother's shadow dancing crazily on the wall, the points of her kerchief looking like two horns. Her eyes glinted frighteningly in the dark.

"When is Poppa's yahrtzeit? Tell me, Momma! When is Poppa's yahrtzeit?"

"God help you! It was just not long ago. Did you have a bad dream? Spit three times—Tfu! Tfu! Tfu! May all be for the best. Amen! Amen! Amen!"

I grew up and became an adult. Benny also grew up and became an adult, a young man with a yellow beard. He acquired a little paunch on which he sported a gold chain. Obviously, he was well-to-do, Benny. Once he was a rich man's son, now he was a rich man himself.

We met on a train. I recognized him by his bulging fish-eyes and widely spaced teeth. It had been a long time since we had seen one another. We embraced and were soon reminiscing about the dear old bygone days of our childhood, reminding ourselves of all the foolish deeds we had done.

"Remember, Benny, that Chanukah when you were so lucky at dreydl? Your dreydl kept falling on the *G!*"

I looked at my friend, Benny. He was breaking up with laughter. He held his sides, doubled over, almost choking to death with laughter.

"God help you, Benny! Why this sudden laughter?"

"Oh!" He gesticulated with both hands. "Don't talk about that dreydl! That was *some* dreydl! *Really* a dreydl! That was a pot of gold, pure gold! With such a dreydl it as hard to lose. Whichever side it fell on, it had to fall on the—ha ha ha—on the *G*!"

"What kind of a dreydl was *that*, Benny?"

"That was—ha ha ha—a dreydl with nothing but *G*'s. Pure *G*! A *G* on every side, ha ha ha!"

A Ruined Passover

"REB YISROEL! REB YISROEL? Please, I must know! Can you promise me to have the boy's suit ready for the holidays?"

So shouted my mother to Yisroel the tailor at the top of her lungs because Yisroel the tailor was almost stone deaf. A tall Jew with a long face and with cotton stuffed in his ears, Yisroel smiled half to himself and gestured with his hand as if to say, "Why shouldn't it be ready?"

"So, please, take his measurements, but only on the condition that you'll have it ready for Passover."

Yisroel the deaf tailor looked at my mother as if to say, "What a strange woman! Doesn't she think I heard her the first time?"

He pulled out a long tape measure from his vest pocket, stood me in front of him, and started to measure me in the length and in the width as my mother stood alongside, carrying on: "Longer, much longer! Wider, much wider! Don't make the trousers too narrow! Make sure the jacket has an extra fold in it—at least several

inches so it can be let out next year. Wider! More, a little
wider! That's the way! Whatever you do, don't make the
waist too short, God forbid! Nicely now, with style! More,
more! Don't scrimp on cloth, because a child grows!"

Yisroel the tailor knew very well that "a child grows"
and went right on about his business. Having measured
my arms and legs, he dismissed me with a slight shove as
if to say, "You can go now. You're free!" I very much
wanted the jacket to have a split and a pocket in the back,
which was then in style, but I didn't know whom to ask.
Yisroel the deaf tailor wound his tape measure on two
fingers as he talked to my mother in fragmented phrases:
"A busy time before Passover! . . . Mud—there's plenty!
. . . Fish—scarce! . . . Potatoes—expensive! . . . Eggs—
not to be found! . . . Work—forget it! . . . New
clothes—not a chance! . . . Just patchwork, patchwork,
patchwork! . . . Even Reb Yehoshua Hersh can only afford to have an old coat turned inside out—imagine! . . .
Reb Yehoshua Hersh himself! . . . Such a time—the
world is coming to an end!"

My mother wasn't impressed. She interrupted him in
the middle of his ramblings. "About how much do you
think it will come to, Reb Yisroel?"

Yisroel the deaf tailor removed a snuffbox made of
horn from his vest pocket, cupped his hand and shook
out a little mound of snuff into it, drew it slowly to his
nose, and inhaled the snuff so deftly that not even a
speck fell on his moustache. Then he gestured with his
hand and said, "What does it matter? We won't argue
about it. . . . Did you ever hear such a thing? Reb Yeho-

shua Hersh! . . . Turning an old coat inside out! . . .
God in heaven!"

"Remember now, Reb Yisroel, what I'm asking—not
too tight, not too short, with an extra fold and the waist—
roomy and full."

"And with a split . . . ?" I started to add.

"Be quiet, we're talking!" scolded my mother and
jabbed me in the ribs with her elbow. And to Yisroel, "I'll
remind you again—not too short, not too tight, with an
extra fold and the waist—roomy and full."

"And with a pocket . . . ?" I tried again.

"You won't be still, will you?" my mother warned.
"Did you ever see such a child who keeps interrupting
while grownups are talking?"

Yisroel the deaf tailor tucked the package of cloth
under his arm, passed two fingers across the mezuzah on
the doorpost, and called from the doorway, "Does that
mean you really want it to be ready for Passover? Happy
holiday to you! Goot yom-tov!"

"Ah, here's Reb Gedalyeh! Speak of the devil! I was
just thinking of sending for you again."

Gedalyeh was a shoemaker, an old soldier who had
served his time, whose front teeth were missing and
whose large, round beard had obviously once been
shaven in the middle, where now straggly hairs grew.

"Reb Gedalyeh," my mother said to him, "tell me, can
you promise to make a pair of shoes for my son for Passover?"

Gedalyeh the shoemaker was a cheerful Jew who accompanied whatever he said with a sideways hop. "Oh, you want them ready for Passover!" he said, almost sarcastically, to my mother. "What a surprise! Just about everyone else wants them ready for Passover too. I promised Chaya, Reb Mottel's daughter, two pairs of boots, one pair for her and one for her daughter, so I have that to do. Yossele, Reb Shemele's son, ordered four pairs of shoes for Passover, so I have to make them for him. I promised to make Feigele, Reb Abraham's daughter, a pair of boots a long time ago. Even if the sky were to fall, I'd have to make *them*! And Moishe the tailor asked me to repair his heels and I can't turn him down. Zyma the carpenter needs new soles, which doesn't help my situation. Just today, Asna the widow's girl was pestering me to——"

"So!" my mother cut him short. "Let's be perfectly frank. Does that mean you won't be able to have them ready for Passover? Because if not, I'll call another shoemaker . . ."

"Why shouldn't I be able to?" said Gedalyeh with a little hop. "Just for you, I'll set aside my other work and you'll definitely have your shoes for Passover. Is there any reason not to?"

And Gedalyeh the shoemaker took out a piece of blue paper, got down on one knee, and began tracing my foot.

"Add a few more inches!" ordered my mother. "More, more! Why are you so stingy with the leather? That's the way! We don't want it to pinch his toes!"

"Pinch his toes . . ." Gedalyeh repeated my mother's last words.

"Be sure it's good leather, not second grade!"

"Second grade . . ." Gedalyeh repeated.

"Put on good soles so they won't wear out!"

"Wear out . . ." Gedalyeh echoed.

"And the heels shouldn't come off!"

"Come off . . ."

"Now you can go to cheder," my mother said to me. "Do you see how much trouble we go to for your sake? If you would only want to study, you could become somebody. Otherwise, what will become of you? You'll be a nobody, a nothing, a dogcatcher!"

I myself didn't know what would become of me—a somebody, a nobody, or a dogcatcher. I only knew that more than anything else in the world, I wanted shoes that would squeak. Oh, how I wanted real squeakers!

"Why are you standing there like a lamppost?" my mother called out to me. "Why don't you go to cheder? Go, that's all the clothing you're going to get."

Gedalyeh the shoemaker started to leave but turned around. "That means you really want them ready for Passover?" he said. "Well, happy holiday! Goot yom-tov!"

On the way home from cheder that day, I ducked into the tailor's shop to see about the split and the pocket for my new jacket. There at a large table stood Yisroel the deaf tailor without his jacket, revealing the short fringed ritual garment men wore under their clothing. He was absorbed in his work; several long threads hung around his neck and a few needles were stuck into his vest. He was marking something with chalk, then cutting the ma-

terial with a large pair of English scissors while scratching
his back with a bent middle finger and mumbling to himself in his absent-minded way, "Extra folds they want . . .
it should be roomy . . . make it wide. . . . With what?
. . . out of thin air? . . . You slice your fingers . . . you
struggle . . . struggle. . . . Like they were boiled
meat . . ."

Around the table sat several young apprentice tailors
sewing, their needles flying as they sang a song in unison.
One of them, a freckle-faced, blond youngster with a flat-
tened nose, sang in a strident voice, drawing his needle in
time to the music:

> Oh, ain't you leavin',
> And oh, ain't you leavin' me,
> Ain't you leavin' me far be-ee-hind!

The others joined him with a shrill,

> I'm gonna stab myself!
> I'm gonna hang myself!
> I'm gonna drown myself!
> I'm gonna do myself i-in!

"What's on your mind, young man?" Yisroel motioned
to me.

"A split," I ventured.

"A what?" Yisroel bent over closer to me, cupping his
ear.

"A split!" I shouted out loud so he could hear.

"A split?"

"A split!"

"Where do you want a split?"

"In the back!"

"What do you want in the back?"

"A split! And a pocket!"

"What split? What pocket?" interjected Batyeh, the tailor's wife, a small woman who sat and did three jobs at once: with her foot she rocked the baby's cradle, with her hands she knitted a sock, and with her mouth she argued and complained. "Why do you need a split? Why do you need a pocket? Where do you have cloth for a pocket? He wants pockets? Let his mother give him cloth for pockets, then he'll have pockets! How about that, pockets!"

I was beginning to regret the whole thing. What if my mother were to find out about it?

"So you really want a split, eh?" Yisroel the tailor asked, taking out his snuffbox. "Go home, young man, you'll have your split."

"And a pocket too?" I said to him, putting on a sad face.

"Go home, young man," Yisroel said again. "I'll see to it that it's just the way you want it."

Joyfully, I ran off to Gedalyeh the shoemaker to arrange for the squeaks in my shoes. Gedalyeh the shoemaker was out. At a bench sat his worker, Karpa, flattening out a large piece of leather. Karpa was a healthy, broad-boned peasant with a pimply face who wore a leather visor over his coarse, black hair.

"What you want, boy?" Karpa tried to say in Yiddish as best as he could. "Speak! What you want?"

He knew a few common Yiddish words and proceeded to rattle them off for my benefit, "Shmata, shlemiel, chutzpah, goniff."

"I would like to talk to your boss, Reb Gedalyeh," I answered in my best Russian.

"Boss go to circumcision," Karpa tried again in Yiddish. "Make kiddush, drink branfy." In order to make sure I understood what he meant, he drew his finger across his throat.

I sat down opposite him on a leather stool and engaged him in a discussion about leather, about heels and soles, about staining and so on, until finally we came around to discussing squeaks. He talked in Yiddish, I in Russian. He couldn't understand everything I was saying, so I used my hands to help.

"I'm talking to you in your own language, fathead," I said in Yiddish, and then in Russian, "Tell me, how do you make shoes squeak? You know, *trrr! trrr!*"

"You better talk Yiddish," said Karpa and licked the leather with his tongue, then made a deep mark on the side of it with his thick, black fingernail.

"How come shoes squeak?" I now spoke in Yiddish. "What's the trick in getting squeaks? What do you put in shoes to make them squeak?"

"Ah, squeaks?" said Karpa. "For to make squeaks you need sugar cube."

"Just a sugar cube?" I wondered. "How come?"

"Sugar cube," Karpa explained. "Sugar—pound-pound, squeak-squeak . . ."

"Aha!" I nodded. "You probably pound the sugar into

a powder and that makes them squeak. Well, and don't you add anything else?"

"Some branfy," Karpa said, mispronouncing the word again. "A little branfy."

"Brandy?" I wondered. "You mean vodka? Why vodka? Sugar I can understand; squeak-squeak! But *vodka?* How does that help make them squeak?"

Karpa made a great effort to tell me in Yiddish so I could understand how the vodka would do the job. "Before you put sugar on soles, you wet with branfy so sugar stick."

"Aha!" I exclaimed. "Now I get it! If there's no vodka, the sugar won't work, and without the sugar, the shoes won't squeak. As it says in the Bible, 'Without food, there is no Torah.' " I opened my wallet and gave Karpa everything I had left from my Chanukah and Purim money. We parted on friendly terms as Karpa shoved his big, glue-stained hand in mine. I hurried home for lunch and from there, sped back to cheder where I bragged to all my friends about the fine clothing that was being made for me for Passover—a jacket with a split and a pocket in the back and shoes that squeaked! Squeaked! Squeaked!

"Momma, no more school!" I ran into the house a few days before Passover proclaiming the great news to my mother that we had been let out of school early.

"Just what I needed! May you live to bring home better news!" my mother scowled, all caught up with preparations for Passover. She and both servant girls had tied white kerchiefs on their heads and, armed with brushes and feather dusters, the three of them were busily cleaning and mopping, scrubbing and scouring, waxing and polishing, getting the house clean and kosher for Passover. Nothing, not a speck of food, not an item of clothing, not a single eating utensil used during the year could be allowed in the house for Passover. All those things were *chometz.* I couldn't find a spot for myself without being told to move. Wherever I sat and wherever I went—no good!

"Get away from the clean Passover cupboard with that *chometz* clothing!" my mother screamed at me with such alarm you would have thought I had lit a match near gunpowder. "Careful, you're stepping on a Passover sack!" and "Don't you even dare to *look* over there, at that Passover borscht!"

I wandered from one place to the next, always underfoot; a shove, a smack, or a pinch always awaited me. "What came over that rebbi of yours? Couldn't he keep you in cheder another day? As if we didn't have enough work to do, who needs you hanging around? Some people's children sit in one place like they're supposed to. Isn't there something better a boy your age can do with himself? Why don't you go over the Four Questions?"

"But Momma," I said, "I already know them by heart."

"So?" said my mother. "Would it hurt to go over them again?"

At last evening came; it wasn't easy, but I made it. My father went around the house with a candle, a wooden spoon, and a feather duster searching out the last of the

bread. I helped him find the bread crumbs which he himself had placed on the window sills as part of the ritual.

"Only twenty-four hours to go!" I thought. "Only one
more night and one more day and then I'll be able to get
all dressed up for Passover like a prince, in a new jacket
with a split and a pocket in the back, and shoes that will
squeak as I walk. I'll bet Momma will ask, 'What's all that
squeaking?' and I'll pretend I don't know what she's talking about. And what about the seder, the Four Questions,
the four glasses of wine, and all the Passover treats: latkes, dumplings, pastries . . ." Just thinking about these
dishes made my mouth water. I had hardly eaten a thing
all day.

"Finish up your evening prayers," my mother said,
"and go to bed. There's no supper tonight; it's the night
before Passover."

I went to sleep and dreamed it was already Passover. I
was going to shul with my father. My new clothes were
crackling, my new shoes were squeaking—Squeak!
Squeak! Squeak! "Who is *that*?" strangers wanted to
know. "That's Mottel, Moishe-Chayim Avraham-Hersh
Reuven's son." Suddenly, from out of nowhere, a black,
shaggy dog leaped up at me—"Bow-wow!"—and grabbed
hold of my jacket with his teeth. My father, afraid to
come near, tried to chase the dog away by making threatening gestures with his hands and shouting, "Scat! Scat!"
The dog didn't obey him and continued to tear at my
coat from behind, right where the split and the pocket
were, ripping off half the jacket and starting to run away
with it. I ran after him with all my might but lost a shoe. I

was left stuck in the mud with one shoe on and one bare foot. I started to cry and scream, "Help! Help! Help!"

I awoke with a start and saw our servant girl, Bayla, standing near me, yanking my blanket off and tugging at my leg.

"It's impossible to wake him up! Come on, get up! Your mother told me to get you up. You have to help carry out the last of the *chometz*."

My father tossed the wooden spoon, the feather duster, and the last of the *chometz* into the oven. The house was officially ready for Passover—clean everywhere, kosher everywhere, the table set, the wine glasses winking at me from across the room. Soon, soon, in an hour, in just one hour, I would be getting dressed for the holiday. But until the tailor and the shoemaker came with my Passover outfit, my mother found time to get me ready for the holiday in her own way. She shampooed my hair with hot, soapy water in which she had dissolved an egg yolk. She combed my hair, yanking it hard. If I so much as cringed, she would jab me with her elbow or slap me. "Stop wriggling like a worm, hear? Did you ever see such a child who can't stand still? You do nice things for him and he still isn't satisfied!"

I survived the shampoo, thank God, and sat at the table in my shirt waiting for my new outfit to arrive. I looked over at my father, who had just come back from the bathhouse, his earlocks still damp. He was sitting bent over a thick book silently studying a portion from the Gemorah, humming and swaying gently.

As I looked at my father, I imagined that nowhere in the world was there a man as virtuous as he, that nowhere in the world was there a more perfect Passover than ours, and nowhere in the world could clothes like mine be found. But why weren't they here yet? What was the delay? What if they weren't ready in time for the beginning of Passover? I refused to even *think* of that! How would I go to shul? What would my friends say? How would I sit at the seder table? God forbid! I'd never live it down!

As I sat considering these grim possibilities, the door opened and in came Yisroel the tailor with my suit. Thrilled to see him, I sprang up excitedly and fell over together with my chair, almost breaking my neck. My mother ran in from the kitchen with a Passover ladle in her hand. "What was that loud noise? Who fell down? Who? It's *you*, is it? May the devil take you, God forbid! A demon! An imp! Did you hurt yourself, God protect you? Serves you right! Don't run! Don't jump! Walk the way you're supposed to!" And to Yisroel she said, "You kept your word, Reb Yisroel—I was about to send for you."

Yisroel gave a half-smile and waved his hand, as if to say, "What did you expect? Did you think I wouldn't keep my word?"

My mother put down the ladle and helped me into the new trousers and then put on the fringed undergarment that she herself had sewn for Passover. On top of that she put on the jacket and seemed content that it was roomy and wide enough.

Immediately, I felt around behind me in the back of

the coat. Oh! Oh! Big problems! A disaster! Not a sign of a split or a pocket! Sewn up, smooth and even, all around!

"What's this bunched-up sausage here?" my mother suddenly wanted to know as she turned me around.

Yisroel took out his snuffbox, cupped his hand, poured in a little mound of snuff, and inhaled it quickly.

"What's this bunched-up sausage here?" my mother repeated more loudly and turned me around the other way.

"That's the extra fold you ordered. Did you forget already?"

"That's some fold!" said my mother, giving me another turn. "It's an awful mess, shameful! Shameful! A disgrace, absolutely a disgrace!"

Yisroel's pride was, I assure you, not injured. He studied me carefully from head to toe like a professor and said that it fit extraordinarily well, couldn't be better. "Such workmanship can't be found even in Paris. The jacket *sings*, as I am a Jew, it actually *sings*!"

"This kind of singing appeals to you?" said my mother and led me over to my father. "What do you say to this song?"

My father turned me around and around, examined the suit, and allowed as how the trousers were indeed a bit too long. Yisroel removed the snuffbox again and honored my father with a sniff.

"Reb Yisroel, don't you think perhaps the pants are on the long side?"

"Ha? What? On the long side, you say? Don't you know what to do? You roll them up!"

"Maybe you're right," said my father. "But what do we do about the width? The legs look like two sacks."

"Some complaint! That's like saying the bride is too beautiful," said Yisroel and took another sniff. "Too wide, did you say? Narrow is worse, a thousand times worse!"

I couldn't stop feeling around the back of the coat, searching in vain for a split or a pocket.

"What are you looking for back there?" my mother said. "Where yesterday went?"

"You swindler!" I thought to myself, looking at Yisroel with hatred. "You rotten, lying, deaf old swindler!"

"Wear it in good health!" Yisroel the deaf tailor said to me after he had settled his account. My father returned to his studies, resuming the same chanting.

"Wear it well!" my mother said to me after Yisroel the tailor had left. She couldn't stop admiring my jacket. "If only you don't start up with any bullies or get into any fights with the peasant boys, you'll be able to wear that suit forever, may you live and be well."

"Well, well, here's Reb Gedalyeh!" said my mother. "Speaking of the devil! Are the boy's shoes ready?"

"What do you mean? Of course they're ready!" said Gedalyeh the shoemaker with a little dance step, holding the polished shoes on his two fingers as one would hold two freshly caught fish. "It's unbelievable! The whole world wants shoes ready for Passover. I worked my fingers to the bone, didn't sleep a wink! Me, when I give my word, neither thunder nor lightning can stop me."

My mother helped me on with my shoes, then pinched and squeezed my feet and asked me if they were, heaven forbid, too tight.

"Too tight?" said Gedalyeh. "It seems to me that you can put another pair of feet in those shoes!"

"Here, stand up!" said my mother. I stood up and pressed down on the soles, hoping to hear them squeak. What! Not a sound out of them!

"Why are you pressing down so hard?" asked my mother. "Don't worry, they're big enough for now, but I guarantee you'll wear them out before Passover, may we live and be well, if you keeping pushing down on them. Now go with your father to Yechiel the hatter and he'll pick out a nice holiday hat for you. But be careful with the shoes! Don't stomp so hard on the soles! They're not made of iron!"

Yechiel the hatter's shop was near our house, right across the courtyard. Yechiel, as luck would have it, was born pale and fair with very light blond hair, but since he always handled black-dyed hats, he was constantly stained. His nose was almost completely blue and his fingers looked as if they had been dipped in ink.

"Welcome, neighbor, come in!" Yechiel the hatter said to us cheerfully. "Who's the holiday hat for? For you or your son?"

"For my son," my father replied proudly. "I want you

to show me something really nice . . . something special . . . you know what I mean? . . ."

"I just happen to have exactly what you want," said Yechiel and took several hats off the shelf, making one twirl around on his finger as he removed it. One after another, he tried the hats on me, stepped back, looked at my face smilingly, and said to my father, "May this year be as blessed as this hat fits him! Well? How do you like that one? That's *really* a hat!"

"No, Reb Yechiel, that's not what I meant," said my father as he scanned the shelves. "I was thinking of a hat that would be . . . *you* know, more 'Jewish' . . . but stylish . . . without any frills . . . well made . . . and . . . and . . . and . . . do you know what I mean?"

"Why didn't you say so?" said Yechiel, and with a long pole, he quickly removed from the top shelf an oval-shaped hat with a colorfully checkered design and a soft brim. He carried it on one finger, spinning it around quickly like a windmill. Then, carefully, he set it on the top of my head so that it barely touched, as if my head were made of spun glass and he was afraid of shattering it. He wished that the year to come would be as suitable to him as this hat was for me. He had, he swore, just one hat like this left. My father bargained with him and Yechiel protested that only to us would he give the hat away so cheaply, almost below cost, may he have a kosher Passover and a healthy life.

I could tell that the hat really pleased my father because he kept coming over to me, admiring it, and smoothing down my earlocks.

"I hope it lasts a summer," said my father.

"Two summers!" cried Yechiel, hopping over to my father. "Three summers! May I live and be well, that's a fine hat! Wear it in good health!"

By the time I reached home, the hat was already down over my ears. I was beginning to suspect that it was a bit large for me.

"Don't fret. So long as it isn't tight," said my mother, pulling the hat down to my nose. "Just don't keep taking it on and off every minute! Don't touch it with your hands! Wear it in good health!"

All my friends were already at shul that evening when my father and I arrived. There stood Itzik and Berel, Leibel and Isaac, Tzadduk and Velvel, Shmaya and Koppel, Mayer and Chayim Sholem, Shachneh and Shepsel, and more and more. All were dressed up in their holiday outfits, all with new jackets, all with new shoes and new hats. But no one wore as long a jacket with a "fold" as mine, no one wore shoes as huge as mine, and I didn't see anyone with a hat as strange as mine. And as for a split, a pocket, squeaky shoes—not at all! I had really been taken in, deceived!

The boys greeted me with laughter. "*Those* are the new clothes you were bragging about? Where's the split in the back? Where's the pocket you said you'd have? How come we don't hear your shoes squeaking?"

I was suffering enough as it was, but they really rubbed salt in the wounds. Each boy humiliated me with his own clever remark:

Itzik said: "What kind of a quilt is that?"

Berel: "A horse blanket!"

Leibel: "A coarse blanket!"

Isaac: "A horse crank-it!"

Tzadduk: "A crock!"

Velvel: "A frock!"

Shmaya: "A petticoat!"

Koppel: "Look at that pair of canal boats!"

Mayer: "And that bat for a hat!"

Chayim Sholem: "A pot for a hat!"

Shachneh: "A noodle bowl!"

Shepsel: "A garbage pail!"

I was so furious that I didn't even hear how beautifully Hersh-Ber the cantor was chanting. I didn't calm down until the congregation was wishing one another, "Happy holiday! Goot yom-tov!" With a heavy heart, I went home with my father, barely able to drag my feet. I felt as if my insides were on fire. I was in no mood to enjoy the four glasses of wine we would soon be drinking, the Four Questions I would soon be asking my father, the Haggadah we would soon be reciting, the delicious peppered fish we would be eating, dipping our matzos in the sauce, the hot dumplings, the Passover pastries and the latkes along with all the other marvelous dishes. Everything, everything seemed so unappealing, dull, ruined, utterly ruined!

At the head of the seder table sat my father, the king, wearing his white linen robe and his velvet Passover hat. He was leaning comfortably on his pile of pillows. Beside

him sat my mother, the queen, in her old-fashioned
dress, wearing her silk kerchief and the fine pearls which
so enhanced her beauty. I, the prince, sat opposite them,
clad entirely in new clothes from head to toe. On one side
of me sat Bayla, the servant girl, decked out in her new
chintz smock and white starched apron which crackled
like a matzo. On my other side sat the cook, Brayna, a
woman with whiskers, wearing a new yellow kerchief on
her head. She held her head in one hand and swayed
back and forth, ready to listen to the reciting of the
Haggadah.

"*Keho lachman aniyah*—this bread of affliction," sang
the king with a pleasant voice, and the queen helped him
raise the matzo platter to show all assembled. Her face
was shining and bright as a star. Bayla lowered her red
hands to her white apron, which rustled like a leaf. As
soon as Brayna the cook heard the first Hebrew word,
she put on a pious expression and screwed her face up,
ready to cry.

Everyone was in a good mood, in fine holiday spirits,
except for the prince who was out of sorts. His heart felt
as if it had turned to stone, his eyes were glazed. Were it
not Passover night, he would have broken down and
cried and perhaps that would have made him feel better.

"*Hashanah avdi*—this year we are slaves," the king
sang out with pride. "*L'shanah habah b'nai chorin*—next
year we will be free."

The king leaned back on his pile of pillows and everyone else followed suit. They all waited for the prince to

rise and ask the Four Questions, which began with *"Ma nishtanah halaylah hazeh—*wherefore is this night different from all other nights of the year?" Then the king would respond by relating the story of Passover: *"Avodim hayinu—*slaves we were . . ." But the prince remained seated as if welded to his chair. He couldn't move.

"Well?" said the king.

"Stand up," said the queen. "Ask your father the Four Questions."

The prince didn't budge. He felt as if somebody had clamped his throat in a vice and was strangling him. He couldn't hold his head up straight. His eyes felt as if they would pop out of their sockets. Two tears, like two pearls, slipped from his eyes down his cheeks and fell onto the Haggadah.

"What's the matter? Why this sudden crying right in the middle of the seder?" the queen scolded me angrily. "Is this the way you thank us for the new holiday clothes we had made for you?"

The prince wanted to stop crying but couldn't; he was too choked with tears. Suddenly the tears gushed out, as if a floodgate had burst.

"Speak! What's the matter with you? What's hurting you? Why don't you answer? Tell us, or do you want your father to put you across his knee and give you a spanking in honor of Passover?"

The prince stood up, trying with difficulty to pull himself together, and stumbled over his words, "Question, I wish to ask you the Four Fathers . . . I mean, Father, I wish to ask you the Four Ques– Que . . ."

The prince's legs buckled under him and he collapsed with his head on the white tablecloth, sobbing and blubbering like an infant.

"A ruined Passover! A ruined Passover!"

The Esrog

MY REAL NAME IS ORI LEIB but I've always been called Leibel, and in cheder they nicknamed me "Leib-Dreib-Obderik." In our cheder every boy had a rhyming nickname: Mottel-Kappotel, Mayer-Drayer, Mendel-Fendel, Chayim-Klayim, Itzik-Shpitzik, Berel-Tzop. How do you like that for rhyming? Certainly Itzik goes with Shpitzik, Mendel with Fendel, and Chayim with Klayim—quite understandable; but how does Berel go with Tzop? And how do you figure Leib-Dreib-Obderik? It drove me wild. I would fight over it constantly and get more than my share of pushes, shoves, pokes, jabs, punches, and socks from all sides. I was made black and blue because I was the smallest one in our cheder, the smallest and the weakest and the poorest—a circumstance that counted for little in Kasrilevka. No one ever stood up for me or defended my cause. On the contrary, if two rich boys beat me up, one straddling me like a horse and the other twisting my ear, a third boy, a poor man's son like myself, would stand alongside, egging them on, chanting:

Atta boy! Atta boy!
Give it to him! Give it to him!
Twist 'em off! Twist 'em off!
Atta boy! Atta boy!

I would lie still as a kitten, but when they finally let me up, I would go off into a corner and cry quietly. Then I would dry my eyes, pull myself together, and slip back with the gang, trying to act as if nothing had happened. So, whenever you read the name "Leibel" in this story, know that it's me.

In appearance, I might have struck you as short and chubby, even fat. But really, I wasn't fat. I was actually skinny. I looked fat because I wore heavy quilted cotton trousers, a heavy quilted cotton shirt, and a heavy quilted cotton jacket. My mother wanted to make sure that I was warm and wouldn't catch cold, God forbid, so she wrapped me in quilted cotton from head to toe. But she didn't realize that cotton batting can come in handy. Cotton batting can be wadded into balls, and balls can be thrown. So I distributed cotton batting to all the boys, pulling it out of my trousers and my jacket until my mother noticed it, and then I received even more pushes, shoves, pokes, jabs, punches, and socks. But that didn't stop me. I went on being the supplier of cotton batting to all comers. Whoever wanted helped himself to my cotton batting, and whoever was so inclined beat me to within an inch of my life.

"Leib-Dreib-Obderik! Serves him right! Serves him right!"

But I had something else in mind to tell you. I wanted to tell a story about an esrog but I got carried away who-knows-where.

My father, Moshe Yankel the clerk, had been working in a tax collector's office for as long as anyone could remember. He earned four and a half rubles a week and was looking forward to getting a raise. Once he received his raise, with God's help, he said he would buy an esrog, that special exotic citron so important to the Sukkos ceremony. But my mother, Batya Beile the clerk's wife, as she was called, didn't count on such good luck. "Cows will have kittens," she said, "before a tax collector will give you a raise." Once, before Rosh Hashanah, Leibel overheard this exchange between his parents:

"I don't care if the world turns upside down, but this Sukkos we must have our own esrog!"

"The world won't turn upside down and you won't have an esrog."

"That's what you say. What would you say if I told you I was promised a bonus toward an esrog?"

"That will be the day. It will go into the record books, I'm sure. But if I don't believe it, don't be too surprised."

"I don't care what you believe. I tell you that this Sukkos we are going to have our own esrog."

"Amen, let's hope so. From your mouth into God's ear."

"Amen! Amen! Amen!" Leibel said to himself and already pictured his father going to shul like a respected elder with his own esrog and with his own lulav, the ceremonial bundle of palm, myrtle, and willow branches.

Then he could promenade before the Holy Ark like the other wealthy Jews who sat near the eastern wall. Leibel's heart was full of joy and pride. He could picture it in his mind. First, as usual, would come Reb Melech the cantor, like a general, step by step, his head held majestically high, chanting in his pure tenor voice, "*Hosa-na, aniyah soarah, hosa-na!*" Behind him followed the rabbi, a frail, perspiring man, his prayer shawl almost covering his face. After the rabbi, the assistant rabbi, a man with a yellow parchmentlike skin, broad shoulders, and a fat belly which quivered underneath his shiny satin gaberdine. Then came the elders, the rich folks, the cream of the congregation, followed by the merchants, who were in turn followed by the small-businessmen and so on and so forth, one behind the other, a rich man behind a rich man, a merchant behind a merchant, each according to his station, each according to his rank, like an army marching to battle. Leibel could see his father slipping in among the finest merchants, holding his esrog proudly.

After Leibel overheard the conversation between his parents about buying their own esrog, he couldn't keep the news to himself. He let it be known in cheder that this Sukkos his family would have an esrog, their very own esrog. But no one believed him no matter how much he insisted.

"What's going on with his father?" the fellows jeered among themselves. "That pauper, that down-and-out pauper is going to buy his own esrog? I bet he thinks it's a lemon or an apple you can buy for a groshen."

The young ones chanted along:

Leib-Dreib-Obderik!
Made up a lie!
Made up a lie!

And along with the jeering and the chanting, they honored him, as always, with pushes, shoves, pokes, jabs,
punches, and socks. This incident really upset Leibel, as
you might expect, and he began to doubt whether his father, a poor man, had the right to desire something
beyond his means. Imagine his surprise when he came
home and discovered Henzel the shochet wearing his
Napoleonic cap, sitting with his father at the table. In
front of them stood a basket of esrogs whose presence
were made known by their heavenly aroma.

The cap which Henzel the shochet wore was the kind
of hat worn in the time of the first Napoleon. In France
the hat has long since gone out of style, but to Kasrilevka
somehow one such cap had found its way, and it belonged to Henzel the shochet. The cap was long and narrow and had a split in the front, and at the base of the
split there was a gold button from which hung two tassels.
I was always fascinated by those tassels. If this cap were
ever to fall into my hands for so much as two minutes,
those tassels would be mine! That was my scheme. But
Henzel never removed the cap from his head, and I
somehow imagined that the tassels, the cap, Henzel's earlocks, and his head had grown together into one piece
because when he spoke and gestured with his hands, his
earlocks would shake and the tassels would bounce in

unison. Reb Henzel the shochet laid out his wares, selected one esrog, and, holding it carefully between two
fingers, brought it over to my father, indicating that this
was the one for him.

"Now, if you take this esrog, Reb Moshe Yankel, you
will get a lot of pleasure from it because it is, I assure you,
a gem, one in a million."

"But is it from the island of Corfu?" my father asked,
examining the esrog from every angle as one does a diamond, his hands trembling with excitement.

"What do *you* think?" the cap replied, shaking with
laughter. "Nowhere else *but* from Corfu!"

My father couldn't take his eyes off the esrog, so delighted was he with it, and he summoned my mother to
come and admire it, beaming as he did so as one beams at
an expensive piece of jewelry or at a beloved, treasured
child. My mother approached silently, slowly reaching
out to touch the esrog, to hold it, but no!

"Easy with the hands! Just a sniff, if you wish."

My mother had to be content with a sniff, but I wasn't
even allowed that much. I couldn't even get close enough
for a look because it was considered too dangerous.

"Look who's here," said my mother. "Just give him
half a chance and the next thing you know, he'll bite off
the stem of the esrog and it will be spoiled for the ceremony."

"God forbid!" exclaimed my father, frightened by
such awful words.

"Heaven protect us!" added the cap, its tassels bouncing.

Reb Henzel provided us with some soft flax in which to wrap the esrog, whose aroma permeated every corner of the room.

Like a diamond or a rare gemstone or a cherished heirloom which has been entrusted for safekeeping, as precious as life itself, so was the esrog treated—tenderly swaddled in flax, as one would a delicate child to protect it from becoming chilled, gently tucked into its nest of flax, and carefully placed in a fine, round wooden sugar box that had been carved and painted. The sugar had been removed with apologies to make room for the beloved guest.

"Welcome, welcome, Reb Esrog! In you go, into the sugar box." Properly blanketed with flax, covered with the lid, placed in the cupboard, the glass door shut, we bid it good night.

"I've got this terrible feeling that this mischief-maker"—meaning me—"is going to be fooling around near the cupboard, God help him, and he just might bite off the stem of the esrog!" my mother warned a second time, took me by the arm, and dragged me away from the cupboard.

Have you ever seen a cat sniffing out some cream? It springs down from the mantel, straightens out its back, paces in circles, rubs itself against the furniture, looking everyone in the eye and licking its fur. So, for a long time, Leibel hovered around the cupboard, gazing through the glass door, smiling at the box which held the esrog till his mother caught him at it and informed his father that the trouble-maker was after the esrog. So he chased Leibel off: "Back to cheder with you! Out of my sight!"

Leibel lowered his eyes and looked down at his feet and ran off to cheder.

In cheder, when we studied the story of Adam and Eve, I used to wonder what would have happened had God placed them in the Garden of Eden without telling them which was the forbidden fruit. The snake would have been powerless to influence Eve to partake of the Tree of Knowledge, Eve would not have offered the apple to Adam, God would not have been angry at them, they would not have been driven from the vineyard, and we might still be strolling in the Garden of Eden to this day. The men would most likely be sitting and studying, the women would be mending socks or plucking chickens, and we boys would most likely be roaming the hills, climbing Mount Ararat, picking dates, eating pomegranates, stuffing our pockets with carob, and swimming all day in Lake Pishun.

Those suggestive words that his mother had uttered to his father, "Just give him half a chance and the next thing you know, he'll bite off the stem of the esrog," worked in Leibel like a poison, entering into his very bones.

From that moment on, the "stem of the esrog" preyed on Leibel's mind, never leaving his thoughts for a moment, coming to him in his dreams, harassing him, whispering in his ear, "Don't you recognize me, silly boy? It's me, me, the stem." Leibel would turn over on his other side and try to fall asleep again but the cajoling wouldn't stop. "Get up, silly, go open the cupboard door, take the esrog out, and bite me off. You will love my delicious taste."

In the morning, after washing up, Leibel hurried off to say his morning prayers, taking his breakfast along with him. On the way out he caught a glimpse of the box which held the esrog through the glass cupboard door and he imagined that it actually winked at him, calling out to him, enticing him, "Come here, come here, young man." Leibel ran off to cheder as fast as his legs could carry him.

One fine morning, Leibel woke up and found he was all alone in the house. His father was at the office, his mother was at the market, the girl who helped out was somewhere in the kitchen, the baby was in the cradle in a deep, smiling slumber, its little hands held alongside its head. "Angels must be playing with the baby," Leibel mused as he washed his hands, shot a quick glance at the cupboard through the glass door, and saw the box. It winked at him, called to him, tempted him. "Here! Come here, young man!" Slowly, slowly, Leibel approached the cupboard, opened the glass door, removed the box—the fine, round, wooden, carved, painted box—raised the lid, and even before he could remove the flax from the esrog, its sharp, pungent aroma assailed his nostrils, the very fragrance of the Garden of Eden. Before Leibel knew what had happened, the esrog was in his hands and the stem was staring him in the face. "Want to taste something delicious? Something out of this world? Come, bite me off! Don't be afraid, silly, no one will ever know, no one will ever tell."

Can you guess what happened? Did I bite off the stem of the esrog or did I restrain myself? I would like to know what you would have done in my place if someone had repeated ten times over that you shouldn't dare bite off the stem of the esrog. Wouldn't you be curious and want to know what the stem of an esrog tasted like?

Moshe Yankel the clerk did his work in an office and was not handy enough to build a sukkah, but his neighbor, Zalman the carpenter, was up to the job. Zalman the carpenter had plenty of lumber for the sukkah and we contributed sheets, pillowcases, and blankets with which to cover the walls. For her part, Batya Beile the clerk's wife would bake him challahs for the holidays. Zalman the carpenter was a recent widower with eight orphaned children. Batya Beile offered to help his eldest daughter, Tzivieh, make the gefillte fish, because no one in Kasrilevka could make gefillte fish like Batya Beile. And bear in mind that it was worth a good deal to have an esrog to share for the ceremony.

"You will have an equal share in the esrog with us," said Batya Beile the clerk's wife.

"Only for the blessing," Moshe Yankel the clerk hastened to correct her.

"What did you think I would do, eat it?" the carpenter retorted.

Zalman wasn't the only one who was looking forward to performing the ceremony in the sukkah. All of his children looked forward to that time as if the Messiah Himself were going to come. What a thrill it would be to hold the esrog in one hand and the lulav in the other and to recite the blessing, *"Al nitelles lulav,"* and to shake the lulav, *Trrrrr!*

"How many days till Sukkos?" they asked one another and counted the days.

The day before Sukkos, Moshe Yankel the clerk was occupied with tying the lulav together—the palm, myrtle, and willow branches—and readying everything in the best possible way for the holiday. The decorated and bound lulav was placed by my father in a corner on top of the cupboard, leaning against the wall where it looked as if it were resting. It wasn't necessary to warn Leibel not to touch the lulav because it was too high for him to reach and even if he were to stand on a stool, nothing would come of it. The stool would likely topple over, he would come crashing down, breaking his neck, get a proper scolding, and have something to tell his grandchildren.

There was another reason why Leibel wouldn't bother the lulav. In fact, he wasn't even thinking of the lulav. All he could think of was the possibility that, God forbid, someone would find out about the stem of the esrog being bitten off. True, Leibel had immediately stuck the severed stem back on the esrog with spit, but who knew how long spit would hold? God Almighty, what would happen? What possible excuse could he give? How would he be able to look his parents in the eyes and tell an outright lie, saying that he knew nothing about it? And why did he have to do it in the first place? What good did it do him? What kind of taste does the stem of an esrog have anyway? It was—phooey!—bitter as gall, horrid, nauseating!

For nothing he had gone and ruined a holy fruit, spoiled an esrog, and such a beautiful esrog. The fruit was useless now. Of this he had been assured by his friends in cheder. Why did he have to do it? What made him do it? He was little more than a murderer, having assaulted a living thing, bitten off its head, and taken its life. Why? For what reason? What had it ever done to him? Wherever he went, he constantly saw before him the decapitated esrog, the mutilated esrog, yellow as wax, without a breath of life, a corpse, a headless corpse.

The esrog came to him in a dream, tugging at his nightshirt, wakening him, "What did you have against me? Why did you bite off my stem? Now I'm useless, useless, useless . . . !"

Leibel turned over on his other side, groaned, and fell asleep again but the voices wouldn't stop. "Murderer! What did you have against my stem? My stem . . . My stem . . ."

At last it was the first day of Sukkos. After an early morning frost, the sun rose in a clear blue sky, drenching the earth in a wonderfully joyous light that quickened one's pulse and filled one's heart with a strange feeling, that singular yearning for a summer that had fled all too quickly. The sun shone but did not warm—"like a stepmother," as they used to say in Kasrilevka. It just wasn't the same warmth as in summertime. One didn't note those special shades of green as in summertime, one didn't hear the peeping of the birds as in summertime. All, all had vanished with the first windy day of Elul, the first month of autumn. Not so quickly would the warmth of the sun return, not so quickly would that special shade of green or that peeping of the birds return. Before that time the earth would be frozen solid; before that time there would be more than enough snowstorms, cold winds, gales, and blizzards. The world would experience its annual icy upheaval before it would again awaken from its frigid slumber, cast off its frozen mantle, and clothe itself in a brand-new green garment, reviving valleys and hills, lakes and oceans, trees and flowers, wild beasts and cattle, people and fowl and all living things on earth.

On that day, Moshe Yankel the clerk arose early to look over the holiday service and to sing through the familiar holiday melodies. On that day, Batya Beile the clerk's wife arose early to prepare the holiday fish, the holiday farfel, and the holiday carrot tsimmes. On that day, Zalman the carpenter arose early to make the blessing on the esrog in the sukkah first so that he could drink his tea with milk at his leisure before dressing for the holiday.

"Reb Zalman is asking for the esrog and the lulav," my mother said to my father.

"Open the cupboard and take out the box, but be very, very careful!" my father said to her and himself placed a stool near the cupboard so that he could reach the lulav. He took the trouble to accompany the carpenter to the sukkah so that he would be present when Zalman fulfilled this important commandment.

"Here now, take it, but gently, and make the blessing on the esrog," my father told the carpenter. "In the name of God, gently."

Zalman the carpenter, God bless him, was a huge man with large hands, every finger of which was capable of knocking down three Leibels with one blow. On each giant finger was a large fingernail, always sticky with glue and stained red with shellac. When he ran his nail over a board, it left a deep furrow as if made by the sharp point of an awl. In honor of the holiday, Zalman had put on a white shirt and a new coat. He had spent hours in the bath scrubbing his hands with soap, ashes, and sand but to little avail. His hands remained sticky and his nails stained with shellac as before.

It was into these hands that the fragile, redolent esrog was entrusted. Moshe Yankel the clerk had reason to tremble with fear as Zalman the carpenter grasped the esrog, gave it a squeeze, and shook the lulav heartily.

"Easy, easy!" my father moaned worriedly. "Now, be sure to turn the esrog so the stem is on top and say the blessing, but gently, gently, for the love of God, gently."

Suddenly Moshe Yankel the clerk's body jerked back and he screamed "Oh!" in such an unnaturally loud and alarming voice that Batya Beile the clerk's wife came running into the sukkah.

"What's the matter, Moshe Yankel? May God help you!"

"You oaf! You clumsy oaf!" he screamed at the carpenter, ready to kill him on the spot. "How could you be so clumsy? What an ox! Is an esrog a hammer? A chisel? A drill? It isn't a hammer! It isn't a chisel! It isn't a drill! You've killed me as surely as if you had slit my throat! You've destroyed my esrog! Look at that poor stem—just look, you ignoramus! Clumsy ox that you are!"

We were all stunned, as if dead. Zalman the carpenter, poor man, was in a state of shock, unable to comprehend how such a calamity had occurred. How did it happen, how did the stem come off? He was almost sure that he had held the esrog ever so gently, barely touching it with his fingertips. A catastrophe! What a catastrophe! Moshe Yankel the clerk was also in a state of shock. He had not even had the chance to take the esrog to shul with him, had not even had the chance to say the first blessing over it, and already it was ruined! Why, why had he allowed such a beloved, treasured, noble fruit into such coarse, clumsy hands? Was this oaf of a carpenter too sick to go to shul and say the blessing over the community esrog?

"You clumsy oaf! You ignoramus!" Batya Beile the clerk's wife wept, wringing her hands. "Why, why did I ever believe we would have a little luck? I should have known better."

Leibel, too, was stunned, in a state of fear and remorse because of his father's woes, his mother's tears, and Zalman the carpenter's disgrace. Leibel didn't know whether to dance for joy that God had performed this miracle on his behalf, saving him from discovery and certain disaster, or whether he should cry over his father's misery, his mother's tears, and the carpenter's disgrace. Or should he throw his arms around the carpenter's neck and kiss him, kiss his calloused hands, his sticky fingers, and stained fingernails because he was his savior, his redeeming angel? Leibel glanced at his father's tragic face, at his mother's tears, at the carpenter's hands, at the esrog lying dead on the table, yellow as wax, without a stem, without a drop of life—a corpse, a headless corpse.

"A dead esrog," said my father, his voice breaking.

"A dead esrog," my mother repeated with tears in her eyes.

"A dead esrog," Zalman the carpenter echoed them, studying his hands, probably thinking, "What a pair of loathsome paws! May they wither and fall off!"

The Goldspinners

Purim is a happy holiday celebrated in the spring. The Book of Esther, which tells about the wicked Haman, is read, people exchange Purim presents of baked goods and sweets, and there are dramatized presentations of the story of Purim.

THE "GOLDSPINNERS"—WHO WERE THEY? Ask something easy, like how they spun gold. They were called by that name in Kasrilevka purely out of envy. They were envied, you see, because they knew how to make money. Don't get me wrong. They were poor people—may it never be your lot—just like the rest of the poor people in Kasrilevka. But when Purim came, they made money hand over fist. The Lord above had bestowed a blessing on each of them, giving to each a special talent, and the world envies people with talent. That fact is as old as the world itself. But instead of wasting any more time on these matters, we'll get right down to our story.

Naftali Long Legs was a Jew with remarkable legs which seemed to start right at his neck. Nobody could ever keep up with Naftali, not because he walked any faster but because his stride was so much longer. One moment he was right beside you and the next he was way ahead of you. Those legs were Naftali's capital, his tools of the trade, his bread and butter—in short, Naftali was a professional errand-runner.

When a wealthy landowner came to Kasrilevka once in a blue moon, Naftali would somehow get wind of it. His long legs would carry him speedily to the inn where the landowner was staying.

"My dear honorable sir, what is your wish?"

And whatever the landowner wished, Naftali would obtain it for him in no time flat: a tailor, a shoemaker, a blacksmith, a servant, a horse, a scythe, a kettle drum, a witch, a curse on his head—you name it! The word *no* was not in Naftali's vocabulary. The only problem was that Naftali didn't have the field to himself. There were in Kasrilevka almost as many Jews as there were errand-runners and more errand-runners than landowners.

Now you can understand how Naftali's legs were like money in the bank. Nevertheless, he still would have suffered had not God in His infinite wisdom favored His beloved people of Israel with Purim—that joyful, lively holiday. During that joyful, lively holiday Naftali's true talent shone forth in all its brilliance and glory. Naftali was a born performer, and his Purim plays were made to order for his long legs.

At first glance, you might think it ridiculous to connect Purim plays with legs, but don't take offense if I tell you that there is indeed a strong connection. Naftali

didn't play the roles of King Ahashuerus or Haman or
Mordecai or Vashti. He played the role of Memuchan,
King Ahashuerus's chamberlain, the man who ran the affairs of the court and palace. Whoever is acquainted with
the story of Ahashuerus knows that the role of Memuchan is a very important one. One could even say that the
whole play depends on him. Who calls Vashti to dance
before the King? Memuchan. Who advises the King what
must be done with Vashti when she refuses to dance?
Memuchan. Who arranges for Mordecai to confer with
Esther? Memuchan. Memuchan was here, Memuchan
was there, Memuchan was everywhere—Memuchan, Memuchan, Memuchan! And you should have seen how our
Memuchan worked those long legs. Here's an illustration:

The door opened and in came the Purim Players with
a big "Goot yom-tov!" Naturally, all the actors had stage
fright and hung back against the wall, their arms hanging
at their sides. But our Memuchan strode out on his long
legs with a sword in his hand and a paper hat on his
head. He took one long step here and another long step
there as he spouted rhymes. Let me tell you a secret: All
those rhymes spoken by Naftali which you will hear were
written by Naftali Long Legs himself:

> I, Memuchan, master of the court
> For crafty old King Ahashuerus
> (And also the master of his sport)
> Was sent to Vashti the Queen
> To command her to dance before the King
> In veils, bangles, and rings

And other shiny, noisy things.
O beautiful Vashti, obey, obey,
The King cannot wait for you all day.

Queen Vashti (Berel Stuffnose) reluctantly tore himself from the safety of the wall and answered him, also in rhymes written by Naftali, in a whining, nasal, singsong voice, like a nervous bridegroom:

Come hither, all ye women of Poras and Modai
And all ye matrons of Shushan,
Listen to my tale and sigh.
In the Megillah I'm always put down,
But the King is really the one to blame.
He's a nasty drunkard without fear or shame.

Memuchan then became all fired up, pacing back and forth on his long legs, reciting rhymes of his own invention:

What do you say to such outrageous stuff!
Well, take it from me, I've had enough!
If I could be sure that the King would not become upset
I'd cut off her wicked head myself without regret.

King Ahashuerus raised his long staff, which was wrapped in gold foil:

As far as I'm concerned, you can execute everyone
So long as you keep the whisky handy to the throne.
Why do all my ministers look like they've been cursed?
Hear now! Let's all quench our thirst!

> So fill your glasses and then shout, "Hey!"
> For now we'll drink and dance and play
> Until the sunlight brings the day!

And the company joined in:

> So fill your glasses and then shout, "Hey!"
> For now we'll drink and dance and play
> Until the sunlight brings the day!

Out stepped Mordecai (Nehemiah the shoemaker), a shabby hunchback with a beard made of flax. He knelt before the King and then addressed Memuchan, blinking his eyes strangely while gesticulating wildly with his hands and singing off key:

Since that day Your Majesty was left a lonely widower
Your royal word went forth alike to lord and commoner
Throughout the one hundred and twenty-seven countries
  of your kingdom
That maidens be brought before you—rich or poor,
  smart or dumb.
O my dear King! Do I have a lovely bride for you!
She's sweet as applesauce, fresh as morning dew,
Her name is Esther,
She has no brother or sister,
No father or mother,
Her nearest birthday is her twentieth,
Not counting holidays and the Sabbath . . .

Memuchan strode back and forth again with fire in his voice:

Hurry! Hurry! Let her come before us
To do a turn before King Ahashuerus,
And if he takes a shine to her,
He will place a crown on her.
And you, Mordecai, for your matchmaking deed
Will be given a haman-tash with poppy seed.
O beautiful Esther, obey, obey,
The King will make you his Queen today!

After the stage was set in this way, the real drama
began. Naftali's legs were stronger than iron to endure
this strenuous Purim undertaking. But out of this effort
Naftali realized a nice bundle of cash because he was,
after all, the director of the troupe, its producer, its
writer, and its treasurer all rolled into one.

"He spins gold, pure gold, that man, when Purim
comes!" So said all the Kasrilevka Jews who simply envied
him, not so much for his talent as for his success in business.

If Kasrilevka consumed as much honey cake, fruit
cake, and angel cake every day of the year as it did on
Purim when people exchanged Purim gifts of baked
goods, then Naftali Long Legs wouldn't have to go
through the trouble of being an errand-runner all year
and an actor on Purim. His wife, Sweet Rivella, as she
was called by everyone, would be able to support him and
his household with plenty to spare. If Naftali was famous
for his legs, then his wife, Rivella, was no less famous for
her hands.

Rivella was a slightly built woman, a thin, tiny creature who, alongside her husband, looked like a plucked chicken. To look at her, who would believe that this little woman was capable of supplying an entire town with sweets for Purim exchanged by the townspeople? It's true there were other women in Kasrilevka who were in the same business, but who possessed such golden hands as Sweet Rivella? Her tortes and her honey cakes, her shtrudels and angel cakes, her poppy seed cookies and gingerbreads, her braided buns had acquired a reputation throughout the world, even as far as Yehupotz, a neighboring town which was in a constant rivalry with Kasrilevka. And how did Yehupotz hear of Rivella? This is the way it happened:

There was this prankster from Kasrilevka, where there are as many pranksters as there are stars in the sky, who decided to play a trick by making fun of the town of Kasrilevka by, of all things, deriding its local products. So what did this prankster do? He mailed a package of Sweet Rivella's Purim cakes as a Purim gift to a rich relative in Yehupotz. In the Purim package he enclosed a letter, very nicely written, in which he asked the rich relative to forgive him for sending such poor stuff. The prankster added that he could find nothing worse in Kasrilevka. So imagine the prankster's surprise when he received a thank-you note from his rich relative with the request that he immediately buy up as much of these baked goods as possible, pack them up properly, and send them collect to Yehupotz. (As you know, rich folks in general, and rich folks from Yehupotz in particular, love to eat and especially crave sweets.) From that time on, whole cases of Rivella's sweets were sent off each year to the rich Yehupotz relative for Purim. And that's how Rivella's fame reached even as far as Yehupotz.

But if Rivella had had to depend on the Yehupotz business alone, she would have starved. The main part of her business was in her own hometown. During the few days before Purim, Sweet Rivella was up to her ears in work. Consider: She alone had to do all the baking, all the shopping, all the wrapping, and all the negotiations with all the housewives. Just to figure up the bills for the orders required the mind of a banker! Rivella had her difficulties, especially with customers like Sarah Pearl, who was rich enough to wear pearls even on weekdays.

"You owe me, Sarah Pearl, for a half-dozen honey cakes with raisins at six groshens apiece. Six times six—how much is six times six? Isn't it thirty-three? And four almond cakes you bought at eight groshens each. It cost me seven, I swear by my health—four times eight is forty-eight. Add two large braided buns without seeds and three small braided buns with seeds and I figure these five items come to twenty-four groshens. It costs me more, may we both be well—five times twenty-four? How much is that? Let's say it was six items, then it would come to a ruble plus six groshens, but since it's five items, it must come to a ruble minus six groshens. So how much is that altogether? Let's see: Thirty-three plus forty-eight equals eight-two plus one ruble and more than half a ruble plus twenty-two minus six groshens, so how much is left? Isn't that a ruble ninety?"

"How about that! What kind of sixty-two? Where did you get sixty-two?" shouted Sarah Pearl, and both women started figuring up the amounts all over again.

"May you live and be well, Sarah Pearl, the total is exactly right: A half-dozen honey cakes with raisins at six groshens apiece is—how much is six times six? Not forty-two?"

"Congratulations! You're doing very well! Just a minute ago it was thirty-three and now it's gone up to forty-two! Not bad!"

Rivella called Naftali away from his work. He was as angry as a hornet.

"What is it with these women? They can't add two and two together. Well? Let's see your figures, but hurry, time doesn't stand still, you know!" Naftali said furiously.

Both women presented him with the figures at the same time. Naftali listened with his eyes shut, counted on his fingers and quickly became confused and angrier. He flew at his wife. "I told you a thousand times that if you don't have the brains to add two and two together, you shouldn't be selling your goods in big amounts. You should sell them one at a time! I'll show you: What do you have there? One honey cake? Give me twenty-four groshens. Another honey cake? Another twenty-four groshens. A braided bun? That's six groshens. Another bun? Another six groshens. See?"

Sarah Pearl, the rich man's wife, wasn't about to allow

herself to be dealt with as if she were an ignorant pauper's wife, but she had no choice. Where else could she buy such delicious baked goods for Purim if not from Rivella? Came Purim and Rivella was the best. Everyone has his time. If you need a thief, you save him from the gallows. That's why everyone in town was so envious of her. "Golden hands . . . the gold piles up . . . both of them fill up sacks of gold when Purim comes."

Some people are blessed with beautiful singing voices, some with artistic hands, and some with dancing feet, but Noah, Naftali's eldest son, was blessed by nature with a talent for carving.

Even when Noah was a child, he was constantly being punished and nagged by his parents: "Did you ever see a boy who goes around day and night cutting and whittling and carving and carving and carving?"

In order to stop the child's nasty carving habit, they sent him to cheder and instructed the rebbi a hundred times to slap his hands if he saw him so much as holding a penknife. Better to make sure he studied the Torah. But the rebbi's efforts came to nothing. Noah left cheder with very little Torah. But he did display a rare mastery of carving. And he carved everything, whatever he laid his eyes on. There were experts in Kasrilevka who claimed that the boy possessed genius; were he to live in a big city, he would surely become . . . well, who knows *what* he might become!

Meanwhile, may his hands wither, on all the pews and all the lecterns in the synagogue, he carved figures of

humans and birds and, forgive me, pigs. For carving pigs
in the synagogue, Noah really caught it from his father,
from his mother, from the rabbi, and from the shul
elders. Whoever was offended by this deed let him have
it.

"Imagine what a boy can do—in a holy place—pigs!"

But that didn't teach our carver a lesson. However,
the spark glowing inside him—that heritage of his biblical
ancestor, Bezalel, architect of the Great Temple—
wouldn't be extinguished. His gift finally shone forth.
Like all such revelations, it came about unexpectedly
through a chance circumstance.

It happened a few days before Purim. He was given a
wooden Purim noisemaker as a gift, the kind that children shake in their hands while the story of Purim is read
in shul. Whenever the name of Haman, the villain of the
Megillah, is mentioned, all the children drown out the
sound of his name by making a racket with their noisemakers. Noah examined his noisemaker from every
angle, quietly taking it apart and putting it together
again. It occurred to him that if he only had something to
do it with, he could make a noisemaker that would put all
other noisemakers in the world to shame. Noah lacked
only two things—material and tools, that is, wood and a
knife. What to do? Well, wood was no problem. Wood
could be appropriated from his mother's woodpile near
the stove. But where could he get a tool, a knife? He hit
on a plan. He would go to the market and sell his present
noisemaker, and with the money, he would buy a knife.

But a misfortune occurred. (Misfortunes always happen to innovators!) The first customer Noah approached took him by the hand and led him straight to his father. "What's going on, Reb Naftali? Your son is selling noise-makers now?"

Of course our innovator had to suffer his punishment before having a chance to explain to his father why he needed the money. Only after Noah had confessed through bitter tears what his reason was, did Naftali, after calling him a dumb ox, buy him a knife and help him select the wood. Noah sat down immediately to his work and labored so intently that in just one day, several Purim noisemakers took shape under his hands, but such extraordinary noisemakers that the whole town came to gape and to congratulate Naftali.

"It's clear, Reb Naftali, that with this son, you have nothing to worry about. He's a moneymaker already!"

From that time on, the entire town, one and all, knew that if anyone wanted the best Purim noisemaker for his money, he would have to go to Naftali's son, Noah, the carver. And no matter how much merchandise Noah prepared, it was bought up instantaneously. Every year, when Purim was over, you could hear Noah saying the same thing: "This was a great year for noisemakers!"

There was good reason for the townspeople to envy Naftali his children. "Not only does *he* earn gold and not only does *she* earn gold, pulling it in from both sides when Purim comes, but they also have to have such talented children!"

. . .

If you want to see something really nice that won't cost you much, then take a trip to our Kasrilevka at Purim time. Stop at whatever inn you like, look outside, and be prepared to see something special. From early morning on you can see boys and girls, wrapped up warmly in shawls, most of them barefoot even though it's still cold out and there are snow flurries, splashing through the mud from house to house. In their hands they are carrying large cakes or platters or bowls covered with white napkins. These are all Jewish children delivering Purim gifts which the Kasrilevka women send one another, exchanging with each other the Purim goodies prepared by Sweet Rivella.

"Itta Leah sent me two braided buns and an angel cake and two almond tortes, so I'm sending her in return one braided bun and two angel cakes and two honey cakes and one almond torte. And Yenta Mirel sent me a shtrudel and two almond breads and two poppy seed cakes and a puff cake, so I'm sending her in return two puff cakes and one almond bread and one shtrudel and two poppy seed cakes."

That's the way the Kasrilevka ladies cleverly figured and combined and balanced their exchanges so that no one would feel slighted and no one would seem too generous—in other words, an equal exchange. And since everyone in town was friendly with everyone else, there were many people exchanging Purim gifts. Even with the help of servants and one's own children, it was impossible to manage. One had to depend on others for all the exchanges. Poor boys and girls who were willing to run errands to earn Passover money were in short supply.

The luckiest were the poor people who had the most children. In Kasrilevka there were many such lucky people. But the luckiest of all were the Goldspinners, who had so many sons and daughters that it was a wonder even for Kasrilevka. I can't even tell you exactly how many they had because you're not supposed to count other people's children. May they just grow up and be healthy. What harm do they do anyone? Wintertime they huddled around the oven like little kittens, and summertime they roamed the streets playing games, raising such a cloud of dust that the street darkened and a passerby could suffocate! Fists would fly and curses were heard that would singe your ears.

But when Purim came, the children felt that they, too, were suddenly worth something—a good deal, in fact! Everyone wanted them for himself. When a Kasrilevka lady put in her baking order to Rivella, she also reserved the time of one of Rivella's children to deliver the cakes. Rivella's children were dispersed throughout the town, carrying napkin-covered trays and bowls full of baked goods. Their cheeks were flushed, their foreheads beaded with sweat, their eyes aglow with excitement. Their paths would cross in the muddy streets but they had not even a minute to stop and peek at what the other was carrying. But in passing, they would hurriedly exchange a phrase or two, so abbreviated that a stranger might not understand altogether what they were saying.

"Fatty! Where to?"

"To Big Leah's. And you, Pigeon-toes?"

"To the old lady with the long nose. Make anything?"

"Not much. And you?"

"I already have a ruble and twelve groshens. And you, how much?"

"No time to count, but more than you, I think."

"Wipe your nose!"

"Break your head!"

And they separated, each going his own way.

The Kasrilevka townspeople had been sitting at their Purim dinner tables for quite a while, singing *"Shoshanas Yaakov,"* having already heartily enjoyed Naftali Long Legs's Purim Players while Naftali's children were still running from house to house delivering Purim gifts and gathering coins from the folks, who enjoyed teasing them.

"Come here, little boy, who are you? Aren't you Naftali's boy?"

"Naftali's."

"Have you put away at least an even twenty rubles?"

"Hee-hee."

"Tell me, don't be ashamed."

"Hee-hee."

"He's giggling, hee-hee, but just look at him. You *know* he'll bring home a pocketful of gold! That's a household of goldspinners!"

All of Kasrilevka had long since gotten up from the holiday feast. Many were thinking of going to sleep, and even more were already fast asleep and snoring loudly after the brandy they had drunk in honor of the holiday which celebrated the destruction of an enemy—Haman. But one family was just sitting down to enjoy their Purim feast, slicing the large braided Purim challah and taking to the food with great good spirit. Those were the Goldspinners.

They were all hungry and tired and their legs ached but each had an interesting story to tell about his day—a raft of anecdotes! Naftali told of his Purim Players and how well they had performed that day, extraordinarily well! Only "Vashti" had stumbled over the lines.

"May he stumble from now till Passover! No matter how many times we rehearsed it so that Vashti should say, 'In the Megillah I'm always put down,' it comes out with his nasal voice, 'In the big illah I'm always but brown!' What kind of 'In the big illah I'm always but brown'? What an idiot! May he rot! But go talk to a stuffed-up fool . . ."

That was Naftali's story. Rivella had even funnier stories about her customers who, it seemed, would do anything to save a little money. One woman decided to steal a fruit cake.

"Imagine that, someone trying to steal from me!"

" 'Madam, how many fruit cakes do you have there?' I asked. She said, 'Four.' I said, 'Well, and what about the fifth?' Her face turned red and she said to me, 'Oh, is that a fruit cake too?' So I said, 'What did you think it was, a grandfather clock?' Said she, 'Oh, I thought it was a honey cake!' Said I, 'So, are honey cakes free?' "

Rivella told her stories and then Noah's turn came. His stories had to do with noisemakers.

"This was a great year for noisemakers! Everyone wanted a noisemaker—just noisemakers and noisemakers and noisemakers! By yesterday afternoon I was already all sold out. This one man kept coming up to me, asking for noisemakers, so I said, 'I'm all out of noisemakers.' Said he, 'That's no excuse, you must give me two noise-makers!' Said I, 'But where am I going to get two noise-makers?' Said he, 'Why don't you give me your own noisemakers?'

"Will you ever stop with those noisemakers?!" said his father and Noah looked down, lowered his head, and blew his nose (under the table). That really tickled the young children. Now it was their turn to relate adventures from their Purim gift delivering. There were so many stories to tell that it would have taken till Passover to finish. But meanwhile, it was still Purim, they were tired from a long day's work, and it was time to go to bed.

The youngsters went off to their places around the stove and soon fell into the sweet, sound sleep of happy children who have had a full, exciting, and profitable day.

It was far into the night; Kasrilevka was long since asleep after the great Purim feast and the Purim desserts. Only two people in the entire town were awake and not even thinking about sleep. They were the Goldspinners, Naftali Long Legs and Sweet Rivella. They had quietly locked the door, drawn the curtains, and sat down with their strongbox. They wanted first to total up the coins that the little Goldspinners had brought in that lucky day, but they couldn't. They figured and figured but they could never agree; either he made a mistake or she made a mistake. Each blamed the other.

"Did you ever see such a woman who can't add two and two!" said the husband, and the wife replied, "If you're so smart, you count it, big financial expert!"

"You count it! You know better!"

"No, you count it! You know better!"

It was the time to settle the accounts and to decide what was needed for the family and what they could afford: shoes for themselves, jackets and dresses for the children—that was number one! How about matzo for Passover? How about goose fat? A crock of borscht? A sack of potatoes? It was amazing! No matter how many times they calculated, no matter how extravagant and spendthrift they wanted to be, the money was always just enough for shoes for themselves, jackets and dresses for the children, matzos for Passover, goose fat, a crock of borscht, and a sack of potatoes.

Both of their faces were flushed, their eyes glistened, their cheeks glowed, and their hearts swelled. Both of them felt that the world which God had created was, after all, not such a bad world and the people in it were, after all, not such bad people. However, it did hurt them that their own people were envious of their success. If someone else had a good day, one good day, it was so heartily resented!

"May Kasrilevka burn to the ground! A town of begrudgers!" said Naftali, and Rivella came to the defense of the town of Kasrilevka: "Poor people, for God's sake . . ."

"Poor people, she says. To her everyone is poor, heh-heh! Kasrilevka people—paupers! Beggars! Penny-pinchers! Egotists!"

"Bite your tongue!" said Rivella, frightened by her husband speaking so bitterly.

From a distance they could hear the crowing of a neighbor's rooster, an old rooster with a worn-out voice. He would start enthusiastically in the upper registers but by the time he reached the low notes, his voice would give out.

"Cock-a-doodle-dooooo . . . oo . . . oo."

It almost sounded as if he were asking himself a question: "Old fool! Why are you screeching?"

The sky was beginning to turn blue. Dawn was breaking. The day was beginning.

The Passover Exiles

The weeks between Purim and Passover are spent cleaning the house from top to bottom to make sure that everything is free of any trace of chometz, *or grain and yeast products.*

"THANK GOD WE'RE FINISHED with Purim and we have just enough time to get ready for Passover."

So said my mother to herself the morning after Purim as she went poking through every corner of the parlor, turning about like a hen looking for a place to lay an egg. A few days later two wooden blocks with some hay on top suddenly appeared in a corner of the room and on the wooden blocks was a spanking-new keg of Passover borscht, covered with a thick white linen cloth. It would be left there to ferment slowly so that when Passover came, it would be ready to eat. In the meantime, it was strictly off limits.

My father and I were summoned and warned repeatedly that we shouldn't dare go near, shouldn't dare look, shouldn't dare sniff around "in that corner." Immediately thereafter, the door to the parlor was shut and both of us, my father and I, were further instructed in a firm but gentle manner to remove ourselves and whatever belonged to us from the parlor and not to return until Passover.

From that moment on, the parlor took on a most attractive character in my eyes and I was drawn to it like a magnet, longing to take a peek "into that corner," if only from afar. Standing on the other side of the door while munching on a thick slice of bread smeared with chicken fat, I peered into our sunny parlor and delighted in the tawny spruce wood sofa, shiny as a fiddle, the three-legged semicircular table, the oval, finely beveled mirror, and the magnificent biblical painting on the eastern wall, marking the direction to Jerusalem, that my father himself had executed when still a young man. My oh my! What you couldn't find in that painting! Bears, lions, wildcats, eagles, birds, shofers, menorahs, esrogs, Passover plates with Stars of David, decorative dots, buttons, little wheels covering every inch. It was unbelievable that a human hand could have depicted a whole world of different things, almost beyond what the eye could take in. "My father is a genius!" I thought. "Such skill, such originality!"

"Get away from the parlor door with that bread, you rascal! Get away immediately!"

So said my mother, grabbing my left ear with two bony fingers as she delivered me to my father.

"Here, just look at this heir of yours. With that thick

slice of bread in his hand, he was over *there*, standing and *looking* at the Passover borscht!"

My father put on a solemn face, shook his head, pursed his lips, and clucked with his tongue, "Tsk-tsk-tsk! Get away from there, you good-for-nothing!" And when my mother turned away, a knowing smile played on my father's face, but when she turned back, the stern look reappeared. He took me by the hand, sat me down on a stool beside him, and told me I was not even to look "in that corner"—it was forbidden.

"Not even from far away?"

But my father was no longer listening to me. He was already deeply engrossed in his Bible study, chanting under his breath. Quietly I stole off to the parlor door to peek in through a crack at the magical room where everything was so beautiful and clean. New pots and crockery stood on the floor, and a cleaver, a chopping block, and two wreaths of garlic hung on the wall.

"The parlor is ready for Passover—for Passover! For Passover!"

"Would you mind taking yourselves and your books into the large bedroom?"

So said my mother, all dressed in white, a white kerchief on her head, a long stick in one hand, and a new feather duster in the other, stretching her neck and tilting her head back to inspect the ceiling.

"Sossil! Where are you hiding with that brush? Come in here, girl! Get to work!"

Sossil, the maid, her head also covered with a white cloth, made her appearance with a wet brush and a pail of whitewash. The two of them looked like ghosts in white shrouds. Sossil smeared the ceiling back and forth with the wet brush: *Fliak! Fliak!* Both of them worked like angry bees.

But to stand and observe this rare comedy wasn't a pleasure long allowed me. First, I was told in no uncertain terms that a boy shouldn't be standing watching while people were whitewashing the walls for Passover. After that, the advice turned more serious.

"Look here, how's about getting back to the bedroom," my mother said, taking my arm and steering me there. But I wasn't quite ready to leave and so moved out of her reach only to bump into Sossil. Sossil immediately pushed me back to my mother:

"How come you're always underfoot?"

"Go to your father, for pity's sake!" said my mother, pushing me onto Sossil, who pushed me back to my mother, saying:

"I never saw such a pain-in-the-neck in my life!"

"Can't get rid of him!" said my mother, swatting my behind while Sossil grabbed me and daubed my face with whitewash. Dissolved in tears, I tumbled into the bedroom and into my father's arms. My father tore himself away from his studies, tried to console me as much as he could, sat me on his knee, and was soon deep in his studies again.

·   ·   ·

"I beg your pardon, sir. The madam said, would you mind moving from here into the small bedroom."

So said Sossil to my father as she came in covered with whitewash like a ghost, lugging her cleaning paraphernalia. We had to move ourselves, books and all, into the small bedroom which was no bigger than a closet. There was room enough for just one bed in which I slept with—please don't tell anybody—Sossil, the maid. Sossil was, you understand, a relative who had been with us for years and years from before the time I was born. It was in her arms I grew up, she always said. Were it not for her, she always said, I would not be alive today. Whatever ailment was going around, whatever sickness or rash, I was the first to get it, she always said, and it was she who pulled me through all those catastrophes. "Is this a way to repay me? Doesn't he deserve a spanking?" she always said.

So saying, she gave me a push or two and pulled my hair for good measure. And—would you believe it!—no one stopped her! Neither my mother nor my father took my part. Whatever Sossil wanted to do with me, she could—just as if I belonged to her and not to them.

In the small bedroom I huddled in a corner, sitting on the floor, and watched my father as he stroked his forehead, chewed on his beard, and swayed to his own drawn-out chanting of the text: "And so it is said . . ." But in came Sossil with her paraphernalia and politely told us once again to get our belongings together and move out.

"But where to?" asked my father, startled by her request.

"How do I know where?" said Sossil, standing in the middle of the room with her brush.

"Into the pantry!" said my mother and entered with her long stick now topped with the feather duster, looking like an enemy on the attack, weapon in hand.

"It's as cold as ice there now," said my father, trying to play on her sympathy.

"So freeze!" said my mother, unmoved.

"People freeze outside, not inside," added Sossil and started to splatter the dry walls with the wet brush. And we had to move ourselves from the small bedroom into the even smaller pantry where we at once began to shiver. Here it wasn't easy for my father to sit and read his books. The pantry was a tiny, crowded, dark room with barely enough space for two people. But for me it was paradise. After all, the pantry was lined with shelves— great for climbing! True, my father wouldn't let me climb on them. He said I might fall and hurt myself. But who listens? No sooner was he into his books than—aha!—I was up on the first shelf, and from the first shelf on to the second shelf, and then to the third.

"Cock-a-doodle-doo!" I crowed at the top of my lungs to show my father my great achievement. I stood up straight and cracked my head on the ceiling so hard that my teeth rattled in my head. My father was taken by surprise and cried out. Sossil, with my mother right behind her, came running and both of them gave me what for.

"How can a boy be so childish?" complained my mother.

"A boy? He's a devil, not a boy!" Sossil added, meanwhile forewarning us that we would soon be asked to move into the kitchen because the house was already more than half-ready for Passover.

There I found Moshe-Ber with the thick eyebrows sitting with my father on a bench. They were not studying now but were sharing instead their bitter experiences. My father was complaining about the Passover exile that he had been enduring for several days now.

"We're nomads, wanderers, driven from one place to the next!"

Moshe-Ber said that was nothing compared to his woes; his situation was far worse.

"My wife drove me out of the house altogether!"

I looked at Moshe-Ber with his beetle brows and could not for the life of me imagine how a man like him, so large and with such thick eyebrows, could be driven out by anyone. Little by little, the two men returned to their customary study routine and odd-sounding talk: Rambam . . . Kuzari . . . Philosophy . . . Spinoza . . . and so forth—words that were gibberish to me.

Of far greater interest to me was the gray cat sitting on the hearth grooming herself. Sossil used to say that when a cat washed itself, it meant that we could expect a guest. Now, how does a cat know when a guest is coming? I went over and started to play with the cat. First I tried pressing down on her paw with my finger. She wasn't in-

terested. Then I tried to teach her how to "beg" standing up on her hind legs. Still not interested.

"Sit up! Beg!" I commanded her, rapping her on the nose several times. But she only shut her eyes, turned her head aside, and stuck her little tongue out, making a peculiar face as if to say, "What does this boy want from my life? Why has he latched on to me like this?" That hurt my feelings. What a stubborn cat! I pestered her so long she scratched me with her sharp claws and I screamed out loud, "Ow-w! Ma-ama!"

My mother and Sossil came running breathlessly and they took turns scolding me, telling me I should know better than to start up with cats. To them, one measly cat is the same as "cats."

"Go wash up," my mother called out to my father, "and we'll go down to the cellar to eat supper."

Sossil grabbed a poker and started to move the pots around on the big stove without so much as a glance at me, my father, or Moshe-Ber. Soon she let Moshe-Ber know that he had no business visiting just before Passover. It seemed to make more sense, she said, for him to stay home rather than get in other people's way in their houses. Moshe-Ber took the hint and said good-bye, and we went down to the cellar for our supper.

I really couldn't see why my father was making such faces, shrugging his shoulders and muttering under his breath:

"Still wandering! Always wandering!"

What's the tragedy in eating one supper in the cellar?

What's wrong with the smell of pickles, fermenting cabbage, and sour milk? What's so terrible about taking two overturned barrels, laying a noodle board across them, and using that as a table while using other barrels for chairs? Quite the opposite. To me that's a lot better and a lot more fun. That way you can roll around the cellar on the barrel. So what if you fall down? You get up and roll around again. The only problem was that Sossil had her eye on me, making sure I didn't roll myself around.

"He's thought up another trick!" she cried. "He's just dying to break an arm or a leg!"

That's ridiculous! Why would I want to break an arm or a leg? I don't know what Sossil wanted of my young life. She was constantly persecuting me, making everything seem worse than it was. If I ran, she said that I'd crack my skull. If I touched anything, she said I'd break it. If I sucked on a button, she got hysterical: "That crazy child will choke himself!" That's why I used to get even with her when I got sick. The minute I felt a little queasy, she would make a terrible fuss over me and do whatever I wanted.

"Now take the child and go upstairs. We have to clean out the last bit of bread and leaven from the cellar."

So said my mother after saying grace, and before my father could ask her where we could possibly go, she anticipated the question and said, "For a few hours up to the attic."

"Because we just washed all the floors and they are still wet," added Sossil. "Just make sure this wild one doesn't fall down the stairs and break every bone in his body."

"Bite your tongue!" my mother said sharply, and Sossil pushed me on ahead of her to get me out of the way a little faster.

"Come on, slowpoke, hurry up!"

My father walked behind me and I could hear him grumbling under his breath, "To the attic, of all places. What an exile!"

What a peculiar man my father was. He was told to go to the attic and he still wasn't happy. I don't know. If I had my way, I would like it to be Passover every week so we could climb up to the attic more often. The climb itself was a thrill. Any other day of the year, if it were my last wish on earth, they wouldn't let me make that climb. But there I was, scampering up the stairs like a demon. My father tried to catch up with me, warning, "Slow down! Be careful!"

How could I slow down? Who could even think of being careful? I felt as if I had sprouted wings like a bird and was flying. I was flying!

Do you have any idea what could be found in our attic? Treasures! Real treasures! Broken lamp globes, cracked pots, old clothes so threadbare you couldn't tell whether they were men's or women's. An old fur piece which disintegrated at the merest touch, like snow, loose pages from Hebrew texts, a burned-out samovar chimney, plumes, a rusty sieve, and an old lulav lying full length on the floor. And the beams! And the rafters! And the roof! The roof was made entirely of shingles and I could touch it with my hands. No small matter, to be able to touch a *roof* with your hands!

My father sat himself down on a plank, gathered up the loose pages of the books, and started putting them together while becoming deeply absorbed in their texts. Meanwhile, I stood next to the small attic window which overlooked the entire town of Kasrilevka, laid out below me as if on a platter—all the houses and all the roofs—black, gray, red, and green. The people down below were walking about looking like midgets and I imagined that there couldn't possibly be a better or more beautiful town than ours in the whole world. In all the courtyards I could see the townspeople washing, scrubbing, scouring, cleansing, and making things kosher. Sparing no effort, they lugged huge vats of boiling water, steam-heated irons, and hot glowing bricks from which arose a cloud of white vapor. The cloud of vapor swirled about and soon dispersed, like smoke. There was a hint of spring in the air. Little rivulets of water ran in the streets, goats bleated, and an old Jew, wearing makeshift boots held together by rope, was urging his white horse through the deep mud. That was poor Ezriel the coachman. He was whipping the horse, which could barely drag its legs through the thick mire. Ezriel was delivering a load of matzos, which reminded me that we already had our matzos a long time. They were locked away in a cupboard, covered with a white sheet. We also had a basket of eggs, a whole jar of Passover chicken fat, two wreaths of onions hanging on the wall, and many more good things for the beloved holiday. I reminded myself of the new clothes which they promised would be ready in time for Passover and my heart swelled within me.

"Sir!" a voice reached us from below. "Be so kind as to go out in the courtyard to air out the books!"

My father stood up, spitting the words out in rage. "Phoo on all this! Will this exile never end?!"

I still couldn't understand my father. Why wasn't he happy? What could be better and more exciting than to stand outside and air the books? I hurried away from the window and bolted out of the attic door and—*bumpety-bump!*—head over heels, I tumbled all the way down the stairs!

What happened next, I can't say. I only know that it took me quite some time to recover from that tumble. They say I almost didn't make it. But, as you can see, I am strong and healthy, may it never be worse. Except for a tiny scar on my face and some shortness of breath and an occasional blinking of the eyes when I speak, I'm as healthy as you.

The First Commune

LET ME TELL YOU something: There is not a trouble in the world to which a person cannot grow accustomed. You'd think that nothing could be worse than a toothache. Nevertheless, I can cite as evidence what happened to my rebbi, Reb Monish. He used to say that were he, God forbid, to get a toothache, he would go out of his mind. And, as it is written in the Bible, thus it came to pass. The time came when a tooth of his began to ache. At first he howled unnaturally, climbed the walls, hopped about the house, and sent all the cheder children home. In the morning, when we returned to cheder, we found him moaning quietly with one cheek wrapped up and his lip swollen. On the second morning, both cheeks were wrapped up, his face glistened as if smeared with butter and he sat subdued, quiet as a mouse, not a peep out of him.

"Rebbi, what's new with your tooth?"

"*Which* tooth?" our rebbi replied with a miserable little smile. "Every one of my teeth, blessed be His name, is aching now."

I'm telling you this story so that you won't be surprised to discover that we finally became accustomed to living in Hershke Mamtzes's house, almost forgetting that we had once lived in our own house, a beautiful house with a courtyard, a garden, a sukkah, a separate pantry, and—well, you name it. True, my mother would still become tearful and let my father know that there was not so much as one inch of storage space. To this my father would respond either not at all or with a deep sigh. But if she really nagged him, showing him how in a proper household one had to have a little storage space, at least a bit of shelf for something, he would finally reply, "Don't sin. Thank God for what we have."

That was his response to everything: to the fact that three housewives had to cook at the same stove, to the fact that all three families had to draw water from the same pump and dispose of waste in the same garbage pail, to the fact that there was only one coop for all the fowl, and to the fact that if one of the goats caused some damage, there was no way of knowing whose it was.

"I beg your pardon, Tzivieh Leah, but your goat will be the death of me. She ruined my milk bucket today," my mother complained to our landlady.

"Didn't your goat break my window pane yesterday?" retorted Tzivieh Leah, a fat woman with a deep voice.

"How do you know it was *my* goat that broke your window pane?" my mother countered.

"How do you know it was *my* goat that ruined your bucket?" replied Tzivieh Leah.

"It certainly wasn't *my* goat!" interjected the third

housewife, a small woman with black eyes whose name was Perella but who was called "Sparks" because she flared up quickly and as quickly died down—exactly the opposite of her husband, whom we called "*Really Moishe.*"

Those who would believe that three housewives who cook at the same stove, draw water from the same pump, and deposit refuse in one garbage can would constantly quarrel are greatly mistaken. True, it was not all love and kisses; one couldn't say that they loved one another so much that they couldn't bear to be apart. Human beings are, after all, just that—human beings. They love one another best at a distance. Those old comforting tales about how one day we will all live together as brothers, share one communal purse, beat our swords into plowshares and our weapons into pruning hooks never to wage war, never to slander or to be spiteful but to live in Utopia—that will only happen when the Messiah comes. Till that time, three housewives living together under one roof and cooking at one stove will inevitably quarrel, insult one another, and occasionally do even worse.

Of course, Tzivieh Leah, Hershke Mamtzes's wife, was a special case. She was, after all, the landlady of the house: she owned property and so expected everyone to pay her respect. You didn't dare speak to her unless you started with "I beg your pardon." She was able to have her way with my mother, who used a deferential tone with her.

"I beg your pardon, Tzivieh Leah, but the garbage pail is full to overflowing."

Or: "I beg your pardon, Tzivieh Leah, but your child has made a mess over there."

Because of my mother's tact, Tzivieh Leah thought the world of her and made sure to tell her so whenever the landlady was quarreling with Perella, the third house-wife.

"Do you know, Batya, dear heart," she would say to my mother with a sweet smile, "do you know why I love you so much? Because you aren't like 'Sparks.' " Perella, getting the point, would then say to my mother, also in a voice as sweet as sugar:

"Do you know, Batya dear, why *I* love you so much? Because you don't own a shack with the paint peeling from the walls and with a leaky roof and because you don't think you are God's gift to the world."

That's how both women would complain to my mother about each other while telling her why they loved her, enumerating all of her many virtues.

My mother's greatest virtue was her genuine love of peace. She would change the subject rather than take sides.

If not for my mother, it would have been a battle royal. Even so, she was forced to witness ugly scenes, to give ear to bitter complaints, and literally to pull these two women apart when they became angry. At those times, she said, they were worse than wild beasts, ready to bite off each other's nose or scratch each other's eyes out.

Only I knew how dearly it cost my mother in health. More than once I found her sitting and crying (she cried over everything), bemoaning her fate. No sooner would my father come in than she would dry her eyes as if nothing had happened.

"What's the matter?" my father would ask her anxiously.

"What do you mean, 'What's the matter'?" my mother would reply innocently.

"Why have you been crying?"

"Who, me?" My mother would try to look happy as the tears slipped from her pretty eyes down her lovely pale cheeks. If I hadn't been embarrassed to do it in front of my father, I would have thrown my arms around her neck and kissed away every tear.

All together we were seven boys in this three-household family: Hershke Mamtzes's four sons, two red-heads and two dark-haired boys—Isaac, Itzik, Hilik, and Israelik; *"Really* Moishe" 's two boys—Yoelikel and Shoeli-kel; and me—Avrahamel. In addition to the seven boys there were six girls: two of Tzivieh Leah's daughters, both with blond hair—Itke and Baylke; and four of Perella's girls—Reiselleh, Foigelleh, Hannahleh, and Yen-telleh.

The boys and girls fought like cats and dogs. We hated each other so much that we couldn't even stand the sight of one another. If something broke, the boys blamed the girls and the girls blamed the boys till we came to blows. The boys pulled the girls' hair and the girls screeched so loudly that Hershke Mamtzes would come running. He was an angry man who detested squabbling. With his open hand he would slap as many of us as he could reach, saying as he did so, "Pitch-potch! Down a notch!" Luckily, "*Really* Moishe" would intercede and yank the boys out of Hershke Mamtzes's reach.

"Let's *really* put an end to this now!"

He was a curious fellow, this "*Really* Moishe"—a man with a childlike soul. He could spend entire days and nights with us children, helping us to make, build, put together, or take apart things. It goes without saying that when it came to puttering, "*Really* Moishe" was something of a master craftsman. How could he stand by and simply watch while someone else was whittling, sawing, or making something?

"Here, give it to me, you good-for-nothing, and I'll show you how you *really* use a whittling knife!"

But that was nothing. Just between us, "*Really* Moishe" never thought it beneath him to tuck the hem of his long coat into his belt and join us kids in a game of hide-and-go-seek, Johnny-jump-up, or hopscotch. And playing with him was, I tell you, a treat. So what did God do? He gave him a wife, Perella, who didn't let him play with us. What a tragedy!

It has long been known that all great ideas come about unexpectedly, as if by chance. And so it was with the idea for the commune, which was born unexpectedly, quite by chance. This is how it happened. Soon after Purim, the grownups were figuring out how much flour each family would need for Passover matzos, and an extraordinary coincidence came to light. It soon became plain that we all needed the same amount, no more nor less. Here's how it added up: My mother, my father, and I were three. We were expecting guests—my older sister, Asna; her husband, Daniel; and their three children— from a small town in Bessarabia, so you have a total of no less than eight people. Figure Hershke Mamtzes and his wife and their four sons and two daughters—there again you have exactly eight. Now take *"Really* Moishe" with his wife, two boys, and four girls—again eight.

"Wonder of wonders! A miracle from heaven!" the men exclaimed jokingly.

"It's got to be Fate!" the women added, more seriously.

"Listen to this, my friends, I have an idea. Wouldn't it make sense if for these eight days of Passover we would all join forces and celebrate together?" I think it was *"Really* Moishe" who said that, and Hershke Mamtzes added immediately:

"Yes, kind of a partnership, it's known as a cooperative, but whatever you call it, let's do it together."

"Some people call it a commune," my father contributed, and *"Really* Moishe" presented us with an explanation illustrated by gestures:

"Commune means: What's mine is yours, what's yours is mine—one pot, one purse, one voice."

"And especially on Passover," all the men said at once, "when all Jews eat one bread—the simple matzo—when all of us drink the same raisin wine—four glasses full—

when we all eat the same green vegetables and horseradish, and when all of us recite from the same Haggadah. Passover is really the best holiday. On Passover, all Jews would do well to have a commune."

The men glanced furtively at their wives—what would they say to this plan? But the wives wisely kept their silence. They were probably thinking, "Why should we stick our necks out? You men want a commune, so have a commune. If it doesn't work out, you can't blame us." In short, the women worked it out rather diplomatically, as women generally do, and the plan for the commune was adopted—not all at once, but gradually.

First of all the three women together bought a sack of flour and baked their matzos at one time at the bakers. This year the matzos turned out better than ever. They brought the matzos home and wished one another well, hoping that they and their husbands and children would all live and be well till the next year when they would bake matzos together again. It was so heartwarming to observe the camaraderie and affection among the wives, as if they had never bickered, never gossiped or even so much as exchanged an angry word. Not just the women, but the men and we youngsters that day felt happier than we had since we started living together under one roof. It was a miracle. Even Hershke Mamtzes, who was always in a bad mood and grumbling at the world (because at one time his in-laws had tried to take his house away from him), this day was unusually genial; he didn't smack us, saying, as was his habit, "Pitch-potch! Down a notch!" and was even humming to himself. Even Tzivieh Leah's voice was that day somehow lighter and softer. In a word, a good angel had alighted on Hershke Mamtzes's house. Its spirit descended on the household.

Having finished with the matzos, the women together put up a crock of Passover borscht, the crock provided, naturally, by "*Really* Moishe," and again they wished one another well, hoping that they and their husbands and children would all live and be well till the next year when they would put up a Passover borscht together again. The house was filled with a happy holiday spirit. After that they all bought a number of chickens and two turkeys. God had provided a real bargain. A crazy peasant was asking only ten gulden for the two turkeys, which were as big as calves. They tossed all the chickens into one coop (repaired, naturally, by "*Really* Moishe"). The turkeys were allowed to roam free about the house, and for us children it became a great game. We chased the turkeys, teased them, and whistled at them as they squawked, "Gobble-gobble!"—and no one stopped us. The wives again wished one another well, hoping that they and their husbands would all live and be well till the next year when they would buy such excellent chickens and turkeys for Passover together again.

They then bought three sacks of potatoes for cash and dozens of eggs at a low price—three gulden a dozen. God had sent them a peasant woman with eggs—God bless her—and the wives laughed at the silly woman as again they wished one another well, hoping that they and their husbands and children would all live and be well till the next year when they would buy such fresh eggs together again.

Need I go on? A sack of Passover coals for the samovar was purchased for a song, it's a shame to say for how little; horseradish and parsnips—all at half-price. "A Passover of real bargains!" the women declared as they laughed, and we young folk whistled at the turkeys and the turkeys answered, "Gobble-gobble!" It was obviously the greatest idea in the world to be working together as one.

"Commune? You ladies have been playing at commune?" the men teased.

But the women said straight out that they wouldn't mind having "commune" all year round. They were in favor of the idea, the men certainly were, and we children—well, what do *you* think!

Only the fish, the meat, and the wine remained to be bought on the last day. Who else but *"Really* Moishe" took it upon himself to buy the fish because where in the world could you find such an expert when it came to buying fish? He would bring home fish that were *really* fish! The wine, chopped apples, and nuts were left entirely to my father as he was the wine specialist. The koshering of the dishes and silverware were assigned to the boys; the girls were given other chores: helping their mothers to scrub, scour, and polish. We boys rolled up our trousers and went off to the pond with the dishes, happy and excited. In short, it was a merry time, all of us busy, all hands occupied, no one with a moment to spare as we disposed of the last of the ordinary bread, went to the bathhouse, came home, dressed in our holiday clothes, and began the preparations for the seder.

As you would expect, "*Really* Moishe" set up the tables and chairs, laid out the wineglasses and silverware, and arranged pillows in heaps on the men's chairs. These were the hesev-beds, which, according to Passover tradition, would permit them to recline on their elbows like kings of old. Anyone who missed "*Really* Moishe"'s bustling around that evening, missed something *really* special. His cheeks were flushed, his hat had slipped down over his ear, and one half of his moustache, the long side, seemed to hang down farther. He looked like the captain of a ship, the general of an army. He wouldn't allow anyone else to touch a thing. By himself he carried in the chairs, by himself he set out the wineglasses, the salt water, the chopped apples and bitter greens. By himself he prepared the four chairs for the men to recline on (my brother-in-law, Daniel, was also counted among the men). When it came to the heaps of pillows, he ordered us to bring in more and more pillows.

"More pillows!"

"Here's another one!"

"More pillows!"

"Here's another one!"

"More pillows!"

"Why do you need so many pillows?"

"More!"

Four tall mounds of pillows grew before our eyes. Did I say mounds? Four tall *towers*, so tall that when the four men returned from shul, they literally had to scramble up to the top, and when they reached the top and were seated, they were afraid they might fall off.

The first to climb up was our landlord, Hershke Mamtzes. He didn't complain at all about the height of the pillows; he just shrugged and muttered angrily, "Wh-what a hesev-bed!"

"Ha! That's *really* a hesev-bed!" Moishe cried out to him with the satisfied smile of a great artist who is proud of his work.

"Let's just hope it doesn't wind up like your sukkah," retorted the landlord sarcastically.

"I was thinking the same thing," said my father, clambering onto the cushions, holding on to his belt with both hands and stamping down the cushions as one does hay on a wagon.

"If you want something done, do it yourself," interjected the landlady spitefully, and "Sparks," defending her husband, said to Moishe angrily:

"You always have to show off, don't you? I wouldn't lift a finger to fix up their pillows. Let them do it themselves!"

Understandably, Tzivieh Leah wasn't going to let this go unanswered and so she said to my mother in an artificial tone:

"Do you see, Batya, dear heart, 'Sparks' are flying already."

And "Sparks" leaned over to my mother and whispered in her ear for all to hear, "Do you hear, Batya, my love, the tea kettle, praised be God, is boiling already."

All of us could sense that a cloud was slowly descending on Hershke Mamtzes's house. The happiness and the liveliness that had prevailed before Passover was disappearing—vanishing, vanishing with the wind and the smoke.

"May you both be strong and healthy, Tzivieh Leah, I beg your pardon, and Perella, honey. Don't forget that it's yom-tov, a holiday, and we are sitting together at one table," my mother said softly, and her face was so full of sorrow and anguish that my heart almost broke.

I had noticed during the candle blessing that she was crying—crying for her own house, the one we had lost, crying because we had to share the holidays with such crude people and had to sit with them at one table, at one seder. Just a year ago we had a little nicer table, a little richer seder. A year ago my father was the only king and my mother was the only queen and I was the only prince. Today, all crowded together were several kings, several queens, and many, many princes, and all the princes were dressed up in holiday clothes as fine as mine and perhaps a little finer. No, say what you will, it wasn't the same as last year's Passover. It wasn't last year's seder.

Even though there were many princes sitting at the table and all were dressed up for the holidays as nicely as I was and perhaps a little nicer, nevertheless I felt that I was set apart from the others. Even though there were several kings and several queens, nevertheless I felt that my father and my mother were not like the other mothers and fathers. If the others were kings, then he was a king above the other kings because he was the handsomest and the most refined of them all. My father recited from the Siddur, conducting the ceremony like an elder, like a general, and everyone looked to him to know what to do next. Even my mother set an example for the women as she read her own fat prayer book and turned the pages with her slender fingers as her pale face glowed like the sun. Picture it: Even my sister, Asna, not a bad-looking woman, couldn't hold a candle to my mother. What a pity that from all her crying, she had developed dark circles under her eyes. What a pity that from all the cooking and scrubbing, her pretty hands had become calloused. What a pity that because of my sister Asna's wedding, she'd had to sell her rings, pearls, and earrings and couldn't show off her true beauty. We praise the beauty of Rachel, Queen Esther, Shulamit from the "Song of Songs," the Queen of Sheba—but they are just fantasies. Give my mother back her rings, her pearls, and her earrings and then you will see true beauty! But it's no use. The rings are gone! The pearls are gone! The earrings are gone! Gone! Sold!

"Kid-duu-shh!" chanted the king of kings—my father, that is—as he sat up with difficulty from his pile of pillows and held his wineglass in one hand while supporting himself on the table with the other. He tilted his head back, shut his eyes, and began the beautiful Passover

benediction over the wine with its moving Passover variation—but with a certain sorrowful intonation. No, it was
not the same melody he sang a year ago at Passover. I
imagined that in my father's kiddush I could hear a plea
to the Heavenly Court of Judgment, a plea for our old
house, for my mother's rings and her pearls and her
earrings, and for all the other troubles, griefs, and heart-
aches that God had dealt us this year with His broad
hand.

Like all great ideas, so too the greatest misfortunes
that occur in the world often start with a trifle, a foolish
incident. So it was that the commune I'm telling you
about had its sudden downfall at its very birth over nothing, over a foolish incident. This is how it happened.

As soon as my father finished saying the kiddush and
sank back onto his heap of pillows, both my brother-in-
law, Daniel, and our landlord, Hershke Mamtzes, each
thinking it was his turn to say the kiddush next, stood up
at the same time, then hastily sat down again, their faces
reddening with embarrassment.

My father indicated to Hershke Mamtzes by sign language and sounds (because during the kiddush you aren't
supposed to speak), "Nu-oh!" That meant he would be
honored if he would make the kiddush next. Hershke
Mamtzes replied, motioning with his hand to my brother-
in-law, Daniel, "Ee-oh!" That meant, "Look at that young
upstart, thinking he's old enough to say the kiddush." My
brother-in-law responded with a shake of the head, "Ee-
ee!" That meant, "Let someone else make the kiddush

next." "*Really* Moishe" put in his two cents' worth (he always loved to get into the act) and gestured with his hand, "Me-oh-nu!" Translated, that meant, "Make up your minds, one or the other." My father replied with a wink of the eye and a "Ma-oh-ee!" meaning, "If not this one or that one, then *you* make the kiddush first."

I don't know what was so funny about all this, but we children suddenly found that we couldn't keep from laughing—and what laughter it was! We suppressed it behind our hands, afraid to look at one another lest we burst out laughing. But how long can a human being control himself? A human being is not made of iron, particularly when he is surrounded at the table by so many silly, noisy, mischievous no-goods who know what it means to laugh. It didn't take much more than a hiccup or a cough to make any one of us lose control. At such moments, I tell you, it was awful; we was playing with fire, because the more we held it in, the more likely we were to explode. You can prove it with your own friends. Just make one rule—no laughing at the table—and you'll see what will happen. At first they'll try to hold it in as long as possible and then there will be such an outburst of laughter that you'll finally burst out laughing yourself. I don't have an explanation for this; I'll leave it to the experts to explain this phenomenon, while we return to our kiddush.

With God's help, the kings completed the kiddush and it was now the children's turn. Hershke Mamtzes's eldest son, Isaac, stood up and started to chant in a choked voice as if someone were strangling him. So his younger brother, Itzik, let out a little high-pitched "*Kchi!*"

This made the third brother, Hilik, laugh out loud, and he was followed by the little one, Israelik, and after them by the rest of us. Isaac was caught right in the middle. There was no going back or forward. It was painful to look at his flushed, anguished face. Hershke Mamtzes sprang to his feet and slapped him on top of his head and sent him away from the table, saying, as was his custom, "Pitch-potch! Down a notch!" and motioned to Itzik to stand up and make the prayer.

Itzik jumped up like a demon and started to recite the same prayer, but so loudly and so eagerly that he was startled by his own voice and tried to lower it by a tone. One of the bunch went *"Hic!"* which made Itzik unable to speak at all because he started to choke. So the poor boy got slapped on the head by his father, Hershke Mamtzes, the same punishment as for Isaac, along with the "Pitch-potch! Down a notch!" and before we knew it, the third son, Hilik, was standing in his place.

Now this Hilik got halfway through the prayer and couldn't go on. Somehow his eye was caught by my brother-in-law's three children and when he saw the three of them holding their noses, blowing up their cheeks like chipmunks, he was at the point of exploding. And in this way, one after another, each child received his punishment from Hershke Mamtzes—"Pitch-potch! Down a notch!" and had to surrender his place to the next one. Finally it came to *"Really* Moishe" 's children, to Yoelikel and Shoelikel. When Yoelikel got up to recite the prayer, he couldn't even get out the very first word, and dissolved in laughter right on the spot. Everyone started to giggle. Big and small were laughing: my mother and my father and "*Really* Moishe" and all the women. I imagined that even the wineglasses, the dishes, the spoons, the lamp, and the walls—everyone and everything—were gripped by laughter.

Only Hershke Mamtzes with the angry eyes was not laughing. He allowed Yoelikel to laugh a little longer, then stood up angrily and—apparently forgetting that Yoelikel had a father of his own, may he live to be one hundred and twenty years, a father who also had hands and could deal with his son as he saw fit—slapped Yoelikel on top of the head, along with the same "Pitch-potch! Down a notch!" as with his own sons. The whole gathering sat stunned. Naturally, this incident mostly inflamed Yoelikel's mother, "Sparks," whose eyes flashed as she said to Tzivieh Leah:

"Could you please inform your husband that his hands should only wither?"

It didn't take Tzivieh Leah long to think of an answer. She said to "*Really* Moishe" in her deep voice:

"Could you please inform your wife that her nasty mouth should only shrivel?"

I can't describe what then took place. I mean, I can, but I don't want to. It's not fitting . . . better to be silent.

The following day, at the second seder, each family sat separately at its own table and celebrated the seder as God commanded. Although still having to sit together in one room, in Hershke Mamtzes's living room, they made sure to turn their backs to one another, in a huff. They could hardly wait till the last day of Passover in order to divide up the remaining matzos, the chicken fat, the eggs, the potatoes, and the green vegetables. Even the crock of borscht had to be poured into separate pots. The women lost no opportunity to blame one another or to insult the men.

"Communes they wanted! Madmen invented them and idiots follow blindly! Communes! May all our enemies live in communes!"

After Passover, my father explored the entire city, looking for another house to rent, and *"Really* Moishe" soon followed suit. Tzivieh Leah suddenly softened her manner and Hershke Mamtzes said casually that immediately after Shevuos, we should all live and be well, he would start repairing the leaky roof. But it didn't help one bit. My mother told my father that under no circumstances would she remain in this house, even for free. She would rather, God forbid, live in the street than in Hershke Mamtzes's house.

And that's what became of the first commune in Kasrilevka.

Glossary

Borscht: A soup made of cabbage and beets at Passover, usually allowed to ferment for several days in a crock or keg.

Carob: A sweet wild pod, also known as St. John's bread.

Challah: The braided Sabbath or holiday egg bread.

Chanukah: The Festival of Lights celebrated for eight days in December. Commemorates the successful revolt of the Maccabees against the Syrians in 165 B.C.E.

Cheder: Room in the rebbi's house where children were taught Hebrew, prayers, and the Bible.

Chometz: Any foodstuff made from grain or yeast products. Before the start of Passover, every remnant of this must be removed from the house.

Dreydl: A four-sided spinning top, played with by children during Chanukah.

Esrog: A large, lemonlike aromatic citrus fruit, used together with the lulav (see below) in the synagogue procession during Sukkos, at which time it is blessed. The stem or apex is the most important part of the fruit, for if it breaks off the esrog is no longer considered to be valid for the religious purpose.

Farfel: Noodle dough, in pellets.

Gefillte fish: Holiday fish croquettes made of spiced ground fish.

Haggadah: Book of the Passover home service read during the two consecutive seders on the first two nights of Passover. It starts with the youngest child asking the head of the family the Four Questions. The answers relate the story of the exodus of the persecuted Jews from Egypt and their subsequent liberation.

Haman-tash: Three-cornered, filled cake eaten at Purim.

Hesev bed: The heap of soft pillows that men lean on during the seder at Passover.

Kaddish: Prayer recited by mourners after the death of a close relative.

Kiddush: Blessing recited over the wine at the beginning of the Sabbath or holiday evening meal.

Kosher: Food or drink that Jews are permitted to eat when proper special regulations have been followed in its preparation.

Latkes: Potato pancakes, traditionally eaten during Chanukah.

Lulav: Palm branch, tied together with sprigs of myrtle and willow, used together with the esrog during Sukkos to symbolize the harvest.

Matzo: Traditional unleavened flatbread eaten during Passover ꞏ memorate the years the Jews spent wandering the desert.

lled-up piece of parchment inscribed with pas-
m Deuteronomy, placed in a container and nailed

in a slanting position to the right-hand doorpost of Jewish homes and synagogues. A devout Jew will kiss his fingers and touch the mezuzah upon entering a building.

Megillah: The Book of Esther, the story of Purim, written on a scroll and read aloud in synagogue. Whenever the name of Haman, the villain of the story, is read, the children drown out the sound of it with noisemakers.

Menorah: Candelabrum holding candles for Chanukah.

Passover: Festival celebrated for eight days, commemorating the Jews' exodus from Egypt where they were slaves. Generally takes place in April.

Purim: A March festival, celebrating the downfall of Haman, the villain who tried to destroy the Jews, as told in the Book of Esther. A joyous holiday, marked by parades and costume parties, gift exchanges and dramatic renditions of the Purim story.

Reb: Mister, a respectful term for a man.

Rebbi: A teacher, generally of the children in the cheder.

Rebbitzin: The rabbi's wife.

Rosh Hashanah: Jewish New Year.

Seder: Passover celebration of the first and second evenings at which the Haggadah is read around the family supper table. The Four Questions are asked and answered; the Passover story is told; four glasses of wine are drunk; matzos, chopped apples, and bitter greens are eaten to symbolize various aspects of the history of the Jews fleeing Egypt.

Shabbos: Sabbath, starting at sundown Friday night and ending at sundown Saturday night. The day of rest and worship for Jews.

Shamesh: Candle used to light the other candles of the menorah during Chanukah.

Shevuos: The Feast of Weeks, a religious harvest holiday.

Shochet: Ritual slaughterer.

Shul: Synagogue, prayer room.

Siddur: Prayer book.

Sukkah: Home-made shed or lean-to behind the house, made of crude lumber and topped with green branches in which the family eats its meals during Sukkos. It symbolizes the dwellings used by the Jews during their wanderings in the desert.

Sukkos: The fall harvest festival, commemorating the Jews' living in crude shelters (see above) during their wanderings.

Tsimmes: Vegetables simmered with honey or sugar.

Yarmulke: Prayer cap worn by Jewish males.

Yahrtzeit: Anniversary of a person's death.

Praise for *Watch You Bleed.*

"The gold standard of rock biographers. . . . A behind-the-scenes story that's at times tawdry and titillating, harrowing and hilarious."
—*The Boston Globe*

"Rampant rockin' sex . . . a lurid tell-all . . . explosive." —*New York Post*

"Five stars! Stephen Davis's real coup is to show how Guns could be electrifying one moment and spectacularly stupid the next. You might not like Axl Rose upon finishing the book, but you may understand him better."
—*Mojo*

"The Guns N' Roses story by the guy that wrote *Hammer of the Gods*."
—*Classic Rock*

"Stephen Davis—America's rock biographer." —ABC News.com

© DOUG TILLOTSON

Stephen Davis is one of America's preeminent rock journalists. His many rock biographies include *Jim Morrison: Life, Death, Legend* and the *New York Times* bestsellers *Walk This Way: The Autobiography of Aerosmith* and *Hammer of the Gods: The Led Zeppelin Saga*. He lives in Massachusetts.

Watch You Bleed

THE SAGA OF
GUNS N' ROSES

STEPHEN DAVIS

GOTHAM
BOOKS

GOTHAM BOOKS
Published by Penguin Group (USA) Inc.
375 Hudson Street, New York, New York 10014, U.S.A.

Penguin Group (Canada), 90 Eglinton Avenue East, Suite 700, Toronto, Ontario M4P 2Y3, Canada (a division of Pearson Penguin Canada Inc.); Penguin Books Ltd, 80 Strand, London WC2R 0RL, England; Penguin Ireland, 25 St Stephen's Green, Dublin 2, Ireland (a division of Penguin Books Ltd); Penguin Group (Australia), 250 Camberwell Road, Camberwell, Victoria 3124, Australia (a division of Pearson Australia Group Pty Ltd); Penguin Books India Pvt Ltd, 11 Community Centre, Panchsheel Park, New Delhi–110 017, India; Penguin Group (NZ), 67 Apollo Drive, Rosedale, North Shore 0632, New Zealand (a division of Pearson New Zealand Ltd); Penguin Books (South Africa) (Pty) Ltd, 24 Sturdee Avenue, Rosebank, Johannesburg 2196, South Africa

Penguin Books Ltd, Registered Offices: 80 Strand, London WC2R 0RL, England

Published by Gotham Books, a member of Penguin Group (USA) Inc.

Previously published as a Gotham Books hardcover edition.

First trade paperback printing, September 2009

10 9 8 7 6 5 4 3 2 1

Gotham Books and the skyscraper logo are trademarks of Penguin Group (USA) Inc.

Copyright © 2008 by Stephen Davis
All rights reserved

ISBN: 978-1-592-40500-8

Printed in the United States of America
Set in Cremona
Designed by Sabrina Bowers

While the author has made every effort to provide accurate telephone numbers and Internet addresses at the time of publication, neither the publisher nor the author assumes any responsibility for errors, or for changes that occur after publication. Further, the publisher does not have any control over and does not assume any responsibility for author or third-party Web sites or their content.

For Vicky Hamilton

"Women hold up half the sky."
—Mao

CONTENTS

INTRODUCTION

$\mathcal{S}$ome think the legend of Guns N' Roses began in the nighttime Los Angeles of 1985, a distant echo of West Hollywood's neon-lit Sunset Strip. Others think it should begin ten years earlier, at the confluence of two Indiana rivers, the Wabash and the Tippecanoe, in the 1970s. But in this telling, the GN'R saga begins in gritty New York, in upper Manhattan, on a sweltering, run-down street in the late afternoon of a summer day in 1980.

Actually it could begin way below the actual city street, in the deeply recessed concrete canyon of the Cross Bronx Expressway, which is where the two young hitchhikers from Indiana decided to get out of the car. It had been a good ride until then, a straight shot from the Ohio line across I-80, Pennsylvania, New Jersey. Bill Bailey and his friend Paul, both eighteen, had left central Indiana via I-65 thirty hours earlier and were making good hitching time toward their first visit to New York City.

The Ford Econoline van that had picked them up crossed the Hudson over the majestic George Washington Bridge. They were on I-95 now. Crossing on the upper deck, looking south, they could see the Empire State Building and the twin towers of the World Trade Center shimmering in the summer haze. Bill Bailey looked up and saw they were passing a sign that said LAST EXIT IN MANHATTAN. He said, "Hey, man. Let us off, OK?"

"I can't pull over," the driver said. He was an electronics salesman on his way to Providence. They were now headed east in the deep-walled pit of the Cross Bronx Expressway.

Bill asked, "Where's the next exit?"

"Way the hell up in the East Bronx."

The hitchers looked at each other. All they had were their backpacks and maybe thirty bucks between them. "Let us off here," Bill said.

"Man, are you sure? It'll be hard to get out of here."

"Yeah, let us out." Just then, traffic slowed into the constipation typical of I-95 as it crosses New York City. The boys jumped out. Cars honked at them as they inched along the sheer walls, looking for a way out. Drivers laughed at them, told them they were fucking insane. A trucker blasted his air horn and they jumped at the sound. The walls of the roadway were at least a hundred feet high, and all they could see were the tops of the buildings up at street level.

After a while they found the service ladder and scaled the wall, a thousand horns blaring far below, emerging into immigrant New York City, circa 1980: Calcutta on the Hudson.

To Bill and his friend, it was bedlam, a Caribbean neighborhood in Washington Heights with a funky street scene of bodegas and shouting kids playing under open hydrants, crones yelling out of windows in Spanish, idlers under shop awnings, hustlers working the corners of 177th and Broadway. Bill and Paul, from Tippecanoe County in Indiana, were the only white faces in a sea of black people, Puerto Ricans, Jamaicans, Dominicans, Muslim women in veils, Haitians, Hindus, Chinese shopkeepers, and lots of kids immediately picking up on two white boys who'd just climbed out of the hellish Cross Bronx like hayseed mountaineers in cowboy boots, blue jeans, and very long straight hair. The boys just stood and gaped, checking out this scene. "Rapper's Delight," bass-heavy hip-hop, blasted out of a bodega speaker. Lurid graffiti covered every flat surface. Kids were busting moves—break-dancing—on the sidewalk. Bill Bailey had never seen this before. Basically, there weren't any black people in his part of Indiana, so they might as well have been in Senegal.

Now an old man limped over to them. He gave them the once-over, seeming to linger over Bill's cowboy boots. Bill was becoming uneasy now, his friend noticed, which was never a good thing, because, when agitated or upset, Bill's behavior could get a little out there. Finally the old man spoke, or rather squawked, in a high-pitched shriek.

"DO YOU KNOW WHERE YOU ARE?"

The boys, taken aback, just looked at him.

"I SAID, *DO YOU KNOW WHERE YOU ARE?*"

Bill Bailey said, "Uh, we're just trying to get to . . ."

"*YOU'RE IN THE JUNGLE, BABY!*"

Bill Bailey—the future W. Axl Rose—just stared at him in wonderment. And then the little old man wound himself up to his full fury and told these white boys what they could expect from New York City at the tail end of the seventies: years of bankruptcy, endemic crime, corruption, decadence—the gateway to the eighties and the scourge of AIDS. He told it to them straight from the gut:

"*YOU'RE GONNA DIE!*"

Sometimes, legends come from true stories, and this is one of them.

Welcome to the jungle.

I'm looking forward to people doing a book
about us that has a lot of stuff in it
that never happened.
—Axl Rose, 1986

Every Angel is terrible.
—Rainer Maria Rilke

Watch You Bleed

Chapter One

HARD ROAD TO HOLLYWOOD

You can still see the shadow from when the
Zeppelin floated over America. It took like
Islam in the desert.
—Michael Herr

ACTS OF THE APOSTLES

*A*nd as Led Zeppelin floated over America in the seventies, its shadow darkened the country's heartland the deepest. All the great English bands of that era—the Stones, The Who, Bowie, Queen—found their largest, most slavering audiences in the middle of the country. It was no accident that the greatest American rock stars of the eighties were born in the Midwest and grew up with lethal doses of the mighty Zeppelin and the other rock bands. Madonna was from Michigan. Prince was from Minnesota. Michael Jackson was born in Gary, Indiana, in 1958.

Four years later, Axl Rose was born a hundred miles south of there, in Lafayette, Indiana, on February 6, 1962. His mother, Sharon Lintner, was unmarried, only seventeen, and still in high school. Her pregnancy was an accident and unwanted, at least by her family. The father was William Rose, a troubled and charismatic local delinquent of maybe nineteen. The baby, born with bright red hair, was baptized William Bruce Rose.

It is not known whether Axl's parents ever married, since a marriage certificate has proved elusive to researchers, but if they did, it was probably a shotgun-type affair and the marital relationship was an on-and-off thing. The baby was often cared for at his Lintner grandparents' house in Lafayette, in an atmosphere of barely stifled hostility toward his no-account father.

In 1964, when the little boy was two, his young parents split up, and the father acted out his own scenario of revenge when banned from the house for hurting Axl's mother. He apparently abducted his son, and may even have molested him. Whatever really happened to the little boy, it was never spoken of again by the family, which treated these incidents with denial and shame. Bill Rose then disappeared from Lafayette, and never returned.

The following year, Axl's mother married a man named Stephen Bailey and moved with him to a house on 24th Street, on the east side of Lafayette. Bailey adopted his pretty young wife's son and gave him his last name. So William Rose became William Bailey, an identity he lived with until he angrily cast it away, fifteen years later. His mother had two more children with her husband, so Bill was raised with brother Stuart and sister Amy. They lived in town but worshipped at a clap-and-shout country church on a gravel farm road in another part of Tippecanoe County. Bill Bailey's stepfather was deep into Pentecostalism, the "old-time religion" that forbade drinking and listening to rock and roll, as well as most of life's other pleasures. His almost total immersion in hyperpuritanism would prove crucial for the child who became the greatest rock star of his generation.

Lafayette, Indiana, was and is a pleasant, small manufacturing city along the banks of the Wabash River. The land had been part of the three million acres the Shawnee Indians sold to the United States in 1809, as the Northwest Reserve of the Ohio Territory. Two years later the local chiefs, Tecumseh and his brother Tenskwatawa—known as "The Prophet"—realized they'd been cheated and began raiding. They were defeated in 1811 by General William Henry Harrison, who went on to be president for a month before dying of a bad cold.

A frontier speculator paid five dollars for the land and laid out the town in 1824, naming it after the Marquis de Lafayette, the French hero of the American Revolution who happened to be making a triumphant progress through America at the time. The riverbanks were low, convenient for loading and unloading supplies, so commerce came naturally. Lafayette became the seat of Tippecanoe

County in 1826, and the town was thriving by the time of the Civil War in 1860. Slavery was illegal in Indiana, and the state sent regiments of its sons to fight for the Union cause. Yet in the aftermath of the bloody war, with a comparatively tiny black population, racism was prevalent in the towns and farm communities. Membership in the Ku Klux Klan was a path to respectability in some Indiana towns in the 1920s.

Lafayette prospered as a manufacturing town. Chicago was 120 miles to the northeast. Indianapolis was 65 miles south. Factories opened on the east side of the river. Purdue University opened on the west side in 1869. The huge courthouse that dominates the main square went up in 1884, a Victorian wedding cake of architectural styles, from Gothic Revival to neobaroque. Young Bill Bailey would become familiar with the imposing building and its stern judges during his future career as one of Lafayette's most annoying teenage offenders, following in the footsteps of his real father.

*R*eligion in that part of the country was mostly the mainstream Protestant denominations until the Great Depression of the 1930s turned the social contract inside out. Factories closed, the crops failed, and the dust blew north from Oklahoma. The banks went under, and money basically disappeared. It took a resilient people to survive this economic disaster, and some, especially in the Midwest, found their strength in the charismatic ministries of the Pentecostal movement.

Open your Bible to the New Testament, the second chapter of Acts of the Apostles. In the first chapter the risen Christ gives various instructions to his disciples. In the second chapter the disciples are gathered for the Jewish holy day of Pentecost. The holy spirit comes over them, falls upon them with "tongues of fire," giving them sudden power to speak in various languages, so those from Cappadocia heard Jesus proclaimed in Cappadocian and those from Phrygia heard it in Greek. Some thought this a miracle. Others sneered that the apostles were drunk on new wine because they were dancing and carrying on and speaking in strange tongues. That's when Simon Peter took over, explaining that they were not drunk, but, rather, they were filled with the Holy Spirit. "In the last days it will be, God declares, that I will pour out my spirit upon all flesh, and your sons and your daughters shall prophesy, and your young men shall see visions, and your old men shall dream dreams. . . . The sun shall be turned to darkness and the moon to blood before the coming of the Lord's great and glorious day. Then everyone who calls on the name of the Lord shall be saved." By the end of that day, three thousand new souls were added to the Christian church.

This story became the basis for a new, more passionate form of American worship that sprang up in Kansas in the early 1900s and flowered during the Roaring Twenties and the later desperation of the Great Depression of the thirties. Pentecostals, interpreting the Bible literally, accepted Christ as the savior of humanity and were compelled to share the faith before the Last Days, when the "Born Again" will be whisked to heaven in the Rapture. In these churches, the Devil was as real as God, so most of human culture was inherently sinful, because it brought pleasure. The archetypal Pentecostal was a humorless scold, but the church services often exploded in a wild collective joy that brought freedom and abandon in worship. Music flowed through everything, and people "spoke in tongues" when rationality failed. Healings, miracles, and exorcisms were normal events. Aimee Semple McPherson became the archetype of the Pentecostal woman preacher portrayed by Sinclair Lewis in his novel *Elmer Gantry*. The Pentecostals were truly populist, and way out in front of the mainstream churches on issues of gender equality and racial diversity. McPherson's powerful ministry, one of the first amplified by radio, would have been barred by the Methodists, the Baptists, and other mainstream denominations, because she was a woman. Even old class distinctions tended to blur in the new churches built among the cornfields and pastures, well outside of town. The gospel-infused singing was loud, raucous, the ancestor of the "praise music" phenomenon currently in vogue in many mainline suburban churches. It was religion as charismatic theater—performance and presentation. Some Pentecostals are "Holy Rollers," enraptured with the Holy Spirit that filled Jesus's disciples. Some handle poisonous snakes, or walk on hot coals, almost daring the Lord: gambling with pain and death for the sake of Jesus.

Stephen Bailey took his family to church at least twice a week, sometimes more. This was how Axl Rose grew up, in the middle of the conservative, puritanical American heartland in the 1960s and 1970s.

DEVIL VISIONS

When Axl's mother got rid of her baby's sociopath father and married a Pentecostal martinet, it meant her son would be raised under a harsh regimen of discipline, serial church attendance, and what Axl later described as regular beatings and psychic abuse. The sensitive boy responded to this immediately, suffering nightmares and other symptoms. Sometimes Bill's dreams were so disturbed he fell out of the top bunk in the room he shared with his sister. Later in life, he said he had suffered seizures. Once he awoke on the floor, bloody because he had pierced his bottom lip with his teeth. In his early school years at Oakland Elementary, he wonderingly described for his parents vivid night visions of being a baby and living in a house with his mother and another man, a strange man who did bad, bad things to him. Bill Bailey had no idea that Stephen Bailey was not his father. (He called him Dad.) His parents told him the visions were false, placed there by the Devil to scare him. But the boy somehow remembered something important, and knew that the visions were true. Years later, Axl remembered: "This was a mystery I tried to uncover since I was a little kid, you know? 'Cos as a kid, I was always told it was the Devil who made me know *for sure* what the inside of a house looked like that I supposedly never lived in. But I *knew* I did. I *knew* I'd lived in this house when I was a little kid. Weird things like that happened to me all the time."

The family went out to their country church, about eight miles outside Lafayette, as much as they could, anywhere from three to six times a week—but at the very least on Sunday morning, Sunday night, and Wednesday night. There wasn't a choir as such; the whole congregation sang out the old hymns—"Come to the church in the wildwood, come to the church in the vale." Young Bill Bailey had a sweet, melodious voice and could be heard above the rest of the believers. Later, he sang in a gospel trio with his sister and brother, and the piano lessons his mother bought for him led to his playing in church. "This was a Holy Roller, Pentecostal, hell-raising revival," he later told an interviewer. "We had tent meetings, we had healings; we saw blind people read; people would talk in tongues; there were foot washings, the whole bit." Youngsters were expected to preach as early as ten years old, so after winning a series of Bible contests—correctly identifying chapter and verse—Bill was invited to sermonize one Wednesday night, perhaps his first exposure to performing before a full house. He thought he had seen real miracles when cripples got out of wheelchairs and walked, but he kept being disappointed that nothing like that ever happened to him. "I knew more gospel songs than anybody else," he said later, "but if there's a god up there, I don't know him. I didn't have a clue about it."

The family's religious life dominated the Bailey household. There was no record player, and the radio played only on Sunday afternoons, when Mom and Dad shut the bedroom door after lunch and had their "special time." "We'd have television for about a week," Axl remembered, "and then my stepdad would throw them out because they were satanic." Everything was evil. Women were temptresses. "I remember the first time I got smacked for looking at a woman. I don't know how old I was, or what [show] I was looking at, but it was a cigarette ad on TV with two girls coming out of the water in bikinis. I was just watching this—not thinking, just watching—and my dad smacked me in the mouth, and I went flying across the floor."

His teachers noticed Bill's singing voice early on. "When I was in first grade, I wasn't allowed to cross the street until I sang an Elvis Presley song. In third grade, at recess, the teachers would put me on a tree stump and make me sing Top Forty and Elvis songs for the younger kids. I loved to work on the harmonies, and I was always getting into trouble for singing everyone else's parts." Almost everyone who went to school with Bill Bailey remembers him singing on the playgrounds.

Bill was expected to be a good student and so brought home straight A's until he was about twelve. But a bad grade, rude behavior, or a sarcastic remark could bring a violent response from Dad. Trying to bang out Led Zeppelin's raunchy "D'yer Mak'er" on the family piano brought on a sneak attack that knocked Bill off the piano bench. Axl later characterized his stepfather as "a paranoid control freak."

And he learned to live with it, for as long as he had to. Years later, he would become (unusually) inarticulate when trying to explain what he had been through. "If a kid is getting beaten, and someone offers help, and the kid just fucking *goes off*... a lot of the time the punishment is just compounded. Instead of helping the kid, and trying to break through to him, it was like, *'No, this is a problem, right now! Do you understand me?'* But that does not fucking work. Commands like SHUT UP and SIT DOWN are outdated if you are trying to help someone."

Often Bill lost himself in music. Years later, he wistfully recalled how the melodies and feelings expressed in the songs he liked became like friends when he was a child. "I heard 'D'yer Mak'er' [in 1973] and I was hooked," he said later. "It blew my mind, and after that I was a Led Zeppelin freak. [Referring to Jimmy Page] I thought, *How does he write like this? How does he feel like this?* I mean, everything around me was religious and strict. This song got into my thoughts and stayed there. It got me into hard rock, big-time. It was like, *How does he think like this*, you know?"

*B*ill was an outsider in school. In the sixth grade at Sunnyside Middle School, he was forced by his parents to wear starched white shirts, buttoned to the neck; black polyester trousers; white socks, black shoes. "I was an outcast, a totally fucking little nerd," he recalled, "because my parents made me dress weird and forced me to get a bowl haircut. Nobody else looked anything like that. The cool kids thought I was a hick. It was totally fucking embarrassing." Then there was the religious thing; winning Bible quizzes in a down-market church was decidedly uncool. If Bill tried to change anything about this, like growing his hair a little, or sneaking a cigarette, a whipping would fall on him like a tongue of fire.

Sometimes, when he was bullied and tormented by Dad, he instinctively turned to Mom for help. But she was afraid of her husband and couldn't help her wild-hearted son. She had her own problems. "I remember watching something horrible happen to my mother when she came to [help] me," he said, twenty years later. "And I got a lot of

violent, abusive thoughts towards women out of watching my mom
with this man.

"I was totally brainwashed in a Pentecostal church," Axl said in
1992, after intensive psychotherapy. "My particular church was filled
with self-righteous hypocrites who were child abusers, child molest-
ers. These were people who'd been damaged in their own childhoods
and lives. These were people who were finding God, but still living
with their damage and inflicting it upon their children. I'm not against
churches or religion, but I do believe . . . that most organized religions
make a mockery of humanity."

Yet somehow, out of this repressive childhood came an instinctive
realization, a *power,* a precognition of his future might. Singing all
the time, preaching to rapt, perspiring believers, playing piano at his
family's church, Bill Bailey learned how to work an audience, how to
handle himself before a crowd, how to manipulate the fervor of the
faithful. Pentecostalism already had major rock star affinities. (Little
Richard was now a Pentecostal preacher. Soon Al Green would open
his own tabernacle.) Ten years later, Axl recalled: "I realized something big—that I could *get up there,* in front of an audience, and direct
whatever message I wanted to give them—*forcefully.* It was something
I had in me. I could *do* this, and they would fucking *respond*! I could
sing in front of people!"

But he couldn't sing in front of his stepfather. One day he was in
the back of the car and Barry Manilow's big hit "Mandy" came on the
radio. Bill started to sing along with the song's catchy, highly suggestive chorus, and Dad turned around and smacked Bill in the mouth
for singing that "evil" song. The boy put his tongue to his lip and
tasted his own blood.

In 1974, when he was twelve, Bill Bailey was secretly listening to his
little radio under the covers one night. The number-one single was
10cc's "I'm Not in Love." Bill loved this ballad with its synthetic effects. When "Benny and the Jets" came on, Bill smiled with pleasure.
The song, from Elton John's *Goodbye Yellow Brick Road* album, was a
faux re-creation of a stadium concert, with ambient baseball-park
echo and the unholy roar of an immense crowd of rock fans. Bill

Bailey was transfixed by Benny and began having visions of himself onstage in a sold-out Dodger Stadium, before a hundred thousand crazy fans, singing his own songs and enjoying the adulation and power of the supreme preacher of the age, the Rock Star, performing for the largest audiences in history. "That's when I decided," he later said, "that I wanted to play a song I was proud of in front of big crowds. The way ['Benny'] was recorded made me want the stage. It made me think about a concert and being onstage and the way it would sound in a room, things all miked out.... Plus it reminded me of the glam scene that was going on around America, and the clubs and bands I would read about in *Creem* magazine and stuff like that. That's when I got the [Elton John] piano book, and was trying to learn the songs, and discovered the guy was playing ten fingers of the weirdest chords in the world. Elton's singing is amazing, and that piano solo can't be touched. It was a huge influence on me."

THE WILD BOY OF LAFAYETTE

*W*hen it was time for Bill Bailey to rebel against his parents, his church, his school, the whole social order—he did it big. This was in 1976, the era of *Frampton Comes Alive* and Fleetwood Mac's new lineup. Stevie Nicks was singing "Rhiannon" on the radio. The Eagles were huge, beckoning America west—"Welcome to the Hotel California"—the way the Beach Boys had a decade earlier. Soft rock was big. So was "Free Bird." Jimmy Carter, a Georgia peanut farmer, became president after defeating Gerald Ford. The former Georgia governor Carter had been endorsed by the Allman Brothers Band. Democrat spin doctors made sure America knew that Carter and his sons listened to Led Zeppelin on the campaign bus.

On the other side of Lafayette lived Jeffrey Isbell, a quiet music fanatic who played drums. Born in Florida in 1962, he moved to Indiana before starting school. There was Indian blood on his father's side. They lived "so far out in Bumfuck" that he had to ride his bike to someone's house for ten miles in any direction, all on gravel roads.

When Jeff's parents split up, he moved into Lafayette with his mom and brother Joe. He was guided toward music in part by his grandmother, who played in a little group with her friends. He asked for a drum kit when he was thirteen, and the family got one for him. His best friend had some older brothers who were the local hooligans. They rode bikes, got drunk, fought each other like mad dogs. He remembered, "They'd have these bands play at this old farmhouse, with a barn like an airplane hangar. So I'd be hanging out there, getting shit-faced, and when they'd got so drunk they couldn't play, they'd go, 'C'mon up here, little kid, and play the drums.' So that was my first adrenaline rush. Other than that, my life was completely boring."

Then he met Bill Bailey. On the first day of ninth grade, he was sitting in class and heard a commotion. "I hear this noise going on in front, and then I see these fucking books flying past, and I hear yelling and cursing, and then a scuffle, and then I see him—Axl—and this teacher's bouncing off the fuckin' door jamb. And then he was gone, tear-assing down the hall with a whole bunch of teachers running after him." Jeff (a.k.a. Izzy Stradlin) laughed at the memory. "That was the first time I ever saw him."

When things calmed down, Bill and Jeff became friends, bonding over music, skateboards, and a caustic distaste for everything Indiana. Izzy recalls: "We were long-haired guys in a high school where you were either a jock or a stoner. We weren't jocks, so we ended up hanging out together." To Jeff, three months younger than Bill, Alice Cooper and Zeppelin were cool, but the Rolling Stones were gods, and the slim, dark-haired teenager patterned his look and attitude on the glowering Glimmer Twin, Keith Richards, and also on Keith's American counterpart, Aerosmith's Joe Perry. Bill and Jeff both loved Aerosmith, America's hometown band, a band that kids in Indiana could actually see, unlike dinosaur bands like Zeppelin that lumbered through the big cities only every few years. Aerosmith stayed on the road all the time in the seventies, played hard rock in Stones and Yardbirds mode, and made deep impressions with their albums of the era: *Toys in the Attic* (1975), *Rocks* (1976), and *Draw the Line* (1979).

Bill was heavy into flamboyant Elton John, and knew every track on Elton's first seven albums because he studied them. To develop his voice, he'd lock himself in the bathroom and sing along with *The*

Eagles Greatest Hits. He and Jeff liked the big English bands of the day: Bowie, T. Rex, Queen (especially *Queen II*), Electric Light Orchestra (especially *Out of the Blue*)—Bill saw ELO play in Indianapolis. And they were knowledgeable about second-division UK bands, especially Nazareth and Thin Lizzy, featuring Phil Lynott's skewed stories and twin guitar attack. They stayed up late on weekend nights to watch the syndicated network TV music shows—*In Concert* and *Rock Concert*. Axl: "In Indiana, Lynyrd Skynyrd were considered God to the point that you ended up saying, 'I hate this fucking band.'" But everyone turned the radio up when "Free Bird" came on.

Then there was AC/DC: raw power from Down Under with a guitar hero who dressed like a schoolboy and a singer whose ghastly scream could saw a tavern bar in half.

So rock fanaticism brought two dissimilar personalities together. Bill was hot-tempered, restless, random, trouble-prone. Jeff was cool, reserved, sarcastic, organized, with an unshakable conviction and a steely determination that he was born to be in a band. All through high school they played together in garage bands. At first Jeff played drums and Bill sang and played piano. Then Bill moved to bass and Jeff sang. Later Jeff played bass and Axl sang. But there were no gigs for them, no place to play unless they could talk someone into renting a hall and throwing a dance. The local bars featured only country groups or cover bands—"which we hated at the time," Izzy recalled. "When you're sixteen, you hate everything you see when you live out there."

Axl said it wasn't much of a band: "We'd do one gig in, like, six months."

Bill managed to keep up his piano lessons. "But I really only played my lesson on the day of the lesson," he remembered. "The rest of the time I'd just sit at the piano and make up stuff. To this day, I still can't play other people's songs." On the day of his piano lesson, he always detoured into a nearby pharmacy, where he sneaked a peek at his favorite magazine, *OUI*, an edgier version of its sister monthly *Playboy*. *OUI*'s younger centerfolds attracted younger "readers."

When he was fifteen, Bill Bailey started to vent his anger and act out his frustrations by getting in some serious trouble. His juvenile records are sealed, but he began to get arrested for petty crimes like possession of alcohol, loitering, or just mouthing off to the cops whose job it was to keep Lafayette's bored, unruly teenagers off the streets. After two years in high school, he'd been busted at least four times and was hated by the local cops, who thought he was crazy. They even arrested him for drinking in his own family's backyard. There were a couple of detectives who really hated him for his drunken personal insults as well as his general attitude of total disrespect. Once, while being arrested in someone else's car, Bill asked them when they were going to stop harassing him, and they told him they would leave him alone after they'd run his sorry ass out of town.

"I was one of the craziest of my friends," he said years later, "but also one of the smartest, so the cops figured I was the ringleader. The first time I got drunk I was sixteen. I was with these three guys, and I had never smoked pot or taken any drugs before. We bought a case of beer, we bought ten joints, and I bought forty Valiums—10 mg. Valiums for five dollars apiece. I ate ten of 'em, drank a bunch of beers, and we smoked all these joints. Then we went to this rock concert downtown, at the Morris Theater, where Roadmaster was playing. They were like the biggest local band we had.

"At the theater I was acting up, and this girl goes, 'You are just too fucked up.' So I tore up her ticket and threw it at her. Then I went over to the front of city hall and directed traffic for a while. Then I threw a beer at this fucking cop, so my friend grabbed me and put a different jacket on me and snuck me back into the concert.

"It was packed. I walked in and tripped over another friend, who was passed out in the aisle. Then this other guy stands up, looks at me, and says, 'What the hell are you looking at?' He was this big ugly guy so I hit him as hard as I could. I saw his teeth go down his throat, so I ran."

But the night was still young. "I fell out the window of a two-story building and broke my hand. I broke into an insane asylum, broke in one side and out the other because I couldn't figure out how to get around this building. I wrecked a bicycle that had no brakes under a train. Then my friend Paul found me and put me in his car, and then I went flying over another car, and then my friend's dad came running out of the house from across the street. He wanted to shoot my other friend because he thought somebody was out to kill me. It was a very exciting night. In fact, I went and got drunk the next day just to forget about it."

"Axl was a *serious lunatic* when I met him," Izzy said, years later. "He was just fuckin' really bent on fighting, and destroying things. Somebody would look at him wrong, and he'd start a fight. And you think about Lafayette, man, there's like *fuck all* to do.... If it wasn't for the band, I just hate to think what he'd have done."

*P*unk rock hit Middle America in 1977 with seismic fury. The records didn't sell all that much, but the culture did wonders for negative teen spirit. The Sex Pistols' *Never Mind the Bollocks*, with its screaming guitar attack and anarchist snarl, was huge. The Clash were next, along with Generation X, Subway Sect, and the Slits. The Ramones blasted out of New York and played in Indianapolis. Bill and Jeff got cassettes of the Ramones' first two albums and spent hours learning the easy, three-chord songs. Also that year, the group Boston set a historic sales record for a band's first album. "More Than a Feeling" was on the radio constantly. Bill loved the album and learned most of the songs.

Jeff Isbell hated Indiana and wanted out. He wanted to go to Los Angeles and start a band. It was all he could think about. Bill Bailey was supportive. He told Jeff that the band they would have together would someday break Boston's sales record by many millions of albums. He could see it, almost touch it, this golden destiny in the West. He had a recurring dream of living in a big house in California with a view of the blue sea, whose walls were covered by framed gold and platinum albums.

Meanwhile they were still in high school, and it was the usual nightmare. Bill Bailey sang in the chorus, and they did Handel's *Messiah* at Christmas. The school was fanatically anti-punk. Everybody loved the Rolling Stones until one night in 1978 when the Stones were playing on NBC's *Saturday Night Live*, promoting *Some Girls*, with the whole country watching. Insanely, lewdly, years after the glam vibe had peaked, Mick Jagger tongued Ron Wood's face during "Shattered." Suddenly, the Rolling Stones were branded as gay in the high schools, and everyone who still liked the Stones was a fag.

*T*hings started to go really badly for Bill Bailey when he was sixteen. He was going through his mother's drawers one day and came upon some old papers. His mom's high school diploma had a different name on it from her maiden name. Insurance papers described him as not the son of his dad, Stephen Bailey, but of someone named William Rose. He read in these papers that his real name was William Bruce Rose.

He confronted his mother, and she told him the truth—or at least some of it. When his dad came home from work, they had a meeting of sorts. His parents told Bill that his real father had hurt his mother and was no good. And they just didn't want to talk about him—ever. Bill asked where his real father was, and was told that they didn't know, and didn't want to know. Bill was getting the idea that something terrible had happened with this guy, and was in effect told that, yes, something very bad had happened, but they wouldn't tell him about it. Bill noticed his mother's eyes would grow black with fury whenever he mentioned his real father.

He went to his relatives, his uncles, but no one would tell him anything except that Bill Rose was a bad actor, a troublemaker, and was more than likely dead. If he tried to say something at home, they told him, "Your real father does not get brought up."

All the same, Bill Bailey changed his name. He told friends that from now on, he wanted to be called W. Rose. For a while he wanted to be called Babe. One of the short-lived local bands he'd sung with was called AXL, which then became his moniker. When the band broke up, he kept using the name, and styled himself "W. Axl Rose."

Bill's mood swings became more violent and uncontrolled, and some of the kids in school were afraid of him. Some of the Lafayette cops were afraid of him. A psychiatrist noted Bill's high IQ and decided his behavior indicated intermittent psychosis. His arrest record grew longer, and his grades dropped way down. Then, toward the end of his junior year, in 1978, he dropped out of high school. He set up his own little school at home. He moved a piano into his room so he could practice in private. He filled his room with art supplies, which in turn attracted friends who came over after school to draw and paint and listen to music. His parents wanted him to go back, but he refused. He was often seen reading in the public library on school mornings, buried in a book for as long as his limited attention span allowed. "Basically," he said later, "I started to put myself through Axl's school of subjects that I wanted to learn about."

Those few people who knew him well thought Bill Bailey was actually a pretty good kid at heart. Monique Gregory, one of his friends from that era, provides a snapshot of Axl's dropped-out life: "[We liked] Axl's bedroom because he just had mattresses sitting around and drawing pads and his piano, so you could get really artistic in there. He practiced his piano a lot, just sat down and played the most beautiful things, especially a lot of Elton John. His creative side was just so intense, it grounded the little group of people that gathered around him."

The following September, he tried to return for his senior year. But after some fights and another arrest, everyone agreed that he leave Jefferson High and try something else. Everyone suggested that Bill "get some help," but it is unknown whether he received any significant professional counseling in this period.

Jeff Isbell, meanwhile, kept his grades up and graduated from high school in June 1979—the only original member of Guns N' Roses with a diploma. He kept hanging out with Bill Bailey, rehearsing "Jumpin' Jack Flash" ad nauseam. They studied the new bands, especially Cheap Trick and Van Halen, and Jeff kept talking with Axl about being in a band together someday.

True to his word, sometime late that summer, Jeff Isbell packed his guitar, his drum kit, a guitar amplifier, and his clothes into an old car and left Lafayette, headed for Los Angeles to be a rock star. (It would take eight years to make this happen, but Jeff did it.) Bill Bailey would have waved good-bye to his friend, but he was spending the summer in the county jail. He didn't trust the public defenders, and his family was fed up and wouldn't pay for an attorney. He'd tried to plead on his own behalf, but the judge had seen enough of Bill Bailey and locked him up. When Jeff Isbell lit out for the territory, Bill was doing three months in jail because he didn't have the money to pay his fines.

Later, in 1986, when he was just starting to make his mark in the world, W. Axl Rose summed up these turbulent years:

"You know, I grew up in a place where I got sick of being made fun of by straights. I had real long hair. I got kicked out of my house when I was sixteen because my dad was real strict and I wouldn't cut my hair. Then they called me a drug addict, when I was actually running cross-country and completely into living healthy. So I left home, got into beer, drugs, and went to jail about twenty fucking times, and five of those times I was guilty of what they busted me for—disturbing the peace. The other times were for the simple fucking reason that the cops fucking hated me. But I always kept my hair long. When I went back to high school, where I knew that certain people had had respect for me—some of the athletes and student council types—and suddenly, they didn't! They thought I was a fuckin' hippie! But I wasn't really friendly with the hippies because I liked all kinds of music. If you thought Devo or the Sex Pistols were good, you were a punk rocker. If you liked Bowie or the Stones, you were a fag. So now, to them, I was now a hippie punk faggot, you know? All at the same time."

SLASH'S BIG AWAKENING

While Axl and Izzy were enduring excruciating adolescence in Indiana, Slash and Steven Adler were hanging out in actual Hollywood and dreaming of what they instinctively foresaw as certain stardom for themselves and their future band.

They were three years younger than the Indiana boys, both born in 1965. Steven, born in Cleveland, came to Los Angeles from Ohio with his family when he was a baby. Slash was born Saul Hudson in England, in Stoke-on-Trent, one of the Staffordshire "Potteries." His parents were both artists. Tony Hudson was English and Jewish, a talented art director who specialized in album design. His mother, Ola Oliver, was a black American costume designer who worked in the theater and in the rock world. When the Hudsons moved to L.A., they settled in the musical haven of Laurel Canyon, in the hills above Hollywood, and pursued their careers. Tony Hudson designed platinum-selling album jackets for artists like Neil Young. His most famous album design, Joni Mitchell's *Court and Spark* (1974), was for their Lookout Mountain Road neighbor David Geffen's record label, Asylum Records. (David Geffen once babysat for tiny Saul as a favor to his parents. Twenty-five years later, when Guns N' Roses was the baddest band in the world, Geffen joked to his executives that he had diapered the reptilian Slash when he was a baby.)

Ola worked with major black seventies rock stars like Chaka Khan and Diana Ross, as well as touring groups like the Pointer Sisters. She made stage clothes for Ringo Starr and Carly Simon. Big rock stars like Ron Wood and Iggy Pop were always in and out of the Hudson household. Drink and drugs were a normal part of the family's diet. Young Saul showed early artistic flair and could draw as soon as he could pick up a pencil. As a child, he contributed animal drawings to an unpublished book of neighbor Joni Mitchell's verse called *The Bestiary*. (Mitchell was living in David Geffen's house in this period.) Saul was fascinated by dinosaurs and snakes and liked to draw the small lizards that had been living in the hills above Hollywood for millions of years.

In 1975, Ola started working on the costumes for David Bowie's sci-fi movie *The Man Who Fell to Earth*. The Hudsons split up around then, and Saul's mom began dating Bowie, who was in his blatant coke-freak "Thin White Duke" persona. Slash remembered: "She was making all his clothes, and I fucking *hated* it, because he took the place of my dad. It was still the age of free love, and you didn't say no. I was sort of young, but this still was weird. [Bowie] had this little white Mercedes, and this huge fuckin' house up in Bel Air that he rented while he was in L.A. His wife was there too, with their son Zowie, and I'd have to hang out with them. They'd take me up there, and I'd think: *What the fuck is this? Why does he have such a big house?* All the to-do he would put into everything . . . It was just fucking ridiculous."

So Saul Hudson grew up in a louche Hollywood milieu that prepared him for a later life with an alternate persona, someone called "Slash." "I grew up in a kind of rebellious hippie household," he said later, "and I was given a lot of freedom as a kid. Like my parents were always telling each other to *'fuck off,'* which is an English thing; so when I started saying it, *'fuck off,'* when I was, like, seven or eight, people thought it was funny.

"My parents were always supportive of me, whatever I did," he recalled. "And I really love them for that."

Slash got his nickname from the renowned character actor Seymour Cassel. "I was friends with his kids, and he used to call me 'Slash,' because I was an aspiring guitar player, always hustling, never stopping to hang out. To him, it looked like I was always in a hurry, so he started calling me that, and it stuck."

With lots of parental love but little actual supervision, Slash was one of the semi-feral lost boys of Hollywood, sometimes staying out all night, sometimes hustling Quaaludes or scalping tickets to club shows, or just hanging out in the parking lot of the Rainbow Bar and Grill on the Sunset Strip, waiting to see who came out and what happened when the club closed at two in the morning. And there were serious sightings, since the Rainbow was the Hollywood "local" of visiting English rockers: members of Zeppelin and their teenage groupies; the Stones and their girlfriends; Elton and his gay entourage; Slade; the Sweet; Judas Priest.

Slash's grandmother, also named Ola, was the anchor of his childhood. A serious lady who could curse like Richard Pryor when provoked, she kept an eye on Saul, and even gave him his first guitar. "I used to fuck up around the house, and she'd chase me around the couch. She'd freak out when I played 'Black Dog' really loud." But this no-nonsense woman was extremely loving and supportive of her grandson, and provided the kind of backbone and background that he would need to survive on the streets of Los Angeles a decade later.

He later mused that he was lucky to have grown up in such an absurdly self-indulgent and ego-driven world. "I watched all this heavy shit go down, all the time. I watched people go down. And I learned from it."

Slash claims that he started drinking when he was about twelve. "I like being drunk," he explained in 1990. "It helps me. It brings me out of my shell. It's a habit I picked up when I was twelve years old." His father, he added, was a heavy drinker. "I had total freedom, all the time," he said. "I used to not come home for weeks."

Up to that point, he'd been unpopular at school. "I had really long hair, and the schools I went to were filled with the kids of bankers and real estate agents. [One exception was Lenny Kravitz, who went to grade school with Slash.] So I was just too weird, had a different background, and never really fitted in," he recalled. "But when I was thirteen I just thought, fuck it, and didn't care about it any more. Then all of a sudden I started becoming popular because I was playing the guitar. It was really strange. All the kids around me changed. Then I stopped even caring because I was into hanging out by myself and practicing guitar."

*O*ne day in 1977, Slash was racing his BMX bike with some other kids at Bancroft Junior High in Hollywood. There was another kid there, on a skateboard, who was busting moves to impress the girls who were watching. But he lost control and smashed his head on the way down. Slash walked over to see if the kid was OK. This was Steven Adler.

They both went to Bancroft but didn't really know each other. However, both were heavy into music and liked some of the same bands (Steven liked KISS, Slash didn't), especially local gods Van Halen, still playing high schools and beach piers in 1977. Steven took Slash to his house on North Hayworth Avenue. He showed Slash his electric guitar and plugged into this little amp. Slash remembers: "He just plugged in and turned all the way up and banged on it—real loud. I was fuckin' just fascinated by it."

Steven Adler was a very Hollywood, very seventies, very post-hippie type of kid: funny, relaxed, happy-go-lucky; an innocent-looking simpleton who walked to eighth grade in the morning, smoking a joint. ("The first time I got wasted, I was eight years old. I smoked some pot in my grandmother's bathroom.") With his wooly blond curls, saucy strut, and vacant blue eyes, he was very attractive to the local gay predators. Steven told an interviewer, "When I was twelve, thirteen years old, I was living in Hollywood, off Santa Monica Boulevard and Fairfax. And Santa Monica Boulevard was a very gay neighborhood...where guys pick up guys for, like, sex...So Slash lived on Sweetzer and I lived on North Hayworth, and there were a couple times that I was on my way over there, walking down the street, and I got a blow job from some guy. I was, like, thirteen years old. I used to walk around with a fucking hard-on, you know, twenty-four hours a day. I was, like, a teenager...and your girlfriends aren't doing it yet . . . and so I was partying with somebody, and I got a blow job. I was thirteen. What? I'm the only one?"

*O*ne night Slash sneaked out of the house to sell Quaaludes outside the Starwood nightclub, and then later he ended up on Hollywood Boulevard, an all-night sleaze bazaar of peep shows, porn shops, liquor stores, hustlers, and whores. It was deep Hollywood, but very alive, and drew the down-and-out from all over, and those who loved them. "I was walking by this hamburger stand at, like, three in the morning. A small crowd had gathered, and there was this crazy fucking guy, on acid or something, who'd decided that he'd fucking had enough, and he was going to beat someone up. He went after the wrong guy, I guess, because he got knifed, right in front of me, and then he was, like, *laid out* on the fucking sidewalk, man." He smiled at the memory. "And I've been on Hollywood Boulevard ever since."

*W*hen Slash was thirteen, he experienced what he later called his "Big Awakening."

"I'd been trying to get into this older girl's pants for a while, and she finally let me come over to her house. We hung out, smoked some pot, and listened to Aerosmith's *Rocks*. It hit me like a ton of fucking bricks. I sat there listening to it, over and over, and then totally blew off this girl, who was annoyed. I remember riding my bike back to my grandma's house, somehow knowing that my life had changed. It was one of those moments that brought clarity. Now, maybe for the first time, I passionately identified with something."

According to Slash, he discovered what would become his signature sound by listening to Aerosmith's two guitarists, Joe Perry and Brad Whitford, the reigning American masters of the guitar style known as "flash." Flash guitar was pioneered in England by the Yardbirds and The Who, in 1965. Flash was explosive musical energy, released as a blast of white sonic heat. It was feedback and drone with R&B overdrive. Flash was a way of holding the guitar, usually low-slung, and moving with it, acting out the raw power of the music:

Jeff Beck playing his guitar behind his neck, Jimmy Page's gunfighter boogie. It was Jimi Hendrix setting his Stratocaster on fire.

Slash went to Tower Records on Sunset and expertly shoplifted a cassette of *Rocks*. "The key to *Rocks* is the first two songs: 'Back in the Saddle' and 'Last Child.' That combination basically ripped my head off." (But the song he actually liked most was "Nobody's Fault.") "Aerosmith had this very intense vibe—aggressive, drugged-out, psychotic—but at the same they had a Stones-y blues thing going on. There was just nothing cooler than Aerosmith coming out of America at that point."

In late summer 1978, Slash went to see Aerosmith play at a nearby festival, with Van Halen and Ted Nugent opening. "They [Aerosmith] were *incredibly* loud, and I barely recognized a note, but it was still the most bitchin' thing I'd ever seen. I totally identified with Joe Perry's image, both visually and sound-wise. He was streamlined, in a way that reminded me of Keith Richards. He always looked completely fuckin' wasted, and had this 'careless' guitar style that was really cool. But I was also into Brad Whitford's guitar solos, and eventually [Whitford] had a more direct influence on the way I play than anybody realizes. And anyone who sings needs to be exposed to Steven Tyler.

"Classic Aerosmith—they were our teenage heroes. I grew up on the Stones, Dylan, the Kinks, Zeppelin, but when I discovered this one Aerosmith record, I related to it on a different level. The decadence, the sloppy guitars, the huge drums, the screaming...The whole of it did something to me. They were the template for what I do...as well as most other bands that came after us—Soundgarden, Alice in Chains, Nirvana, Pearl Jam. We all owe a serious debt to Aerosmith."

The next time Slash shoplifted cassette tapes from Tower Records, the security guard stopped him at the door. They took him upstairs to the office, which had a one-way mirror overlooking the selling floor. They searched his jeans and found the tapes. He told them he just forgot to pay. OK, they said, pay now and you can go. He had no money. They threatened to call the police. Then they told him to call home so his parents could come and pay for the tape. He called home, and his mom—who often shopped at the store and was known to the

staff—arrived and paid for the tapes. The manager told her that her
son was banned from Tower Records—a serious indignity in West Hollywood.

In 1978 the Pasadena band Van Halen released their first album.
They had been playing (as Mammoth) since 1974 but came alive
only after hiring singer David Lee Roth (who had actually failed his
first audition with the group). But Roth had his own PA, so they
eventually let him into the band, which he renamed after the Van
Halen brothers, because it sounded cool. The *Van Halen* debut album was a sensational, hard-rocking bitch slap against punk rock,
with Eddie Van Halen acquiring immediate and awesome street
cred for deploying the most innovative arsenal of guitar techniques
to appear on the scene since Jimi Hendrix. Van Halen helped develop string-tapping and shredding—the speedy, hypertechnical picking style that injected a shot of meth into heavy metal and which
millions of would-be guitar gods would soon start slaving to master.
Eddie's technical genius and musical chops, plus Roth's hearty vocals, athletic showmanship, and long blond locks established Van
Halen almost overnight as Hollywood's top-dog band and America's
latest response to the mighty Zeppelin (which, unknown to all, had
already played its last American shows). Van Halen ruled the Strip
as Slash was growing up, and Eddie Van Halen had an incalculable
influence over him, as he had over every young guitarist in the
country for the next ten years.

Stevie Adler switched to drums around the time he and Slash
started ninth grade at Fairfax High in Hollywood. (They also cut their
wrists and rubbed them together, according to Adler, becoming "blood
brothers.") With so many show business families living nearby, the
school was bursting with talented kids, and the two pals quickly
joined one of the school's two rock and roll bands. (The other starred
super-talented guitarist Tracy Ulrich—the future Tracii Guns.) But
Slash and Stevie mostly cut school and hung out, smoked dope, did
poppers, jammed all the time, and actively talked themselves into the

total assurance that they and their band were destined to be major rock stars when they grew up.

"I *always* knew it, since I was ten years old," Adler said—thirty years later. "Me and Slash grew up with each other. We've known each other since we were eleven years old! I gave him his first guitar, and showed him his first chords. The whole Guns N' Roses trip—that was *our dream* that we dreamed. We ditched school every fuckin' day, and all we did was talk about putting a real rock and roll band together. The best fucking band anyone had ever heard. Make a record. Travel around the world. Fuck all the girls we can.

"What still fucking kills me is that our dream came true! But there was *never* a doubt that we weren't going to do it, or that it wasn't going to happen."

Steven Adler dropped out of Fairfax High in the tenth grade. Slash stayed until his junior year, then just stopped going. Slash began playing in a band called Tidus Sloan. It was 1982, and the fugitive W. Axl Rose was on his way to Hollywood, waiting to be born.

THE HISTORY OF SUNSET STRIP

The old Chevy Impala carrying Jeff Isbell, the future Izzy Stradlin, somehow made it across half of America to Los Angeles, and within three days resourceful Jeff was in a band with a paying gig. Usually, for most musicians arriving in Hollywood in obsessive pursuit of their silk scarf fantasies, this kind of progress took much longer, or never happened at all. First you settled in somewhere, usually a cheap motel. Needing to make connections, you checked out the bulletin boards at the Guitar Center or Tower Records. You perused the classified ads in *Music Connection* and *The Recycler.* You hung around The Troubadour, the fabled music club on Santa Monica Boulevard. Most of all, after midnight, you made the scene on the legendary Sunset Strip, still Hollywood's nighttime playground after fifty years.

The Strip had been American rock and roll's HQ since 1964, when two reputedly "connected" guys from Chicago opened the Whisky a Go Go in an old bank building at Sunset and Clark. Until then, the Strip's former Old Hollywood and fifties/Ratpack glamour had faded after Frank Sinatra and his cronies moved their acts to Las Vegas's casino lounges. The Whisky, patterned on sophisticated Parisian discotheques of the early sixties, where adults danced to pop songs, was an instant sensation when house band Johnny Rivers—stolen from Gazzari's nightclub just up the street—began to have hit records. Swingers packed the place. Steve McQueen had his own booth. So did Warren Beatty and other New Hollywood stars. John Lennon and Paul McCartney hung out at the Whisky with Jayne Mansfield. It was the hottest nightclub in America, and spawned dozens of other clubs along Sunset Boulevard, which needed new bands to fill them. The Byrds exploded on the Strip in 1965, followed by Sonny and Cher, The Mamas and the Papas, the Doors, Buffalo Springfield, and literally hundreds of other bands. On weekend nights, younger kids poured onto the Strip from the upscale suburbs and the San Fernando Valley. They hung out ten deep on the sidewalk and spilled into the road, annoying the sheriff's deputies and creating a whiff of antiauthoritarian tension. There were so many kids—barefoot girls blowing bubbles, long-haired guys with guitars—that people had a hard time getting from one club to another. You couldn't drive west on Sunset at night because it was too jammed. A week of riots erupted in 1966 over cop harassment, one of the first instances of sixties kids defending themselves against the police in the streets. Hollywood smelled tear gas for the first time. The whole scene was sexy, exhibitionist, and volatile. Featured in magazines and broadcast on television, the new Sunset Strip set the tone for youth entertainment for the rest of the country, and began to draw ambitious young musicians from all over.

The Rainbow Bar and Grill opened up the street from the Whisky and was soon a clubhouse for visiting rock stars. A few doors away, one of the old clubs reopened as the Roxy Theater, which became, along with the Troubadour, the premier band showcase in L.A. Now the folk rock hippies of the sixties gave way to the hard-rocking neon angels of the seventies—underdressed, amoral glitter kids in spandex, stacked heels, and big hair. The organic scent of reefer was replaced by the acrid odor of cocaine. The punks brought heroin into the scene a few years later. The Whisky and other clubs survived the punk slump in the late seventies by booking new bands, often on a "pay to play" basis, in which the band hired the club to book them and were paid with the door receipts. Now it was up to young musicians to lure an audience. Unsigned bands learned to promote themselves with street buzz and "flyering"—creating eye-catching photocopied leaflets—which became just as important to new bands as rehearsing and looking ultra-cool.

The Strip saw it all come and go. Country rock, glam, Rodney's English Disco, reggae, disco, punk, new wave, the Runaways, power pop, heavy metal. When Izzy and then Axl arrived from Indiana in the early eighties, the Strip was at the beginning of another upward thrust that, by the end of the decade, saw its hair metal energy assume a huge slice of not just the counterculture, but mainstream American culture as well. Not since the eighties has there been another era when so much of the mass market share—how kids looked, what they saw on TV, what they heard on the radio, what they bought in the record stores, what they read in magazines—derived from one specific street.

*W*hen Izzy got to town, the serious L.A. punk bands—Black Flag, X, the Blasters, Social Distortion, Fear—were still dominant. On his third day in town, he made a connection with some guys, went to see them, had a play, and was hired. "Since I had a car and a drum kit, I was an asset." The next gig was that weekend in a warehouse loft in L.A.'s then deserted downtown. "We're getting ready to go on," Izzy recalled, "and the rest of the band show up—completely in drag. I mean, lipstick, mascara, pink spandex tights, high heels. This was my band, but they'd forgot to tell me there was like a motif, you know?"

Izzy shrugged and took the stage in his Keef-looking outfit of white shirt, dark vest, cool scarf, cloth cap, his guitar slung low. "And it was like, slam music. BAM BAM BAM BAM. We made it through about three songs" before the local skinheads and Fear fans charged the stage and started spitting on the band. It was a punk chaos of curses, chairs, and bottles flying through the smoky air. Someone cut the lights. Someone called the cops. The bass drum got kicked in by a linebacker in Doc Martens. Izzy: "I stepped back and saw they were *beating the living fuck* out of the band. I grabbed a cymbal stand, took a few swings, and slipped out the back door.

"That kind of broke me into the way things were out here." It was simple: If you were in a band, you were at war. It was cutthroat competition, dog eat dog, with no quarter asked or given. Other bands would kill you if they could—or at least send you packing with your tail between your legs, back to the nowhere from which you'd arrived. "After that, I had no problems with how anyone looked or sounded, or if they didn't like you. So I guess it was a good way to break the ice."

ONE IN A MILLION

*B*ack in Indiana, Bill Bailey was restless. His family wanted him to finish high school, go to college. Everyone said Bill had such a good mind. His friends knew he was too big for Lafayette; some of them urged him to leave and find himself. But Bill Bailey wasn't ready to go just yet. He and a friend hitched to New York and back. He often hung out at Arni's, his fave pizzeria, on Elmwood Avenue. (Arni's upstairs seating area was called the "Toys in the Attic Room," in homage to Aerosmith.) Bill got himself arrested some more, mostly for petty crimes, but now the Lafayette cops were really out to get him.

"Once this girl picked me up in her mom's car. She was sixteen, maybe seventeen, and her mom reported the car stolen." The mother was horrified when someone called and said they'd seen her daughter in a car with Bill Bailey. The police stopped the car in West Lafayette, near Purdue. Axl was driving. "They tried to get me for grand theft auto, contributing to the delinquency of a minor, statutory rape—and I never even *touched* this girl. After they filed charges against me, I went over to her house and we had a little party. I left town after that."

This was late in 1979. Axl decided to hitchhike to Los Angeles and try to find Izzy. Izzy's mom told him that she didn't have a phone number for her son, who had purposefully dropped out of touch with his family. Axl thought he could probably find Izzy on his own, since he had a postcard Izzy had sent him from L.A. with a return address in Hollywood. He stuffed his backpack with a change of clothes and some cassettes, and put his thumb out on the entrance ramp to I-65. The first guy that picked him up took him up to Chicago and then all the way to St. Louis.

Axl remembers this with horror: "My first ride—this guy—told me I could crash on the floor of his hotel room. I was like, nineteen years old, very naïve, and very tired. So I basically passed out, but I woke up a couple of hours later with this guy trying to rape me." Axl shoved the man away, and he fell to the floor. As he got up, Axl reached into his backpack and grabbed his straight razor. "He came at me again. I went running for the door. He caught up with me, and I pinned him between the door and the wall." Axl held the razor up to the guy's face and hissed, "Don't *ever* touch me. Don't ever *think* about touching me. Don't touch yourself and think about touching me. *Nothing.*" The man ran out the door, leaving a badly shaken Axl to himself. "I'd almost killed this man, I was so frightened. I felt so violated. [Back then] I didn't know that I felt so violated because of what had happened to me in my childhood, and what I had pretty much buried—and didn't even remember."

Axl grabbed his stuff and fled into the night, sleepless, with no place to go, in the middle of nowhere, somewhere outside St. Louis. Shivering in the cold wind as the sun came up over the river, he stuck his thumb out and kept heading west.

He got to L.A. eventually, and was dropped off near the downtown bus station late at night, where Axl—this slender, red-headed kid in cowboy boots and very long hair—was confronted by a midnight carnival of sleaze. A boom box was blasting "The Message" by Grandmaster Flash and the Furious Five: *It's like a jungle sometimes / It makes me wonder / How I keep from going under.*

"I'd never been in a city this big before. Black people kept coming up to me, trying to sell me joints and stuff. I saw this huge black dude with a fucking Bowie knife take a boom box off this Chinese guy." He looked around. The sidewalk was thick with hookers, beggars, dope dealers—most of them black. People were shouting in Spanish, in Chinese. Latinos jostled him off the sidewalk by an all-night burrito stand. He tried to orient himself, get directions, but couldn't get a straight answer from anyone. "When I finally sat down, after walking in circles for three hours, the cops came by and told me to get off the streets. The cops down there have seen so much slime that they figured that if you had long hair, you're probably slime too."

Finally, someone took pity on the kid. "I was fortunate enough to have this black dude help me find my way. He guided me to the RTD station and showed me what bus to take. He wasn't after my money or anything. It was more like, *'Here's this new kid in town, and it looks like he might get in trouble down here. Let me help him get on his way.'* You could kind of say that he was—one in a million."

Axl searched for a week but couldn't find Izzy anywhere. When his money ran out, he hitched back to Lafayette. (Izzy later remarked: "He just had no fucking idea how *big* this place was.")

Bill Bailey kept working at music with his friend Paul Huge. Together they wrote a stupid, misogynist punk song called "Back Off Bitch." Axl somehow thought it was a cool song he could take with him to Los Angeles, when he moved there for good.

Axl turned eighteen in February 1980. After that his police records indicate numerous arrests and at least ten days in the county jail for criminal trespass, public intoxication, vagrancy, assault and battery, marijuana possession, car theft. So Bill kept leaving town for short periods in L.A., where he kept searching for Izzy wherever young musicians hung out: Canter's Deli on Fairfax; Tower Records on Sunset; Ben Frank's coffee shop. Sometimes, in the parking lot behind the Rainbow at two in the morning, he would hear things like: "Izzy from Indiana? He left an hour ago." Or, outside the Cathouse, where the white-hot Mötley Crüe was packing 'em in: "Izzy? Yeah man, he was here last night. We couldn't get in, so we hung out on the sidewalk."

Finally, in April 1980, on a rainy Easter Sunday morning, groggy Jeff Isbell woke up to a persistent knocking on the door of his little apartment. He had just gone to sleep, having played drums all night in a band called the Atoms. When he opened the door, Bill Bailey was standing there, dripping wet in cowboy boots, having walked for miles in the rain, carrying nothing but his soggy backpack. "Uh, well, Izzy," Axl said, smiling. "I've only been looking for you *at least* a fucking month."

Axl Rose said later that over the next two years he made eight round-trips between Indiana and Los Angeles, usually on a bus. What he later described as "very bad experiences with homosexuals" led him to avoid hitching if he had the money to ride the bus. On one of these long-haul rides, he heard some music in his head, some piano chords vaguely related to an old Elton John song, and wrote down the approximate notation in the notebook he was carrying. This Greyhound revelation was the beginning of the epochal late GN'R ballad "November Rain."

Finally, sometime in early 1982, things came to a head for Axl in Lafayette. "Me and my friends were always in trouble. Fuck, man, we'd get in trouble *just for fun.* There was nothing else, for kids like us. But with me, it finally reached a point where I just realized that I was going to end up in fucking prison, because I just kept fucking with the system."

During the summer of 1982, Axl said: "This guy and I got into a fight. I hit him, and he pressed charges. Later we got friendly, and he tried to drop the charges, but the state [attorney] wouldn't let him do it."

These assault and battery charges were eventually dropped, "so they tried other charges. They tried everything! Once you've pissed off a detective, it's like a fucking vengeance rap back there [in Indiana]. I'd already spent three months in jail, so now they were trying to brand me as a habitual criminal, which could mean, like, *life in prison.*" A public defender eventually managed to get the assault charges dismissed, but ancillary charges against Bill Bailey were pending, so the judge decided to keep him out on bail.

But then Axl skipped town, forfeited his bail, and lit out for the territory—a great American tradition. "I left town, and came to California," he recalled. "They ordered me *not* to leave, but I left anyway. My lawyer [eventually] took care of it. I didn't go back to Indiana for a *long* time."

So W. Axl Rose went on the lam. Even years later, even at the height of Guns N' Roses' greatest success, whenever Axl Rose returned to Lafayette to see family and friends, he kept a low profile and carefully avoided any contact with the police in his hometown.

Chapter Two

A GHOST SENT TO HAUNT US

**This band comes from zip.
We built it from nothing.
—Izzy Stradlin**

I WANT MY MTV

*A*xl Rose arrived in Hollywood with an Indiana girlfriend in December 1982, just as a colorful and ironically sleazy new scene along the Sunset Strip was beginning to take shape.

The roots of what became known as glam metal were in the East: the New York Dolls, Aerosmith, KISS, Boston, Cheap Trick. Led Zeppelin had retired from the arena after drummer John Bonham drank himself to death in 1980, leaving an immense gap for some lucky band to fill. Los Angeles musicians like Van Halen mutated these influences with the noisy British metal revival bands of the late seventies (Judas Priest, Ozzy, Iron Maiden, Def Leppard, Scorpions), and the chemistry ignited a new Hollywood rock underground characterized by garish costumes, overblown hair, feminizing makeup, frenetic stage shows, pain-level volume, and outrageously decadent public behavior usually involving drugs, alcohol, and ego trips. When Axl blew into town like some rough beast in dusty cowboy boots, many of the key players were already on the scene.

By 1982 Mötley Crüe had replaced Van Halen as true rulers of the Sunset Strip, simultaneously killing off the L.A. punk bands almost overnight. Crüe was four local musicians copying Eddie Van Halen's guitar anthems while decked out in stiletto heels, spandex, hair spray, hot-pink pants, and generous lashings of lipstick, rouge, mascara, and kohl. Presenting themselves as cheap hookers or drag queens, they were mediocre players but put on a loud, intense rock show that packed clubs like the Whisky, Club Lingerie, and the Starwood. Vince Neil had good stage moves and long blond hair puffed up high on his head like David Lee Roth. Drummer Tommy Lee played his ass off. Nikki Sixx thrashed his bass guitar until his fingers bled. Guitarist Mick Mars chopped out chords like he was cutting meat. Everybody knew Crüe was a mediocre band, but its show was a sensational revival of the New York Dolls' glam act, ten years after the fact.

Other bands on the scene included Great White, a Zeppelin cover band that succeeded in writing its own material and often gigged at the Troubadour; W.A.S.P., whose singer, Blackie Lawless, threw bloody chunks of raw meat at the audience and acted out gruesome torture rites with half-naked models stretched on a rack while the band cranked out heavy metal riffs; Ratt; Quiet Riot; Dokken. Up-and-coming new bands included Slayer and Metallica. Extremely influential glam band Hanoi Rocks arrived from Finland and captivated the Strip with its extreme hair. The band that became Poison drove in from Pennsylvania. Stryper and Warrant were on their way too, both from way out of town. These were the bands that would be magnified by the new medium of cable television until their music—variously glam metal, hair metal, girl metal, heavy metal—took over rock music later in the decade.

But in 1982, the L.A. band explosion was still underground. None of the glam bands were signed to major record labels. The new MTV cable channel was mostly putting British new wave bands—Haircut 100, Flock of Seagulls, U2—into heavy video rotation, and old school rock still dominated the radio, with Boston's J. Geils Band ending up with a simultaneous number-one single ("Centerfold") and album (*Freeze Frame*).

All this was shaping up amid a confusing period of transition for America, and even the world. Politically conservative governments—Reagan's in America, Mrs. Thatcher's in Britain—had taken power in the West in a backlash against socialism and even some cherished liberal ideals, beginning the eighties economic boom that would bury European communism later in the decade. Music that had been immensely popular in the seventies faded away. Punk rock sold out.

Disco developed AIDS. Reggae died with Bob Marley in 1981. The musical slate was clean, waiting for new stars. A few months later, Persian brown heroin, carried by refugees from Ayatollah Khomeini's revolution in Iran, killed star comedian John Belushi in a Hollywood bungalow, an indication of the sleazoid underbelly of stardom always in play in Los Angeles. A few years later, the AIDS virus killed "free love" and the so-called sexual revolution. Soon, according to Nancy Reagan, it was "Just Say No" to drugs. There was ultra-hot Madonna, dripping with sex, appearing on MTV, and begging her fans to use condoms in order to save their lives.

Some think that the L.A. glam bands of the eighties were an appropriate, *Dada* expression of youthful outrage at Reagan-era prudery and censorship. But reasonable, rational pundits of youth culture couldn't even have a conversation with a faggot-looking, heroin-smoking, tattooed rock star in leather and spandex, coming on like a white punk on dope.

But this was exactly what the programmers at MTV in New York were looking for, and this would impact the scene on the Strip by projecting its anarchist, dragon-chasing style into every upscale household in America. Beginning in 1982, MTV completely changed the equations of the American music business. It started in Houston, when local radio stations began getting massive requests for the new British boy band Duran Duran. The promo guys at the band's record label quickly discovered that the requests came only from the part of the city that was wired for cable TV. No kids on the other side of the tracks, the side without cable, had even heard of Duran Duran, who then rose to planetary fame on heavily rotated videos featuring cute guys, girls in bikinis, sailing yachts, and exotic locations. Before MTV, kids who loved a new band had to pay to see it play, just to find out what the band looked like. After MTV, the kids immediately knew what the band looked like, and if the look was wrong, they wouldn't pay to see them. Then the band wouldn't be on MTV anymore.

Michael Jackson filled the pop idol gap of the early eighties, but only because his record label forced MTV to play the groundbreaking videos made to accompany his new album, *Thriller.* Despite Michael's dancing and the brilliance of the *Thriller* music (which featured some Eddie Van Halen guitar solos), MTV was slow to show his videos because its audience was totally white. The cable companies hadn't yet bothered to wire low-income black neighborhoods, and MTV's audience research showed zero interest in seeing black stars on the channel. Media critics accused MTV of blatant racism. The channel responded that it had no black audience. Eventually, the label threatened to pull all the company's videos off the channel and complain to regulatory agencies. MTV relented, and Jackson's hot stuff—"Billie Jean," "Beat It," "Thriller"—dominated the music world of the early decade and propelled *Thriller* into the biggest-selling record ever.

SECTARIAN MUSIC CULTS

*L*ate in December 1982, Axl Rose, fugitive from justice, and his Lafayette girlfriend, Gina Siler, arrived in Los Angeles, having driven across prairie, mountains, and desert in her car. She'd met him a year or so earlier when he'd arrived at her seventeenth birthday party in dark glasses and a raincoat with the collar pulled up, looking like a spy. He'd explained that he was trying to avoid the cops, who were looking for the kids who had smashed most of the plate glass store windows on Main Street the night before. "They're out to get me," he drawled, "but I'm fucking innocent." Gina said that she bailed him out of jail several times in Lafayette.

In January 1983, Gina enrolled in a community college on L.A.'s west side and got a part-time job. She rented an apartment in an old building on Whitley Avenue in Hollywood. Axl kept his things at her place and lived there on and off. "He knew he wanted to be in a band," she said later. "He was made to be a musician—nothing else." She loaned him her car when he needed to get to a rehearsal and paid for Axl's first tattoo, the Thin Lizzy rose on his right shoulder. They were supposed to be engaged, but when they fought, which was often, or when she was just sick and tired of supporting him, she would throw him out. So Axl often roamed around Hollywood all night. Sometimes he crashed with Izzy or a girl, or slept on the streets, sometimes on a bench or behind a Dumpster.

By 1983 Izzy had established himself as a capable and ambitious presence on the scene. Cool-looking, understated, organized, with hair dyed jet-black, he'd played in several groups around town, starting as a drummer with a punk band, Naughty Women. Later he played drums with the short-lived hard rock band the Atoms, and after that played bass with a local metal band, Shire. He took up the guitar after that, he said, because it was easier to write songs that way, which was the only real way to make money in the music business. On nights when his band wasn't working, he hung out in the melee of kids in the Rainbow parking lot, trying to make connections.

With Axl now permanently living around West Hollywood, he and Izzy started jamming again. They talked about doing a band called Rose, but other young L.A. players, whom Izzy introduced to Axl, ridiculed him (behind his back) for his hayseed demeanor and especially for wearing cowboy boots. Everyone said that Axl looked like he'd just got off the fucking bus. Axl recalled: "In Indiana I was labeled a punk—a punk rocker. When I moved to L.A., the punk rockers called me a hippie, and basically told me to get lost."

The fabled Hollywood rock scene, Axl quickly learned, which had spawned such legends as the Byrds, the Doors, and the Eagles, was now in fact a highly ideological battleground of sectarian music cults.

"One of the first things that happened was I tried out for a punk band, but I didn't make it because they thought I sounded too much like Robert Plant"—the Zeppelin vocalist currently reviled by ultra-orthodox punks as a boring old fart in the same pathetic league as Elton and the Stones. "I was really bummed," Axl recalled. "I really liked that band, and thought I had a gig."

*M*eanwhile his family was pleading for him to come back to Lafayette and finish high school. It was "Come home, Bill, and we'll pay for college." Although he ignored this, he kept in touch with his family when he could. Axl later told an interviewer that he spent the next two years hanging outside the Hollywood rock clubs, totally ignored by everyone, from the bands who played there to the fans that crowded in on weekend nights. Lurking in the shadows near the Whisky, the Starwood, the Roxy, the Cathouse, Radio City, the Stardust Ballroom, Axl would watch as Mötley Crüe members were mobbed on the sidewalk, or as larger-than-life David Lee Roth, almost a cartoon of a rock star, arrived in his big Mercedes with its kustom-kulture skull-and-bones paint job, two MTV-ready babes on each arm, a goofy smile on his mug, and a big tip for the parking valet.

"What I remember about that time is standing outside the Troubadour for two years, and *nobody* talked to me," Axl said. "But then, I didn't really know what to say to them either, so . . . you just watched and learned for a long, long time."

Axl and Gina were always broke, hardly even had enough to eat. Cheap wine—Night Train, Boone's Farm, Thunderbird—was their main fun. Eventually, Gina Siler got tired of being abused when she argued with her crazy boyfriend. "He'd be in fights a lot," she said a few years later. "I don't think he was even conscious of what he does, or how angry he gets. I always thought there was something chemical that happened to him when he got angry." She would notice a serious change in Axl's eyes and features when he was about to lose it. "And when you see that coming across the room, coming at you, it's frightening as hell. And I'm not very big, and that made it worse."

After five months, Gina broke the bogus "engagement" between her and Axl and moved out. Izzy moved into the apartment on Whitley Avenue for a while, as he and Axl kept jamming, trying to get something together.

In early spring 1983, Axl answered a classified ad for a singer in the local trade paper, *Music Connection,* and quickly joined Rapidfire, a new band put together by guitarist Kevin Lawrence. In May, Rapidfire performed a weeknight pay-to-play gig at Gazzari's, next door to the Roxy on Sunset Boulevard. This was Axl Rose's first-ever show on the Strip. The band covered Stones songs and other warhorses, but Axl and Kevin Lawrence also wrote some new material. Five of these songs—"Ready to Rumble," "All Night Long," "The Prowler," "On the Run," and "Closure"—were recorded on May 25, 1983, at a demo studio near Santa Monica Boulevard. Rapidfire posed for glossy promo photos. Someone tried to shop these tapes to the record labels but couldn't get past the receptionists. Axl quit Rapidfire, the first band that he actually recorded with, sometime that summer, and resolved to concentrate on working with Izzy, who was starting to show the early stages of becoming one hell of a songwriter.

IRIDESCENT GHOST

$\mathcal{S}$o between 1983 and 1985 the jumble of young musicians that would eventually congeal into Guns N' Roses interacted in a confusing sequence of events that involved multiple bands, crossed and double-crossed alliances, serious dope dealing, abandoned loyalties, blatant careerism, manipulation of friends, abuse of girlfriends, fortuitous accidents, and a messy collaboration between Lady Luck and The Hand of Fate. When it was over, almost no one could look back and say how it happened.

One of these musicians, Chris Weber, saw it all firsthand and was there at the beginning. He grew up in West Hollywood and went to Fairfax High with Slash and Steven Adler, who were in the class ahead of him. Slash and Steven had one of the school's two bands, Road Crew. Fairfax High's other band was Pyrrhus, fronted by Tracii Guns. In 1983 Chris had been playing guitar since he was nine. His extremely supportive parents bought him a three-quarter-size Les Paul hollow body guitar, and at sixteen he started playing in local bands as a hot young lead guitarist inspired by Jimmy Page. Chris was very much the teenage rocker, with cool leather clothes and teased-up hair dyed blazing white like the guy in Hanoi Rocks, the Finnish band transplanted to Hollywood in a whirlwind of glam.

"That time [1983] was like Disneyland in Hollywood," Chris recalled. "Lots of new young musicians forming bands, with the *image,* the way the band looked, much more important than the music." The look was glam; the sound was metal lite. You didn't have to be a master musician to get on MTV; you just had to look cool. "There was a whole sea of bands, flyering, competing. Hollywood was completely plastered with flyers and posters of new bands working to get noticed.

"I was friendly with Tracii Guns from high school and playing in bands. Tracii met Izzy, who immediately asked Tracii to do a band with him. Tracii said, 'No, I already got a band.' Because Tracii was *really* good, really a prodigy. He could play like Randy Rhoads [Ozzy's guitarist]. That was his hero. Tracii told Izzy: 'No, I can't start another band, and I can't put you in my band because, like, it is my band and I am the guy. But I have this friend named Chris who is real good and maybe you and him can try to get a band together."

Tracii Guns called Chris Weber. "I got this guy that I met—Jeff. He's a guitar player, he's got a killer look. Don't know if he can play but—*great look!* I want you to check him out."

That weekend, Tracii introduced Chris to Izzy in the Rainbow's parking lot.

"That was the main place where you met people if you were too young to get in, like me, or couldn't sneak in, or had no money. If you wanted to be part of the scene on the Strip you'd hang out in the parking lot before, during, and after the evening. At two in the morning the club opens up into the lot and all the people in the bar and restaurant come outside and hook up, pairing off with whoever they're going to go home with or have a party with. Girls, guys, whatever. A lot of strange shit happened in that parking lot."

They sat and talked in the bed of Tracii's dad's pickup truck. Chris was impressed by Izzy, who was four years older but who treated him like an equal. "I was just blown away," Chris recalls. "I mean, Izzy was just about the coolest thing I'd ever seen in my life. He had this aura about him, with dyed black hair—what they used to call 'black blue'—and he was a really nice guy who wasn't into playing a role or pretending he was someone else, like so many of those people. Izzy dressed cool. He smoked cool. He was great. You could see that he was going to be a huge rock star someday.

"He asked me, 'You wanna start a band?' I said sure. He said, 'OK, come over to my house tomorrow,' and I went there and we started writing songs together. Izzy was still learning to play guitar—he couldn't really play yet—well, he played bass—but he did have the coolest guitar, this black Les Paul Custom.

"Izzy was living downstairs from this mad Russian called Gary, a keyboard player who was dying to be in the band, but Izzy wasn't about to have keyboards. I mean, forget it. He was adamant that the model for this band was the New York Dolls, or Aerosmith. We were talking about what kind of band this was gonna be, what type of players he wanted, and he said, 'I've got this friend, Bill, that just came in from Indiana, and he's gonna be the singer.' I just said, OK. He explained that Bill sometimes stayed there with him when he wasn't with his girlfriend, but now he was at her place, so we went over to the girlfriend's apartment at Whitley and Franklin, to meet Bill."

It was a burning hot day. The old, decrepit Hollywood apartment house had an ancient elevator, with a sliding metal gate, which slowly clanked its way to the top floor. Izzy then led Chris up a dark flight of creaky wooden steps. When they opened the door to the roof, Chris was momentarily blinded by the intense sunlight. It was so hot that the black tar on the roof was almost bubbling.

"At first I couldn't see anything. When my eyes adjusted, there was like this white, iridescent figure. As we got closer, I could see he was wearing a pair of little white shorts—nothing anyone in Hollywood would ever wear. He had white skin, very pale, and bright red hair, real long. Izzy mumbled, 'That's Bill.' And Bill got up and walked over to us. I remember that he looked almost translucent.

"He said, 'Hi, my name's Bill Bailey,' and stuck out his hand. Izzy was Jeff. You could tell right off they'd obviously had a long relationship, like brothers. And now we had our singer."

Chris and Izzy started writing together, often at Chris's family house in Laurel Canyon. Chris's dad had a four-track tape recorder, and within a few days the two guitarists started to get some songs down. One inspiration was the new Aerosmith album, *Rock in a Hard Place,* with replacement guitarist Jimmy Crespo filling in for the departed Joe Perry. (Chris: "A *great* fuckin' record.") Then Izzy moved in with Axl after his girlfriend, Gina, fled for her life.

When Axl left Rapidfire, Izzy and Chris thought it was time to show him what they'd come up with.

"When we first brought the song ideas to him, they were just hooks and melodies. He started singing along, using these lyrics he'd written in a notebook. He started out singing real low, a low baritone, kind of a growl, a little like the voice he used later for 'It's So Easy.' He'd sing that way on the melody, but then, when he went into the chorus, he did the high falsetto—that scream of his. Then he went down low again to sing the melody.

"Me and Izzy looked at each other. Jesus Christ. That's the sound! You gotta sing like that all the time! I said, '*That's it!* Can you do the melody with that, the high voice?'

"He goes, 'Whoa—I don't ever sound like that.' And of course he could, so we kept that sound because we loved it. It was such a power-ful voice that he hardly needed a microphone. It was like an air raid siren or something. So from then on all the songs we wrote were in that high register. We encouraged that voice as the sound of the band, or it never would've sounded anything like that."

*A*xl and Izzy were now twenty-one, old enough to get into clubs and order drinks. The first time they tried this, dressed in their cool-est outfits, Axl having put up his hair with enough Aqua Net to sup-port a bridge, something cool happened. He later recalled, "At that time, after Mötley Crüe's first album came out and everyone was wearing leather and studs, Izzy and me walked into the Roxy—one of our first times—and I remember Vince [Neil] and Nikki [Sixx] watch-ing us, and then fucking *leaning over the rail* [of the VIP section], try-ing to figure out just who the fuck we were. We laughed ourselves sick about that, but then it took three fucking years to start getting accepted in L.A."

In late May, they snuck underage Chris Weber into the joint.

"One night I was sitting in the Rainbow with Axl and Izzy, and David Lee Roth comes up and starts talking to us. Die happy! He's chatting away, dispensing huge rock star vibes, asking us about the band, giving us advice about some big rock festival. Then he started to leave, but turned around and said, 'Have a *great* show, you guys!'"

Later they found out that Diamond Dave had thought he was talking to Mötley Crüe.

A.X.L. / ROSE

*B*oth Van Halen and Mötley Crüe performed at rock music's pivotal event in 1983, the second US Festival, held at a remote desert site in San Bernardino County at the end of May. The two massive US Festivals were organized by Steve Wozniak, one of the founders of Apple Computer. (The founding Apple geeks were such music fans that they named their company after the Beatles' record label, resulting in decades of legal wrangling that ended only in 2007.)

Slash, almost every young rock musician in L.A., and 300,000 other SoCal headbangers attended the US Festival on "Heavy Metal Sunday" (May 29), when Van Halen headlined a program that started with Quiet Riot at noon and proceeded through Mötley Crüe (promoting *Shout at the Devil*), Ozzy Osbourne, Judas Priest, Triumph, and Scorpions. Van Halen, on the end of their *Diver Down* tour, with "Pretty Woman" a number-one record, pretty much ruled the festival, but there was an underlying sense that the event had been heavy metal's last crunch. Metal was definitely going in a new direction in 1983, with Metallica's brutal speed metal and Slayer's astounding thrash assault carrying the banner for a new age of rock.

Later that summer, Axl and Izzy were evicted from 1921 Whitley Avenue. They lived off girls, peddled drugs, pulled shameless scams. "You drifted around," Axl said. "You stayed in friends' garages. You slept in cars. You drifted around and tried to stay one step ahead of the sheriffs." Like many other young rockers in L.A., Izzy was now dabbling with heroin: the inexpensive, powerful brown-colored dope smuggled in from Iran.

"Then," Izzy recalled, "we were just slumming it, here and there. We started writing songs in this roach-infested pad off Franklin Avenue, doing speed like there was no fucking tomorrow. Night after night, we would just pump out this fast, upbeat, insane music. I'd tell the club owners that we were playing these huge parties and could easily draw five hundred people. When only twenty kids showed up, they'd get hugely upset and we wouldn't get paid. But we were slowly getting something together."

When they got evicted again, Chris Weber invited Axl and Izzy to move into his parents' house. "We had a big house in Laurel Canyon, up near Mulholland Drive. So we lived up there, worked on songs, and recorded demos on our four-track machine for maybe six months in '83 and '84. Axl and Izzy slept in the spare bedroom. Everyone got along, and we just kept going."

By the end of 1983, they had enough material to record five songs. "You needed a demo tape to get shows, but we had zero money. I went to my parents and explained we had these songs, and we needed to make a demo tape and have some pictures taken. They were financing everything anyway—they were really into it—so my dad booked some studio time, paid for it, paid for the actual tape. We needed a drummer, so we found this guy Johnny Kreis from an ad in *The Recycler*. We only met him for the first time when he came in and set up his drums in the studio where we were cutting the demo." Fortunately, Johnny Kreis was competent and had come to play.

The band that became Hollywood Rose recorded five songs at a now-defunct sixteen-track studio in Hollywood in late January 1984, just after Crüe singer Vince Neil smashed up his car while on a drunken beer run and killed his passenger, Hanoi Rocks drummer Nick "Razzle" Dingley. This cast a brief pall over the Hollywood glam scene. Hanoi Rocks was extremely cool and indeed rocked like a bastard, but sympathy was generally in short supply in the Hollywood sleaze jungle, and then people just forgot about it. Somehow, Vince Neil got off with only eighteen days in jail, but Hanoi Rocks never recovered, its potentially brilliant career cut short by a member of a competing band.

Axl, Izzy, Chris, and Johnny Kreis cut five songs in one furious daylong session. The two guitarists laid down the bass tracks over Kreis's improvised drums. "Killing Time" was a hard-rocking drone, similar to Aerosmith's version of "Train Kept A-Rollin'." Axl deployed his Robert Plant—like wail, spiced with the occasional screech: "I make my living—killing time." A primitive two-guitar riff ignited "My

Way Your Way," written by Axl and Izzy (which later appeared as "Anything Goes" on *Appetite for Destruction*.) "Rocker" started with Axl drawling, "Take one—yeah . . . play the rhythm." He then supplies some crazed bleating and squawking as two guitars weave in and out of each other. The track ends with Axl cackling like an evil spirit gloating over a dead rocker's body in a wrecked car.

"Shadow of Your Love" was a driving, post-punk rocker that banged like a screen door in a hurricane. Axl's future trademark yowl is already in place as he screams out angry threats and declaims, "I'm not standing in the shadow of your love—never again." The final track cut that day was the best. "Wreckless Life" featured Chris Weber's fuel-injected dragster of a guitar riff, with Izzy's rhythm guitar droning like a radio wave from another planet. "Wreckless Life" described the romantic outsider's precarious existence on the mean streets of Hollywood after midnight, a savage netherworld where anything that didn't kill you made you stupid or crazy. The song was a killer, so strong that it became the mainstay of the band's set in the next few months and then survived to make it onto *GN'R Lies* as "Reckless Life" almost five years later.

Chris Weber remembers, "We kept rehearsing, now with Johnny Kreis. [His band name was Johnny Christ.] He lived out in Orange County but didn't seem to mind the slog into Hollywood every day. The bassist was a friend from the Troubadour, named Andre Roxx. About a month later, we played a few shows as a band called A.X.L. The letters were pronounced, like Ay-Ex-Ell."

The first gig was at a club called the Orphanage on Lankershim Boulevard in North Hollywood. "A few people actually showed up," according to Chris. "We just went over there with a pickup truck, set up, checked the sound, went in the corner and had a soda, went up and played. Then we went home. That was the first show."

To try to get some buzz going, the road crew even spray-painted the name *A.X.L.* on the huge billboard overlooking Sunset and Doheny, at the west end of the Strip, and took pictures of it.

"But then something got Axl pissed off—and he quit! He told us, 'Fuck you guys. I'm not gonna play with you fuckers anymore,' and walked out. I was shocked. We'd recorded already. It was even funnier because he was still living in my parents' house.

"A couple days later, Axl came back. He wanted back in. But Izzy said, 'If you wanna come back we gotta change the name of the band.' He said, 'You can come back but we're changing the name of the band to Rose.' I went along with Izzy, and Axl caved, so for the next few gigs we were Rose."

In those earliest shows, people noticed that Axl Rose was pretty much devoid of image or a stage persona. He concentrated on getting the songs right, with none of the serpentine dances or furious thrashing that made him famous later on. When the band played fast and hot, Axl jumped in place, holding on to the microphone stand as if for dear life. From the beginning, Chris Weber was stunned by Axl's stark intensity.

"Axl was so full of pent-up energy that he would shake, literally tremble, when he got up there. It's hard to describe, but it was almost like a convulsion happening to him—or like he became possessed. He'd be letting this energy out, and I could see him just vibrating. It would actually be kind of scary, seeing someone evoking all this power, energy, and emotion."

*R*ichard Weber, Chris's dad, took some pictures of the band rehearsing. Axl is in full-metal lead-singer crouch. Izzy's on his knees, emoting with the guitar. Big-haired Chris is shredding. Bass and drums complete the eight-by-ten glossy. In March and April 1984, they designed some flyers, plastered them all over Hollywood, and played a few gigs as Rose, opening for other unsigned bands at the Troubadour, the Country Club, and Madame Wong's West. The flyer read:

> **Rose—There [*sic*] Living Fast and they'll DIE YOUNG!!! / see them now ! / 10:00 APR 1ˢᵗ [1984] / TROUBADOR [*sic*] / 9081 Santa Monica Blvd. / NO AGE LIMIT / $2 admission w/ coupon [flyer] / 2 drink minimum.**

The gigs went down pretty well. They did a bunch of covers and their new songs for about a dozen kids. Then the band broke up temporarily when Izzy joined the band London, a veteran L.A. band started in the late seventies by Blackie Lawless at the Starwood. It lasted until about 1981, at one point including Crüe bassist Nikki Sixx. The band was revived in 1984, recasting itself as a glam metal band fronted by singer Nadir D'Priest. Slash had played with London for a few weeks that spring because Road Crew was unable to get paying gigs, but quit when he couldn't take D'Priest's girlish posturing. Izzy then joined London on rhythm guitar because he needed money.

At this point Tracii Guns saw an opportunity and stole Axl, who, it was generally agreed, was potentially the best singer on the L.A. scene. Tracii and Axl started a new band called L.A. Guns, with bassist Ole Beich and drummer Rob Gardner. They worked on some songs, sounded pretty good, and even opened for London until Axl and Izzy decided to stop competing against each other and put Rose back together.

1984

It was the year that Prince, the elfin twenty-six-year-old rock star from Minneapolis, broke through with dazzling music, omnisexual imagery, his movie and album *Purple Rain*, and a songbook that included "Let's Go Crazy" and "When Doves Cry." It was the year that Apple introduced the Macintosh computer, the spearhead of the personal computing revolution that (no one could yet predict) would destroy and replace the recording industry within two decades. Ronald Reagan would be reelected president. A year later Mikhail Gorbachev would take over the Soviet Union, and the end of the Cold War was in sight.

In 1984 Slash and Steven Adler were both nineteen and scuffling around the Hollywood band scene, trying to get something going. They jammed together as Road Crew, a band with a name only. They took out ads in *The Recycler* and *Music Connection,* carefully calibrated classifieds that listed their influences and needs, specifically a bass player and a lead singer. To make ends meet, Steven had a bunch of little jobs around Hollywood. Slash lived at his grandmother's house and sometimes with his girlfriend, Yvonne. He worked at a clock factory and part-time at the Centerfolds news-stand on Fairfax.

Despite Road Crew's not-happening status, Slash was acquiring something of a name on the Strip. Rock connoisseurs who'd seen him jamming, effortlessly, bare-chested behind a curtain of frizzy black hair, could see that Slash was star-quality material, and he was occasionally invited to audition for various bands that he wouldn't be caught dead in.

Like Poison.

Back then, not long after MTV began broadcasting, and kids could see for the first time what the new L.A. glam bands looked like and understood (to their astonishment) that even crap bands like Ratt could get on television, every ambitious young bar band in every American burg began having silk scarf fantasies of their own. The boldest and most shameless of these bands abandoned their dreary rust belt homes and lit out for the territory. One of these bands was Paris, from Harrisburg, Pennsylvania. Paris was Bret Michaels, Bobby Dall, Rikki Rockett, and Matt Smith. They loaded up in an old Ford Pinto. A week later, Paris wound up in Hollywood, where the car died. Then they changed their name to Poison, aiming for a glam look and a party sound. Since singer Bret Michaels was unusually pretty, Poison wanted to position itself somewhere between the New York Dolls and Duran Duran.

Poison lived and rehearsed in a hovel behind a dry cleaner's shop on Palm Grove Avenue. They struggled for months, making flyers, hanging out in the club parking lots, trying to get noticed. Just after connecting with their first manager, guitarist Matt Smith announced he was quitting and going home. His girlfriend was pregnant and it was the right thing to do. Anyway, he told them, he was tired of living like a pig.

Poison held auditions for a new lead guitarist. The guy who played in the Joe Perry Project almost got the job. Others tried out, because word on the Strip was that Poison was serious, record labels were interested, and the band could be really big. One of the guitarists who showed up to audition was Slash. He didn't even bother to say hi to the guys in the band. Long black hair covering his face, he just plugged in and started shredding.

Rikki Rockett said, "The guy I really liked was Slash. People we trusted recommended him. This was before he was in Guns, obviously, but he had that same look back then. He was very cool, with that Rolling Stones–type cool of his. He came to our rehearsal room and played every song we had, note perfect. He was very rock and roll." Poison all but offered Slash the gig. But Slash was put off by Poison's glam ambitions—the costumes, the makeup, the cheesy stage show. While he was thinking it over, CC Deville came in and auditioned for Poison with teased pink hair and the basic riff of "Talk Dirty to Me."

Bret Michaels later remembered: "At the time, I argued for Slash. Our management wanted him in the band. But Slash wanted to have dual guitar situations, and we weren't looking for that. Then CC came in, but me and him didn't get along from the start. Rikki and CC loved each other, but me and Bobby couldn't stand him. There was just something about him. So we made the right decision for us and for Slash, but it's been a fiery ride."

So Poison hired CC Deville, and soon was signed to a major label record deal. But Poison was so manufactured, so conspicuously obnoxious, so blatantly derivative of earlier bands that—within a year—Guns N' Roses would carefully position themselves as the antidote to Poison's toxic glamour.

Some time late in 1984, Slash got a phone call from someone who said he'd got the number from someone who'd said Slash might be looking for a bass player.

It was Duff. Duff McKagan.

Mike McKagan was a twenty-year-old, six-foot-three-inch blond bassist from Seattle. Even on the street, he looked every inch the rock star in leather trousers, ripped T-shirts, biker boots, and Russian military cap. He told Slash that he'd been in L.A. for a few months and was looking to get into the right band.

He was born in Seattle in 1964, one of eight children in a Catholic musical family. His older siblings were hippies, so Duff grew up listening to Sly Stone, Hendrix, the James Gang, Vanilla Fudge, Led Zeppelin. He later said his father, who sang in a barbershop quartet, gave him his first drink—some Hawaiian moonshine—before he was ten years old. It was his first time drunk.

He was fourteen years old when the punk and new wave bands hit Seattle, and he started drumming in bands, using the *nom de punk* "Duff"—a name he'd been called by his family since he was two years old. He later estimated that over the next four years he played in thirty bands around Seattle. He played in neighborhood bands the Vains and The Living. At fifteen Duff joined the hardcore band Silly Killers and moved to San Francisco. When that didn't pan out, he returned home, switched to guitar (he wanted to play like his hero Johnny Thunders, late of the New York Dolls), and joined the band Cannibal.

Then, in December 1980, when he was almost seventeen, Duff joined the Seattle new wave band the Fastbacks—first as a roadie, then on drums, playing his first show with them at the Gorilla Room in Seattle. Six weeks later, in January 1981, the Fastbacks recorded four songs at Triangle Studios in Seattle. The band opened for ex-Runaway Joan Jett in March 1981, but Duff had to quit the band in July because he was too young to be in clubs that served liquor. A couple of months later, there was controversy in Seattle when the alcohol licensing authority shut down the Gorilla Room, the punk scene's main venue, for letting underage kids in the club. Michael McKagan had been identified as one of the teenagers caught in the club.

In 1982, Duff joined punk band the Fartz, which then changed its name to Ten Minute Warning when bassist Steve Fart took his amp elsewhere. This band, inspired in part by Black Sabbath, sounded like punk rockers flirting with psychedelic jam styles. When drummer Greg Gilmore joined, Duff switched to guitar. They opened for hardcore Henry Rollins, who compared them to a punk version of Hawkwind. This lineup recorded, but the music wasn't released and the Fastbacks broke up in late 1984. Around this time, Duff turned down an invitation to join a visiting UK punk band, Angelic Upstarts, as their drummer because they were going home to England and Duff didn't want to leave America. Instead Duff and Gilmore decided to move to L.A. and try out the febrile glam scene that was spreading up the coast as bands like Crüe and Stryper worked their way through the Pacific Northwest in a tacky blur of hair spray, spandex, and sweat.

In Los Angeles, Duff styled himself a bass guitar player since there was no use competing with the many flash shredders along the

Strip. "There were millions of great guitar players there already," he told an interviewer. "So just to get a fuckin' foot in the door, I decided to get a bass and an amp and go down to L.A. that way." Duff's older brother Bruce had taught him the rudiments of the bass, and he was more than competent. Plus, Duff already looked like a rock star.

"I called Slash," Duff said, "thinking that with a name like that, he'd be this older punk guy. I could barely understand him on the phone because he spoke so quietly. But he said their influences were Aerosmith, AC/DC, Alice Cooper, Motörhead; so I thought: *Cool. I'll try it out.*

They met up at Canter's Deli on Fairfax, a late-night Hollywood rock and roll hangout. (Slash was best friends in high school with Mark Canter, the son of the deli's owner.) Slash looked at Duff and almost did a double take at the tall dude with short, spiked hair colored in lurid stripes of red, black, and blond. He was wearing a long red-and-black leather trench coat and sported a padlock on a neck chain. "So I walk in there," Duff recalled, "and instead of some old punk, it's Slash and Steven and two girls, and they were all completely fuckin' *wasted.* Their girlfriends immediately thought I was a fag, because of my hair." Slash's unshy girlfriend, Yvonne, asked Duff if he was gay.

Later Duff recalled: "When I met Slash for the first time, it was weird, 'cause I'd never met guys like this—L.A. locals, you know? We went out that night and got drunk." An immediate problem for Duff was that he hated Steven Adler. "He was a real little asshole," Duff said later. "He had a double [bass] drum, all these drums and shit, and he was just a little asshole. I love him now [1989] to death, but he'll tell you himself that he was just an asshole then."

But Duff and Greg Gilmore hooked up with Slash and Steven Adler, and they jammed together a few times. Duff asked Slash about a singer, and Slash told him that he was hot to steal the singer from this other local band, L.A. Guns—a dude called Axl Rose—who Slash thought would be a perfect foil for himself in Road Crew.

Duff proved to be a much more professional musician than Slash and Steven were used to, and they deferred to him instinctively. Duff was much more into punk rock than they were, and Slash thought Duff's hero worship of Prince was a little strange, but Duff "joined"

Road Crew, still a band without a gig, to the extent that he rehearsed with them and hung out. (These early Road Crew sessions gave birth to Duff's jangling guitar riff that would become "Paradise City" three years down the road.) Greg Gilmore then moved back to Seattle, where later he would figure in some of the early nineties grunge bands. Eventually Duff left the Road Crew brethren to pursue other opportunities—none of which panned out. Just in case something happened, Duff kept Slash's phone number in his wallet.

HOLLYWOOD ROSE

*M*eanwhile, in the winter of 1984, Izzy and Axl were still in different bands, each wary of competing against and maybe even upstaging the other and maybe causing the other to fail somehow, which would be a big drag, given the history of their friendship.

Someone who saw all this is Robert John, a young photographer who went on to travel with Guns N' Roses as their exclusive eye and trusted friend for the rest of the original band's career. Born in Alabama in 1963, Robert came to L.A. with his family as a child and turned his family's Kodak box camera into a hobby. By 1983, when he met Izzy Stradlin, he was taking pictures of the bands on Sunset Strip.

"I was friends with Chris Holmes, who played lead guitar for W.A.S.P., and one night he asked me to come to the Troubadour and take pictures of the band. At most clubs, the kids would jam in near the stage and it was like a crush. But W.A.S.P.'s stage show was such a gross-out that the audience at the Troubadour would actually *back away* from the stage. I mean, they had a [torture] rack, and they brought out a [nearly] topless girl wearing a leather bondage hood. And they'd pretend to cut her throat—right?

"Anyway, her name was Laura, and I started going out with her. It turned out that her ex-boyfriend was Izzy. Laura introduced me to Izzy one night at the Troubadour when he was in the band London. We hit it off right away, and became friends."

Izzy told Robert about another band he was in called Rose, with his old friend from Indiana, Bill Bailey, who right then happened to be the lead singer of L.A. Guns, which was Tracii Guns's hot new band. Izzy mentioned that L.A. Guns was opening for London the following weekend and he should come to the gig and take some pictures.

Robert John went to the club where the bands were playing, and Izzy introduced him to Axl Rose. "I shot both bands," Robert says, "but then there was this brawl backstage when Axl and Nadir [D'Priest] got into a fight. It turned out there was this major feud between them over the fact that they're doing the same chick at the same time." Nadir said something, Axl swung at him, and then the road crews got into it. After that, Robert didn't see Izzy and Axl again until they were in Hollywood Rose together.

Circa March 1984, Axl left L.A. Guns before Tracii Guns could fire him.

Axl later explained, "During the time I was in L.A. Guns, Izzy and I were doing stuff on the side and kind of calling it Guns And Roses. Finally I got myself kicked out of that band [L.A. Guns] by putting on a pair of ripped-up black jeans and a biker jacket that I'd spray-painted pink and black, putting up my hair, putting full makeup on, and running all around the stage and into the crowd one night. The guitarist freaked out 'cause it was his band and he was used to getting all the attention. So, before I could say to him, 'I fucking quit,' he kicked me out. I just said, 'Yeeahhh!' It was great!"

Then Izzy left London. They called Chris Weber and said they wanted to put Rose back together and try to do something with the demo they had recorded early in the year.

Chris remembered: "Then we changed the name of the band to Hollywood Rose because we found out there was another band in Orange County that was already called Rose. This was right out of [the movie] *Spinal Tap,* which had just come out. Then we stumbled across an album by another band called Rose, from somewhere else. And then there was [punk band] Rose Tattoo, which we were all very fond of. So, for the rest of 1984, we changed it to Hollywood Rose and played under that name."

HELL REVISITED / WITH HOLLYWOOD ROSE / 9:00 FRIDAY MARCH 16TH [1984] / $4 W/ FLYER / MADAME WONG'S EAST / 624-5346 / 949 SUN MUN WAY / L.A. / Warning: The Surgeon General has determined that Hollywood Rose Is Dangerous to Your Health / but worth the risk.

Two weeks later, Rose landed an opening gig at the Troubadour.

Rose—There [*sic*] Living Fast and they'll DIE YOUNG !!! / See them now! / 10:00 APR 1st / TROUBADOR [*sic*] / 2 dollar off coupon / no age limit / 2 drink minimum

From its earliest days, the band presented itself, without apology, as a toxic squad of gonzo degenerates. Izzy Stradlin was almost openly involved in the surge of the Persian brown-colored heroin that had flooded into the L.A. rock scene, as both a user and a small-time dealer. As far as is known, Izzy was never a major supplier but instead was a small-time purveyor of heroin to the local rock community—which paid for his own use of the drug. Axl Rose has said he used heroin on occasion, beginning in those days, but never developed a habit. Chris Weber got totally hooked. In any case, it was widely known in contemporary L.A. music circles that Izzy was a go-to guy for a taste. When, for instance, Joe Perry came through L.A. with his own band in 1984, he was referred to Izzy as a reliable source of star-quality heroin.

Four years later, Izzy's band would be opening for Joe's.

Robert John continued, "The next time I ran into Izzy, he told me about Hollywood Rose. So I went to see them at the Troubadour. There were maybe twenty-five or thirty people there. I went backstage and Izzy introduced me to everybody. This must have been when I met Axl. Much later, he told me he was worried that I was one of Izzy's 'shoddy' friends of that time." Meaning that Axl thought Robert was one of Izzy's dope customers. "Izzy had a much darker side to him back then, so Axl was kind of right to be wary."

The problem that Hollywood Rose faced, in the summer of 1984, was landing a gig. The band had a good demo, decent street cred, but no place to play. The only way to get noticed, the only way to land a deal with a record company, the only way to hear your band blasting out of KNAC-FM, 105.5 on the dial, while cruising down the boulevard was to play live and get the scumbag record execs to come down and hear (and especially see) what you were doing. But the reality was that the Hollywood music clubs depended on local talent agencies to supply them with hot bands that brought customers into the venues. If a band didn't have an agent, the band starved to death.

Axl and Izzy did some rudimentary market research and discovered that two young women effectively controlled the booking of bands into the local rock clubs. So Axl Rose went into action and called Vicky Hamilton, a booking agent at Silverlining Entertainment in Hollywood. It was the call that made his career.

*V*icky Hamilton was from Indiana, like Axl and Izzy. She was pretty, blond, ambitious, extremely open, unusually kindhearted, and already knew her way around the scene. She had managed local bands back home in Fort Wayne, before lighting out for the territory to stake her claim in the gold mine of rock. She arrived in Los Angeles in 1981, when the Pretenders were on top of the charts. She worked as a waitress at Gazzari's on the Strip, and at the Palomino Club in North Hollywood, and then landed a gig as a record buyer at Licorice Pizza, the record store across the street from the Whisky a Go Go on Sunset Strip. There she met Crüe bassist Nikki Sixx, who liked to hang out in the store, and then got involved with Mötley Crüe as assistant to the band's first manager. Then she was involved with Poison before they signed their recording contract, and may have arranged Slash's audition with the band. Of late she was working with Stryper, a pretty but mediocre band from Orange County who were trying to position themselves as a Christian-metal act, an implausible but ultimately semisuccessful gambit. Vicky's association with Stryper got her an agent job at Silverlining.

Vicky had been living in the San Fernando Valley. She moved to Hollywood to be closer to her new office, sharing an apartment on North Clark Street, just a few steps from the Whisky at the corner of Clark and Sunset, with Jennifer Perry, who booked bands into the

Troubadour. Together, the two housemates joked, they controlled the night in Hollywood as far as bands were concerned.

One day Vicky got a phone call at Silverlining:

"Hi, Vicky. My name is Axl Rose, and I'm the lead singer of the band Hollywood Rose. You might not have heard of us yet, but we're going to be the biggest band in Hollywood. You were recommended to me as, like, someone to help us get some gigs."

Vicky had heard come-ons like this before. She said, "Well, OK, but do you have a demo tape that you can send in for me to hear?"

Axl replied, "Yeah, of course. How about I just come there, now, today, and play it for you?"

Vicky was charmed. This was more boyish enthusiasm than she was used to in Hollywood. Maybe it reminded her of Indiana. She repeated that Axl should just mail her the tape, and he asked why. She said, "Well, for starters I don't have a stereo here to listen to a demo on."

"That's OK, no problem. I'll bring a boom box. It'll be cool."

Vicky thought, *If the guy's that persistent, let him come.* And she gave him directions to the agency. Two hours later, Axl and Izzy were in the lobby.

SHE SCREAMED AND KICKED

*A*xl and Izzy showed up at Silverlining Entertainment with their demo tape, a stolen boom box, and some snapshots of Hollywood Rose. Axl did the talking. Izzy interjected when he had something to add. Vicky Hamilton sat with them in the lobby of the agency and tried not to seem too impressed. "But I was just *blown away* by the demo," she said later. The hard rhythms and crashing guitars of "Killing Time" and "Wreckless Life" were pure murder, better than anything she'd heard lately from a new band. "Then I heard that voice. Oh, my God. It had this incredible power and presence. I immediately realized that what Axl had said to me on the phone about being the biggest band in Hollywood was really just the beginning of where this band was headed."

With a handshake to seal the bargain, before she'd even seen the band perform, Vicky Hamilton agreed to start booking them. The first time she saw Hollywood Rose was at Madame Wong's, where they opened for Candy, a popular local band. She got chills watching Axl grab the tiny audience's respect and hold it for forty-five minutes. Hollywood Rose did their songs and a bunch of covers like "Jumpin' Jack Flash" and Aerosmith's fiery anthem of teen ambition, "Mama Kin." Axl didn't yet have any of the stage moves that he later made famous, Vicky recalled. "Mostly he just pogo'd, you know? He jumped up and down. [The pogo had been invented by one of Axl's idols, Sid Vicious.] But it was still contagious."

What impressed Vicky was her own gut reaction to the band. It was "the feeling I get in my stomach when I first see a band that's going to make it." After hanging out with them, she knew for sure. "They were definitely outlaws, totally the real deal. I thought, 'This may kill me, but they're so great. I have to do it.'"

She got them several more shows over the next few months at respectable venues: the Country Club, Dancing Waters, the Music Machine. On July 10 they played the Troubadour for the first time, billed as "The New Hollywood Rose." (Their flyer, which featured a cartoon of a bosomy woman holding a whip, warned: TWO DRINK MINIMUM ENFORCED AT THE DOOR.) Meanwhile the young musicians scuffled for money and were living hand-to-mouth. Axl and Izzy had moved out of Chris Weber's family home and were at large. For a while, Axl lived on the street, in abandoned apartments and behind Dumpsters, hustling, scrounging, getting by on roughly $3.75 a day, just enough for a meal of biscuits and gravy at Denny's, plus a half-pint of cheap wine. This long period of homelessness, he later said, was something Axl Rose took particular pride in.

"It's not like we're the most intelligent bunch," he later told *RIP* magazine, "but as far as street sense—hanging out, doing drugs, partying, girls, and shit like that—it's like we purposefully put ourselves through street school. I never knew how to pick up chicks, so I used to stand outside the Rainbow and watch how it goes down. I didn't know shit about doing drugs, so I learned what's safe, and what's not, how to get them, how to do it properly, and everything else that's involved. Basically, what it came down to was, we learned how to survive."

* * *

hen Chris Weber's grandfather died, and Chris moved into his house. "It was just below the Hollywood Bowl," Chris recalled. "Izzy stayed there a lot, and sometimes Axl and one of his girlfriends. The place had a good atmosphere, and Izzy and I wrote a bunch of songs there." One of the numbers they worked on turned into the young Guns anthem, "Move to the City."

On Wednesday, August 29, The New Hollywood Rose played at the Troubadour. The hand-drawn flyer featured cartoons of the band and a girl's hand holding a whip. A quatrain verse, under the whip, was a band manifesto on its shameless treatment of the girls they sponged off:

**SHE STEPPED INSIDE THE DOOR
AND WAS QUICKLY LAID UPON THE FLOOR
SHE SCREAMED AND KICKED AND RAISED A FIT
BUT WAS LATER HEARD TO SAY—SHE LOVED IT**

Two nights later, on August 31, Hollywood Rose played at an after-hours party at Shamrock Studios on Santa Monica Boulevard. The band went on at two in the morning in front of a room packed with Strip kids who'd heard that the "new" Hollywood Rose was one hot baby band.

Around this time Izzy, who was effectively the band leader, got a nibble from a record exec. "I never even thought about a record deal," Chris Weber says, "until one day Izzy showed up and said, 'I got a guy at Columbia Records who wants to meet us.' So, a few days later, we went to Century City, where their offices were, all of us completely dressed to the nines: high heel boots, hair sprayed straight up to the ceiling, at, like, eleven in the morning. I remember that Axl needed some serious coaching on how to do his makeup, but Izzy had been tutored by Gary, the guy he used to live with, and showed everybody what to do. Axl's look, especially the big hair, was Izzy's concept. The whole look of the band—and later Guns'—was all Izzy."

They played the demo for the A&R guy at Columbia. He said he liked it, said he would be in touch, but they never heard from him again.

Vicky Hamilton continued booking Stryper into the rock clubs until they fired her for being insufficiently Christian. Her downfall was not joining the band's backstage prayer circle before the shows. (Stryper told Vicky, "God told us that your values are different than ours.") One of the last shows she booked for Stryper was at the Music Machine in West L.A. in the autumn of 1984. She put Hollywood Rose on the bill, along with a new band, Black Sheep, featuring Slash on lead guitar. "I remember introducing Slash to Axl that night," she said later. "I had to talk him into this, because Slash was so shy. Who knew that this would be history in the making—the beginning of Guns N' Roses?"

It wasn't exactly, but it pretty much was the end of Hollywood Rose because Chris Weber quit the band right after. "I left for a bunch of reasons," Chris recalls. "For one thing, I was only seventeen. They were much older, and the drug thing was huge because Izzy was in the business. Then I got into a fight with Axl when we played the Music Machine with Stryper. I swung around onstage and hit Axl right in the face with the neck of my guitar. It wasn't the first time this had happened, and he got mad. It kind of broke up the band as far as I was concerned."

Chris knew Slash from Fairfax High, and thinks Slash might have played guitar in Hollywood Rose for a couple of gigs after he left the band. Chris says also that Axl rejoined L.A. Guns and cut some tracks with Tracii Guns before they were a signed band, using some production money that Tracii somehow got.

At the end of 1984, Vicky booked Hollywood Rose into a New Year's Eve show at Dancing Waters, a "crazy club in San Pedro" with an indoor waterfall and a hard rock clientele. According to Chris, Slash couldn't make the gig, so Izzy called and invited him back in to do the gig. Chris rehearsed with the band and thought it sounded great. Friends of the band thought it was Hollywood Rose's greatest moment, with the band's cover versions paling in comparison to the heat generated by their own songs, especially "Wreckless Life," "Shadow of Your Love," and "Move to the City."

"After that New Year's show, and after I'd taken a rest from the band, I sort of hoped that we could start the whole thing going again.

Hollywood Rose was such a great band, and people were talking about us. But the idea didn't catch on, and things moved on. I went to New York for a while, and dabbled in dangerous stuff. When I came back, I was still friends with Izzy, and Izzy was still in the [heroin] business. Then I kind of went into that business with him, working for him, actually.

"But then I really didn't miss being in that band. We wrote a lot of music together, had a lot of dreams, and did a lot of playing. In the end, it worked out for the best, because they made a lot of great music with Slash—God bless 'em. I still cherish my friendship with Izzy, because he just could not have been any cooler. You know how they used to spray CLAPTON IS GOD on the walls in London? That's how I felt about Izzy. I didn't have any brothers or sisters. Izzy, to me, was like the greatest big brother that you could ever have."

Chapter Three

THE TREACHEROUS JOURNEY

*Who wants to be this jaded at the
beginning of their career?*
—Slash

SHARK ISLAND

*G*uns N' Roses finally came together in 1985 after years of trying, but this was also the year whose various events would very much shape the destiny of the band. The AIDS virus now began to kill hundreds of homosexual men, opening their community to plaguelike conditions that eventually claimed tens of thousands of lives and then spread into the general population. War in Central America and strife in Iran sent human waves of immigrants to southern California, until already disaffected young men like Axl Rose began to feel like strangers in their own country. Famine in Ethiopia aroused the dormant consciousness of the rock music world, leading to massive public concerts that gave the old rockers a final chance to prove they still had relevance in a music business now dominated by post-punk bands and rappers.

At home in Los Angeles, even a great band like Guns faced withering competition. Mötley Crüe still ruled the Strip, but Poison quickly got a record deal and began working on their album. New bands like Jet Boy, Faster Pussycat, and Shark Island were coalescing at the same time as Guns and competing for the same gigs at the same clubs. There was even a nagging question within the music industry whether a hard rock band, no matter how talented, could survive in a climate where the Big Four of Thrash—Metallica, Megadeth, Anthrax, and Slayer—were among the biggest acts of the day. Even Axl Rose liked to listen to Metallica's song "Fade to Black" before going to bed, usually around dawn. He said later that his interpretation of the song's theme of suicide and redemption gave him hope that the next day would be better than the one he had just struggled through. (Metallica later revealed that "Fade to Black" was actually about the band's gear getting stolen, but no matter.)

Then, later in the year, a group of Washington politicians' wives, outraged by what their kids were listening to, began a campaign to censor rock songs, specifically targeting some of the Sunset Strip bands. This led to congressional hearings and the first ratings system imposed upon popular music since the days of "race records" earlier in the twentieth century.

In retrospect, 1985 was a perfect time for a band of nihilistic provocateurs like Guns N' Roses to come along.

At the beginning of 1985, Axl Rose was working with Tracii Guns and Rob Gardner, trying to get something together. Any time line for this period, when bands and loyalties and promises shifted like the Santa Ana winds, must be said to be thinly sourced and unreliable, but Hollywood Rose was finished for good, and talented, ambitious Tracii Guns was trying to steal Axl from Izzy. At the same time, talented, ambitious Slash was trying to steal Axl for Road Crew. Everyone on the scene knew that talented, volatile, even fucking crazy Axl Rose was the alpha dog, the most important lead singer and front man on the Strip. Anyone who could control his energy, indeed, anyone who could ride his cyclone, was going to rule the Strip someday, and then the world beyond.

In March 1985, Axl and Izzy decided they had to work together again. Izzy persuaded the Troubadour to book a weeknight show for the new group. Needing a star-quality lead guitarist, Axl then stole Tracii Guns from his own band. They rehearsed with drummer Rob Gardner from Hollywood Rose and bassist Ole Beich from L.A. Guns. They sat around trying to think of a name for this new band. Axl wanted something evil, like Poison or Anthrax, something that made you sick and then killed you. Izzy suggested AIDS as a joke, but he was taken seriously until he protested that he didn't mean it. Then someone came up with Heads of Amazon, which was rejected as uncool. Eventually they decided to combine L.A. Guns and Hollywood Rose, which is what they were doing anyway. Soon a crudely drawn flyer was plastered all over Hollywood:

"ITS [sic] ONLY ROCK N ROLL" / L.A. Guns and Hollywood Rose Presents [sic] the band GUNS 'N' ROSES / March 26th / Doug Weston's Troubadour / 10-pm / 2$ with flyer.

This new band played the usual covers of Stones, Zeppelin, and Aerosmith, Hollywood Rose's greatest hits, and featured instrumental jams starring Tracii. That first night, there were only a couple dozen people in the club. Only four had paid to get in; the rest were friends of the band.

Nobody was really happy about this. Axl and Izzy knew they were now a team, but Tracii seemed less than committed. They didn't think Ole had what they wanted in a bass player, so they put an ad for a new one in *Music Connection*. Then Izzy heard that Ole had seen the ad and was quitting the band. But the same lineup played its second gig at the Radio City, a rock club near Disneyland in suburban Anaheim.

Then something crucial happened. Photographer Robert John took Axl to see a group he was shooting: Shark Island, the house band at Gazzari's on the Strip. Shark Island was supposed to be a great metal band, but they were too fond of melodies, plus their hair was all wrong, and so they would never break out of the L.A. metal circuit. But Richard Black, Shark Island's lead singer, was a charismatic front man with killer stage moves, the kind of small-venue choreography that could make a packed club break out in a communal, drenching sweat and get the joint rocking on its foundations. Axl watched Richard Black with total fascination and then proceeded to appropriate his act.

Vicky Hamilton, among others, is adamant about this. "People who were around then have been saying for years that Axl ripped off all Richard's moves. In the early days, Axl just would pogo. He hopped up and down like a rabbit. He never did that great swagger thing until later."

According to Robert John, "In Hollywood Rose and L.A. Guns, Axl jumped straight up and down, holding onto the mike stand for balance. Axl later admitted that he got that whole snake move, that S-curve, from Richard. He once told me that he even wanted Richard to somehow get credit for this. Most of Axl's moves"—the headlong run across the stage, the furious stomp, holding the mike stand straight out with both hands, the blatantly sexual snake dance—"that's all Richard Black."

"He was *brilliant*," Vicky says of Black, "and he got totally ripped off."

Axl went back to see Shark Island at Gazzari's several times. One night he and Tracii Guns got onstage with Shark Island and jammed on Led Zeppelin's "Rock and Roll."

Richard Black remembered all this with resignation. "Once when I went over to Axl's house, he was playing a video of me. There were half a dozen tapes on top of his TV, marked 'Shark Island.' I don't want to come across as a whiner, but sneaking a video camera into a concert to record somebody is a big thing. [Axl] scooted in and took advantage of my shtick. I felt ripped off, but I was powerless to stop him. . . . I figured he might've [given me credit] when Guns N' Roses made it, but he never did."

WHERE EVERYONE'S SMASHED

Then, in May 1985, the Guns N' Roses ad for a bass player in *Music Connection* was answered by Duff McKagan. The ad had called for a "heavy punk metal glam bassist." They wanted, Axl later said, "someone who wore makeup and put their hair up. That was the first 'glam' ad I think I ever saw. And then we quickly got rid of that [concept], but it stuck."

Duff showed up with his bass guitar and his amp and they jammed. Tracii wasn't sure about Duff, but Axl and Izzy took to him immediately. The tall musician in the red-and-black leather trench coat with hair dyed in various DayGlo colors looked like he'd been sent over from glam central casting. Even better, he was a schooled musician who could actually count off a song. He could be the band's musical director, something they sorely needed. But Duff took a hard look at the band, and almost didn't take the job.

"So I got together with Axl and Izzy," Duff said. "They had a band and they asked me, 'Can you come and play bass for us?' The group was already called Guns N' Roses, but there was another guy on guitar and a different drummer. To me it just seemed like a real iffy band because nothing was really happening."

Duff was not impressed by the group's low spark. He was also unsure about Axl, who seemed raw and unprofessional to him. "I was like, 'He's good, he can really sing, but I don't know.' We had these other two cats in the band, and the band was just not clicking the way it needed to. Actually, that lineup [of Guns] was pretty bad."

Rehearsals would be called, but people wouldn't show up. There was none of the cohesion Duff knew a successful band needed, and with no forthcoming gigs, Duff began to lose interest. He'd been through this kind of thing many times before, with many different bands. He later told British interviewer Mick Wall: "Like, I would hardly show up for rehearsal myself, and that is not like me. I am always the first guy to show up for rehearsal and always the last to leave. . . . I was beginning to wonder why I was bothering with this band."

But Duff decided to commit to Guns and started using his connections to set up its first road trip. He called in some favors at home and got his new band a series of paying gigs up and down the northwest coast with his old band, the Fastbacks, scheduled to begin on June 8, 1985. Then Vicky Hamilton booked the band into the Troubadour for a warm-up show on June 6.

But, suddenly, Tracii Guns and Rob Gardner quit Guns N' Roses—three days before the tour was supposed to start. At a band meeting to plan logistics for the Seattle trip, Tracii blithely told the others: "Uh, we don't know if we wanna do it." Tracii later said that he didn't like the direction the band was going in.

Duff was "fucking shocked, man. I could not *believe* that these two guys just pussied out. I was like, *'OK—fuck you.'*" Duff was now in a jam. If he didn't show up in Seattle with his new L.A. band, it would look bad at home. He had two days to find a drummer and a lead guitar. Then he remembered Road Crew. Duff talked to Axl and Izzy, who already had played with Slash. What else were they gonna do? So he found Slash's number and called him up.

Slash and Steven were still struggling as a two-piece band with no prospects. "The main problem," Slash recalled, "was we had this great little band, but we'd never been able to find a singer." Slash had played a few gigs with Black Sheep, but it hadn't worked out. When Duff called him and asked him to join Guns, Slash accepted the offer, but in the back of his mind Slash saw the gig as a way of eventually stealing Axl Rose for his own band.

Slash said he "didn't want to work with Izzy at all. I didn't want to work with *any* other guitar player, because I'd never done it before . . . [and] I couldn't be in control of what was happening, guitar-wise. What I wanted was to get Axl away from Izzy, which was just fucking impossible. Then I got this call, and they said, do you want to come back and play with us? At first I didn't want to do it, because Axl and I had been through some bad times together."

Slash had indeed played a few gigs in Hollywood Rose after Chris Weber left the band. For a while, he even let Axl crash at his grandmother's house. Axl slept in Slash's bed while he was working at the newsstand. When Slash came home, he woke Axl up and they went off to rehearsal. But one day there was a problem when Ola Sr. wanted to watch TV and asked Axl to remove himself from her sofa. Axl told the old lady to go fuck herself. Slash heard about this, and on the way to rehearsal he suggested to Axl that he ought to apologize. Axl got a weird gleam in his eyes and began to rock back in forth in the passenger seat. Then he jumped out of the moving car, which was doing about 40. He disappeared down a side street, and Slash didn't see him for a while. At their next gig together, Slash quit Hollywood Rose after Axl brained a rowdy fan with a beer bottle. Then Slash and Yvonne broke up for a while, and Slash found out that Axl had fucked her in his absence. At the time, Axl was an assistant manager at Tower Video on Sunset, so to make things up to Slash, Axl got him a job there. This lasted until Axl got fired for screening porn films in the store during evening hours.

In the end Slash decided to join Guns. "But then I did it, and began working with Izzy, because that was what was happening. It was the only band I could find, that I could actually relate to."

Adler was much more pumped. "I said to Slash, 'If we get *that* singer, and *that* guitar player, we'll have ourselves one *kick-ass* band.'"

The first rehearsal of the new band was at a studio in Silver Lake in May 1985. Someone distracted Steven Adler while Izzy and Duff hid all the extraneous drums from Steven's kit, reducing an almost comical metal setup to a more primitive, punk simplicity. Duff remembered, "The moment that we fuckin' slammed into our first chord, there was something. And we all knew it." At first, Axl was just standing there, holding a beer and leaning against an amp, listening to the group's sonic chemistry; and then he started singing. Duff: "All of a sudden, Axl *clicked*. He was right in there, man. It took something for Axl to click, and it took something else for Slash to click, but when it did, it really did.

"We were only twenty years old," Duff said, "but we already considered ourselves real veterans. It felt like, 'This is the band, this is it. This is what we've all been searching for.'"

Slash and Steven rehearsed with Axl, Izzy, and Duff for two days. There was some consternation among the old Hollywood Rose gang because they hated Slash. "We all thought he was a smart-assed little prick," Robert John says. "The crew called him 'The Snake' behind his back," because he was creepy and an egomaniac. "We got to be good friends later on, but we just hated each other in the beginning." The other problem, Slash said later, was that Axl didn't like Steven Adler. But Slash and Adler were a package deal; they came together, and Axl acquiesced on the drummer as something of a favor to Izzy.

Guns N' Roses' first show with its new lineup took place at the Troubadour, opening for another unsigned band, on Thursday, June 6, 1985.

A ROCK N ROLL BASH WHERE EVERYONES [*sic*] SMASHED / GUNS and ROSES / TROUB. JUNE 6–10 PM.

The flyer featured an early attempt at a band logo, with crossed Lugar pistols flanked by what were supposed to be roses but looked more like cabbages. Tracii Guns, who had either quit Guns N' Roses or been pushed out (according to some) in favor of Slash, queried Izzy Stradlin about the wisdom of their keeping the old name of the group. Izzy told him they were fucking keeping Guns N' Roses, and besides, Izzy said, it didn't really matter—it was only a band name.

The afternoon of the gig, Slash went over to Melrose Avenue, lined with hip boutiques and pre-owned clothing shops, and bought a black, broad-brimmed, crowned hat at Leathers & Treasures. It was a conscious visual homage to Jimi Hendrix, and the early antecedent to the top hat that would become his trademark later on.

Only a dozen people saw the debut of Guns N' Roses' new lineup, but those few never forgot it. Guns played louder than bombs. Axl had teased and sprayed his hair way up, and deployed his flamboyant new stage moves. Izzy was in a white shirt and vest, a walking clone of Keef, laying down skilled rhythm licks. Duff teetered in cowboy boots, anchoring the band with his bass, singing backup to Axl's howls. Slash—bare-chested, sweating profusely—was alternately riffing and playing intricate solos, really showing off. Presiding over everything was Steven Adler on his drum riser, flailing with his sticks, his long blond ringlets shaking around his smiling face, looking like a kid in ecstasy under the club's lone spotlight. If anything, Steven provided a splashy, onstage visual foil—like a junior David Lee Roth—to Axl's menacing prowl around the stage.

They played some Stones, some Sabbath, "Mama Kin," Rose Tattoo's "Nice Boys," and Hollywood Rose songs. There was a smattering of applause. The next day they packed their gear into a rented van and headed north to Seattle on the first Guns N' Roses tour. Their saga had now truly begun.

"THE TREACHEROUS JOURNEY"

*G*uns N' Roses borrowed someone's car and started driving north, Duff at the wheel. Their gear went with their two roadies in a borrowed van that had left town earlier in the day. The band was so numb and stupefied on drugs that they hardly even knew where Seattle was. Duff had told them: "Yo, Seattle, man—it's fuckin' right on top of America!" And Izzy had said, "Hey, cool, let's just fuckin' *go*."

The band was truly psyched. They were "on the road" at last. Izzy had been dreaming about being "on tour" since he was twelve years

old. After Seattle, they were supposed to play shows in Portland, Eu-
gene, Sacramento, and San Francisco. These shows were decent
$300-a-night gigs, their first shows out of town.

Two hours later, north of Fresno, the car broke down. Duff pulled
over. Smoke was seeping from under the hood. Around them was
nothing but deserted farmland and scrubby desert. This was before
cell phones. Guns N' Roses was stranded on the highway.

Someone mentioned turning back and going home. Izzy said that
there was no fuckin' way he was going back to Hollywood. He got his
guitar case out of the trunk and stuck his thumb out. The rest followed,
abandoning the still smoking car, and started walking north. No one
picked them up. They were, Slash says, "dressed to the fuckin' hilt" in
full rock regalia, ready to go onstage. The summer sun baked them in
their leathers. They had no water. According to Slash, he and Izzy and
Steven were all using heroin, so one or more of them was probably
withdrawing from drugs. They waited for a ride. And waited.

And waited. Cars and trucks whizzed by, contemptuously. Off came
the jackets and stage gear. After many hours in the desert, as the sun
was setting over the low hills in the west, a truck driver finally stopped.
He said they could ride in the back of his empty eighteen-wheeler.

Twenty hours later, in the middle of the night, the trucker dumped
groggy Guns N' Roses at an interstate exit. They were a sight, according to Duff: "Five guys in tight striped pants and boots in the middle
of fuckin' Oregon." They kept hitching.

Izzy recalled that finally "two ex-hippie girls from San Francisco
picked us up." They were just like Thelma and Louise. "First they
passed us, but then they remembered back, in the hippie days, when
no one would pick *them* up, so they came around again and stopped,
and we piled in." Guns was starving, weak from hunger, and asked the
women if they had anything to eat. The one who wasn't driving produced some "radical" pot brownies, and they kept heading north.

Forty hours after they left Hollywood, Guns N' Roses arrived in
Seattle. The band was exhausted, dehydrated, but just in time for their
first gig. The flyer read:

**ROCK THEATER / Guns and Roses with Fastbacks plus 5150 /
The Omni Room / Sat. June 8.**

But there was no sign of their gear or their roadies. Guns N' Roses had to borrow drums and amps from the Fastbacks. Duff was embarrassed. The poor, bedraggled Gunners were totally wasted. They stunk.

Izzy said, "We played. There were ten, maybe twenty people in the place. We hadn't rehearsed that much. We didn't get paid. It was downhill from there."

Actually, they did get $50, plus food and drinks from the waitresses at the Omni Room who took pity on them. And when they learned the van carrying their gear had broken down near Santa Barbara and wouldn't arrive, they were informed by the Fastbacks' manager—who pegged them for pathetic losers—that the rest of their "tour" was canceled.

The band recuperated from what Slash called "that treacherous journey" at the McKagan family home. It was in Seattle that Axl Rose started writing lyrics about the life they'd been living on the streets of Hollywood—a hothouse world of hardship and competition, a subbohemian demimonde where the only decent meal came from street charity, and the evening's high was a dollar bottle of cheap fortified wine—Night Train or Thunderbird. The reality of "Hollywood," for Axl Rose, was making love to an overweight, insecure band groupie from Nebraska so he could stay at her place long enough to get his clothes washed and take a shower. Axl Rose's "Hollywood" was a heartless battleground where the Malthusian drill was the survival of the fittest, a place of high-risk, semidesperate fun and games, whose losers wound up back home in Bumfuck—or ended up blue and dead, tied off on the bathroom floor.

The song Axl began to write, on what the band called The Hell Tour, eventually became "Welcome to the Jungle."

Guns had no money, and no way to get back to Hollywood. They were so far from home that even degenerate, polluted, quake-prone L.A. looked to them like Paradise City. They thought about borrowing enough from Duff's family to take the bus. But, Duff recalled:

"Eventually, we bummed a ride back to L.A. with this chick who was a junkie. It was horrible. But the thing was, this is where the band like, *bonded*. We all stuck together." For the first time, Duff thought: *This is real.*

Steven agreed. "A lot of guys who might have been in the band at that time would have wimped out, you know? Just gotten on a plane home before we were halfway there."

"No one died, no one fainted," Slash said. "We all survived. And we pushed ourselves that way ever since."

Izzy: "And from the day we got back to Hollywood, it was like: whatever goes down, y'know, we were still united . . . in this conflict against—*fuckin' everything!* Guns N' Roses' motto, from that day to this, has been: Fuck *everybody.* Fuck everybody—*before they fuck with you.* Fuck the whole fuckin' *world,* y'know? Just let's keep moving."

Izzy thought the Hell Tour had been a test, a rite of passage, for the band. They had suffered together. They had thirsted in the desert. It was fucking biblical. They could have died. They had sucked in Seattle and had been rejected. They straggled back home, a defeated platoon, dead broke. But then, after their humiliating adventure, after they had been on the road and eaten shit, the sleazy jungle of the Hollywood rock scene didn't seem so bad after all. It seemed, instead, like . . . home.

Axl Rose was now, finally, convinced that Guns N' Roses was his band. A short while later, he told an interviewer: "We went through *so* many different people. Guns ended up being the people we most believed in. We *believed* in each other. We were like a family back then."

A LIVING HELL

*A*fter Seattle, Guns rehearsed for a few days in a semipro studio in the Silver Lake district, near Echo Park, that was owned by local musician Nicky Beat. According to Slash, this was "where the whole band really came together" around Izzy Stradlin's songs: "Think About You," "Don't Cry," "Out ta Get Me." They also worked on the earliest parts of "Rocket Queen" and "Welcome to the Jungle."

In the summer of 1985, Izzy Stradlin rented a moldy rehearsal space for his band. Instead, with nowhere else to crash, most of the band started to live there. In Izzy's mind, Guns had actually moved up a notch in life.

Guns' new headquarters was a small storage area the size of a one-car garage, behind 7508 Sunset Boulevard. The rent was $400 a month. The dimensions of the space were roughly twelve feet by twelve feet, with just enough room for a couch (scrounged from a dead guy's stuff found on the street) and what meager gear they possessed. Izzy and the roadies stole some lumber from a nearby construction site and built a loft that had enough space for maybe three malnourished rockers to sleep in. Their gear was stashed beneath the loft.

Their storage space opened onto an alley that the City of Los Angeles officially designated "Lot Number 619." It was near the intersection of Sunset and Gardner, a musical neighborhood that included the Guitar Center; various new and used instrument shops, including Sam Ash and the Mesa/Boogie amp store; and various crucial support businesses such as Sunset Strip Tattoo, the Sunset Grill, Mory's Pizza, and El Compadre—"Fine Mexican Cuisine." The neighborhood baked in the California sun under looming billboards, towering royal palm trees, and the arid, cone-shaped Hollywood hills.

There was no bathroom, no shower, no kitchen, no air-conditioning, and the summer heat was stifling. Izzy described the place as "a fucking living hell." Slash hated it. Sometimes, to get away from the squalor, he slept down the road in the Tower Records parking lot, where he felt safe. "I'd fuck girls," he told *Rolling Stone,* "just so I could stay at their place." If they had enough cash to buy hamburger, sometimes they burned Steven's drumsticks to grill the meat on a hibachi stolen from someone's backyard. When it rained, the roof leaked and their gear got wet.

"We had zero money," Duff fondly recalled, "but we could usually dig up a buck and go down to the liquor store for a bottle of Night Train wine that would fuck you up for a buck. Five dollars and we'd all be gone. We like *lived* on this stuff."

"Our studio—it was basically a fuckin' uncomfortable prison cell," Slash said, "but God, did we sound *good* in there. We're a loud fuckin' band, and we don't compromise the volume for anything." They'd pound away with a couple of Marshall amps in the tiny hovel, and they could be heard ten blocks away. "It was cool, because all the fuckin' losers from Sunset Boulevard and all the other bands would come over to hang out."

These other bands included Faster Pussycat, Black & Blue, Redd Kross, Thelonious Monster, and Jet Boy. Todd Crew, who played bass with Jet Boy, was friends with Slash and Duff. Local musician West Arkeen was tight with Axl, as was *RIP* magazine writer Del James. Robert John was always around with his cameras. Don Henley, the Eagles drummer who was making a solo album, dropped by and wrote his song "Sunset Grill" about the serious moral decay he saw in the alley behind the restaurant. Even guitar legend Joe Perry turned up one night to cop some of Izzy's brown Persian heroin. (This was considered to be beyond awesome by the band. Within a few months, Perry cleaned himself up and re-formed Aerosmith. According to contemporary Sunset Strip lore, he was inspired to do this by the adamantine rock and roll energy, plus the general adulation for early period Aerosmith, that he encountered in Hollywood in 1985.)

That's when Guns started to have impromptu parties in the alley outside their lair. Izzy ran his heroin enterprise from the room, which the band decorated with posters, pinups, hard-core porn, flyers, and whatever they could find. Their scene immediately attracted feral party girls, some of them extremely young, many dressed in the lacy corsets, tiny leather skirts, fishnet stockings, and Doc Martens boots of the day. The girls in turn attracted guys in other bands, and kids who wanted to look like they were in a band. Musicians, pimps, deviants, dope dealers, and street-level artists and actors started hanging out. Some nights, as the summer of 1985 wore on, noisy crowds of partying kids jammed into Lot Number 619 while Guns rehearsed inside. Pretty soon all the drinking, drugging, smoking, whoring, fighting, and extra-loud music began to attract the attention of the L.A. cops and the West Hollywood sheriff's deputies. Young girls started claiming that they'd been molested. Teenage kids from the Valley claimed they had been mugged, rolled, ripped off, sold bogus drugs. Sirens pierced the sultry summer evenings as ambulances arrived to pick up overdose cases. Guns N' Roses began to get a serious negative reputation in local police precincts.

To its general discredit, the band used girls ruthlessly. Then they threw the bones out the window. Some of them used drugs, big-time. Slash began a major heroin habit at this time that lasted for years and would almost destroy Guns N' Roses. Steven Adler later claimed that he was pressured to use heroin by some of his bandmates.

"We sold drugs," Izzy later admitted—with no apology, with even a hint of pride. "We sold girls. If one of the guys was fucking a girl in our sleeping loft, we'd ransack the girl's purse while he was doing her. We *managed*."

Axl agreed. "There was a lot of indoor and outdoor sex. There was sex in cars. People would show up at all hours, and we'd talk the girls into climbing into our loft, and someone would hit the light and go, 'All right! Everybody in the loft—*get naked or leave*.' This one girl, she fucked almost the whole band, friends of the band, and the band next door. Two days later, she comes back and goes, 'Axl, I'm having your child.'"

For every girl run through by the band, three more showed up the next night—rarin' to go. The band had its own semi-reserved table at the El Compadre cantina on Sunset. "We used to sit here in the corner," Slash later whispered to London writer Mick Wall, "because it was the best spot to get a blow job under the table without anyone else in the room knowing. Or else [we'd] take 'em in the toilets out back."

When exhausted or strung out, Izzy liked to crash in the cramped, narrow space between the back of the urine-soaked couch and the roach-infested wall of the building. A friend of the band remembered that Izzy could be lost in there—for days. "You'd just see his head appear occasionally to check out what was going on. I'd say, 'Izzy—you OK, man?' He'd go, 'Uh, yeah,' then disappear again."

On Saturdays the Salvation Army gave out free food to Hollywood's homeless and indigent at their mission on Vine Street. Guns N' Roses was often there, lined up with the local bums, junkies, winos, and tramps. Duff McKagan preferred the fare at Rage, the notorious Hollywood gay bar, which had a five o'clock buffet. Guns N' Roses was a regular. They all loved Rage. "You got all the food you could eat for a dollar," Duff recalled. "You clenched your butt cheeks and ate. They had delicious fried squid!"

Axl was revolted by all this. "At one point we had the band and four other women living in this one room. The nearest bathroom had been destroyed by people throwing up. I used to shit in a box and throw it in the trash, because the bathroom was so disgusting."

Slash said later that their squalid rehearsal room was a kind of negative inspiration: "Basically, it was just down to a poverty thing. That's where [our] fuck-you attitude comes from. We'd rehearse in there; sleep in there. It got hectic: you're not showering, you're not getting enough food. You do what you have to do, to survive." One time, Slash and Izzy were both fucking a girl in their loft. Izzy wasn't wearing a condom, and he pulled out of the girl and ejaculated on Slash's leg. This was when Slash knew they had to find new quarters.

This whole scene was also where the legendary Hollywood street buzz about Guns N' Roses started. People started to talk about the crazed, dangerous scene at Sunset and Gardner—a vile supermarket of sex and drugs and rock and roll, something down and dirty and alive. The band lived like swine, drank too much all the time, didn't practice safe sex, worried about AIDS, openly dealt dope. They'd go to the clubs, get people to buy them drinks, and act like assholes. "We'd just go out at night," Axl said, "like *annihilated,* pass out our flyers, and just make sure everyone in the fuckin' room knew that we were there."

It got so stupid that Axl's obnoxious behavior caused him to be formally banned from the Rainbow Bar and Grill for two years.

Axl Rose loved being down-and-out. He dug the whole romance of skid row. Five years later, he reminisced: "Every weekend, the biggest party in L.A. was down at our place. We'd have five hundred kids packed in the alley, and our old roadie was selling cold beers for a buck, out of his car trunk. It was like a bar. Older people bought whiskey for younger ones. . . . If there was a problem with someone, they'd be 'escorted' out. We'd fucking drag 'em down the alley by their hair, naked, and leave 'em in the street. We could do whatever we wanted, at least until the cops showed up.

"The funny thing is," Axl said wistfully, "we almost miss it." It was when Guns was really more of a gang than it was a band. It was the best years of their lives. In 1991, when he was one of the biggest (and one of the most miserable) rock stars in the world, Slash reminisced, "For years I lived out of a duffel bag—and I was happy."

"We were like a gang," Steven confirmed. "That's how we thought of ourselves. *We play rock and roll music, and we will kick your ass.*"

*T*he part people forget about Guns' famously decadent rehearsal space was that they did manage to actually rehearse there. Duff and Steven jammed together almost every day, playing along to funk numbers by Prince and Cameo, especially Cameo's "Word Up," getting into hard rock grooves that almost *swung*, an extreme rarity among L.A. bands of the day. (Duff McKagan would later say that "Rocket Queen" was mostly based on Cameo's groove.)

*V*icky Hamilton kept booking Guns into clubs as an opening act for other bands. On June 28, they played the Stardust Ballroom at Sunset and Wilton in Hollywood. In July they were working at Raji's, a dive bar on Hollywood Boulevard. Slash had snorted too much smack and was blowing chunks of vomit behind his amplifiers. While Guns was playing "Don't Cry," a new ballad and the first song the band had written together, members of Thelonious Monster started heckling. When a bottle sailed past Axl's head, he retaliated by smashing Monster's Bob Forrest in the face with his mike stand. Then Axl jumped him and they fought until the bouncers pulled them apart. "They were intoxicated," Axl told *L.A. Weekly*, "and I was completely straight and playing. They were throwing beer bottles at us. If somebody does that, I hit 'em with the mike stand. I don't care if *my mother* came up and started punching me. I'd hit her with the fucking mike stand too."

*O*n July 25, 1985, Axl watched the daylong Live Aid concerts at his friend West Arkeen's apartment. The biggest bands in the world had sold out Wembley Stadium in London and a football field in Philadelphia. It was so huge and so hyped that even Led Zeppelin reunited for the day.

The giant charity concerts supposedly raised a lot of money for African famine relief, but in reality the whole thing sucked. Duran Duran was awful. Led Zeppelin was worse. Mick Jagger performed a lame solo act with Tina Turner. Bob Dylan, supported by Keith Richards and Ron Wood, was embarrassing. When Michael Jackson and a choir of pop stars performed Jackson's hideous famine anthem, "We Are the World," Axl turned to West Arkeen and said that he thought this was the worst rock star bullshit—*ever.* It was the same Boring Old Fart crap that the original punks had so loathed and denounced. Later Axl recalled the scenario:

"We were writing off-color [lyrics] at the time. We were dealing with a situation that was really heavy, ugly, and scary, and so we were making light of it. . . . There was a lot of confusion about a lot of issues. We were being told, 'we are the world.' But we knew it wasn't fuckin' 'we are the world.' It was 'we are the world' for a chosen few, who did a nice little song or something, but down in the streets, it was *war.* That was being just glossed over—the same old shit."

Axl swore that if his band ever made it big, he would never get caught making a fool of himself at some dumb benefit over which he had no control.

FUCK LIKE A BEAST

*G*uns continued working in the late summer of 1985, playing at the Troubadour, the Roxy, the Water Club, and the avant-garde club Scream in downtown L.A. They opened for Poison several times, a band Guns despised for being so phony and so self-consciously glam in all the wrong ways that they gave the whole scene a bad image. Poison's singer, Bret Michaels, retaliated by dissing Guns onstage as an unsigned band of degenerates.

One time, after Michaels had slagged Guns, Axl confronted Poison backstage and told them, to their face, that they sucked. Bobby Dall, whose band already had a record deal, replied: "Maybe fucking so—but you *gotta* suck, sometimes, to make it in this business—*and you guys will never make it at all.*"

This stuck in Axl's craw. Sucking was against everything W. Axl Rose believed in.

Despite this conflict, Vicky Hamilton recalls, the band scene on the Strip in the eighties was mutually supportive. "Many of the people who were part of that big hair scene knew each other, and tried to help each other's bands. Axl, for instance, liked Faster Pussycat, and kept after me to book them gigs or manage them."

"It's like a family," Duff told the *L.A. Times.* "If you don't support your own scene, your trip is not going to happen. You've got to support your friends. You can't go out there and say, *'We're the best. Screw you all.'* You've got to say, 'Look, these guys are good too.'"

As the buzz about Guns and their increasingly frenzied and violent shows began to spread beyond West Hollywood, club owners noticed that the band drew an unusually diverse crowd. Years later, Slash remembered that "the word got out that there was this new band, and we'd got this audience in L.A. from all the different scenes: old-school rock and rollers, the punks, high school teenyboppers, model chicks, drug dealers. It was *great.*"

Now Guns N' Roses was working on building a homicidal set list, alternating badass covers (Rose Tattoo's "Nice Boys," "Jack Flash," "Mama Kin," "Heartbreak Hotel" as Elvis Presley never conceived it) with redeveloped Hollywood Rose numbers ("Reckless Life" and "Anything Goes") plus some of the new songs they were writing in their little studio: red-hot "Move to the City," early versions of "Welcome to the Jungle," Izzy's new "It's So Easy," growled by Axl in a low voice, and the ballad "Don't Cry," the only song that Guns played at less than ears-bleeding volume.

Guns began their sets with a recording of "What's That Noise" by Stormtroopers of Death, the Anthrax spin-off band whose new album *Speak English or Die* was close to Axl's heart for its blatant racism and anti-immigrant lyrics. Living on the streets, Guns came into conflict with the immigrant merchants—refugees from Ayatollah Khomeini's Islamist revolution—who were taking over the gas stations and convenience stores along the Hollywood boulevards. With his long red hair, flash clothes, total poverty, and bad attitude, Axl Rose was constantly hassled by Iranian shopkeepers, thrown out of fast-food joints, and refused service in stores managed by recent arrivals to what was derisively called "Teherangeles." Some of these ugly scenes got semiviolent, with the police arriving soon after. Axl would scream at troublesome Persian shopkeepers to fucking go back where they came from, and take their fucking shitty brown dope with them, or at least learn to speak fucking English if they were going to rip off real Americans in the land of the free and the home of the brave.

Despite being something of an immigrant to L.A. himself, Axl's attitude toward the Iranians, Asians, Latinos, and the other nationalities that made up the weird mix of Los Angeles would get him and his band in trouble with the politically correct a few years later.

*G*uns opened the show for some other bands at a Hollywood benefit for comedian Jerry Lewis's "Jerry's Kids" charity on August 30, 1985, at the Stardust Ballroom. Poison headlined the show, which also featured Ruby Slippers, the Joneses, and Mary Poppins. The next day, Guns played the Roxy Theater on Sunset Strip for the first time. The Roxy, along with the Whisky down the street, was the Strip's premier showcase, where visiting bands did club-size concerts for fans and the music industry. (Slash had designed a flyer for this gig, describing the band as "Diamonds in the Rough." For days prior to the gig, Slash and Izzy had tramped up and down West Hollywood and into the Valley with staple guns, tape, and bottles of wine, insolently defying a new city ordinance forbidding band flyers on the streets.) Adrenalized by this gig, Guns played loud and fast, with Slash running around the stage, his hair flying, a whirl of flop sweat and wicked-sounding power chords. People said it was the best show the band had yet played.

*M*eanwhile, rock music was put on trial by Congress in September 1985. Alarmed by sexy videos on MTV and the overt violence of the metal bands, a group of powerful Washington wives calling themselves the Parents Music Resource Center (PMRC) persuaded a congressional committee to hold hearings to determine if popular music should be censored and graded for content with a ratings system like the movies. Sunset Strip bands were specifically targeted for wallowing in filth. The defining moment of the hearings came when Tipper Gore, wife of Tennessee senator Al Gore, and Janet Baker, wife of Reagan's secretary of state, held up a big enlargement of W.A.S.P.'s album, *FUCK LIKE A BEAST,* as an example of rock gone haywire. There were gasps in the hearing room as the committee beheld the image of a tortured woman on the album jacket. Such music, it was argued, should be labeled as "offensive" so that parents could monitor what their kids were exposed to.

A few days later some musicians, including Frank Zappa, John Denver, and Twisted Sister's Dee Snider testified against censoring music, which only reflected the society that created it. Said Zappa: "The PMRC proposal is an ill-conceived piece of nonsense, which fails to deliver any benefits to children. [It is] the equivalent of treating dandruff by decapitation." Eventually, the music industry caved, and a black parental warning label later appeared on all of Guns N' Roses' albums when they were released.

"Welcome to the Jungle" read GN'R's flyer for the band's next show at the Troubadour on Friday, September 20. Axl's signature song was finished by then and was already causing girls to start screaming when Slash's guitar stutter began the set. The band's reputation was now exploding. By the time Guns went on at eleven P.M., the kids in the old folk club were packed together like goats.

Also in the house that night was Poison, about to start recording their first album, *Look What the Cat Dragged In.* Poison made the mistake of bringing Ric Browde, who was producing their record, to see Guns N' Roses at the Troubadour that night.

Browde and Poison were already at odds over what the record should sound like. "It didn't help," Browde later recalled, "that the first night we started recording, Bobby [Dall], Bret [Michaels], CC [Deville], and I went to see this unsigned band at the Troubadour, and they just—blew me away." Later, after a few drinks and whatever, "I told Poison that—no matter how many records they sold—they would never be as good as this unsigned band we'd just seen, who were called Guns N' Roses."

It was, perhaps, the wrong thing to say. Poison hated their producer from then on.

THE "RAPE" OF MY MICHELLE

There were people in Hollywood who thought Guns N' Roses was a righteous band just because Guns kept insisting they didn't give a shit. They told people they just wanted to play music and have fun and didn't care about a record deal. They had decided early on not to scam their way into highly desirable weekend shows (like Poison did). Axl Rose was actually proud of Guns having worked their way through the system: starting out on Monday and Tuesday "pay to play" nights, where the band basically rented the room and had to sell its own tickets (which is where the hard work of flyering and street promo really paid off), then moving to Wednesdays and Thursdays while building an audience. Axl believed they had to "play weekdays. Play everywhere, and from there, work our way to a headliner slot [on weekends]. We did that, and it took a long time."

But then, like any band, Guns had to change its fuck-all attitude about recording. As their buzz kept surging, as people started to see the balls-out authenticity of their presentation, with Slash in full fury and Axl screaming on his knees until his face reddened with blood and the cords of his neck tightened like steel cable, as they got better and tighter, the band began to realize they couldn't move up out of the clubs until they signed a contract to make a record with one of the corporate record labels of the day.

Eventually, around October 1985, they started to ask Vicky Hamilton about this. She had been involved in managing Crüe, Poison, and Stryper, and knew all the key players. She had been booking the band for about a year through various lineups but had never had any interest in managing them until Slash had joined Guns the previous June. She told Izzy that she could take them around to talk to the labels—if they really wanted her to be their manager. This was a slightly touchy subject, since they didn't have management yet, but it was made clear

to Vicky—and was understood by the industry—that if she got Guns N'
Roses a good record deal, she would manage the band.

Guns needed a demo tape, so they recorded five songs at a little
punk rock studio in Hollywood. Duff McKagan said that would-be
Guns producer Black Randy from the band Metro Squad paid for the
session, which cost about $300. Several different GN'R demos from
this period exist, but the most likely songs on this tape were "Jungle,"
"It's So Easy," "Nightrain," "Move to the City," and "Reckless Life." Vicky
remembers that they were cut "live" in the studio and approximated
the explosive energy of the band in concert. She started circulating
copies of the tape to a few label people she knew would be interested.

Duff says, "Then we just kept playing. We did Mondays at the Troubadour. Then we were doing Tuesdays." Guns opened for a lot of speed
metal bands. "That was like God for us at the time, just opening for
bands at the Troubadour. We were all like, 'Wow—we're making it!'"

Guns played again on October 18 at Chuck Landis's (packed)
Couxntry Club in Reseda, and then at Radio City's Halloween show in
Anaheim. In mid-November, flyers started appearing in Hollywood
and shopping malls in the Valley announcing the band's next gig:

**ADDICTED—Only The Strong Survive—Guns N' Roses—Friday Nov.
22—Troubadour 10:30 PM—$6.50 / 1 drink minimum.**

Above the photo of a glam-looking, even an almost Poison-looking
Guns spitting melon seeds was the band's new, Slash-designed logo.
This was a crude rendering of crossed .44 Magnum revolvers, the famous death-dealing weapon of vigilante vengeance wielded by Clint
Eastwood in the massively popular *Dirty Harry* movies, the .44s in the
logo being entwined with thorny rose briars that ran along the long
barrels of the revolvers.

This show was part of an experiment, to see if two clothes-deprived
girl dancers would contribute anything to the show. This was Axl's
idea and was abandoned after only a few gigs.

*T*wo of the girls who hung around the Guns' "decadent little sweat-
box" of a studio would later be immortalized in song. Barbi Von Greif

was a cute little pixie and the creative equal of anyone in the band. A sometime exotic dancer who worked in pasties, a self-described "wild child," she was involved with both Izzy and Axl at various points, and influenced Axl's hair and makeup in those days. Axl later said Barbi had unmatched instincts for what was cool in the nexus of music, drugs, and style. One of her ambitions was to have a band of her own, and the name of the band would be Rocket Queen.

Then there was a teenager named Michelle. According to most accounts, feral child Michelle, prime Hollywood jailbait at fifteen, followed Axl into the band's room on the wrong day in December 1985. Axl was in one of his moods. He grabbed Michelle, tore her clothes off, threw her out into the alley, and locked the door. They didn't have sex, at least then.

Later, speaking to *L.A. Weekly,* trying to defend or at least describe Guns' bad reputation, Axl told his version. "One time this hippie chick wandered into our studio and started fucking with our equipment, trying to break stuff." Someone suggested calling the cops, because the girl was on dope, screaming for attention, out of her fucking mind. But Axl warned that the cops would just turn the situation around and hassle them for picking on this poor underage waif. "So eventually she wound up running down Sunset naked, all dingy [stoned], doesn't even know her fucking name."

Later that day the police showed up, then fire trucks arrived. They were looking for Axl, who was hiding behind the amps with another girl. The cops lined up everyone else outside and brought in Michelle, who was hysterical and crying rape, but then she identified somebody else as Axl, which the cops knew was all wrong.

Axl laughed at the memory. "Being bad is such a fucking rush! While the cops are out there harassing everybody, asking their stupid questions, I'm with this girl behind the amp, and we start going at it. *That was the rush!* I fucking got away with it! It was really exciting!"

Even more exciting was what the police told Guns: Even discounting the rape charge, just having sex with an underage girl was good for prison time in California. The cops told them to have Axl turn himself in, and left. Soon after this, Slash heard that he was going to be charged with statutory rape as well. Then the band learned that the LAPD's vice squad was interested in Guns' extra-musical activities and wanted to question them about rumors that they were pimping for certain girls. Then Axl heard undercover cops were doing surveillance on their alley, looking for him because Michelle was sticking by her rape claim and wanted to press charges.

"They were talking a mandatory five years," Axl said. "It kind of settled my hormones for a while." The band canceled a December 20 gig at the Music Machine because Axl was a wanted man.

He took to the streets. He slept under the canopy of the loading dock at Tower Records. A Dumpster behind Sunset Plaza offered shelter. He was hassled in gas stations for trying to use the bathrooms. He was locked out of a 7-Eleven convenience store for the way he dressed. An Iranian pizzeria owner threatened him with a butcher knife. One time Robert John was driving Izzy somewhere. "We stopped at a red light. A homeless person was asleep on a bus stop bench. 'Oh look,' Izzy said, just kinda matter-of-factly, 'there's Bill.'" Indeed, W. Axl Rose was taking his rest on Sunset Boulevard that evening.

*L*ate one night, Vicky Hamilton answered the phone at her apartment at 1114 North Clark, just up the hill from the Whisky a Go Go. Saul Hudson was on the line. "Vicky—you gotta hide Axl," he rasped. "The cops are swarming us, looking to bust his ass."

Vicky asked how long Axl needed a place to hide. "Just a day or two," Izzy said. Soon Axl arrived, under cover of darkness. He swore to Vicky that he hadn't raped that girl. *"Great,"* thought Vicky, *"I'm harboring a rape fugitive."* A day or two later, around the time another statutory rape charge was filed against Slash, Guns abandoned their studio in the middle of the night and moved in with Vicky too. She and Jennifer Perry shared the apartment's single bedroom, while the band crashed in the living room amid their instruments and gear. They stayed in Vicky's place for the next three or four months while she shopped the band to record labels, continued as their booking agent, and negotiated her handshake management agreement with the now truly outlawed Guns N' Roses.

The rape charges against both Axl and Slash would eventually be withdrawn. The rumor on Sunset Boulevard was that Axl had sex with Michelle's mother, who convinced her daughter to let the matter drop.

Chapter Four

VICTORY OR DEATH

A band is an extreme form of
co-dependency, to use a recovery term. It's
like a marriage without the sex, without
the ceremony, without the love, without the
children, without the golf, without the
Sunday lunches, without the in-laws. When
you put a band together, you tend to accept
that this guy in the band can do the job.
But, God! They're so weird. And if you get a
hit, you're stuck with this weird person for
the rest of your life.
—Pete Townshend

THE DANGEROUS ALTERNATIVE

In January 1986, the word was out on the Strip among the glam rockers, the Aqua Net set, the pretty punks, the teenage wannabes: Their favorite band, Guns N' Roses, was on the lam. But this street buzz actually helped Guns in certain circles: the doubters who called them Whines N' Posers and Lines N' Nosers and the jaded cynics in the record business who were slow to buy into Guns' being the real deal, a trueborn bad boy band—which, if it were true, would make the group's fortune, because a *real* bad boy band hadn't come along since the Sex Pistols, ten years earlier.

The new "Move to the City" leaflets were gaffer-taped, illegally now, on trees and streetlights along Sunset, Hollywood, and Santa Monica boulevards. They advertised the band's next show at Doug Weston's World Famous Troubadour on January 4.

Get Yourself Together / Drink Till You Drop / Forget About Tomorrow / Have Another Shot / Sat. Jan. 4ᵗʰ 11:00 / $2 off with flyer.

The band picture shows Slash in his black hat for the first time. Guns slouches like sheep-killing dogs in the bombed-out rubble of a construction site at Sunset and LaBrea. "Move to the City" was scrawled on the wall as graffiti, reflecting the song's popularity on the street and its currently hot prospects as the band's first single—if they ever got signed to a record deal. At the bottom of the flyer, reflecting the band's fugitive status, was a tongue-in-cheek appeal to their growing fan base:

Send donations to: Guns N' Roses / Keep Us Out of Jail Fund / 9000 Sunset, etc.

There was some concern that Axl would be arrested at the Troubadour, but the cops never showed up. Some thought they had either stopped believing that anyone had been raped, or just stopped caring about it.

Two weeks later, Guns played an incandescent show at the Roxy before a throbbing audience completely in sync with the life-or-death performance by the band. They all wore heavy makeup: all kohl eyes and lipstick. Axl wore his new S&M outfit: black vinyl pants, open at the crotch, which he covered (barely) with a leather bikini bottom, black leather riding boots, black leather vest open to reveal his newly pierced left nipple, lots of silver-and-leather bracelets, mirrored aviator shades, patent-leather motorcycle cap of the type made popular in the fetish clubs and gay bars. When the cap came off, Axl's red hair burned orange under the stage lights, teased to the max and standing tall. ("The only reason I put my hair up," Axl said at the time, "was because Izzy had these pictures of Hanoi Rocks and they were cool. And because we hung out with this guy who studies hairstyles in *Vogue* magazine and was into doing hair.")

Thrashing around the stage in a dead-eyed shaman's trance for some songs, deploying his snake hips, microphone stomp, and other choreography, Axl proudly showed off his recent tattoos: a lush brunette under the rose on his right shoulder; the cartoonlike rocket queen, wide-eyed, on his left shoulder; above another tattoo that looked like a military patch, a red zipper bisecting a yellow shield over the scrolled motto: VICTORY OR DEATH.

Slash played his thunderous solos in a pair of jeans, sneakers, and a winged Aerosmith logo shirt. Bright metal conchos circled his black top hat. Izzy stood to Axl's right, playing in his usual loose shirt and a slouch hat, the gold ring in his right nostril reflecting the spotlight. Duff, the second voice in the band, was to Axl's left, in punk regalia and a Russian Red Army soldier's hat with crossed swords above the brim. (This was somewhat appropriate since Duff also had a bottle-a-day vodka habit.) Steven, on his drum riser, was constantly on the move, fidgeting with spare energy, a hairy, smiling, golden presence keeping slightly behind-the-beat time and looking like he was having the time of his life. The whole band played in front of a new white banner heralding Slash's crossed Colt .44s entwined with thorny roses. Guns N' Roses looked and sounded like a gang of bastard angels come down to earth to save rock and roll from the eighties.

*A*fter that Roxy show, Guns mania started to surge with an unstoppable momentum. Nobody in Hollywood had ever seen such a feeding frenzy for an unsigned band before. Six months after wandering in the desert, only half a year after they'd become brothers on The Treacherous Journey, still living for the most part on the street, Guns N' Roses looked and sounded like the Next Big Thing. Others saw it as like the Second Coming. Joe Perry later said that Guns N' Roses was the first band since Led Zeppelin that made him think of Led Zeppelin.

No one who saw it happen ever forgot what it was like in those early months of 1986. Vicky Hamilton lived through it: "They got popular the old-fashioned way—all word of mouth. Basically, people couldn't stop talking about them. It was that intense. We'd look at each other and say, *God—this is happening fast.* I mean, the early shows they had twenty people, then a hundred people, then, in a *very* short time, they had like *hundreds* of people showing up for their gigs. Then there were these *huge* lines at these clubs, and people couldn't get into the venue." Kids hung out near the clubs they played just to be near the energy, to talk about the band with other fans who couldn't get in.

"The crowds were building," Robert John said, "building, with every gig. There were lots of good bands around, but [Guns] were drawing comparisons to Zeppelin, the Stones, Aerosmith. There was this feeling in the air that something important was happening. The main talk was all about Axl—that he was dangerous, volatile, very rock and roll, running around, in your face, trying get a reaction, piss you off, pumping with energy."

Axl said that "all of a sudden we heard there was this nationwide buzz about us among record executives. And since a lot of them lost their metal acts, we suddenly became talked about and sought after."

"We had this edge," Slash told VH1 years later. "We had this unpredictable, scary thing about what we did. We didn't give a fuck about anything around us. There were no holds barred. And Axl, as volatile and complicated as he is—all the things you might find complicated or difficult about Axl is what fuels him to be such an amazing performer and such an amazing songwriter."

Up till then, all this was happening below the media radar. There were a few reviews of club shows in 'zines and alternative papers. One writer called Guns "a dangerous alternative to makeup metal groups like Cinderella and Poison."

"Makeup and spandex and crap," Axl spat, "we didn't go that route. We just went out and played rock and roll."

THE BADDEST BAND ON THE PLANET

*L*ate January 1985. They may have been the baddest band on the planet, and they may have been the current rulers of Sunset Strip (mostly because Mötley Crüe were away on a long tour, and no one took Poison seriously because they sucked and had pink hair). But the sad truth was that Guns N' Roses was dead broke and living in their agent's living room—all except Duff, who was staying with a Hungarian girl named Katarine in groovy Laurel Canyon.

Guns needed some cash to keep going. The amps and other gear were battered and needed constant repair. They needed a van. They needed drum heads, guitar strings, clothes, food, and drugs. Duff had a telemarketing job. Slash sponged off exotic dancers at strip joints like The Body Shop and The Seventh Veil. His stripper girlfriends usually lived in decent motels or respectable shared apartments. Slash got fired from the clock factory because he spent all his time promoting Guns on the pay phone. At this point, Slash was already working his ass off for the band: promoting, designing, flyering, making the phone calls, and, as he said, "having sex with the right people." Steven Adler had a bunch of different part-time jobs as a dishwasher, janitor at a bowling alley, pizza maker, landscaper. Izzy worked briefly in a guitar store, but mostly peddled smack. Izzy was later described by Doors manager Danny Sugerman as being "remembered on the L.A. junkie scene as a consistent face among customers for the Iranian brown heroin that was flooding in back then."

Axl also did some telemarketing, and reportedly worked nights at various stores. When the weather was mild, he slept in back of Tower Video, under the rear staircase. He and Izzy also volunteered for medical tests conducted at UCLA, in Westwood, where they made eight dollars per hour smoking cigarettes for science.

Mostly, they scammed chicks. If a girl wanted to come over, she couldn't arrive empty-handed. Groceries, alcohol, drugs, and sex were casually accepted as tribute gifts to the band. One of Duff's hustles was to call up some band-crazy girl. "You go: 'Look, my bass was just shipped from somewhere, and they forgot to loosen the strings, so the fucking strings broke, and I need a new set, so can you lend me twenty dollars, please?'"

Nor was Slash too proud to beg for money in the bars. "I used to go to the Whisky and the Rainbow and the Roxy a couple nights out of the week, and fuckin' just panhandle money from everybody." He would whine that the band's rental van got towed, and that he lived way the fuck out in Silver Lake, and the only way he was gonna get home was if you gave him twenty bucks to help him out. "It sounds pretty scummy," he said later, "but sometimes it got to that point."

According to Axl, they sharpened their survival skills in this period by constant reality checks. "What we did was fucking yell at each other like crazy, kick the shit out of each other if somebody's fucking up, doing too much drugs. We'd go, YOU'RE BLOWING IT, DUDE! WE HAVE NO FUCKING TIME FOR THIS!...It's like we don't want to fuck anybody over in the band, we just want to scare the shit out of each other because we don't want to lose what we have."

Asked a year later about rumors that the band dealt drugs, Axl was unusually candid. "We're all wasted," he replied, "and we were exploring drugs. We talk openly about it, but then that was just what was happening. Not a lot of people knew about it, but then big bands started coming around and wanting to score off of us—and we needed money, sure....So, it became something that we found ourselves in the center of. That was when it got messy."

"They were all party animals," Vicky confirmed, but she says she never saw any needles around her apartment. "My only involvement in that part of their lives was driving Izzy to rehab." Guns N' Roses may have been the band with the worst reputation in L.A., the band most predicted to die, but a few industry veterans already realized that Guns could also emerge as the band with the stamina, the vision, the ambition, and the internal cohesion to get really big.

And then some people just cherished Guns for giving the conflicted, often phony Hollywood band scene the sulfuric stench of authentically damned youth. Everyone talked about this. No one had been this publicly fucked up since those late sixties days when giants like Brian Jones, Jim Morrison, and Janis Joplin staggered across Santa Monica Boulevard, asking only to be shown the way to the next whiskey bar.

*A*fter a month Guns N' Roses living there, Vicky's apartment was in rough shape. Her landlord sent her an eviction letter. The neighbors were up in arms about the scarecrow-looking junkies littering the stairs and the riffraff playing Metallica records at top volume late at night. Gear was stacked to the ceiling. The apartment's floor was an unhealthy miasma of overflowing ashtrays, pizza crusts, beer cans, liquor bottles, soiled underwear, and drug paraphernalia. "We, like, *destroyed* her apartment," Axl said with a smirk to English writer Sylvie Simmons. "We were like five bags of garbage all in one room, and the girls coming over." The girls were wary about even cleaning up because Izzy sometimes scrawled lyrics to new songs on the bottom of pizza boxes.

With his usual mean-spirited candor, Axl bit the hands that fed him: "It got really crazy, really rude. These two girls were like guy-crazy and band-crazy, and there was no way that any guy in any band was gonna be caught dead with either of them, especially us." He went on to accuse Slash of working this situation for all it was worth.

Barbi Von Greif remembered it as "a twenty-four-hour-a-day party, literally. They had Tupperware [containers] full of cocaine, everyone strung out, using Ecstasy, always a song written on a pizza box, a few bodies on the floor" just lying where they blacked out.

Vicky Hamilton knew she was just weeks away from getting Guns their record deal, but the scene in her flat was now so crazy that she was thinking of moving to a hotel until she finally got the band signed and they could get a place of their own.

WE'LL BE DAMNED

The mad scramble to sign Guns N' Roses to a recording contract began in earnest in February 1986.

Vicky Hamilton was already taking Guns to meetings with record labels when the band started living with her in late 1985. When she started to manage the band in 1986, she borrowed $25,000 from Howie Huberman, who owned the music store Guitars R' Us, to finance a signing campaign and buy gear and clothes for the band. (The store's name would be echoed in the way the band decided to standardize the spelling of its name around this time.) Vicky kept booking them into cool shows, sometimes with Lions & Ghosts, a shoe-gazing band that Vicky loved but that annoyed Axl.

Vicky thought she was managing Guns, but the band actually had other ideas and also worked on their own behalf. Axl and Izzy wrote a letter to L.A. promoter Kim Fowley, a twenty-year veteran of the Hollywood pop scene. The letter, described as "grandiose on one hand and endearingly naïve on the other," stressed the band's impeccable street cred and defiant antiauthoritarian stance. They told Fowley with total seriousness that they were only out to please themselves and that anyone who didn't get this was their enemy. Fowley was interested enough to see Guns play at the Roxy and to offer Axl a publishing deal for his songs.

Axl told Vicky about this one night at the Troubadour. He told her that Fowley had offered him $2,500 each, for publishing rights to three songs. Dead-broke Axl Rose thought this might be a good deal. Vicky was shocked. "Axl, are you crazy?"

"Ah shit," he said. "I can write a million songs." Fowley, who was now talking up Guns as the next big thing, was so furious at Vicky for killing this deal that he followed her into the club's ladies' room, screaming at her for helping Axl protect his interests.

There was another five-song demo tape, cut with producer Spencer Proffer, around this time that included the ballads "Don't Cry," "Patience," and "Used to Love Her." But the band argued with Proffer: The tracks were too polished, too clean, and didn't represent their raw, saw-toothed sonic attack. Then Paul Stanley, who played guitar with KISS, started courting Guns—showing up at gigs, making noises about wanting to produce the band.

"Slash had him come over," Axl told *Hit Parader,* "and I sat down and talked production with him, and played him the demo. He immediately wanted to rewrite two of our favorite songs, so it was over right there." After that, Axl wouldn't talk to Stanley. He wouldn't even look at him. Then Stanley started hearing that Slash was spreading the rumor that Stanley was gay. Stanley thought this was funny, since Axl was performing in fetish clothing and heavy makeup. Slash later temporized that Stanley was a nice guy but didn't have a clue about what Guns was.

By then, there were lots of requests for publicity photos of Guns N' Roses and press-ready biographies of the band. Vicky duly sent out a 1985 shot of the band by Robert John and the following band bio:

GUNS N' ROSES

Wild abandon & streetwise composure are encompassed by the music of the savvy & sexy guns n' roses. rising from the hollywood underground, the band has confidence, raw power, and the authenticity of actually surviving the streets. A power based in the hard knocks depths of reality let [*sic*] the music of the band exude confidence in themselves and their music.

Izzy Stradlin and W. Axl Rose played together and separately for ten years before forming guns n' roses in the spring of 1985. Soon added were the duo of Slash and Steven Adler, who had worked together for over five years. Duff McKagan on bass completed the gang. His previous experience in guitar, drums, and vocals cements his place in the band.

Guns n' roses is the combination of individuals and personalities that each member has been striving for since their long ago start in rock & roll. Perhaps selfish in the fact that they please themselves first, this enables the band to play music they truly believe in. Guns n' roses runs on the pure strength of emotion and feeling as can be seen in their highly visual and energetic performances. They aren't afraid to be themselves and refuse to compromise their stance and beliefs for anyone or anything. They've paid their debt to society and are ready to take on the world. . . .

In the words of Axl Rose:

"We'll be damned if it isn't everything we can give, or there's no point in existing."

By mid-February 1986, the sixties-era veteran executives who ran the major record labels in Los Angeles—CBS, ABC, RCA, London, Capitol, Chrysalis, Atlantic, Warner/Reprise, Elektra/Asylum—were being told by their spoiled, streetwise teenage kids that they were total boring losers if they didn't make a deal with Guns N' Roses. In the high school parking lots of Hollywood, Beverly Hills, Brentwood, Sherman Oaks, Malibu, Van Nuys, Encino, and Orange County, the kids talked about no other band. The men who ran the labels in turn told their people that their jobs now depended on getting Guns' palsied signatures on one of their abusive, exploitive recording contracts. In the relatively small Los Angeles record business, anxiety polluted the already compromised atmosphere.

At first Vicky thought that Elektra Records would sign them. The label had done well with Mötley Crüe, but despite a slew of promises and missed deadlines, the label did not come up with a deal. The truth was that the record executives had heard all about Guns N' Roses and were terrified of being associated with the band. Their reputation preceded them like a bad smell. Some streetwise young record people had been to the band's parties in the alley behind their studio and seen the junkies and the drunks that hung out with the band— some of whom were actually in the band. The word was that when Guns flamed out, as was inevitable, the band would take you and your career with them. They all asked each other: Would *you* sign five maniacs with no management, a declared problem with authority, some of whom were known to be junkies, a band that seemed determined to destroy itself, to a major label record deal?

*V*icky was shopping the demo tapes now full-time. Elektra Records loved the demo. Vicky brought Elektra exec Peter Philbin to a Guns show, and the next day all the other labels started calling nonstop about Guns. "That's when we found out that all the record executives knew each other," Axl said, "and if one guy wanted us, they all did. So they started fighting with each other." In the heat of battle one night, Axl swore an oath, to an attractive and flirtatious female A&R executive, that Guns would sign with her company if she would walk down Sunset Strip, stark naked, for at least three blocks. The woman smiled and said she would think it over.

One sunny winter afternoon, Vicky walked Axl, Slash, and Duff down Sunset Boulevard to a meeting with Chrysalis Records. Duff's piled-up hair was dyed neon green, and he looked eight feet tall in his boots. Slash was in top hat and leathers, his black curls veiling his features. Axl was in his regular gay biker regalia, but with a bandanna over his long red hair. Vicky was thrilled to see their glam apparition actually *stopped traffic* when they crossed the street to the label's offices at Doheny and Sunset.

They took the elevator to the top floor and were ushered into an office with a panoramic view of Hollywood and Los Angeles. Chrysalis was a British label with a cool track record: Jethro Tull, Blondie, the 2-Tone ska bands, Billy Idol, "New Romantic" bands Ultravox and Spandau Ballet. The company had pioneered music videos. Any new band would want to sign with them.

Axl put his boots up on the executive's desk. Vicky remembered: "This guy [Ron Fair] was desperate to sign them. He was shouting that Guns *must* be on Chrysalis. At one point he grabbed a yellow legal pad and a Sharpie pen, drew a giant dollar sign on a blank page, and thrust the pad at Axl, like he was showing him the money that the band was going to get if they signed with him."

Axl had been in Hollywood a few years now. He just looked over at Vicky and said, with a snort: "Is this guy fucking *nuts,* or what?"

Duff claimed that "the fuckin' Chrysalis brains" offered Guns $750,000 to sign with the label. "We just said, *'Yeah, but have you ever seen us play?'*" Chrysalis said no, not yet. Guns and Vicky were out of there fast.

"So we just kept playing," Izzy recalled, "and we didn't go away, and we just made so much fuckin' noise in the city that the labels started to come to see *us.*"

Vicky scheduled meals with record people with expense accounts at all the best restaurants. Izzy loved this. "We made them take us all out to dinner for a few weeks. We'd order all this food and drinks and tell them 'OK, *now talk.*'" Guns N' Roses started eating well for the first time in years. Suddenly it was prime filet of beef au jus and the finest champagne, lobster flown in from Maine, thick steaks at The Palm, multiple trips to the loo for gleaming rails of Peruvian blow, Alaska king crab, aged veal, and vintage wines, more cocaine, followed by every dessert on the menu and bottles of four-star French cognac and Cuban cigars smuggled in from Tijuana by pregnant Mexican girls.

"The buzz got out," Slash said later, "and we kept getting invited to meet these idiots from the record companies." At one lunch with a label's A&R staff, Slash described Guns as being a little like Aerosmith, and Axl as a little like Steven Tyler. "And the [A&R] chick goes, 'Steven who?' All of us just looked at each other." No one could believe this. Slash broke the long silence that followed. "Can we have another round of those Margaritas?"

The band drank deeply on corporate music's tab and gorged on the freshest, most exquisite, most expensive sushi that Beverly Hills had to offer. When, a month later, they signed their deal, master manipulator Slash told Vicky he wanted it kept secret for as long as possible so the other labels would continue entertaining them in the high style to which they'd become accustomed. Slash, high on the unique magic of the moment, already knew that it would never be quite like this for Guns N' Roses again.

For most of these companies, the real truth was that despite all the industry hype, as Slash later said, "Nobody *really* wanted to sign us—to deal with us—produce us—to manage us—and even the fuckin' club owners were scared of us too." Conventional wisdom in the executive suites of Hollywood held firm to the notion, not altogether wrong, that Guns N' Roses was a ticking bomb that could blow at any moment. The fuse was already lit and sizzling down to the head of the barrel.

It was David Geffen who finally took a chance on them.

"JUST ONE"

David Geffen was forty-six and the chief of his own premium record label, Geffen Records. He'd started in the mailroom of a talent agency in the sixties, and then became a talent manager for some of the singer/songwriters, like Joni Mitchell and Jackson Browne, who emerged from an earlier, post-folk era at the Troubadour Coffee House.

Geffen started his first label, Asylum Records, in the early seventies, and the label evolved into the premier artistic platform for some of the major stars of the decade, including Mitchell, the Eagles, and even Bob Dylan for a time. (As already noted, Slash's father designed the album jacket for Joni Mitchell's most successful Asylum album, *Court and Spark,* in 1974.)

At the height of this success, Geffen was diagnosed with cancer and stepped down from Asylum. But in 1980 he came back with a new label. Funded by Warner Bros., Geffen Records let its founder—a legendary deal maker—maintain complete control while retaining half the profits. David Geffen then built one of the most successful record companies in history. The label hit gold immediately that summer with disco queen Donna Summer. Geffen then released *Double Fantasy* by

John Lennon and Yoko Ono in December 1980, two days before Lennon was murdered by a fan in New York. Lennon's last record sold millions internationally and gave Geffen the label's first number-one album and single. The biggest rock and pop stars now flocked to the label: Elton John, Cher, Don Henley, Neil Young. Whitesnake filled MTV's Zeppelin gap and went platinum. In 1985, Geffen signed the re-formed and newly sober Aerosmith—still superheroes to Guns N' Roses. The former "toxic twins" Steven Tyler and Joe Perry now attended Alcoholics Anonymous meetings and had begun working with outside songwriters to create the music that would pump their comeback into the record books within a few years.

Now David Geffen, who watched MTV like everyone else in the business, wanted an L.A. metal band with big hair and a snotty attitude. Geffen personally hated the likes of Mötley Crüe, but he wanted a crüe of his own. His most successful A&R executives, like the bearded John Kalodner, who was working with Aerosmith, began to tell David Geffen about Guns. The only problem was that no one wanted to stake their career on an unstable group of Sunset Strip desperados.

A year earlier, Geffen had hired twenty-five-year-old A&R whiz Tom Zutaut away from Elektra Records. Back in 1982, Zutaut was working as a sales assistant for Elektra in L.A. after migrating from suburban Chicago, where he had grown up. Cherubic, baby-faced, often dressed in preppy rugby shirts, Zutaut prowled the Strip by night and heard the unsigned Crüe. Immediately he was a believer. But the older A&R guys at Elektra ignored the pathetic rantings of a pudgy clerk from out of town, so Zutaut went over their heads to the label boss, infuriating everyone but signing Crüe and earning himself a wall full of gold disc awards by the end of the following year. Now his mandate from Geffen was to find another Mötley Crüe, and they'd better be good.

Zutaut heard of Guns N' Roses for the first time the previous year, when he walked into hipper-than-thou record store Vinyl Fetish on Melrose Avenue and asked the facially accessorized guy at the cash register if he'd heard of any great new bands.

The guy looked at Zutaut and said, "Just one."

Guns N' Roses' main chance boiled down to a single show on Friday, February 28, 1986, at the Troubadour, promoted by Vicky Hamilton as a showcase to the record companies. Since they were basically auditioning for employment and the very future of the band, everyone except Axl got drunk, did heroin, snorted coke, or all of the above. The band turned its amps to what was estimated by audio engineers present that night as 130 dB, or roughly the sound of a loaded Boeing 747 waiting to take off.

When the band began its set (with Axl's autobiographical "Out ta Get Me"), the label people stampeded out of the club. Vicky recalled, "I was standing out there with twenty A&R people whom I'd invited, because it was so loud inside. I had four or five labels throwing bids at me, and the numbers were getting bigger. It was even loud *outside*. Tom Zutaut came up to me and yelled in my ear, 'If that guy can really sing, I'll sign them.' I yelled back, 'Don't worry—he can sing!'"

Zutaut went back into the Troubadour as Guns N' Roses blasted their way through "Rocket Queen," "My Michelle," "Think About You." The band was brilliant; the energy was convulsive. Even the jaded industry people in the room were moving and jiving, and the kids who'd paid to get in looked like monkeys in the jungle after the bananas had fermented.

After the band walked off, Zutaut went outside. He was careful to tell colleagues from competing labels that he thought GN'R totally sucked. Worst band ever. Dope fiends. Head cases. Never make it off the Strip. He found Vicky on the street. She handed him a copy of their demo tape. Still dazed by the volume, Zutaut whispered, "Get them in my office tomorrow."

But tomorrow was Saturday. "Oh yeah. I'll call you on Monday." Zutaut didn't call, but on March 5, the following Tuesday, he wrote a note to Vicky asking to speak with her and to talk with the band.

"The next night," Vicky recalled, "they went over to Tom's house [in Beechwood Canyon] and he played Aerosmith records for them all night long." *Toys in the Attic. Rocks. Draw the Line. Aerosmith Live.* Zutaut was extremely knowledgeable about Aerosmith minutia and secret lore, such as guitar gods Joe Perry and Brad Whitford not playing on their second album because the label considered their sound too raunchy. (The guitar parts were overdubbed by New York studio pros Steve Hunter and Dick Wagner instead and passed off as Aerosmith.)

Guns *loved* Aerosmith. Aerosmith was now signed to Geffen, beginning a comeback that would soon become historic. Ergo, Zutaut told them, Guns N' Roses should be on the Geffen label as well. It seemed logical to everyone.

Vicky: "And the next day, they were like, 'We're signing with Geffen!' I said, 'Are you crazy? All these other labels are *killing* each other over you. There's a *feeding frenzy* out there.' Axl just looked at me and said, 'We're signing with Geffen.'" It was a done deal.

Zutaut had told them that they were the loudest band he'd ever heard. They liked that he said that. He said they were even louder than AC/DC. This impressed them. Zutaut told them he wanted to record them in London. He mentioned Bill Price, who'd done the Sex Pistols. They fucking *loved* that. Axl told him about the other labels that were after them, about how he thought they could be immense, in the right hands. The next day, Zutaut said, he went to the office and told David Geffen: "I just saw the best rock and roll band in the world. I think they could sell more records than any band other than Zeppelin or the Stones." Geffen reached for the phone and told Legal to draw up the memos.

Zutaut knew this—signing Guns N' Roses—was a huge deal. It was a risk, since Geffen wasn't known for releasing debut records by new bands. But there was a downside: Three of them were openly using heroin, the singer was nuts, and the bass player was an alcoholic. It could all go terribly wrong.

There was something else as well. For the next few days, Zutaut got nervous every time he looked out his office window at 9130 Sunset Boulevard. He was worried he would see that woman from Chrysalis, walking naked down the street for at least three blocks.

*A*xl, meanwhile, was getting even weirder than usual. Everyone noticed it. Living with him for several months, Vicky soon learned to detect a blossoming manic episode, or some other mental status change, by the look in his eyes. If a strange light was shining in Axl's blue pupils, things could get very weird, very funny, or very scary—very quickly.

"He was so damaged," Vicky recalled. "Today you'd call it bipolar.

He was either childlike, or a dog from hell. I loved him dearly, but I also felt sorry for him because he could not trust anyone and already had big issues with paranoia and control."

Vicky had one of the few VCR tape machines around, and Axl would spend hours, even whole nights, staring at porno tapes starring underage Traci Lords, and commercial videos featuring extreme violence.

"He used to rent those *Faces of Death* videos," Vicky says, "and he'd sit there and stare at them forever." These consisted of real-time footage of people dying in accidents, being executed, getting killed, or committing suicide. "You'd see people's eyes being gouged out, or people smashing the heads of monkeys and eating their fresh brains." Robert John hated it when Axl watched these things. "I was horrified. But Axl was *laughing* at this stuff. It was so sick I had to leave the apartment when they were on."

Vicky added, "The other video he really loved was the Sex Pistols' version of 'My Way,' with Sid Vicious singing. Axl would yell, 'Rerun that! Rerun it! Yeah!'

"He watched MTV a lot, I guess to see what was going on with other bands. He liked Stevie Nicks's videos, taped them off the cable, and watched her to see how she moved. Then he started to try some of her ballet-style spins onstage, which was pretty hilarious."

By this time, she said later, Vicky had stopped trying to figure Axl out. "At times he's the sweetest boy you could know, but when he gets mad he's like a top spinning off. He's not consistently evil, but not consistently nice. It's two distinct personalities."

She actually found him scary. But then, everyone did.

Guns played the Music Machine on March 11, and then opened for Johnny Thunders at Fenders Ballroom in Long Beach on March 21. Thunders, an ex–New York Doll (real name: John Genzale), was in the throes of the acute heroin addiction that would later end his life in a New Orleans rooming house. He was also a founding father of what they were doing, and a post-Stones, pre–punk culture hero to Guns, and they told him so, and posed for photos with him.

The paperwork took a few weeks to happen, during which the

band starved and went into serious debt with its drug suppliers. If the deal fell through, some local musicians were going to have their fingers broken—or worse. Then there were problems with the paperwork. Slash didn't want his real name to appear on the contracts, or on the check, because he didn't want David Geffen to know whose son he was. Axl's real name was still William Bruce Bailey, and the label wouldn't sign a deal or write a check to someone using a stage name. So the lawyers had to get the name legally changed to "W. Axl Rose." Then there was the question of semi-outstanding rape charges in West Hollywood that Geffen's lawyers discovered during due diligence. (Izzy: "We're going: rape charges? *What rape charges?*") And then it turned out that William Bruce Bailey had served jail time in Indiana and still had outstanding warrants for his arrest in Lafayette for stuff like grand theft auto, assault, jumping bail, etc. It was a big and expensive hassle, but the lawyers took care of it all.

Guns was represented by Peter Paterno, an entertainment lawyer well known in the music business. Vicky had asked Paterno to represent both her and the band in negotiations with Geffen. He explained that he could not represent both, as this would be a potential conflict of interest. So he quite sensibly chose to represent the band, which, she was to learn, was basically the end of that phase of her managerial career.

Guns was due to sign at the Geffen Records offices on March 26, 1986. They weren't actually signing recording contracts that day, but just a "memo deal" that would lead to the real contracts later on, if Guns defied conventional wisdom and made it through the next few months alive. An advance of $75,000 was now due the band: half on signing the memo deal, half when the real contracts were executed. This meant that each member of Guns would receive a check for $7,500 both times they signed. It was a big day. It was the beginning of everything their band had worked for. It was the rock and roll dream coming true for them.

Vicky Hamilton knew the truth. It was the end of Guns as what they had been—an authentic L.A. street band. Already she could see what would be lost, and what would happen. She later said that she cried the day Guns N' Roses signed with Geffen Records.

DRINK YOUR FACE OFF

*L*os Angeles is most beautiful in the spring, when the arid vegetation blooms bright green and the bushes flower into shades of magenta, blue, and red. Before the smog settles, the hillsides glow in morning light. Snowcaps gleam on the far San Gabriels, the air is fresh and blue from Pacific zephyrs, and the beach beckons you west.

But W. Axl Rose's contact lenses were missing, which was making Guns N' Roses insufferably late to a crucial business meeting.

Vicky Hamilton remembers that "the day we were supposed to sign with Geffen, Axl couldn't find his contacts. He accused Slash of taking them, or misplacing them, and then he flipped out and left the house." Now it was someone else's problem. "Me and Slash just looked at each other. He said, 'We gotta find them.' So we went through all his pockets and then found the lenses on the floor. I looked at the clock. They—David Geffen, Tom Zutaut, [company president] Eddie Rosenblatt—were all waiting for us, and we were now an hour late. I'd had nightmares like this."

Slash was standing by the window, looking down Clark toward Sunset. He said to Vicky, "Come here, check this out."

Vicky looked out the window. Just down the hill, a hundred feet away, Axl was sitting cross-legged on top of the Whisky a Go Go, in a meditative pose, facing away from them, toward Hollywood. The Whisky had been closed while the building was undergoing renovation. Axl had climbed scaffolding that ran up the back.

They managed to coax Axl down from the building. They walked the two blocks to Geffen's office. They were two hours late, but the signing was uneventful. Corks were popped on good champagne. Slash was identified as "Stash" on the contracts and the check.

*T*he band continued to crash at Vicky's place for a while, until she realized that she'd been left out of the deal and wasn't going to be the manager of Guns N' Roses. There was talk of a management "consultancy" for her with the band, but delays were said to be unavoidable and the band was looking for management elsewhere. She reminded everyone that she had gone into debt. The lawyers asked her to be patient. Meanwhile she kept booking GN'R into shows, and the band proceeded to binge on their cash advance. Vicky took it all in. "They never had any real money before, and suddenly it was *'life's a party now.'*"

The band's trusty drug dealers got paid off. Slash said they spent their money on dope and motel rooms. Axl said he bought clothes and took people out to some rad restaurants. They took cabs everywhere. Steven ate breakfast at Hamburger Hamlet every day for a week. A month after they'd signed, Slash told an interviewer who asked him what it was like, finally, to be off the streets: "Our attitude hasn't changed at all. The only difference I can think of is that now I can fuck up and get away with it."

On March 28, Guns was back on Sunset Strip for a pair of shows that had sold out the day after the first red flyers went up:

DANCE YOUR ASS OFF / DRINK YOUR FACE OFF
GET YOUR ROCKS OFF /
GUNS N' ROSES
2 SHOWS! / 8 &10 PM / ROXY THEATER

The late show was videotaped with two cameras and is the best documented record of the band's early shows.

The house is black. The band takes the stage. Girls up front shriek. Sound of deafening guitar chords. Axl greets the crowd. "Welcome to the Roxy! Thanks for coming. Is everybody nice and relaxed?" He's in his crotchless leathers with a thong, the vest, the patent-leather cap. Among the accessories hanging around his neck is a silver Acme Thunderer, a sports referee's whistle. He apologizes for being so late, explaining that their van was pulled over by the fucking cops, who held them and searched them for drugs. "THEY'RE OUT TO GET ME," Axl screams, and he was right in the sense that Guns soon became an even bigger cop magnet than before. The song features the pelvic serpent, lots of mike handling, and a red-hot solo from Slash.

Then right into "Welcome to the Jungle," performed with lots of snake hips, flashing lights, and—already—broad, arena-style stage moves from Slash and Duff. Axl pointedly caresses his leather thong as he sings about "my serpentine." During the song's Zeppelinesque middle section, Axl plays tambourine and maracas as Slash and Izzy conjure the stygian murk of the La Brea Tar Pits via distortion, reverb, and feedback.

During the blackout between songs, Axl promotes their show scheduled for next week when the Whisky will reopen. Faster Pussycat will be the opening band. Vicky had fought Axl over this, but Axl had insisted. "They're good friends of ours," he tells the girls up front. "Whyntcha all come down for that."

Guns then tears into "Think About You," with Izzy singing backup, really into it, with Axl throwing his shades away. Scream city. The drummer is a blur of hair and arms. Slash's licks have a touch of lightness to them that recalls Jimmy Page at his most subtle.

Bang into "Rocket Queen." It's big-haired Duff in the spotlight with Steven. The two-part song is already a formatted set piece, with Axl dominating the rocking first half before Slash's guitar slithers and hisses. The anthemic second half features Axl deploying various dance moves with and without the mike stand. The second guitar solo is a rock-style clinic showcasing various shredding techniques of the day.

Axl disappears and Slash comes to the front, tells the girls that are calling out to him to shut up, and introduces "Nightrain" amid clouds of dry ice. The kids watch in inert silence as Slash mounts the drum riser and blazes into the main riff while Axl comps with maracas. The band adds to the dynamism of the rock song with multiple stage transpositions. When Axl goes into his high kick at the climax of the song, the room almost implodes with released energy.

Blackout. The road crew hold flashlights so the band can do lines of drugs arranged on top of the stage amps.

Amid some portentous, horror-show rumbling from the two guitars, Axl next dedicates "My Michelle" to Tom Zutaut and begins the song with a scream that could have emerged from the fires of a Pentecostal hell. The song is about the barely legal girl who had cried rape. It describes her dysfunctional Hollywood family, her decadent teenage promiscuity, her issues with narcotics, her difficulties with personal boundaries. But it also looks upon her with a loving and compassionate sympathy, as if they see her as a sisterly reflection of themselves.

Duff and Izzy both sing on the chorus; the bridge is played mad-crazy up-tempo; Axl bangs a cowbell during Slash's brief but ballistic solo, and the number finally crashes into its rip-roaring coda.

Blackout. Slash swaggers up to the mike. "So, Roxy—what's happening? I know this place is empty. [Chides audience:] I've heard it *much* louder than this." Axl takes over: "This song means a lot to me. It's called 'Don't Cry.'" The mid-set ballad is sung in a crooner's voice for the first verse, but Axl does the second part in his "choked scream," a voice that seems to express a soul in existential despair and on the threshold of disintegration. Slash plays a subdued, deep blue guitar solo with a fresh cigarette burning through the curtain of black hair that covers his face.

Then into "Back Off Bitch": driving and mindless punk rock, with Slash singing on mike with Axl on the chorus. Slash then steps up to introduce the set's last song: "OK, we're gonna leave you with one last tune.... This song's about a little trip we took.... I don't think that anyone else has ever been there.... It's called 'Paradise City.'"

This is Guns' memoir of the treacherous journey, the Hell Tour, the feeling of being so far away. Izzy lays down some big chords while Slash plays the song's banjo breakdown of a theme. Then Axl blows his silver whistle and is off and dancing in his rough-trade leathers, shades hiding his features, sweat running down his exposed belly into his crotch. (This was an intense male sex show for the kids up front.) As the energy builds higher, Izzy doffs his jacket and chops out notes in white blouse and vest. Then Axl is on his knees for "so far away," screaming pure murder, then begging to be taken to a place of safety and familiarity—to be taken home.

Strobe lights blinding everyone during the ride-out. Band walking off. Slash: "G'night!" Drumsticks arc through the smoky club air, en route to fans eager for souvenirs. Everyone is stone deaf.

ANOTHER VERSION OF THE AYATOLLAH

*G*uns' first formal encounter with the media went really badly. Until recently, the group had been an underground cadre, a guerrilla band operating behind enemy lines and below the radar. A few local photographers had picked up on them but no major media, because there was no point in giving publicity to a new band with no record label to buy adverts in your magazine, or airtime on your station.

In early April 1986, *Music Connection,* the L.A. weekly magazine, sent reporter Karen Burch to interview Guns. The band had been promised the cover of the magazine. Twenty years later, her published text is the clearest available window into the days when GN'R was still a band of outlaws in the forest—"one for all, all for one"—robbing from the rich (record companies) and giving to the poor (hairy band guys).

Karen started out her dispatch by making it plain that she had heard the latest GN'R rumors: The rape charges against them were dropped; the band had trashed the ladies' room at the Roxy on a night they weren't even playing; a raging Axl had heaved a bar stool through the mirror. The street buzz said that Guns were now banned from the Roxy. She called the club, and they said it was true about the ladies' room, but no one had been banned. *Are they,* she asked herself, *this year's model of the perennial L.A. bad boy band?*

She found them still living at Vicky's place, amid wall-to-wall amps, guitars everywhere, brimming ashtrays, garbage. At that point, Vicky's management contract with the band was still up in the air. The phone rang every two minutes during the interview. Slash answered: "Grand Central—hello? Barbie? Oh, Christine—yeah, this is Slash. No, don't call *here* again, call me at that other number." Slam. Friends and roadies were in and out. A green gallon of cheap white wine was going around.

Axl did most of the talking, speaking softly and seriously. Izzy would break in with sarcastic asides, cynical jokes, and open hostility. He would deflect her questions with: "Ask another," "We don't care about that," "That's a stupid question," "No one gives a fuck about that," "Next," "Fuck you and your magazine."

Duff looked drunk. Steven Adler seemed impatient to hook up with this cute young girl that was hanging around. "Slash's role," she wrote, "is that of general troubleshooter and band mediator."

She started by asking their ages, and it went downhill from there. She watched them stiffen. Their eyes narrowed. They cast sidelong glances at each other. They looked at her: daggers.

AXL: "Sure, we'll reveal our ages."

DUFF: "Yeah, we don't care. I'm nineteen."

AXL: "I'm twenty-four."

SLASH: "No, Duff is twenty-two and I'm nineteen."

IZZY: "This really does not fucking matter."

SLASH: "Just fucking tell her."

IZZY: "Axl isn't really twenty-four. He's a million years old! He's seen fucking everything!"

VICKY: "C'mon—go with the real ages here."

IZZY: "What's the bullshit with the ages? That shit doesn't matter to us."

SLASH: "Izzy is twenty-three and Steve's twenty-one."

IZZY: "Just print that for the Rainbow so they'll let us all in."

SLASH: "Please—just don't ask us where we're from."

IZZY: "Yeah, fuck that. There'll be no shit in there about me being from Indiana, which deserves fucking nothing. It was a worthless fucking city. It's shit."

SLASH: "Can you print, like, 'Indiana sucks'?"

IZZY: "The fact that I'm from Indiana has no business being in my career."

It went on from there. The band didn't want to discuss their record label at all. Questions about their "image" brought snarls and rude remarks. But Slash eventually described Guns as "a hard rock band with an R&B base. It's not a glam band. It's not a heavy metal band."

Axl mentioned their sources. "We listen to funk, disco, metal, classical. We listen to soundtracks, old blues, fifties stuff, sixties music. We're influenced by all of it. We're trying to be as sincere as we can with our music without claiming that we're the originators of anything." He added that the new songs they were working on all had a heavy edge to them.

She asked about songwriting. "We all write," Axl answered. "I write the majority of the melodies, and we work on everything else."

Slash said that Axl wrote all the lyrics and they all collaborated on the rest.

Axl continued: "We write in vans on the way to shows. We write songs when we're hanging out on the corner waiting for someone to buy a bottle. Yeah—waiting for alcohol."

"If I can speak for everybody," Slash said, looking around at his already bored bandmates, "the whole point is that we want to reach a lot of people. We want to be a . . . worldwide exhibit! We don't have to be *accepted*, we just wanna be a band that's fucking out there."

Slash's inspiration sent Axl into a self-defining soliloquy:

"I live for the songs," Axl said. He paused. His tone changed, darkening. He seemed in a trance. The rest of the band woke up and leaned in to listen. "If I go through a bad time . . . well . . . *anything* I have to go through is worth it if I can get a song out of it. If I slept in a parking garage, and I hated it, and I wanted to give it all up . . . but I just kept going . . . and I got a song out of it, from the experience . . . then I'm so glad that I had to go through a ton of shit. . . .

"When I'm onstage, that's when I take what I'm worth to the public. I bring out everything I've worked on for the past month, show the people my songs, and give that feeling to them.

"When I'm singing a line, I'm thinking of the feelings that made me come up with the song in the first place. At the same time, I think about how I feel singing those words *now,* and how those words are gonna hit the people in the crowd."

(This description of the lead singer's time-bending conscious experience of singing onstage at a rock concert is almost unique in the movement's history.)

Axl described the toll these feelings took on his body and mind. The band had all noticed how he would tremble after good shows. "I usually have to have someone stand beside me when I come offstage, because I can't even tie my own shoes. I've gone through so many thoughts onstage." He described looking out at a crowd of 700 and knowing 300 of them. He loved some, hated others, was in debt to this one, had slept with that one—ten times.

"You see all this stuff, plus—you're thinking about the feeling in the music. I put *every possible thought* I can, into every performance and every line."

The room was quiet. They were listening carefully. Time stood still.

"And that's why I might be known as . . . *histrionic.* Because I go all out."

* * *

*W*hew. Who's got a fag, then? No one? Vicky came up with some cash and Steven and Duff left on a Marlboro run. Karen Burch went to the bathroom. While she was out of the room, they recorded some vulgar sexual suggestions on the tape for her to discover later. When she returned, she was shocked to find that Axl had broken her cassette recorder. He explained that he was going to leave a message on the tape, but he pushed the wrong buttons and the thing is fucked. Sorry. Vicky came up with another machine, and the interview continued.

DUFF: "We're doin' what we wanna," *glug glug,* "and we're pulling it off."

IZZY: "We sell out every fuckin' club in L.A. that we play."

SLASH: "Listen, I don't care if you think I've got a bad attitude, or if I'm being big-headed about it, but this is the only fuckin' band that's come of L.A. that's *real*—and the kids know it."

Karen asked how the band got along with each other. Slash said that they didn't have many friends outside of the band.

AXL: "We're a family."

DUFF: "When we go out, there's nobody else we would have more fun with. If someone's not there and then they show up, it's like . . ."

AXL: "Great—you're here! Let's go! Rape! Pillage! Destroy!"

IZZY: "That's our motto."

Axl said that he thought the band would stay together as long as there was a spark between them.

IZZY: "Till we die, and then some."

Steven said that even after they died, they would still be together.

SLASH: "Yeah, I mean . . . I loved my dog. . . ."

IZZY: "But then he died, and now you have Steve."

STEVEN: "Hey—fuck you!"

AXL: "And we don't share girlfriends."

This set Slash off. He explained that they *had* girlfriends, some-where in the past, but they had gotten rid of them when the band started to happen. "They're a pain in the ass," he opined about the girlfriends they'd had. "They take up too much fuckin' time, and they have their own ideas which they're constantly throwing in your face."

Asked if they were as "bad" as people said they were, Slash re-plied, "We are."

Duff added, "We have no choice."

Axl concurred: "Trouble? All the time."

The reporter gave everyone one wish. Steven wished for peace of mind. Izzy said he wanted a Maserati. Slash wanted an endless supply of Marlboro cigarettes. Duff just wanted to have the GN'R record out, and to be on the road.

Axl was more prophetic. "I think that . . . I don't like that question. It's ridiculous because we are *working* on getting everything we want. If I had my wishes, I'd want all the money there is. I'd want power and control over everything there is, and third, I'd want all the wishes there are to have."

Slash summed this up. "Axl is just another version of the Ayatol-lah."

The other version of the Ayatollah then tried to spike the interview. He had hated the whole thing. He tried to sabotage the photo session for the promised cover story. He began calling Karen Burch and threatening her, almost daily. He had the band's lawyer call the maga-zine. When the story was published on April 14, 1986, it carried a disclaimer: "This issue's cover [photo] and cover feature are running against the wishes of Guns N' Roses, according to W. Axl Rose."

Then Axl sat down and composed a long, angry, highly rhetorical, turgidly pompous, and self-righteous letter to the editor, complaining about the interview and offering a fascinating glimpse of his thinking at the time. The letter was published with a rebuttal from Karen Burch a few months later, on August 4.

Axl began by chiding the magazine for sucking up to the music industry. He continued:

Did it ever occur to you that I am trying to do exactly as I choose by the only road I have found? ... Freedom of choice is a concept in which each member of Guns N' Roses shares a commitment. We are our own political party within a government just as any small business. ...

I realize in a world or particular reality where the pen acts, and so often is in actuality, as the knife, we all fall beneath the blade of personal opinion. No one escapes hypocricy [sic].

The attitude of Guns N' Roses in contact is relatively simple to understand. Honesty and the fulfillment of commitments to the best of abilities within the realm of our survival hold the key. In an attempt to communicate with us, you violated our basic laws of a well-balanced relationship with any outside organization, or individual for that matter.

The letter continues for ten more long paragraphs. The mag, he claimed, violated a verbal agreement giving the band complete control over the story and the cover. He accused the writer of betraying them. "The unrecorded sexual prodding of the band by Karen Burch resulted in the accidental breakage of the reporter's tape recorder by Guns N' Roses. Responsibility for this incident is a matter in which I ask myself if I should accept. Perhaps under different circumstances I would, but as of now I won't."

Axl finished up by insulting the poor guy who shot the cover, which he hated. "His insincerity and lack of personability resulted in chaos in the studio. I apologize for not walking out, there is no acceptable excuse." He complained that the magazine gave off a "stench." He concluded by denying that Vicky Hamilton got them their record deal, or even had much to do with the band.

Axl Rose's difficult relations with the press, which have lasted his whole career, stems from this earliest band interview. In his letter he predicted that his feelings would never change. "It's a shame our first contact with the press should leave such a foul taste in my mouth."

"As for the foul taste in Rose's mouth," Karen Burch replied: "May I suggest he try a little soap to wash away a severe case of sour grapes.

Concerning the stench he's left with, it's merely the bad smell that plagues those who harbor a rotten attitude."

HOLLYWOOD BUNGALOW

**WHEN WAS THE LAST TIME YOU SAW
A REAL ROCK N' ROLL BAND......
AT THE WHISKY A GO GO?
GUNS 'N' ROSES
SAT. APRIL 5TH
DOORS OPEN 8:00 PM
One night only, one show only
Tickets on sale night of show only
1ST COME, 1ST SERVE
THIS COULD BE
YOUR LAST CHANCE!
ALSO THE WETTEST,
WILDEST BIKINI SHAKE OFF OF 1986
WITH A $500 CASH PRIZE TO THE WINNER**

The reopening of the Whisky, where in olden days the Byrds and Love and the Doors had entertained, was a big deal. Guns would be playing their third gig as a signed band, and the stakes were high on a Saturday night. Axl had fought to get Faster Pussycat on the bill, was stressed by a million things, and was preoccupied with a young model named Erin Everly, who wasn't like the strippers, teen Madonna clones, and female whack jobs that hung around the band in their street days.

Then Axl lost his money. He'd basically been on the run for a few years now, living under a false name, and he didn't have a bank account. His name change became legal only a few days before they signed and got their checks, so Axl hadn't had time to set up an account. He could not cash a check in Los Angeles. The result was that he demanded his $7,500 in cash. He later told friends that he carried the money in his boots for a week.

Then, in true hillbilly fashion, Axl hid the money under the couch where he slept in Vicky's living room. The next morning, he'd forgotten where he'd put it. He went ape and accused Vicky of stealing his money. He swore he was leaving the band and stormed out. Vicky turned the apartment upside down, and found the money—stuffed in a dirty sock that had been stuck into the springs of her sofa.

Meanwhile, Axl had proudly relayed his Hollywood success story to his mother back in Lafayette. A few weeks later, his stepfather, Stephen Bailey, showed up to check things out. Axl told Vicky that he saw this as maybe an opportunity to "patch things up with Dad." Vicky told Axl that, from what she'd heard of him, she thought Mr. Bailey was there to get control of Axl's career. This pushed Axl's always tender paranoia button, and Axl raged out on Vicky, cursed her, called her names.

Later, she says, he told her that she had been right.

*O*n the day of the Whisky show, Axl was crashed out on Vicky Hamilton's couch, trying to sleep through a hangover. Vicky recalled: "He was on the little couch as opposed to the big couch, lying next to the coffee table, which was covered in beer cans and bottles. That afternoon, we were supposed to go to a pre-show meeting at Geffen. I said to Steven, 'We gotta go, can you wake Axl up?' So Steven grabbed a garbage bag and started throwing the cans in, making a racket."

Axl opened one eye. He whispered, *"Stop it."*

"Steven kept it up with the bottles. One broke on the glass table. Next thing I know, Axl is up, just in his briefs, and he grabs this big wooden table and heaves it at Steven," who ducked out of the way. The fight spilled out into the hall, where Axl pushed Steven into the fire extinguisher, which got knocked off the wall and started spurting on its own; then back into the apartment. They were wrestling and Steven shoved Axl into the glass table, which shattered under their weight. "Then Axl's on top of him, kicking his ass."

Suddenly the door opened and Slash walked in with Yvonne. Axl was on top of Steven, landing blows to the head. The living room was trashed, broken glass, the TV knocked over.

"Slash goes, 'Oh great, Axl—why don't you just fucking *kill our drummer* the day of the showcase?'

"But then," she mused, "you know, they were always *very* rough on Steven, who was the youngest in the band."

An hour later, Axl and Steven hugged and said they loved each other, and went on to do a killer show at the Whisky.

$\mathcal{F}$or a short time, it looked like Guns would be managed by old Hollywood pro Arnold Stiefel, whose main client was Rod Stewart. Stiefel signed the lease for a band house that was quickly trashed. Someone ripped the toilets out and threw them through the windows. The sinks were full of shit. Stiefel almost fainted when he went into the house. Tom Zutaut: "They would just get in these drug rages, and just go berserk." When the landlord gave him the $22,000 repair bill for the house, Stiefel dropped Guns N' Roses from his client roster.

With no professional management yet in sight, Geffen's A&R department took over temporary custody of Guns N' Roses. The label assigned Teresa Ensenat to work with them, although Vicky kept booking their shows. (Vicky had also received another eviction notice from her fed-up landlord.) Teresa rented a house for the band on Fountain Avenue, near La Cienega in West Hollywood. The band, the roadies, and some friends moved into the little bungalow, and immediately began to drive neighborhood property values down with all-night parties, loud music, unmuffled cars, and the jagged sound of breaking bottles and the occasional gunshot at three o'clock in the morning. The cops were annoyed by the complaints they were getting about Guns' appearance in a quiet neighborhood, and they kept watch (sometimes undercover) on the band's house for the two months that they lived there.

Vicky Hamilton was eventually placated with a job at Geffen Records. She was hired as an independent street scout with a mandate to find new bands for the label. She was assured that Guns would pay back the funds she had borrowed to further their career, but it didn't happen. Vicky Hamilton had a big heart and an old-fashioned, highly romantic rock-and-roll vision—that the fame and the joy were more important than the money.

*A*xl didn't like the new band house. His (padlocked) bedroom was an oasis amid viral squalor. For a time, he kept breaking into Vicky's apartment and crashing on the couch, where he could get a good day's sleep. "He knew I was working for Geffen," she says, "so he knew he could get away with it." This went on until Vicky was evicted in June.

Axl stopped speaking to her. She waited three years to sue, and then filed papers against them in financial desperation only after ungallant Axl Rose said unkind things about her in the press.

Others felt differently, and felt guilty too. Everyone knew Vicky got the band their record deal. Steven Adler later protested his innocence in this matter. "Vicky Hamilton—awesome woman! I wanted her to be part of it after we signed—because *she got us signed*. What happened was not my idea, and I did not have enough say-so in it [to do anything about it]."

Slash: "We lived at her house, and she busted her ass twenty-four hours a day. She couldn't pay her rent because she spent all the money she could get her hands on trying to get us off the ground. She was the only person that—way back when we were doing our first gigs—she'd say, 'You guys are great, you're gonna make it.' I've gotta tip my hat to her."

*T*om Zutaut now had to find a manager for Guns, someone the label could work with, and then find a producer to bring their music to the market. The label's first choice to manage Guns was Tim Collins. He was a former Boston booking agent who had worked on Joe Perry's solo career, and then had helped reunite the fractured and polytoxic Aerosmith. Collins then convinced that band to get treatment for their various addictions and helped them stay sober—which was considered a great miracle by industry people who knew how crazy Aerosmith had been in its early days. Aerosmith, reborn, was currently recording for Geffen, and their new music was running hotter than ever. Run-DMC was about to release its sensational hip-hop mash-up of Aerosmith's "Walk This Way" (which would top the charts and own MTV)

In 1984 W. Axl Rose and Izzy Stradlin formed a band with sixteen-year-old L.A. native Chris Weber and called it Hollywood Rose---the direct precursor to Guns N' Roses.

Chris and Axl, hair up

Hollywood Rose---Chris and Axl---gigged at Hollywood club Madame Wong's West.

Jeff Isbell, Bill Bailey, and Chris Weber in West Hollywood, 1984

Jet Boy was another band on the mid-eighties Hollywood rock scene. Their bass player, Todd Crew, was friends with Guns N' Roses and later worked for them. His 1987 heroin overdose in Slash's hotel room was a traumatic event for the band.

Jet Boy—guitarist Billy Rowe, bassist Todd Crew, singer Mickey Finn—at L.A.'s Club Lingerie, October, 1986 (above)

Todd Crew

*Crucial Guns collaborators West Arkeen and Del James play with Duff McKagan's pickup band, Drunk Fux, at Coconut Teaszer, Hollywood, May 1987.

*Tom Zutaut and Vicky Hamilton, circa 1986

*A*xl Rose wrote "Sweet Child of Mine" for his girlfriend (and later wife) Erin Everly in 1987. Photographer Neal Preston made these intimate portraits of the couple at home in 1990.

Steven Adler

was a Hollywood kid who fell into Guns N' Roses because he was a middle school friend of Slash. His splashy, highly visual drumming was crucial to Guns' early presentation.

Right: Steven Adler, circa 1987

PHOTOS ABOVE AND BELOW BY GENE KIRKLAND

Above: Steven Adler, circa 1989

PHOTO BY GENE KIRKLAND

Right: Steven, circa 1988

Duff McKagan,

a punk rocker from Seattle, joined Guns N' Roses in L.A. and became the band's musical director.

Left: Michael "Duff" McKagan, circa 1988. **Below, left:** Duff, 1990. **Below, right:** Duff, circa 1992.

ALL PHOTOS ON THIS PAGE BY GENE KIRKLAND

Izzy Stradlin

was the beating heart of Guns N' Roses. The epitome of rock-and-roll cool, he quit Guns in 1991 because he thought the band had gotten too big.

Above, left: Izzy, circa 1987; above, right: Izzy, circa 1989; below, left: Izzy, 1988

Slash

Hollywood street kid Saul Hudson—"Slash"—moved from racing BMX bikes to practicing guitar, and became the last axe hero of the rock movement.

Top: Slash, acoustic, 1990

Slash

Slash from the mosh pit at the Santa
Monica Civic Center, January 1988

PHOTO BY GENE KIRKLAND

PHOTO © JANISS GARZA

later in 1986. Geffen hoped that Tim Collins, whose personal quest for sobriety bordered on the messianic, could work the same kind of rehabilitative magic on Guns N' Roses. But Tim's newly sober client, Joe Perry, was skeptical about sharing a manager with guys he used to buy dope from.

Tim Collins remembers, "I flew out to L.A. to meet with Guns. I didn't really want to manage them, but there was some subtle pressure for me to take a look at doing it. John Kalodner [Aerosmith's A&R executive at Geffen] told me that David Geffen really wanted me to manage Guns, and we all lived in fear of David—fear and admiration.

"I knew Tom Zutaut a little, who was handling Guns for Geffen. He was a great guy, a character, kind of a younger version of me, but crazier. We hung out at his house in the Hollywood Hills one night, and he took me out back and showed me the place where the spaceship had landed and Jesus Christ came out and spoke to him.

"Tom took me to this showcase that Guns were playing at the Whisky. There were a lot of industry people there, and Guns were so loud, way above the pain threshold. I was deaf after the first song. Tom took me backstage to meet the band after the show, and I remember how intense that was. I was a veteran of a thousand backstages, but Guns had a different kind of vibe—not evil, but violent and somehow threatening. You could feel the danger around this band. The roadies running around were intimidating. There were a lot of girls—crazy, kinky, lots of bare skin, some of them very young. The whole thing was dark, exciting, and a little scary. My own sobriety was recent, and I immediately felt the narcotic vibe of this band, and knew that I was now at risk for a serious relapse if I wasn't careful.

"Tom Zutaut introduced me to the band. They knew why I was there, but didn't seem to care that much. Slash shook hands but wouldn't make eye contact, hiding behind that curtain of black hair. Duff was drunk, beautiful, slurring his words. He was almost naked in the dressing room, with a girl hanging on him in a little erotic kind of scene. Steven was sweet, childlike, wasted. Izzy Stradlin was aloof, incredible in his poise, obviously the sanest of all of them and the brains of the outfit.

"Axl Rose was in a room of his own. Roadies and girls were dashing in and out, but Axl seemed very calm. Vicky Hamilton introduced us, and Axl showed me that he was in control, *not* wasted. I explained why I was there, and invited him and the band back to my hotel later to have something to eat and talk about their future.

"I was staying at Le Dufy, an apartment hotel in West Hollywood. The whole band came over with Tom Zutaut, and we stayed up and talked until dawn. They ordered from room service and the bill came to just under a thousand dollars. They smoked a lot of pot on my suite's little balcony. I remember that I was drinking a lot of water, trying to lose some weight, and that I had to pee all night. But I couldn't get into my bathroom because Izzy was in there with the door locked—for hours!

"Finally, well after sunrise, they left. At last I got into my bathroom and found blood dripping from the ceiling and walls. I thought someone must have died upstairs, but no. I called up Joe Perry in Boston and told him about the blood. 'One of them is a junkie,' Joe explained. 'He was mainlining in your bathroom.' Then Joe asked me, 'Are you *seriously* thinking of managing them?'"

Tim told Joe Perry that he had decided that he wasn't going to work with Guns. "Good," Joe said.

"Frankly, I was scared of them," Tim says, "and scared for Aerosmith's hard-won sobriety at that point." No rock band had ever kicked drugs and then gone on to be bigger and better than their original selves, which was Collins's ultimate goal for Aerosmith. To take on Guns would be a Herculean task that might put his main clients at risk. "I called David Geffen and told him I didn't want to do it. He beat up on me, gave me lots of agita. He said I was crazy, that Guns was going to be immense, maybe the biggest band in the world. I countered that if I took them on, I would relapse, and Aerosmith probably would too, and that he'd lose a lot of money in the end."

Geffen paid the large room service bill from the meeting. Later Duff explained to Tim that they weren't being intentionally bratty. "It's just what we were used to"—slopping at the industry trough—"and what we were at the time"—drunks with an attitude.

Finding a producer for Guns would be no easier. Tom Zutaut's idea of recording in London, and perhaps even breaking the band in

England first, as Jimi Hendrix had done, went as far as contacting Bill Price, the British producer/engineer of Sex Pistols fame, who had already heard the buzz going around London and New York (courtesy of Kim Fowley, according to Slash) about this potentially major new rock band in California. Price, in demand as an engineer because of his work on the first Pretenders album, began negotiations to work with Guns at Wessex Studio in London, where *Never Mind the Bollocks* had been cut. "I'd heard demos [from Guns] that sounded great," Price said. "I was really looking forward to doing it." Then wiser heads at Geffen realized that throwing a new band, especially this new band with no management and no discernible discipline, onto the streets of London with a recording budget was not a happening idea. "Geffen got cold feet," Price recalled. "They quite rightly didn't want to let them out of their sight. David Geffen himself insisted that the record was made in Los Angeles. Geffen asked me to go to Los Angeles to make it, and I turned him down." Price had a young family, and Wessex was too hot a studio to leave behind for an uncertain period in L.A. Price would have made his fortune, but he was properly stoic: "*C'est la vie,* mate."

Then they got Mötley Crüe's producer, Tom Werman, to go hear the band. "He came down to our rehearsal," Duff said, "then he covered his ears and left." Game over.

Rick Nielsen, Cheap Trick's guitarist, might have had designs on producing the band. He invited Guns to his house and made the mistake of issuing a tequila challenge to Slash. What happened next is unclear, but there was a brawl, and the neighbors called the cops. Nielsen said that he thought he'd had a fight with Slash. Izzy said that Nielsen assaulted them in a drunken rage, and that he had kicked the cheap trickster in the balls. "I didn't kick him hard," Izzy told *Rolling Stone.*

Chapter Five

APPETITE

Kids need a band like us.
—Duff McKagan

THE HARDEST ROCKER-LOOKING DUDE

*I*n May 1986, Guns N' Roses was terrorizing the neighbors around the band's skuzzy house on Fountain Avenue. Slash even annoyed his own band with his brainless habit of throwing empty Jack Daniel's bottles against the house's back wall in the wee hours—at all hours, in fact—since he was using heroin and living on vampire standard time. The group's creative energies nominally went into writing material for their album while they waited for their record label to find a manager and producer for them. Mostly they stayed as stoned as they could.

Some members of the band had their own rooms. Slash's had a tank for Clyde, his beloved pet snake. Izzy's was an opium den. Others crashed out where they could. The roadies had the living room, sort of. There were girls all over the place. Izzy's clients came and went all night. West Hollywood deputies were constant visitors. (Once they came looking for the Whisky's expensive sound-mixing console; it had vanished from the club, and a police informant claimed he'd seen it in Izzy's room. The club had a $2,000 reward out on the street, no questions asked, but Izzy denied everything, and it was never seen again.)

Axl often got tired of all this, padlocked his room, and could be found instead at the biker house on Santa Monica shared by West Arkeen, writer Del James, and other Harley enthusiasts. A recent addition to the band's entourage was Todd Crew, the bassist with the San Francisco glam band Jet Boy, which had relocated to L.A. and landed a recording contract with Elektra. Everyone in the GN'R orbit dug linebacker-size, full-sleeve-tattooed Todd Crew.

"Toddy was such a cool guy," Steven Adler says. "We had a lot of fun with him. He was like a hardcore-looking rocker James Dean. I mean, James Dean was all cool and slick looking, right? But Todd was, like, Dude! He was the hardest rocker-looking dude, but he was just as cool as James Dean."

But Todd was also an occasional client of Izzy's and had just been fired from Jet Boy for preferring mainlining heroin to rehearsing with his band. So Guns gave him a job on the crew, and he moved in with them too. Duff McKagan and Todd Crew formed the cover band Drunk Fux, which played a gig on May 10 at Night Train on Sunset. The flyer read:

L.A.'s premier [*sic*] of—In Their Never Ending Battle Against Sobriety—DRUNK FUX—(Feat. Members of Guns N' Roses) and Other Notorious Drunkx.

Drunk Fux lasted about a year until Guns went on the road, and was mostly a way for Duff to blow off steam. West Arkeen and other local musicians played in Drunk Fux whenever a rare gig materialized. Mostly it was an excuse to get loaded and play before an audience with Todd.

*S*ometime in June, Guns recorded a long demo tape supervised by Manny Charlton from the Scottish rock group Nazareth, a high school favorite of both Axl and Izzy. Guns reportedly attended all seven of Nazareth's southern California gigs in June, and Axl asked guitarist Charlton to supervise a recording session. They cut twenty-seven songs at Sound City Studio in Hollywood, including early versions of "Paradise City," "Back Off Bitch," "The Garden," "Sentimental Movie," "Crash," "Bad Obsession," "Anything Goes," and "Just Another Sunday." Axl also played an early version of "November Rain" for Charlton, telling him, "I'm saving this one for the second album."

Later that month, Guns hosted a barbecue at their house. It was one of the major glam freak shows of 1986, since in addition to some strippers, club waitresses, leather fetishists, and friends of the band, members of almost all the other L.A. bands showed up. Faster Pussycat, the newly reconstituted L.A. Guns, Redd Kross, Social Distortion, Shanghai, Angel, Prodigal Sons, Ratt, Cinderella, Hanoi Rocks, even a couple of gross-out champions from W.A.S.P. were all represented. Jet Boy wasn't invited. Poison knew better than to show.

The social pathology of the other bands, their contemporaries and competitors, was carefully monitored by Guns, who were all interested in the social delineations of the scene and were anxious to distance themselves from the dreaded glam label that was already being branded on the band. To a reporter from the rock mag *Concert Shots* who turned up at the party with a tape recorder, Slash whispered: "If you put us side by side with an actual glam band you'll see a big difference. We wear leathers and jeans. Their hair is always spiked up, and they have a full-time makeup job. And they wear a lot of frilly stuff. But no matter what we wear—even if we wear the same things as a glam band, there's a fucking difference."

"We just had a barbecue," Axl said later, "and the glamsters are not really the majority of our crowd. They don't fit in. You don't see them at our parties, not that they're not invited. They just don't fit in. At our barbecue the people who showed up weren't talking about fucking fashions. We were talking *music,* songs, and material that we're going to work on. I mean, we're listening to *blues tapes.*"

Slash was dismissive about most of his peers. "What's wrong with the whole L.A. scene is that so much of it is just a front. There's so much falseness in the way all these bands take on a certain style that's supposedly 'in.' All the basic stuff, what's real important—they miss. They spend most of their time getting their 'image' down. What's that? So I have to say, the glam scene's cool, and there are bands that we like, but as a whole it's pretty false."

Slash took pride in his band's audience. "Come down to our shows and watch us," he challenged. "You'll see that there's every different kind of fan at our shows. We got hard-core metal heads, hard-core punks, all kinds of people. There's that whole white-faced makeup with the black hair scene, and there's all the really young kids that have just gotten out of high school.

"The cool thing," Slash murmured in his low voice, "is that, in reality, you can't put a label on us." He was right. They were a mash-up of everything they loved about rock. There was no other young band quite like Guns N' Roses. Slash loved that part the most.

The summer of 1986 was a hot one in Los Angeles as Guns kept playing. They did a show with punk band Social Distortion that turned ugly. The crowd of young punks didn't like rock bands and started throwing beer cans at Guns when they went onstage. The kids up front were spitting on Slash. "They just hated us," Axl recalled. "So we started throwing their shit right back at them and spitting back on them, and they loved it! They started cheering. Here were these skeptics, throwing shit at us, but we won them over."

The flyer for Guns' July 11 show at the Troubadour said "Farewell L.A.," as if the band were still leaving to record in London after the show. (This plan had been abandoned by then.) Guns was almost the Troubadour's house band now, a far cry from a year before. "Every time we played there, we'd get a ton of people who were determined not to like us," Axl recalled. But now they were cool. At the July 11 show, Axl spoke to the audience. He explained that they were making a record for Geffen, but that they were also going to release an indie LP first, so their real fans could get a taste. This would be a sort of authorized bootleg, using material from the raw demo they'd recorded with Manny Charlton.

The crowd cheered at this news. "It was the greatest feeling, having these people react positively. They wanted it. They seemed so thrilled that they could get an album of our stuff."

The idea for the so-called indie release was Geffen's. The band now had a national reputation but no producer, no record, nothing to sell. They were half a year away from finishing their first album for Geffen, and they might well be old news by then. Putting out an EP on the band's fake "independent" label in 1986 was a way of getting music to the market while holding fan interest for the debut album in 1987. No one was going to question any decisions Geffen made for the band anyway, since they were still looking for a manager. The label seemed almost infallible in those days; they had signed Aerosmith, whose new version of "Walk This Way" with rappers Run-DMC was then in major rotation on MTV and at the top of the sales charts.

Other bands like Poison and Cinderella were already cutting records and going on tour, but by that summer, Axl claimed that Guns was the top band in L.A. He told an interviewer: "What we've done for bands in L.A. is to create a reason to stand up for themselves and their music. You don't have to be 'commercial.' Elton John was considered noncommercial at one point, and he couldn't get signed. Then in 1975 he was the epitome of commercialism. Are you gonna tell me that 'Someone Saved My Life Tonight' is an actual, written-for-radio type of song? Look at Metallica. We're nothing like them, and we play nothing like them, but we do have this similarity."

Slash picked up on the similarity. "Metallica is one band that's gotten through, doing what they want, and we're another band that's done it, and there's gonna be another band after us. And someday you're gonna see a bunch of kids who are a lot rougher and tougher than anybody expected. It's gonna take a lot of people by surprise. *[Cue gangsta rap.]* We're not trying to change the fucking world. We just really want kids to be more aware of what's going on around them."

REHAB SHOW

*G*uns N' Roses played the Troubadour again on July 20, 1986. The flyer for the Saturday night show was to the point:

FRESH FROM DETOX
GUNS "N" ROSES
'REHAB SHOW'
TROUBADOUR
8:30 PM
$2.00 off with this ad

The band figured that since everyone knew about their public, hard-core drug use anyway, why hide it? *Let it rock!* Junk was part of the deal on the streets of Hollywood. Alcohol flowed through their music like a Russian river of Stoli; and their rabid Saturday night audiences were as stoned as they were (possibly excepting Axl, who sometimes performed stone-cold sober, but who was so juiced with adrenalized fury that no one noticed).

Guns thought "Move to the City" was their big jam, but for many of their fans, "Think About You" was one of the highlights of their set. It was one of the earliest GN'R songs where the band's brutal punk rock attack was offset by the (incongruously) tender and loving nature of Axl Rose's vocal. It was a real love song, delivered with undisguised yearning and a classically romantic sensibility. (Tracii Guns claimed, "It's about a girl named Monique, who we all dated. Axl has a tattoo of her on his arm.") This tension—a street gang singing about love, and meaning it—would become the booster rocket that eventually blew Guns into its stratospheric orbit.

This new catch in Axl's voice, this unexpected tenderness from a demonic performer, developed around the time that Axl got seriously involved with Erin Everly. Erin was beautiful, tiny, and when she swayed with the music, the world turned all around her. She also was descended from rock-and-roll royalty. Her grandfather, Ike Everly, was an old-time country music star from Kentucky who was a regular on the Grand Ole Opry. Her father, Don Everly, was half of the Everly Brothers, the godlike duo of early rock and roll. (Don Everly's flamboyant rhythm guitar performances inspired many of the future British Invasion guitar heroes when the Everly Brothers toured through England in the late fifties and early sixties. Keith Richards copied Don's windmill technique, swinging his arm in a big circle and cuffing the strings. This was quickly appropriated and trademarked by The Who's Pete Townshend, who made a career out of the windmill move.)

Axl Rose and Erin Everly had met earlier in the year at a club in New York, where she was working as a model, and they started seeing each other that summer. She moved to Los Angeles to be with him, and then he moved into her apartment. Erin continued to do modeling work to pay the rent. The relationship would last for four tumultuous years, and would inform almost every Guns N' Roses song throughout the original band's career.

No one thought it would last. Axl and Erin fought in public. She was a daughter of Beverly Hills (her mother was actress Venetia Stevenson), and he was a self-described "hick ass" from nowhere. She was intelligent and well brought up, while he was half savage and just in from the reservation. She had a nice place to live, and he was used to roaming between band houses and crash pads. She was seminormal, and he was certifiable. Nevertheless, those who knew the couple thought their bond was intense. "She was a sweet girl," a friend of the couple said. "She was nice, the opposite of Axl. When it was good between the two of them, it was very good. When it was bad, it was horrible. You wouldn't even believe what they ended up putting each other through."

*S*ummer 1986. Night. The Rainbow Bar and Grill. Metallica's smash album *Master of Puppets* rocks the house. Axl, sipping a Long Island iced tea, is interviewed by Jory Farr of the *Daily Press,* who asks him about performing in a Scottish kilt, showing his legs, and wearing a black leather g-string. Wasn't that a little . . . gay?

"I wear what I want to wear, and I don't want to analyze it, 'cause I might be scared. *[!]* Yes, I like to put my hair up, and wear makeup. But when I first came out here, I thought stage clothes and makeup was a false image, something only gays did. But I was naïve."

Guns had gotten some bad reviews lately. "They write that I'm a histrionic singer, which means I overact. Or they say I'm a jaded poseur. But that's bullshit! Anyone who knows me knows that whatever I do is real. Everything the band does is real." Axl said he hated critics anyway and didn't really care what they wrote. (This was not true.)

On his band: "Our favorite music is hard rock—with a blues edge. We used to call ourselves a heavy metal/punk band, [but] I saw a fusion coming together a long time ago. . . . The blues edge, the blues riffs, the blues feeling; we're trying to put that back into the music."

*W*ith a little money in his pocket that summer, Axl got into more scrapes on the street. Most involved aggressive merchants (mostly immigrant Iranians) giving him a hard time in their Hollywood stores.

One day Axl and his brother went to a gun shop to buy a stun gun, because: "We were headlining the Whisky [where Guns had some trouble recently], and things were getting out of hand, so I figured, 'I'll buy stun guns. We won't have to break their jaw. We'll just zap 'em, and someone will carry 'em out.'"

Axl and his brother walked into the gun shop, and Axl said, "Excuse me, sir, can I see a stun gun, please?"

The middle-aged gun dealer checked out Axl: long red hair under a silk bandanna, mirrored aviator shades, leather jacket, slept-in clothes. He snorted, "Listen, son, I don't need your god-damned bullshit. Why don't you just get the hell out of here?"

Axl: "My brother said, 'Look, he just got signed, he can buy ten of these.' And the guy said, 'I don't care. I'll sell them to you, but not to him.'" So the brothers walked out in a humiliated rage. "That happened to me a lot," Axl said later. "I *never* understood this. If I'm breaking the law, fine. But why, when I'm just being a nice guy?"

Another time, Axl and Slash were in a grocery store and got into it with the manager, a rude, swarthy, six-foot Iranian who looked like he'd been a torture specialist in the late shah's secret police. When Axl gave him some attitude, the big foreigner grabbed a carving knife and came out from behind the counter.

"He chased us outside with a butcher knife because he didn't like the way we were dressed," Axl said. "Fucking scared me to death." Axl hated being frightened. It made him mad. He grabbed the top of an orange plastic garbage can and went right back at the Iranian with this shield, screaming *"COME ON"* and cursing in full rage-out mode. "I did *not* want to back down from this guy," Axl said. Shouting in Farsi, the Iranian backed into his store and locked them out.

A few days later, Axl's attempted use of the toilet of the gas station at La Brea and Romaine ended in Axl threatening the Iranian manager with blowing up his gas pumps. The police arrived almost immediately, but Axl had beaten a strategic retreat. These and other incidents of harassment from people Axl considered less than American culminated in his writing a new song at West Arkeen's apartment one day. Axl was playing West's guitar and watching the fearsome comedian Sam Kinison's HBO special while trying to write a simple, raunchy song using some of Kinison's fury and screech.

Sam Kinison was a kindred spirit to Axl Rose. He also was a former Pentecostal preacher, and his routines featured intense ranting punctuated by his trademark primal shriek. The rock stars of the day loved him. Kinison was obsessed with AIDS, and he blamed homosexuals for ruining sex for everyone. (This attitude was also rife among the younger rock stars, the first of their profession to fear the plentiful and random sex with willing girls that was, traditionally, one of the perks of the trade. Slash, already infected with various venereal diseases, was very worried about catching AIDS.)

Axl and his pals had also been talking about West Arkeen getting robbed of ninety-eight cents by two black hoodlums on Christmas day, the year before, and about Axl being hassled in downtown L.A. by hustlers at the bus terminal.

Axl remembered, "I started writing about wanting to get out of L.A. for a little while. I'd been downtown to the Greyhound [bus] station. There're a large number of black men selling dope and stolen jewelry, and most of the drugs are bogus. Rip-off artists misguide young kids getting off the bus, not knowing where they're at, trying to take that person for whatever they've got. That's how I hit town, man."

Axl could play only the top two strings of the guitar; but, sitting there, he managed to write the first bits of a new song. "Niggers and police," it began, "get outta my way." Somebody laughed at this, but West encouraged Axl to rock on. "Immigrants and faggots," the second verse began, "they make no sense to me / They move to our country / And spread some fucking disease."

That's how "One in a Million" came into being, during that hot, smoky L.A. summer of 1986. Axl Rose may have been about to grasp the stardom of his childhood dreams, but inside Bill Bailey was a black well of resentment that would ignite into national controversy when Guns released the song, two years down the road.

Axl wasn't the only angry one in the band, which sat for an interview with *L.A. Weekly*. Slash came out swinging.

"The kids just wanna be fuckin' *free*," he murmured. "They wanna go out and have a good time. They don't wanna be told what to do. And one of the outlets for that is rock and roll bands, and the whole rock and roll way of life. The only place kids can go is out to see a band, and get away from the fuckin' teachers, and their scumbag parents, [and] all the authorities who tell you what the fuck to do. You go to a show to let it all *go*. All the opposing forces, all the cops and teachers, and all that shit; they all come down on you, and it causes havoc. Then they come down on the people that influence the kids—like the bands."

Axl agreed that life was hard. "More things in life—mine anyway—piss me off rather than make me happy—really heartfelt happy, like overwhelmed with joy. You can have a girlfriend or a wife, but you can count on your fingers the times that are so beautiful that you remember them—forever. It's harder to write about those beautiful experiences. Those times are so short."

Slash wasn't finished. "How happy can you be when you're living in L.A.? Like, you're looking at a tree, and there's a dog pissing on it, and there's some whores in front of it, and the air's filled with smog."

"That's the stuff I write about," Axl said. "To some people, that's depressing, but that's what I am, and that's what I deal with."

INTERVIEWER: "What's next year's thrill?"

IZZY: "A platinum album, or something. Just to get on the road and play."

AXL: "A world tour. Playing with all these bands we've listened to for years. Getting an opportunity to play with people we respect. To go out there and kick as much ass as we can."

SLASH: "If and when we get to open up for AC/DC, that will be a fucking turning point in my life."

IZZY: "I'd even open up for Mötley Crüe."

AXL: "The ultimate for me would be to open up for the Rolling Stones. Yeah!"

IZZY: "That would be *it*."

UNDER NEW MANAGEMENT

Conventional wisdom about Guns N' Roses holds that Mike Clink wasn't anyone's first choice to produce the band's crucial debut album.

But in the summer of 1986, Guns was on a band-wide bender, staggering through a noisy and drug-addled public binge in Hollywood that was impossible to ignore. This meant that none of the key record producers of the day was anxious to spend the next year in an airless studio babysitting five degenerates.

Tom Zutaut found Mike Clink. He had begun as an engineer at the fabled Record Plant studio in L.A., home to the Eagles and other mastodons of California pop. He was mainly known for being the engineer who worked with producer Ron Nevison, who'd done KISS, Europe, and Ozzy. By 1986 Clink had recorded Metallica, Heart, the Babys, Eddie Money, and Jefferson Starship. He had just switched over to producing, and was known in the industry for a no-nonsense approach to potentially unruly bands, a daily work ethic, and staying out of the way of the music. Best of all, he wasn't intimidated. Mike Clink liked Guns N' Roses, and he wanted the job.

Guns started recording with Mike Clink in early autumn 1986, right after opening for Lords of the New Church at Timbers Ballroom in Glendora. They worked first at Take One Studio, then at Rumbo Recorders, a modest (and inexpensive) studio in Canoga Park, way out in the San Fernando Valley. (Rumbo was owned by Darryl Dragon, the Captain of the pop group Captain & Tennille.) Mike Clink had been immediately impressed by the band's battle-worn gear—old amps, beat-up drums; Slash's guitar still had the original strings it came with. This indicated to Clink that Guns really was a band from the streets. Slowly, Mike Clink and Guns started building a debut album, song by song.

Slash later reported: "How did Mike Clink handle us? With kid gloves. He totally kept us at arm's length. We were all young and excited to be doing our first record. That was a time when we were partying extremely hard, but when we were in the studio we were actually pretty much together. Just a bottle of Jack Daniel's—no doping and all that stuff."

The whole band knew that for them the stakes were high. There would be no second chance if their record sucked. "We were really hard workers," Duff remembered. "We rehearsed twice a day. When we had to be on, we took it very seriously."

But then heroin addiction threatened to take the band down.

Slash turned blue one night at their house. He was revived, but rumors quickly spread through Hollywood that one of Guns had died. There were other street bulletins that the band had broken up after a loud public row at the Club Lingerie. Axl threatened to walk out almost every day. At Geffen, the executives started to get scared. Some thought that signing Guns had been a mistake. The total budget was $375,000, an unusually large amount for a debut album at the time. It would cost a lot to make Guns' record and then promote them, but meanwhile the band was on a suicide watch. Further rumors spread that Geffen would not sign the second half of the deal, the actual recording contract, unless Guns N' Roses cleaned up its act.

Slash, it was true, was a stone junkie by then. "There was a point," he said later, "when I fucking stopped playing guitar, and didn't even talk to my band, except for Izzy, 'cause we were both doing it." For three months that summer, Slash hardly left the band house except to walk to the market for cigarettes. One night he was found lying in the gutter, barefoot and unconscious, on Hollywood Boulevard. Someone helped him get home. At a photo session organized by Geffen, Slash had to be literally held up by someone crouching behind him, so he wouldn't fall down.

Steven Adler, according to band insiders, was using. Duff was downing a handle of vodka per day. Axl holed up with a girl and a bag of heroin for three weeks. (Axl reported that they listened to all the Led Zeppelin records, over and over again.) Izzy was dealing dope—so openly that *Spin* magazine sent a New York writer to report on the heroin underworld from which Guns N' Roses was supposedly rising.

In truth, a heroin epidemic had gripped L.A.'s bands since the post-punk explosion in the early eighties. The first to OD had been L.A. proto-punk hero Darby Crash of the Germs. Then it was John Belushi's turn, after being shot up with a brown heroin speedball in 1981. Rather than a warning, this was seen as an invitation, or a challenge. "Heroin was huge with the L.A. punks in the early eighties," Axl said. "Then it went away for a while. And then, all of a sudden, when the heavy metal bands came in, it got real big again."

Then Axl reported, with astonishing candor: "Well, it was *Izzy* that brought it back."

By all contemporary accounts, Izzy Stradlin's addictive coolness was *extremely* influential in the L.A. band scene. If Izzy was doing heroin, it was obviously working for him, and his band. Other groups looked at Guns: Four of them seemed strung out, but they could see that Guns was still a killer rock band with a high-end record deal. This made the "junkie musician" persona even more attractive. According to Doors manager Danny Sugerman, who claimed that he bought drugs from Izzy: "Hundreds of competing musicians [in Los Angeles] now steeped themselves in smack, hoping to achieve the same alchemical transformation from starving unknown to rock superstar."

When it was reported to Geffen in late August that the Guns sessions were stalled—Slash was basically not showing up at the studio—Tom Zutaut went into action.

"Tom was a nice guy," Vicky Hamilton said, "but he could also be manipulative and even vicious when he had to be." He began to insinuate to Axl, who seemed the Gunner most in control of himself, that the band's future was in jeopardy. A hundred thousand Geffen dollars had been spent already, with little to show for the money. A former Geffen executive recalled: "Tom basically threatened them. He told them the label was scared shitless, and that people's jobs [at Geffen] were on the line. He read them the riot act—as much as you could with them. He told them the deal was off, unless they kept their bad habits in some kind of check."

Years later, Zutaut told VH1: "I was worried about them even surviving, because you can't tell junkies or drug addicts to just stop taking drugs. They probably laughed when I told them, 'Hey, guys, you're going to be the biggest band in the world. You don't need to destroy it with this crap.'"

"The only thing that really stopped me [from abusing heroin]," Slash recalled, "was a phone call from Duff, saying, *'You've alienated yourself from everyone.'* And since they're the only people I'm really close to, that really affected me, and I finally quit."

At least for the time being.

"If I remember correctly," Izzy said, "at one point they [Geffen] wanted to drop us." Tom Zutaut had to be forcefully persuaded by the band not to ditch them. Both Slash and Izzy went into rehab, which didn't exactly work, but at least the sessions could start again later in 1986. A little time went by, and there were no more warnings from Rumbo Sound. Everyone at their record company was shocked and pleasantly surprised when Zutaut's strategy seemed to work, and the band managed to pull itself together long enough to make *Appetite for Destruction.*

*I*t's an accurate measure of the dread that Guns N' Roses inspired in the music business that it took Geffen five months to find a manager for a group that would be the biggest band in the world. Eagles manager Irving Azoff passed. Tim Collins said no. Doc McGhee said forget it. Every reputable talent manager Tom Zutaut contacted turned him down flat, or didn't return the call. No one wanted to risk their careers trying to manage this band, especially since the word on the street was that the lead singer was really crazy, and the rest were dope fiends.

Slash admitted, "We got restless. We got signed, they gave us a bunch of money, put us in a house. We didn't go out and do any gigs.... So we got fucking bored to death and started doing a lot of drugs, drinking a lot, tearing up houses. So just about every single manager was scared shitless. And it was bad. We were starting to fuck up."

"We couldn't get a manager to save our lives," Izzy said later. "They'd just look at us and leave." One candidate arrived for an appointment with Slash and Izzy, who had been on a buying trip to Mexico. "We'd just come back from Tijuana," Izzy recalled, "with a case of tequila and that black tar heroin that was the thing of choice back then. The guy took one look at us, and split. Not a word was spoken."

But finally Zutaut made the right call, and in August 1986, Alan Niven signed up to manage Guns. Niven managed the hardworking metal band Great White, and agreed to manage Guns only at the strong(-arm) urging of David Geffen. Alan Niven was basically a head-banging Kiwi (from New Zealand) with long stringy hair. He'd helped get the Sex Pistols signed to EMI ten years earlier, which gave him instant cred with Slash and Duff. Niven dressed in well-worn leathers and could have passed for a European biker dude. He was intense, angry, a brawler. "He was a throwback, even then," a Geffen exec recalls. "He was a more raw version of Spinal Tap's manager— totally dead-on." His management company, Stravinsky Brothers, had an office in the Orange County surf town of Hermosa Beach. Niven got the job managing Guns N' Roses by default—no one else wanted it—even though Axl didn't like him.

"Actually, Axl didn't *hate* him," Robert John says. "It wasn't that he didn't like Alan. It was more that he didn't *trust* him. With Axl, it was always a question of trust, or it wouldn't work."

The whole band hated Great White.

But the label told Guns that it was now or never, and Alan Niven seemed enthusiastic. He courted them with home deliveries of pizza, beer, Jack Daniel's, and hardest-core Swedish porno mags and videos. He showed them what a classic, old-school rock "minder" could do for them. The tough-guy patter and knowing accent was a plus. Finally, to seal the bargain, Niven took the band to the legendary West Hollywood joint Barney's Beanery, where Jim Morrison hung out and Janis Joplin liked to drink when she wasn't shooting smack in a motel room down the street. Niven, often described as brash and abrasive, impressed Duff and Slash with his alcohol intake. Even Izzy thought he'd do: "Alan Niven became like the sixth member of the band. He saw us and said, 'Well, they are a mess,' but maybe he'd been there once himself. The truth is, he was a major factor in getting this band out of town."

Much later, Alan Niven told Guns biographer Mick Wall that for him, the whole thing was a shot in the dark. "When I signed this band," he said, "I didn't know what to expect. I thought the first album might sell a couple hundred thousand copies. If you'd told me there was a hit single on it, I would've laughed in your face."

This was probably why Axl Rose didn't like Alan Niven.

RIOT AT STREET SCENE

*G*uns N' Roses may have been in a sort of prefame limbo in the late summer and autumn of 1986, but despite all the pressures of addiction, alcoholism, mania, and rehab, the band never turned in anything less that a great show. Guns was on fire every night when they took the stage, sweating out the toxins poisoning their almost bare bodies in the heat, sound, and fury of a full-throttle rock show.

In August they signed the final contract with Geffen Records. The sixty-two-page document had been drafted by Jeff Fenster, a young lawyer for Warner Bros., whose employees helped Geffen in back-office matters as part of their distribution agreement. The band knew Fenster because he sometimes DJ'd at one of their hangouts, the Scream, a rock club in an old downtown hotel ballroom. Soon Fenster—tangentially one of their attorneys—would soon be blowing his blues harp with Guns on Sunset Strip as well.

Slash was relieved at the signing. He told a trade paper reporter, "It's what procured the other half of our money." Axl said it was a big day in his life. The former William Bruce Bailey legally changed his name to W. Axl Rose in order to sign the contract. Axl reported that David Geffen had congratulated them on becoming "indentured servants" to Geffen Records.

They sold out the Whisky on August 23. They opened for Ted Nugent at the Santa Monica Civic Center on the 30th. They sold out the Roxy the following night. The flyer advertised them as *The Band That Wouldn't Die*. Axl was still mostly performing in his backless patent-leather gear and biker cap, the costume of a gay punk, sometimes channeling Freddie Mercury's unambiguous stage moves, emoting furiously on "Out ta Get Me," "Think About You," and everything else. Sometimes he exchanged the fetish pants for a Scottish kilt in the Campbell tartan. The shows left everyone who saw them breathless.

On September 15, Guns N' Roses headlined "Street Scene," a summer concert series in a downtown Los Angeles park. Only a few hundred had attended the previous concerts, but 5,000 kids showed up to see Guns perform outside on a platform stage. It started well, but then it went wrong when Axl began to give one of his badass preludes to "Out ta Get Me." These antiauthoritarian screeds about persecution and paranoia, directed to an already alienated young audience in a grating, highly aggravated whine, were just part of the show in a rock club. But, in a public park, it sounded more like a blatant invitation to throw something at the police.

Four songs into their set, Izzy Stradlin looked up from his guitar strings and saw a riot beginning at the edge of the crowd. People were throwing empty oil drums at the cops. The kids up front overwhelmed the security, broke down the barriers, and started climbing onstage. Axl saw bedlam in the form of hundreds of people looking up into his face and screaming at him, trying in some way to communicate—what?

"The crowd just went bananas," Axl told *Hit Parader.* "All these kids—punk rockers, heavy metal kids—just goin' nuts. If I would have said, 'Tear up downtown,' all of downtown L.A. would have been rubble!"

The band wanted to keep playing, but the fire marshals stopped the show. "We were gonna get fried by the electrical system anyway if we stayed onstage," Axl recalled. The band took off. It took the cops four hours to clear the park of unruly Guns N' Roses fans.

The San Fernando Valley town of Reseda cracked down on band flyers that fall. It was a blow to the bands, because Chuck Landis's Country Club was a major venue for unsigned acts like Guns. Now, if a band defied the town fathers and flyered the strip malls and the streets of Reseda, they found their Country Club gigs canceled when they showed up to play. True to form, this didn't deter Guns, whose yellow flyers were brazenly plastered up and down Ventura Boulevard like a case of municipal acne:

FRIDAY / OCT. 18 / CHUCK LANDIS' COUNTRY CLUB / GLAM NITE / WITH GUNS 'N' ROSES / NO AGE LIMIT.

Other flyering bands had their gigs canceled, but tickets to Guns had sold out in a day, and the show went on as scheduled. They opened for Red Hot Chili Peppers at UCLA on October 31, a Halloween show. The last gig of that tumultuous year was in Long Beach, where Guns opened for the Dead Boys. Guns N' Roses wouldn't play again in public for four months. They spent this time working on their stopgap faux-indie record, and writing and recording their ultimate masterpiece.

L.A. ROCKS: "You've been labeled as Bad Ass. Why?"

IZZY: "Body aroma. Our armpits stink."

AXL: "We don't like to lay down and die."

DUFF: "We're the only band I know that will say no to a very good opportunity—but later we'll shit in your face."

IZZY: "Yeah, there's the benders, and then there's the bendees."

SLASH: "And we're not the bendees." (Laughter)

There was a lot going on with Axl, between his band and his love life, but he remained upbeat and realistic when he talked to the press. "I have something I want to do with Guns N' Roses," he told the *Los Angeles Times*. "It's a part of me that I want to get out and take as far as I can. It can be a long career, or it can be a short, *explosive* career. I don't really care—as long as it gets out, and it gets out in a big way."

*A*xl loved anything to do with the Sex Pistols, according to Robert John. The balls-out anarchy of the group and its annihilating blitzkrieg bop were what made Axl love the whole punk thing in the first place. And Sid Vicious, the Pistols' bass player who famously immolated himself and OD'd in New York after (supposedly) killing his girlfriend, held a special place in Axl's perverse pantheon of heroes. So when the movie *Sid and Nancy* was playing in Hollywood, Axl and a gang of friends went to a screening.

It was one of those nights. They all—Axl, Robert John, Tracii Guns, and some girls—got stoned on heroin. They planned to see the film and go on to the Troubadour afterward. The movie turned out to be a bummer—Slash had worked on the set as an extra when it was being shot—but that was only the beginning. On their way to the club after the movie, their rented van slammed into a car crossing Santa Monica Boulevard. The driver of the other car was apoplectic that he'd been rear-ended by what he thought were drag queens. The cops showed up so fast, there was barely time to stash the drugs on top of the car tires before the deputies frisked and harassed them for an hour.

Guns recorded a bunch of material for their EP in October. They played some of their ferocious early Hollywood Rose material and some of the punk and classic rock numbers they covered in their shows. They cut an acoustic guitar version of "You're Crazy," which Axl, Izzy, and Slash had written just after they'd been signed by Geffen earlier in the year, and a new song of Izzy's called "Patience." Much of this material was recorded at Take One Studio in Burbank by engineer Hans-Peter Heuber and later mixed down by Heuber and Alan Niven. Four tracks were released in December 1986 on a vinyl EP titled—after many band meetings that turned into aphasic encounter groups—*LIVE ?!*@ LIKE A SUICIDE.*

Guns' pretend-indie label was also called UZI Suicide. The theory behind this, according to Alan Niven, was that since the whole band was assumed to be monumentally self-destructive, they might as well run with it.

Since the EP was disguised as a genuine indie-style, post-punk release, Geffen pressed only 25,000 copies. The jacket featured a big-haired color shot (by Robert John) of Duff and Axl in a red fog of sprayed hair. The back cover, by Jack Lue, was everyone's favorite Guns photo. It portrayed them in an alley, insolently arrayed on someone else's customized muscle car, in full glam jacket. Steven, Slash, and Duff all rock black leather trousers. Izzy leans into Axl. Axl's crucial "look" was styled for this session by the rocket queen herself, Barbi Von Greif, who tucked his white leggings into his battered cowboy boots, teased his hair like a human dandelion in full weedy flower, and applied an expertly sinister maquillage that made him look, as they used to say about Keith Richards, "elegantly wasted."

The vinyl record itself, snapped up at the record stores on Sunset and Melrose as an instant collectible and heard by only a few thousand local GN'R fans, was an incendiary roadside bomb of a rock record. The two Hollywood Rose tracks and the two cover versions completely summed up Axl and Izzy's westward journey and subsequent apprenticeship in Hollywood's demimonde, and specifically channeled the superheated sonic revolution of the Sex Pistols in a way that no other American band had yet managed to achieve.

It starts with one of the roadies—Jason, Ronny, Danny—introducing the band to a fake audience that approximated a rabid Guns crowd in a Sunset Strip rock club: *"HEY FUCKERS! SUCK ON FUCKIN' GUNS AND ROSES!"* The band crashes into "Reckless Life" with the casual abandon of *Toys*-era Aerosmith, very punk with a growling, two-chord riff and vocals screeched like a ruptured duck. The difference between punk and Guns was Slash. Rock god guitar heroics had been anathema to the original punks, who viewed virtuosos like Clapton and Page as false idols needing to be reviled and smashed. Guns took this to the next step, deploying the stark minimalism of the punk arrangement with a blues-based guitar soloist who had grown up with Joe Perry, Brad Whitford, and Steve Jones. The track ends with a brief Viking wail in the style of early Robert Plant, evoking the Zeppelin mindscape of dungeons and dragons.

Next is a speed-demon version of "Nice Boys," originally by Australian rock band Rose Tattoo, with lots of buzzing guitars, bad attitude, and stop-time dynamic in the rhythm section. Chris Weber's "Move to the City" had made the jumps from Rose to Hollywood Rose to Guns N' Roses and was one of the flash points in their live show. The track starts in a blaze of deliberately sloppy guitars before Axl issues his strident challenge to live a reckless life in the street as opposed to the brain-dead existence of teen suburbia. The song then moves through different sections that interlock into a dramatic climax that brings the fake house down in an ecstasy of canned applause.

Steven Tyler's "Mama Kin," which even predated 1972 Aerosmith, closes the record. "This is a song about your fucking mother," Axl sneers with total contempt. Guns punks up the old song, taking it faster than Aerosmith did, Axl even copying Tyler's "black" voicing from the original version. It is a faithful recitation of classic material and an explicit homage to Guns' main inspirers. It speaks volumes to every adolescent loser whose main ambition was *"Livin' out your fantasy / Sleepin' late and suckin' weed."*

Live ?!@ Like a Suicide* was the band's first blow against the empire. The back cover made it clear that this limited edition was mainly for those who had believed in them back when: "This album is dedicated to our friends, for support in the streets as well as the stage."

People who knew the band well, or at least some of them, say Guns N' Roses never sounded this good again.

LOOK OUT, WORLD!

*G*uns N' Roses' ten thousand fake-indie EPs sold out immediately.

RIP, a new music magazine started by Althea Flynt (wife of *Hustler* publisher Larry Flynt) to chronicle the throbbing glam metal scene, was enthusiastic:

"Look out, world! From the sleazy, slimy depths of Hollywood's backstreets crawl Guns and Roses [*sic*], one buncha joltin' mo fo's who play uncluttered, ball-crushing, Led Zeppelin–style rock 'n' roll. With dual guitars, screeching Steve Marriott–like vocals, and thunderous drumming, these guys are the epitome of young, snotty rock stars."

The New York rock mag *Circus* weighed in: "The rock world doesn't need another 'bad' boy band, but from a look at the charts, it does need this L.A.-based quintet. While they aren't particularly original, they manage to parlay only average talent (and above-average ego) into some truly manic punk/R&B/glam/metal noise that's guaranteed to piss off your folks (and half your friends as well)."

Geffen's promo people sent review copies of the EP to the London rock press, which printed unqualified rave reviews in early 1987, basically predicting the Second Coming of Rock. Mick Wall, writing in the English metal magazine *Kerrang!,* called the record "the choicest side of lowlife rock 'n' roll to emerge out of L.A. since Mötley Crüe's *Too Fast for Love* in 1981."

Most reviewers in America immediately likened Guns to their main inspirers, Aerosmith, which was generally fine with both bands.

In interviews, Guns insisted that *Suicide* didn't represent the direction they were taking on the real album they were making. Slash said that *Suicide*'s only purpose was so "all the people who saw us from the beginning should have a chance to get our early stuff on record. It's like an expensive dedication to all the kids who helped us get along when we had no money, and were living in abandoned apartments."

Axl Rose felt differently. He hadn't really been in favor of the project. "The EP's just a piece of shit compared to the album," he said early in 1987, while they were making *Appetite*. "It's the most contrived piece of shit that we've done yet. It ain't no 'live record.' If you think it is, you're crazy, or stupid. What we did was go into a room, record ourselves, and put fifty thousand screaming people on top." He basically thought the whole thing was dishonest and a sell-out, but the record label had insisted that the band maintain some kind of street presence while it was holed up in studios, making their album.

But, for GN'R's fans, the UZI Suicide EP is the only record of what the original band really sounded like, before the deluge of fame and fortune that followed. Record dealers and collectors compete ferociously for scarce and highly valuable copies of the band's first attempt to get recognized beyond the wall of dry mountains east of Los Angeles.

*G*uns and Mike Clink recorded the basic tracks for *Appetite* at Rumbo and Take One studios in late 1986 and early 1987 amid all sorts of rumors concerning the demise of the band. Word along the Strip was that Guns had AIDS. It was said that their album wasn't being recorded in London because Guns had been prevented from entering the UK. Geffen had dropped them. Slash died of an overdose. They broke up before, or after, a wild show at the Club Lingerie.

JOURNALIST: "Did you really break up then?"

SLASH: "No, we didn't break up. We just had a long talk; sorted out a lot of shit."

AXL: "There was conflict, disagreements [about drugs]. I thought it was one of the worst shows we ever played. But the next day we had to have it out. A lot of things went to our heads, because this is all new to us. If we did break up . . . *who else* are we going to play with—that we really value as much as we value each other?"

DUFF: "We're not the most relaxed guys. We're not fuckin' [contemporary MTV soft rockers] Mister Mister, y'know? We don't just wear these clothes to play shows. We're living it! So things like this are bound to happen. We think for ourselves and we fuckin' don't let anybody tell us what to do."

SLASH: "We are a very tense bunch of people, when you get down to it."

AXL: "We've very explosive. It gets put into our music. And after that Club Lingerie show, it was like starting all over again. Most of us have worked together for three years. We've exploded on each other many times, and we always came back."

But there was still a lot of dread at Geffen Records about the band. A former A&R executive recalls that the band was always in trouble. "They were in fights in clubs and were forever getting kicked out of the Rainbow and the Cathouse. They were having sex with porn stars. They were openly using hard drugs. They were operating with no restraints. You would go over to their house, and there would be semi-naked girls running around in various stages of distress. Once they arrived at the [Geffen] office, late for a meeting, with a naked girl wrapped in a shower curtain—she was still wet. The whole deal, to us at the company, seemed out of control. There was a real belief at the label that Axl, the most important member, was simply not going to make it out alive. I remember one long discussion at Geffen where someone, possibly David Geffen himself, or maybe his hatchet man, Eric Eisner, said: 'We must record *everything they do*—rehearsals, sound checks, concerts—*now,* because this band is going to be incredibly popular, and they're going to be incredibly short-lived. One of them is going to OD before it's all over.'"

*A*ctually, the recording sessions for *Appetite for Destruction* went off without much of a hitch, mostly because Mike Clink made it clear to the band that professional musicians, who were being paid to record an album of original songs, should not fuck up.

Clink had been everyone's last choice to produce, but he turned out to be brilliant. He tried, ideally, to limit tracks to a single take. They called him Mike *"That was it!"* Clink. His philosophy was to capture the ferocity of the band in full manic episode, not tame the music for commercial release. "It's an instinctive thing," Clink said—umpteen million albums later. "You just *know* when a song is as good as it can be." Guns manager Alan Niven later said that Clink was crucial to the success of their album: "I simply cannot imagine another human being having the patience to get that record made."

Mike Clink: "They came in—many, many times—well hungover."

Slash spent his late nights at the Rainbow. "After terrorizing Hollywood all night, we'd still, somehow, have to get up, and be at the studio by twelve noon. And mostly we did it."

One of the first decisions was whether or not to use Steven Adler on the album. "Everybody loved Steven," a Geffen exec said, "because he was a sweet little puppy dog, and an important part of their stage act. He was the least fucked up guy in the band, but also the least talented musically. There was serious talk at Geffen that Guns should record with another drummer, but it never went beyond that, and Steven played on the record."

The band worked hard. As Slash said, Mike Clink treated them with respect. If one of the musicians was fucking up and not able to perform, Clink quietly made them aware that there was something that could be done better in their performance. He'd give them an opportunity to practice and focus and hone it down, and then record the track later, when they were feeling better. Clink had the ears to take a song like "You're Crazy," which Izzy, Slash, and Axl had written on acoustic guitars, and develop it into a searing rock blaster that would be a centerpiece on the album.

The band had something like thirty different songs when the sessions had started the previous summer. But none of their ballads—"Don't Cry," "November Rain"—would make it onto an album that turned out to be the hardest hard rock album since Led Zeppelin's blistering *Physical Graffiti* in 1975. Tom Zutaut was adamant that Guns save their ballads for later, when they had a bigger audience. Some new songs were written while they were working in the studio, including Izzy's thunderous "Mr. Brownstone" and "Sweet Child o' Mine," Axl Rose's tribute to the voluptuous Erin Everly.

The famous guitar figure that begins "Sweet Child" started off as a joke. Slash was playing this circuslike riff in the studio as a funny warm-up hook, but Clink got it on tape and Axl loved it. He was reminded of a poem he had worked on but had reached a dead end with. "Then Slash and Izzy got working together on songs, and I came in. Izzy hit a rhythm—and all of a sudden, this poem popped into my head." It turned out to be, as Axl admitted, the first positive love song he had ever written—the (bi)polar opposite of "Back Off Bitch" and Axl's other paranoid, woman-hating screeds.

Slash later recalled how his tossed-off lick penetrated Axl: "What started out as a fuckin' joke for me turned out to be a huge anthem for Axl . . . regarding the relationship he was in at the time. I know that it was one of the most heartfelt moments in his life."

People who knew Axl Rose believed that Erin Everly was the first person he had ever loved unconditionally. That's where "Sweet Child o' Mine" came from. And Axl really wanted to get the tone of the song down right.

"I'm from Indiana," he told an English rock writer at the time, "where Lynyrd Skynyrd was considered God, to the point that you ended up hating them, right? And yet for 'Sweet Child o' Mine,' I went out and bought some old Skynyrd tapes, just to make sure we captured that down-home, heartfelt feeling."

THE SEX TAPES

*S*ome of the songs on *Appetite for Destruction* were developed with input from West Arkeen, whose role in the album was big enough to have the band describe him as "GN'R #6" in the record's credits later in the year. Arkeen, born in Paris in 1960, was a little older than Guns, and more accomplished as a musician. He'd been raised in San Diego and taught himself guitar by practicing with a metronome in his family's home. Inspired by Hendrix, John Lennon, and Ted Nugent, he moved to L.A. in 1981 to work in the music industry. He befriended first Izzy and then the rest of the band. With his long blond hair and Gallic intensity, he looked like a medieval troubadour plunked down on the Sunset Strip. He was a mainstay of Duff's party band, the Drunk Fux. (Guns also had a song about West. Actually it was about his penis. "It's named after this guy West Arkeen," Duff told Mick Wall, "who writes with us sometimes. He's a real little fucker, right? But his dick, it's only about this long, but it's like *this* wide, man! So he's got the girth, right? So we call this song 'Girth.'") If anything, Arkeen was the band's reliable, cool, enigmatic older brother. Duff looked to him for ideas, tunings, voicings on guitar. In 1986 they wrote "It's So Easy" together.

Axl contributed a verse to "It's So Easy," but it was mostly Duff and West. As Duff said later in 1987, "Me and West had a special time in our life when we were really inspired by tequila. He was teaching me different guitar tunings, and we were sitting around a lot. Before we got signed, people and girls wouldn't give you the time of day. Then we got signed, and all of a sudden the girls started coming over, bringing booze and dope and whatever, and they'd fuck you, and they'd suck your dick, and it got to be ridiculous. We couldn't even believe this! That's what 'It's So Easy' was all about."

"West Arkeen was super-talented," a friend of the band recalls. "He was also a strange, shadowy figure—very private and withdrawn. A weirdo. But Axl rated him—highly. You'd see Axl playing stuff for West, to get his opinion on what they were doing. This was rare because Axl was such a perfectionist and didn't really trust anyone else. West Arkeen was the exception to that."

The *Appetite* sessions were, in every way, a complete rethink of Guns N' Roses. Their live act was purposefully shambolic, "out to lunch" as Axl put it. "Visually, we're all over the place, and you don't know what to expect. But . . . how do you put that on a record?"

Mike Clink's tactic was to let Guns be themselves. He didn't try to impose anything on them, other than to help them make an album that would sound like what they were. The most important thing about the band's (and Clink's) vision of their music was the experimental, improvised, newly episodic rendition of the songs. "Jungle," "Rocket Queen," "My Michelle," and "Paradise City" were given new dimensions in the studio as Clink and the band began to apply Led Zeppelin's lessons of light and shadow to the tracks they were recording.

"That's why we went with Mike Clink," Axl said later. "We went for a *raw* sound. We knew the way we were onstage, and we knew that the only way to capture it on the record was to make it somewhat 'live': doing the bass, the drums, and the rhythm guitar at the same time. [We recorded it] a bit faster than you play it live, OK, so that brings some energy into it. Getting the best track, adding lots of vocal parts and overdubs with the guitars. I mean, there was a definite plan to that."

"*P*aradise City," the song that would put Guns on the radio, was an example of how songs got built. It came from the original Hell Tour to Seattle, when Guns found itself improbably homesick for gritty Hollywood. Then there was the general folkloric, romantic yearning for home comfort, a simpler life, a place where the girls are pretty and didn't give you herpes. Axl told *Kerrang!* about the recording process: "I came up with two of those first vocals—there's five vocal parts there— and they sounded really weird." Then Axl and Clink experimented, putting two of the weirdest tracks together—"the two most obtuse ones." Clink didn't like it, but he was diplomatic. He listened and told Axl, "I don't know about that, man."

Axl: "I'm like, 'I don't know either. Why don't we just sleep on it?'" The next day, Axl called Clink and said he still wasn't sure. "But [Clink] goes, 'No, now I think it sounds cool.' So now, he was the other way! So we put three more vocal parts on it, and then it fit. The whole point is, that wasn't how we had it planned. We don't really know how it happened." ("Paradise City" is also the only track to prominently feature a synthesizer, at Axl's suggestion, according to Clink.)

In his mind, Axl divided "Paradise City" into verses and choruses. "The verses are about being in the jungle," he said. "The chorus is like being back in the Midwest, or somewhere." It reminded him of being a small child, looking at the immense sky in total wonderment. "There are parts of the song that have more of a down-home feel, and when I started putting down the over-layers of my [five vocal tracks], it seemed that it came out like some Irish or Scottish heritage."

*A*xl Rose's vision for "Rocket Queen" was typically perverse. It was, at least in its balladlike second half, an anthemic song about hope and friendship. But Axl also heard some porn in there, and was determined to tape a sex act in the studio and use the orgasmic cries of a woman in ecstasy (or pain) in the song. Mike Clink later told an interviewer: "The guys were taking turns fucking this girl in the studio.

Those are actual sounds of sex, live on the tape." A former Geffen executive claims that Axl fucked two or three girls at least two or three times at Rumbo Sound, without being satisfied with the results. Assistant mixing engineer Victor Deyglio had to run in to adjust the vocal microphones when the mikes were disturbed while Axl and the girls went at it in the darkened studio. One of these girls was Steven Adler's sometime girlfriend, a nineteen-year-old stripper named Adriana, who was getting back at Steven for cheating on her. As the tape was rolling, Axl barked at her: "C'mon, Adriana! Stop faking—make it real!" When Steven Adler found out about this, he freaked out.

Axl: "I wrote that song for this girl, who was going to have a band and call it Rocket Queen. She kind of . . . kept me alive for a while. The last part of the song is my message to this person, or anyone else who can get something out of it."

Naturally, rumors about the band's sex tapes were circulating back in Hollywood. Axl didn't bother to deny the story. "For that song, there was something I tried to work out with various people—a recorded sex act. It was supposed to be somewhat spontaneous, but premeditated. Something I wanted to put on the record. . . . It was a sexual song, and it was a wild night in the studio."

"*M*y Michelle" started out as a kind of sweet tribute to Axl's teen girlfriend, Michelle Young. She was still a friend of the band, and she did drop the rape charges when Axl asked her to. One night, Axl and Michelle were on their way to a gig when Elton John's "Your Song" came on the car radio, and Michelle said she'd always wanted to have a song written about her. So Axl wrote a song for her, and then realized that the lyrics had no basis in reality. So he rewrote them, depicting "Michelle" as a teen prostitute from a sleazy, broken family, with a taste for heroin and cocaine. He spat the words into the mike at Rumbo, wearing shades under a blue bandanna and a T-shirt knotted at the waist. His cowboy boots were accessorized with chains, dog collars, leather straps, and silver.

Despite Michelle's miraculous redemption at the end of the song, the rest of the band thought the new lyrics were too harsh. Axl said, "Slash and some other members of the band said that [the lyric] was too heavy to say about poor, sweet Michelle. *'She'll freak out, dude!'* But it's a true story. It describes her life. This girl leads such a crazy life—doing drugs or whatever—you don't know if she's going to be there the next day. . . . Every time I see Michelle, I'm so fucking relieved."

This debate about the lyrics to "My Michelle" went on for what Axl estimated was about three weeks. Finally he called her up. She came to the studio and he read her the lyrics, then he played her the song. Axl told her he wouldn't put it on the record, like it was, without her approval. Axl went on: "And she was *so happy* that someone just didn't paint a pretty picture. It was a real song, about her. She *loves* it. Even her dad loves it!"

"NIGHTRAIN"

*A*gainst all rational expectations, and in defiance of conventional wisdom, Guns N' Roses laid down the basic tracks for *Appetite for Destruction* with relative ease. For the band, the songs represented the best of what Duff later called "two years' worth of music." The sessions at Rumbo also took place in sleepy Canoga Park in the San Fernando Valley, an hour's ride from the temptations of Hollywood if the traffic was bad (and it usually was). "The girls and the dealers and the parasites couldn't really bother them, because they were cutting way out in the valley," one of their friends said. "It made for a more concentrated effort."

Everyone was impressed by Slash, who was supremely focused on getting the songs down and the guitars to sound the way they should. Slash had traffic issues of his own, since he smashed up the band's leased equipment van, which at one point was photographed in the parking lot of Take One Studio (in Burbank) with a broken electric guitar poking out of its shattered windshield. This was a rented Gibson SG whose technical problems whetted Slash's appetite for destruction. Eventually, Slash cut most of the tracks with a Les Paul copy plugged into a Marshall amplifier. He would work in the late afternoon and evening. Then Axl would come in and sing until dawn, which meant that Mike Clink was working eighteen-hour days.

Slash was throwing down masterfully in the studio, playing his ass off. The album seemed to mean everything to him. He later described the songs as "a storybook of what this band went through in Hollywood, trying to survive, from the early eighties to when it was finished." Slash was officially supposed to be off dope, but he and his snakes (Clyde and Cranston) were taking shelter at roadie Todd Crew's place, and Crew was openly using heroin, so Slash's drug status was an open question.

But Slash's devotion to the album never flagged. He was a trueborn rock soldier. "Slash was a *dedicated* player," Robert John said. "If he'd feel sick onstage, he'd go and throw up behind the amps, [then] come back onstage and keep playing. If he was soloing and his cigarette dropped down his jeans—*Dude! You're burning up!*—he'd finish that solo—in pain."

People were in awe of Slash. Axl called him his favorite cartoon character. He had this almost mythological vibe, half man, half beast—the centaur of rock.

The only nonmember of Guns N' Roses to play on the basic album tracks of *Appetite* was Jeff Fenster—one of the band's lawyers.

Fenster was thirty-three at the time, a transplant from New York and a graduate of Columbia Law, who had landed a job at Warner Bros. Records when it was run by Mo Ostin and Lenny Waronker (now considered the label's golden age). Fenster had met Guns because he also moonlighted as a disk jockey at Scream, the ultrahip downtown club where the band hung out to listen to the latest sounds—so-called industrial music and new bands like Ministry.

"My day job was at Warners," Jeff recalls, "but one of my hobbies was deejaying at brat-pack parties in Hollywood and at the Lhasa Club, where alternative bands like Hüsker Dü would play. I must have met Guns at Scream, near MacArthur Park, where Jane's Addiction got its start. Guns played there too, and in fact they were supposed to be part of an album I was involved with, *The Scream Compilation*, which showcased the bands that were playing at Scream. Jane's Addiction's first single was on the album, but then Guns got signed to Geffen, and they wouldn't give us a track for our little indie project.

"Back then, there were five cool bands working in L.A.—Guns N' Roses, Faster Pussycat, L.A. Guns, Poison, and Jet Boy. Poison had a record deal, but they were like the 'joke band'—except that it was well known in Hollywood that Poison got more, and better-looking, girls than the other bands. [One of their flyers notoriously read: **GIVE ME LIBERTY OR GIVE ME HEAD.**] But I remember seeing a battle of the bands at the Whisky one night—maybe it was all five of these bands—and Axl Rose stood out so completely as the alpha dog of this scene. He had a 'bad boy' persona, but he was also sensual, *really,* and almost feminine in his moves, and the way he presented himself. He was clearly the avatar of the L.A. bands of that era. And then there was Slash, instantly recognizable as a kind of rock archetype, but who was also the best guitar player in town.

"I worked on the band's record deal because Warners helped out Geffen as part of their distribution deal. I was the junior guy at Warners, and when it came time to do the Guns N' Roses contract with Geffen, they gave the job to me. Guns' deal [with Geffen] was nothing special—either it was for two albums, firm, or for one album with an option. I don't remember. The whole thing, including the band's advance and album budget, was a few hundred thousand [dollars].

"I must have met the band through Tom Zutaut and his assistant, Teresa Ensenat. Somehow I made them aware that I also played harmonica, and I began to hang out with them at their band house, which was everything you might have heard—naked girls, plenty of dope, loud music, breaking glass, complaining neighbors, the cops arriving to restore some semblance of order. Maybe we jammed while they were rehearsing, and eventually Axl asked me to play harp on their song 'Nightrain' at some gigs they were playing. The first one was at Madame Wong's, and then I played the Troubadour with them. Then they asked me to play with them at the Whisky a Go Go.

"So I get to the Whisky, which was probably one night in the summer of 1986. I was so psyched. How many lawyers get to play with their bands? I go upstairs to the Whisky's little shithole of a dressing room, and I find Axl sitting there, with two strippers. He gives me a high five, and he says to the girls, 'This is our friend Jeff. He's going to play with us tonight. I would appreciate it, very much, if you would take him into the bathroom and help him relax.'

"So I went with these two girls, and they basically 'serviced' me"—with double-headed oral sex. "Then Guns went onstage, and when it was time for 'Nightrain' they called me on, and I played with them. The audience—lots of girls—was rabid. *Bonkers.* I was ten years older than the band, but Guns were sort of *goofing* on it—that their label's lawyer could do this. They gave me a harp solo, like we'd done before." The whole thing was so utterly cool that Jeff Fenster could hardly believe it was happening.

A few weeks later, Axl called Jeff and asked him to come out to the studio to play harmonica on "Nightrain" for their album. So one night after work, Fenster drove out on the Ventura Freeway to Canoga Park and met the band at Rumbo.

"It was pretty low-key," Jeff recalls. "Rumbo was way out in the Valley, a nice and old-fashioned studio, very analog, wood paneling. The whole scene was peaceful, rather than decadent. They played me some stuff—I think I heard 'Welcome to the Jungle' and 'Mr. Brownstone'—and you could not help but be impressed."

Jeff laid down a couple of harmonica tracks for "Nightrain," and that was basically it. Mike Clink told him: "Great job. You're good."

"Mike Clink was totally laid-back," Jeff says. "He was very cool, very calm. You have to remember that expectations were low here. It was like: This is another Sunset Strip band like Mötley Crüe. Where does this fit? Does it fit at all? No one knew for sure."

A month or so went by. Jeff Fenster heard nothing. Then, in the spring of 1987, Axl Rose called Jeff and asked him to come to New York, where *Appetite* was being mixed. Axl wanted Jeff to play his harmonica part on "Nightrain" again, only this time a little differently.

Chapter Six

THE BIG GUNS N' ROSES ADVENTURE

Soon we'll be the meanest, nastiest, sexiest
band in rock and roll. We're not glam,
we're not punk, we're not heavy metal. It's
a rock and roll band—first and last.
—Axl Rose

HARP ON HARD ON

Guns N' Roses, its crew, management, A&R people, assorted hangers-on, and certain girlfriends relocated to the island of Manhattan in early 1987 to mix and sequence *Appetite for Destruction* at Media Sound Studios, near Carnegie Hall in Midtown. Everyone was excited about the rawness of the tracks they brought with them from Los Angeles. Some thought a recent song by Axl and Izzy, "You Could Be Mine," was a potential first single. (It was left off the album.) They got a great take on "Back Off Bitch," but that wouldn't make it either. "Paradise City" with its bluegrass banjos and exile's lament—"so far away . . . take me home"—was loved by all. "Mr. Brownstone," originally written by Izzy and Slash on acoustic guitars while stoned on heroin, was now a dynamic speed-ball rap set to an atomic Bo Diddley beat. In addition to tracks like these, most of the acoustic songs (like "Patience") that came out later on *GN'R Lies* were also developed in this rabidly creative period.

Axl Rose was confident they had something. "I just want this to be the biggest-selling debut album by a rock band—*ever*," he said.

"I think it's gonna fucking kick *ass*," Izzy predicted. "Listening to the playback, it's against the mainstream grain. You'll either love it or hate it, which is OK, as long as you *notice* it."

There were major problems too. Steven Adler mutinied after someone whispered something in his ear about the publishing rights to the band's songs. "Publishing"—the ownership of songs—was and is the only sure thing for any rock musician whose touring days were limited and whose record company would certainly cheat him blind in the unlikely scenario that the record would sell enough for the advance to "earn out."

Steven Adler was the drummer in Guns and an important part of its presentation, but he hadn't written any of the songs, and almost hadn't even played on the record. Nevertheless, he threatened to quit unless he was cut in. This made Axl furious.

"At one point," Axl later fumed, "in order to keep this fucking band together, it was necessary for me to give [Adler] a portion of my publishing rights. It was one of the biggest mistakes I've ever made in my life. But he threw such a fucking fit." This was at a band meeting at their hotel, the Milford Plaza. Steven Adler told them he wasn't going to stay in the band if he got stiffed. And it worked! Guns was quietly advised by the A&R people at Geffen that their album could be delayed, or even not be released at all, if Adler left the band and then sued them. So Steven Adler successfully held them up, and for once the drummer was cut in on the songwriting credits.

In 1991, Axl estimated that this had cost him $1.5 million. (It's probably doubled since then.)

One day in January 1987, Jeff Fenster was in his office at Warner Bros. when he got a call from Tom Zutaut in New York. Axl Rose wanted him to come to New York, where they were mixing their album, and rerecord his harmonica solo on "Nightrain." This surprised Jeff, who thought he'd nailed his part at Rumbo. But no. Axl had another part in mind, which would be explained to Jeff once he arrived in New York. Then Jeff had to explain to his bosses at Warner that he was expected to fly to New York (on the band's Geffen recording budget) and redo his harmonica part on Guns' record.

When Jeff arrived at Media Sound a few days later, Axl and Tom Zutaut met him at the studio. Axl sang the new harmonica part to Jeff, but it was hard to play. "It had this double bent note that you could do on a chromatic harmonica," he recalled, "but was almost beyond my ability on the blues harp I was used to playing. It took me a while to get anywhere near what he wanted."

While he was working in the studio's live room, Jeff saw the rest of the band come into the control room. Then, through the thick glass, he saw Axl talking to this young girl, real pretty and very sexy. Then the door to the live room opened and the girl came in, carrying a newly cracked bottle of Jack Daniel's. She wore the briefest of skirts. Axl spoke to Jeff through the headphones he was wearing.

"Jeff, this girl is a good friend of ours, she just flew in from L.A., and she's gonna dance for you while you're playing." The idea seemed to be inspirational; that Jeff would do his best while an exotic dance unfolded before him. And so, between deep swigs of Jack, the girl began to move. Off came the blouse, then the miniskirt. More ample draughts of Jack as she handed the bottle to Jeff.

"She's dancing for me—drunk," Jeff recalls. "She's down to bra and panties. I'm getting excited. Then she stops dancing and says to me, 'That's as far as I go—unless you take off *your* clothes too.'"

Within a New York minute, Jeff was wailing on his harmonica wearing only his striped boxers, socks, and sneakers.

"By this time she was pretty much naked, and of course quite drunk. We had finished the bottle of Jack. Then she collapsed on the floor. But she was awake and writhing around and looking at me, so I got busy, and then I was on top of her, and then my face was in the place, and she was into it, and so was I."

As Jeff was about to consummate this exciting new relationship, he felt a hand prodding him from behind. He tried to ignore this, but someone was definitely poking him in the back. The girl was moaning, begging for it now. "C'mon, honey, what are you waiting for?" Now someone was shaking Jeff's shoulder; someone else was pulling him off this tumescent young woman who seemed to crave his blues-playing manhood.

It was Axl. He said, "Uh, Jeff—I'm sorry, but *I'm* gonna fuck this girl now. It's for the record. We're putting it on the record."

Unknown hands pulled Jeff upright. The roadies were laying a blanket down on the floor. An engineer brought in a microphone on a low tripod and placed it next to the blanket. As Jeff was ushered out of the live room, he heard the girl say that she wasn't going to go through with this—unless they cleared the studio of everyone except the engineer in the control booth. She got her way.

Now Jeff found himself in the studio lounge—"pissed off, really annoyed, still aroused." Zutaut explained they were trying to put sex noise on a track called "Rocket Queen." Jeff asked who the girl was, and was told she was a Sunset Strip regular and good friend of the band's, and they'd flown her in for this session. Meanwhile, the sounds of Axl doing this girl were piped into the lounge. Then Zutaut could stand it no longer, and he sneaked into the control room, crawling on all fours, and watched the action between Axl and the girl while crouching behind the console.

The session was a success. Mike Barbiero chopped the girl's operatic orgasms into three separate tracks, at least two of which would appear on *Appetite.*

Jeff Fenster was in a state. "So I'm in the lounge, steaming. The girl comes in, very drunk still, wearing only a sweatshirt and [Axl's] cowboy boots. She looks at me and says, 'Why didn't *you* fuck me?'"

After this session, Jeff, the band, and the girls trooped into Wolf's Delicatessen nearby. The girl who had danced for Jeff, and then played her part on "Rocket Queen," was buoyant, lively, very cool. They ordered some food. An hour later, after drinks had spilled, customers had complained, and matzoh balls had been flung around the restaurant, they were thrown out. They could pull that shit at Canter's in Hollywood, but not in any New York deli.

A month later, Mike Clink called Jeff Fenster to say sorry, but his harmonica solo would not be on the album. Both Slash and Zutaut had signed off on it, but then Axl had decided it wasn't right.

When the album was released that summer, Jeff was credited as "Jeff (harp on hard on) Fenster." (Victor Deyglio was credited as "the fuckin' engineer" for his work on the sex tapes.)

"L.A.'S SCUZZIEST SCUMBAGS"

Guns N' Roses was back in Hollywood by March, when it played two gigs on Sunset Strip. The first was at the Whisky on March 23. The intro tape was Stormtroopers of Death's "What's That Noise." Roadie bawls, "GUNS N' FUCKIN' ROSES!" They open with "Reckless Life," molten metal and crystal meth. Soon they're all shirtless. Izzy scorches his big white Gibson, prowling the backline, staying out of Axl's way as the almost spectrally slender singer stalks the stage in a pair of skintight purple leathers and tatty cowboy boots. Slash, stinking of booze, plays his black Les Paul behind his curtain of hair, jamming like a demon, soloing with concentrated ease. "It ain't my fuckin' fault that the PA sucks in this place," Axl complains, before the band rumbles into "Welcome to the Jungle." The choreography is all there now: the knee drop when the jungle brings you down, the crotch tug at the mention of his "serpentine," the crucifixion at the end with spread-out arms, blue with tattoos. "Nightrain," "You're Crazy," "My Michelle." British writer Paul Elliott described the show as "pissing raw depravity" and the songs as "bullets from a misfit's heart" and "anthems to the estranged."

The garish pink flyer for the second March show, at the Roxy on the 29th, advertised, under a band photo and logo:

GEFFEN RECORDING ARTIST / GUNS & ROSES / 1 FINAL BLOW-OUT SHOW / With FASTER PUSSYCAT / EVENT WILL SELL OUT.

Faster Pussycat, self-proclaimed "wild, reckless Hollywood boys from Hell," opened the show before a squirming crowd of cute teenage girls. Guitarist Brent Muscat was himself so cute he melted the first seven rows of chicks right into their nylons. Singer Taime Down's high-treble vocal propelled cover versions of the Stones' "Star Fucker" and "I'm Your Venus" by the Shocking Blue. They announced they'd just signed with Elektra Records.

An hour later the crowd was foaming for GN'R, bursting with anticipation, but the band took the darkened stage amid sound problems, feedback, and confusion. A furious Axl could be heard yelling, "What the fuck is that noise?" But then, according to local 'zine *L.A. Rocks*, "they quickly got under way into their own world of rock that made the entire audience feel like they were on drugs. Their constant playing and the finishing of their album has honed these heart-throb musicians to a fine edge, and Axl's high-pitched voice is so perfect and strong that it doesn't bother my ears like it used to. It even gives me goose bumps when he goes over the top of the screaming lead guitars, and 'Nightrain' sounded so good I became a GN'R fan all over again. Now it's your turn. Check um out."

But now it wouldn't be easy for their local fan base to see them anymore. These were the end of days for Guns N' Roses as a club band. Their original genius had been in the streets. Now they were going on tour, leaving town. They'd be playing for strangers now, not for their friends, lovers, and dope dealers. There would be no more flyers for the band plastered around Hollywood and the Valley.

Meanwhile, the work the band and its technicians had done in New York was being sequenced, and the word began to trickle down that Guns' record was all killer, no filler. Tom Zutaut insisted that there be no ballads on what he viewed as the hardest-rocking album in years. There was some opposition to this, but Zutaut held firm and was supported by his boss. "Guns wasn't exactly David Geffen's thing," a former exec says. "He'd been Joni Mitchell's manager, and liked Bob Dylan, Neil Young, like that. But he truly believed in his people, and believed A&R ran the company. He backed his people, like Zutaut and John Kalodner, to the hilt. Geffen was famous as an A&R-driven label."

One of Zutaut's early ideas was to break the band in London first, and so Guns was booked into London's legendary Marquee Club for three nights in late June. To this end, Geffen publicist Bryn Bridenthal began arranging for British rock journalists to interview the band on its home turf in order to increase their UK buzz factor in advance of their arrival.

*I*t was around this time that Axl got the iconic tattoo that covered most of his right forearm. Designed by Bill White and inked by Robert

Benedetti at Sunset Strip Tattoo, the artwork was a variation on the Teutonic cross with the five band members portrayed as death's-heads on the cruciform. Axl was in the middle with red hair and a biker cap. Izzy was on top; Slash was on the bottom with his concho-ringed top hat. Steven and Duff flanked Axl, like the two thieves crucified with Christ. The new tattoo was such a bold statement that it drew much comment and admiration. Axl said later that he got the tattoo so he wouldn't look so much like a fucking chick when the band went out on tour that summer.

*L*ate in March, the guys in Guns were drinking at the Cathouse on Sunset, which twenty years earlier had been the London Fog, whose 1965 house band was the Doors. The Gunners' street cred was now immense. The hipsters who owned the Cathouse were glad to have Guns holding court in the place, and someone sent a bottle of Jim Beam to their table. Within an hour, the club's chairs had been reduced to firewood, someone had a pool cue broken over his head, and the band was thrown out of the club.

The next day was 70 degrees of late winter sunshine at the band's small, flaking white-frame house off Santa Monica Boulevard. A reporter and a photographer from the British music paper *Sounds* arrived at noon to find the band waking up. Their old cars lined a street of trim houses. The band's uncollected garbage, several empty beer kegs, and some broken chairs sat in the small front yard. A neon Miller High Life beer sign flashed in the front window. The band posed for photos on roadie Todd Crew's big Harley motorcycle stored on the front porch, while its owner shot dope in the filthy bathroom. A rough mix of *Appetite for Destruction* blasted out of the house and could be heard two blocks away. The neighbors call the cops—again.

Three black-and-white LAPD cruisers pulled up. One cop got out and stepped across the garbage, broken glass, and litter and addressed the band from behind his mirrored aviator shades. "Where's the party?"

"Uh, we ran outta beer," Duff tried. Someone inside turns the music way down.

"Sure," said the cop. "Try to keep it down, OK? We'll be back to check in half an hour."

As the officer turned to his car, Axl yelled, "Hey, how about if we take a couple of pictures on your car. You don't mind, do you?"

The cop said to go ahead, and the band was pictured leaning on the Ford police battlewagon. "That was the third bunch of cool cops in a row," Axl said later.

The interview took place inside, which was in typical disarray. "It's the West Hollywood sheriffs that we hate," Izzy said. He looked gaunt, fidgeted a lot, chain-smoked. "They the worst fucking pigs I've ever known." Duff passed out on a bed. Axl, shirtless under a fluffy fake-fur jacket, did most of the talking. Slash hid behind his mask of black curls and stuck to one-liners. Steven Adler mostly listened.

"Axl's voice is soft, deep, slightly rasping. Axl enjoyed opening up, and the others tended not to compete." Axl answered every question put to the band except one, when Alan Niven tells him that details of legal problems with their ex-manager shouldn't be on tape. The reporter had asked about rumors that Vicky Hamilton was suing the band for a million dollars.

The reporter, Paul Elliott, asked about "the scene" in L.A. This was approaching the height of the eighties glam metal era, when the Strip's lurid underground culture was broadcast nationally on cable television and basically moved from a small, decadent, drug-soaked counterculture to what passed for mainstream rock in America, within the space of a year.

The question seemed to rile the band, perhaps because they knew that the roiling Hollywood post-punk scene that had nurtured them was already dead, the clubs that provided them with vital support were already passé, and their album hadn't even come out yet.

Axl told *Sounds* he thought the L.A. scene was in a state of decline. "It's died a bit," he allowed, "and I think the reason why is . . . us." The others nodded. Axl explained that when they started headlining the clubs they used to pay to play in, they brought in local bands to open for them—Jet Boy, Faster Pussycat, L.A. Guns. "And it kinda created this scene, where we were pretty much the top draw.

"Then we quit playing for a while to work on our record, and the others started headlining. But some of them haven't been quite as cool about helping other bands out. We always tried to help others because . . . I wanna see a really cool rock scene here. I wanna be able to turn on the radio and not be fucking sick about the shit I'm gonna hear."

Axl pointed out that now they were playing with Jet Boy and Faster Pussycat again. But both bands had signed record deals, "so, it's all starting up again, but only for a couple of gigs. That's basically all the scene that there is here, right now."

Izzy: "Our scene is dying because the four other bands got signed."

Slash: "The thought of the L.A. scene makes me wanna hurl. L.A. is considered a pretty gay place, and we take a lot of shit from people thinkin' we're fuckin' posers."

"Poison fucked it up for all of us," Axl said sadly. The first post-Crüe L.A. band with a record out, the first to get exposure on MTV, the first to be reviled as empty and stupid, Poison boasted to America that they ruled Sunset Strip. "They said that everyone in L.A. was following their trend. What a fuckin' joke!"

The band was clearly pumped about their record. "We've got our progression planned out," Axl said—"how we're gonna grow. This record's gonna sound like a showcase. I sing in, like, five or six different voices, so not one song's quite like another, even if they're all hard rock." Axl said that in the last year he'd spent over $1,300 on cassettes: "Everything from Slayer to Wham!, to listen to production, vocals, and all that."

Slash laconically observed that Guns was the only real rock and roll band to come out of L.A. in ten years. "Van Halen was the last."

Izzy: "Mötley Crüe was more teen metal. We got a more roots-oriented sound than most other bands here. The only reason we got labeled with that 'bad boy' shit is because the other bands in L.A. are such fuckin' wimps."

And the Aerosmith comparisons?

"That's OK," Axl said. "In my mind, the hardest, ballsiest rock band that ever came out of America was Aerosmith. I liked that they weren't the guys you wanted to meet at the end of an alley if you'd had a disagreement. I always wanted to come out of America with that attitude."

Sounds concluded with its reporter's analysis of the band he termed "L.A.'s Scuzziest Scumbags":

> Survivors, scavengers, sexists, sleazeballs, brats, bums, bad apples . . . but not originals. If there's a familiarity about Guns N' Roses it's hardly surprising. The motions they're going through are old but tireless. These five are simply the latest in a long line of no-goods upholding a great, glorified, and greedy tradition. And in a year when raising hell has regained some of its former glamour, Guns N' Roses are calling the shots.

A NIGHT AT SCREAM

*A*pril 1987. The hottest club in L.A., if not the world, is Scream, a warren of themed rooms carved out of the ballroom of the old downtown Embassy Hotel at 607 S. Park Street. Scream had opened a year earlier as one small room on Monday nights, and drew fifty hipsters on a good night. Now it opens at eleven P.M. on weekend nights and draws its capacity of 1,200, with another thousand waiting on Grand Avenue to get in. For a ten-dollar membership and entrance fee, they get as many as three local bands, often Faster Pussycat, Jane's Addiction, Jet Boy, or L.A. Guns. DJ Mio Vukovic spins hard rock platters from the sixties and seventies at the pain threshold: Sweet, Slade, T. Rex, Aerosmith, Free, Steppenwolf. The Kinks are huge on the Scream dance floor. Current, retro-rocking bands Sisters of Mercy and the Cult are acceptable. Requests for something by Duran Duran or Brian Eno draw contempt.

Trend spotters abound. Malcolm McLaren, impresario of the Sex Pistols, is in from London to see what he can steal. Beastie Boys producer Rick Rubin has flown in from New York specifically to spend a night at Scream and to see Guns N' Roses play.

Every night Scream fills its little rooms with different stuff. Tonight there are music rooms, video rooms, a room with nothing but a large white animal skull. A large room contains a fifty-piece piccolo band from Watts who have rehearsed there for eight months. The tattoo room lets you in only if you already have impressive body art. One room contains a man dressed as Jesus crawling around with a full-size cross on his back, asking anyone who comes in to buy him a drink. Another room contains a large Canadian bear, seemingly tame, with its handler. Another room is alive with hundreds of scorpions on the floor. In another, patrons can get their legs shaved for a dollar.

It's also a drug supermarket. On offer are Valium, Quaaludes, amyl nitrate poppers, and lots of heroin. Cocaine was too expensive for most, but Scream regulars substituted a product called Ener B, a vitamin B-12 nasal gel that provides a strong energy rush and even hallucinations. Makeshift bars set up in dark corners sell cans of beer to anyone with a fake ID. The look is black, trash, and leathers. The club is packed with bimbos, fashion victims, punks, young hookers, and various rock stars in waiting, including some of Guns N' Roses, who have reluctantly appeared at Scream in response to Geffen's strategy of having English writers interview them prior to their London shows.

At midnight the man from *Time Out* ("London's Weekly Guide") arrives. On the way to the club, his Geffen escort mentioned that the label was betting the band would be huge, and also that some of them wouldn't live long enough to cash their first royalty checks. When our scribe gets to Scream, he realizes he has met, or at least seen, some of Guns before, a couple of nights earlier, at the Cathouse. When he went there, two people had really stood out. "One had [Marc] Bolan-style hair, a mucky face, and big boots, and spent a fair part of the evening jumping on wooden chairs until they splintered. The other had long, matted, yellow and black hair, and spent forty unhappy minutes whirling around on his back, weeping about guitar insurance. These two fine specimens [were] Slash and Duff, guitarist and bassist for Guns N' Roses."

Problems arise immediately. Guns think Scream is now totally passé, like, over, and they all want to split. Plus the band seems genuinely frightened of a psychopathic skinhead stalker called Animal, and nervously wonder if he might try to murder them. Wily predator Slash gets twenty dollars off the reporter in the first five minutes. He gives it to a girl, supposedly to get some "special" Mexican beer for them, but she never comes back. They tell him they are leaving, but Axl, accompanied by the lovely young daughter of Don Everly (still something of a god in England), invites him to the band's headquarters the following day, to do the interview.

*N*ext afternoon. Eighty degrees and California sunny, meaning a thick haze of smog and drifting smoke from the scrub burning in the hills over Hollywood. The sky looks white rather than blue.

"Along with ten friends, roadies, and groupies, they make their daytime home at a place called the Hellhouse, a filthy, blitzed suburban bungalow in an otherwise pristine street of well-kept houses in West Hollywood." The sheriffs arrived three times during the interview, which lasted just over an hour—once because a neighbor complained that they had parked a car on the lawn; once to warn that there would be arrests if there was any more bottle smashing; and once to bust Candy, a friend of the band who had pulled up in her car. The cops found no drugs, but one officer managed to get Candy's phone number, and promises to call.

Inside the house, Slash is resting on a grimy mattress on the floor, surrounded by dirty clothes, empty bottles, broken garden chairs, and garbage. A fat, nearly naked roadie is slumped in an armchair, head lolling back, looking very dead except for his gross snoring. Slash gamely makes conversation: he just broke up with his stripper girlfriend, mostly because her boobs were too big. "What do you do with them? Flop flop flop. I had to let her go." He also mentions that she gave him crabs, from which he is in recovery.

Alan Niven arrives, described as "the band's English manager (i.e., real-life *Spinal Tap*)." Niven cautions that Guns didn't think *Spinal Tap* was funny. Niven allows that the record company is nervous about the band. "Half the time, Geffen are thrilled with them, and half the time, they're scared shitless." He confides that the band was almost fired last year and had to clean up their act.

Asked about their bad boy image, Slash bristles that it is not an image but their daily reality. He insists the band is actually dangerous:

> You get warned that when you go on the road, people will try to push
> shit on you—drugs and booze. They should be more worried that

we're gonna push shit on them. Me and Duff, man, we have been in this drinking phase for about two years now. When we get up in the afternoon to do the sound check, we drink so much that we can't play because our hands are shaking like fuckin' windmills. So . . . what happens? We drink some more until we're fine, and we wake up the next day with the same fuckin' floozie, and you don't know her fuckin' name, and you've got some weird fuckin' shit oozing out of your dick, and your bed's all wet from pissing in it, and you go [to the floozie]: 'Will you do me a favor and find me some booze and a fuckin' pizza?'

Soon Axl Rose arrives. Slash, casually but with undisguised malice, introduces him as "the most temperamental fucking . . . meanest little fuck—*in the world.*"

Axl comes out swinging for the London press, which, he has been advised, needs a good editorial hook if the band wanted publicity when it got to England. He had asked what English people held sacred. Someone said they really loved dogs. Now he is quoted thus: "I'd just like to say that I have a deep personal disgust for small dogs. I have some *serious physical problems* with them. Everything about them means I must *kill* them. I must."

This doesn't sound right, or anything like W. Axl Rose, but the quote was published, and duly provided the tabloid newspapers with headlines when the band showed up in London two months later.

Axl wasn't in much of a mood to chat. Asked about writing songs, he managed: "Sometimes, six lines take two years. It just has to say *exactly* what I mean. Sometimes I write these great words and hear this fabulous music in my head, and I think 'Wow—this is really happening. This is better than Led Zeppelin!' Then I go home and put on a record and I realize, shit, it *was* Led Zeppelin."

Axl's arrival ratchets up the tension in the Hellhouse by a factor of ten thousand. Slash suddenly seems quite stressed, and the general vibe gets weird, and it becomes clear that Slash and Axl don't get along. Pushing on, *Time Out* asks about the band's influences.

Slash: "We all have 'em. It would take until Tuesday to name them all."

Someone pointed out that it *was* Tuesday.

Slash: "Look, we can sound like AC/DC, the Mahavishnu Orchestra, Aerosmith. We can sound like what's-his-name, that fuckin' idiot that plays guitar real fast . . . Al DiMeola, that's right. And you put that all together in your head, then you bang your fuckin' head like this [thump, thump], and then, maybe, you go get a new tattoo, and then, *bang,* out comes Guns N' Roses songs."

Axl shakes his head at this drunken rant. This puts Slash uptight. He drains his bottle of Jim Beam and gets up to break the glass. They can see the sheriffs beginning to cruise down the street again. Axl tells him not to smash the bottle.

SLASH: "I *got* to, man!"
ALAN NIVEN: "Oh, come on now, Slash!"
DUFF: "Please don't . . ."
ROADIE: "Don't, man. I have to live here."
SLASH: "I *got* to!"
AXL: "Only do it up and across the street."
SLASH: "I *want* to do this."
AXL: "No, no—you don't live here anymore."
SLASH: "Just against this fuckin' wall here. I just wanna break it."

The cops slow down in front of the house. Alan Niven turns pale.

Slash: "Just this little wall. Hello, wall." He smashes the bottle down. Shards of glass scatter everywhere. Slash seems immensely relieved. If the cops heard anything, they ignore it and drive on.

The article concludes with an interesting observation about L.A. that spring:

Both [Guns] and [Scream] represent something of a new musical era in L.A. People that you meet are awfully proud that L.A. is no longer in the musical shadow of New York. London and Manhattan have never spoken highly of the spaced-out West Coast scene, and even more seldom in positive terms of anything happening hard on the streets, but attitudes are changing. Sure, at one end of the city you get the beach and the tan. But downtown and in West Hollywood, you get maniacs with guitars that can break bones at twenty paces.

One can pay this band the greatest compliment of all. They are not in it for the videos and the career moves. They live this stuff, and they live it because it's money for booze and chicks for free.

THEIR ONLY GOOD ALBUM

*M*ay 1987. Guns N' Roses have thirteen songs, mixed down and ready to go, for their debut album. After they throw out "You Could Be Mine" for having a different vibe from the other relentless, slamming hard rock songs, they have twelve, which are now sequenced in Los Angeles. The running time of the album would be just over 58 minutes.

"Welcome to the Jungle" opens the album with its whole lotta guitar stutter, a specific tribute to the original blitzkrieg riff on Led Zeppelin's "Whole Lotta Love." The Zeppelin vibe continues with the moaning winds of the long journey to metal hell, and then the serious crunch begins with Axl's explicit invitation to sell you dope or "whatever you may need." The jungle that they come from, he warns, will bring you to your knees. The very sexy girl gets her props, and now it's time to make her scream, in the form of a loop of live studio sex during Slash's orgasmic guitar serenade. The bridge takes us down, suck-down, before the turnaround and the white-noise "middle section"—another homage to Jimmy Page's guitar vortex from "Whole Lotta Love." And then: "You know where you *are*? You're in the *jungle*, baby. You're gonna *die!*" The song concludes with Axl's threats of violence and shame, warnings of failure and doom, and vivid premonitions of death if the inexorable laws of the jungle are violated.

This opening track was GN'R staking its claim as alpha predators of the Hollywood scene. They can get you high while warning you that, sure as shooting, you're going to die. Their taunts, their threats, warnings, and dire prophesies both repel you and draw you into their orbit, until you're an aspiring feral creature of the jungle yourself.

"It's So Easy" comes next, sung by Axl in a low growl while the two guitar players do an early Rolling Stones imitation of Chuck Berry's basic groove. The lyric describes the decadence of hyperavailable sex, and evolves into a distastefully crooned power ballad bridge. The verses drip with more threats and snarling contempt. Axl insults your sister. He wants only money and anal intercourse from her. You want to kill him. He provokes a fight in the wet streets—*Fuck off!*—outside a nightclub at three in the morning—"See me hit you / You fall down"—but when you try to get your hands around his neck, he ducks behind a linebacker-size black bodyguard and is hustled into the back of a vulgar stretch limousine and fades, screaming "It's so fuckin' easy" into the night.

"Nightrain" begins with a cowbell and, like the real thing, you get a quick, cheap buzz that gives you a wicked headache later. There are motherfuckers and pimps in the verses, and then you find yourself on Sunset Strip, loaded on Ecstasy and waiting on the corner while a girlfriend buys you some cheap wine. Slash's solo is pure Stones (of the Ron Wood era), and then there's a torrid swerve into Axl's crazed, staccato screaming—it's like Page and Plant for retards—and then more heavy metal guitar (Slash and Izzy trading phrases) to the fade.

Bang into "Out ta Get Me," Axl's paranoid scenario about his years on the run. "They break down the doors / And they rape my rights but / They won't touch me." Izzy riffs on rhythm guitar with Steven's drums while Slash flies over them like a buzzard, and you can hear the jail door clang shut.... Axl screams and shrieks in paranoid panic, while the band provides a honky-tonk drone in open G. The lyrics throb with a desperate scenario of pursuit and escape, Axl having lived for years with various Indiana arrest warrants hanging over his head. It's the ultimate adolescent complaint, "something I been building up inside"—whether it's about the cops or the parents. "They're out to break me...I'm fuckin' innocent....So you can suck me!" The song ends with fanfare, and then Axl concludes with a triumphal sneer that sent a message to everyone who persecuted him during his troubled life: "Take *that* one to heart."

"Mr. Brownstone." Now the album detonates like a car bomb in a shopping mall. There's blood everywhere. It's Bo Diddley on crack. An explicit homage to Aerosmith's "Walk This Way," Slash inverts Joe Perry's signature riff while the rapped-out lyrics brilliantly echo the syllabic intricacy of Steven Tyler's original. The story of the band's gradual, insidious slide into full-bore dope addiction—"I used to do a little, but a little didn't do it, so the little got more and more"—was a stupendous re-creation of the junkie mentality in blank verse. It was also, of course, a raw confession of drug addiction to Mr. Brownstone, the dark Iranian heroin that was the smack of choice of Guns' opium eaters. (Axl reportedly found the lyrics in Izzy's room when the band was clearing out of one of its Hollywood hell hotels.) Axl uses an almost operatic voice—"He's been knockin' / He won't leave me aloooooooone—no no no"—that he never used again, and Slash's soaring, utterly inspired guitar solo invoked the blue velvet of heroin oblivion. "Mr. Brownstone" portrayed "that old man"—addiction to smack—as a demon to be avoided by anyone wishing to have a real life. The song was written by Izzy and Slash, but Axl added his own vocal tag at the end, one that doesn't surface on the album's lyric sheet: "I shoulda known better, I wish I'd never met her / I'm leaving it all behind." The Aerosmith homage of "Mr. Brownstone" even extended to the idea of giving up drugs, and was even played out in the Tyler-esque tag at the end of the song: "Yowzah!"

The pace of the album now changes with the banjolike electric guitar intro, like the beginning of an old Appalachian ballad. "Paradise City" is a plea for home comfort, green landscapes, and wholesome, pretty girls—a world away from the scabrous references of the band's other songs. Sustained power chords set up the song, and then Axl's party whistle signals the down-and-dirty riff that pushes the verses. The urchin of the first verse morphs into the career criminal of the second. In the third, he's in the gas chamber as the lethal pellets drop. "So far away" from home and family, with Captain America, lone biker symbol of lost freedom, now an old joke, one can only plead and beg: *Please* take me home. After a final squeal, the quest for paradise turns into a frantic drag race, on the double, with Axl echoing the epic wail of Robert Plant on the speeding chorus. Slash plays like there's a nitrous oxide hookup on his Les Paul, shredding, faster, faster. Axl is frantic now, meaning it: "I wanna go! I wanna go! I wanna go! Won't you please take me home?"

The dark, doom-laden guitars and ceremonial cymbals that open "My Michelle" spell trouble. Right away, Mommy's underground, Daddy is a porn mogul, and poor Michelle is a coke freak and a slut. Again the song starts slow while Axl tells of a lost teenager on the fringes of Hollywood vice, but as the story develops, the tone of the lyrics change to love and compassion—notably unusual for a band that was lumped in with mindless glam metal. Then the band shifts into rave mode, and Michelle cleans up in the last verse. A self-described accurate portrait of a troubled girl, one that began with sneering contempt, finishes in a display of touching empathy, hope, and redemption. As the guitars weave down into their final crash, Axl tells her to not stop trying to be good, and exclaims, after a cool, serpentine guitar tag: *"Michelle!"*

This heavy-metal tenderness extends into "Think About You," in which a cowbell starts a jet-fueled rocker about the infatuation of early love and shared moments of bliss. Axl opens his heart in his most touching lyric—"There wasn't much in this heart of mine / There was a little left and babe you found it"—yowling and mooing in his bipolar crooner persona. Meanwhile, the guitars twine and chime like victory bells—"think about you, honey, all the time"—and, as Axl pledges his final troth, his never-ending passion, Guns seems to explode into a manic rave that goes back, even beyond the Zeppelin's era, to the misty days of the early Yardbirds, ancient founders of the hard rock movement. The chiming coda then jumps forward in time to echo the sonic ambience of the late Zeppelin masterpiece, *In Through the Out Door.* Axl's whispered exhalation at the end releases, with great relief, the bittersweet memories of "the best time I can remember."

"*Sweet* Child o' Mine," the song that got Guns on MTV and the radio—a year later—continues the tender, loving run of songs. It begins with Slash's circus riff, which started as a jokey warm-up (and which Slash later claimed he hated). Through power chords and building drums, Axl takes us to his crying childhood in a corny but sweet telegram of memory. After the chorus, the next verse is the intimacy of his mother's hair and the safety of her embrace when the tornados and cyclones bear down on the child's riverside town. The vocals are way up in the screecho-sphere for the poetic verses, lower for the declarations of love—"sweet child . . . sweet love of mine." The rhythm is bump-and-grind, and the guitar solos recall the familiar cadences of the Allman Brothers. Ultra-traditional, unabashedly sentimental, "Sweet Child" has namesake affinities with classic seventies southern rock, even recalling "Sweet Home Alabama." But then, ominously, the song changes course. As Slash draws Jurassic pterodactyls with his guitar, Axl asks that age-old question "Where do we go now?"—fifteen times. There is, of course, no reply. It is a new American generation asking itself what comes next in what Bob Marley had called "this world of competition." As the guitars begin to rave again, Axl's caterwaul singing reveals the agonized uncertainty and emotional vulnerability of so-called Generation X, trying to figure out just what the hell is going on in a world where sex is death and acid is rain. "Sweet Child" is the closest thing to a traditional romantic ballad on the album, but, as if unable to contain itself, Axl's poignant love song morphs into one of the greatest rock moments of Guns' decade.

"You're Crazy" is Axl's other side, the one most people see: abusive, accusatory, vengeful. It's a coked-up take on the Sex Pistols reference, blazing with sonic fury, with verses veering from heartfelt love to accusations of treachery, some seemingly from a point of view alternating between a boy's and a girl's. The song slows for Axl's growled, sarcastic repetitions of "you're ffffuckin' crazy," and then its dueling guitars take over and Axl Rose can be heard screaming a blood-eagle all the way to Valhalla. A slower crazy coda sets up another riffing end and crashes to a halt in a fireball of twisted Strip metal.

Crash into "Anything Goes," originally "My Way Your Way" by Hollywood Rose, written by Izzy and Chris Weber. A sleazoid slide guitar and a sirenesque wail introduce a song that describes the rubbery sex scene on Hollywood Boulevard, a fetish world of bondage, "discipline," anal sex for sale—a pre-AIDS teen worldview from 1983. "Panties 'round your knees / With your ass in debris." Axl squalls out the chorus with a feline edge, and the full band blasts into a hard-rocking tag that blows up at the end.

Many Guns N' Roses fans feel that the group saved the ultimate masterpiece of *Appetite* for the end of the album. "Rocket Queen" is really two songs: The first describes an edgy relationship, rough sex, violence, and despair; the second radiates care and concern for a girl who's a friend and a confidante, and a loving, explicit warning about the dangers of heroin. The song—the longest on the record—starts with drums and a cathedral of dark chords, signaling a major statement to follow. The razor and switchblade threat display in the first verse leads into the chorus, where *queen* is rhymed with *obscene*. The next verse describes a jaded sensibility with a high-value demand for dope in the burned-out, false paradise of Hollywood. There's a classic Slash guitar solo and then a section of Axl murmuring sexual love moans—more guitars—and more pillow talk and orgasmic cries from the live-sex tape sessions—*Mmmmmf . . . oh . . . uh . . . UH, UH, Uh Uhhh . . .*

The great and precious rocket queen is getting fucked on the floor. Welcome to the jungle.

At which point "Rocket Queen" shifts into what at first seems like a middle-eight bridge but which becomes a different song, a change of heart from callousness to tenderness and public acknowledgment of the queen's great value and influence amid her loneliness and vulnerability as a woman in a predatory scene. As this feeling builds, Axl deploys his rawest, screechy-baby voice with ever-increasing intensity, and after another guitar aria, Axl issues his epochal promises to the rocket queen of unending fidelity and concern: "All I ever wanted / Was for you / To know I care."

*A*ppetite for Destruction was the only great album that Guns N' Roses would ever make. (Some—even some GN'R fans—argue that it was also the only *good* album the band ever made.) It was among the last classic rock albums to be mastered with vinyl in mind, its two-inch analog audiotape edited by hand with a razor blade, its final tracks mixed down by five people manipulating faders at a noncomputerized mixing board. *Appetite,* with all its incongruities and surprises, dodged the stupid posturings of eighties glam metal, and staked its claim with the classic pose of the hard rockers—a tough take on romantic love—and a unique solidarity with the female aspect of the gritty underworld of this band. *Appetite* has zero affinities with the outside world. Other than "My Michelle," nothing in the album's lyrics refers to another human by name. Nothing refers to any specific place, product (other than Night Train wine), episode, or any cultural "signifier" of any kind. Like Led Zeppelin a decade earlier, this band barely exists outside of its own zone, a naked tribe barely touched by contact with traders and missionaries from the outside world. *Appetite for Destruction* is a hothouse universe of its own device, and a visionary restatement of what it meant to be an American rock band, one that would go unchallenged—at least until Kurt Cobain and Nirvana broke the mold, three years later.

THE VIOLENT, MOODY ONE

*B*ut in May 1987 it was Jon Bon Jovi, another rocker from New Jersey, on the cover of *Rolling Stone*. Almost every high school in (white) America themed its senior proms that spring around either of their singles, "You Give Love a Bad Name" or "Livin' on a Prayer." Their 1986 album *Slippery When Wet* was flying out of record stores by the millions. To serious rock fans, Bon Jovi's anthemic songs and gauzy music videos were the anti-punk embodiment of current corporate rock. But idol-looking Jon Bon Jovi soared above his concert audiences, godlike, on a trapeze wire, and radio was beginning to play the new single, "Wanted Dead or Alive." Everybody hated Bon Jovi—except the kids.

In many ways, especially musically, Guns N' Roses tried to style themselves as the anti–Bon Jovi. But they had a little more respect for Cinderella, now one of the hottest bands playing on the Strip, whose original lineup had been discovered in Pennsylvania by Jon Bon Jovi. Migrating to L.A., Cinderella picked up drummer Fred Coury, who had been in the band London with Izzy Stradlin. Cinderella's album *Night Songs* came out in 1986. With Cinderella opening for Bon Jovi that winter, it sold three million copies. Even Axl Rose respected that.

*A*ppetite for Destruction was originally the title of a painted cartoon by the artist Robert Williams, whose background was in California car culture, *Zap Comix*, and other underground art of the sixties. The image depicted a horrific street scene that tantalized a death-porn obsessive like W. Axl Rose. This allegorical painting depicts three figures. A teenage saddle-shoed girl is down on a sidewalk, her panties pulled down below her knees, her exposed breast bleeding from a wound, her head lolling back, white-eyed with shock. She's a street vendor, selling little red robots called Mr. Mini-Mites, but she has just been attacked, and possibly raped, by a revolting predator robot with a lightbulb for a head and camera lenses for eyes. As he stands over his nubile victim, destroying and stomping her little robots, he raises his hideous head to behold her scarlet avenger—a fence-leaping, four-armed, knife-toothed chromium sphere exuding multiple death-head spermatozoa and guided by three tiny homunculi. It's the fractional moment before a terrifying death, the just deserts of a lethal appetite for destruction.

This image was on a postcard that Axl had bought at Tower Records on Sunset, and the name of the picture seemed, perfectly, to fit the band's bad-boy street rep. Axl wanted the image on the album jacket, and reproduction rights were duly purchased from the artist. But then there was a problem with Geffen's legal department, and with some of the people in marketing as well. The lawyers thought the image was too violent in the wake of Tipper Gore's congressional hearings and was also possibly obscene under the existing laws of some states. The salesmen said, accurately, that the "big box" stores in the Bible Belt and the South wouldn't like the half-naked girl with her pants pulled down. But the band dug in. Somehow, Teresa Ensenat walked the lurid, risky cover of *Appetite for Destruction* through Geffen, where pretty much everyone else thought it was probably a big mistake. The album's final release date, postponed from May, was set for July 1987.

In June 1987, Vicky Hamilton sued Guns N' Roses. (The papers were served on Slash at the Cathouse.) There had been some back and forth in the press, where Axl had claimed that she was never really the manager of the band. Vicky just laughed at this and said to ask anyone how Guns got their record deal if she hadn't helped. Everyone in Hollywood knew she was right, and that she'd been ripped off by a bunch of lowlifes and assholes. At length, there was a settlement. Vicky got $35,000. After she paid back the 25K she'd borrowed from Howie at Guitars R' Us, she had enough left to settle into a new apartment and continue developing new talent. Axl Rose left obscene messages on her answering machine, and Vicky kept the tapes.

Guns N' Roses wasn't playing much, and two or more of them were chasing the dragon—smoking heroin—but at least there was some muted excitement about their upcoming gigs in London, later in June. The band, or at least Slash, who didn't mind bantering with the rock press, did a lot of interviews. To *Metal Edge* he described Izzy Stradlin as "the quiet, reserved one." Axl was accurately described as "the violent, moody one." Duff was "the alcoholic." Steve was "the cute one." Slash said he was "the businessman of the band." He also said they were all dead broke, having spent their advance money on equipment and recreation. He insulted Poison, never missing any opportunity to dump on a band for which he once auditioned.

The band's first national exposure in the rock press was in the old school New York teen mag *Hit Parader* under the headline, "Latest L.A. Glam-Metal Unit Sets Out For Big Time":

"Whaddya get when you throw together the raunchiness of Mötley Crüe, the stylin' and profilin' of Hanoi Rocks, and the most primal elements of the Stones? Well, when you shake 'em all together, and toss them out on the burning streets of L.A., you get Guns N' Roses."

This goes on, name-checking Aerosmith and complimenting the band on eschewing spandex, makeup, and hair spray. "We never planned our look," Izzy lied. "We wear tight pants and boots, but that's what we've always worn."

Axl considered this, and added: "When I came out to L.A. five years ago from some hellhole in the Midwest, I was wearing cowboy boots and everyone said I looked like I just came off the boat. Now you look around and everyone's wearing them, so now I guess I'm driving the boat.

"Right now," he went on, "the biggest thing in L.A. is all these bands coming out with these hard luck stories: 'We've been through this; we've gone through that.' It's all bullshit! *We* lived it, not them! I lived on the street for five years until we got signed. I never lived in one place for more than two months."

At this, a tired-seeming Slash, who had seemed to be asleep, piped up: "We had no fucking place to live, man. We'd walk up and down Hollywood Boulevard and visit every porno store, 'cause they stay open twenty-four hours."

The rock fans of America better be prepared, the magazine editorialized, because this was no slick, prepackaged act. "They're entertaining and unusual—the kind of band that sets the trends for years to come."

"We want to stay one step ahead of everyone else," Axl concluded. "We know this is our big chance and we're sure not gonna blow it."

RIP magazine's first feature on the band, "Guns N' Roses: Live Like a Maniac," in the May 1987 issue, was a band interview, minus Slash, at their old hangout, El Compadre, on Sunset.

RIP: "They are gut-level rockers who live on the streets of Hollywood and put their experiences to music."
AXL: "We slept behind fucking garbage cans. We've fucked in the backs of cars because that's where we lived."
DUFF: "So when we see some fucking punk faggot from Beverly Hills walk into the Troubadour with spikes in his hair, we just want to smash his fucking face in. We've been doing this too long for people to call us fucking 'Guns and Poses.' We're not fucking posing!"
IZZY: "The estimated time of death in this band is twenty-nine, and that may be pushing it."

[The waiter arrives.]

DUFF: "Two double margaritas with salt."
IZZY: "Gin and tonic."
RIP: Why twenty-nine?
DUFF: "To die. My doctor told me I have the liver of an eighty-year-old."

[The waiter tries to leave.]

AXL: "Wait! Wait! Wait! [He glares at the waiter with contempt.] Did you get my order? I want a Long Island" [iced tea with vodka].

RIP: How does drinking affect your music?

STEVEN: "It fucks it all up, man—but not Duff, though. He can't survive without a drink first thing in the morning."

DUFF: "I know that if we play good, there's a possibility someone will give us more beers."

Asked to describe their record, Axl said, "It's just rock 'n' roll. Some of it is aggressive, some of it is fucking mellow. Some is sexy and sweet."

"It's a summary of our lives," Izzy added. "We just put in whatever comes along, y'know, like: *'I used to get up about seven, and now I get up about nine'*—that's seven o'clock at night."

Steven: "Then head up to La Brea and Sunset."

Izzy: "Get in the van. Play a show."

"He's just jacking you off," Axl told the interviewer.

"No I'm not," Izzy protested. "That's the lyrics to one of the new songs ['Mr. Brownstone']."

The band was asked what kind of impact they wanted to make.

"Like a fuckin' warhead," Izzy said.

Duff: "I want to cause serious sludge in the FM [radio] bullshit."

Axl: "We'll be the meanest, nastiest, sexiest hard-core street band in rock 'n' roll. We're not glam, we're not fucking punk, we're not heavy metal. It's a rock 'n' roll band, first and last."

Several more rounds of margaritas, gins and tonics, and Long Islands later, the interview wound down with a long debate about crab lice. Izzy said that they'd all had crabs. Axl said he'd rather have crabs than any of the other shit that was floating around. Steven said he'd be glad to get crabs. Duff claimed that "if you take a crab off yourself, and someone else who's got crabs, and put them in a jar, the crabs will fight each other to the death."

Parting words for *RIP* readers:

AXL: "Do your breast exercises and get that vaginal control."

STEVEN: "Do anything you want, as long as you think good, and do it for yourself. And don't give up!"

IZZY: "Never miss Chanukah."

"THE BIG GUNS N' ROSES ADVENTURE"

June 1987. Three weeks before Guns N' Roses was due in London, Axl got into a fight with a sheriff's deputy outside the Cathouse, and he was beaten so badly that he ended up in the hospital for three days, attached to electrodes and various machines. "I got hit on the head by a cop," he explained later, "and I guess I just blacked out. Two days later I woke up, tied to the bed with wires running into me." Axl claimed that he couldn't remember what had happened to him, but he thought that he'd had some kind of berserk episode, and suggested that electroshock therapy had been used to calm him down.

After he got out of the hospital, Axl had Bob Dylan's song "Knockin' on Heaven's Door" in his head. Slash explained: "It was on Axl's mind, and on my mind. But I never wanted to play it with the band, because I thought too many people [had] covered it. But one night Axl came over to this place where I was staying, and he said, let's *do* it." Slash and Axl worked out Guns' arrangement of the song right there, and brought it to the band when they rehearsed for their British shows. Slash started playing the chords. Steven Adler thought it was a new song until, halfway through, he realized it was Dylan's.

The band and its entourage, including photographer Robert John, flew to London on June 15. In those days one could still smoke on trans-Atlantic flights, and so Slash, who wasn't feeling very well, got drunk, passed out with a lit cigarette in his hand, and set fire to his seat, which smoldered for a while before the flight crew dragged Slash out of the chair and dumped water on it.

None of the band had been to England before (except Slash, who was born there). In their first days in the city, they walked around, drank in pubs, and visited the Soho offices of WEA (Warner-Elektra-Atlantic), the Euro division of Geffen's parent company, where Izzy and Slash were photographed on the WEA roof, chugging from a bottle of Glenlivet scotch whiskey. Robert John snapped Axl in a grocery store, smirking over a package of Spotted Dick, an English dessert. They were taken around to Denmark Street, London's Tin Pan

Alley off of Charing Cross Road and home to music stores and publishing companies. Someone who knew that Izzy was a Stones fan
pointed out that one of the guitar shops in Denmark Street had been
Regent Sound, the recording studio where the Rolling Stones' first
records were cut in 1963. In another shop, Slash was inspecting a
vintage Gibson SG guitar when he suddenly collapsed, a victim of
alcohol, jet lag, and the flu. They took him back to the hotel and
poured him into bed for two days of rest. He'd been drinking for five
days straight.

Nobody felt good. The change in time zones felt weird. Steven
Adler, normally placid, even made some stupid remark to Robert John,
who had paid his own way to London to document Guns' crucial English debut. Robert recalled when this happened: "Suddenly Duff just
lost it, and grabbed Steven by the neck and slammed him against the
wall. 'Would you shut your fucking mouth? 'Cause Robert's over here
helping us—*for free*. And you're giving him shit? You're 'Mister fuckin'
rock star' now?' They were all pretty tense at the beginning of that
trip."

They had reason to be. The London shows were their European
debut—a big deal. If they fucked up, or did lousy shows and got shitty
reviews, it would impact their album's release and affect how much
effort the label would promote it. British radio wouldn't touch the first
single, "It's So Easy" / "Mr. Brownstone" (released on June 15), because the lyrics to "Easy" were obscene and "Mr. Brownstone" seemed
to promote drug use. So Geffen was counting on the band to generate
enough buzz with their Marquee shows to get the UK media interested in them, which would hopefully spur the American rock press to
take a closer look at what was thought to be yet another annoying
glam band from L.A.

(Geffen Records was much more proactive with Guns in England.
The label also released a twelve-inch vinyl record with the two A-side
singles plus two added tracks: "Shadow of Your Love" and "Move to
the City" from their UZI Suicide EP.)

Actually, the London papers were already interested in Guns.
Time Out magazine's profile of the band had just been published, with
Axl claiming an urge to murder small dogs, and Slash explaining that
the band were major lush alcoholics. These lurid details were repeated

by the London tabloids, with headlines like: L.A. SLEAZE ROCK; LINES AND NOSES; LOCK UP YOUR DAUGHTERS; and SELF-CONFESSED POODLE KILLER. The music weekly *Sounds* gave the single a positive review, calling it "glassy-eyed gutter-crawl boogie." The London *Star*: "A rock band even nastier than the Beastie Boys is heading for Britain." One paper opined that Axl's putative hatred of dogs could provoke a backlash against the band.

On June 18 the band did a sound check at the Marquee. Alan Niven had told Izzy that the Rolling Stones had played their London club debut there, which was true enough, but the Stones had played at the original basement room, which had started on Oxford Street as a jazz club in 1958. Guns was playing at the Marquee's second location, in Wardour Street, Soho. After the sound check, the band was driven over to Tower Records' flagship UK store, in Piccadilly Circus, to buy some music. Slash bought a Damned T-shirt. Izzy got two Rolling Stones tapes—*Sticky Fingers* and *Some Girls.* Axl bought a cassette of the Eagles' *Their Greatest Hits,* and then felt dizzy and weird from jet lag and the antihistamine he was taking to ease the congestion in his nose and throat.

While he waited for the others to pay for their tapes, Axl sat down on the steps outside Tower's cassette department and put his head in his hands. Suddenly, three store security goons grabbed Axl and hauled him to his feet without identifying themselves. Axl started cursing them, and they frog-marched him out of the store. Alan Niven intervened, and an ugly scene played out, involving some shoving and so much screaming and cursing that the police soon arrived. Tom Zutaut eventually helped calm things down.

"The cops are kind of different here," Axl said the following day. "When they turned up at Tower, Alan told them, 'Take your hands off me.' And they did! Now, back in L.A., the cops won't take shit like that from anyone. They'd bend you over the front of the cruiser and put a gun in your ear."

*G*uns' first show at the Marquee on June 19 totally sucked. The room was packed with very drunk kids and media people, and was unbearably warm. "It's good to be in fucking England—finally," Axl told the crowd before the band blasted into "Reckless Life." The response was a barrage of heavy plastic beer glasses, human snot, and other stuff. "They're throwing *rigs* at us," Steven shouted, as a just-used hypodermic needle bounced off his snare drum. Another almost put out his eye. London had shown Guns something the band had not seen before. After "Out ta Get Me," Axl and Izzy both had audience-derived mucus gobs in their hair. (They were later told this treatment was standard when Iron Maiden played the club.)

Axl: "Hey! Hey! Fucking cut it out! If you want to keep throwing shit, we're gonna fuckin' leave. OK? Think about it." Another beer glass whizzed past his head and crashed into one of Steven's cymbals. Axl: "Hey! Fuck you, you pussy."

But the snot and unguided missiles slowed, and the band went into its transgressive sex boogie "Anything Goes." It was now broiling on stage. Axl was having trouble breathing and took off his shirt, which had a naked woman and the words FUCK DANCING / LET'S FUCK. Between songs, Axl shouted to Izzy: "It's like we're in hell!" The customers were palpitating and a couple of girls fainted and had to be carried off. Both Slash (naked from the waist up) and Duff (black Harley shirt) stage-dived into the seething crowd, and the intensity kept building with "Welcome to the Jungle" and "Mr. Brownstone." To calm things down a bit, Guns played "Knockin' on Heaven's Door" for the first time in public. (Written for the 1973 Western film *Pat Garrett and Billy the Kid*, Bob Dylan's ballad portrayed the dying words of an Arizona deputy, gunned down by the Kid and ready to enter the next world.) Axl turned the morbid song into an audience sing-along ("hey hey, hey hey hey") and sarcastically dedicated the song to Todd Crew, who, unable to score any heroin, had drunk himself blind and passed out backstage, missing the whole performance. (Alan Niven wanted to fire Todd, but Slash protested that Crew was his best friend and insisted that he had to be kept on.)

After the show, the band had a visitor. Ian Astbury was the leader of the Cult, a storming rock band (originally from Yorkshire) that deployed a Zeppelin-style attack (cut with a Doors-like mystique), and which was becoming wildly popular in mid-America. Axl told Astbury that they were disappointed with their show, but Astbury told them he *loved* what they were doing, and right then offered Guns the opening slot on the Cult's North American tour later that summer. This was huge news for them. For Axl, it made up for the general slagging the band received in the London media for their first show. "So fuck those assholes who wrote bad things about us," Axl later said.

The second London show, on June 22, went a little better. Alan Niven kicked Todd Crew's ass, and he did his job. The band was getting over jet lag and general malaise and again turned the packed Marquee into a steam bath. They partied at their hotel afterward. The hotel asked them to check out the next day.

There was still another Marquee gig scheduled for June 28. So Guns moved to a rented flat in Kensington, and Slash and Axl did a fresh bunch of interviews with London music writers intrigued by what they'd seen. Guns had dropped into a fallow period in the English rock scene, and there wasn't much happening except for new bands like the Blow Monkeys. So Guns was able to attract attention just by coming to town. (Some attention was unwanted, as when Slash got into a fight at a party for the premiere of *Hearts of Fire,* a movie starring Bob Dylan.) They were asked a lot about the glam scene in Los Angeles and were careful to insult and put down Poison in almost every interview. As *Nazareth's Greatest Hits* played on his hotel room sound system, Axl tried to explain Guns to *Kerrang!*: "We have pieces of everything in our band, and we try to bring it all out, rather than limit ourselves to one frame.... You don't see this much anymore. Queen used to do it, and Led Zeppelin, but now people tend to stay in one vein.

"I sing in about five or six different voices. It's all part of me, not contrived at all. There's two guitar players, that play very different from each other. One [Slash] plays an eighties blues [style], and the other guy [Izzy] is completely into Andy McCoy [from Hanoi Rocks] and Keith Richards, and they've figured out a way to fit it together."

They put a test pressing of *Appetite* on. Izzy listened intently, and then commented, "This record is gonna fucking *fly*. It's against the mainstream grain. You'll either love it or hate it—which is good, as long as you notice it."

"You can't really hate us," Slash mused, "because this band is for real. Regardless of whether anyone likes us, we're gonna just keep on keepin' on, and still do what we do. We want to tour. We want to travel and continue the big Guns N' Roses adventure. And indulge ourselves. And fuck a lot!"

The final London show was on June 28, and Guns dominated. Axl's cobra dance and high-kick stomp exploded the Marquee. He dedicated "Out ta Get Me" to "all the fucking critics in the back." They played "Knockin' on Heaven's Door" again, with Slash taking beautiful bluesy solos. The gig was superb and, like the earlier shows, was recorded by Tom Zutaut. (Some of these performances were released as single B sides, and as part of picture discs, in Europe over the next two years.) The last encore was a really raunchy version of AC/DC's "Whole Lotta Rosie," which climaxed with Slash and Duff again diving into the swirling melee from the knee-high stage.

*A*xl Rose wanted to make sure the British music scene remembered his band, so he was deliberately provocative in the interviews. "We're a *bad boy* band," he emphasized. "We're not afraid to go to excess with . . . substances, or sexually, or anything else. We're always going to be at odds with people about something, and we're not afraid to be that way. Why? The reason is that the bands who made it real big are the bands who were *that way*—not afraid. And Guns N' Roses plan on making it—*real* big."

And so Guns went home after two weeks in London. They had arrived, billed as alcohol-soaked sociopaths and dog butchers. They left as what some people saw as the most sensational rock band in the world.

KNOCKING ON THE GATES OF HELL

*J*uly 1987. Guns N' Roses flew to New York to make an appearance at the New Music Seminar, an important trade show for new bands and the record labels that owned them, as well as an important fringe of baby bands looking for bookings and managers. Guns checked into the Milford Plaza Hotel, a popular musicians' haunt where quality dope could be copped in the bar.

But Guns didn't play at the New Music Seminar, whose central venue, the skanky punk club CBGB on Manhattan's skid row, currently featured the usual kind of groups that would never, or barely, make it to the big time: Fetchin' Bones, Mojo Nixon, Zeitgeist, Agitprop. The major buzz at the seminar was R.E.M.'s surprise 1987 indie breakthrough (via college radio), which had given all the young bands new hope. Vicky Hamilton was in New York on July 8 and went to the album release party for *Velvet Kiss*, the debut album by L.A. shoe-gazers Lions & Ghosts, a band being promoted by its record company as "the next R.E.M." Some of Guns were at the party, along with Todd Crew, who seemed wasted (actually looking dead). Vicky watched as the once beautiful Todd stole a case of beer from the party and disappeared.

Later that night, Slash, Todd Crew, and the glorious L.A. porn star Lois Ayres were doing smack in Slash's hotel room when Todd nodded off in a heroin coma and fell out of his chair. A few minutes later, the phone rang in Robert John's apartment in Los Angeles. The photographer had flown directly home from London to get his film rolls of the Guns N' Roses debut at the Marquee processed and ready for sale. To complicate things, Robert had also had a major fight with Todd Crew, who had been living with Robert and his girlfriend, Shannon, over Crew's excessive drinking and drugging. Robert picked up the phone.

It was Slash, who whispered: *"Robert, it's about Toddy, man. . . . He's like, OD'ing. What? He's turning . . . blue. No, he's not breathing. I think he's gone. What do we do?"* Robert told Slash to dial 911, and then call right back. Slash hung up, but he never did call back.

Todd Crew died at the Milford Plaza that night, and everyone went into what passed for shock in the world of Guns N' Roses. News of Todd's death got back to Hollywood's rock demimonde immediately, and there were torrents of bad blood on the Strip after members of Jet Boy put out the word that Guns—especially Slash—was maybe to blame for the popular musician's death.

A few days later, Todd Crew's mother called Robert John. She had heard that her boy might have died in New York, and she wanted to know if it was true.

Later in the year, Slash was full of regret. "I still can't believe he died in a hotel room in New York a while back. We'd wanted to cop some stuff, and he got it right there. He went out...I tried to bring him back...it was horrible. And he was like my best, best friend. That really fucking scared me. I had a habit, and I finally stopped it."

(Not really.)

Axl had his own regrets. He'd seen how fucked up Todd Crew was in London, and instinctively knew that Todd was going downhill. Axl stayed away from heroin. He hardly ever even smoked pot, according to Robert John. Like the others, Axl was filled with remorse. "I regret not talking to Todd before he went to New York," he said later. "I'd felt a massive need to talk to him, out of concern for his well-being. But I was not...*aware* enough, to realize that I didn't have the time that I thought I did. I thought I'd have time later...."

Chapter Seven

THE REAL RAUNCH REBELS

It was the right band at the right time at the right place. It just happened to hit the youth of America in a certain way.
—Slash

IN THE HANDS OF THE REAL RAUNCH REBELS

The mighty *Appetite for Destruction* was released by Geffen Records on July 21, 1987, and . . . pretty much . . . nothing happened. Except for some minimal airplay in southern California, radio ignored the record. MTV didn't spin the video of the first single into heavy rotation because there was no video to rotate. There were no ringtones to download because there were hardly any cell phones, and no such thing as ringtones. *Rolling Stone* didn't care. The editors, in New York, thought Guns was just more lame-ass poison from L.A., and besides, they already hated Poison, who *were* in heavy rotation on MTV. The cursing and violence of its lyrics earned *Appetite* the horrible little black-and-white warning sticker, the fruit of the PMRC, which read: PARENTAL ADVISORY / EXPLICIT CONTENT.

The album's reception in England, where heavy metal was more mainstream, was better. In England, there was no pathetic warning label. *Kerrang!*: "Rock is at last being wrestled from the hands of the bland, the weak, the jaded, the tired, the worn, and being thrust back into the hands of the real raunch rebels." The rest of the English music press was just as enthusiastic.

The reason *Appetite* didn't pass the who-cares test in America was that the competition was so intense. Aerosmith's big comeback album,

Permanent Vacation, had great songs like "Angel" and "Rag Doll" on it. Def Leppard from Sheffield, England, owned hard rock radio with the album *Hysteria* and the single "Pour Some Sugar on Me." W.A.S.P., Anthrax, Heart, and White Lion all had strong albums out. Wendy O. Williams and her band, Plasmatics, were on TV a lot, along with Night Ranger and Europe. U2's theologic rock basically ruled MTV in prime time. Lesser bands—Keel, Loudness, King Kobra—were also trying to push up from below. Cinderella and Megadeth were competing for the same audience as Guns. It truly was a jungle out there.

*T*here were some people, though—mostly industry insiders in Los Angeles—who had an inkling of what would eventually happen. Jeff Fenster, now an executive with Geffen Records, remembers hearing an advance cassette of *Appetite* early in July. "I was driving around L.A. with Mark Babineau, the head promo guy at Geffen, and we were blasting the stereo, really cranking Run-DMC and the Beastie Boys. Then Mark put the Guns tape in and 'Welcome to the Jungle' started up, louder than I'd heard it before. It just sounded so immense. We sat there and listened. How many bands made you think of Led Zeppelin? I remember thinking, *Holy shit!* This could be an incredibly huge record."

*G*uns N' Roses was idle in July, barely playing at all until its fabulous opening slot on the Cult tour started in August. It was an immense drag that Todd Crew had OD'd in Slash's hotel room, and some old friends of the band were blaming Guns for his death. No one had tried to do a fucking thing for the downward-spiraling Crew; but then, other members of the band and its entourage were almost as strung out as Toddy had been.

The temper of the times was evident in the downcast interviews the band did around then. Talking about "Rocket Queen," Axl explained: "I'm singing as if it's me, OK? But it's really about this girl I know. I'm singing as though I was in her shoes, and then, at the end of the song, I'm singing it *to* her.

"The girl it's about...her life is history now. I mean, she's alive, but she's an addict, and there's not that much left of it [her life].... Since I've been in L.A., I've lost five or six friends, people that I used to hang with—every day. It's a really fucked thing, man."

*A*lmost from the start, there was a problem with the *Appetite* album cover. Robert Williams's nightmare cartoon was bordered on either side by the band's name and the album title. The back sleeve featured Robert John's studio shot of the band: Steven, Slash, Duff, and Izzy recline on an oriental carpet. Slash has a bottle of Jim Beam whiskey between his legs. Duff (listed as Duff "Rose" McKagan) holds a bottle of Stolichnaya vodka. Axl stands behind them, somewhat removed, holding a bottle of beer. Except for Steven, they all look stoned or drunk.

In America, the big chain stores—especially K-Mart, and Wal-Mart in the South—had serious problems with the album's artwork. They objected to the lurid rape scene and the violence, and started returning the offensive albums to Geffen's distributors. In Britain, the ubiquitous W. H. Smith chain banished the album, and even the Virgin Megastore on Oxford Street in London refused to display the album when it released in August. There ensued a mad scramble at Geffen Records, and hectic meetings with the band. Axl protested that he'd submitted the original cartoon as a joke because he couldn't think of anything better, and then was really surprised when the label went for it. Then a Geffen art director checked out the big new tattoo on Axl's right arm—the multiple death's-head cross with the Celtic ribbons—and suggested that this logolike tattoo art be the new cover illustration. This was OK with Axl, so the cross design was redrawn, and the Williams cartoon was relegated to *Appetite*'s inner sleeve. The initial release was pulled, and the redesigned albums were shipped to the stores in September.

*A*ugust 1987. Guns filmed their first music video, for "Welcome to the Jungle," at the Park Plaza Hotel (on the site of the Ambassador, where Robert Kennedy was assassinated in 1968, now demolished) and in a studio at 450 La Brea. Directed by Britisher Nigel Dick, the video begins at the bus station in L.A. Young Bill Bailey steps off the bus with his shabby suitcase, and in case you didn't get that he was a hayseed, he's actually sucking on a wheat straw. A slick city hustler, played by Izzy Stradlin, offers him something, but Bill shrugs him off. A hooker walks by. Then the song starts and Guns are onstage in front of a crowd of chicks. Axl's hair is way up, and Slash is the Mad Hatter. Axl's moves are subdued for the camera, the band's lupine sexuality tamped way down so they could get on TV. The concert footage is intercut with violent imagery of police abusing their authority in California, Belfast, Israel, and South Africa. The gyrelike middle section depicts psycho Axl tied to a chair, bound in a straitjacket, electrodes attached to his head like the Droog in Stanley Kubrick's film *A Clockwork Orange*. Axl is being forced to witness the *Faces of Death* snuff films that he obsessively watched when he lived at Vicky Hamilton's flat.

Nigel Dick wanted to cut some scenes of the band with a pretty girl into the video. Steven Adler: "Think about this: Guns N' Roses, one of the coolest, biggest bands in L.A., and we're filming 'Welcome to the Jungle,' and none of us could think of a girl to be in it with us. [The band was too broke, and the video budget too small, to pay someone to do it.] Nobody could think of a girl. So I go, 'Let's get Julie Angel, man. She's got a great ass!'"

Julie was actually Steven's landlord, since he was crashing at her and her friend Lisa's apartment, sleeping on a futon in their laundry room. "I had a TV, and I had the cable put in, and I had my own little door. They were my roommates. They were the greatest girls."

Steven called Julie, asked her to be in the video, and she said OK. "And I say, 'We'll be by to pick you up in ten minutes.' And that's why she was in the video, because none of us could think of a girl, except, well, obviously—me."

The *Jungle* video ends with Axl, no longer a hick but now a contemporary L.A. rocker, watching his own video through a TV store window. When it ends, he turns on his heel and walks off into the sultry Hollywood night.

Guns N' Roses may have been one of the most telegenic bands to come along in years, with a sex-bomb singer, a bassist who looked like

Duff, and a guitarist who looked like a stoner cartoon. "Welcome to the Jungle" may have been one hell of a rock song, but its violence-obsessed video version hardly ever got played on MTV. When it did, it would be heavily cut and censored, and even then it took one hell of an intervention, almost a year down the road, to make any airtime happen at all.

THE CULT CHANGED THE LAMINATES

*I*n August 1987, Guns N' Roses launched itself into North America, opening shows for the Cult, beginning in Halifax, Nova Scotia, on August 14. The band knew they had a big problem with *Appetite*'s cover art when there were no albums in the record stores in Halifax, and it was explained the jacket had been judged indecent. The tour, gathering a wobbly momentum, then moved west through Quebec and Ontario, down to Detroit, Michigan, on August 21, and continued through Alberta, Winnipeg, Calgary, and Vancouver through the rest of the month. Guns was so completely cash-starved that ever-resourceful Izzy Stradlin took to scalping concert tickets outside Guns' band bus so that the band could at least get something to eat after the show.

But they played their asses off, spicing their hard rock attack with "Don't Cry" and other ballads. They covered "Nice Boys" and sometimes "Mama Kin." They started performing "Used to Love Her (But I Had to Kill Her)," and the kids would laugh and clap at the new song's macabre premise. They kept "Knockin' on Heaven's Door" in the set as a sing-along and kept dedicating it to Todd Crew, even though they had agreed to try not to do this anymore because it bummed them out afterward.

Axl: "If we get through the whole song, as soon as it's over, one of us goes to the microphone to dedicate it to Todd. We can't seem to break away from it. I'm told by a friend of mine, someone who would know, that we won't get over it until it happens again."

Axl was rapping to the audiences on the Cult tour, introducing the band, hyping *Appetite,* really drawing the kids in between songs. His rap just before "Mr. Brownstone" was frank and to the point in almost every show. While refusing to condone or promote drug use, Axl also pointed out the dangers of heroin. This was necessary because many of the band's new fans interpreted the lyrics as meaning that life got easier and more fun (sleeping later, better transport) when dancing with Mr. Brownstone.

"Some people think we're condoning heroin," Axl told an interviewer around this time. "We did this one show [in London], and they were throwing needles on the stage. So now I do my little thing about how it's your responsibility to actually wake up the next morning. I don't rehearse this or anything. I always do it a little differently. I show them where I'm coming from. I'm not saying, 'Go do heroin.' And also, you know, I *do* care about the audience. I'd like to think that if people are going to do . . . whatever, after the show, maybe . . . in the back of their heads—if they're having fun and going, *'Yeah—Guns N' Roses'*—they'll say to themselves: 'Maybe I won't do as much, because tomorrow I have to . . .' You know what I'm saying?

"I had it happen to me with Todd Crew," Axl concluded, "and I don't want to see it happening to . . . other people." [This might have been a reference to Izzy and Slash.]

Asked if Crew's death had changed any of his opinions, Axl replied: "No, it didn't make me change my opinions. It just makes me be a little more careful sometimes." Axl thought for a minute, then whispered, "I get really freaked out by the Todd thing."

So it was in the steamy summer of 1987, touring with the Cult, that Guns N' Roses quickly came into their own as a touring rock band. They were beginning to move toward what they would become—the biggest band in the world. And, of course, Guns started blowing the Cult off their own stages, sometimes to the point where the English band didn't want to play after Guns had elicited many encores and massive chanting after their sets. This is when the Cult's roadies began sabotaging some of Guns' performances.

The Cult was a good second-division English rock band, but it was six years into its career, and for them, it never got better than this. (Drummer Matt Sorum was not yet in the Cult. The version of the band that toured with Guns N' Roses in 1987 had Les Warner on drums). The group had first been called Southern Death Cult in York-shire in 1981, and then mutated into Death Cult, a band on the fringe of London's early goth scene. Ian Astbury and guitarist Billy Duffy then changed the band's name to the Cult, and (influenced by Jim Morrison) expanded their lyrical interests to Native American sha-manism. After 1985, "She Sells Sanctuary" and "Love Removal Ma-chine" both made the charts, and the band's Doors-like attempts at audience orgasm got them strong road followings in the American and Austro-Asian markets. In 1987 they were touring behind a new album, *Electric*, and the single "Wild Flower."

Ian Astbury dug Guns N' Roses. Axl later said that Ian (bandanna wrapped around head, mirrored aviator shades) spent more time in Guns' pharmacopeia-ready dressing room than in the bitchy ambi-ence of the Cult's. Early in the tour, there had been talks between Axl, Ian, and Billy Duffy to try to write together, but then nothing came of it. The truth was that no English band could afford to be upstaged every night by an American supporting act whose album wasn't even on the charts. This humiliation would get back to London via the road crew and the tour staff, and the Cult would lose industry cred in cru-cial markets like Europe and Japan. So the Cult's roadies began fuck-ing with Guns N' Roses while they were onstage.

Jeff Fenster saw some of these shows. "This tour was a big deal for Guns, the first time they were outside their Sunset Strip comfort zone, the first time playing for arena audiences." Now they were opening in Canadian hockey rinks, often without sound checks or any respect from the venue or anyone else. "The Cult roadies kept fucking with Guns N' Roses, even though everyone denied it, because Guns was blowing the Cult away, every night. Sometimes they'd just pull the plug on Guns. It could get really petty and stupid like that." Most of this involved minor damage to Guns' gear, or the backline going dead as "Welcome to the Jungle" was set to tumble onto the rabid audiences.

But Guns never complained, and just kept getting better every night. On September 2, they crossed back into the United States and started a run down the West Coast—Seattle [Duff: "It was fuckin' hec-tic, man: the whole family was there."], San Francisco, Santa Cruz, San Diego. On September 5, there was a fiasco at the Long Beach Arena, near Los Angeles. This was Guns' big local homecoming, a huge deal for the band, and their guest list was long and relatively lustrous, with a nice party planned for backstage after the show.

Slash: "The night before we played, I walked around with one of our roadies until, like, six in the morning. Then we walked about eight blocks to get breakfast at Denny's, and on the way there, you could see Long Beach [Arena]. Zeppelin played there, man. Everyone had played there. And I remembered all the times I'd gone down there, scalping tickets, or getting in line for Aerosmith tickets, getting sick, throwing up. And the times I'd been there for AC/DC and stuff. And all of a sudden . . . *we're playing there!* I just looked at the place. It's sitting there, at dawn. This is 'sensitive' bullshit, but . . . it was a fuckin' trip!"

In the true spirit of rock music, the Cult then sabotaged Guns' homecoming. The Cult's tour management decided to cancel all backstage passes for the Long Beach shows, and also changed the tour's laminated IDs—at the very last moment, without telling Guns. No one said why, and it was the first and only time they did it. The guys in Guns N' Roses and their crew could barely get into the venue. "There wasn't any reason given," Axl said later. "It was Guns N' Roses territory, and right then, *we* were the big heroes. It was more the [Cult's] management than the band. And it wasn't like, 'The Cult fucked us' [as had been reported in the L.A. music press]. But everything just got really uncomfortable. It was a really weird aura. Even [the Cult] felt kind of weird."

Guns didn't play that great, and only a few of their guests got backstage afterward. It was an insult, a fucking outrage. Guns' management tried to intervene, but was strong-armed and ignored. The tour then broke for a few days, and resumed on September 11 for five more shows in the South.

After San Antonio, Austin, Dallas, and Houston, the tour ended for Guns at the Saengar Theatre in New Orleans on September 17. As soon as Guns took the stage, Ian Astbury showed up at the side of the stage and began throwing food at them. A pie whizzed past Slash's head while he was soloing on "Move to the City." Then the Cult's crew chief came out with a broom and started sweeping the stage like a janitor. Then, while Steven was trying to play "You're Crazy," they came out and dismantled his drum kit and carted it offstage.

But Guns had their revenge. When the Cult came out and tried to mystify the Cajun kids with their hokey Navajo act, Guns lined up above the drum riser with post-shower towels duct-taped to their heads, like Iranian sheiks, and started grinding out what Axl called "this stupid Egyptian dance. Then we fuckin' covered them with gobs of cottage cheese and wads of gook we made from the deli trays—guacamole, hummus, egg salad. Then Ian got Steven naked—all he had on was the towel—and carried him around the stage on his shoulder."

Guns then left the stage, but their revenge was still coming. After the Cult started their set, a tiny Stonehenge was lowered onstage—a direct reference to the pathetic fate of the hapless movie band Spinal Tap. Then the Guns road crew came out, wearing masks of Joe Piscopo, the *Saturday Night Live* comedian, and danced around the mock Stonehenge like the dwarves in the film. It was Guns N' Roses' sarcastic kiss-off to a downwardly mobile English group, and it probably stung the Cult not a little.

Both bands were glad to see the last of the other. A few days later, Guns returned to Europe and continued their run for the roses. As for the Cult, their 1987 tour eventually wound down in Australia, where, somehow, 30,000 pounds' worth of touring gear got wrecked, preventing the Cult from touring in (extremely lucrative) Japan, where they were big. (No one would rent them new equipment.) By then, *Electric* had sold platinum numbers in England, and about three million units worldwide. The main trouble for the Cult was that the band members were barely speaking to one another, and their glory days were almost over.

Music Connection: "Was the Cult intimidated by your success?"

Duff: "No! They supported it 100 percent!"

THE WHORES IN THE WINDOWS

The original idea for October 1987 had been for Guns N' Roses to open a series of European shows for rip-roaring Aerosmith, whose hard-won sobriety and improbable showbiz comeback had just been ratified by the success of their album *Permanent Vacation*. For Geffen Records it was a heaven-sent double bill. For Slash it was a dream come true, a Euro tour with his teenage heroes. He proudly called it "the bill from hell." The halls were booked, the tickets printed, and some concerts sold out in an hour.

Then Aerosmith pulled out at the last minute. Their manager, Tim Collins, recalls, "There were all sorts of reasons for this. I forget what the public excuse was. But the real deal was that some of our people thought it was an insane idea to throw our band into the arena with a bunch of drug addicts and drunks. Aerosmith had less than two years' sobriety at that point. We had them going to Alcoholics Anonymous meetings even while they were on the road, and the whole band was responding to this self-imposed discipline—beyond all our dreams. So we felt that the situation was fragile enough without exposing the so-called Toxic Twins to the most negative role models in the industry. I think the thing that sealed it, that made us cancel that tour, was when Joe Perry told me that he used to buy drugs from Izzy Stradlin when Guns had that scene in the alley behind Sunset. Whoa! Hello? I don't think so."

So Guns decided to do a few dates in Europe anyway, on their own, but as headliners instead of the supporting act. They invited Faster Pussycat, whose debut album was just out, to open for them, and began what was described on the concert posters as "Destruction '87," a downsized Guns tour of Germany, Holland, and England, beginning on September 29, 1987. The first gig was at the Markethalle in Hamburg, the German port city where the Beatles had honed their act. Arriving a day early, some of the band visited Hamburg's notorious red-light district, where they were fascinated by the full-figured women of many nationalities selling themselves in shop front windows. Back at their hotel, Faster Pussycat's drummer passed out in Slash's room after hanging around Guns all day, which the band thought annoying. So Slash and Izzy completely wrapped him in duct tape, like a mummy, threw him in the elevator, and pressed DOWN.

The German kids immediately loved the band, and the local press thought their gear—black leather biker vests, skintight jeans tucked into badass cowboy boots accessorized with spurs, kerchiefs, chains, and jangly bangles—were the epitome of au courant L.A. glam. The next night, September 30, they played at the Tor 3 club in Düsseldorf. The energy was so high that the cops had to deal with some smashed windows and overturned cars in the streets surrounding the gig.

On to Amsterdam via Lufthansa. The taxi driver taking Izzy to the hotel gave him the lowdown on Holland: "Like the cabby said, 'Speed limit? What speed limit? Who gives a fuck? Prostitution? Who cares? It's legal here! Drugs? Who cares? You can buy anything you want here! What do you need?'

"It's the most degenerate place I've ever been to," Izzy concluded— approvingly.

Slash loved Amsterdam. "All the cool stuff is just in one section of the city," he explained later, "like there's only one Hollywood Boule-vard. Not all L.A. is like that, and not all of Amsterdam is like that ei-ther." The night before the gig at the famous Paradiso, the band was escorted through the city's hooker quarter, where girls for sale lounged in windows. (Some of them were knitting and reading books.) "Let me tell you," Slash said, "you can almost tell what country you're in by the size and shapes of the women." They were big in Germany, more pe-tite in Holland. "They have every age, shape, race, and size—in every conceivable outfit: leather, corsets, lace. Whatever you need."

The band especially dug the hash bars of Amsterdam, where you sat down; ordered Nepalese, Lebanese, or Moroccan hash from a menu; and smoked it with a cup of tea. They couldn't believe this. Slash: "I walked into this one hash bar, looking for Steven, who had disappeared. The air in there was like fucking paste. And there was my drummer, slumped in a corner with a fucking hookah tube in his mouth—totally gone."

The show went down great at the Paradiso. The kids were bon-kers. Before the second song, "Move to the City," Axl vented about some negative comments about Guns that had run in the British music press. He told the crowd that he'd been reading about what some old-school rock stars had been saying about his band. He mumbled that Guns wasn't trying to be anyone else. "And people like Paul Stanley from KISS can just go and suck my dick! [Cheers.] And some of these old guys . . . they say we're ripping them off . . . Maybe they should just listen to some of their old albums, and maybe they should fuckin' remember how to play 'em." [More cheers.]

They flew to London the next day. WEA had just released "Welcome to the Jungle" as a single.

*A*nd on to Newcastle on October 4, and then to Nottingham, where they arrived late that night. Axl went off at the band's old-fashioned hotel because there was nothing to eat, and he was desperate to talk to Erin back in California. But the call wouldn't go through, and no one would help him, and he was having difficulty making the connection on the phone in his room. He was getting madder by the minute. After he complained about it, the hotel shut his phone off completely. So Axl ripped the phone out of the wall and fired it down the stairwell at the uncooperative receptionist. It took all the diplomatic talents of Guns' new tour manager, former security guy Doug Goldstein, to keep the hotel from evicting them.

Robert John wasn't on this trip, so Guns was met at the venue, Nottingham Rock City, by George Chin, one of the best rock photogs in England. George quickly picked up the vibe that the band had a ganglike impenetrability, and that, on this night at least, Axl Rose was extremely angry at something that had happened earlier. When the band took the stage (Axl in white jeans, pink bandanna, white Zurich Tattoo Convention shirt), Chin was astonished at the sheer intensity of Axl Rose, close-up. "That night at the show," Chin recalled, "it was the first time I ever saw a singer sing out his anger onstage. It was raw vocal power, a performance where Axl strutted and stomped and swiveled until what was bugging him was out of his system, and the anger spent."

Guns had the crowd jumping from the moment they crashed into "It's So Easy" and kept them panting through ninety minutes and two encores. They did a runner to their tour bus, but their new, pumped-up fans surrounded the bus and started rocking it, almost tipping the bus over as the band tried to escape the venue.

Again, there was trouble in the streets of Nottingham after the show as the audience left. It was almost as if Axl were transferring his own rage onto the people who had come to see him perform, and the more impressionable ones now carried some of his raging psyche with them in reverse catharsis.

After shows in Bristol and Manchester (where a fan gave Slash a ticket for the canceled Aerosmith/Guns tour, and the band played a shortened set for many empty seats), the tour wound up at the legendary Hammersmith Odeon, the West London theater where the Clash and other Brit rock icons made their bones. George Chin was working backstage: "I was hired by *BURRN!,* the Japanese rock magazine, to shoot a cover of Axl for the January 1988 issue. When I got to the theater, the Geffen publicity people warned me that Axl was in one of his moods. Then Axl showed up, looking kind of puffy and hungover, wearing an ugly black German army beret tilted to one side. He reminded me of an IRA type, without the dark glasses." George could tell that Axl felt horrible and didn't want to be there. He was mostly unresponsive and just glared at the camera. Chin knew that Axl was quick to anger and offense, that the pictures would be bad, and so gave up after one roll. "Later, when I showed him the pictures, he immediately agreed to a new session. He reappeared a bit later, in a better mood and with a revamped look. A large silver cross hung from his neck. He'd wrapped his head in his trademark bandanna, and after he warmed up a bit, he agreed to take off his black leather jacket and fold his arms to emphasize his unique tattoos. I knew that was the shot for the magazine cover. So did he, and he started using that pose when he had to be photographed—something he really grew to hate."

George Chin also shot a series of Axl and Izzy together backstage, and came away impressed with Izzy's sense of cool. "You could tell they were really good mates—very loyal to each other. Axl respected Izzy's opinions and ideas, especially musical ideas. You might hear the others slag Axl about this and that, but never Izzy—even if he was pissed off at him. I thought Izzy the epitome of a real cool dude."

The Hammersmith show, which came 200 seats short of a sellout, had to be a masterpiece because every important rock writer and disk jockey in England was there—and the band pulled it off. Slash played in a blue denim vest over his black leathers and took solo after looping solo, showing the bluesy side of GN'R to the Brits. Axl worked in a Mickey Mouse shirt with his lurid arm tattoos shining almost neon with perspiration. The band played everything they knew, and the audience wanted more, so they did a few covers, like Black Sabbath's "It's Alright." Slash sounded unusually bitter after

"Knockin' on Heaven's Door," when he dedicated the song to their dead friend. The showstopper in Hammersmith was "Rocket Queen" toward the end of the set. The already long song was extended to an atomic jam, halfway through, with Slash arched backward, soloing with one boot up on the stage monitor. Suddenly the drums shifted into a deafening cannonade, and the guitars shut down and the rest of the band disappeared during the drum solo. They let the tension build for a minute, then Izzy came out and jumped on the drum riser with a pair of sticks, beating out a counter rhythm. Then Duff appeared on the other side and started pounding away with sticks of his own. Then Axl materialized, playing Duff's bass guitar, and Slash again took center stage and brought down the house with a firestorm of Hendrixian fury. The cheering afterward was long and sincere. Some of the kids and media people who crowded onto the District Line's late trains after the concert were saying it was the greatest rock show they'd ever seen.

The reviewers now tried to outdo each other in describing the heavy-osity they had experienced. London *Star*: "The world's most outrageous band." *Kerrang!*: "This outrageous wrecking crew, with no pretentions and the rawest sound around, are the best new act heard in ages … the group who come closest to capturing the real essense of hard rock … arguably the most dangerous band in the world." *Sounds*: "A depraved Hollywood garage band, a toxic cocktail of their influences, the nearest thing to a street band from a city of freeways, and the worm at the bottom's their own." *Metal Hammer*: "Guns N' Roses stands alone as the finest hard rock band on the planet."

They stayed in London for another day or two. Geffen wanted them to do a quick tour of clubs and theaters in the Northeast that would last through the rest of October, so there was no time to return to California. The night after the Hammersmith show, Slash went to a party for Bob Dylan in Kensington. Someone later asked Slash if he'd had a chance to speak with Bob, whose "Knockin' on Heaven's Door" was becoming a staple of Guns' live show. Slash regretted that he hadn't had a word with Dylan, but the evening hadn't been a total waste, because he'd drunk five bottles of very good French wine.

*G*uns left London with a huge reputation to defend, having been called the most dangerous band in the world. They had to live up to this now. And Slash was, in his laconic way, thrilled. Later, speaking to English journalist Mick Wall, he explained: "For me, and I know for Izzy too, packing your gear and going over to England is the fuckin' epitome of what the rock and roll gig is all about." Wall thought this sounded a little strange, but Slash was adamant. "No, man, seriously; the British fans are so fucking *balls-out.* We feel that if you can be good in England, if you go there and are well received, it means you can play *anywhere else in the world,* you know what I mean?"

PISSING ON HAMMERJACKS

*O*ctober 1987. Guns N' Roses began a two-week tour of clubs in the college-heavy northeastern United States, beginning at Long Island's Sundance club in Bay Shore on October 16. After the next night's gig at a club at the Allentown (Pa.) airport, the band fetched up at Hammerjacks, the famous Baltimore club where all the hair metal bands played. Izzy Stradlin, normally Dr. Kool, made a negative connection with the place almost immediately.

Axl: "Izzy—he's not usually the one to cause any trouble at all, but he got totally annihilated at this place called Hammerjacks—the most fucked place I've ever played. First, they got about thirty [uniformed] security guys that look like West Hollywood sheriffs. And Izzy got in arguments with them early in the day about some bullshit they were giving our crew, who were just trying to do their jobs. So Izzy got drunk, and was really hating this club. Then, right before we played, and there are more hassles, and Izzy's fucking sick of everything, he walked into the club manager's office and just whipped it out and pissed all over the guy's desk—with the guy sitting there! It just blew their minds. Then we go on, and Izzy is so drunk we had to turn his guitar down, and when he realized what was going on, he unstrapped the guitar and threw it into the crowd."

It took more of Doug Goldstein's persuasive talents to retrieve the guitar and then avoid the Baltimore cops arresting Izzy for indecent exposure and urinary assault.

The next night, at a Philadelphia club called The Experiment, people in the crowd threw hypodermic needles at the band. The roadies and minders who picked them up said they smelled like heroin.

After gigs in Albany, New York, and suburban New Jersey, Guns returned to Manhattan, where they taped a segment for MTV's *Headbangers Ball,* the cable network's heavy metal programming that ran after midnight so as not to corrupt the children with satanic hard rock. Three months after the release of *Appetite,* Guns was still (barely) relegated to MTV's overnight metal ghetto, mostly because of the album's stall in the upper atmosphere of the *Billboard* chart, but also because radio wasn't playing the record and there were zero requests for the *Jungle* video. (The video for Guns' future second single, "Sweet Child o' Mine" was probably shot by Nigel Dick before the band went to Europe. *Sweet Child* featured grainy, fleeting black-and-white images of Erin Everly, cut into color tape of the band performing the song in an L.A. rehearsal hall.)

But Tom Zutaut and other Geffen personnel kept bugging MTV about Guns, so the network booked the band into its West Side taping studio on October 24, the night after Guns sold out shows at Manhattan's Ritz nightclub, the city's major rock venue of the eighties, located in an old Masonic auditorium on 34th Street. After miming to tapes of "Jungle" and "Sweet Child," the band was directed to create some mayhem to go with their "so-called bad boy image." They thought that this suggestion, coming from the obviously gay director, sounded a little smarmy, so the band and the crew proceeded to tear down the whole set.

Then *Appetite* started to climb the charts a little, reaching number 64 by November 1987. Only twelve radio stations in America were playing the record, but on half those stations, Guns was the most heavily requested band. Also a serious buzz began in the retail industry that this album was a sleeper, could sell tonnage if MTV really got on it. So Geffen Records picked up their option and started talking about the second album. But Slash was adamant that he couldn't write while on the road. Izzy, who wrote much of *Appetite,* was in no shape to think about writing another record. Axl Rose told the label that the band had a lot of songs and that the next real Guns N' Roses record would probably be a double album. So it was decided to release the four UZI Suicide tracks, plus a bunch of acoustic tracks the band would record in Los Angeles after they got off the road. This would be released the following year, and Guns N' Roses would record its "official" second album in 1989. "If they're still around," Geffen executives whispered to each other, some without much hope.

*O*n to gigs at the Chance in Poughkeepsie, New York; Lupo's Heartbreak Hotel in Providence, Rhode Island; the Paradise in Boston; and L'Amour in Brooklyn. (Guns was following the basic Northeast club itineraries that had worked well for the fledgling Police in 1977, U2 in 1980, and many other bands in breakout mode.) The band was fried, having had only two days off in two weeks, right after Europe. They checked into the dowdy but inexpensive Gramercy Park Hotel on 23rd Street.

There was some mayhem the day after the band checked in. West Arkeen was traveling with Guns, and learned that his father had died of a heart attack. A message had been left for Arkeen at the hotel, but the clerk at the Gramercy Park's front desk didn't give it to him. Axl: "So West went down and yelled at the guy, and the guy jumped over the counter and hit him. Then two other guys jumped West and worked him over. So he came upstairs and got me, and I went down and was confronted by two big guys holding blackjacks. So I grabbed this big metal sign and we had a little showdown." An enraged Axl held his ground, told the hotel goons to back off, and they did. The cops arrived and calmed things down without any arrests.

On October 30, the band rehearsed an acoustic set (without Axl) at CBGB's Record Canteen, the punk club's record shop, located a few doors down on the Bowery, Manhattan's skid row. The club, decorated for Halloween, had a tiny stage and could squeeze in about a hundred kids if the fire marshal wasn't around. That night Axl showed up with West Arkeen and an entourage that included his girlfriend, Erin Everly, tiny and gorgeous in long curly hair and black jeans. A video crew taped the band's showcase performance and subsequent press conference.

When the band came out to scattered applause from the young and mostly girly audience, they struggled to get seated in an acoustic configuration, with various crew and friends of the band seated behind them. Steven played tambourine in the absence of his drum kit. When they were almost set, Axl came out and sat down, wearing a black Bauhaus shirt, his long red hair under his pink bandanna, aviator shades covering most of his face. "This mike is a piece of shit," he drawled. The girls kept calling to Slash, resplendent in his denim-over-leather garb, Metallica shirt, black top hat. Girls: "Slash! Slash! Slashy, baby!"

Slash: "What? What? Shut up!"

Duff chugs beer. Then he counts off the acoustic version of "You're Crazy," played as a folk-rock ballad while Axl sways reptile-like in his chair. "That's the way it was written," he tells the girls after the song ends. Then he tells them the band is going to release an EP of some of the acoustic songs they were playing for them "in about a year," and that the next song is going to be on that record. Then Guns lurches into "One in a Million," which, Axl mentions, the band has played only once before in public. They chug the angry, racist, homophobic, immigrant-hating verses along, with musical director Duff using body language and eye contact to signal a slower tempo as they reach the chorus. The "police and niggers" line draws silence from the kids, who haven't heard this before, but the lines about faggots and "some fucking disease" elicits embarrassed laughter. Another unfamilar song, "Used to Love Her," introduced by Axl as "not really a song, but kind of the way you feel sometime," draws excited female giggles when Axl sings about how he used to love her, but he had to kill her. Meanwhile, on the landing above the stage, Erin Everly dances her own serpentine choreography. When the cameras pan up to her, she stops and moves out of sight.

There's a little break before "Patience." Slash swigs deep from a bottle of Jack Daniel's. Axl checks recently reworked lyrics from a sheet of paper. Guns played this almost every night in Europe, so the song is right and tight. The guitars improvise a little coda that could have been on *Led Zeppelin III,* an acoustic brew from the misty mountains of ancient Wales.

This is followed by a thrilling version of "Mr. Brownstone," with Axl rising out of his seat in restrained abandon, and his girlfriend writhing behind the band in her own sultry majesty. Then Axl stood up for the last song, "Move to the City," and performed his trademark cobra dance as his band burned, quietly but forcefully, in full but contained sonic fury.

The show over, the band gets up amid a clatter of instruments bumping against folding metal chairs and microphones. The girls shout to Slash that he promised them some of his newly customized guitar picks, and he grins broadly and gives them the finger. "Yes," they yell. "Do *that* to us." He just laughs, and joins his bandmates at a table down in the record store, where they start to sign albums and, blinded by TV lights, offer comments on various topics.

Asked to sign a copy of the UZI Suicide album, Axl nudges Slash. "This picture of us . . . I was sober that day, but I look . . . *annihilated.* It comes from hanging out with Barbi [Von Greif]." She had done his hair and makeup for Richard Lue's 1986 back cover photo (which many fans feel is *the* classic image of Guns N' Roses). "No one else has that mentality, of understanding the connection between drugs and rock and roll. She's so smart. She knows how to do it."

Since MTV is filming this, Axl drops a broad hint. "What I *really* want is to open for U2."

Asked about the unfamiliar acoustic songs they'd just performed, Axl answered: "Well, other bands like us are scared to venture into anything but hard rock. They're afraid to be . . . wimpy. But us, we'll do anything we want to."

Slash was asked about how they got together. "They were the only other people I wanted to form a band with," he claimed, ostentatiously chugging from a bottle of Jack.

Axl: "We're like a family. We believe in each other. It's almost like a family thing."

The next question was about Tipper Gore's campaign against obscenity in rock music. Izzy mumbled about it being about somebody's [Al Gore's] wife.

AXL: "I don't care about the PMRC."
SLASH: "The more stickers they put on the records, the more records we sell."
AXL: "It's the classic teenage rebellion thing."

For the next month, November 1987, Guns would be opening for Mötley Crüe, and they were asked about this. Slash explained that label politics were involved. "We were supposed to start this tour, but the label thought [David Coverdale's] Whitesnake would be cooler. But then Whitesnake got big and started to headline, so now it's our turn.

"They [Crüe] like us, and we like them. They're rolling out the red carpet for us—more lights than usual for an opening act, more [stage] monitors. They're really helping us with this."

Someone asked about Guns' general philosophy. Axl and Slash were sitting next to each other. Slash was gulping down serious glugs of Jack.

Slash: "This thing is legit. It's not pretentious. It's not aimed at Top Ten radio. It comes from the heart of it."

Axl: "We care enough about each other to keep each other in line. [He nudges Slash.] Like I saved this guy's life a couple of times already this week." Axl took a drag of his cigarette and smiled. Slash looked sheepish and turned away slightly, obviously embarrassed at having been dissed for turning blue in their hotel two nights earlier.

Asked about their recording plans, Axl replied: "We've told Geffen that we'll record a double album when we're done touring. We're already writing stuff. We've got about forty songs we believe in."

After a digression about his tattoos ("I wanted to show it [his rose tattoo] to [Thin Lizzy's] Phil Linnott, but he died on me"), Axl complained bitterly about their recent touring conditions with the Cult: "We're renting the whole floor of the hotel. We're playing a big show—ten thousand people—and they won't let us into the [hotel] restaurant because of the dress code. Some guy making eight dollars an hour, telling us to get lost..."

Axl was asked to say something about himself. He replied: "I'm like, fucking schizo! But, you know," he laughed, "I can turn it on and off."

And in the blink of an eye he was gone.

WHERE'S MY VODKA?

*N*ovember 1987. Guns N' Roses open for Mötley Crüe at the Municipal Auditorium in Mobile, Alabama, beginning a tour of the American South with the most popular of the L.A. glam bands at the zenith of their career—the *Girls Girls Girls* Tour. Like with the Cult, Guns was opening for a band that would never get any bigger than this, a band Guns would soon consign to the compost pile of rock history. Meanwhile, at least at the beginning, the Crüe tour was a gas. Relations between the Sunset Strip musicians and veteran road crews were friendly. There was tons of brown Persian heroin available, for those with a taste for it. Slash, Steven, and Crüe bassist Nikki Sixx formed a little clique that raised hell in the hotel bars after the shows, and then retreated to forbidden pleasures in party suites upstairs. Some of these scenes got so scary that Mötley Crüe's management warned Slash to his face that his band would be fired from the tour if Nikki Sixx was supplied with any more narcotics from Guns' mobile pharmacy.

Mötley Crüe's singer, Vince Neil, later described Axl Rose (improbably) as "a shy, humble guy who was a lot of fun to be with," and said that Axl asked him for advice about his throat, which tended to close like a vise after an hour of screaming his lungs out. Axl was now having fairly serious trouble breathing during shows, and he began to resort to oxygen breaks in the dressing room during Slash's long guitar solos, which got extended for this purpose.

The tour moved through the mild weather of the South in November—the Cajun Dome in Louisiana; Lake Front Arena in New Orleans; Mississippi Coliseum in Jackson; North Carolina; Savannah, Georgia; South Carolina; and back to Atlanta, where Axl was arrested onstage on November 20.

The trouble started with a sadistic security guard at the venue, the Atlanta Omni, who hassled Axl as he was walking in the back door that afternoon for the band's sound check. That evening, as the band was about to go on, Axl and the guard got into it again, curses were exchanged, and Axl sucker-punched the guy in the face. Ten minutes later, during "Mr. Brownstone," Atlanta police officers stormed the stage and hauled Axl away.

It was probably the first onstage arrest of a rock star since the legendary days of Jim Morrison—twenty years earlier.

Road manager Doug Goldstein had to think quickly. Guns was contracted to play for forty-five minutes or the band didn't get paid. He asked roadie Big Ron (or, as Slash called him, King Kong Ron) to go onstage and sing, and Ron did what he was told. They played "Communication Breakdown" and "Honky Tonk Women," the only songs the roadie knew. While the cops interrogated Axl backstage, Slash played long, doodling guitar solos. Steven Adler played the longest drum solo since John Bonham died. Guns' show sucked, but the sparse crowd had come to see Mötley Crüe anyway. According to court records, Axl later pleaded guilty (in absentia) to assault charges, and paid a small fine.

*O*n November 24 and 25, the tour played two shows at the Civic Center in Lakeland, Florida. MTV, late to play Guns but now infected by the industrywide buzz about the band's incendiary live shows, sent a crew to Lakeland in another attempt to do something with Guns, since the channel had deemed the CBGB tapes too crude to put on the air.

Appetite was now a semirespectable number 61 (and climbing) on the *Billboard* Hot Hundred album chart and MTV now wanted the band. The only problem was that Guns N' Roses was completely fried after a full month on tour—something Guns hadn't done before—and the band was in no physical condition to be profiled on MTV. Slash and Steven (and Nikki Sixx) were in a heroin club together. Izzy was only just coping. Duff McKagan was, daily, guzzling a gallon of Russian vodka. Only Axl Rose wasn't using smack or drinking to blackout.

He liked cocaine, but it hadn't turned him into an idiot, mostly because he had to protect his throat and didn't do that much.

Guns N' Roses was a young guitar band, in its first year on the road, and so it wasn't real pretty backstage. Or apparently onstage either, since the band wouldn't let MTV tape their Lakeland shows. Indeed, the MTV video crew was kept away from the band until the last possible moment, just before the second show on November 25. Tape is rolling, and we see Steven at a set of practice drums wearing a hat with two beer cans on either side, from which tubes lead down to his mouth. Duff McKagan, visibly drunk, staggers in and bawls, *"Where's my vodka?"* He looks at the camera and, stupidly, says, "Fuck!" Pan over to Slash, in full Slash regalia. "Have a drink," he offers, slurring. Axl, rocking his pink bandanna, turns up in the dressing room at the last minute and the group takes the stage. They let the video crew film only a few minutes of "It's So Easy," Duff singing backup with Axl on the chorus.

During Guns' set, MTV interviews Doug Goldstein: "... about two hours' sleep a night ... the craziest guys I ever worked for ... they keep me hopping all the time ... gotta make sure I have enough alcohol ... doesn't matter if its eight A.M., or whenever ..."

The dreaded band interview is filmed in the meet-and-greet lounge after the show. Mötley Crüe can be heard pounding away dimly in the background. Guns are trashed, sprawled in telegenic disarray on the couch, except for Axl, who sits upright, sober and coherent, and noticeably somewhat apart from the wasted rabble of his band.

Wearily, Axl tries to help: "Tom Zutaut signed Crüe, Tesla, Dokken ... got us the money we needed and the freedom we wanted ... also was a helping hand in making the record.... The other labels didn't seem to have a clue." Asked about "Welcome to the Jungle," he tells the story of being lost in New York City on his first visit there, and of the old man who told him that he was in the jungle and that he was going to die. "True story," Axl concluded.

Slash tries to comment on this, but he seems tired, uses *fucking* as an adjective every third word, and finally laughs at his own befuddled crudeness.

Izzy [helpfully]: "Hey, it's just street language . . . how we talk."

Duff [schwacked]: "They're real-life stories, these fuckin' songs."

Slash [trying]: "The band . . . and what we fu—, what we believe in, is more important than a . . . a . . . a fuckin' sticker, on an album."

Axl winds up the discussion about profanity: "Look, we just don't give a fuck. The next album might not have any [cursing], just because we didn't write it that way."

*S*omeone at MTV cut this footage into a half-hour segment called "A Night in the Jungle." When it was screened for the channel's executives, the band was deemed too obscenely wasted to be shown in prime time. According to MTV's (chaotic) archives, the segment was shown a year later, at three in the morning, and then filed away and forgotten.

*A*fter a few more stops in Florida, Mötley Crüe's tour wound up its southern leg and both bands returned to Los Angeles. Guns was basically homeless, so their management installed them in the Franklin Plaza Hotel, a favorite Hollywood hideaway for vagrant glam metal bands. In a few days, Guns was going back out on tour, opening shows for Alice Cooper for the rest of 1987.

Slash and Nikki Sixx had gotten to be good pals during the *Girls* tour, road warriors who shared their dope and liked to go out and party afterward. One night in early December, Nikki set out for the evening in a silver stretch limo, with presents for Slash: an antique beaver fur top hat (which he'd paid a *lot* of money for) and a limited edition "presentation" gallon jug of Jack Daniel's whiskey. He stopped at a dope dealer's place—the guy was annoyed by the cop-magnet limo idling out front—and picked up a few bags of heroin after sampling the product. This caused Sixx to throw up in the limo, blowing colorful chunks of puke all over the beaver hat, which he still gamely presented to a revolted Slash, along with the gallon of Jack. Certain members of Megadeth were also in residence at the Franklin Plaza, which made for a party.

According to Nikki, they all did drugs until their minds went blank. Then they piled into the foul-smelling limo and went to the Cathouse, where they drank deeply and held court, until it was time for the next fix. They jumped back into the limo, trailed by carloads of excited teenage Crüe fans from the Valley, and ended up in Slash's room at the Franklin Plaza. The earlier dope dealer was waiting for them, newly supplied with what he described as "especially sweet" Persian brown. Nikki was too far gone to inject himself, so he asked the dealer to do it. As Slash watched, the dealer tied off Nikki's arm with rubbing tubing and shot the Persian smack into a vein. As the strong heroin began to course through his bloodstream, Nikki turned blue and fell out of his chair.

"Oh no," Slash murmured. "Not *again.*" Slash's girlfriend dialed 911 while Steven Adler dragged Nikki Sixx's azure corpse into Slash's shower and turned on the cold water.

The ambulance arrived a few minutes later. They found Nikki dead on the floor of Slash's bathroom. His heart had just stopped, and some roadie-looking guys were trying CPR and yelling, "We're losing him!" They carried Nikki into the ambulance, past his horrified, crying young fans, and plunged two adrenaline needles directly into his heart. This saved his life.

Slash was profoundly shocked to see this happen again, but it was also great material. The rest of Mötley Crüe's tour was cut short. Slash dined out on Sixx's gruesome OD for months, and he didn't let it stop him from nursing a bad habit of his own for at least another two years.

THE DECLINE OF WESTERN CIVILIZATION

$\mathcal{D}$ecember 1987. Two months of Guns on the road, playing the shit out of their album, push *Appetite* to number 59 when sales surpass 200,000 units. Geffen's promo people maintain that the band's fetid reputation as neobarbarian rapists and pillagers has actually helped sell records. Tom Zutaut tells a skeptical Geffen staff meeting that he predicts *Appetite* will go AOR Top Ten, and that Guns N' Roses will be headlining within six months. "*If* they can get on MTV," someone temporizes. "*If* they're still alive in six months," whispers another.

Music Connection runs a second Guns interview early in December, the hatchets between Guns and the mag having been buried. (The writer of *MC*'s first, controversial band profile left town in the wake of the article.) Axl phones his part of the interview from New York. Chatty and honest, he confirms a rumor that Guns might tour with Aerosmith in 1988. He says that some reviewers' comparisons of Guns to Aerosmith and Led Zeppelin are flattering, but not the end of the world. "Lately, we listen to Metallica all the time. What is cool is that those guys listen to us all the time. Right before we went out on tour, I was in Chicago and Lars [Ulrich, Metallica's drummer] was trying to reach me, and my girlfriend gave him the numbers of the rest of the band, and they all went out and got wasted together—without me." (One can only speculate how Erin was made to suffer for this.) "Where Metallica is amazing is the realness, the sincerity. A lot of their stuff is more dark, getting out their anger, and we do that in our way too."

Asked if Metallica-style speed metal could influence Guns' next record, Axl's answer was interesting about the internal workings of his band. "Oh. Well, before Slash really knew who Metallica was, we had some very heavy material backlogged. But we didn't put it on the record because Slash and I didn't think [our] band had the ability to play that material—at least at that time. Not back then, no. Like, Izzy has his own style of guitar playing, and we didn't want to tell him, 'Oh, you can't play this, you're not in the band.' Because what he was playing worked perfect for other songs. So we just decided to take the time and progress on our own. So now everybody writes. We write songs we'd never record. Wait'll you hear this new one we've got, 'Cornshucker.' We're going to come back to L.A. and put some more stuff down, because we're going to put out an acoustic EP."

On record reviews: "I was just reading a [critic] Robert Christgau review on Faster Pussycat [in *The Village Voice*], but it wasn't about how great Faster Pussycat is. It's about how stupid Guns N' Roses is; how we should just fuckin' shoot ourselves. People like that . . . don't take the time to get into it. I think there's a lot in our record to explore—different little parts in every song. They *could* hear this, if only they'd just do their job and *listen* to the fuckin' record. I mean, I'm trying to do *my* job—as hard as I can. I want the writers to do theirs too."

Axl was asked about Guns' next album (which wouldn't come out for another four years). He replied that there would be some serious ballads next time, "because we have eight written, and we believe in all of 'em. I like to write real emotionally. I can dig down way deep inside myself." He mentioned "November Rain" as being ten minutes of acoustic guitars, and perhaps an orchestra, with himself playing piano. Axl insisted that he would quit music altogether if "November Rain" wasn't eventually recorded the way he wanted it. He also mentioned "Don't Cry" and "Patience."

At the end of the interview, Axl said he was sick of L.A. and wanted to move to New York. "I want to explore things again," he said—wistfully.

*A*fter speaking with Axl on the phone, writer Katherine Turman troops over to Geffen and meets the rest of the band. She finds them sprawled in a conference room overlooking Sunset Boulevard, bathed in bright early winter light. Between long pulls from a bottle of Jack Daniel's, Slash tries to get money off her, ostensibly for Mexican beer, but she's been warned about this gambit, and says she's broke. Her report: "Slash is cunning, street-smart, manipulative, and funny.... Bassist Duff 'Rose' McKagan is helpful and courteous; drummer Steve Adler is goofy and sweet; guitarist Izzy Stradlin seems preoccupied, but occasionally he chimes in intelligently." The interview meanders drunkenly:

INTERVIEWER: "How are English audiences different?"
SLASH: "Not to put these bands down, but Poison and Ratt and a lot of other L.A. bands do not go over well there. They told us this. So it was nice to be from L.A. and be totally accepted. We had to do three encores at Hammersmith last month."

The band is asked if Axl always introduces "Mr. Brownstone" with his rap about not killing yourself with drugs, while not pretending to be "antidrug" either.

SLASH: "In one form or another. He really just says, 'Think for your-self.' He tries to get that across, because he fuckin' believes it, and I only fuckin' imagine how many fuckin' punk kids don't really understand the words and think it fucking advocated drug use."

ADLER: "At our first gig in the UK, a couple rigs came flying onstage."

DUFF: "Oh, man!"

SLASH: "But there was this one English girl who thought the song was about groupies!" [They began to tease Slash about fucking her.]

INTERVIEWER: "Do you feel some responsibility toward your audi-ence?"

SLASH: "No. We're just telling them, 'It's not our fault.' We're not gonna fuckin' preach. You have to understand what the lyrics say, if you're gonna take them seriously."

INTERVIEWER: "What about . . . your whole lifestyle?"

SLASH: "That's another interview."

INTERVIEWER: "As kids, didn't you look up to bands and say, 'I wanna be just like that'?"

GN'R: "Yes!"

SLASH: "Everyone wants to get on our cases because we're real honest and out in the open [about drug use], while everyone else is get-ting into MADD [Mothers Against Drunk Driving] and the PMRC, and anti-this and anti-that, and you can't fuck without a rubber. And, *we're not like that.* We're fuckin' . . . *out in the open!* It's just like a bad kid in school—the more they tell you not to, the more you're going to do it. But look—we don't tell anyone to do anything, or to take us too seriously, because even we don't take ourselves that seriously."

*I*n those days Slash had a girlfriend, not a groupie, but a real friend: someone he counted on. When he was in Los Angeles, on the loose between tours, he always carried her name and phone number on a piece of paper in his pocket. On several occasions, she received late-night calls from concerned people who had found Slash—passed out, sometimes in the gutter, once shoeless, having been rolled and robbed by whomever he was last drinking with at the Cathouse or the Rainbow. Slash was twenty-two years old.

There was beginning to be ugly talk about Axl and Erin and serial abuse. The year before, Erin's best friend walked in on Axl beating Erin, and she called the police. When the deputies arrived, Axl hid behind the door and Erin told them it was a false alarm. Then the couple fought at a crowded barbecue at a house in the Hollywood Hills. "He was beating her," a witness said, "and pulling her hair. He was like a rabid dog." Erin told her friends she loved Axl but was frightened of him. There were also people who felt that she provoked Axl, and that Erin could give as good as she got. The police were called to the couple's home so many times that one of them, Mike Ascolese, received an album credit on *Appetite*.

Guns N' Roses played two final shows with Mötley Crüe in Texas, early in December 1987. (Slash trashed his hotel room in Dallas with such violence that the hotel called the police. The band had to run away, without checking out, to avoid arrest for aggravated vandalism.) They were desperately hoping to pick up another tour (Slash: "No one wanted to go home") but nothing was quite working out. David Lee Roth, who'd left Van Halen and was touring on his own, already had an opening act. Guns almost went out with AC/DC; the two bands loved each other, but the money AC/DC was offering amounted to disrespect. Then the band flew to San Francisco to appear, briefly, in a new Clint Eastwood movie, *The Dead Pool*. In the annals of eighties pop culture, almost nothing is stranger than the confluence of Guns N' Roses and Dirty Harry Callaghan.

*D*irty Harry was Eastwood's signature character as an actor over the course of five films between 1971 and 1988: a San Francisco homicide detective who doubled as a vigilante to rid his city of scumbags and the lowest of human vermin. Dirty Harry's trademark weapon was the long-barreled .44 Magnum revolver on which Slash had based the Guns N' Roses logo two years earlier. And this was not lost on Clint Eastwood's son Kyle, who lived in L.A. and was a fan of Guns N' Roses. So when the script for the final movie in the Dirty Harry series called for a sleazoid punk band, Kyle Eastwood convinced his dad to cast the obviously up-and-coming Guns in the film. They also made a deal with Geffen to use "Welcome to the Jungle" as a recurring theme in the movie.

The band and its management were not shown the script and were kept in the dark about the movie's plot. (They would regret this later.) All they knew was that they were portraying the band of a dead rock star, whose murder Dirty Harry was trying to solve. Guns appeared in only two scenes, including the rock star's funeral. Slash's top hat stands out, seen from afar, but the band had no lines to speak. The director told them just to stand there, look cool, and never look at the camera.

*A*fter two days, Guns joined the Alice Cooper tour for the rest of December. Axl missed the first show in Santa Barbara, and the band almost got fired. But the rest of the tour went smoothly through the Midwest—some of Axl's family came to the Chicago show—and then back to southern California. Cooper's management were floored by the amount of hard-core, X-rated partying in Guns' dressing room, and rumors about them began to fly around the U.S. rock circuit like bats at sunset. Alice, himself an alcoholic and just recovering from a freebase habit, told his manager that, before the tour ended, he thought one of Guns would end up in the coffin Alice was using as a prop in his decades-old rock horror show.

But actually Guns, embarrassed by their early no-show, was on what passed for its best behavior. "They behaved like complete professionals," one Cooper associate said. "Not one trashed hotel room." This tour finished with four nights in Pasadena, California. Steven Adler missed some of these when he injured his hand after reportedly punching a streetlight in a rage at something. (The streetlight turned into a "bar fight" when Geffen's spin doctors translated it into a press statement.) Steven Adler was replaced for a few shows by Fred Coury (from Cinderella). With a different, energized drummer, Guns N' Roses was so hot that many fans left after its show, and Alice Cooper found himself playing to many empty seats. (Around this time, Guns went into the studio and backed Alice singing his warhorse "Under My Wheels," later used in the sound track for the lurid rock documentary *The Decline of Western Civilization: The Metal Years.*)

Guns finished 1987 with a New Year's Eve gig at Glamour, a tacky new club in West Hollywood. Later, after midnight, Axl and Erin ended up at another club, the Central, where he sang "Honky Tonk Women" with the house band at dawn.

*I*t had been a fateful, even triumphant year for Guns N' Roses, but one marred by death and overdoses. The real party hadn't even started yet. At that point, at the dawn of 1988, nobody could possibly envision just how big this band was going to get.

Except for W. Axl Rose. He later claimed that he'd known it all along.

"It was the right band at the right time in the right place," Slash said later. "It just happened to hit the youth of America, a certain way. I had no expectations for it to become such a global event."

Chapter Eight

MONSTERS OF ROCK

"We smell the fear."
—Slash, 1988

GLOBAL EVENT

January 1988. It was the beginning of the year when Guns N' Roses would take over what remained of the rock music movement. Prodded by management whose philosophy was to push the band to make some serious money before one (or more) of them died, Guns worked so hard that year that it did almost kill them. Some people who were close to Guns say that the band never really recovered from the extreme efforts at self-medication undertaken in 1988 to extend themselves and their protean energies closer to their ever-explosive young audience.

The irony was that Guns' youthful appetites ran counter to the prevailing winds of late-eighties hard rock and heavy metal culture. Inspired by Aerosmith's seemingly miraculous recovery from decades of addictions, other bands took note. Most of Mötley Crüe entered rehab in January. *Circus* magazine quoted Great White's singer, Jack Russell, as typical of some rock veterans' new attitudes: "I realized that I could go out and do drugs every day of my life, and I could die. Or, I could go out and play rock-and-roll music, and make myself and other people happy."

No one in Guns N' Roses felt this way.

* * *

On January 5, Guns opened for Great White, their manager's other act, at the Santa Monica Civic Center. Two days later they went into the studio with producer Mike Clink and recorded (at least) five acoustic numbers for an EP that Geffen wanted to release as a stopgap between *Appetite for Destruction,* now rapidly climbing the rock charts, and the next "official" Guns N' Roses album, which Axl was already saying wouldn't be ready for another two years. (Actually it was more like three years.)

These early 1988 acoustic sessions produced some of Guns' most popular, and most controversial, songs. Most dated from the months before and during the 1986 sessions for *Appetite.* "Patience" was a sweet little ballad written by Izzy Stradlin well before many of the *Appetite* songs. "Used to Love Her," by Izzy and Slash, was the jokey ditty about killing an annoying girlfriend, which Guns had played a few times in public. "You're Crazy" had been written (mostly by Axl) in the spring of 1986, just after the band had signed with Geffen. The 1988 version tried to capture the original, organic feel of the acoustic guitar song that had mutated into a viciously hard rock number during the *Appetite* sessions.

"One in a Million" was Axl's diatribe against hustlers, homosexuals, and immigrants that he had written, mostly as a joke, while watching a TV tirade by Pentecostal comedian Sam Kinison in 1985. The original idea for the song was supposed to be comedic, but in the studio Axl changed the tone from a smirk to a snarl that italicized his politically incorrect racial and social views. His use of the taboo word *niggers* was immediately troubling to Slash (whose mother was black) and to Geffen Records; but Axl stuck to his guns, and the song would take on a (negative) life of its own when *GN'R Lies* was released later in 1988.

This short, hours-long recording session, later described by the band as drunken, also included "Cornshucker," a dirty, less-than-magic rock song that was never released by the band. These tracks would be worked on sporadically for the next eleven months before being released at the end of 1988.

* * *

On January 14, Duff's pickup band, Drunk Fux, was revived for a gig at Coconut Teaszer in Hollywood. The Fux were most of Guns without Axl, along with West Arkeen and writer Del James, with whom Duff shared an apartment in Hollywood. They played the usual punk rock Drunk Fux stuff and some of Guns' recent acoustic material—"You're Crazy" and "Used to Love Her"—which made people laugh. Duff sang lead on punk gems like the Misfits' "Attitude." A week later, Guns N' Roses played a similar set at the Cathouse on Sunset, causing serious Strip gridlock as kids who were too young to get in—like Axl five years earlier—impeded traffic on the busy boulevard outside the club.

Ten days later, Guns played a post-midnight set at Limelight, a desanctified church turned nightclub (and dope bazaar) on Manhattan's West Side. On February 2, the band performed for a sold-out crowd at the Ritz on 34th Street. This gig was filmed by MTV.

It was a freezing night in New York. The show had sold out in minutes, and the icy sidewalks were thick with people trying to get in—somehow. Inside the old Masonic theater, both floor and balcony were packed. Guns' big new logo banner hung impressively behind the drum riser. Backstage, Slash was furious about some problem and told Doug Goldstein that he wasn't going on. But Goldstein made something happen, and there was a shout when the lights went down and some top-hatted tuning chords blasted out of the speakers.

"Please welcome L.A.'s hottest band—GUNS AND ROSES!!"

The big crowd surged forward as Guns stormed into "It's So Easy." Axl was snarling, slapping hands with those crushed against the stage. He had been asked to play down the "so fuckin' easy" line so MTV wouldn't have to repeatedly bleep the opening number, but he ignored this in favor of connecting with the kids in front of him. Axl was in a golden snakeskin jacket and leather trousers, skintight. Izzy wore a Byronic white shirt and black vest, a cloth cap over his eyes. Duff rocked a black leather suit. Slash wore his button-decorated denim vest over leathers. Steven was a flouncing mop of blond curls under the spotlight, all smiles as usual. "Thank you," Axl said after "Easy" crashed to a halt. "They're filming tonight for MTV. Are you gonna help me rip the roof off this place tonight?"

RRRRAAAAAAAAAHHHHHH!

Steven began some Bo Diddley thunder as Mister Brownstone reared his ugly head. Izzy sang the chorus with Axl, and Saul Hudson bent way back and tore off a sirenlike guitar solo. He finished the song with his head resting on Axl's shoulder, indicating that any backstage problems might have been forgiven.

Now Axl, looking wide-eyed, even a little manic, spoke to the audiences: the one in front of him and the one who would be watching later on cable TV (if they didn't cuss too much).

"I want to dedicate this next song . . . to the people who hold you back. To the people who tell you how to live. To the people who tell you how to dress. To the people that tell you how to talk. To the people who tell you what you can say, and what you can't say . . . *I PERSONALLY DON'T NEED THAT! I DON'T NEED THAT SHIT IN MY LIFE!"*

Working himself up now, banshee-voiced and wild-eyed, Axl spat out the rest of his artistic manifesto:

"These people *bring me down.* These people, they make me feel like someone is . . . *OUT TA GET ME!"*

The band swung into the tune. Axl grabbed a water bottle off the drum riser, flushed out his mouth, and went into a high-kick routine that got an intense mosh pit going in front of the crowd. He deployed his serpent strut, inflaming the crowd even more. Duff sang on the "they can't touch me" part. As the band built its show, the atmosphere became thick with human sweat and pungent pot smoke.

It was also getting hot, and the band's jackets came off, revealing various T-shirts, carefully chosen for coolness. During Slash's crazy carousel of a guitar figure introducing "Sweet Child o' Mine," someone threw a condom onstage. Axl opened the foil with his teeth and blew the thing up. Then he let it fly and launched himself into a manic whirlpool, flouncing around the stage, arms akimbo, legs stomping to the music. He performed "where do we go now?" on his knees, as if in prayer, drawing the crowd's energy into him like the former Pentecostal preacher he had once been. It was a brilliant, wickedly intense performance, and the audience cheered for a full minute.

Axl's intro to "My Michelle":

"This is for a girlfriend of mine, and she gets hassled a lot because no one really believes it's about her. And now she's out there signing autographs, if you can understand *that* one.... And this is for people that... if you have something that fills your life, fills your space, but deep down inside you know it ain't right... don't *ever* give up hope. There's something out there, and all you have to do is just—hold on and believe.... This is a song called 'My Michelle.'"

The song's doomy intro evolved into another heaving cauldron of humanity as Axl danced with his mike stand held high over his head. This caused the temperature onstage to rise to almost 85 degrees, and all the band (except cool Izzy) took off their shirts. They were all soaked in sweat, and they toweled off while Axl introduced the next song:

"About five or six years ago, I hitchhiked here [New York] and ended up stuck out in the middle of nowhere.... We climbed up out of the freeway, and this little old black man comes up to me and my friend; we're wearing backpacks, with about ten bucks between us, and he goes: [shrieks] '*You know where you are?* [crowd cheers] You're in the *jungle*, baby! [louder cheering] You gonna *DIE!*'

"That's a true story," Axl mentioned, as Slash swaggered into a da-da-da/da-da-da guitar stutter. "That ain't no lie, so... *WELCOME TO THE JUNGLE, RITZ!*"

What followed was a hypersonic, throbbing reminder that the streets weren't safe anyplace, that the law of the jungle will bring you to your knees, and that Guns was the new Godzilla of Rock.

"Knockin' on Heaven's Door" was next, and its sheer boredom provoked an audience melt-away to bar and toilets. After a real loose sing-along (Axl: "We're the sloppiest band in the world"), Axl introduced the band. Duff was called the King of Beers. Axl said he'd known Izzy for thirteen years. And the drummer was Steven "Popcorn" Adler. "And last, but definitely not least... In a world that he did not create... but he will go through it as if it was of his own making... He's half-man, half-beast... I'm not sure what it is, but—*whatever* it is—it is *weird*, and it's *pissed off*, and it calls itself—*Slash!*"

Big cheer. Slash—bare-chested, lighting a fag—strolled to the mike as Axl disappeared. "All right... Shut up. I'm gonna intro this song, and not say anything offensive so we can get on TV. This song is *not* about drinking, or drug addiction, or anything like that. This song is about a walk in the park—and it's called 'Nightrain.'"

Axl came back in a black coat over a Thin Lizzy T-shirt, wearing a black leather cap. Dancing with a renewed energy that might have owed its source to the hill country of Peru, he high-kicked like a Radio City Rockette during Slash's bluesy guitar solo. Then they went right into the last song of their regular set, "Paradise City," and fans started trying to get onstage. During the guitar solo, there was a scuffle just under the stage and Axl got a crazed look on his face and dived right in. Doug Goldstein and roadie "King Kong Ron" went in after him while Slash kept shredding and finally got their singer back on the stage, where Axl finished "Paradise City" with renewed intensity, the whole place roaring out "Take me home."

The encore was "Rocket Queen," but Axl abandoned the stage after the first verse, leaving the band to jam the first half of the song without him. Then he came back out, lit a cig from the one dangling from Slash's lips, and began his cosmic cobra slither, dancing furiously alongside Slash's clanky riffing during the second-section solo. But before the end of the song, Axl raged out at something he didn't like on the side of the stage. He fired his mike at the annoyance and stormed offstage in the other direction. Guns N' Roses finished "Rocket Queen" without him, then walked off to prolonged cheers and shouting.

LITHIUM DREAMS

*F*ebruary 1988. Guns began their first tour as headliners at the Crest Theater in Sacramento on February 4, and things were looking good for the band. "Welcome to the Jungle" was on the radio a lot, and *Appetite* was climbing the chart. Old-school L.A. punk band T.S.O.L. was opening a series of shows that would play around California and Arizona. (T.S.O.L. was coy about its name, which supposedly stood for "the sound of liberation.") British post-punkers Zodiac Mindwarp were occasional "Special Guests" on some shows.

Guns was playing well, but people were starting to worry about Axl Rose, who seemed wiggier than usual. He and Erin Everly were sweet together when they appeared in public, like backstage at the Celebrity Theater in Anaheim, where Guns was playing, but then they fought terribly at Axl's apartment at 3rd and Sycamore. (The décor featured a giant movie display of Arnold Schwarzenegger.) It may also have been around this time that Axl learned from a family friend that his real father, William Rose, was probably dead.

Then Axl missed the first show in Phoenix, Arizona, where Guns was scheduled for two concerts on February 12 and 13, 1988. Axl didn't show up. For a while it seemed like he'd disappeared. Frantic phone calls were unreturned. Erin said she didn't know where he was. Hoping he was just late, opening band T.S.O.L. went on and played its forty-five-minute set, then an hour of Led Zeppelin classics until Axl finally called and said he wasn't going to make it. (There was a story that he told Doug Goldstein he was quitting the band, but Doug kept it from the others because they were so upset.)

The Phoenix shows were canceled and the band went into a downward spiral. They knew that a no-show was immediately reported to the concert industry, and their future bookings would suffer as a result. They talked about firing Axl. Duff drank a gallon of vodka that night. Slash went berserk. Later he said it was the lowest he ever went, "a fucking little episode in Phoenix where I flipped out on coke, destroyed a hotel room, and was all bloody, running around the hotel naked and shit." Slash was so scary that the crew couldn't control him. The hotel called the cops, who arrived with paramedics. When the hotel staff saw what Slash had done to his room, and all the blood in his bathroom, "some people wanted to press charges, but fortunately I lied my way out of it." (This involved a spurious claim that Slash had been attacked and would sue the hotel chain if he was arrested.) They let him go. King Kong Ron slept in the hallway outside Slash's new room so the cat in the hat couldn't escape.

Axl arrived in Phoenix the next day. He seemed tired and shifty, and was reticent about where he'd been. The band was told they had lost the highly coveted opening spot on David Lee Roth's tour because of Phoenix. The meeting broke up and the band went back to L.A., feeling bitter and broken. This was a huge tour for them that Geffen had been counting on, and they lost a lot of work that spring. People at Geffen stopped talking about Guns opening shows on Jimmy Page's tour for his solo album *Outrider.*

For three tense days, no one talked. Finally Slash and Axl spoke on the phone, then Slash and Izzy met with Axl and heard his reasons for missing Phoenix. Axl was contrite but still had his attitude. They could fire him, he told them, but who the fuck were they gonna get? So it was patched up, but with injured feelings and barely concealed anger all around.

"That was no big deal," Slash later told Mick Wall, "except when you cancel a gig, it starts this whole big upheaval. Everyone freaks out. The press plays it up. We weren't really scared the band was falling apart; we were just pissed off at Axl."

*O*ne of a bunch of promises and compromises Axl Rose agreed to in the wake of the Phoenix crash was to have a psychiatric evaluation. "Hey," he laughed to his manager, "everybody already knows I'm crazy." But management exercised some leverage and got Axl to a psychiatrist at UCLA Medical Center.

There Axl took some tests, talked to the psychiatrists, told them about his childhood, the twenty arrests, and received a clinical diagnosis of manic depressive disease (today known as bipolar disorder), a form of psychiatric illness sometimes manifested as wild and convulsive mood swings, from the highest elation to abysmal depression—and then back again. Axl was prescribed lithium, a recently developed mood stabilizer in 1988 (and still widely used to treat so-called Bipolar I).

Axl wasn't in the least shy about this, asking friends questions about lithium, often mentioning it to interviewers in the next year. Axl began taking the drug, it is thought, in March 1988. Sometimes he didn't like the way it made him feel, and so he didn't always take his daily dose of lithium. As a result, the people around never knew which version of Axl Rose would turn up, or if he would turn up at all.

A year later, in 1989, Axl tried to explain it to Del James. "I went to a clinic, thinking it would help my moods. The only thing I did was take one 500-question test, filling in these little black dots. All of a sudden I'm diagnosed: manic depressive! *'Let's get Axl on medication!'* Except the medication didn't work. But it helps keep people off my back, 'cos they figure I'm 'on medication.'"

Axl also spoke to *Rolling Stone* about this.

"A lot of the things about my mood swings are like...I have a temper, and I take things out on myself. Not physically, but I'll smash my TV, knowing that I have to pay for it, rather than going down the hall and smashing the person I'm pissed off at.

"I can be happier than anybody I know. I can get so happy that I'll cry. And I can get completely opposite, upset-wise." Axl said that he didn't think the lithium was doing much for him. He mentioned seeing *Frances*, a recent movie about the film-noir actress Frances Farmer, who had been institutionalized because of emotional outbursts. "I always wonder if, like, somebody's gonna slide the knife underneath my eye and give me the lobotomy. I think about that a lot."

On the last day of March 1988, a month in which the band didn't work, Guns N' Roses appeared on Fox TV's *Late Show*. In their acoustic guitar configuration they played "You're Crazy" and "Used to Love Her." It was a low-key but totally controlled and brilliant performance, with Axl leering wickedly as he told of killing his girlfriend and burying her in the garden—only to hear her still complain. It was not politically correct. Fox's studio audience loved it.

The band was broke from not working, but *Appetite* had now sold half a million albums. The band was told that they would be awarded gold albums.

One day Izzy Stradlin, with hair cut shorter than usual and deathly pallor intact, left his apartment on Hollywood Boulevard, boarded the Sunset Boulevard bus for eighty-five cents, and got off at Sunset and Gardner. "I went down to see our old studio on Sunset by the Guitar Center," Izzy told an interviewer. "An old friend of ours lives there now. We paid $400 a month for this 12 by 12 room with no shower." Izzy looked around the place with evident nostalgia. When *Appetite* went gold, he thought he'd be able to buy a car and bid the bus fare-well. But no. "Then I found out there's more to it than that. We have to pay everyone back first. Then it's like we get a check every six months, or something fucked like that."

Inspecting Guns' old lair, Izzy was amused to discover that "this girl, Michelle, still has her name and phone number carved into the wall. God, that place was a riot back then. When you consider that, we're all doing a lot better now than we ever did before."

WHAT DIFFERENCE IS MONEY GOING TO MAKE?

*A*pril 1988. MTV broadcast Guns' February 2 Ritz nightclub show on its late-night metal program, *Headbangers Ball*. It was the show's highest-rated episode to date. Then Axl Rose raged out when he heard the way Geffen had edited "Sweet Child o' Mine" for release as *Appetite*'s second single. The label thought "Sweet Child" was make-or-break for Guns N' Roses. *Appetite* was starting to really sell, but "Welcome to the Jungle" had flopped as the first single, failed to get on the radio, and the video had been rejected by MTV. (When MTV finally began playing *Jungle* in regular rotation, seven months after its release, the network demanded changes in the video's violent content.) British di-rector Nigel Dick had apparently shot some scenes for the *Sweet Child* video late in 1987. Further footage was also done at the Ballroom in Huntington Park on April 11, 1988. Nigel Dick was bored at the shoot. The band was all dolled up, and Axl was dancing seductively in his leathers and denim. Dick was staring at his monitor, thinking that the video was going to suck and that the band's look was so ordinary. But some of the girls from Geffen were peeking over his shoulder. When the camera held a tight shot of Axl, one of the girls sighed, *"This is so fucking cool."* This was an instant attitude adjustment for Dick, be-cause the girls so obviously appreciated that Axl Rose was really, re-ally hot.

* * *

he single release of "Sweet Child o' Mine" now had to be extremely radio-friendly, so Tom Zutaut cut the album track from almost six minutes to just under four. When this was played for Axl, he was incandescent with rage that no one had consulted him. He got even angrier when he was accused of being in a mood swing. That was bullshit, he later told *Rolling Stone*. "When something gets edited, and you didn't know about it, and the song is real important to you, you *lose your mind*. And of course, it's like, 'Axl's having a mood swing.' Well, 'mood swing,' my ass. This is my single, and they chop it to shit."

The A&R people and his manager tried to placate him. "They said, 'C'mon, Axl, your vocals aren't cut at all.' But my favorite part of the song is Slash's slow solo; it's the heaviest part for me." He lashed out at the execs about the greed of moronic, corrupt radio. Shorter songs meant more time for commercials. He ranted about the radio version of Eric Clapton's "Layla" ("not that any of our songs compare," he temporized), which left out the climactic piano part at the end. Later he told an interviewer, "When you get the chopped version of 'Paradise City' or half of 'Sweet Child,' you're getting screwed."

Stardom was starting to get to W. Axl Rose. "With all this pressure," he explained, when something like this happens, "it's like I'll explode. And so where other people are going, 'Oh well, we just got fucked,' Axl's going *God damn it* and breaking everything around him. It's how I release frustration. That's why I'm pounding and kicking all over the stage."

*A*ppetite for Destruction entered *Billboard*'s Top Ten album chart late in April 1988. In May, Guns was picked up by Iron Maiden's North American tour as opening act. The two bands didn't get along.

Iron Maiden was, along with Judas Priest, an exemplar of the so-called New Wave of British Heavy Metal: late seventies bands that followed Led Zep into the breach clad in black leather and studs, selling horror and monster themes to pumped audiences of mostly young males. (Def Leppard, currently the biggest band in America, even with a one-armed drummer, was part of the younger end of this movement.) But Maiden wasn't selling that many tickets and needed

about-to-surge Guns to fill some of the empty seats they had played to
early in the tour.

Guns picked up the Iron Maiden tour in Iowa late in April and
stayed in the Midwest until the headliners took a break early in May.
Guns took the opportunity to sell out theaters in Boston, Philadelphia,
and New York. Axl was late to their sold-out show at the Felt Forum,
the theater under Madison Square Garden, and his people were freaking because every minute past an eleven P.M. curfew would cost the
headliner thousands of dollars in union overtime and fines.

"I was late because I'd passed out from drinking Night Train and
doing an MTV interview," he told *RIP* magazine. When Doug Goldstein got him on his feet, "I showered, did my vocal exercises, and got
dressed within fifteen minutes and went to the gig." Guns got out of an
$8,000 overtime bill only because the barricades in front of the stage
were set up wrong, and they weren't reset by the time he arrived.
"People wonder why bands don't play longer. . . . There are nights
when we want to play all night long, but we just can't afford to."

The Iron Maiden tour now moved north, through the Canadian
Maritimes and west to Calgary and Vancouver. Guns was playing to
the same kids who'd come to see the Cult the year before, but now the
kids seemed more excited to see them. They played a new rap-rock
song for two weeks on that tour, announced as being on a forthcoming
album, but it was never heard of after the tour ended.

"Sweet Child o' Mine" was released as a single in late May. It got
on the radio right away. The radio programmers of 1988 liked it for
the same reason—thuggish rockers singing a tender song—that their
older colleagues liked the 1964 Rolling Stones. "Sweet Child" got into
the Top Forty very quickly, and at Geffen it was hoped that Guns had
their first hit single.

By the time the tour reentered the United States, Maiden and
Guns had stopped saying hello. With Guns on the bill, the concerts in
California and the Pacific Northwest had all sold out. So many kids left
the arenas after Guns' set that local promoters started telling Guns
(according to Slash): "You guys shouldn't be opening for Maiden, because you could headline here." Iron Maiden was mad as hell. The
opening act was bigger than the headliner, a nightmare scenario for
any major band.

Guns was playing well, but Axl's voice was giving out, and they couldn't wait for the tour to end. After the show at Seattle Center Coliseum, Duff and Slash were reportedly arrested after a bar fight. Things were so loose that Duff then left the tour for a few days to marry Mandy Brix, the blond singer of L.A. girl metal band Lame Flames. (The courtship had been short.) The Cult's bassist, known professionally as Haggis, filled in for Duff for the rest of the tour.

Axl's voice went out completely during a show in Mountain View, California. Slash had to play guitar solos to fill the spaces where Axl couldn't sing. Next day, Axl went to the doctor, and the band drove to Sacramento and set up their gear. They played the sound check and waited for Axl. An hour before they were supposed to play, Doug Goldstein got the call: Axl wasn't coming, and the doctors told him not to finish the tour.

The doors had already opened and there were hundreds of kids in front of the stage. When the road crew went out and began taking down Guns' huge banner, the kids started freaking. Slash: "I had to go out in front of—I think it was like 22,000 kids—and go: 'Axl's voice isn't working right at the moment, so, um, we're not going to be playing tonight.' They just went nuts."

Axl Rose showed up ten minutes later, very subdued, and they drove all night, straight back to Los Angeles.

*O*n June 8 and 9, Guns and Maiden were to play two sold-out shows at Irvine Meadows, a 17,000-seat venue near L.A. But Axl quit the tour, supposedly—so Maiden was informed—after he'd been diagnosed with polyp growths on his vocal cords. (This often happened to those who screamed for a living.) On June 8, L.A. Guns opened the show instead. Slash and Izzy joined them for a jam at the end. The next night, to try to placate their disappointed fans, Guns N' Roses—without Axl Rose—walked onstage after L.A. Guns had finished and blasted into a hell-fire "It's So Easy" with Duff on lead vocals. "I was never so fuckin' scared in my whole life," he said later. Guns N' Roses then quit the Iron Maiden tour.

A few days later, in his room at the Continental Hyatt House on Sunset, where he was registered as "Mr. Disorderly," Slash told Mick

Wall: "The afternoon we found out we were quitting the Iron Maiden tour, I grabbed every bottle of Jack I could find . . . and took it all back to the hotel. That was five days ago, and I've been living off it ever since."

Asked about the band's burgeoning success, Slash was annoyed. "All you can talk about is money"—he rolled his eyes—"and that's where I get lost. I mean, look at me [well-worn jeans, lived-in Zeppelin shirt, old boots]. That's all there is. That's all there's ever gonna be. I don't even like the idea of going into a fuckin' dressing room and changing into different clothes just to go onstage and play. Give me a roof over my head and something to drink, and I've got everything I need. *What difference is money going to make?*"

WE SMELL THE FEAR

*A*round this time, June 1988, Poison threw a party at London, a sleazy West Hollywood club. Slash attended with his bodyguard and Mick Wall, who was covering Guns for *Kerrang!* "C'mon, man," Slash taunted. "Let's go start a fight. I'll take care of you."

With the sudden uptick of press interviews being done by Slash, the de facto spokesman for Guns N' Roses, came incessant attacks on Poison, who were the main butt of the whole Guns N' Roses joke—the band that Guns did not want to be compared to. Everyone in L.A. hated Poison, but only Slash had the public platform to make this hatred real.

At the party, nursing a bottle of Jack Daniel's, Slash explained this. Guns and Poison had sometimes played together at the same small clubs around L.A. in 1985, when all the baby bands more or less helped each other. But Poison had a different attitude, especially when they opened the show.

"Every time those assholes went on first," Slash said (between generous draughts of Jack), "Bret Michaels would end their set by announcing that the band was having a big party, and everyone was invited. And the people in the kind of dives we were playing in those days didn't have to be asked twice to go to a band party, and within minutes the whole fuckin' club would empty out. [Poison] were always pulling sneaky, shitty little stunts like that. That sucks, man.... I think they must be insecure about their talent."

Later on, Slash met CC Deville but couldn't penetrate his thick Brooklyn accent. "I could not understand him, what he was saying, and that pissed me off. The next day I made the mistake of mentioning it in a magazine interview. They turned one sentence about CC Deville into an entire article."

Slash also claimed, perhaps jokingly, that he threatened to shoot CC Deville when the Poison guitarist started wearing a top hat onstage. Now the rock press was reporting that both bands received occasional death threats from fans of the other.

Mick Wall had noticed the tension that swept through the party when Slash walked in. Was Slash aware of this? "Oh, yeah. Good. [They're thinking:] 'Oh God. Slash is here, or Axl is here, and they're gonna smash the place up.' The only time it ever happens is with these fuckin' assholes out there who try to fuck with you.... It's the same thing as being eaten by a wolf. We smell the fear."

Slash enjoyed the party, which produced no violence or even social intercourse other than brief hellos between Slash and Bret. Slash danced around with his bottle of Jack. When he slumped against the wall, he held it in his arms like an infant.

Shortly after this, Poison was at a Mötley Crüe show at the Forum. The after party was also attended by Guns' ace publicist Bryn Bridenthal (who would soon work full-time for David Geffen). After some strong drink, Bret Michaels and Bobby Dall recalled some of the recent public insults and scathing put-downs directed their way by Guns N' Roses. (Axl: "We don't associate ourselves with glam because that's what Poison associates themselves with. I've told those guys personally [that] they can lock me in a room with all of them, and I'll be the only one who walks out.")

So the two gentlemen from Poison, their lip-glossed manhood duly challenged, reluctant to be locked in a room with W. Axl Rose but still hell-bent on revenge, took their righteous fury out on Guns by attacking their publicist. They staggered over to Bryn Bridenthal at this party and began insulting her, even threatening her if she couldn't get Guns to stop slagging their band. Then, to emphasize their strong feelings in this matter, they threw their drinks in her face. The affair came to a halt. No one could believe how lame this was. Someone called the cops. The police asked Bryn if she wanted to press charges, and she said yes. Michaels and Dall were arrested and charged with assault and battery. Later Bryn Bridenthal filed a civil lawsuit against them as well. The judge ordered them to apologize, and their lawyer sent her a form letter.

*W*hen he wasn't out carousing, Slash was living in a hotel off Sunset and keeping his head down. He split up with a girlfriend he'd been having problems with. He spent a lot of time in various VD clinics. He worried (not a whole lot) about contracting AIDS. "I was dating a porno chick," he recalled, "as well as this sweet little jailbait junkie girlfriend." He tried to cut down on heroin. He read the two major works of the French writer Louis-Ferdinand Céline, *Journey to the End of the Night* and *Death on the Installment Plan*. ("He's got one of the most bitter fucking...most *negative* outlooks on life I've ever read.") He went out occasionally with one of his harem of renegade strippers, or: "I get really drunk, and then I get to the hotel and I'll pick up the first chick I see." In the morning he would have an anxiety attack about getting AIDS. "Slash," he'd say to himself, "you've gotta watch out, you're playing with death." He told Mick Wall: "What can I do? If drinking doesn't get me, AIDS will. It's like a fucking ghost sent to haunt us. I have this underlying fear, all the time. If anything—*any-thing*—goes wrong with me, I think, *Oh shit. This is it!*" At one point Slash discovered that a starlet he'd been fucking had done sex scenes with John Holmes, a porn actor who had recently died of AIDS. Panic city. "Everyone should realize that as soon as David Lee Roth or Gene Simmons or me goes down with it, then we're all gonna go. It's gonna be like 1989, 1990—the year all the rock stars died!"

Asked about the immediate future, Slash answered that the band would record their new album in the fall of 1988, but then he allowed that there was always the chance there would be no band, that total collapse was right around the next curve. "This might sound negative, but I'd rather be as good as possible, in the amount of time that we can do it, and do it to the fucking hilt. Then—fall apart, die, whatever. I'd rather do that than five or six albums, ten albums, and end up like fucking KISS."

Mostly he sat around and waited. "I'm 125 percent band-oriented. Everything I do is geared to that. When we have time off, I can't focus on anything else. I used to collect snakes, but I don't have the time to look after them now. So I just go out and get drunk all the time, and wait for the next gig."

*E*arlier in 1988, Tim Collins had a problem. As Aerosmith's manager, he needed a strong opening act for his band's big summer tour. Aerosmith would be touring for their big comeback album, *Permanent Vacation,* packed with hit singles, and was also immense on the street from their epochal appearance in Run-DMC's rap-meets-rock video for their cover of "Walk This Way." Tim was getting pressure from Geffen to put Guns on the tour, but Tim was worried.

"Everyone wanted Guns on our tour. Their A&R man, Tom Zutaut; ours—John Kalodner; and even David Geffen himself. Geffen was usually very hands-off with the younger bands on his label, but he got involved with Guns when MTV was slow to play 'Sweet Child o' Mine.' David's people—Kalodner, Eddie Rosenblatt [president of Geffen Records]—begged David to intervene. I was told that he personally called the head of MTV and the chairman of Viacom to complain, and of course they started playing 'Sweet Child o' Mine' in prime time, and look what happened.

"Anyway, there was a lot of pressure to have Guns on the tour. I didn't know what to do. Aerosmith was only a year into complete sobriety, and Guns N' Roses were public drug users. Our guys had bought drugs from their guys before. Aerosmith's last tour had been a failure, and we couldn't let it happen again. I was worried also that Axl Rose might blow Steven Tyler away. Steven was tired from the stress of recovery. He looked fat, bloated. And Axl was in the prime of this furious intensity that he had. In the end, I decided to take the chance, but only when Joe Perry said he wanted to do it. Joe wanted Guns' audience, and Geffen wanted ours for Guns.

"The funny thing was Alan Niven was being difficult, and their [booking] agent didn't want to do it either. Niven kept saying that Guns didn't need Aerosmith. He kept saying that Guns was going to be the biggest band in the world. (He was right!)"

But Geffen kept insisting that Niven and Collins have a meeting and make a deal.

"So I go to meet Alan—at his gun club in Orange County. But hey, I'm teachable, and he taught me how to shoot, and we sort of bonded over this. His price [$5,000–7,000 per show] was high for what was still considered an unknown band, but we ended up making the deal for Gun to tour with Aerosmith over the course of three months that summer."

*G*uns was happy about this. "They were like our teenage heroes," Slash admitted. But what Tim Collins didn't know was that Axl's voice was gone. He could hardly speak, let alone sing. People were worried. When he tried to sing for the throat doc, only hoarse subsonics came out of his head. Axl's throat had closed down with polyps and swollen tissue. If he needed surgery to remove the polyps, they had to wait ten days for the swelling to subside, and then two weeks more to heal. There had been talk of going to Japan at the end of June to promote a (cool) Japanese Guns N' Roses compilation album that had been released in April and was selling well. This trip was rescheduled for later in 1988. (The Japanese album mashed up UZI Suicide tracks, *Appetite* tracks, and live cuts from the Marquee in 1987.)

"We're looking at two weeks of anxiety," Slash told an interviewer, "if the operation goes well, and Axl stays out of trouble. Basically, we have three months on the Aerosmith tour coming up, and I do not want anything to fuck with that. Of all the tours we've done in the last year—besides the Monsters of Rock thing in England that we're doing this summer—*that* is the tour that really means something to us. Us and Aerosmith!"

Asked if Guns had any cool new songs, Slash mentioned "You Could Be Mine" and "Patience." And he said he felt that things had really changed for his band and for himself.

"A year ago, people treated us like garbage because we had the worst reputation in town. Now they act like we're larger-than-life heroes *because* we have the worst reputation in town." (This was true. No one had outperformed Guns in the bad-boy stakes since 1985.) "This makes me feel awkward," Slash murmured, appreciating Guns' unsubtle shift (felt only by the five of them) from authentic rebels of the street to cartoon characters on MTV. "It's made me about 50 percent more cynical than I was last year."

A CHANGED MAN

July 1988. Almost all of Axl Rose's different persona voices—insane preacher, nuclear crooner, screechy baby—came back, reportedly without surgery. A rumor spread that Axl had gone into rehab for cocaine dependency, but apparently it wasn't true. Another spread that Axl was dead—not true. But W. Axl Rose came into the summer of 1988 a changed man, as far as his band was concerned. The throat doctors had told him that he had to curb his appetite for destruction if he wanted to keep his voice. The biggest change was that Axl began to separate from the others and no longer traveled with the band.

After two makeup shows in Phoenix, Guns N' Roses joined the Aerosmith tour in progress at the Poplar Creek Music Theater in Illinois on July 17. Axl had his own bus. The band had theirs. This raised eyebrows, as it usually meant the band members hated each other. Actually, it was Izzy Stradlin's idea, so that Axl's titanic mood shifts could just blow through and not inflict casualties.

Axl later explained it to Del James as a function of taking care of business. "After shows, I can't afford to go out and party like the other guys. There's been several times when I had to leave the bus because of... 'nerves,' you know what I'm saying?" Implying that his major drug use was in the past, Axl went on: "It's impossible to sit there [on the band bus], completely straight, listening to someone who is completely annihilated, go off about some stupid fucking bullshit." Axl also pointed out that the band were a little older now, and needed their space. "We all used to live together, but now we've outgrown being crowded in together. Not because we don't like each other; we just have different lifestyles."

How different?

"Well, I don't abstain from doing drugs, but I won't allow myself to have a fucking habit. I won't allow it. I'll have done coke for three days, and my mind says, *'Fuck, No.'* And I'll refuse to do coke that day, because . . . I know that if I *do* it, I won't be able to hit my goals with what I want to do with this band."

Axl got used to this new separateness quickly. While the rest of the band caroused in bars, Axl remained in his hotel room. Often on that tour, he arrived half an hour before the show and got himself ready to perform by listening to "The Needle Lies" by Queensryche, or something from Metallica.

*A*erosmith was ready for Guns N' Roses to join the tour, but not without trepidation. First, *Appetite for Destruction* was roaring up the Top Ten, way ahead of the record the Bad Boys from Boston were promoting, and Geffen execs were predicting Guns would have the number-one album in the country before the end of July—while they were still opening shows for Aerosmith. Tim Collins knew that under these circumstances, any competent band management would try to renegotiate Guns' deal, and this could significantly alter Aerosmith's financial end of a long and grueling tour.

Tim Collins also didn't want newly sober Aerosmith infected by the junkies and alcoholics in Guns. "We were all worried," Collins recalls, "and we were overcontrolling, because we had to make this work. We had all these crazy meetings with our sobriety consultants and security people, and we decided we had to keep the two bands apart. We devised this 'containment plan,' which divided the backstage area between the bands. We let Guns have their drugs and booze in their area, which we had guarded so stuff couldn't leak out. We timed it so Aerosmith arrived at the venue while Guns was onstage. We told Guns they had to leave as soon as their set was over. The backstage areas were divided by walls of tarps, and our security people [headed by a moonlighting Arizona state trooper] insured there would be no interaction between the bands. We only did this for the first couple of weeks, until we could see what kind of shape Guns was in."

And it wasn't real pretty. "They were totally wasted all the time. You looked in their eyes—not Axl, but all the others—and they basically looked dead." One never saw Slash's eyes at all, or even his face. "We'd see Guns straggling through the hotel lobbies, looking like—not just gypsies, but ragged, *strung-out* vagrants. Their luggage was embarrassing: shopping bags, backpacks, shipping boxes wrapped with duct tape. It was actually kind of depressing, so we decided to leave things [backstage] as they were, and then see what happened as we stayed on the road with them."

Guns went into action even before the tour started. They tried to check in early at a chain hotel outside of Chicago, but the front desk gave them a problem. Voices were raised. Security was called. A problem was averted—by inches. Later that night, Axl was sitting in the hotel bar with some friends who'd driven from Indiana to see Bill Bailey's band open for Aerosmith. A drunken businessman, part of a group with serious asshole issues, passed a remark about a girl with one of Axl's friends. Then, loudly, he told Axl Rose that he wasn't taking any crap from "some Bon Jovi look-alike."

Whoa! Axl smashed him in the face. The police arrived and arrested Axl and Steven Adler for assault. Later the same evening, stone-drunk Slash passed out in the same hotel bar, where he was discovered, under a table, by Doug Goldstein, who had Ron Stalnaker throw Slash over his shoulder and carry him up to his room. While underway, Slash pissed on his faithful minder. After depositing Slash into bed, propped up on his side with pillows so he wouldn't choke on his own vomit like Jimi Hendrix or John Bonham, Ron slept outside Slash's door to prevent further escape.

Tim Collins: "When Guns N' Roses joined us, we'd already been out [on tour] with other bands—White Lion, Dokken. When Guns came along, we noticed the difference immediately. They had a hit single [with 'Sweet Child']. They were on MTV much more than we were. Suddenly Steven Tyler wanted to meet them. But we had this major segregation strategy going. I'd lie to Steven: 'Oh, Guns? Sorry—they left the hall already. You'll see them in Cleveland.'

"Meanwhile, they were incredible! Guns N' Roses now had the same intensity that Aerosmith had back in 1975, a real rock-and-roll band—big-time." Joe Perry got to a few shows early so he could see Guns. He wanted to see what Aerosmith had to follow. Tim Collins: "I'd stand there at the side of the stage, with Joe Perry and Brad Whitford, and we'd watch Slash and Izzy giving each other these looks of semi-disbelief that they were being observed, and maybe judged, by their old heroes.

"Believe me, it made both bands play *much* better."

AMERICA'S SWEETHEARTS

On July 23, 1988, after Guns N' Roses' fourth show on the Aerosmith tour, at the Show Me Center in Cape Girardeau, Missouri, Guns learned that their debut album, *Appetite for Destruction*, was the number-one album on *Billboard* magazine's Top 200 album chart, beginning that week.

Tim Collins: "This totally blew our minds, even though we knew it was coming. It was almost epic. Suddenly, our opening act was bigger than we were. This had never happened to us before. We were slightly in awe. Even Steven Tyler, who had seen everything twice over, was impressed."

Guns was impressed too, and a little amazed. "I'd always figured we'd just be a cult band," Slash admitted.

Izzy Stradlin was annoyed because he was an artist, a purist, a sex pistol, and it definitely was not a cool, punk thing to have this big a fucking success. This wasn't necessarily what Izzy had wanted.

Axl called his mother, back in Lafayette, and told her the news.

Steven Adler was out of his mind with pride and joy.

Duff was astounded, but not surprised, because "Sweet Child o' Mine" was blaring out of every car radio in every town they raided. Even Duff's legions of thirteen-year-old nephews in Seattle had started

listening to his band, along with their heroes Metallica and Def Leppard.

Duff, to *Circus*: "That song ['Sweet Child'] was written—like, three
chords—in five minutes. The vocals were sweet and sincere. The guitar lick was meant to be a joke. We thought, 'What *is* this song? It's
nothing. It's filler on the record.' We never had any idea of making it a
single."

Guns was actually shocked at what happened when "Sweet Child"
came out and started getting airplay on MTV in May and June. "We
had *no idea* what it would do for the album," Duff reported. "You
should have seen the fucking difference [in crowd reaction] before,
and after, that single came out. Before, only the people in front even
knew who we were. They came to see us because they were our fans,
all two dozen of them. Afterwards, when [we played 'Sweet Child']
everybody was on their feet with their cigarette lighters switched on.
It was amazing, night and day. It happened that quickly."

Like Izzy, Duff thought that having a huge hit record was dodgy,
in the classic punk worldview. He was almost apologetic. "We're a
rock-and-roll band. We've *never* written a song for commercial purposes.
We fucking *despise* that. But . . . it just happened. It certainly did."

*A*nd it was a great thing to have happen, the massive 1988 success
and ascendancy of Guns N' Roses—if you loved rock music; if you
loved hard rock music; if you loved metal; if you loved punk; if you
loved old-time traditional American cussedness; if you thought that
all the crap, bubble gum, and sludge on eighties radio and MTV—most
of it "produced" by two British hacks from the discredited progressive-
rock era, Phil Collins (ex-Genesis) and Jeff Lynne (ex–Electric Light
Orchestra)—"sucked a big dick" (as Izzy Stradlin put it in *Rolling Stone*
that month).

Slash was on top of this. He whispered to *Circus*: "Compared to
everything else in the eighties, we *do* stand out. There aren't many
rock bands as hard as us, shooting for total commercial acceptance."
Slash, unlike Izzy or Duff, was not conflicted about world domination.
"There's an element in our music that can reach a whole different, and
much wider, audience."

(Slash said this three months later, in October 1988, after *Appetite* had sold five million units in three months.)

Appetite for Destruction, some savants say, saved rock music: because the classic form (Stones/Yardbirds/Zeppelin) had pretty much croaked in the late eighties, an era when Paul Simon's appropriation of South African choral music was a major happening and tedious groupings of older stars like the Traveling Wilburys (George Harrison, Bob Dylan, Roy Orbison, Tom Petty, and, inevitably, Jeff Lynne) got huge play in the media because nothing else was happening.

For their fans, Guns N' Roses was the anti-eighties. To younger kids, born in the seventies, they were a magical and alive synthesis of the greatest rock bands: the Stones, Yardbirds, and Zeppelin; Aerosmith, AC/DC, Sex Pistols; all the bands that would never play in your town. Guns reminded their young audience of the raw power, the immense emotionality, and the spacious psychic landscapes to be discovered in a great rock band in full fury. Some rock historians still wonder what would have happened if Guns had failed, or self-destructed earlier than it did. Some think rock music would have withered on the vine, and might have died.

*M*eanwhile, Aerosmith—to its credit—was not exactly getting blown off its own stages. Their classic two-guitar attack now held two generations in thrall, and new songs like "Dude (Looks Like a Lady)" and the ballad "Angel" brought in rabid new fans. Aerosmith boss Joe Perry carefully checked out his opening act and noticed that Guns had some ragged nights: "They had plenty of attitude, but I thought they handled their new stardom really well. You could tell when they had a bad night, but they were always on time and always gave their best.

"Axl really knew how to work an audience. I noticed that their crew taped foam rubber around everything that he might touch—teleprompters, his mike stand—to make sure he wouldn't break anything, or hurt himself. We saw that [Axl] was basically let out of his cage, and then thrown onstage. The sheer fury of it was almost naked. The thrill was, what was he going to do next?

"We respected them after we saw them. They had that solidarity, like a gang that played music together, which is just what you want in a band. They showed us how rock could move forward. People were saying you couldn't get any better than the Stones, or Zeppelin; and [Guns] came along and inspired people. You think it's all written, but it's not. There's always another way to twist those three chords around."

*B*y the end of July, Tim Collins decided to let go of some of his backstage control, because rock protocol now required it. "Guns N' Roses was, temporarily, bigger than my band," Tim recalls. "They just *exploded*. It was a really intense period for everyone. So after a while, we let them [Guns] come over and say hello [to Aerosmith]—if they [Guns] weren't fucked up, or strung out. But they were respectful toward what we were trying to do, so it was all very low-key. They drank and smoked on their side, and when they came over, they left their stuff in their area.

"Axl seemed to be sober, but wasn't claiming to be. He came over the most, and Steven [Tyler] befriended him, in a way. Axl already knew me, so sometimes we would take Axl's psychic temperature—what we called his 'weather report'—which could most often be described as 'agitated depression.' You couldn't help feel for him. I probably knew at the time, through the management grapevine, that he had been diagnosed as manic depressive, and was supposed to be on medication—a mood stabilizer.

"Anyway, Steven would talk to Axl about things that Axl found interesting or helpful. Then, almost invariably, Alan Niven would come over, speak with Axl about some problem, ratchet up the stress, and Axl would throw him out. I felt sorry for [Niven], though; he was working with a singer who had a serious mental illness, but who was also a genius. I could empathize with that."

Right after *Appetite* went to number one, Tim Collins got a call from publicist Bryn Bridenthal, whom he had hired to work the tour. "*Rolling Stone* is coming. We've got the cover!" This was great news. A *Rolling Stone* writer would join the tour in Detroit, and Aerosmith was promised the cover of the legendary magazine for the first time. Geffen executives were enthused. It looked possible to them that Aerosmith might actually pull off the most daunting maneuver in showbiz: the comeback. David Geffen was a generous boss, and there might be star-quality bonuses at the end of the year.

THE DEVIL WITH THE LES PAUL

*I*t was the best of times; it was the worst of times. Guns N' Roses was about to become the first rock band in a generation to have a number-one single and album at the same time. *Appetite* had sold 2.5 million units and was surging ever higher. (Axl insisted that their framed platinum album awards feature the censored Robert Williams cover.) But W. Axl Rose and the rest of the band fucking freaked when *The Dead Pool*—their Hollywood movie debut—was released that month. The movie made Guns N' Roses look like chumps and losers. Clint Eastwood used them as examples of everything that Dirty Harry hated, especially the decadent, drug-sodden, cryptosatanic L.A. hair metal subculture. Guns N' Roses, the number-one band in America, was ridiculed and depicted as human filth on the silver screen. Their big song, their very anthem, "Welcome to the Jungle," was used, abused, and degraded. In the film's climax, as avenging angel Dirty Harry is about to blow away the psychotic killer, he enters a room where "Jungle" is blasting out of a boom box. He looks at it with lip-sneering distaste and, despite being low on ammo, levels his .44 Magnum—the same weapon on the logo banner Guns played in front of every night!—and destroys the machine playing Guns N' Roses' hit song.

Someone asked Axl about *The Dead Pool.* "We got fucked in the ass," he replied. Someone got a message to Kyle Eastwood, warning him not to come around Guns anymore.

*T*he Aerosmith/Guns tour stayed in the Midwest through the end of July 1988: Texas, Kansas, Iowa, Wisconsin, where they played the Alpine Valley music venue in East Troy. Axl liked it around there, and thought about buying land when the checks started arriving later in the year. After shows in Michigan and Ohio, Guns N' Roses went home, so to speak, to open for Aerosmith at Market Square Arena in Indianapolis, Indiana.

Axl actually did go home on August 3, the day after the show, being careful, he told an interviewer, to avoid any contact with the cops in Lafayette. (Bloody-minded Izzy Stradlin couldn't be bothered with Lafayette, and stayed with the tour.) Guns was a red-hot topic in Lafayette, with "Sweet Child o' Mine" on TV and the radio, especially at Jefferson High after people started seeing Jeff Isbell and Bill Bailey on MTV. "Don't look up to him," some of Bill's old teachers told their students. "He didn't do well here." The old Bill Bailey stories went around again. He dropped out, they said. He was nothing but bad attitude. *Don't look up to him.* (This negative buzz was even reported in the Lafayette *Journal & Courier.*)

An urban legend in Lafayette features Axl taking his family and some friends to dinner at Arni's pizzeria on Elmwood Avenue that evening. The large party went up to the Toys in the Attic Room, where a nervous teenage waiter tripped over Sharon Bailey's purse and dumped a large tray of sodas all over Axl and his guests. The kid was mortified, but Axl said the purse shouldn't have been there, and they cleaned it up without any fuss. (The waiter's colleagues accused him of spilling the sodas on purpose, but this wasn't the case.)

It got a little crazy after that. Guns' two buses made the all-night run from Indiana to Philadelphia for two shows beginning August 4. But arena security at the Philadelphia Spectrum was reluctant to admit Axl's bus to the load-in area because they were expecting only one bus from the opening act. Axl got off the bus and the situation deteriorated into shouting and threat displays. Axl's brother, Stuart Bailey, was working for his brother and tried to calm things down but got shoved aside for his trouble, and the two brothers were soon surrounded by a dozen scumbags wearing the same T-shirt and some off-duty members of the notoriously violence-prone Philly cops. Axl was grabbed by the cops and roughed up. An arrest was narrowly averted by the timely arrival of reinforcements in the form of Doug

Goldstein and the road crew, but curses were exchanged and W. Axl Rose was in a state. The vibrations backstage at the Philadelphia Spectrum were toxic when Guns took the stage at eight o'clock.

Axl, still enraged by the parking lot episode, wearing leather GN'R colors and a bandanna, roared right into "It's So Easy." The whole band played into the high energy of the full house—a rarity for any opening act. The chicks were screaming, and not just down front. Halfway through the song, Axl noticed that a bunch of the security goons he had confronted outside were now "guarding" the stage in front of him. Some of them were looking at him the wrong way. When Guns finished the song, Axl strode to the lip of the stage and looked down: "[unintelligible] . . . parking lot attendant—*FUCK YOU!*" Axl gave him the finger. Steven Adler started the Bo Diddley beat. Duff, in a black leather cowboy hat and a CBGB shirt, picked it up. The whole arena was rocking. Izzy was gesturing through sustained chords and, as always, sang the chorus with Axl, now rocking a backward leather baseball cap over his head shmatte. Slash, in a fringed black leather jacket over a Batman shirt, squeezed off notes like tracer rounds. When they finished, the roar was ungodly.

Axl then told the audience about his adventures in the parking lot. ". . . parking security . . . like, me and my brother against fifteen guys from parking security—who were a bunch of assholes. . . . This cop comes and grabs me—the guy with long hair—and throws me over a rail! . . . I ain't crying about that. . . . What I'm cryin' about is, how could he tell that the kid with the long hair was wrong, man? [crowd roars] How did he fuckin' *know* that the kid with the beer in his hand was wrong? The best quote [from the cop] is, 'Fuck your civil rights. I'm the law.'"

The Philadelphia audience, who knew about their police force, let loose a big noise. Axl looked down at the glowering goons in front of him with total contempt, and let fly: "Luckily, we got out of this bullshit, and I'm gonna end this story so you won't have to hear me talk all night. . . . But anyway, it's assholes like this that gives us the fuckin' majority of all the fuckin' problems we have. So we're gonna dedicate this next song . . . to that little altercation in the parking lot . . . *and to these assholes down here* [he gives the finger to the line of goons below him] that are . . . OUT TA GET MEEEEEEEE!"

Guns ripped into the song as a veritable shower of fabric—mostly shirts, bras, panties, and banners—poured onto the stage from the kids up front. Instead of the usual "and you can take that to heart," Axl finished the number with a pointed invitation to the now livid security team: "AND YOU CAN SUCK MY DICK!"

Axl, winded and sweaty, next introduced "Patience" as a new song written by Izzy and Duff. He performed his trademark snake sway, drawing a barrage of female screaming. Izzy supplied the high harmony vocal on the chorus. Slash's blues-metal solo channeled James Marshall Hendrix by way of James Patrick Page.

Next, Axl introduced the band in a fake New Zealand accent. "On the rhythm guitar is Mr. Izzy Stradlin. On bass guitar is the King of Beers, Mr. Duff 'Rose' McKagan. On drums is mobile home-headed, nowhere-going Mr. Steven Adler [huge crowd roar]. And the devil with the Les Paul . . . straight from hell . . . *Mr. Slash!* . . . and he will talk to you now."

Slash (cigarette dangling; hair covering face, bare chest dripping with sweat):

"Hey, fuckin' Philadelphia—are you having a good time—or what? [Immense crowd roar.] I don't got a whole lotta time, but I just want to say: you guys came out here and sold out two fuckin' shows . . . so . . . shut up! *Quiet!* So, what I'm saying is . . . Philadelphia kicks fuckin' *ass!* . . . So . . . this is my chance to play the guitar. . . . It's 'coke time' for anyone who doesn't feel like hanging out."

This led into a shredding version of the guitar intro to "Sweet Child o' Mine," the number-one hit single in America, here an energy volcano, sparked by Axl's furious microphone dance in the "where do we go now?" section. Pandemonium at the Spectrum! Afterward, Axl thanked the audience:

"Well, thanks to people like every one of you there . . . You made a dream come true for us [huge crowd roar]. . . . You made a record that nobody wanted to fuckin' touch [roar], and nobody wanted to deal with . . . You guys! You people! You took it straight to number one! [big roar] I want to thank . . . *you* . . . for that! [huge roar] And . . . if you haven't gone to see the new Clint Eastwood movie, don't fuckin' bother! *It's a piece of shit!* [crowd roar] They gave us money, and we gave 'em this song, and we got fucked up the ass! And now I get to go: WELCOME TO THE FUCKING JUNGLE, BABY!"

Axl played the song in his leather cap, grabbed his crotch while thinking of his serpentine, worked himself into such a fury that he fell down while dancing through the middle section. After this he again spoke: "We got a lot of staff from our record company here tonight.... We wanna thank everyone from Geffen Records, because either to-day, yesterday, or tomorrow *Appetite for Destruction* is going triple platinum [three million units sold]. Thank you! [immense roar from crowd]

"So I guess Bobby Dall was wrong," he continued. "We're having a little ego here.... I kinda like what we do up here.... See these guys? These guys are my favorite band! [big cheer].... Anyway, Bobby Dall from Poison, he said, 'You gotta suck to make it.' [booing, with some cheers] ... Well ... *HE CAN SUCK THIS!*" [grabs crotch] [big cheer]

The last number before the encores was "Used to Love Her" in a country rock arrangement, with Axl in a cowboy hat, making throat-slitting motions during "but I had to kill her." After Slash's solo, Axl's lyrics made some people laugh: "She bitched so much / She drove me nuts / But now we're happier this way."

A BRUTAL BAND FOR BRUTAL TIMES

*A*ugust 6, 1988. Guns N' Roses opened for Aerosmith at the Sara-toga Performing Arts Center in upstate New York. The outdoor shed was brimming with kids who charged forward as soon as Guns lit into "It's So Easy." From the stage, the musicians beheld an awesome spec-tacle of fan mania as human waves from the back surged and crashed over those in front in order to get closer to the band. Down in front was a roiling whirlpool of kids eddying around itself, while frantic se-curity guards reached over barriers and pulled frightened girls out of a seething pit. Axl stopped the show after "Mr. Brownstone" and asked the kids to cool down, but every new song brought more crazed, tribal behavior. Right before "Jungle," Izzy walked over to Axl and rasped, "This is going to crack." When fans began sprinting onstage, the band bailed out.

After their set, they walked past the medical tent, where medics were tending to those injured in the melee. There were dozens of them, and a lot of bloody faces. Guns hadn't quite seen this level of rock bedlam before, and spoke to each other about it afterward. "After we got offstage, the medic's booth outside was just loaded with kids," Slash said. "Man, they were fucking dropping out there. It made me remember when I used to go to festivals and it was heavy. You had to be strong. When the whole crowd sways, you have to hold on to your own and go with it. It's *rough* out there. It's like the world is about to explode. It came back to me when I saw those kids, all bloody."

Izzy: "Yes, there was nearly a riot [in Saratoga]. But I get off on that vibe, where anything's just about ready to crack. When there's like twenty thousand people and they have three security guys. God—that was fucking intense, man. It was just on the fucking edge of twenty thousand people coming down on the stage."

*A*erosmith, meanwhile, took all this in with a certain degree of awe. Joe Perry told his manager that Guns was drawing a crazier and more authentic rock and roll response from their audience than Aerosmith was. It was making Aerosmith feel like a heritage act. Not only that, according to Tim Collins:

"In August, Guns now had the number-one single, the number-one album, and the most requested video on MTV. They were going through the roof. *Rolling Stone* joined the tour, and ended up putting Guns on the cover, not Aerosmith. (I caught hell for this from my band.) Business-wise, we were nervous about all this, because we expected their manager to want to renegotiate our deal with them. At every show, we waited for him to bring this up, ask for maybe $25,000 and a percentage, but he never did. But at the same time, Alan Niven was obviously angry about the deal, and every night he got more and more belligerent toward me, yelling at me, picking fights about stage space. We'd tell him: 'Joey Kramer's not gonna move his drums for Steven Adler. Joe Perry isn't going to move his amp for anyone.' There were a lot of little scuffles over power. We would have done the $25,000, but he never asked. Frankly, I think he was sticking to his original bargain because he had a code of honor that a deal was a deal."

*A*ugust 13, 1988. The last night of a three-night stand at the Pine Knob Music Theater in Clarkston, Michigan, near Detroit. Rob Tannenbaum, a reporter for *Rolling Stone,* was (with some trepidation) let into Guns' dressing room for some post-concert backstage atmosphere.

Izzy was slumped in a corner, draining a second bottle of wine, cranking up the Stones on a boom box. He paused to inform the reporter that "Rock and roll in general has just sucked a big fucking dick since the Sex Pistols." Slash, the designated interviewee, his copper skin still moist from performance, was wearing only a pair of shorts and cradled a bottle of Jack. Axl, resting from the show, wore jeans, cowboy boots, and a shirt that said WELCOME TO DETROIT / MURDER CAPITOL OF THE WORLD.

Slash and Axl were trying to be interviewed. Slash explained their old connections to Aerosmith: "Our guys were selling drugs to their guys." Izzy cranked up the volume for "Stupid Girl." The stress factor in the room was getting to the hair-trigger level.

Guns' show had not gone well. Slash had to be carried onstage by the crew. When they carried him off at the end, he passed out. (This was, according to crew members, more normal than not on this tour.) Then the stage monitors failed. The band ended their show five minutes early because of this. Axl had then put his boot through the dressing room wall. While they all sat there, trying to be cool for America's most famous rock mag, a commotion ensued in the hall outside as their sound mixer and a bus driver were noisily fired for incompetence.

This embarrassed Izzy, who decided to put on a show for *Rolling Stone.* He grabbed a bottle of vodka, shouted "Violent mood swing!" and smashed the bottle on the far wall. "Mood swing!" shouted Axl, leaping from the couch. He grabbed a vase filled with fresh roses and hurled it into the wall after the vodka.

All this smashed glass did little to relieve the tension in the room. Slash told how he expected to die in the inevitable L.A. metal band AIDS epidemic, "since we all fuck the same chicks." He talked about his drinking problem. "It's the only thing that brings me out of my shell enough to be able to deal socially."

Duff came in and noted that his bottle of vodka was shards of broken glass. Izzy was still blasting the Stones at top volume, which was annoying Slash. Duff stormed out. "This is entertaining," a somewhat abstracted Axl Rose said, adding: "Drug use is not in the past. We scare the shit out of each other, because we don't want to lose what we have as a family."

Izzy cranked up the sound for "Some Girls." Slash and Axl yelled at Izzy, who became remorseful. "Fuckin' Duff, man," he said. "I shouldn't break his vodka. I know how much he loves that stuff."

" $\mathcal{B}$ ut Guns N' Roses don't play heavy metal [opined *Rolling Stone,* in their cover story on the band, published later in 1988]. They play a vicious brand of hard rock that, especially in concert, is closer to Metallica than heavy metal. They are a musical sawed-off shotgun, with great power but erratic aim—they veer from terrible to brilliant in a typical set, often within a single song."

The magazine pointed out that most metal bands base their imagery on a fantasy world that has no relation to the reality of their teenage fans. The fans have nothing in common with David Lee Roth and the other rock stars of the day, but Axl Rose and Co., in their early twenties, still remembered what it was like to be seventeen, and took the trouble to communicate the contradictions of adolescence in a language teens could understand. Guns was compared to Public Enemy, rap artists who projected a hard edge while promoting self-improvement, and the early Rolling Stones, who also sang about hostility and spite. "And if the Gunners go beyond the Stones . . . it's because times are rougher; they are a brutal band for brutal times. Unlike the Stones, they don't keep an ironic distance between themselves and their songs."

Slash explained: "Our attitude epitomizes what rock and roll is all about. At least, what *I* think [it's] all about, which is all that matters. Some bands go out, and the whole thing is completely wrong, but they can put on a good show anyway. We're not like that." Slash showed the reporter his bruised right hand, swollen from cuffing his guitar during the three Detroit shows. "See this? We *bleed,* and fuckin' sweat for it, you know? We do things where other bands would be like, 'Get the stunt guy to do it.'"

"*W*as I, like, a major dick last night?" *Rolling Stone*'s interview with Slash was conducted early in the afternoon, with Slash nursing a hangover. The night before, Slash had done vodka shots in the hotel bar until he slumped in his chair, out. Ronnie Stalnaker ("His job is to follow me around when I'm drunk") took Slash up to his room, where—now revived—Slash threatened to throw his furniture through the windows. After putting Slash to bed, the burly minder removed the TV from the room and slept outside the door yet again.

"I'm one of those blackout drunks," Slash admitted. "I get so fucked up I don't remember anything. I probably give the impression of being a real asshole most of the time, but I'm really not that bad."

Rolling Stone noted that the Aerosmith/Guns bill was a great success since the concerts consistently sold out. For a couple of hours, the only supervision was the security staff. "You can get a warm, flat Miller Lite for $3.75 if you're over 21 or if one of your feet touches the ground." It was here that Guns N' Roses found their mass audience. Aerosmith was the headliner and was applauded and loved, but the kids regarded them as history, like the Doors or the Dead. "Their response to Guns' set was much more powerful, and demonstrated an unusual emotional connection with their songs and attitude."

"The sincerity of the band shows," Slash explained. "That's why the crowds are so fuckin' violent. I don't condone violence and riots, but it's part of the energy we put out."

Axl: "At times, like in Philly, I could easily start a riot. I mean, it's great watching 'em go crazy and beat each other up, but I don't want to see people get hurt."

"I guess we're playing with fire," Duff acknowledged. "It seems like a violent incident is inevitable, the way the Stones were destined to have an incident like Altamont"—the fateful 1969 California concert where a gun-toting fan was killed by bikers in front of the stage while film cameras rolled. It was, Duff said, a scene he'd viewed a hundred times while watching the Stones' concert film *Gimme Shelter.*

MONSTERS OF ROCK

*F*riday, August 15, 1988. Guns N' Roses' buses drove to New York after the Detroit shows. "Paradise City" was chosen as the next single, and in Manhattan the band was joined by Nigel Dick's video crew, who filmed them walking the summer streets in the city, shopping for guitars at the legendary Manny's on West 48th Street, and playing their sound check at an empty Giants Stadium across the river. The next night's show would be the apex of the Aerosmith tour, playing before 80,000 fans, the biggest audience Guns had yet faced. And Deep Purple was opening the show, not Guns N' Roses. After that, the band would fly to England on the supersonic Concorde and play way down on the bill at the Monsters of Rock festival, the biggest metal and hard rock showcase of them all.

Next day, the band was filmed playing to the nearly sold-out football stadium. Axl wore a new white leather suit (with band colors on the back of the jacket) when they got to "Paradise City," which normally finished their show. By then the big, seething crowd in the open field had pressed up against the stage, with thousands of raised arms saluting Axl in national socialist mode as he skip-jived across the stage, and Slash ran wind sprints across the lower catwalk while spewing "atomic hyper-crunch guitar riffs" with his black Les Paul. (He was wearing a T-shirt that read: POISON SUCKS.)

Two days later, on August 19, Guns was filmed boarding British Airway's Concorde aircraft in New York for the three-hour flight to London. The atmosphere in the plane's small cabin was festive, with a meal served on elegant china and the curve of the earth visible through the Concorde's tiny portholes. (Slash got drunk and went to sleep.) From London the band was bused (with a small video crew) on a luxury coach to Leicestershire, in the English Midlands. The band was billeted in a staid country house hotel near the raceway where, on the following day, the mighty monsters of rock would lay waste beyond the ramparts. After the sound check, Slash spent his entire stay in his room, doing press and radio interviews. Axl was in seclusion with a sore throat. Izzy was carrying around a 16mm Bolex camera the video crew had loaned him.

Most of Guns spent the evening drinking quietly in the hotel's paneled bar, absently listening as a hard English summer rain poured down outside the open windows.

*M*onsters of Rock was the biggest outdoor rock show in England, the descendant of the big seventies festivals at Reading and Knebworth House. Since it usually rained all summer in England, these large August parties usually turned into Woodstock-style mud baths. Since 1980, Monsters had been held at Castle Donington Motor Race Circuit, a hot rod track near Melton Mowbray. Dedicated to metal bands and hard rock groups exclusively, the day-long concerts typically attracted an average of 40,000 fans for the eight summers it had operated. But the heavy-duty 1988 Monsters of Rock lineup—Iron Maiden, KISS, David Lee Roth, Megadeth, and opening act Helloween—reportedly drew more than 100,000 British metal fans. (Estimates of the crowd size at Castle Donington that day—August 20—vary between an official low of 107,000, and what the veteran American road crews thought was upwards of 25,000 more by the time Guns took the stage at two P.M.)

*T*he morning of August 20 was rainy, raw, and rotten. The first downpour started at one o'clock, just as Helloween (a German KISS clone) began their set. It rained furiously for half an hour, and a burst of wind blew one of the massive stage-side video screens off its scaffolding, sending it crashing to the ground without injuring anyone. A visible shudder passed through the soaked kids in front of the stage. When Helloween finished its set, the hillside in front of the stage was a sea of red liquid mud.

No one had told Slash (top hat, black leathers over *RAW* magazine shirt, cool silver snake charm hanging from his neck) about a cherished Monsters of Rock tradition called bottling. By the time the band appeared at the side of the big stage, 100,000 fans were packed together, standing in ankle-deep ooze. With no place to piss, the fans simply filled empty plastic soda bottles with urine and then threw them as far as they could. Dozens of these sailed through the air at any one time, not all with their tops on, creating a steady yellow drizzle over the crowd. Waiting to go on, Slash took a swig from a bottle of beer that he found in the floor, only to spit out a wretched mouthful of English urine.

It proved to be that kind of day for Guns N' Roses.

The sky was low and dark, but at least the rain had stopped. Guns was announced, to tepid applause from the cold, wet crowd, and they banged out "It's So Easy." The fans came to life. Girls on their boyfriends' shoulders waved crude banners lettered WELCOME TO THE JUNGLE. Then Izzy began "Mr. Brownstone," and the entire hillside started to dance. Axl danced around, unshaven, in a black leather vest, cowboy boots, and black leather trousers ripped from knee-dives onstage. His red hair was under a blue bandanna and a backward black baseball hat. He wielded the mike stand like a javelin and performed his narcotic gliding shiver, now familiar to fans from the videos. The huge crowd went wild, and thousands at the top of the hill pushed downward to get closer to the action.

Between songs, Axl yelled to Izzy that this scene was fucked up. Axl could feel something wasn't right. He made some off-mike remarks to the people in front of him, telling them to calm down. Slash: "We just looked out there, and it was like, *Oh fuck!*" To cool things off, they began the acoustic version of "You're Crazy," but it didn't help. Suddenly there was a violent human surge from stage right, and the impacted kids in front compressed into a deadly swoon. Upturned faces turned into screaming ovals. About twenty feet from the stage, clearly visible to the band, a hole opened in the crowd, and in a flash several faces disappeared. Then the hole vanished, immediately covered by a violent mosh pit. The band could see that the fallen people could not have gotten up. Izzy stopped playing and was gesturing wildly. Slash [to *Kerrang!*]: "It looked really hectic from right up above it. We could see that surge. You could see this 'force.' And they're just... people, y'know?"

The band stopped playing. Cursing, red-faced with fury, Axl stood at the edge of the stage and told people to calm down. Slash and Duff were pointing at the place where the hole had been, and yelling to get those people out. Slash said later that they had stopped playing because they were scared shitless by what they had seen. Now, in the band's pause, several filthy bodies, some of them limp, were pulled out of the thick red muck by security and passed along to the medics.

It took a few minutes for things to get sorted out, but then Slash started the banjolike intro to "Paradise City," and the show continued. As the song built, the crowd got rowdy again. During "so far away," the entire hillside turned into a mosh pit, much to the delight of the video crew capturing the day for Guns' next video. But then more bodies starting coming over the front barrier, and one bloody, dead-looking girl got Axl upset. He stopped the show for a second time.

"Hey! Hey! Cut that shit out, OK? I'm taking time out from my playing to do this, and that's the only fun I get all day."

They finished the song and blasted into "Welcome to the Jungle," anxious to get the hell out of there. The sky turned dark gray with storm clouds. "Jungle" whipped the crowd into more pagan savagery, so the band again tried to cool things down with the new song "Patience," which was received with sodden indifference.

After this, Axl spoke to the now quieter throng, thanking them for helping make the next song Guns' first hit single in England. Slash's carnival intro to "Sweet Child o' Mine" got the biggest cheer of the day. The band lurched through the number, and left the stage. "Have a great fuckin' day," Axl told the crowd, adding "—and try not to fucking kill yourselves!" Then he too was gone. Backstage, while doctors worked frantically on five muddy, unconscious bodies laid out on the ground, Alan Niven told the worried promoters that Guns wouldn't play an encore.

*   *   *

$\mathcal{P}$eople who had seen Guns in England the year before were impressed. Their British photog, George Chin: "They were no longer like any other L.A. band; their whole image had moved far away from the glam thing. Their show was better now, faster, more frenetic. Axl looked tired, much thinner. Everyone said they were the highlight of the day." They would have gotten great reviews if no one had been trampled to death.

$\mathcal{I}$t started to rain again after Guns' set, so the fans on the upper hillside thinned out a bit, giving the people down front room to breathe. That's when someone noticed a hand sticking out of the mud, about twenty feet from the stage, where the hole in the crowd had been. A shout went up, and people began frantically digging in the muck. A body was pulled out, and then, sickeningly, another. Both were squashed from being stomped repeatedly by the jumping crowd. Rushed to the backstage medical area, both were immediately declared dead. Sixteen-year-old Alan Dick was identified by papers found in his pocket. The other corpse was so mangled that it took his family to identify the teenager, Langdon Siggers, by the tiger and scorpion tattoos on his arms. Tour manager Doug Goldstein, who had been in front of the stage, told George Chin not to tell the band that anyone had died if he saw them back at the hotel.

Guns wasn't informed until later that night. In the bar, Slash noted that Alan Niven was really bummed out about something, and demanded to know why. Slash later told VH1: "Our manager told us later, in the pub. And we just went from like an all-time high—something you can't compare to anything—to an all-time low."

The events at Donington were headlines in the next day's British papers, with the London tabloids quick to blame the band. *The Mail on Sunday* headlined them as "The Most Dangerous Band in the World." A year earlier, the British press had welcomed Guns N' Roses as new avatars of rock. Now they turned on the band. Several papers reported that the stage had collapsed and that Guns refused to stop playing, which had no basis in truth. No one reported that the band had stopped the show twice. These unfair vilifications and outright lies were repeated for several days, and Axl began to really hate the press in general.

No one was ever arrested or charged with the deaths of the two boys. But Monsters of Rock was canceled in 1989, and it took the promoters two years to get another license from local authorities, and then only after they agreed to a crowd limit of 70,000.

Guns flew back to New York on the Concorde and rejoined the Aerosmith tour. They carried back from England a new kind of knowledge, serious information based on personal experience. Not only had they witnessed the death of two of their fans; but—as had happened at Altamont—their film crew had captured the event on camera.

Two months later, Slash told Mick Wall he still felt terrible about the dead kids. "What bums me out the most is, whoever it was who was, like, *standing on top of somebody* . . . You can't stand on somebody and not know they're there. They were so self-involved and selfish that they *had* to be close to the stage, and somebody was gonna suffer for it, and have to die under their feet in ten inches of mud." Slash took a drag of his cig. "The craziest ones are always gonna be the ones in the first fuckin' twenty rows," he whispered. "They're the diehards."

Duff McKagan was honest about what he felt: "Whatever anyone says or writes about the incident couldn't make us feel any worse. It weighs very heavily on us. We don't fucking care about the media making us the scapegoats. But that thing will haunt me forever. It's strange how tragedy and pain seem to dog our career."

THE SADDEST FUCKING DAY OF HIS LIFE

*L*ate August 1988. Guns N' Roses, freaked out by the disaster at Donington, flew to New York, then to Boston for three nights of shows near headlining Aerosmith's hometown. Guns had no rest after England and were brain-fried. Several were dependent on heroin to ease the dislocation, the jet lag, the merciless touring schedule at the end of their time with Aerosmith. They jokingly wondered who would crack first, or just die. Photographs of the band in late August 1988 show a haggard troupe of exhausted kids. Bon Jovi's album *New Jersey* had knocked *Appetite* off the top of the charts. Some of Guns N' Roses shows around then, and into early September, were thought by Steven Tyler to have been less than magical. A veteran junkie rock star, Tyler knew exactly what was going on with his careening opening act.

During a final plunge into the middle of the American summer— Ohio, Missouri, Tennessee—Izzy Stradlin invited English photographer Ian Tilton into the band's tour bus. Izzy led him to the toilet, and suggested—with an almost emotional pride—he document the massive turd that Izzy had produced and wanted to preserve for posterity.

The tour returned to California on September 4. Three days later in Hollywood, they played "Welcome to the Jungle" live at the MTV Video Music Awards telecast and, a few minutes later, accepted a little chrome MTV spaceman trophy for "Sweet Child o' Mine," chosen as Best Video by a New Artist. They did their best to look elegantly wasted at the podium, but nobody cursed and they didn't get bleeped. The ratings for the show were the highest ever. When the single version of "Paradise City" was released a few weeks later, MTV put the video into heavy rotation. Guns' young audience, now seeing itself for the first time (in colorful Giants Stadium footage, intercut with grainy black-and-white scenes of the Castle Donington chaos), made "Paradise City" the most requested video in MTV's history.

Hollywood was Guns' home turf. And now, as Duff McKagan publicly affirmed, they could afford *much* better dope. During their California shows in the first two weeks of September, part of the band was grooving on high-quality Persian heroin. Duff enjoyed Russian vodka. Axl, according to people who worked with him, stuck to cocaine.

Guns drummer Steven Adler revered Steven Tyler and the rest of Aerosmith, and respected their public commitment to sobriety as an alternative to degradation and death. But he was also a twenty-three-year-old rock star, and he sometimes "did a little" now and then. Then he did a little one night in California, which he remembered with grief twenty years later:

"That last night when we played with Aerosmith at Irvine Meadows— and I was riding my scooter around [backstage]—and I rode up the ramp where the trucks come down. And I ran into the bass player from T.S.O.L. And I said hi—because I knew him—'cause I was friends with his drummer—that's why I wore the T.S.O.L. shirt in the 'Sweet

Child' video. And I go, 'Hey, dude!'—his name was Roach—and I said, 'Roach, what's happenin', man? How you doin', man?' He said, 'Oh good, hanging out.' I said, 'You got tickets, passes [to the show]?' He said no, so I reach in my little hippie shoulder bag and give him tickets and passes.

"So I go, 'Where're you going now?' And he goes, 'I'm gonna score some dope.' And I did heroin one time before—with Izzy and Slash—and I was never *so sick* in my whole life. But this was three years later—and I didn't even think about it—and totally forgot how sick I did get. So I said, 'Here. Here's twenty bucks, get me a little too.'"

Roach came back with a taste for Steven, who snorted it in the toilet. Then Steven was reminded of a meet-and-greet that the two bands were supposed to do for some Hollywood types who'd come out to see the show. At least Steven wasn't sick, which was a relief, but he was *way* fucking stoned.

"And that's when I walked into the room, and Steven Tyler saw me. And that's when it ... oh God!"

Veteran user Tyler immediately intuited that Steven Adler was clobbered on heroin, and let Adler know that he knew with a grimace and some unsubtle body language. Adler could see the disappointment (and maybe the envy) on Tyler's face, before the Aerosmith star turned away in evident contempt.

"Oh man," Steven Adler told the Metal Sludge Web site in a 2006 interview. "That ... ah ... umm ... that was the saddest fucking day of my life."

*S*eptember 1988. The epic Aerosmith/Guns tour was in its last days. At the L.A. shows, Guns joined Aerosmith onstage for "Mama Kin," the only time the two groups played together. Guns was told by its roadies that Aerosmith *never* watched an opening act from the side of the stage. Slash: "But for us, they were there almost every night [at the end of the tour]. The first time I saw them watching us play, it fucked with my head. It was weird."

The tour finished at the massive Texas Jam festival in Dallas. Both bands appeared on a bill, headlined by INXS, which also featured

Iggy Pop and Ziggy Marley. In the dressing room before the show, Aerosmith thoughtfully presented Guns N' Roses with end-of-tour gifts: complete sets of gold-tinted aluminum Halliburton cases, the ultimate in high-end travel accoutrements. (Not everyone thought this was cool.)

Guns was elated that the tour was over. They had been on the road for nine months. "Sweet Child o' Mine" was the number-one single in America. They hated INXS and thought of bailing out of Texas Jam. "What are they gonna do," Izzy asked in the dressing room, "kick us off the tour?" They had agreed to do this show long ago and had dreaded it ever since. "I hope we learn a lesson from this," Axl mused. "Don't do something just for the money, 'cause it ain't gonna work."

A lot of people wanted Guns to stay on the road even longer. *Appetite* was approaching five million in sales; the band was told it could set a record for a debut album if they kept touring. Backstage in Dallas, Slash told *Musician* magazine: "The promoters, the booking agency want us to keep going. We're getting offers to headline the [L.A.] Forum, Madison Square Garden . . . but we knew this has to end. And Axl's voice is getting to the point where he can't keep going. Everyone's been having a good time, but the thing is: we're burned out."

Duff threw a football around with the road crew. Steven Adler banged his sticks on chairs and tables, drinking royal jelly syrup. (He told British journalist Paul Elliott that it "builds up come in your balls.") Doug Goldstein's shirt said GET OFF MY DICK. (A few days earlier, Axl had approached Goldstein and asked if the other guys felt he had become a prima donna. "I haven't changed, have I, Doug?"

Goldstein put his arm around Axl. "Of course not," he replied soothingly. "You're the same prick you've always been.")

It was Slash's twenty-third birthday, and a cake was delivered to the dressing room in care of Peter Cottontail, Slash's hotel name. The icing spelled out HAPPY FUCKIN' BIRTHDAY YOU FUCKER.

*G*uns played second, as the rainy remains of Hurricane Gilbert soaked the stage into a Slip 'n Slide mat. Axl performed in a leather hat, a snakeskin jacket, and his leather codpiece. Two songs in, Axl realized the band wasn't fooling anybody. After slogging through a mistake-riddled "Mr. Brownstone," Axl snorted: "Guess I could use a little, huh?" He made some disparaging remarks about INXS singer Michael Hutchence, but they didn't come over clearly on the stadium's echoing PA system. Halfway through the set, Axl said: "I apologize if...I...sound like shit...but, too many planes...*and too much co-caine* [crowd roar]...But... *YOU KNOW WHERE THE FUCK YOU ARE?* [gladiator-scale crowd roar] *YOU'RE IN THE JUNGLE, BABY!... YOU'RE GONNA...DIE!!!!*"

It was ragged, but it worked. Way back in the stands, girls wearing Guns shirts screamed like Beatles fans while their guys pumped their fists. But up close, Axl thought his band sucked. He glared at them, stumbling around the stage like winos and barely turning in a professional concert. "Guess nobody here wants to play today," he said in disgust. Then he kicked a stage monitor that didn't seem to be working. (Slash: "Usually when we get in that situation, we get very punk. We *blaze,* even if we don't play that good. But we didn't do it today [in Dallas]. We fucking cracked. We didn't take over.")

"Sweet Child": Forty thousand Texan fans sang the "where do we go?" part with religious fervor—as if Axl Rose might know the answer. Then the band was seen arguing onstage. Tapes of the set reveal raised voices off-mike. They played a truncated version of "Paradise City" and waved good-bye—less than forty minutes into a contracted seventy-five-minute set. Duff smashed his bass guitar. Slash walked up to the microphone and delivered a curse-filled screed that nobody really got. No encore. Backstage, one of the promoters muttered: "Does it get any worse than this?" But out on the field, in the stands and bleachers, the big crowd was still cheering for Guns N' Roses, and begging for more.

W. AXL ROSE THROWS HIS BOMB

Guns N' Roses recuperated from exhaustion and various states of drug dependency over the next couple of months, in the hot L.A. autumn of 1988, a season made unusually hellish by the smoky fires in

the dry hills above Hollywood. The flames were fanned by the seasonal, mysterious Santa Ana winds, which blew the toxic exhaust of
the city back onto itself from the east. In southern California, the
winds had long been associated with psychic disturbances, bad luck,
and bummers. Coming events during the remainder of 1988, and well
into 1989, would not leave Guns N' Roses unscathed.

Slash moved into a rented apartment. As Guns' spokesman, he
spent a lot of his time talking to interviewers curious about the reality
of the world's most dangerous band. "I liked it when young kids loved
us and we were still sort of underground," he told writer Mark Rowland. "Now, we're sort of a circus act for normal people to go: 'Look at
them fall down! Isn't that cute?' . . . The fact is that we're sensitive
people, man. That's why, for one, I drink so much, and why Axl flies
off the fucking handle, and has these huge fits of total fucking depression. Because we're still living life, and sometimes that's hard to deal
with. . . . There's no big macho scene in this band. Duff is married. Axl
loves his girlfriend very much. No one [in the media] wants to know
about that, because it's not 'Guns N' Roses' for anything like that to
happen."

Duff moved back in with his wife. (They fought a lot.) Steven got a
place of his own, but then got so crazy with nothing to do that he actually asked Alan Niven for a roadie job with Great White, just so he
could be back on tour—someplace that was organized, and had a disciplined structure. Otherwise, "Stevie" was just out there, all alone by
the telephone, and all the dope dealers had his number.

Izzy lived with his girlfriend, whom the band hardly knew. One
day he showed up at a photo shoot for the cover of *Musician* magazine. He had come on foot, and arrived on time. The *Challenger* space
shuttle had recently exploded, killing the crew, and Izzy observed that
the chances of getting GN'R together in one room about equaled those
of the next space shuttle. Duff, Slash, and Steven called in periodically
to see if Axl had shown up. Two hours went by. Izzy and his girlfriend
chatted with Mark Rowland. Asked what he did on tour, Izzy said he
often wandered the streets of strange cities by himself. "He's a loner,"
the girl said. "He wants to buy a house in the desert, away from
people."

"I enjoy life more now," Izzy admitted, when asked about Guns' success. "I'm not so pissed off all the time. When you got no bread, drug problems, and winos in your alley throwing up, it tends to aggravate you. Now I can live like a normal person. For the ten years I've lived here, I've never had a bed. I just bought a futon, 'cause I'm used to sleeping on the floor."

Izzy mentioned that his father had turned up at one of the recent shows. It was the first time he'd seen him in eight years. "He comes walking backstage, unannounced, out of the blue. It took a second or two to recognize him. It was a real trip, but it wasn't . . ." Izzy decided that was enough about that. "Well, I don't want to get into it. I mean, in ten years I've only been to Indiana twice. I don't keep up like Axl does. I don't even know anyone there anymore." Prodded a little, Izzy admitted some affection for the place: "Well, when I look back, I do see some kind of stability that comes from growing up in a fucking cornfield. You're 'at one with the earth.'" He laughed at this irony. "You don't give a shit about much. It's a simple life."

How did that explain Axl? "Well, that has a lot to do with how he was brought up, and how he sees things." Izzy thought about his old friend a moment. "He's very uncompromised. He's the first one to say, 'Fuck this.'"

After waiting three hours, Izzy got ready to go. "I know this guy [Axl]," he told the photographer. "If I don't leave now, and he does show up, I'll have to wait *five* hours next time." Axl never showed up. He skipped another shoot the following week. He bagged an interview appointment. The publicists wrung their hands. "It's not personal," they soothed. "It's just his way."

But Axl was taking care of business when he had to. He was staying at a hotel, or with Erin. He was looking for an apartment in a secure building. He went to another band's promo party and hung out with Slash, something they rarely did anymore. He cut a backing vocal for Eagles drummer Don Henley's new record. He went shopping for a car, the faster the better. He was in the studio with Mike Clink, tinkering with his vocal tracks for Guns' forthcoming, already controversial album. He was on the phone all the time, fighting with the label, his management, the lawyers, and especially his band, fighting with every fiber of his being to get the song "One in a Million" on the album—uncensored.

* * *

*G*effen wanted the new Guns record out by the end of the year, while *Appetite* was still a Top Ten record and the buzz on the band still smoldered from their grand theft of the Aerosmith tour. (Around this time, Alan Niven sucker-punched Tim Collins in a Beverly Hills restaurant, because he thought Collins had tried to steal his band, and had insulted him with the gift of the expensive luggage to Guns.) At the same time, the cutting-edge label was worried that some of the material on the album would provoke a backlash that might not be worth the trouble of ever releasing it. The firm's legal department reportedly advised Geffen against putting out the album as Axl Rose was demanding it be released. There were even members of the band who had serious misgivings about what Axl was doing.

The record had a working title: *The Sex, The Drugs, The Violence, The Shocking Truth.* The first side had the four songs from the UZI Suicide EP ("Reckless Life," "Nice Boys," "Move to the City," "Mama Kin") and four songs that originated in the "acoustic" session recorded early in the year. The first was "Patience," written by Izzy, whistled by Axl, a soft song to a sad woman, asking for time, with a Dobro-like guitar solo. Axl shifted voices from metal crooner to screechy baby on the song's coda, tacked on later to combat ballad boredom. "Used to Love Her," the song about killing an annoying girlfriend, was like a funny fake Eagles song (written by Izzy and Slash). "You're Crazy" transposed the metallic screed on *Appetite* into faux southern rock and a bluesy R&B jam with some nice picking.

But "One in a Million" was something else. It started out like "Jumpin' Jack Flash" with a rocking beat, dark chords, folkish strumming. Then Axl threw his first bomb, at the dreaded bus station downtown. *"Police and niggers, that's right, get out of my way."* He doesn't want to buy any fake gold chains. On the chorus, he changed the point of view to what seems like the sarcastic comments of his friends back in Indiana, who taunt him as an egomaniac, who hope that they see him before he dies.

The next bomb went off in the second verse. "Immigrants and faggots" were taking over America and spreading "some fucking disease." The shooting star in the chorus had just about enough of what the eighties were offering up. Slash played an acoustic guitar solo and then Axl warned off the Klan and the "radicals and racists" who might try to exploit the complex set of images he was singing. In a scream, he raged that he was just a small-town white boy who was venting his anger. The Indiana chorus then reminded him that he was much too high, and concluded: "Maybe someday we'll see you, before you make us cry." The song trails off—"much too high, much too high"—on a stressful single piano note, played through the fade.

The furious energy and the lurid phobias of "One in a Million" bothered everybody, including Axl, who was compelled by his demons to defend it to the death. Usually songs like this appeared on indie records by Nazi skinheads or Serbian death metal bands. Nobody saw the point of the biggest band in America putting out blatant racism, homophobia, xenophobia, and then denying it was what it was. David Geffen was gay. Slash was half black, and his father was an immigrant. (He told an English writer that he was ashamed to have his mother hear the song.) One of Duff's brothers had married a black girl. (Upset, Duff said that he had black family members who wouldn't like what his band was putting out.) But Axl stood by his great hateful rock song, and even staked his career on having it his way. "One in a Million" would close *GN'R LIES*, unmolested, or there wouldn't be an album at all.

Slash later recalled: "There's a line in that song . . . police and niggers . . . that I didn't want Axl to sing. . . . But Axl's the kind of person who will sing whatever it is that he feels like singing. So I knew it was gonna come out, and there wasn't anything I could do." Slash argued that it was crazy to ask for trouble like this. "There's a point where making a statement is cool, and there's another point where you do things that aren't necessary and you're just asking for trouble. To intentionally put yourself in a position like that is not cool."

A compromise was finally reached when Axl agreed to apologize in advance for the song—on the album jacket itself. (He later claimed this was his idea.) The cover was designed to look like a sleazy London tabloid newspaper, with headlines screaming of sex and violence ("Sue's toes shot off by snatch gang"), and even a parody of *The Sun*'s "Page Three" nudie pix on the inner sleeve. Axl indeed wrote the wretched, snarling copy himself for the cover's apologia for "One in a Million":

Ever been unjustly hassled by someone with a gun and a badge? . . .
Been to a gas station or convenience store and treated like you don't
belong here by an individual who can barely speak English? Hopefully
not, but have you ever been attacked by a homosexual? Had some
so-called religionist try to con you out of your hard-earned cash? . . .
This song is very simple . . . my apologies to those who may take
offense.

As a summation of W. Axl Rose's (and William Bruce Bailey's)
experiences and worldview, this apology is nonpareil. As a statement
on an album jacket, it was without precedent. (It also wasn't the only
one on the record. Explaining the sentiments behind the misogyny
and sexism in "Used to Love Her," the jacket copy read: "Wife-beating
has been around for 10,000 years.") But it placated the lawyers and
marketers at Geffen, who signed off on the content, and the label
scheduled what would be called *GN'R Lies* for release in early December 1988.

When "One in a Million" provoked a furor in the press early in
1989, no one even noticed the apology at all. *Lies* peaked at number
two on *Billboard*'s chart and began to sell in the millions, chasing *Appetite* into the Top Ten within days of release.

HARD ROCK HEROES

*N*ovember 1988. Until *GN'R Lies* is released later in the month, the
talk of the rock world is Keith Richards' ultracool solo album *Talk Is
Cheap*. The Rolling Stones had been moribund during most of the
eighties. They hadn't toured since 1982, or even put out a decent album in years. The once sacred and invincible Stones were floundering
in internal feuds and personal acrimony. Mick Jagger was making irrelevant solo albums and insipid videos, while Keith Richards writhed
in embarrassed discomfort. Finally convinced to make an album on
his own, Keith came up with a funk-heavy backing band and a
mojo-laden book of songs, especially "You Don't Move Me," an explicit

attack on his onetime partner and glimmer twin. *Talk Is Cheap* was a critical success and sold well. Keith toured America and got great reviews. (But Richards, widely considered the Old Oracle of Rock, a Druid priest of the music's essential genius, publicly disrespected Guns N' Roses around this time, via anti-glam, anti-metal [and anti-rap] remarks published in the UK rock press.) But somehow Keith's brave album, which had attacked his bandmate head-on, provoked a Stones reconciliation a few months later in 1989, an event that would have repercussions for both the Rolling Stones and Guns N' Roses later that year.

*G*uns N' Roses was on the cover of *Rolling Stone* #539, dated November 17, 1988. The photo (taken at a New Jersey biker bar at dawn, before the Giants Stadium show the previous summer) was a miasma of teased hair, ripped jeans, tattoos, and attitude. The headline was HARD-ROCK HEROES. The magazine brazenly anointed the band as the saviors of rock music: "Finally, some bad boys who are good." Axl Rose was portrayed as pale and fragile offstage, almost "angelic," a sensitive soul whose musical tastes ran to George Michael, Frank Sinatra, the Raspberries, Philip Glass, and existentialist sound track maestro Enrico Morricone. But: "Onstage, releasing years of anger, he's a remarkably charismatic figure. He sings savagely, abusing his vocal cords, working the crowds with unequaled ferocity."

Slash on Axl: "He does a lot of weird shit that no one understands."

Axl spoke about a "new" song he was working on, working obsessively, an eight-minute ballad called "November Rain." It was going to be the big statement on Guns' next "real" album, and Axl was already worried about it. "If it's not recorded right," he said softly, "I'll quit the business."

Asked about the deaths at Monsters of Rock, Axl declined to accept responsibility. "I don't know what to think of it," he replied. "We didn't tell people, 'Drink so much alcohol that you can't fucking stand up.' I don't feel responsible in those ways. I don't want people to get hurt. . . . We want the exact opposite."

The band was all over the rock press in late 1988, glowering from the covers of *Circus, Musician, NME, Hit Parader, The Face, RIP, RAW,*

Kerrang!, Spin, and every rock mag in Europe and especially Japan. Axl warned their readers that there were songs on their upcoming EP that would "freak people out," but he said he didn't let anyone's reaction influence him. "People look over your shoulder and go, 'I don't know if you should say that, man, 'cause that's a little *heavy.*' But I don't worry about that. I don't want to censor myself, before I bring a song to the band." Axl also said that he was writing a lot of ballads, and that for their next record, Guns would try to make the longest record they could.

On writing songs: "Slash sits with his guitar. I run through some ideas as he plays, then we connect the pieces. Izzy and I write a lot of fun stuff real quick off the top of our heads." Axl said he wrote lyrics by himself. "It has to be a real situation, but it's still an abstract version. I want to write about the last two years—people I've met, situations that I've been in."

How is he dealing with the band's success? "Right now, it's hard, man. It's gonna take a little time for me, from living like a rat in the streets, to being able to manage my accounts, find places to live, buy houses. I'm getting a place here [in Los Angeles] and in the Midwest, and eventually I'd like to live in New York and get ideas for songs on the street." The main thing, he said, was to "get myself stable, 'cause we have another record to make, and I really want to make that record. It's like a dream. We get to be 'the big talent artists,' respected by people in the business." Axl said he wanted to record as many new songs as possible, maybe even make a double album, "so if anything happens to the band, it'll still live on for a while. . . . I just hope I'll write the kind of music that sticks around for a long time, whether you hear it on the radio or not. That's what I want: to be part of a band that gets a little place in history."

Axl also mentioned (to *Musician*) that he had just bought a customized Corvette Sting Ray sports car with a four-cam Chevy engine that, he proudly insisted, could do 180 miles an hour. Some dreams, at least, were coming true.

Slash did most of his interviews over the telephone. But he met a reporter from New York at the Hamburger Hamlet, just off Sunset, early one autumn afternoon, and blearily ordered a double Stoli screwdriver. He explained that he'd switched to vodka after drinking a bottle of Jack Daniel's a day for the past five years. "I've been up since five this morning doing interviews," he sighed. "Guy called me from Brazil. The album's fucking fourteen months old, but it just opened at number seven in Brazil, and it's number four in Greece. In fucking Holland, it's like number ten. So I've had to do all this."

Slash had a glib spin for the press, but it was already out of date in 1988. "We're like this mirror of what kids really go through, the reality of the teenager: having to work nine to five, or having shitty parents, or dealing with cops, authority. . . . So we're very close to the kids we play for. . . . Rock 'n' roll is a rebellious thing, getting away from authority, getting laid, getting drunk, doing drugs at some point. We're that kind of band, and there's not too many others." Asked about deadly Donington, Slash sounded almost proud. "Most rock concerts are safe as pie," he sneered. "We're doing something more . . . unpredictable, . . . that has a certain amount of . . . recklessness."

Slash, no fool, was still promoting Guns in late 1988 as the insurgent street band it had once been—in 1986. He didn't foresee that—shackled by fame and hype—Guns N' Roses' era as sonic avatars of "the street" was already over. His band would rarely ever play for "the kids" again—unless they could afford a ticket in the local basketball arena or at a gigantic football stadium on the outskirts of town.

*B*y the end of 1988, Guns had two albums in the upper reaches of *Billboard*'s chart. They had outdone their boyhood heroes, Aerosmith. And indeed, the competition had been murderous during the year that Guns exploded: U2's *Rattle and Hum,* Metallica's *And Justice for All,* George Michael's *Faith*; the mega-selling *Dirty Dancing* sound track; Bon Jovi, INXS, Def Leppard. Metallica's *And Justice for All* went platinum within days of release, with virtually no commercial airplay. But Guns had bucked all the so-called trends and transcended the music establishment's lack of street cred and woeful misreading of fan psychology. Hard-rocking Guns had shoved old-school hard rock (with a bipolar glam-blues spin) down the throats of the high school kids. They had forced mainstream America to accept them, on their own terms.

All the rock mags did end-of-the-year polls, and multi-platinum Guns consistently won as best new group. "It doesn't feel like we're a new group anymore," Duff told *Circus*. "We've been through so much shit. Even before [*Appetite*] came out, we didn't feel like a new band. Now we're dealing with all the things a regular band would, after its first album—apart from the fact that it sold so much. It's a strange feeling."

*I*n mid-December, Guns fulfilled its postponed commitments in Japan. They played arenas in Tokyo and Osaka, and made in-store appearances at record chains in both cities. There was no dope available in Japan, so the band binged on Suntory whiskey. Duff and Slash were registered at hotels as the Likesheet brothers: Luke Likesheet and Phil Likesheet. Before playing the Budokan Arena in Tokyo, the band and its entourage were dinner guests of the legendary Japanese concert promotor Sejiro Udo, who had brought the Beatles to Japan in 1964. Before then, no rock band had ever defiled the Budokan, which was built as a martial arts theater and was held sacred by devotees of jujitsu and other fighting techniques. "Mister Udo," as he was known to the western bands he promoted, had received serious death threats at the time, but the Beatles played the Budokan anyway, and now the big room was the most important showcase venue in the country. Guns N' Roses had sold out the hall in half an hour. (During dinner, Axl reportedly asked Udo-san if he had any advice for the band. The inscrutable Tokyo gangster of rock sagely answered that long-term relationships were very important for success.) On December 10, 1988, Guns played a fast, punkish, superheated show at the Budokan, played as if for their very lives. The (very young) fans screamed as if for their own lives. The next day the Tokyo newspaper *Asahi Shinbun* called Guns the best rock band that had ever played in Japan. Meanwhile, the road crew heard that Axl had locked himself in his Tokyo hotel suite and was refusing to speak to anyone.

Guns next played two shows in Melbourne, Australia. On December 15, Axl's introduction to "Mr. Brownstone," a long and rambling disquisition on drug use and free will, seemed to condone and glorify heroin addiction, which was an actionable public offense. Someone at the venue complained to the police. A warrant for Axl's arrest was reportedly prepared.

The next concert was in Sydney, where the press printed some unwise comments by the tour's opening act, local heroes Kings of the Sun, to the effect that Guns N' Roses owed a lot to Australian rockers Rose Tattoo. This sent Axl into a fury. At the show that night, he spewed invective against Kings of the Sun, whose loyal fans heckled Guns for the rest of the concert. This scene got real ugly, and at one point a furious Axl was prevented from diving into the crowd and going after a heckler only after Izzy grabbed his arm and suggested he cool it.

Guns flew to New Zealand for a December 19 concert near Auckland. There they learned that an overzealous prosecutor in Melbourne had issued a warrant for W. Axl Rose's arrest on a charge of (supposedly) promoting drugs. The vice squad was watching the band's hotel to arrest Axl when Guns passed through Sydney on their way home. The band's return journey from the far side of the world was rerouted to avoid Australia.

Chapter Nine

MAJOR PSYCHO TIME

**The urge to destroy is also
an urge to create.
—A. Bukunin**

STATE OF SHOCK

The year 1989 was hard for Guns N' Roses, five young men struggling under the daily burden of living up to being The World's Most Dangerous Band. But the year was totally epochal for almost everyone else in the world. The astounding and unforeseen collapse of European communism took the West by surprise when the Berlin Wall was knocked down. This was followed over the next two years by the (mostly nonviolent) demise of repressive regimes in Russia, Poland, Czechoslovakia, Hungary, and the rest of the former Warsaw Pact. Russia split into republics: Georgia, Ukraine, Latvia, et al. Yugoslavia self-destructed into a genocidal race war. This whole thing, Keith Richards theorized at the time, had evolved because of the subversive influence of rock and roll. It was, Richards claimed, the cultural artillery of blue jeans, the backbeat, long hair, and "no satisfaction" that finally pushed European communism onto the trash heap of history. (The following year, when the borders opened from the East, thousands of pilgrims descended on Jim Morrison's grave in Paris to pay their respects to the fallen poet of rock. On the July 3 anniversary of his 1971 death, they refused to leave the cemetery in the evening, partying wildly until the riot cops showed up with tear gas and batons.)

In the hermetic Hollywood world Guns N' Roses inhabited, 1989 was the year of the Rolling Stones' rebirth, when the band that had inspired Guns reformed after seven years of rancor. David Bowie had a terrific new avant rock band, Tin Machine. Madonna still ruled the dance floor. Her former protégées, the Beastie Boys, ruled the high schools now. NWA (Niggers With Attitude) from L.A.'s Compton area were the big stars of rap. Great White was blasting out heavy metal on the road via constant touring. New Kids on the Block owned Top Forty radio. The Cult's album *Sonic Temple* was big in L.A. There was also a new, head-banging metal band called Skid Row: three kids from Philadelphia discovered by Jon Bon Jovi and teamed with a white-hot lead singer from Toronto—Sebastian Bach. Early in 1989, there were people on Sunset Strip already predicting that Skid Row was going to be the next Guns N' Roses.

The real Guns N' Roses was off the road, and in a state of shock. In January 1989, Axl had Alan Niven fire most of the road crew and almost everyone who had worked for the band up till then: security, stagehands, photographers, stylists. There were rumors that Axl also wanted to fire Niven, who had never recovered from his handling of the Aerosmith tour and was now disliked at Geffen, but it was reported that Axl was talked out of this by the lawyers. Jeff Fenster, now working at Geffen Records as an A&R executive, says that Axl also wanted to fire Tom Zutaut as well. Jeff Fenster (and others) say that Axl wanted new ears at the label, and that he (and others) were approached to work with Guns on their next album. But Zutaut had gotten Fenster his job at Geffen, and Fenster had to remain loyal. (He also knew better than to work with the volatile Axl Rose, who he thought was a genius but totally unstable.)

So Axl began the year by cleaning house. Almost all the familiar faces were gone. The first new hire was a guitar tech for Slash. This was Adam Day, a young L.A. crew guy who jumped from tour to tour. He got the job because he'd worked for George Lynch of Dokken, whose playing Slash appreciated. Adam Day not only got the job but also moved into Slash's rented house in North Hollywood as a sort of permanent minder for Slash and his growing reptile zoo.

And Slash needed the company, because he was totally bummed.

There was nothing for him to do but drink and cop dope. He was totally disillusioned. "We'd been on the road," he recalled, "and we'd heard that we'd sold a certain number of records.... And the pace is what was exciting to us. We had no other life. Then—bam—it all comes to a screaming halt. You don't have your crew guys to take care of you. The maid doesn't come in to clean up. You lie in bed, waiting to go to the gig, but it's not gonna happen.... Then we went back to Hollywood, and it's the same shit—living in a cheap apartment and doing drugs all the time—except now I didn't even want to go out because people would recognize me." Soon the panic set in. Slash told *Rolling Stone,* "We got off the road, and it was like the wind and fucking tumbleweeds. People moving into houses, and buying cars and shit. It didn't kill us, but there was a lot of pressure, and the people around us wouldn't leave us alone. They thought we had bad attitudes, but... we were really fucking unhappy. It was depressing because the sense of... *abandon*... was gone. We thought we were streetwise, and hip to things, but we were really naïve. That's where [success] screwed with us, because it totally took our innocence away."

Slash wasn't alone. They were all bummed. Duff was drinking vodka heavily, and fighting with his young wife. Izzy isolated himself and his girlfriend, Dezi, from the others. Steven Adler was using heroin, cruising the Strip in his new Mercedes-Benz, enjoying all the attention and adulation due to a local rock star on his home turf (except when Stevie was hiding out from the dope dealers he owed money to). Axl, extremely depressed, moved himself and his framed gold and platinum albums into a luxury apartment in West Hollywood, whose walls were either all mirrors or all painted black. The floors and ceilings, even the refrigerator was black. For the next two years, as he later recalled, "I lived in a black room, with blackout curtains. Sometimes it was really good, and sometimes it was a nightmare. I tried to put my head together and find answers, because I couldn't find a reason to stay alive." He and Erin Everly often fought like tigers, at least until the screaming and shouting got crazy and Axl started breaking stuff, and either Erin or the neighbors called the cops.

On January 30, Guns was due to perform at the American Music Awards, held at the Shrine Auditorium in Los Angeles. They rehearsed "Patience," the new (and only) single from the *Lies* album, but on the day of the show, Steven Adler was reportedly receiving treatment at the Betty Ford Clinic for heroin addiction. Don Henley played drums instead, the telecast went on as planned, but now Axl Rose was mad as hell. He was getting tired of this band of junkies and alcoholics. He told a Geffen executive that pretty soon the other guys in Guns N' Roses were going to have some hard fucking decisions to make if they couldn't pull themselves together.

February 1989. *Appetite for Destruction* was at the seven million sales level and still in *Billboard*'s Top Five, eighteen months after its release. Then, early in the month, *GN'R Lies* surged into the Top Five as well, and Guns became the first band since 1984 to have two albums that high in the charts. This, despite the press-driven controversy over Axl's lyrics to "One in a Million." Nobody "got" the song as an artistic expression of frustration and the realities of life in urban America. Far from it: Nobody could believe the coolest new rock band in the world was actually calling black people "niggers," disrespecting the cops, bashing immigrants in general and Iranians by name, and raging against homosexuals and blaming them for the AIDS epidemic. No rock star, not even arch-controversialist Jim Morrison, had ever before gone this far in putting what he really felt on the line to the enormous rock audience.

Mainstream press reaction was predictable. The editor of *Billboard* let fly: "['Million'] is still a piece of racist, gay-bashing garbage, a brainless screed . . . affronting any human person who believes in art's mandate to articulate the Truth." (No one had ever heard of this mandate before, but no matter.) Radio wouldn't touch the song. Even some of the (advertising-dependent) rock mags questioned the band's judgment. Slash was embarrassed in front of his family and was in semi-hiding. When *Lies* had come out, he called his mother: "My mom, who is black—right?—was in Europe, and it was the first time we had talked in ages. I asked if she'd heard the EP yet, and she said no. But later my little brother came on and told me she *had* heard it, but she was so shocked that she didn't know what to say to me on the phone. I understood it. There's nothing that I can say in the press that's gonna cover it up."

Axl Rose stayed on the sidelines that winter and watched the furor unfold around "One in a Million." The gossip columns said that Guns would be dropped from performing at an AIDS benefit associated with the openly gay head of their record label. (Axl noted, with all due irony, that Geffen was making serious money off the record, as sales of *Lies* broke the two million mark.) Axl pointed out that he had already apologized—on the fucking album cover! He told friends he was proud that he'd gotten the (normally stupid) hard rock audience thinking about what the song meant. He told one interviewer that that song was about someone who had to take a side against bullshit and injustice. He told another that he thought the whole thing was "a strange amount of power to share." Charged with homophobia, Axl defended his artistic rights: "The song is very generic. It's very vague, very simple. It was written that way. It was like, 'OK, I'm writing this song—*the way I want to.*'" Axl spoke for the record about a West Hollywood deputy sheriff who told him that he had arrested an HIV-positive male hustler, only to see said hustler again working Santa Monica Boulevard the next day. Axl explained to an English metal mag that he had never experienced racism until he came to Los Angeles, and even described another possible interpretation of "One in a Million," this one involving his own black angel: an older black man who had noticed Bill Bailey's primal confusion at the now archetypal downtown bus station; a kindly sort of African American tribal elder who had helpfully guided the furious and humiliated country bumpkin to where he needed to go. "Maybe *that* guy was the one in a million," Axl suggested. Nobody believed a word of it.

On February 18, Guns gathered to shoot the "Patience" video at the Record Plant. As the band strummed acoustic guitars (and Adler idled with a lone drumstick), Axl whistled the intro and slithered his way through the lyric, which he read from a sheet of paper. Additional scenes shot by Nigel Dick featured ghostly images of people moving through hotel corridors, and a disheveled Slash in bed, fondling a large snake and entertaining a series of well-stacked girls in stripper lingerie. The video helped propel "Patience" into *Billboard*'s Top Five again, when the single was released later that spring.

PANDORA'S BOX

*M*arch 1989. The "Paradise City" single hit the American Top Five. FM stations played the entire seven-minute version. Top Forty radio, again to Axl's displeasure, broadcast an edited version.

Del James interviewed W. Axl Rose for *RIP* magazine at Axl's black and mirrored apartment. By then Axl had grown a full red beard and a moustache. He proudly displayed his new gun collection, including a riot-grade shotgun, a 9mm pistol, and an Israeli-built Uzi submachine gun. He explained that he'd gotten into a disagreement with someone whose house he was trying to buy and just felt like arming himself with an Uzi. Axl and Del talked about the pending wrongful-death suit against Judas Priest, after a young American metal fan killed himself, and his family blamed Priest's satanic lyrics. All the L.A. bands were out on the road, except for Guns. Slayer and Motörhead were on tour. Danzig was opening for Metallica in Europe. Hollywood was now the music industry's assembly line, pumping out big-haired product for the unslaked cravings of metal fans around the world.

Axl liked Del James and gave him a good interview. He described his clinical diagnosis of manic depression and became the first rock star to admit he took medication for his mood shifts. He said he was toning down the illegal drugs, leaving that to the rest of the band. He explained all the Axl-is-dead rumors, saying it was because he liked to disappear for a few weeks at a time, just lying low and trying to digest what was going on around him. He tried to explain "One in a Million," doing a cheesy Iranian accent in imitation of the dark-skinned store managers he so hated. He denied that the band was raking in millions and provided a cogent lesson in band economics. He talked about a new song of Izzy's the band was working on, "Double Talkin' Jive."

Axl said he was sad that Slash had to drink so much, but he understood it. "Once you reach a point where you're multi-platinum, all of a sudden you're dealing with major record executives, and lawyers and managers, and MTV and everything else. You start becoming one of those people you thought you were against.... Slash probably wouldn't drink so much if he didn't have to deal with all these people. He's able to quietly drink his bottle and talk to them. If I got that drunk, I'd just tell everybody to get the fuck out of my house."

Axl told *RIP* that he was scared of getting AIDS. He emphasized again that he didn't use drugs. "I can't hide in drugs anymore," he said. "And I have shows to do. I won't touch drugs because it fucks up my throat."

Advice to *RIP* readers: "My advice is don't get a fucking habit, don't use anybody else's needle, and don't let drugs become a prerequisite for having a good time. Do things in moderation, and just be careful." The April 1989 issue featured Axl on its cover, with the big black barrel of the riot gun rising out of his crotch, aimed obscenely at the reader.

*L*ate March 1989. Slash had left the first apartment he lived in that year. It was a constant debauch, with the cops there almost every night. So many people crowded in that Slash usually bolted after midnight and slept on friends' couches. One of his fave crash pads was the West Hollywood house of publicist Arlett Vereeke, who worked for David Lee Roth at the time. Interviewers would call, looking for Roth. Slash would answer the phone: "No, he's not here, but I'm Slash from Guns N' Roses, and I'll do the interview."

In March, Slash rented and moved into a secluded house at the end of a dirt road, high in the hills above Hollywood. The road was so bad that cab drivers made him walk the last fifty yards. A limo almost went over the cliff one night. The view after dark spread out below like a broad lagoon of twinkling stars. (He never saw the view in the daytime.) The main room, done up in deep-purple drapes, contained stacks of red Marshall mini-amps and loads of collectible guitars. Pandora, Slash's brand-new eight-foot python, was in her glass case. The other snakes were cared for elsewhere while the house Slash had bought on the other side of the hills was being readied for him.

Three in the morning. The TV was on, a rerun of *Dynasty* flickering without sound. Videocassettes included *Richard Pryor Live, Scarface, Animal House, Sex Boat.* Kitty Kelley's biography of Frank Sinatra was open on the coffee table. Slash (Metallica shirt, black jeans, bare feet) poured interviewer Mick Wall a Jack and Coke. "I got bored with the vodka," he explained. When Slash vanished into the bathroom and emerged with renewed energy and fresh quotes, Wall assumed he was doing lines of cocaine. Slash confirmed this. The phone never stopped ringing. Guitar tech Adam was sleeping downstairs.

Wall asked what Guns was doing. "Writing and rehearsing," Slash answered. "Supposed to be, anyway." He said he had new songs Axl was excited about. "Izzy's got a few. I had him over here and we managed to get them on tape. Hopefully, Axl will come over in a coupla weeks and start putting melodies and lyrics to this stuff." He said that at one point he and Axl were going to rent a house together and write some songs, but no house they looked at was big enough for both of them.

The truth was that success had driven the band further apart than was easily fixable. Slash was miserable. He had to deny the band was on a high. "Actually, it's not a high anymore. The initial high was those first few tours; that was the best of it. Now we're off the road and we have a lot of money and we can do whatever we want. Except—there's nothing I want to do, except go back out there and fuckin' play. I just want to get back on the road. Now I just go out to a club, and end up leaving drunk and totally depressed. It's really a pretty traumatic experience.... It gets to be a little lonely after a while."

The phone rang again. No one answered.

Mick Wall suggested that Slash seemed bitter about Guns' success. Slash looked away. "It's like the songs we wrote when we were nothing, and being fucked with all the time, and hassled, and we were outsiders and the underdogs—those experiences provided us with all the material we needed for the first album.

"Now, though, it's like the amount of bullshit we have to put up with, and the amount of crap we have to take from people has changed. You can't find people to be close with, and maintain any sort of normal lifestyle. It makes you bitter, and you start to write in that vein. So there's no lack of material: it just sort of shifted from one fucked thing to another."

It wasn't all bad. Slash had been voted best guitarist of the year in *Kerrang!* and *Circus*. The Gibson guitar company wanted to market a Slash-model Les Paul guitar, with a special Slash pickup, "and shit like that. That, to me, is an amazing compliment. It actually means something to me, you know?" But something didn't quite feel right to Slash. "It's like this one album has taken us as high as we can possibly go—*on one fuckin' record*. It's scary, man." What if there was no second record? Slash told Gibson that he wouldn't do these endorsements until the second record was done, and the next Guns N' Roses tour started for real.

"I mean, look what happened to Aerosmith. They were huge, and then, all of a sudden"—he snapped his fingers—"gone. No matter who you are, one band doesn't make the world go round, and you can't take yourself so seriously to think that it does."

The phone kept ringing. The doorbell sounded. "Shit," Slash muttered. "I didn't really feel like company tonight." It was Izzy Stradlin at four in the morning, after the Hollywood clubs had closed, with an entourage that included rocker Billy Squier, whose Zep-style songs had dominated radio and MTV five years earlier. Mick Wall observed, "[Izzy] pranced into the room like a man trying to avoid a minefield, floppy cap yanked down over his eyes, cigarette smoldering between thin pale lips, the face and hands as gray as a ghost's." Izzy made straight for the kitchen. "You got any more vodka?" he bawled at Slash.

Slash ignored this. "That's OK!" Izzy shouted. "I found it!" Slash ushered Izzy and his entourage downstairs so he could finish the interview. He told Mick Wall that Guns was thinking about an offer they had received from the Rolling Stones to open for them in Los Angeles, when the Stones hit town on their (much-rumored) comeback tour of the United States later in 1989. The tape picked up the raucous party now raging downstairs, with Izzy and Billy singing and playing guitars. Slash padded into the kitchen in hope that they'd left him his bottle of Jack Daniel's. Izzy came up to get Slash's twelve-string Martin guitar, and glided downstairs with it. The phone rang again. This party went on for two more days, until everyone collapsed.

LET'S MILK THIS SUCKER

*M*ay 1989. "Patience," the first single from *GN'R Lies,* was released in England and was an immediate hit. In Los Angeles, rumors continued to swirl around the dormant Guns, improbable stories of death and debauchery. Axl and Slash were both said to have died. One story had Steven Adler kidnapped by the drug dealers to whom he owed big money. Another had an enraged Duff McKagan going after said dealers with a shotgun, drunkenly barging into a ranch house in the Valley where he thought Steven was being held, and realizing he was in the wrong house when a startled senior citizen started dialing 911.

Izzy Stradlin, wisely, left town for a while. He traveled around Europe with his girlfriend and stayed only in sporadic touch with the Guns office.

The persistent rumor was that the Rolling Stones were coming to town for four nights later in the year and would be playing the massive Los Angeles Coliseum. The Stones were cutting a new album—*Steel Wheels*—that would hopefully bring the epic band back from the dead. The local angle was that Guns N' Roses was offered all the L.A. shows, but the band kept denying these rumors through Geffen's spokespeople. Geffen was also fielding repeated requests from *Rolling Stone* magazine to interview Axl. He finally agreed when the magazine promised that they would put Axl on the cover, by himself; that the interviewer be his friend Del James; and that GN'R's official lensman, Robert John, shoot all the photographs, including the sacred cover.

Del James arrived at Axl's West Hollywood condo late in the day, in the middle of May. Axl and Erin had fought the previous evening, and his apartment was still a battlefield. The big mirrored wall in the living room was shattered. An acoustic guitar was a pile of tragic splinters in the corner. Axl's framed gold and platinum albums, which had neatly adorned the walls along with various plaques and awards, were scattered around the floor, most beyond repair. Someone had kicked in the expensive stereo. The telephone had been dropped off the twelfth-floor balcony. Axl's immense, uncontrollable rage still hung in the air, like stale tear gas.

He wouldn't say what the fight had been about. Now, Axl explained, he was trying to calm down, get a handle on things, write some songs and try not to be just another "rich asshole," as he put it. He'd achieved his teenage ambition, he said, which was to outsell Boston's 1976 debut album. (*Appetite for Destruction* was now at the twelve million sales mark.) He was regrouping now, trying to be the CEO of Guns N' Roses, learning to pay attention to things like marketing and merchandise.

Mostly he was writing songs, or trying to. The label wanted another record, and fast. "They're all saying, 'Let's *milk* this sucker.'" Axl was pleased that the new music was richer for him than the old songs: more emotional, more nuanced. For the first time since he left Indiana, he was able to afford a piano, and a place to play it. ("For years I couldn't even figure out where I was sleeping on any given night, let alone having a piano.") Writing on piano brought out ballads, not rock songs. He mentioned "November Rain" and "Don't Cry," but in almost the same breath worried (and rightly so) that *Appetite* would be "the only good album we'll ever make."

Axl was tired of trying to explain "One in a Million," since whatever he said, about a song that nobody understood, only seemed to make his critics hate him more. He did confirm that the band had been dropped from a Gay Men's Health Crisis benefit that David Geffen was affiliated with.

Axl insisted he wasn't anti-homosexual, that he was just proheterosexual. He didn't believe in bashing gays. "The most I do is—on the way to the Troubadour in 'Boystown' [West Hollywood]—I'll yell out the car window. *'Hey—why don't you guys like pussy?'* 'Cause I'm confused. I just don't understand it."

Axl said he had sex as often as possible, and gave a clue to his recent domestic disharmony. "I'm a person that has a lot of different relationships. It's hard to maintain a one-to-one relationship if that other person isn't going to allow me to be with other people. I have a real open, hedonistic sexual attitude. Just because you're not totally in love with a person doesn't mean you don't like them. You can think they're attractive, and you want to touch them, have a great time with them. Love and lust go hand in hand, like good and evil."

Asked about music, he mentioned Derek and the Dominoes, Todd Rundgren, the Bar-Kays, "the first Patti Smith." He was just getting into the Cure, and liked Soundgarden for its singer, Chris Cornell. His desert-island disks were the Sex Pistols and *Queen II.* He said that no formal offers had yet been made for Guns to open for the Rolling Stones later that year. He said he liked hanging out at the beach in the evening. He indicated he'd made up with his stepfather, who he claimed was a fan of the band's. He proudly said he had bought a couple of suits (and was photographed in one of them for *Rolling Stone's* cover—for which he also shaved his beard.) When the interview was published the following summer, it ended with Axl's biggest regret.

"That I didn't talk to Todd Crew before he left for New York."

In June, Axl and Slash were working on songs in Chicago. Axl wanted a change of atmosphere, and he loved Chicago. It was the Big City when he was growing up down the road in Indiana. Tim Burton's *Batman* had just opened, and Axl went to see it a couple of times, and tried to perfect the fiendish laugh that Jack Nicholson had developed for the Joker.

They worked on Axl's two related power ballads, "November Rain" and "Estranged," at a rehearsal studio above the Metro night-club. These were his autobiographical epics of love and loss, as straight from the heart as anything he'd ever written. "November Rain" was an older song, "Estranged" more recent. Both reflected Axl's turbulent relationship with Erin Everly. Axl previewed the songs for Indiana friends and visitors from L.A. on a grand piano in the middle of the large room. Meanwhile, Slash was beginning to work out the beautiful guitar melody he put onto "Estranged" later, in Los Angeles.

* * *

*A*xl was also writing songs with West Arkeen during the blistering California summer of 1989. In July, the two musicians appeared at the Scrap Bar in Hollywood. With Arkeen accompanying him on guitar, Axl sang two songs, both ballads he'd written with Del James: "The Garden" and "Yesterdays." The session was taped by MTV and parts were later used in their GN'R *Rockumentary*. Axl was also seen in various New York clubs that summer and early autumn, partying hard with some of the Cult, reportedly having an affair with a very hot young Chinese girl while staying at the Mayflower Hotel near Central Park. One night, after he'd taken her along to a Michael Monroe (ex-Hanoi Rocks) video shoot, she could be heard yelling at Axl in the hotel corridor, complaining that he had fucked her only once that day. Soon, all the *"How Fucked Up Is Axl Rose?"* stories began wafting out of nighttime Manhattan like malign vapors.

August 21, 1989. Slash got onstage with Great White at South Street Seaport in Manhattan and banged out some Stones songs. On the 26th, Axl joined Tom Petty at the state fair in Syracuse, New York, and performed Petty's hit song "Free Fallin'" and Dylan's "Knockin' on Heaven's Door." This created a small stir, since Petty was a client of L.A. talent manager Irving Azoff, and Axl was rumored to be thinking of dumping Alan Niven. But nothing immediately came of it.

*A*ugust 27, 1989. Izzy Stradlin was on a plane heading to L.A., where he was supposed to work on Guns' next record, and he was none too happy about it. He was also drunk. He lit a cigarette. "I was smoking, and the stewardess came over, and I must have told her to go fuck herself." Then Izzy's bladder demanded attention, but there was a long line waiting to use the toilets. So Izzy, unable to contain himself, snuck into the plane's little galley, unzipped, and let flow into the trash can. When this was reported to the pilot, he put the aircraft down in Phoenix. Izzy was escorted off the plane, arrested, and charged with interfering with the flight crew and public indecency. "I remember thinking, 'Uh oh, I just fucked up again.'" This quickly got into the papers. Suddenly, Izzy Stradlin was looking at six months in jail because he had a prior arrest for drug possession in L.A. (A Geffen publicist helpfully suggested that urinating in public was just Izzy's way of expressing himself.)

NOT YOUR THINKING MAN'S DRUG USER

*T*wo weeks later, September 1989, Izzy was in Los Angeles, staying in a hotel near Venice Beach. His urine was being tested for drugs, so he was trying to stay clean. The phone rang at four o'clock one morning. Slash was calling from a pay phone. He'd been pulled over for driving stoned but somehow talked the cops into letting him go. Izzy later said, "This was when he was doing a lot of heroin, right? So he showed up at dawn, fucked out of his mind, and I let him stay the night. The next morning I found two rigs stashed in the closet. I told him, 'Listen fucker, I got my own problems and I can't have this shit around.' I was on probation for six months at the time."

One night Izzy was holding court at the Cathouse, when he was approached by Sharise Neil, the blond, big-breasted, mud-wrestling wife of Vince Neil, lead singer of Mötley Crüe. Vince was out of town, and the un-shy Sharise tried to chat Izzy up, but he allegedly rebuffed her with the same charm he had displayed to the airline girl, eight miles high.

So she told her husband that Izzy, "all fucked up," had hit on her, pulled her shirt down, exposing her. She told Vince that she had slapped Izzy, and that Izzy had kicked her. Everyone in the Cathouse saw this go down, she claimed. Vince reflected on this, and swore revenge.

On September 11, 1989, Izzy and Axl appeared at MTV's Video Music Awards at the Universal Amphitheater, where they accepted a statuette for Best Heavy Metal/Hard Rock Video (for "Sweet Child"). Later in the program Izzy and Axl joined Tom Petty and the Heartbreakers on "Free Fallin'." As Izzy was coming off the stage, he handed off his guitar and was then smashed in the face by a pudgy, long-haired figure that jumped out of the shadows. It was Vince Neil, who blurted words to the effect that Izzy had besmirched the honor of his wife. Izzy went down. Vince's ring had cut his lip. Neil was dragged away and thrown out. Axl chased after him, shouting death threats. Neil claims he offered to fight him, and that Axl backed off. "Just don't fuck with my band again, OK?" Axl said, according to Neil, and walked away.

Neil later claimed that Izzy apologized to his wife. But it got into the press and set off an embarrassing catfight after Axl started using interviews to suggest a duel between himself—"knives, guns, fists, anything"—and the cowardly bushwhacker from Crüe. Vince Neil and Nikki Sixx said some shit of their own. Of course, fists never flew, and they all looked like girls to the readers of *RIP, Raw, Metal Edge, Smash Hits, Kerrang!, Circus, Hit Parader,* and the other mags on whose covers Axl appeared over the next year. (Also Duff and Slash were annoyed because they were known to party with certain Crüe members. Tommy Lee was even a Drunk Fux one night.)

September 1989. Guns was supposed to be making its next album with Mike Clink. Axl was telling the press that they had thirty-five songs and were going to make the longest album they could. Forget about it: Axl and Slash weren't speaking to each other, and Steven Adler couldn't play the drums. Duff was drinking, and he and Mandy weren't getting along. The band never saw each other. There was no new album.

Slash: "The band got separated. We'd written the first album when we were living in one room. Now we're getting our homes. Slash here, Axl there. Duff's here, and I don't know where Steven lives. It's like, 'Duff, can we come over?' And he goes, 'Well, the gardener's coming today.' This was a new experience for us that took a long time to adjust to."

Slash was also adjusting to becoming, as he later put it, "a major heroin addict." His beloved grandmother had died in the summer, making matters even worse for Saul Hudson. Heroin helped him get through this shattering loss. But to his mates, the narcotic was sapping the energy of the band. Axl was said to be extremely angry. Even veteran user Izzy Stradlin was amazed: "[Slash] was a mess. He's a great guy and all, but he can't monitor his own intake, with the result that he's always fucking up big-time: leaving dope on the table when the cops come by; nodding out into his food in restaurants.... Slash is *not* what you'd call your thinking man's drug user. He's real careless ... doing really shitty things—like OD'ing in other people's apartments. A lot."

Slash was so out of it that he would borrow friends' cars and forget where he had left them. He would troll the Rainbow, trying to borrow cash so he could score. It was embarrassing. His manager and friends tried to force him into rehab programs with the same people that had helped Aerosmith, but Slash always left early. Alan Niven and his wife took Slash into their home and endured a days-long cold-turkey detox marathon. Slash relapsed immediately. Then, just before the Stones shows—the biggest performances of Guns' career so far—Slash started being found late at night, unconscious, lying in the gutter outside various clubs, sometimes minus watch, wallet, and cowboy boots.

"It was getting to be a real disgrace," photographer Robert John says. Around this time, he went up to Slash's house on Walnut Drive to shoot a cover story for *RIP*. Slash excused himself to take a shower, and never came back. Robert found him, smacked out in the shower, smoking a cigarette. He took a couple of rolls of Slash naked, under the spray, eyes shut in a blissed-out poppy reverie. The magazine ran the pictures a few weeks later as an honest depiction of the life of an American rock star.

*B*ack in the early summer of 1989, Axl basically said that the band should go cut the album without him, and he'd do his vocals when they had the tracks down. By some accounts, Duff, Slash, and Steven Adler worked sporadically in Chicago for several months that year. "We waited for Axl and Izzy," Duff remembered, "but Axl had some reasons for not coming out. He was waiting for us to do our trip, as musicians. Izzy ... was having a hard time with life at that point and was traveling around Europe. So the three of us sat in Chicago for three months, and kinda got suicidal. But we also got some shit done, and I think we even might have gained some edge [after a long lay-off]."

Axl told Mick Wall that the band had fought like dogs in Chicago, and even blamed himself. He said he'd called Slash from the road while he was driving across the country in his truck, and that Slash complained that nothing was happening. When he arrived, he started messing with Duff's music, tampering with Slash's riffs. "I thought we were on a roll. And then they decided that I was a dictator, right? I'm a 'total dictator' and I'm a 'totally selfish dick.' Slash is like, 'We're not getting nothin' done.' I was like, 'What do you mean—we just put down six parts of new songs!' I thought we were cranking."

In October 1989, Guns N' Roses reconvened in Hollywood to gather what energies remained to the band, so they could support the rampaging Rolling Stones for four nights later that month. Guns had reportedly been offered the opening slot for the whole *Steel Wheels* tour but had declined. Then Guns was offered $400K for two nights in L.A. The two shows sold out in minutes. Two more L.A. concerts were added, with Guns getting $600K in addition. It was the band's ultimate payday, so far. But no one in the band was doing that well, and Axl was soon said to have changed his mind and didn't want to go on. His band had not played together since New Zealand, nine months earlier and, seemingly, a lifetime away. Guns was now second on the three-band bill. Opening the shows would be the virtuosic black metal trio, Living Color, whose guitarist, Vernon Reid, was being egged on by the media to respond to the racism of "One in a Million" from the stage of the Coliseum to 70,000 people.

On October 10, Guns tried to shoot a video for "It's So Easy," in case the old album track had to be the band's next single. The video crew set up at the Cathouse. Erin Everly was to be featured in the video, her costume a provocative black leather bondage ensemble. There were whips on the set. A surprise visitor was Slash's faux uncle David Bowie, who might have had a cocktail prior to arrival. Bowie began to pay close attention to Erin, not realizing she was the crazy lead singer's girlfriend. Axl saw this and was over in a flash: jostling, cursing, pushing, probably not realizing who was hitting on his scantily clad, totally stunning woman. David Bowie beat a hasty retreat, followed by Axl and everyone else. The story made the papers. The video was never finished.

Axl wasn't even sure that Guns could perform by October 18, 1989, the date of the first Stones concert. But rather than rehearse with the band, he accepted *RIP*'s invitation to play at the mag's third anniversary party on October 13. Guns N' Roses went on at one A.M. at the Park Plaza Hotel in Echo Park, near downtown L.A., after fire marshals had evicted a thousand people from the packed hotel ballroom. The band turned in a rusty but credible show, the last gig in a small room that Guns N' Roses would ever play.

Afterward, Axl said something to Izzy about not wanting to open for the Stones anymore. Izzy couldn't believe it. His band could fall apart at the apex of its career. Izzy Stradlin told his girlfriend that it would take a fucking miracle to get Guns N' Roses through the next week.

MIXED EMOTIONS

*I*t was dawn in Los Angeles, a balmy Friday morning, October 18, 1989. Izzy Stradlin's phone rang at six A.M., and he took the call because he knew who was on the other end. Axl Rose, according to Izzy, was "completely hammered." He told Izzy, "I'm quitting." They spoke briefly, then Axl got off the phone.

When Izzy walked into Guns N' Roses' dressing room in the bowels of the Coliseum some hours later, he looked at the band and said, "Fellas, it's gonna be a *long* four days."

W. Axl Rose arrived backstage at the Los Angeles Coliseum early in the afternoon. A Rolling Stones fan since childhood, he had never seen the band perform, had never met any of them, let alone open for them later that evening. Axl watched, fascinated, as Mick Jagger ordered his troops around like a general on a battlefield. The once primal Rolling Stones, originally a five-piece guitar band, now consisted of fifteen onstage musicians, with a touring crew of around two hundred people backing them up. Their stage was a gigantic scaffold that suggested a rusting steel mill, or a launchpad for an obsolete rocket.

Axl Rose noticed that between rehearsing some of the Stones' new songs—"Mixed Emotions," "Rock in a Hard Place," "Terrifying"—Mick reviewed documents from aides, signed checks, took calls from Jack Nicholson and Warren Beatty. Axl also noticed Jagger's new keyboard player, Matt Clifford, who seemed to be the musical director of the Stones—on Jagger's authority. Maybe, Axl considered, he too should have a keyboard player in Guns N' Roses, to keep him on pitch, like Mick did. And maybe if Mick Jagger could be a total fucking dictator, and call every fucking shot there was to call, maybe it could work that way in his band too. Some changes would now be made. W. Axl Rose, son of the late, murdered William Rose—*what had he done, to end up like that?*—must have already had a trick up his sleeve, a card that he was going to play that night, in front of a lot of people.

After their sound check, Axl was sitting around backstage, just observing from atop an amp, when Mick Jagger came up to him. Axl was surprised, because Mick didn't talk to anybody, and no one was supposed to bother him. With Jagger was a mild-looking gent, wearing glasses: Eric Clapton.

Jagger: "So, um, Axl? Ya got inna fight wiff Dy-vid Bowie, roight?"

Axl: "You know? And I'm like . . . I told them the story real quick, and they go off into their own little world, right in front of me, talking from years of knowing each other. *'Well, of course, when David gets drunk, he turns into the bloody devil from Bromley, innit?'* I'm not even in this conversation, just sitting there, and every now and then they'd ask me for a couple more facts, and then go back to bitching about Bowie. I was thinking: *wow!*" Eventually Jagger excused himself, saying he had some paperwork to do.

"He checked everything," Axl said. "*Every fucking thing.* Every little aspect, from what the backup singers get paid, to how much we're paying for this part of the PA. He's on top of it all."

Slash, meanwhile, was having a bad hair day. "At the time, I was at the tail end of a really, really serious heroin problem," he said later. "I felt that we *had* to do the Stones gigs, to bring the band together. No one *ever* saw anybody. I was doing my [heroin] thing; only three of us were rehearsing on a regular basis. I wanted to do the gig—even though our management was against it." Slash later said that he had a clear, prior understanding with the band, its management, and record label, that he would clean up after the concerts.

October 18, 1989. It was a beautiful southern California evening. Seventy thousand rock fans were in their seats when Living Color went onstage in the bright twilight. As expected, guitarist Vernon Reid made some remarks about racism. He said that anyone who called somebody a nigger, especially in a rock song that many people heard, was selling bigotry, and it wasn't cool, no matter how anyone tried to make excuses for it. There was some scattered cheering at this from the crowd, most of whom were white and prosperous, and even possibly felt the same way that Axl Rose did about predatory niggers, AIDS-spreading gays, and uncouth immigrants from Iran.

The vibes in Guns N' Roses' dressing room were subdued. Slash hid behind his hair, noodling on guitar. (He was doing speedballs—heroin and cocaine.) His dealer had a backstage pass. There were three leather-clad horn players (the Suicide Horns) on the gig, anchored by Duff's bother, Matt McKagan, on trombone. Steven Adler was hyper, a little bloated-looking. Izzy kept his head down, no eye contact. They were drinking Jack, listening to the preshow mix tape: Prince, Fear, Faith No More, Live, Metallica, Cameo.

But . . . no Axl Rose. Where the fuck was he?

The Los Angeles concerts were a headline story around America that autumn. People from Axl Rose's past now tried to contact him. Axl was startled when one of these turned out to be an uncle, the brother of his real father, the vanished and presumed-dead William Rose.

"His brother called me," Axl later told an interviewer, "right around the Stones shows, and I had my brother talk to him. I didn't talk to him, because I needed to keep that separation. But I confronted my mom, and she finally talked to me about it, and they told me he was dead. He was pretty much headed for that anyway—a very unsavory character, was what they said." (An investigator later learned only that William Rose had probably been murdered in 1984: shot at close range, and buried in a seven-mile strip mine, somewhere in Illinois.)

Bad timing, as this knowledge sent Axl into a manic downswing. Road manager Doug Goldstein told a reporter that Axl hadn't slept for more than forty hours before the show.

*A*t the Coliseum, they started to panic around six o'clock. Still no Axl. They couldn't find him anywhere. Izzy told Doug Goldstein that he didn't think Axl was coming. Axl didn't answer his phone. Finally Axl picked up, sounding tired and deeply depressed. Someone talked him into doing the gig. Robert John: "We found out Axl was still at home, and Alan [Niven] sent me to get him. I picked him up at Erin's apartment in Beverly Hills. Him and Erin were fighting, or something. He said he wanted to quit the band because Slash wouldn't stop using heroin, but I didn't take it seriously."

Guns N' Roses was introduced at nine P.M., playing in front of the Stones' immense, postindustrial scaffold set. The crowd made a thunderous human noise for their local heroes, the loudest the musicians had yet heard. The first song went off seemingly OK, and then it was time for "Mr. Brownstone," when Axl usually addressed the audience about doing drugs, one way or another. Still wearing aviator shades, looking down while he spoke, Axl stepped to the lip of the stage, adjusted the microphone stand, and blew everyone's mind.

"I just want to say . . . I hate to do this onstage. . . . But I tried—every other fucking way. . . . And unless certain people in this band . . . get their shit together . . . these will be the last Guns N' Roses shows you will fucking ever see." [Big cheer from audience.] The videotape shows Slash holding his guitar, fidgeting, looking down, thinking about walking off and quitting himself, right then and there.

Pacing now, a Pentecostal hellfire preacher scolding his flock, Axl

continued: "'Cause, I'm tired...of too many people, in this organization...DANCING WITH MISTER GOD DAMNED BROWNSTONE!"

This was the signal to start the song, but Mr. Brownstone staggered to life slowly, as the band realized Axl had just threatened to
quit in front of the whole city. This was unprecedented. Mick had
never denounced Keith as a junkie at Wembley Stadium. Paul McCartney had never slagged John Lennon on *The Ed Sullivan Show*. Even
Johnny Rotten's attacks on Sid Vicious were mostly backstage. This
was something new, a public intervention, a humiliating kick in the
crotch that would feel even worse the next day.

The band went into shock, and the rest of the show sucked. When
it was over, they just stayed in their stage places, seemingly stunned,
because no one wanted to confront anyone else backstage. Axl was
overheard telling David Lee Roth that three guys in the band were
smacked out, and then he left the building. They were stunned. No
one could believe the shit that Axl had pulled.

Before the Stones went onstage, Mick Jagger was informed that
Axl might walk out. His lawyer listened to the taped playback of Axl's
remarks, and determined that Axl had only *warned* that "these
shows"—a big payday for Guns—could be the band's last. It seemed
that there was little imminent danger for the Stones: But Rose was famously volatile and had definitely threatened his band—in public. The
Stones' people had a word with Guns' people later that night, quietly
suggesting bone-crushing legal action if Guns N' Roses did not appear,
as contracted, for three more concerts. Guns' accountant reportedly
advised that the band would be liable for almost two million dollars if
Axl canceled.

The Rolling Stones played well that night. Mick Jagger—puckishly—
dedicated "Mixed Emotions" to Axl Rose. "Button your lip, baby."

The Stones received rave notices the next day. Guns' reviews were
tepid, and focused on the racism issue and Axl's public threat. The
L.A. Times wrote that someday the truth would finally come out about
Axl Rose's anger, as if he were hiding some dark and dirty secret. This
made him angry. But Axl's actions had stolen the opening-night buzz
from the mighty Rolling Stones. "A real showman," Mick Jagger called
him later, with a wicked laugh.

The poor reviews prompted Elton John to send an over-the-top floral bouquet to Guns' dressing room on the second night. The note read, "Don't let the bastards grind you down. I hate them all too. Love, Elton."

*G*uns N' Roses' second appearance at the Coliseum took place after intense negotiations—over the phone. Duff recalled, "I was pissed off with Axl . . . because I wasn't one of the guys he was talking about. So I was furious. But the next day we were on the phone together, and it was OK because he explained his reasons for doing it. And he was blowing off a lot of steam about a lot of shit . . . the fact that the band hadn't gotten it together in Chicago, shit like that. So I was mad at Axl, but we got on the phone and really got out what was going on. We don't bottle shit up. It may not have been the right place [for Axl to blow up], but it sure worked."

Slash and Steven Adler, and to a lesser extent Izzy, said they would reform—after the high-risk concerts were done. Slash: "Axl said he wouldn't perform [the second show] unless I agreed to go up and apologize. Which I refused to do." But the next night, Axl left the stage during Slash's customary remarks, about halfway through the set. There was a huge roar as Slash stepped up to the mike. Another seventy thousand people then quieted down and listened as Slash (wearing a Betty Ford Clinic shirt) said his piece:

"There's a lot written about this band and drugs. A lot of it is bullshit. Some of it is true. . . . I remember coming here as a kid to see Aerosmith and Van Halen and the Stones, and dreaming of being up here. Well, last night I was up here, and I didn't even know it. . . . Smack isn't what it's all about. No one in this band advocates heroin. . . . We're not gonna be one of those weak bands that falls apart over it."

Axl then came back onstage and said into the microphone: "I just don't want to see any more of my friends slip away." Then the band went into "Patience," and their set continued.

Slash's sincerity (and evident pain) moved the audience. "I just opened up and said what I felt about heroin, and what it does to people, who it's killed, and how fucked it is. That's what I felt. But I was a junkie at the time. I was even a *cocaine* junkie too. It wasn't an apology. It was sort of an explanation. I said what I said, and Axl came out [onstage], and it was warm [between us], because what I said was totally honest."

That was the spin that Slash tried to put on the episode. But the immediate word on the Strip was that Axl made Slash grovel in front of their fans. It was not a very rock and roll thing to do. Years later, Slash told VH1 the truth: "I knew it was all directed at me, because I was real strung out at the time. But it was probably one of the things that made me hate Axl more than anything. Something I probably never forgave him for, without thinking about it."

*G*uns N' Roses played better on the final two nights of the Stones dates, October 21 and 22, 1989. During the third show, Axl went off into a tirade over a review in the *L.A. Times* that had compared him to the uncontrollable Jim Morrison. "I'm not a fucking racist," he bellowed. "This is fucking art, this is *how I feel.* You don't like it, don't fucking listen. It's real easy. Fuck them [the newspaper], 'cause I'm on this stage tonight."

*M*ick Jagger was impressed by the audience response to Guns, unusually ferocious for an opening band, even a local one, in a stadium full of Stones fans. At the same time, he commented that, like the Clash before them, Guns had a built-in obsolescence factor. But after the fourth show, Jagger invited Axl to join the Stones when they played Atlantic City at the end of their tour. The final show would be a huge event with superstar guests, and would be broadcast for an elite, paying audience on cable TV all around the world. Axl Rose said he would think about it.

MAJOR PSYCHO TIME

*A*fter the Rolling Stones left town, it was quiet for a while. In some quarters, Axl Rose was seen as having (shrewdly) deflected negative attention from his supposed racism by outing his guitar player as a dope fiend. Axl was also admired in certain circles for diverting media attention from the Stones' big comeback onto himself. He told an interviewer that Slash's mother and brother later shook his hand and thanked him for what he did, because Slash was in a twelve-step program by then ("forced into rehab" as he put it), and doing much better.

No one could say the same thing of Steven Adler, who didn't bother to clean up. He just lied to his band that he wasn't doing drugs, beginning a long slide from which he never recovered.

Robert John maintains that many Guns associates thought Axl had done the right thing. "The atmosphere around the band was very tense after the [Stones] shows," he says. "We all saw that Axl was giving a hundred and fifty percent of himself, *every night,* and he wanted the rest of the band to give that too. He was fucking pissed off. Axl finally just got tired of people screwing up. And, yeah, they cleaned up. Or, Slash and Izzy did. But, you know? They just drank more, to compensate."

Jeff Fenster recalls that the incident made obsolete Guns' most prized image of itself: the street gang of drug-dealing desperadoes. "The fallout from this was *intense,*" he says. "People were talking about it immediately. It came as no surprise to some of us at Geffen, because Axl had been complaining—often bitterly—about the drugs for months. Now everybody could see the incredible tension in this band. It was on the record that it wasn't really a gang anymore. A page had turned. Now, Axl was his own gang."

But people close to him knew that this was what Axl Rose wanted now. He'd seen how Mick Jagger controlled a band that was twenty-seven years old, and controlled the Stones' "brand" as well. Axl started telling people not to call him a dictator anymore. "Go work for the fuckin' Rolling Stones for a while," he laughed, "and you'll see what a *real* dictator looks like."

"How we got through those [Stones] gigs, I'll never know," Izzy said later. "There was so much shit raining down on us: Axl's mood to quit, the drug problem, the Steven problem, the racist thing. I even had a court date [for pissing in the airplane trash can] at eight in the morning after the last Stones show, and was looking at six months in the county jail because I had a prior arrest, if the lawyers couldn't take care of it. So it was a fucking major psycho time."

Somehow, Guns managed to stay together—for a while. But, although no one could foresee this at the time, the shows opening for the Stones were the last full shows played by the original five guys in the post-punk guitar band from Sunset Strip called Guns N' Roses.

A few days after all this, David Bowie made overtures to make amends to Axl for hitting on his woman. A rendezvous was planned, through Slash, at a chic restaurant in Hollywood, where Axl and his uncouth entourage (ex-roadies, Izzy) arrived in leather jackets and mirror sunglasses. David Bowie duly arrived at their table and crouched down next to Axl to apologize. Someone bumped Axl's arm, and his hand brushed Bowie's face. Bowie clutched his eye, said "Oh, FUCK!"—as if he'd been blinded, then laughed it off as a joke. Axl thanked Bowie, told him that no one had ever apologized to him before, for anything. Then they went out to the China Club, where they got fucked up. Axl on Bowie: "I never met anybody so cool, so into it [the music biz], so whacked out, and so sick—in my life. I mean, I'm pretty sick, but this guy's just fuckin' *ill*." Talking to veteran rock hero Bowie gave Axl serious pause. "I was thinking to myself, *I've got twenty more years of* that *to look forward to? I'm already like this! Twenty more years?* It was heavy, man."

*A*round this time, someone in Duff McKagan's family—reportedly a brother-in-law—approached Duff with an investment idea. There were some interesting companies starting up in the Seattle area, and if Duff wanted to invest a little money, he might see a tidy profit someday. So Duff gave this relative $50,000. The start-ups turned out to be Microsoft and Starbucks Coffee. Fifteen years later, the payout was said to be around $15 million, and Duff never had to work again unless he wanted to.

*T*he final three American shows on the Rolling Stones' *Steel Wheels* tour were held at the Convention Center in Atlantic City, New Jersey, on three nights in December 1989. Axl had agreed to appear with them, and on the worldwide telecast of the last show on December 20, as a guest artist—but under certain conditions. The main one was that he would choose which Stones song he would sing with Mick Jagger. The second was that Izzy Stradlin appear onstage as well. Since playing with the Stones was an impossible dream he and Izzy had shared since they were fourteen years old in Indiana, Axl decided to make the wish come true for both of them.

Izzy got to Atlantic City first, on December 16. He called the Guns office to find out where Axl was, but nobody knew. They said he might be driving east, but they had no clue. He went to the venue, where the Stones were rehearsing, and was welcomed effusively by Ron Wood, his old customer from the back-alley heroin business. Fellow guest Eric Clapton was rehearsing his guitar solo for "Little Red Rooster." Boogie legend John Lee Hooker was working out his bit with the Stones' rhythm section.

Ronnie Wood asked Izzy what song they wanted to do. "We'd chosen 'Salt of the Earth,'" Izzy recalled, "but they said they didn't know it! I'm thinking, *Fuck, you guys wrote it—over twenty years ago. You gotta remember some of it.*" They took Izzy into the tuning room, a mobile home parked backstage. They put a cassette of *Beggar's Banquet* on a little tape player, and Mick listened to the song with a lyric sheet in his hand. "And I'm there, playing guitar with Keith [Richards], and Charlie [Watts] and Bill [Wyman] are sitting there, listening to it, and I'm thinking, *This is soooooo cool.*

"Finally, we finished the song. They all turned to me and said, 'So where's your singer?' And I didn't have an answer. Axl was late again—real late."

W. Axl Rose arrived in Atlantic City in time for the first concert, on December 17. "He was getting up Jagger's nose by being late," a Guns employee said. "It was a typical Axl gesture, supposedly showing who was really in charge." Jagger in turn sent them up later that evening: "We got some special guests wiff us tonight. . . . They opened for us in L.A. [big cheer] and they've been following us around ever since, in a beat-up old van. . . . And they've come all the way back east to get their tattoos touched up! [Wood smirks at this] . . . Here's AXL AND IZZY FROM GUNS AND ROSES! [loud cheering]"

Axl walked onstage in his full-body skeleton suit, an *Exile on Main Street* T-shirt, and a baseball cap reversed over his bandanna, followed by Izzy with an acoustic guitar. Very animated, deploying his now familiar serpent dance, Axl completely stole "Salt of the Earth," upstaging Mick Jagger in front of a planetary TV audience and injecting some of his scary passion into the Stones' exercise in rock revivalism. Axl also appeared later, toward the end of the Stones' set, to sing backup on "Sympathy for the Devil." He and Izzy repeated this for two more nights in Atlantic City, and then flew back to California to be home for Christmas.

The year wasn't over yet. Duff McKagan kicked his wife out of the house on Christmas day. "She told me that she hated me, and I told her to get the fuck out, and she did. It was the shittiest Christmas I ever had." Duff and his wife had been together for three years, and he was extremely upset. (Axl and Erin reportedly also fought that day.) A week later, Duff stumbled into the China Club on New Year's Eve. Red-eyed, unshaven, disheveled, distraught, he tried to get into the spirit of Bang Tango's set. It was his first night on the town since his wife left. But then someone said something disrespectful to him. Duff handed his wallet to Del James, then turned and smashed this big guy in the face. A brawl broke out, and Duff left just ahead of the cops. Of 1989, he later said that it had been "a very tough year for every single person in the band."

Chapter Ten

RECOVERED MEMORIES

If your finger suffers from gangrene, what do you do? Do you let the whole hand, and then the body, become filled with gangrene? Or, do you cut the finger off? What brings corruption to a country and its people must be pulled up like the weeds that infest a field of wheat.
—Ayatollah Khomeini

THIS IS WHO WE ARE

January 1990. President George H. W. Bush sent the marines into Panama to topple the ruthless, coke-dealing dictator Noriega. The dictator holed up in the Vatican embassy. The Americans got him to surrender by blasting Guns N' Roses and AC/DC tapes at ear-bleeding volume for seventy-two hours straight. The Romanians had just executed their own ruthless dictator, Ceauçescu. The ruthless dictator of Iraq, Saddam Hussein, began to threaten Kuwait and the inbred sheiks who milked its vast oil reserves. And the ruthless dictator of Guns N' Roses, W. Axl Rose, was spotted visiting the grave of Jim Morrison at Père-Lachaise Cemetery in Paris, a sentimental visit by one legendary rock star to the other. Axl left a cigarette burning on Jim's bare tomb.

It was now two and a half years since *Appetite for Destruction*, which was still selling well, but Geffen Records was howling for a new Guns album. Some prescient Geffen execs were already suggesting that Guns (and "hard rock" in general) might be obsolete. In Seattle, the new grunge bands that would eventually displace Hollywood metal in the parking lots of America's high schools were beginning to gel. In England, new groups like Primal Scream and Happy Mondays were trying to create something different: trance rock, hypnotic hardcore. U2's *Achtung Baby* and Aerosmith's *Pump* were both in production, two albums that some fans figure to be the final two masterpieces of the entire hard rock movement that had spanned the past quarter century, from 1965.

*W*hen Axl Rose returned to Los Angeles later in January, the band tried to work at Rumbo Sound. But their essential chemistry had dissipated. Slash seemed better, but Duff was getting divorced and was drinking harder than ever. Izzy Stradlin had quietly quit drinking and drugging, and so didn't like hanging out with his intoxicated comrades anymore. His last drink had been with Keith Richards and Ron Wood. Izzy: "I just reached a point where I said, 'I'm gonna kill myself. Why die for this shit?'" Izzy took off to some place where he couldn't score any dope, and sweated it out. "Then I started drinking, but I gave that up a couple of months later. Alcohol's no good for the American Indian blood I've got in me. I couldn't afford to fuck up anymore. I'd used up all my 'get out of jail free' cards." Izzy would spend much of the next year traveling, visiting Germany, Spain, England, Amsterdam, and Paris. He told friends he missed the drugs sometimes, "but not all the bullshit that went with it—the scoring, the rip-offs, the bad drugs, the day-to-day hassle."

And then there was Steven Adler, deep in the throes of his jaw-dropping, gonzo suicide mission. In the studio, Slash looked at his old pal in disgust as Steven tried to play the drums. Despite his firm denials that he was using heroin, he was nodding off on the drum stool, managing to keep his seat, with his head almost touching the floor. Adler kept saying he wasn't high, just tired. They managed to get him to play semiprofessionally on one song, "Civil War," and then forced him into another rehab. It didn't work either.

Adler later tried to explain this period: "I wanted to get off heroin and . . . Because, I just started doing it with the guys [in the band]. The first day I got sick, I called my manager and said, 'Dude, I feel real sick.' And he took me to this doctor, and this doctor gave me an opiate blocker.... And I got completely so sick, and then they wanted to go in and record 'Civil War.' I said to Slash, 'Dude, I'm so sick that I can't do it right now.' And he said, 'We can't waste the money, we got to do it—*now*.' "

Steven couldn't stop doing heroin, and his life was spiraling down. He was lying to his band and everyone else. There were new, more serious death threats from unpaid dope dealers. Members of the band warned off, and even threatened, the dealers supplying Adler, leading to tension in the streets and the nightclubs they frequented. On advice from their lawyers, Guns removed Steven from the band's limited partnership, and put him on salary. He was informed that he was no longer a director of their company. They gave him an option: If he could clean up enough to cut the record and do the tour, they would make him a full member of Guns N' Roses again. Axl told an interviewer that Steven then cut his wrists. That didn't work either.

*O*n January 22, 1990, Slash and Duff McKagan attended the American Music Awards, produced by rock-and-roll veteran Dick Clark, and broadcast nationally, live, on the ABC television network. Slash later claimed that he and Duff didn't even know that their band was up for any kind of award, so when *Patience* won for best video, they were unprepared to accept graciously. Duff and Slash staggered to the podium, both visibly drunk. Slash unleashed a flow of profanity in his speech, dropping frequent f-bombs, and then he gave the audience, and millions of viewers, the finger as he sauntered off the stage. There was no time delay on the broadcast, and the network reportedly received ten thousand phone calls in protest. Then Guns won another award, and Slash and Duff wobbled to the podium again, and Slash said "fuck" again. Dick Clark was furious, and so was ABC. This was a front-page story in Los Angeles and New York the next morning, and Alan Niven was summoned to Geffen Records for a meeting. Several radio stations had already pulled Guns off the airwaves. According to a former Geffen employee, Niven was told the label was fed up. Niven was informed that, in Geffen's view, he had lost control of his clients, and Guns would be released from their contract, for cause, unless the band cleaned up its act and got the fucking album made.

A reporter asked Slash about this latest outrage. "Sorry," Slash replied, "but this is who we are."

So the ailing band tried to go back to work. They did have the beginnings of some songs. Izzy had "Dust N' Bones," "Pretty Tied Up" (based on a Melrose Avenue dominatrix), and "Double Talkin' Jive." "You Could Be Mine" was left over from *Appetite,* as were Axl's primal ballads: "Don't Cry" and "November Rain." There were "The Garden" and "Yesterdays," both written with West Arkeen and Del James. It even looked like the scabrous "Back Off Bitch" was going to see the light of day. The problem was that they didn't have their drummer. Axl told a friend that it almost felt like they had to start the band over again.

"He just couldn't play," Slash said of Steven. "He was so messed up he couldn't pull off the drum tracks. And he would lie to us. We'd go over to his place and find drugs behind the toilet, under the sink."

*L*ate in January, Axl gave an interview to a British metal mag. He was living at the time in a snug, two-bedroom apartment in a West Hollywood building, where he was feuding with a woman in the adjacent flat. The glass coffee table he had smashed the year before had been replaced, and was full of rock star detritus and overflowing ashtrays. Asked why the new album was so delayed, he tried to explain: "Partly, the answer is drugs. But another reason things have been so hard is this: the first album was built around Axl coming up with one line, or maybe a melody, or how I want to present it, and then we'd build a song around it. Or someone came up with one line, OK?

"On this, Izzy has brought in eight songs—at least. Slash has brought in a whole album. I've brought in an album. Duff knows everybody's material backwards. So we've got like thirty-five songs we like, and we want to put them all out, and we're determined to do that."

About the Stones shows: "I didn't cancel them, because the band would have paid too high a price. I don't want Duff to lose his house because Axl canceled the shows. But at the same time, I'm not gonna be a part of watching them kill each other, just killing themselves off. And it worked, man. It *way* worked. Slash is *on,* like a motherfucker right now. The songs are coming together real heavy. I've written all these ballads, but Slash is writing all these really crunch rockers.

He's got these eight songs that I gotta write words to, and they're badass songs!"

February 1990. Over in North Hollywood, Darren "Dizzy" Reed was being evicted from the apartment he was squatting in. He was a hard-rocking twenty-seven-year-old keyboard player from out of town, who had run through a string of tough luck. He'd known Izzy Stradlin since they'd both arrived in L.A. ten years earlier. He'd played in bands—the Wild, Johnny and the Jaguars—that never got off the ground. (The Wild had rehearsed in the storage room next to Guns' old lair at Sunset and Gardner five years earlier.) Dizzy was almost asked to join Guns in 1985—"they talked to me about it," he said—but he was then injured in a car wreck that mangled his hand. Now, in 1990, Reed rehearsed with Guns and another drummer to see what would happen. Axl told Mick Wall: "Dizzy came in and played three songs he'd never heard before, songs that we never planned to put a piano on—like heavy metal. But he put heavy metal piano into it, and he was amazing."

But Dizzy Reed's money was all gone, and his car had been repossessed. He was jobless, depressed, on foot, and about to be homeless. He called Axl on a Sunday night. "I go, 'Dude, I'm starving, and as of tomorrow I'll have no phone, no apartment, no food, no nothing. If you guys need to reach me, I don't know where I'm gonna be.'"

Axl: "When I found out [Dizzy] was going to be on the streets, I called up Alan [Niven] and said, 'Secure this guy, hire him, put him on salary, and give him an advance so he can get an apartment. Now we have a piano player.'"

The phone rang the next day. It was Alan Niven, inviting Dizzy Reed to join Guns N' Roses, on keyboards. Dizzy accepted, with great relief, and was put on salary, effective immediately. "Basically," Reed told *Rolling Stone,* "they fucking saved my life."

That was it for Guns N' Roses being a guitar band. Now, like Mick Jagger, Axl Rose had a piano player who would help him key his vocals to the right pitch.

* * *

Guns was now informally rehearsing with different drummers. They told Steven Adler he could do the tour, but only if he could do the album. Slash and Duff actually wanted Steven out of the band then, but Axl resisted for various reasons. Robert John: "I remember Slash complained during the rehearsals and recording, about trying to do stuff but Steven was too high to work. They all talked about getting another drummer in there, but I remember that Axl was the last person that wanted to fire him. He thought Steven was an important part of the show. But nobody—especially Slash and Duff—could take it anymore. It was killing the band."

So Guns played with Adam Maples, formerly of the Sea Hags. According to Slash, Maples almost got Steven Adler's job, but then he didn't. Guns also worked for a week in the studio with Martin Chambers, the hard-hitting English drummer who had powered the Pretenders. Guns reportedly recorded eleven songs with Chambers, but the chemistry wasn't right—Chambers was much older, and wiser, and supposedly had an arrogant attitude—and so Guns had to keep looking.

THE CHILDREN INSIDE US

In the California spring of 1990, those around Axl Rose could sense that his troubled relationship with his girlfriend was coming to some kind of climax. One of these people was his manager, Alan Niven, whose home telephone answering machine frequently documented frantic, late-night pleas for help from Erin Everly as she was being assaulted, punched, and even kicked by her raging boyfriend. (One of these phone tapes was allegedly used as sonic undergrowth on a Great White album, a few years later.) Erin later claimed that he dragged her around by her hair, and locked her, naked and shivering, in a closet all night. When she got out of the closet, she later testified, Axl anally raped her. Robert John says that Axl locked Erin in a closet in a Las Vegas hotel suite, and then set it afire. (This copied a scene in

Oliver Stone's recent biopic, *The Doors,* in which Jim Morrison did a similar number on his girlfriend and sparring partner, Pamela Courson.) Slash's girlfriend testified later that Axl threw a television at Erin, kicked her with his cowboy boots, and spat on her while she cried and pleaded not to be hurt. (This woman, Megan Hodges-Knight, also said that when she asked Slash to try to calm Axl down, Slash replied that it would only make Axl behave worse.)

These attacks on Erin allegedly continued through the spring with increasing frequency, until one epic battle ended with Erin in the hospital. This had fatal implications for Axl's band, and almost for Erin herself.

The reasons for their epic fights are known only to the two combatants. The details are murky. "Erin and I treated each other like shit," Axl admitted later. "Sometimes we treated each other great, because the children inside us were best friends. But there were other times when we just fucked up each other's lives—completely." Axl told friends that Erin—doubtlessly provoked—had damaged his beloved BMW on purpose. He beat her up. She tried to fight back. He ripped the phone out of the wall, smashed a glass coffee table, then rampaged through her precious collections of antiques and figurines, breaking everything in a deranged fury of shattered crystal and smashed porcelain. According to Axl, Erin then fled to Steven Adler's house, where Adler injected her with a speedball—a mixture of heroin and cocaine. Erin turned blue in sixty seconds, and Adler dialed 911.

She spent the next few days in a coma, with Axl by her side, begging her to survive. His first impulse had been to murder his junkie drummer. Erin's relatives, the Everly clan, originally from Tennessee, also wanted to kill Steven, or at least fuck him up real good, but Axl pleaded with them not to. Erin's mother wanted to call the cops and have Steven arrested, and again Axl persuaded her that it wasn't a great idea.

Steven Adler later vehemently denied that he'd given any drugs to Erin Everly. Adler claimed that he was in his backyard studio in Laurel Canyon on that evening, trying to write songs with Andy McCoy from Hanoi Rocks. "And [McCoy's] wife, because he lived up the hill from me, comes down to my house with Erin, who couldn't even fucking stand up, barely. She's all like, *blah blah blah.* And I said to his fucking wife: 'What the fuck did you give her?' She said, 'Well, Axl and her got in a fight, and he beat her up. So she came over, and she was hysterical, and I gave her all these pills'—Klonopins and Clonodines and shit.

"These are like major downers, right? And Erin is all fucked up, in my house. I'm going, 'What's wrong with her?' And Andy McCoy's fucking wife is like, 'Blah blah blah, and then I gave her all these pills.'" Then Erin fell down and couldn't be revived. She was lying there, on the floor, foaming at the mouth. Someone gasped, "Holy shit!" Steven picked her up and carried her to his bed. "Then I called the ambulance and saved her life. And the whole time, this bitch—Andy McCoy's wife—is telling me, 'Give her some heroin, give her some.' And I'm like, 'Fuck you, bitch. I'm not giving her fucking heroin.' For one, I only have a little bit left, and if you're a heroin addict, you're not giving your last hit away. Two, this was Axl's fucking girlfriend! And you *never* fuck with your fucking bands' mates, right? Your bandmate's woman—I would *never* do that to anyone. So I called the ambulance and saved her. Then, this bitch [Mrs. McCoy] tells Axl that I gave [Erin] heroin! She told him I gave his old lady heroin! So he called me up, and told me he was coming over with his shotgun, and he was going to kill me. But he never did anything. Hey—*I'm* the one who called the fucking ambulance. I never did anything to Axl, or to Erin. But then he told everybody that I gave her heroin, and almost killed her, but that he forgave me for it. Yeah—*right.*"

*I*n the late winter of 1990, when everyone seemed to be cracking up, Duff McKagan was interviewed by a Japanese rock mag: "In the whole scheme of things, we're just a rock 'n' roll band. We're sitting here, smoking cigs and having a drink, and then we go home and fuck our girlfriends and go to sleep. Then we wake up and go to the studio and work on another song or two. Fuck, man—we're being asked to comment on things totally out of our league, just because we've sold a few records. Fuck, man—*what do we know about Nelson Mandela being free?*"

* * *

*A*pril 1990. All over America, there was a continuing crisis on family farms, where low prices meant the nation's farmers were struggling to survive. The evil specter of heartless "agribusiness" loomed large, as big corporations took over America's precious harvests. Images of bankrupt farm auctions, and the funerals of suicidal farmers, dominated TV news. No one liked this. So Willie Nelson, Neil Young, and others started Farm Aid, a series of annual concerts to benefit family farms. When the fourth Farm Aid concert was scheduled for Indianapolis that year, Indiana native John Mellencamp suggested to the organizers that local heroes Guns N' Roses—the biggest band in the country at the time—be invited to perform.

Axl Rose accepted but so late that his band wasn't on the bill.

After some deliberations and misgivings, Steven Adler played the gig. Considering Izzy Stradlin's airline issues, the band chartered a jet and flew to Indiana on the morning of April 7, 1990.

Pandemonium broke out when Guns was announced. Guns hadn't played in public in six months, since the Stones shows the year before. (Axl and Slash had done an encore with Aerosmith in L.A. the previous month.) It isn't known whether Guns rehearsed for Farm Aid, but they actually played great. As the elated crowd rose in a mighty cheer at this unexpected treat, Steven Adler streaked out from the side of the stage and jumped onto the drum riser.

He didn't make it. The jump was ill timed, or he tripped, and MTV's cable broadcast audience saw Guns' hapless drummer smash himself onto the platform. (Slash: "Steven almost broke his fucking neck.") This was totally mortifying, but Steven recovered quickly, and Axl—in ripped jeans, cowboy boots, and a straw hat—dedicated their performance to his uncle Bob, farming somewhere in Illinois. "This is something new we got," he drawled, and the band launched into "Civil War." The unfamiliar ballad received a respectful hearing, with both Axl and Duff singing, and then the crowd got into it when the song moved into its rocking second section, and the band let loose and Slash shredded into the atmosphere.

The (vague) plan had been to play "Welcome to the Jungle" next, but Axl couldn't resist a dig against Indiana, and called for the UK Subs' hilarious punk nightmare, "Down on the Farm" instead. "This is the only farm song we know," he told the crowd. Steven Adler had no clue whatsoever. He'd never even heard the song before. Adler remembered, "We're onstage, and all of a sudden Axl goes, 'This is a song called 'Down on the Farm.' And I yelled at Duff. I go, *'Duff! Duff! What the fuck is this? How does this go?'* And Duff clapped his hands [in rhythm] and said, 'Just do this'—*boom boom boom*. And that song came out so kick-ass, because I always knew what Duff was gonna play before he played it. It was just so tight. It was wonderful."

Axl sang "Down on the Farm" in a Marlboro T-shirt and a fake cockney accent, dancing madly, snaking his hips as the band blasted out sex pistol rock. The crowd went wild for the snotty, antifarm tirade that ended: "But I'd rather be back in Soho, than down here on the farm—the *fucking* farm." Guns crashed to a halt, and Axl glanced into the TV camera's red eye, slammed the microphone to the stage, and screamed: "THANK YOU—GOOD FUCKING NIGHT!"

No one knew it yet, but this was Steven Adler's last gig with Guns N' Roses.

WHAT'S WITH THE PIANO?

*A*pril 1990. Axl Rose, motivated by what he described as "fear and depression," decided that he must marry Erin Everly right away. He had moved out of their apartment a few weeks earlier. He showed up at her door, unannounced, at four A.M. on April 27, and asked her to marry him. Wisely, Erin refused. He begged her to be his wife. She still said no. He told her he had a gun in the car and threatened to kill himself. What could she do? Axl called Howard Stern's radio show to announce they were driving to Las Vegas and getting married.

On the long drive, he promised to never hit her again, and never to divorce her. Erin and Axl were married in a Vegas wedding chapel on April 28. A month later, Axl threatened to divorce her, and then changed his mind. The glamorous, dysfunctional couple stayed married, for the time being. They fought often. One night she threw her wedding ring out the window. The next day, Axl was seen scanning the ground outside the house with a metal detector. In June, Erin claimed, Axl beat her so badly she ended up in the hospital. Their tormented marriage would provide the basis for many of the bitter ballads and wounded songs which Axl and Guns were trying to mold into material for their long-overdue next album.

*A*round this time, Guns rehearsed with yet another drummer, but this one clicked. He was Matt Sorum, a hard-hitting American rocker who was currently the Cult's (fourth) drummer. Slash had seen him play at a recent Cult show in L.A. and realized he might be the best guy for the job. And Slash was semidesperate, he told friends, because he was convinced that Guns would die if they couldn't find the right drummer. Matt Sorum was a bluff, likeable guy with a heavy bass drum sound, good rhythm, solid drive. He'd been on the L.A. club scene since 1976, playing everything from new wave power pop to a stint with Gladys Knight. Matt Sorum knew how to power a rock band, and best of all, he wasn't a heroin addict. Slash wanted him, and Sorum got the job.

Izzy went to see Steven Adler, and found him at the end of a three-day drug binge, trying to scrape stray particles of cocaine off the floor. Adler was still lying to the band about his drug use, and actually seemed worse than ever. Stories circulated in Sunset Strip's vicious (and often accurate) rumor mill that Adler (or cronies with access to his checkbook) was peripherally involved in financing drug deals, but these remain unproven rumors. Axl Rose seemed to confirm them later, when he told MTV that Steven "couldn't leave his drugs. Then he was involved in other things, beside the band, that were dangerous, and scary. I want nothing to do with him."

Matt Sorum was thrilled to be in Guns N' Roses, the most important American band, on the threshold of a new album and then up to three years of touring all over the planet. But Sorum was also wary, because of the drug milieu the band was notorious for. "I'd dabbled in it like everyone," he said later, "but *nothing* like what you heard they did. When I went into it, I thought I was walking into an opium den." Sorum didn't realize it, but by then the heaviest days of Guns N' Roses' drug use were already in the past.

W. Axl Rose—

the last brilliant front man of the hard rock movement and still the leader of Guns N' Roses in the twenty-first century

*A*xl in his black-leather codpiece at L.A.'s Music Machine, September 1986

*A*xl playing a studio pinball machine, 1991

PHOTO BY GENE KIRKLAND

In 1988, Guns N' Roses opened shows for early heroes Aerosmith. Their forty-five-minute sets established Guns as the hottest new band in America.

Top photo: Axl and Steven Tyler, 1988. Middle: Aerosmith guitarist Brad Whitford, Stevie Nicks, Steven Tyler, and Axl Rose. Stevie visited the tour backstage in L.A. Bottom: Three new members joined Guns beginning in 1991. From left: Drummer Matt Sorum, keyboardist Dizzy Reed, and guitarist Gilby Clarke.

PHOTO BY GENE KIRKLAND

PHOTO BY GENE KIRKLAND

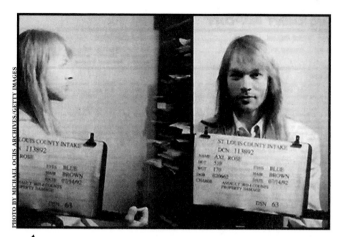

*A*xl was arrested in St. Louis in 1992 for starting a riot the previous year. He paid a fine and served a day in jail.

*G*uns N' Roses, with guitarist Buckethead at left, played Las Vegas in 2000.

*F*rom the 1991 Get in the Ring Tour: three horn-section girls, Dizzy Reed, Gilby Clarke, Duff McKagan, Axl Rose, Slash, Matt Sorum, and Teddy Andreadis

W. Axl Rose outside the Rainbow Bar and Grill on the Sunset Strip, 2003

* * *

June 1990. New Kids on the Block were the biggest act in show business, ruling Top Forty radio along with girl group Wilson Phillips. MC Hammer and 2 Live Crew ruled hip-hop. (The latter had censorship problems, but sales quadrupled.) Hardcore rapper Ice-T asked Axl to do a version of "Welcome to the Jungle" with him, but Axl declined. The Replacements (with Tommy Stinson on bass) were the best new band in the land. Slash sat in with the Black Crowes in New York, joining the white-hot Georgia band for three encores. Guns N' Roses' version of "Knockin' on Heaven's Door" was released on the sound track for a Tom Cruise movie, *Days of Thunder.* It was the first new music from the band in almost two years.

Sessions for the new album stopped that summer, after Steven Adler was fired in July. They were, Slash said, tired of wiping Steven's ass for him. Adler was out of the band, announced a terse press release dated July 11, without compensation or consideration. Slash's sad comment was widely reported: "With Steven, it was sex, drugs, and rock and roll. It was all he lived for. Then it was drugs and rock and roll. Then it was just drugs."

Adler couldn't believe what was happening. Both Axl and Slash publicly expressed contempt for him. Suddenly he wasn't ushered into the Cathouse anymore, but was asked to wait on the rope line with the rest of the hopeful customers. He tried to kill himself. "I had nothing to live for," he later said. "I mean, everybody that I knew, that I thought were my friends, took everything they could from me and . . . disappeared!" His drinking went off the rails. Later in the year, he sued the band for cutting him out, claiming that the band had turned him on to drugs, and then had turned on him. He used so much cocaine that he stroked out, and almost died.

Slash tried to explain this, later in 1990. "Look, Steven was a part of what made Guns N' Roses happen. He had great energy. He wasn't an insanely great drummer, but he had tons of attitude. When the sex and drugs bit went out of control, he went right along with it. But then there's a certain time where you have to control your life. Right? I'm in no position to preach, . . . but you *must* be aware of your own existence, and take care of your own business. You can't be loaded all the time, and expect everything to be okay. Trust me, I know."

Axl was furious about being sued by Steven. "We turned him on to drugs?" he sputtered. "My fucking ass! He said he's sober now, but every time I see him, he's wasted. I don't know what he's on, and I don't care. I lost all concern and feeling for the guy. And I know a drug lie when I see one."

Years later, Slash was asked about the firing by *Mojo* magazine: "Izzy and I went through great pains to get our shit cleaned up, but we could never fucking pull Steven back in, and we really tried. And Axl never really liked Steven, so that was all the excuse Axl needed to fucking fire him. That was the beginning of the end of our little gang, like fucking Robin Hood's merry men."

*T*he final Guns N' Roses song recorded with Steven Adler, "Civil War," appeared that summer on *Nobody's Child: The Romanian Angel Appeal,* an album organized by George Harrison for the relief of Romanian orphans. This was appropriate, since the TV images of the violent Romanian revolution had inspired "Civil War," which began as a ballad and ended as a rave-up. Released in July 1990, it was Guns' first original music on the market since *GN'R Lies* two years earlier.

That summer Axl had been hanging out with Canadian rocker Sebastian Bach, lead singer for multiplatinum metal band Skid Row. Skid Row had the same feral energy (hair, leather, chains, guy cleavage, piercings, light makeup, tattoos, pentagrams) as the early Guns, and the tall, hairy Bach was the clear successor to W. Axl Rose in the Psycho Metal singer department. "Bas," as he was known, and his cute girlfriend, Maria, hung out with Axl and Erin and they all got on great. The extroverted Bach idolized Axl and persuaded him to get out more. On July 28, Bas and Axl showed up (with their ladies, Del James, and Cult shaman Ian Astbury) at *RIP* editor Lonn Friend's birthday party at his home in Culver City. Instead of singing happy birthday to Lonn, Axl and Bas sang a soulful a capella duet of "Amazing Grace" in his kitchen while they were getting fresh beers. Axl then took Lonn out to the car, played the instrumental track of "November Rain," and sang the lyrics into his ear.

A few weeks later, the two couples—Axl and Erin, Bas and Maria—were having supper on the twelfth-floor balcony of Axl's West Hollywood apartment. They might have been celebrating the excitement of Erin's pregnancy—it wasn't really planned—by listening to some new Guns N' Roses mixes at top volume. Suddenly a dozen cop cars appeared in the street below. A few minutes later, there was banging on the door. There had been a noise complaint. Axl narrowly missed arrest, and later had his lawyer file a harassment complaint against the deputies who were bothering him.

September 1990. Guns N' Roses went back into the studio with Mike Clink and without Axl Rose. They recorded more album tracks with Matt Sorum and Dizzy Reed, without vocals or useable mixes. By October, they had almost twenty-one additional tracks, which were given to veteran rock engineer Bob Clearmountain to mix down. A former Geffen executive remembers the chaos: "They had Bob Clearmountain—this great engineer—mixing in one studio while Axl was singing his vocals in another studio, and Slash was doing the guitars [overdubs] in the third studio. It was a recipe for chaos. Bob mixed twenty songs while having no contact with the band. If Slash liked the mix of one song, Axl hated it." In the end, Slash and Axl rejected Clearmountain's "too slick" production values, so they threw all of these mixes out and started over. Axl was adamant that "I just want to bury *Appetite*. I don't want to live my life through that one album. I have to bury it, and do something new."

The people at Geffen were getting alarmed. Their Christmas bonuses were flying out the window. Tom Zutaut was quoted on the reason for the album's delay: "Axl's creative idea of going forward was, 'We can't remake *Appetite*. We have to go in a different direction.'" Many at Geffen Records felt that no one would care about a ballad-heavy album from Guns N' Roses. They decided to approach Bill Price, who worked on *Never Mind the Bollocks,* to mix the record for some fabulous sum that would lure Price to Los Angeles.

Bill Price: "They called me and said it involved about forty songs. It was over-budget, over-time, over everything, but Geffen wanted it finished. They started pressuring me to come out to L.A., but not even to actually mix the record, but to 'audition' for mixing it." Bill Price flew out to California. "Geffen pays for my flight and my hotel, and I do an 'audition' mix of 'Right Next Door to Hell.' It's an up-front rocker, so I did an in-your-face, heavily compressed mix of the backing track, and then added Axl's raw vocal on top . . . so that you could hear what he was singing. Everybody loved it, so they hired me."

Meanwhile Guns' working conditions were weird, since Axl almost never showed up at the studio. "It was impossible to get us all in one room," Slash said. Izzy wasn't around much either, content to let his songs remain in their crude, punkish, four-track demo state. (Axl complained about this, bitterly.) Slash had given Axl the instrumental track for "Coma" that summer, but it took Axl another full year to write the lyrics for the complex song. (Axl said he kept passing out every time he tried to concentrate on the difficult material of the lyrics.) Trying to write together, Axl and Slash communicated with each other only on the telephone. Matt Sorum remembers these recording sessions as "very dark, a lot of just toxic feelings, and the sightings of Axl Rose [in the studio] were few and far between."

Guns had a lot of new songs, but the new music didn't seem to interact with itself in any organic, traditional sense of an "album." Slash later told VH1: "It was all over the place, all this material coming from different directions. It was Guns' version of the [Beatles'] *White Album*—maybe not as good."

Much of Axl's energy went into his epic ballad "November Rain," which Slash later described as "the sound of our band breaking up." Guns had started as a lean and mean guitar band, but Axl's piano-driven, symphonic production of "November Rain" turned everyone off—but himself. He called it "our 'Layla' song."

Slash: "Now we had this piano, and an orchestra, backup singers, and all this kind of crap we didn't necessarily want, as a band; but it was something Axl still wanted, and that's what he got."

Even Guns' new drummer Matt Sorum had second thoughts: "I felt like, I didn't really sign up for *this*—all these ballads. I was hoping to join a badass rock-and-roll band. I was like: *what's with the piano?*"

RECOVERED MEMORIES

*E*rin Everly suffered a miscarriage on October 29, 1990. Axl went to the house in the Hollywood Hills that the couple had been preparing to move into with their child and thoroughly trashed the place. Damages were estimated at a hundred thousand dollars. Axl was distraught. Erin later said she had to sell her Jeep to cover her post-miscarriage hospital bills. It was the beginning of the end of W. Axl Rose's star-crossed marriage.

The next night, Axl fought it out with the unhappy woman who lived in the apartment next door. The issues were loud music, loud arguments, fan mania, and general cretinism. Sometime after midnight, the woman hammered on his door with a wine bottle. Axl took the bottle away from her, she alleged, and cracked her over the head with it. Early in the morning of October 30, Axl was arrested by West Hollywood sheriff's deputies for assaulting this woman. Bail was set at five thousand dollars, and Axl went home. The lawyers took care of it, and all charges were later dropped.

*E*rin Everly left Axl Rose in November 1990, after he beat her again. "Take a good look," she told him, "because you're never going to see me again." The marriage was annulled in January 1991. Erin sold her jewelry and moved into a condo in the Valley. When Axl tracked her down and called her, she moved the next day.

Axl Rose finished the lyrics to "Right Next Door to Hell" and started looking for a house in Malibu. Meanwhile a cot was moved into Rumbo Sound for him, and he basically lived in the studio while doing the vocals and mixes for the new album. On November 9, Axl and Slash teamed up with Sebastian Bach and most of Metallica, and played at *RIP*'s anniversary at the Hollywood Palladium. Axl sang on "Hair of the Dog" and "Piece of Me," stage-dived repeatedly into the mob like in the old days, and then wasn't seen in public again for eight months.

* * *

*L*ate in 1990, Axl was seeing a psychotherapist in an attempt to discover the sources of the torments and mania that made him so volatile and unhappy. He told an interviewer that he had been depressed, and had nearly overdosed on pills. Around this time he experienced a revelation that changed his life, and the lives of his band and the people around him.

America in the early 1990s was fascinated by a series of widely publicized cases in several locations where people undergoing psychotherapy or counseling came to recall childhood abuse at the hands of parents, caretakers, and teachers. Preschool teachers in California and Massachusetts were subsequently convicted and jailed for sexually abusing children—many years, even decades, earlier—when the "recovered memories" of one or more victims proved convincing in court. Sometimes entire communities were stigmatized as satanic covens when people claimed to recall mass orgies of public child rape. More therapists began to practice "recovered memory therapy," based on the belief that adult distress and psychological difficulties may sometimes be caused by sexual abuse in childhood that had been forgotten or repressed.

At the same time, a new mental illness was identified: false memory syndrome, where people in treatment "remembered" childhood sexual abuse that in fact had never happened. Some therapists, it was claimed, encouraged patients to search for repressed memories, often using techniques such as hypnosis. Under therapeutic influence, some patients believed in the reality of imagined events, and came up with horror stories that shattered families and even provoked widely publicized lawsuits against the alleged abuser, usually the father. Claims of innocence were seen as evidence of denial and guilt.

It was in this torrid atmosphere that Axl began to remember bad stuff that he claimed had happened to him. He was driving in his car one day. "All of a sudden the thought crossed my mind," he told an interviewer, "of what had gone on in my childhood and what I had pretty much buried—and didn't even remember. When it crossed my mind, I had to pull over, stop the car, and I just broke down—crying." Axl was seized by a paroxysm of grief. "Such an outpouring had never come out of me before."

Soon Axl started telling people his real father had abused him, and raped him. He told people that his father had fucked him in the ass when he was two years old, and that this was the horrible secret that his parents had kept from him whenever he asked about William Rose. Whether this was a real or false memory, it led Axl to despair and suicidal thoughts. All this led to many years of possibly the most intense course of psychotherapy ever undergone by any rock star, before or after. And of course, the "reversion therapy" he experienced confirmed Axl's worst fears about what happened to him when he was a child.

*D*ecember 1990. At the end of the year, Guns had thirty-five songs they wanted to put out. The band came to the conclusion that Geffen should release these on four CDs that would come in a box. The label said this concept would be much too expensive for their fans. (Slash: "You don't make some kid go out and buy your record for seventy dollars if it's [only] your second record.") They compromised on releasing the songs on two separate CDs, to be released on the same day. After several possible titles (like *GN'R Sucks* and *Buy This*) had been mooted, Axl insisted that the album(s) be called *Use Your Illusion*. Like *Appetite for Destruction, Use Your Illusion* was the title of an illustration, this one by the New York art provocateur Mark Kostabi, who manipulated ancient figures from *The School of Athens,* a mural by Renaissance master Raphael in the Vatican that depicted the greatest philosophers of antiquity.

Geffen hoped that *Use Your Illusion* would be mixed and ready by the spring of 1991. But no one close to the situation had any hope of that happening. A Geffen A&R executive recalls: "This was such a huge record that they wanted it to be perfect. Anytime you're working with a band that big, it'll take some time to mix the record. If you had a mix ready, Axl had to approve it. Slash had to approve it. Tom [Zutaut] had to approve it, the management had to sign off. There were all these different opinions on what this record should be."

The album would be delayed so long that Guns N' Roses went on tour for three months before their albums finally came out in September 1991.

* * *

Christmas 1990. Slash went shopping for sex toys. He had a new girlfriend, a nice house in Laurel Canyon full of kittens and puppies, and was stable and relatively sober. He was mourning the recent death of Clyde, his favorite snake. (He had ten others.) He was rehearsing with Guns and their new drummer for a big show in Rio de Janeiro in January. He did an interview with *Rolling Stone,* on whose cover he appeared the following month. He played a session for Bob Dylan's *Under the Red Sky* album, and others with Lenny Kravitz, Iggy Pop, and Michael Jackson. He got to meet George Harrison (at the Dylan session) and Les Paul, who kindly told Slash he'd be pretty good when he learned how to play. He played rough mixes of new Guns songs for friends: "Dust N' Bones," "Double Talkin' Jive," and "The Garden."

Slash told *Rolling Stone* that the new record would be like cleaning out the closet, and that it would be dark. "There's not a ton of really happy material on it, you know? Most of it is pretty fucking pissed off. Very pissed off, and very heavy." Asked why Guns was so unhappy, Slash responded that their lives were more fun when they had no money, no responsibilities, and just hung out on the street. "I don't trust anyone," he said. "I've had too many friends turn on me."

Asked about heroin, Slash said he didn't want to be another Keith Richards, whom rock fans knew for his drugs as much as for his music. Slash described addiction as "one of the most disastrous things you can go through. It's like sitting on your deathbed all the time."

Regarding Axl Rose, Slash wearily described him as a magnet for problems. "I mean, shit just goes *on* with that guy. He'd tell you the same thing." Slash said that any tension between him and Axl was "in a morbid kind of way" conducive to their artistic collaboration. Slash wasn't shy about expressing his frustration with Guns' situation: "Axl has no idea of what the financial reality is. To spend all that money to make a record is ridiculous. Of course, if I was to say this to Axl outright, he'd say that I didn't know what he was going through, and there would be a fight, right there. . . . We have our ups and downs. We butt heads. So I just sit there, with my head between my knees, freaking out. . . . But Axl's craziness drives me even crazier than it does Axl, unbeknownst to him. And that's the truth."

At the Pleasure Chest sex shop, in Hollywood, Slash and his girlfriend bought Axl Rose a bondage-style straitjacket for Christmas.

MANIC NIRVANA

*J*anuary 1991. W. Axl Rose was reeling from one crisis to another, and was often beside himself with manic behavior. No one had a clue what to do with him. His marriage was formally dissolved in January 1991. Axl was trying to cope with what he claimed were devastating recovered memories of being raped by his natural father when he was two years old. Those close to him felt that his anguish level was off the chart. Then Axl's half sister apparently told him that she, too, had been molested by her father—Axl's stepfather. Axl soon began an intensive course of psychotherapy—five hours a day, five days a week—in an effort to somehow feel better. At one point, desperate to rid himself of demons and bad humors, Axl went through a New Age–style exorcism that, he said later, had cost him $72,000. Afterward, he felt ripped off.

*G*uns N' Roses was now a six-piece rock band that had still never headlined a big tour. Two of them, Matt Sorum and Dizzy Reed, had never played in public with the band, nor had they ever played music at all with the lead singer. This was the group that was scheduled to headline two nights of the Brazilian rock festival, Rock in Rio 2, held in Rio's biggest football stadium. Other headliners included Prince, New Kids on the Block, INXS, George Michael, and A-Ha. (Of these, Guns was the only band to sell out two nights.)

In early January, Guns rehearsed (without Axl) at the Long Beach Arena, and then flew to Rio on the 15th. Axl was registered at the hotel as Bob Omnibone. Slash was Luke Likesheet. Duff was Phil Likesheet. Izzy was Dali Lhama. Matt was Ian Wasasaint. Each musician had a bodyguard, and they needed them because they were immediately mobbed by fans whenever they left the Intercontinental Hotel on Ipanema beach. They rehearsed for two days in a small theater in Rio, again without Axl, who didn't turn up at the band's press conference either. Slash and Duff handled this chore with an interpreter, deflecting multiple questions about the Gulf War by saying Guns wasn't a political band. Meanwhile, Izzy was out by himself, skateboarding anonymously in the hazy summer sunshine. Matt So-rum visited the massive statue of Christ that loomed above the city like a stone god. Photographer George Chin, who had flown in from London to work with Guns, was amazed that Sorum, who had never played with Guns in public, or had even appeared in a picture of the band, was recognized immediately as a Gunner and mobbed on the street.

Slash mostly stayed by the hotel pool, shadowed by Ron Stalnaker, described in the local press as Slash on steroids. (On a day off, they flew to São Paulo to visit an Amazon snake farm.) Duff brought his new girlfriend along, so he mostly stayed in the room with her. Dizzy Reed, who had never toured before with any band, had split with his wife just before Rio and was enjoying the plentiful supply of barely dressed girls who would do anything to get close to anyone even re-motely connected with Guns N' Roses. Dizzy Reed told anyone who would listen that his wildest dreams had come true.

$\mathcal{B}$ut tensions were running high within the band. At a meeting be-fore the first show, Axl demanded that the others (Slash, Duff, and Izzy) sign over the trademark name, Guns N' Roses, to him exclusively. He reportedly threatened not to go onstage in Brazil if this didn't hap-pen, and the paperwork was ready for their signatures. This was a big payday for the band, some of whom were strapped for cash, and Axl knew the others had no choice but to sign control of the organization over to him. It was an extra-classic showbiz power play, down and dirty. It was something, people said as they shook their heads, that you didn't do to your friends. Tom Zutaut later explained to VH1: "In Axl's mind, the name belonged to him. He wanted to ensure the band's sur-vival, even if this version of the group broke up."

$\mathcal{G}$uns' mood turned sour after this, and then got worse. Mick Wall described the vibe in Guns' encampment as one of confusion and dread. Twelve gorilla-looking bodyguards surrounded the band and kept everyone else away. Guns refused to do interviews unless by signed contract that guaranteed the band's publicists final approval of anything published. This was a new order in pop media relations, and it earned Guns the hatred of all but the most slavish teen mags. Then a well-liked Brazilian photographer who tried to snap Slash in the hotel bar was carried out on a stretcher after bodyguards stomped him and smashed his camera. Judas Priest, second on the bill for Guns' second show, let it be known that they had been threatened. Axl would not go onstage unless Priest played a shortened set, didn't use their pyro effects, and played only one encore. Rob Halford couldn't enter on a motorcycle either, as he had been doing for ten years. There was also trouble at Guns' sound check, when Axl noticed that they were being filmed by TV Globo without his permission. Doug Goldstein grabbed the tape out of the camera and was surrounded by stadium employees, who demanded it back. Goldstein tossed the tape to Guns security chief John Reese, who summoned their road crew on the double. Everyone had knives on their belts, and many had been drinking. There was a tense standoff until an interpreter got things calmed down.

The sound check was the first time Axl Rose had played with Matt Sorum and Dizzy Reed, but this essentially new band sounded great anyway. All the same, the crew noticed that Dizzy Reed's keyboards changed the spare, classic two-guitar attack that had made Guns famous. Some of these veterans sadly realized that this band wasn't going to sound quite like the old Guns N' Roses ever again.

*G*uns N' Roses took the stage in front of 160,000 rock fans jamming Maracana Stadium on January 20, after Queensryche, Faith No More, and Robert Plant's band had warmed up the crowd. (Led Zeppelin's singer, touring behind his *Manic Nirvana* solo album, presumably wasn't threatened by Guns.) Axl looked his best, taut and muscled, clear-eyed and trim. He told George Chin that he was doing two hundred sit-ups a day. Izzy's new song "Pretty Tied Up" opened the set. Any doubts about the band's new drummer were dispelled when the denim-clad Sorum expertly hammered out the rhythms for "Mr. Brownstone." His thunderous attack sounded like Bo Diddley with a nitrous oxide hookup, and the whole stadium shook to his expert time.

Axl came onstage in a white leather Guns motorcycle jacket over tight bike shorts in stars and stripes. The jacket came off after two songs and was never seen again (to Axl's fury later). He played the whole show in his shorts and a headband, showing his sinewy legs and thighs, dancing in a pair of bespoke Nike high-top sneakers with his name embroidered in leather on the tongues of the shoes.

"We didn't have a set list for Rio," Duff said later. "We have this 'pick list' we like to use. We told Matt—three minutes before we went on—that he's gotta do a drum solo. [Sorum hadn't done this with the Cult, but Axl needed time to get to the oxygen bottle in his dressing room.] And he fucking pulled it off! Right before we went onstage, the whole band—and this hadn't happened in a *long* time—got together in one room. You could just feel the electricity between us."

The new band played well as Guns blasted through its show. New songs given their public debuts included "Double Talkin' Jive," "You Could Be Mine," "Estranged," and "Bad Apples." But Axl thought the crowd sucked—the "Heaven's Door" sing-along was tepid, at best—and he cut Guns' show by twenty minutes and refused to play a second encore.

They played again in Rio two nights later and knocked 'em dead. There are veteran Guns N' Roses fanatics of long (and train-spotting) standing who maintain it was the band's best show ever. Performances of "Pretty Tied Up," "Double Talkin' Jive," "Estranged," and other new songs rocked the house. The ovations in the big stadium—where Brazil's legendary soccer teams had scored some of their greatest triumphs—were tumultuous. The show was so good, so perfect, that the whole troupe was buzzing afterward. Axl couldn't sleep and decided to have a party in his suite—at dawn. The entire entourage was called from their hotel rooms to the party. Even Billy Idol, staying in the same hotel, got a wake-up call from W. Axl Rose.

WHEN THE MACHINES TAKE OVER

*B*ack in Los Angeles by the beginning of February 1991, Guns spent the southern California winter and spring working on their album and preparing for their first headlining tour. The psychic backdrop to all this was the bombing of Baghdad in February 1991, followed by the carnage of the first Gulf War. Punished for brutalizing Kuwait, an irate Saddam Hussein set the desert oil fields ablaze, blackening the skies over the Middle East, confronting the world with some of the most apocalyptic imagery since Hiroshima and Nagasaki. Axl Rose took this all in, as riveted by these pictures as he had been by snuff videos years earlier.

Since his run-in with his neighbor a few months earlier, Axl had been living in various hotels, often the Sunset Marquis, and his new house in Malibu. After the Rio shows, he basically moved into the Record Plant, where he was recording his vocal tracks. Photographer Neal Preston found him living in studio A, which Axl had equipped with a bed and an exercise bike. "There was also a punching bag," Preston recalls, "and two pinball machines—KISS and Elton John. No one was supposed to be allowed in while Axl was there, but he let me take some photos of him playing pinball. He seemed calm and said he was working hard on their new album." Studio personnel noted that Axl was staying awake for two or three days at a time, seeming to run on sheer adrenaline and nervous energy. Izzy Stradlin, perceived by everyone as the only stable member of the band, was prodded to ask Axl about finishing. "I *tried* talking to him," Izzy said later. "[I suggested] if we had a schedule, came in [to the studio] at a certain time ... And he completely blew up at me."

"There is no fucking schedule," Axl snarled. Izzy never bothered Axl again, and Izzy never worked on the new album again either.

Guns' new music was now in the hands of Bill Price, in from London to mix down *Use Your Illusion*. By March 1991, Price thought he had a handle on most of the songs. He later described his work on one of the most anticipated, preordered albums in the history of sound recording:

"So I spent a very long period in Los Angeles [in 1991], working my way through this huge amount of material. I had fantastic help from Mike Clink, who'd produced the original backing tracks, and day-to-day support from his engineer, Jim Mitchell. Then I had alternate visits from Slash, Axl, and various others, and then I sent everybody DATs [digital audio tapes] for approval.

"Then, having worked through about twenty songs, I had to wait for the next song to be finished. For example, 'November Rain'—which was a bit of a baby of Axl's: I had Mike Clink's original 24-track master, which had just drums and bass on it, and a 24-track slave [duplicate] that had a load of vocal ideas on it, and a 24-track slave that had a lot of guitar ideas on it, and a Sony 48-track slave that had a hell of a lot of vocal and keyboard work that Axl had been doing in his studio. I had another 48-track slave that Slash had been working on in his studio. So I tried a telephonic method of working out which tracks would be used, but I couldn't get anyone to agree on exactly what to use.

"I decided that the only way to do this would be to run them all together. We were in Skip Saylor's studio [Saylor Recording], which had an 84-channel SSL [Solid State Logic]—a pretty big desk. So we hired a bunch of tape machines, and of course they didn't run in sync; but the L.A. rental companies have some very good technical engineers, and soon a hairy bloke in shorts arrived with a homemade interface, and managed to get everything running in sync. Then I could play every track that anybody had recorded on.

"The only real way to find out which tracks to use was to get the entire band in the studio at the same time." Price had no idea what this meant. "It seemed like quite a normal thing to me. When I mentioned this to the band's management, they were horrified. The thought of Guns N' Roses all being in the same room at the same time was too much for them to bear! They warned me against it, but I couldn't think of another way."

When Guns got to Saylor Recording, they checked out the impressive display of linked tape machines. There was this elephant trunk of cables coming through the door, which ended at the mixing desk. Bill Price said that it looked like a science fiction movie in which the machines take over.

"Eventually, they all arrived, and we got down to a mix." Guns was immediately deferential to the man who had mixed *Never Mind the Bollocks*. "They were perfect gentlemen. Axl walked in and said [something like], 'Good afternoon, Slash. I know it's your guitar, and obviously you have the main say in it, but I *do* love that lick there. Do you think we could have it a bit louder?' Total gentlemen. We finally got the mix done.

"But that was just the beginning. That mix [of one song] was on the board for a week. DATs flew back and forth, and harmony lines were being changed and different guitar licks put in. You name it. [*Use Your Illusion*] was about the most complicated mix—musically, technically, people-wise—that I've ever done in my life."

Bill Price kept at it for almost seven months. The process was so slow that, later in the year, Guns would go on tour before their new album was anywhere near finished.

W. Axl Rose had ambitious plans for a series of videos for *Use Your Illusion*. Three in particular—"Don't Cry," "November Rain," and "Estranged"—would have movie-quality production values and link the songs in a trilogy of ballads about the heartbreaking circumstances of Axl's existence. They needed a young actress to play Axl's female foil in the three videos, so they hired the top model in America, the luminous Stephanie Seymour.

At the time she was Warren Beatty's girlfriend—but not for long. She was a twenty-three-year-old brunette beauty from San Diego, with a perfect figure and a three-year-old son from a brief marriage to a local rock musician. (Her affair with Beatty reportedly ended the marriage.) Stephanie had been modeling since she was fourteen, and was known as a hard-partying young woman who also had a spiritual, and even visionary, side to her. She was also a *Sports Illustrated* swimsuit cover girl, and the principal catalogue model for the lingerie company Victoria's Secret. (She was almost not hired because, at five feet ten inches and wearing high heels, she was way taller than Axl.) Cast as Axl's savior-from-suicide in *Don't Cry*, and as his bride in *November Rain*, Stephanie Seymour captured his heart immediately. He called her the night after they first met on the video set, and soon they were seen necking in the front rows of fashion shows on both coasts. Then they were inseparable, and Axl was convinced they were a pair of old souls. He told friends that she was helping him with the things that bothered him, the things that held him back from what he needed to do.

Through a series of "life readings" with a trance medium, Axl and Stephanie were advised that they had indeed been soul mates before, in sixteen previous incarnations. Erin Everly later said Axl told her that he and Stephanie had been sisters in one past life. Axl also told Erin that in a past life he and Erin were Indians, and that she had killed their children, and that's why he was so mean to her in this current life. Axl also told her that he was "possessed" by the malign spirit of John Bonham, Led Zeppelin's drummer, who had drunk himself to death in 1980. (The other guys in Zeppelin had often referred to the uncouth, rapacious Bonham as "The Beast.")

Axl Rose is said to have proposed marriage to Stephanie Seymour soon after they met in the spring of 1991, but she put him off until she got to know him a little more. Seymour was supposed to have ditched Warren Beatty, but some sources suggest that the powerful film star and producer kept his hand in, so to speak. In any case, in the 1991 springtime, W. Axl Rose thought he had finally met the woman of destiny. And indeed, he was publicly desperate for some kind of normalcy. "I'd like to have some security," Axl told Mick Wall. "I've never known *any* security in my life, you know?"

*I*n May 1991, Axl fired Alan Niven, Guns' manager of five years. It was reported that Axl refused to finish *Use Your Illusion* unless Niven was replaced, and that the band went along. Axl later told *Rolling Stone* that he had gotten tired of Niven's combo platter. Photographer Robert John and others close to Guns N' Roses say that Axl had never completely trusted Niven, and Geffen Records executives were incredulous that *Use Your Illusion* hadn't come out by then. Alan Niven had probably had enough anyway. He continued to manage Great White and other bands.

Guns N' Roses' new manager was Doug Goldstein, who had started with them doing security. Izzy Stradlin thought Alan Niven had been shafted, but he tried to spin the news a certain way: "Dougie [Goldstein]'s done a lot of stuff in the last couple of years." This meant that he had taken good care of the band. "Now, he's the guy who gets to go over to Axl's house at six in the morning when the fucking piano is hanging out the window." (This was shortly after a rampaging Axl had indeed tried to ram a fifty-thousand-dollar Steinway grand piano through the plate glass picture window of his Malibu house so that it would smash into fragments as it crashed into the canyon below. The piano was too big for the window, so it just hung there, precariously, until someone dragged it back into the house.) "Now, when we get these fucking calls: *'You hear what happened? Axl did what?'* That's nice, Dougie. *You* take care of it, and call me when it's over."

John Reese replaced Goldstein as tour manager. So, under new management, and while still working on their album with Mike Clink and Bill Price, Guns N' Roses prepared for what would be called the "Get in the Ring Tour," which followed the summer sun around the world for the next twenty-eight months.

HERE'S OUR STAND

*M*ay 1991. Guns N' Roses warmed up for its first tour as headliners with the Top Secret Club Tour, three nights in small venues. The T-shirts made for these dates, echoing the spirit of the old band's street flyers, declared: HERE TODAY, GONE TO HELL. The first show was May 9 at the Warfield Theater in San Francisco with local heroes Dumpster opening. Axl came out swinging in a C.A.M.P. (Campaign Against Marijuana Prohibition) T-shirt and led the band through a wild two-hour rehearsal. Two nights later, Guns played at the Pantages Theater in Los Angeles before an audience of rabid fans and press people who had signed the band's draconian media contract. On May 16, the band played the Ritz in New York City. Part of this gig was filmed for the video of *Illusion*'s first single, "You Could Be Mine." Axl Rose, in stars-and-stripes tights, took a video-friendly flying leap off a ramp at stage left and experienced a horrible pain in his left leg when he landed. After the show he couldn't walk. X-rays revealed a fracture in Axl's left heel. Everyone freaked. The tour was three weeks away. But pro football doctors were brought in, and sneaker designers, and two weeks later Axl began the Get in the Ring Tour wearing a customized, knee-high boot/splint protecting his left foot while the injury healed.

* * *

*O*n a mid-May afternoon a few days before the tour, Axl sat down with journalist Kim Neely at a burger joint in Hollywood and ordered a cheeseburger, french fries, and a chocolate malted. Dressed in tight shorts, customized AXL-emblazoned sneakers, and a black blazer, he held forth on a variety of topics. He was incredulous that Steven Adler was suing the band and making public statements that his bandmates in Guns had hooked him on heroin. Axl described undergoing intensive weeks of psychotherapy that involved five-hour sessions, five days a week. Now well versed in therapeutic jargon, Axl said that he used to despise women, but now he felt differently:

"I had an extremely volatile relationship with Erin," he allowed. "And I was projecting strong negative feelings about myself onto other people. I was attracted to other people with similar dysfunctional traits, people that I was going to end up not getting along with. It wasn't good for me or for them. It made me despise being with anyone, or meeting anyone, or having good thoughts about being linked to someone."

Still, Axl said he was feeling slightly better now. "I'm getting more comfortable with things. I'm still not good at handling stress, and I was told this was because of the way I was raised. My family screwed up any positive or productive form of release. . . . I still have to restrain myself. It's not gonna happen overnight." Asked about his sexual attitudes, Axl replied that he'd been through some ugly and violent episodes in his childhood. "And these affected me negatively. I formed some very strong, serious opinions, and I've been acting on these ever since." The interview ended with Axl's wish that he could be of some use to an organization that dealt with childhood sexual abuse.

*G*uns' first show was at Alpine Valley in Wisconsin on May 24, 1991. Raging hair metal stars Skid Row was opening this leg of the twenty-eight-month tour, and the young headbangers celebrated their good fortune by trashing their dressing room on opening night. The cops guarding the venue wanted to arrest Bas and his rowdy band, but were talked out of it by Doug Goldstein. Skid Row was now what

Guns N' Roses had been four years earlier: brash delinquents who did stupid shit and got in trouble. Guns, on the other hand, were now elder statesmen of rock. They were flying to gigs in the expensively chartered MGM Grand jet, a Boeing 727 outfitted as a flying Mafia bordello with bedrooms, a bar, and lounge; they were sipping champagne and tasting canapés as they soared over America. (Not Izzy Stradlin, though; he was traveling in his own luxurious tour bus, enjoying his privacy, his good-lookin' wife, Anneka, and his hard-won sobriety between gigs, as well as the toys—Harley motorcycles, bicycles, skateboards, model planes—that he carried with him. Axl referred to Izzy as "Mr. Invisible." No one could say what Izzy did in his spare time. His German shepherd dog, Treader, had his own backstage laminate.) So ultimately, for many of Guns' younger fans, it was Skid Row that would provide the taste of authentically damned streetwise anarchy they had paid to experience, as this star-crossed rock tour played the suburban amphitheaters and ball fields of America during that summer of 1991.

But Guns had been rehearsing, and some of the early shows just blasted off. There was no rigid set list, since Axl insisted on calling the songs spontaneously, depending on what he felt like singing. Also, the band was hesitant to test some of their new songs, since the album containing them wasn't out yet. They often started with one of the new numbers, or "Out ta Get Me," and then always "Mr. Brownstone" second in the set; and usually "It's So Easy." Then they mixed things up. A typical set segued into "Attitude," then "Live and Let Die." Then new music: "Bad Obsession," "Double Talkin' Jive," and "Civil War."

Axl then calmed the crowds with "Patience." But "Welcome to the Jungle" now turned whole stadiums into ecstasy raves. Matt Sorum's nightly drum solo gave Axl a chance to get to his oxygen bottle in his miniature hideout just beneath the stage. The band then came back with "You Could Be Mine," a new hard rocker that some fans already knew from the radio. Then a piano was wheeled onstage and Axl sat down to play "November Rain," which was Guns' new, self-proclaimed "Layla" moment, full of Dizzy Reed's synthetic keyboard orchestrations and Slash's sustained, anthemic guitar aria. "Sweet Child o' Mine" followed, another big production, followed by "Heaven's Door" as a sing-along and the climax of the show. The encores were "Paradise

City," played fast and furious, and then the band sometimes sent the audience home with "Don't Cry," reminding their fans that there was a heaven above them.

$\mathcal{I}$t had rained at Alpine Valley, drenching the kids out on the grass. At three the next morning, back at the band's hotel, Dizzy Reed was getting teased about the four wet girls passed out on his bed. ("You can always tell the new guys in the band," one roadie joked. "They get the muddy chicks.") While the crew partied in the hallway, Axl cracked open bottles of champagne for a small group in his suite. At five A.M. he spoke on the record for a couple of reporters covering the tour. He said he owned some land in the area and had wanted to be buried there someday, but now he wasn't so sure anymore.

Heatedly, Axl explained the album was delayed because Guns refused to cater to needy and greedy record executives. "I've watched a lot of bands put out two to four albums, and who cares?" He said he wanted to recapture the purity of heart behind *Appetite for Destruction.* "We didn't just throw something together to be rock stars. We wanted to put something together that meant everything to us." Axl insisted he held the moral high ground: "I've had a good understanding of where I wanted Guns N' Roses to go, and I can't say everyone's had a grip on that. We're competing with rock legends now, and we're honored to be in that position. We want to define ourselves. *Appetite* was a cornerstone, a place to start. It was like, 'Here's our stand,' and we just put a stake in the ground. Now we're going to build something."

Axl acknowledged that Guns had lost a part of its old self, but he said, "There's a lot of desire to keep what we have together. I mean, we already lost one guy. Actually we lost a lot of people—Alan [Niven], certain photographers [who were no longer welcome], certain security, road crew, stagehands [who had been let go]." Axl mentioned that the band's next shows were in Indiana, and there were a lot of people he *wasn't* inviting to the gig, almost as many as he was inviting. He seemed stressed when talking about Indiana. It didn't seem to anyone that W. Axl Rose was looking forward to going home.

LIKE SELLING YOUR SOUL

GET IN THE SHOWER MOTHERFUCKER! commanded the tour info sheet slipped under Guns N' Roses' hotel doors on the morning of May 28, 1991:

WAKEUP—10:00 AM

BAGS IN HALL—10:30 AM

VANS TO AIRPORT—12 NOON

FLIGHT TO INDY—1:00 PM

ARRIVE INDY—2:00 PM

SOUNDCHECK—4:00 PM

SKID ROW—7:15 PM

GN'R ONSTAGE—8:45 PM

CURFEW—11:00 PM

YOU GUYS WERE FUCKING AWESOME LAST NIGHT!

Guns N' Roses played two shows at the Deer Creek Music Center in Noblesville, near Indianapolis, starting on May 28. Axl's home-o-phobia was in florid display after the opening number, "Out ta Get Me." He stopped the show and complained bitterly about the small stage and a 10:30 county curfew on concerts. In a five-minute screed, Axl cursed out the local authorities and said that only a hick state like Indiana had such a stupid curfew. He described friends in Lafayette telling him that when he "bagged out" on the place, it inspired them to get out too. "It seems to me," Axl said, pacing the stage in an American flag jacket, plaid kilt, and headband, "there are a lot of *scared old people* in this fucking state, and basically . . . for two-thirds of my life, they tried to keep my ass *down*." There was a big cheer, and Axl looked down to the kids in front of the stage. "Looks like I got a lot of cool prisoners in fucking Auschwitz here," he smiled. This remark got in the papers, and soon the wire services reported that Axl Rose had compared Indiana to Nazi Germany. He tried to explain it later, to the *L.A. Times*: "I just wanted to tell them . . . that they could break away too."

This concert is thought to have been the first live performance of

"November Rain." Sebastian Bach brought an exotic dancer onstage to grind away during "Rocket Queen."

For the second Indiana show, Axl sent a stretch limo to pick up his grandmother and other family members in Lafayette. (The chauffeur also stopped at Arni's on Elmwood and filled the limo trunk with a dozen fresh pizzas.) The crew marveled that Granny Lintner seemed like an older version of Axl. She also knew the words to Guns' songs and sang along at the gig. After the show, Axl hosted a proper family reunion backstage. But something—perhaps just contact with family members—must have set him off, because Axl was raging when he got back to the hotel. Heavyweight boxing champion Mike Tyson had raped a girl in the same hotel not long before, and Axl had insisted in staying in the same suite. Later that night Axl was heard wreaking fearsome and wanton destruction as he went wild over something he didn't want to talk to anyone about. Doug Goldstein had to pay off the hotel to keep Axl from being arrested.

After further shows in the Midwest and Canada, Guns' jetliner landed in Philadelphia on June 13. As usual, three stretch limousines pulled up to the plane: one for Axl, one for Slash and Duff, and the other for Matt and Dizzy. Two vans carried the managers, assistants, and photographers who traveled with the band. The convoy then proceeded to the hotel or the gig.

By then Skid Row's new record, *Slave to the Grind,* was the number-one album in America, an echo of what Guns had handed to Aerosmith three years earlier. (Slash later said the addition of mad raver Sebastian Bach to this tour added a whole new level of debauchery that Guns hadn't seen in a while.) But there was also serious tension among Guns because Axl had kept crowds in Ohio and New York waiting for more than an hour, refusing to come out of his dressing room until he was ready to perform. (Guns had to pay hefty fines when this caused their concerts to extend beyond local curfews and, especially, stagehand union rules. Axl didn't care. The rest of the band, who were financing his willfully late behavior, cared.)

There had been some worry about Philadelphia, where Axl had narrowly avoided arrest last time, but Stephanie Seymour had joined the tour, which usually served to cool out Guns' neurotic avatar. Axl mentioned the previous unpleasant incident early in the show, which went on smoothly until Axl stopped "Welcome to the Jungle" and tried to cool a violent brawl in front of the stage.

Afterward, the band received the (compliant, bum-kissing) press in a backstage room lit by candles and scarf-draped lamps. Queen and AC/DC were roaring out of huge speakers. Stephanie was rubbing Axl's back as he sat, cross-legged, on the carpet. Duff was saying that he wanted to get off booze and study at Harvard when Guns was over. Matt Sorum, giddy among a lust of lightly clothed groupies, said he felt like Led Zeppelin every time he boarded Guns' luxurious private jet. Slash said he was sick of groupie scenes, and split. Guns' tour contract rider, which specified what was supplied to the band backstage, listed what the band wanted to drink. Axl got chilled champagne and other white wines. Slash's bar included Jägermeister liqueur, Jack Daniel's bourbon, Coca-Cola, and Black Death vodka. Duff drank vodka and cranberry juice. Matt was satisfied with beer. Dizzy was down with Jack. Izzy drank mineral water exclusively.

Izzy Stradlin ("clear-eyed, witty, unpretentious") explained that he'd had his last drink eighteen months earlier, with Keith Richards and Ron Wood. He said he traveled by bus "because if you're driving, it keeps you in touch with the rest of the world." *Rolling Stone*'s Kim Neely noted that Izzy reputedly had written the most songs on *Use Your Illusion,* but Izzy played this down. "I have a few on there," he admitted, but Izzy's spirit was communitarian: "But they all get mixed together. Once they're on tape with Axl singing and Slash playing guitar, I just look at it as Guns N' Roses stuff." He added that he wanted the album out so he could hear the new songs on truck stop juke boxes. "I *never* play our music at truck stops," he quickly added, "but it's a kick to hear Hank Williams and then one of our songs. That's like, *Yeah! We made it!*"

June 16. Guns bypassed Manhattan on this early leg but would play Nassau Coliseum on Long Island the following day. They stayed at the Royalton Hotel in Manhattan, preferred by Axl for its chic décor and dark suites. That night, Axl invited the band to the Old Homestead steak house for champagne and red meat. But Slash thought Axl's invitation sounded more like a royal summons, and he skipped the dinner, preferring to stay in his room, chip heroin, and listen to Metallica, especially "One."

Slash, hiding behind his black veil of curls so his eyes couldn't be seen, told writer Kim Neely he wasn't an addict, though. "I'm no angel, but I know I can't get hooked again. It's an alienating drug, period." He admitted that the stress level in the band was sky-high, and coping with this was terrible for them all. And he could already see the end of the road: "What freaks me out is—if the band falls apart—I'll never shake the fact that I'm the ex–Guns N' Roses guitar player. It's almost a feeling like . . . selling your soul."

At nine that evening, the band was to be shot for the cover of *Rolling Stone* by fashion photographer Herb Ritts. Axl hadn't wanted to do this on the day of a show, but Ritts was in high demand, and it was the only open date he could offer the band. Izzy Stradlin came to Ritts's studio on time, then retired to his bus to read until the other rabble showed up. Axl and Stephanie swanned in—at three in the morning. The stylists did their thing, the six-piece Guns posed for the cover, and then Ritts did portraits of each. Axl sat last for Ritts, and seemed to enjoy the shoot, which ended at six, as rosy-fingered dawn broke over the towers of New York City.

*L*ater that evening, the parking lot of Nassau Coliseum, a big hockey arena in Uniondale, Long Island, was filled with the hot rides of New York's affluent youth: Mustangs, Firebirds, 'Vettes, 3-series BMWs. Inside the steamy arena, the kids cheered through Skid Row's ferocious, no-frills opening set. Five years younger, with a prettier front man who was described as genetically engineered for the job, Skid Row wowed 'em without lights or anything but a stripped-down massive attack. The kids loved the chants Bas led them through, arena mantras such as "One, two—fuck you!" They liked Bas's AIDS KILLS FAGS DEAD T-shirt. (Sebastian Bach was by then serving three years' probation for throwing a bottle back at a kid in Springfield, Massachusetts, and braining an innocent girl instead. She sued, and Bas had to pay her everything he earned on that tour.) Now the kids waited for Guns to come on. And waited. And waited some more.

Airborne from Manhattan via helicopter because the Long Island

Expressway looked like a parking lot, Axl arrived onstage two hours late, and the sold-out, roaring Coliseum went bright with flashbulbs and lighters as the band took the stage. Axl (in his stars-and-stripes stage clothes) was raging out. He was annoyed at the record company, the New York critics who had disrespected their out-of-town shows, and at photographer Herb Ritts. After the first song, Axl apologized:

"Yeah, I know, I know. It sucks.... If you got any real complaints, you could do me a favor.... You could write a little letter on how much that sucked and send it to Geffen Records.... And you can tell *those people* to get the fuck out of my ass." (Soon "those people"—a row full of Geffen staffers near the stage—reportedly got a message "from a certain dressing room" that their laminates were no good backstage after the show. So the Geffen employees walked out, earning Guns undying, institutionalized contempt from many of the people charged with selling their records.)

Axl was just getting warmed up. After "Mr. Brownstone," he told the crowd not to buy *Rolling Stone* with the band on the cover. "Steal it," he counseled eighteen thousand Guns fans. But Axl's evident fury gradually built into a blistering, balls-out concert, with liquid electric blues from Slash and Axl's manic rock eurhythmy. Halfway through, before a sequence of new music, Axl told the crowd: "The new record is delayed again.... Geffen Records told us they wanted to change the [band's] contract, and I'm deciding: FUCK YOU! [big cheer] ... And since I don't have the time to do both—go back there and argue and bitch with them, or be out here on tour ... I guess we'll just be on tour, and have a good time, and ... FUCK THEM!" This also drew a big cheer. Axl went on: "It's a shame, but ... So, we'll play a lot of the new shit tonight, and it doesn't really matter, does it?"

Guns crashed into "Live and Let Die." Later, during "Patience," a bottle landed at Axl's feet, and he told the crowd to beat the living fuck out of anybody throwing stuff at the stage. He threatened to leave if anything else landed, and the fans took him at his word. The rest of the show included Axl's barbed comments about *The New York Times,* the New York weekly *Village Voice*, and a *Philadelphia Inquirer* critic who had praised Guns, but slagged local band Skid Row. Axl Rose seemed to be paying careful attention to Guns' press notices. Unique among rock stars of any era, Axl began to use his concert pulpit to attack, by name, writers and critics who dared to speak their minds about what *RIP* magazine was still calling "the reigning band of rock 'n' roll."

COMBAT ROCK

July 1991. "You Could Be Mine," Guns N' Roses' first single from *Use Your Illusion*, was released early in the month. The song was linked to the Arnold Schwarzenegger action movie *Terminator 2*, and the future governor of California had appeared in the video. "You Could Be Mine" was less a radio grenade than Geffen had hoped, because Guns' old-school hard rock sound was being quickly eclipsed (even drowned) by the new "alternative," heroin-fueled sound of Seattle—*grunge*. The important new bands of 1991—Nirvana, Pearl Jam, Soundgarden, Stone Temple Pilots—recycled Led Zeppelin's sonic undertow with lyrics of tortured ambivalence and subversive nihilism. The new music was perfect for an era when the Beatles' "Revolution" was used as an advertising jingle, and the Gulf War—with its smart bombs and unmanned drones—was being reported as if it were a video game. Within a few months, Nirvana's Kurt Cobain was branded as the voice of his generation, and suddenly Axl Rose's personal problems seemed irrelevant to anyone but himself. Some of the new grunge heroes actually made Guns look conventional, and square. Where Axl Rose had attacked homosexuality, Kurt Cobain French-kissed his bass player on *Saturday Night Live* and played MTV's *Headbangers Ball* wearing an evening gown.

Even as *Use Your Illusion* was being mixed, it was becoming clear to certain Geffen executives, especially those working with the label's grunge signing, Nirvana, that Guns N' Roses' new album might already be obsolete. Soon America's hard rock radio stations would change to the "alternative" format, leaving rock bands like Guns scrambling for airtime. Nevertheless, Guns fans and retailers still wanted the album(s), advance orders were in the multimillions, and the band kept Bill Price busy while they were out on the road.

Bill Price recalled: "They still hadn't finished the album when their massive tour started. Mike Clink was on the road with the band, recording them whenever he could. I was back in L.A. at the mixing desk, waiting for DHL [courier] to bring my next tape through the door. So the last half-dozen songs were recorded, overdubbed, vocal'd, and guitar'd in random studios dotted around America, when they had a day off between gigs. My mixing mode switched to flying around America with pocketfuls of DATs, playing the mixes to the band backstage—great fun, actually. They kept me quite busy."

*D*uff McKagan said later that Marlboro cigarettes had offered Guns a $20 million sponsorship deal for their tour, and that the band had turned it down. They all smoked, Duff said, but that didn't mean they wanted kids to smoke too. Nevertheless, Axl Rose appeared at many of that summer's shows wearing an oversize shirt with the brand's red logo on his chest.

*I*n interviews, Axl referred to touring as the "combat zone" of his already conflicted life. He was way late for many shows, and some concerts sucked. Tour manager John Reese said that on any given night, Guns could bore you to death or treat you to the best rock concert you've ever seen. Axl's psychotherapist, Susan London, a youngish and attractive woman, came on the road sometimes as part of Axl's large entourage, and the crew learned that Axl did better when she was around. If nothing else, his friends told each other, Axl's therapy had helped him with the crushing depression that had made him want to kill himself in the past. "I get mad because of fear of my own weaknesses," he said. "Mine happen to involve what I do, and what I do is sing and run and get my picture taken." Asked about his large support staff (psychotherapists, his sister Amy, bodyguards, stylists, assistants, physical therapists), Axl replied, "I've always needed high maintenance to keep my act together. Nothing really comes naturally, except the desire to sing." He also said that he felt trapped by his destiny. "What am I gonna do—go to Paris and write poetry? Look at art museums, and hope that *not* going after what I set out to do, didn't eat me alive?"

* * *

July 2, 1991. Axl Rose hated the vibrations of Riverport Arts Center, a new amphitheater near St. Louis, Missouri, as soon as Guns took the stage an hour after the band was supposed to go on. The old river town's summer heat and humidity were intense, enervating. Security at the venue seemed unusually laid-back, and Axl had been unnerved upon arrival by an anxious fan backstage. Once the show started, he saw a security goon shove a young girl, obviously hurting her. The temperature onstage was a hundred degrees. He noticed cameras in the crowd, which he hated, and then saw people drinking beer from verboten glass bottles, a couple of which soon hit the stage near Duff McKagan.

Then, his anger rising uncontrollably, Axl watched as a local motorcycle gang seized the area in front of the stage, shoving kids aside and muscling out the security goons. This was ninety minutes into the gig. The biggest and meanest biker started shouting Axl's name, trying to get his attention. Axl stopped the show and let the biker hand him a business card. Then the biker whipped out a video camera and started taping. Furious now, Axl stopped the show and ordered the camera confiscated, but no one was about to venture into a beer-sodden Missouri biker gang and try anything suicidal.

Combat rock! Axl Rose flew off the stage, through the air, and landed in the midst of the gang. He somehow clamped onto the biker with the camera, and called for help. The band stopped playing and looked on helplessly while the venue security grabbed and manhandled Axl instead. Axl lashed out at one of the guards, and the melee was out of control until Guns' bodyguards got Axl back onto the stage. But he had lost a contact lens and could barely see. The bikers were still down front, and the security guards seemed to be laughing at him. It was an outrageous situation. Axl said, "Well...thanks to your lame-ass security... *I'm going home!*" He slammed down the mike, hard, and left the stage.

The hapless promoter turned the houselights on ten minutes later, as if the show was over—a major mistake. The kids sensed a rip-off and freaked. They started throwing bottles, then chairs; the more drunk ones took off their shirts and charged the stage. "I went back-stage," Axl said later, "and found another lens. It was getting crazy, and we decided we were going to go back out and try to play because we didn't want anybody to get hurt." With hundreds of kids now oc-cupying the stage, it was announced that the concert would resume if they returned to their seats. No one budged. Fires were lit. Whole rows of seats were lifted up and marched toward the stage to be used as fan artillery. Then someone mounted the stage with a fire hose and started spraying the rioting fans, which broke the whole thing down into chaos. The cops briefly took control of the stage, pepper-sprayed the kids down front, and then retreated completely. Slash: "The whole place was destroyed. It was the scariest thing I've ever seen. Back-stage, people on stretchers, all bloody, really gnarly. We're in the dressing room, listening to hell."

Later Axl told MTV: "Yeah, I jumped offstage, and things went haywire after that. I could've handled it better, but at that point no-body was handling anything. So I took it upon myself..."

The promoters blamed Axl for starting the riot and suggested to Doug Goldstein that he get his band the hell out of there. As Guns was rushed to an anonymous van under a bottle barrage, police sirens and the sounds of arson and vandalism filled the humid night. John Reese told the band to keep their heads down and ordered the driver to get them out of Missouri before anyone had time to charge Axl with anything. Guns' equipment and some instruments were in splinters. As they crossed over the Mississippi River for the safety of Illinois, Guns N' Roses said very little. John Reese later recalled: "I just told the driver to head for the nearest state line—fast. Here's the biggest band in the world, laying down flat in the back of a van to escape arrest. We drove straight to Chicago without stopping. It was just insane."

It took riot cops three hours to restore order. They arrested twenty, and ambulances carried sixty injured people to hospitals. Damage to the new amphitheater and the surrounding area was esti-mated in the hundreds of thousands of dollars. The St. Louis papers headlined the riot the next morning, and within hours Axl Rose's in-temperate stage-dive in a torrid Midwestern shed was national news.

FREEDOM OF EXPRESSION

Summer 1991. Guns N' Roses was barnstorming around America's stadiums, arenas, and coliseums with various degrees of artistry. (The band was competing with the first Lollapalooza Festival, a new traveling circus for alternative and indie bands with more street cred than Guns had.) Some nights, Guns rode white-water sluices of hard rock brilliance; others were like the dreary gig in Charlotte, North Carolina: After playing two new songs that nobody knew, Axl insulted the audience for their lack of appreciation and then basically pouted for two hours, which kept the fans *off* their feet. He then apologized for his behavior and stated that there were no "fake orgasms" on his stage. The kids who'd paid their allowance money for cheap seats wouldn't have minded fake orgasms, which was better than two hours of boredom.

After the St. Louis debacle, the tour's July Fourth Chicago concerts were canceled, which gave Guns and Skid Row almost a week off. The road crew had to scramble to build a new stage and find new gear to replace what had been trashed. The St. Louis prosecutor charged Axl with three counts of assault and one count of property damage in connection with the riot there. These charges carried three years of jail time, and were taken seriously by Guns' legal staff. The case was eventually settled, but Guns N' Roses never returned to St. Louis.

Axl Rose used this downtime to polish vocal tracks for *Use Your Illusion*. Axl brought in Blind Melon singer Shannon Hoon to sing high harmonies on many of the new ballads. Hoon was from Lafayette, Indiana, like Axl and Izzy. (Hoon was also supposed to be distantly related to Axl, and he also had a similar rap sheet for petty crimes while in high school.) He had followed Axl to Hollywood and eventually made contact with him after Blind Melon's four-song demo got a half-million-dollar advance from Capitol Records. Shannon's ethereal, boy-soprano voice smoothed out Axl's screechy yowls on crucial new songs like "The Garden" and "Don't Cry," and gave Guns' new ballads a silvery, slightly spooky edge of their own.

* * *

*T*he tour resumed a week later in Dallas with two shows at the Starplex Amphitheater. Axl as usual was seething with rage: All that week he'd been watching a CNN report that he'd started a riot in St. Louis. It was a big story on the twenty-four-hour cable channel, and every time Axl saw it, he just got angrier.

The first Dallas show, therefore, began more than two hours late. The band was primed, ready to rock, and was then kept waiting: an excruciating internal humiliation for a top, world-beating rock band. Matt Sorum muttered that he wanted to punch Axl out. Guns went on at eleven-thirty that night. After the first few songs, an obviously agitated Axl spoke to the audience: "Sometimes . . . it's hard to figure out why we get up onstage to do this, because . . . sometimes it's fun, but . . . other times it takes all the fucking physical energy we've got, to get up here, and do what we do for a living."

He complained about CNN: "They're talking about, *'And in the band, they have a recovering heroin addict, and once Axl Rose was seen driving down the street yelling obscenities at his former wife.'* . . . What the *fuck* does that have to do with St. Louis?"

People down front were yelling song requests, but Axl was just getting warmed up. "Now, at the same time . . . that this won't have an effect on Dallas, and it *shouldn't* affect me, *it fucks with rock and roll*—in general. Because, *who are the main people* that watch these news things, and read this shit? They're all in their forties to fifties, sitting there, eating their fucking bran flakes and drinking their coffee."

Axl said he wasn't knocking getting old, but old people shouldn't deny young people their essential humanity. He said he was worried that old people would read shit about the band, and if their kid liked Guns, "he's gonna get smacked upside the head or something." (Which is what had happened to Bill Bailey, years before.)

Axl finally got to his point: "And that [the kid getting smacked] really makes me go, 'Fuck, what's the point?' We're up here, and what we are doing . . . is something that is fucking *dying in America*—it usually stays underground and doesn't get as successful as Guns N' Roses—and that's freedom of expression. And basically, that's all we fucking are. Guns N' Roses is just a prime fucking example of freedom of expression." Big cheer at this. The rest of the show went off great, with Axl and Slash racing up and down the stage's high-tech steel ramps and expending enough energy to light the city for the rest of the night. After the show, Matt Sorum burst into Axl's inner sanctum. Sorum complained bitterly about starting so late, but Axl was in a conciliatory mood, and managed to put the band's new drummer firmly in his place.

It had been a hard week that had taken a heavy psychic and financial toll on the tour. So Axl's posse of therapists, counselors, and psychics decided that it would be good if he could tell the band and the crew that he was sorry about what had happened. Words are painkillers, he was told, and at the end of the day it would help him feel better. So, after the second Dallas show, Axl invited the entire crew to dinner in a private dining room at their hotel. Supported by his therapists, Axl stood up and apologized for his behavior: being late, raging, arrogant; being a dick (as he put it); starting a riot. Everyone applauded when he was through.

But two nights later in Colorado, it all happened again. They could only shake their heads. Izzy Stradlin was stoic. "We've got the gigs booked," he said, "and so we'd best show up and play. Besides, I don't want to be on CNN anymore."

*B*ackstage in Denver: Slash and Duff sit in Guns' lavishly appointed suite, dismantled and rebuilt for each gig. It has comfy furniture, a big sound system, lots of video games, a bar and buffet. The crew hates it because of Axl's strict order not to dismantle anything until he has left the building after the gig, which could be at the break of dawn. Slash and Duff are checking out the girls near the stage, using a live video feed, assigning interest on a scale of 1 to 10. (Duff: "Cool tits! Nine!") Roadies are dispatched to the lucky little ladies with laminates for after the show. Izzy plays a video game in the corner, virtually incommunicado. Axl is out of sight.

The band went on two hours after Skid Row had finished. "You Could Be Mine" was followed, as always, by "Mr. Brownstone." "Live and Let Die" was rough and ragged musically, but five big floodlights flashed blinding strobe rays at the audience from behind the band during the hammered chordal slabs of the chorus. Everything was going OK until Axl gave the microphone to Izzy for "Dust N' Bones." Two bars into the song, Axl stopped the show to ream out some poor kid who'd given Axl the finger. Axl called him fucking scum, a dickhead, a fucking asshole, a motherfucker, and a motherfucking asshole. Izzy, interrupted, just looked on, almost beyond belief. When Axl calmed down, they finished the number. The next song was "Patience."

Oliver Stone's movie *The Doors* had come out recently, and Axl had seen it several times already. In Denver, between songs, he paced the stage nervously and spewed against the media. "Well, they fucking killed Jim Morrison, didn't they? And now ... *they're trying to kill me!*" Some critics pointed out that Axl's notorious habit of starting concerts late was an attempt to copy Morrison's habit of doing the same thing. But no matter how weird things got onstage, the old stuff usually won the crowds over in the end. The band bore down on "Rocket Queen," "Sweet Child," and "Paradise City," and on some nights they played the stars from the skies.

At the makeup Chicago concerts, Axl went off on his family in a furious fifteen-minute tirade that was mostly unintelligible. Some in the audience thought they had heard Axl say that he'd been sexually abused, and his sister had too. There was a big contingent from Lafayette at the concert, and they (and many others) were shocked by what they heard. Axl was not apologetic. "I got these heavy phone calls from people in my family. They said, 'How could you do that to your poor mother?' Fuck that, man. How could she ever have gone outside the house, when she knew all about the shitty things that were happening to me back home? ... People want me to keep quiet, but I'm gonna talk about this. I'm gonna *attack* those motherfuckers. And I'm the *last* person they ever expected to be crawling up their asses."

*G*uns stayed on the road for the rest of July, mostly in the western states, finishing in California. Axl got in trouble with the road crew in San Francisco because he kicked a roadie who'd scrambled onstage to pick up a microphone that Axl had knocked over, and he had to apologize later. They finished with four sold-out homecoming nights in Los

Angeles. (The last gig ran three and a half hours, the band's longest ever.)

During the run-up to these shows, Axl and Slash finalized the vocal and guitar overdubs to their two new albums. The last song they worked on was the hellacious "Get in the Ring," a venomous challenge to critics, cops, anyone foolish enough to step in the way of Guns N' Roses' pitiless run for the rainbow. Axl formally signed off on the final mix DAT on July 28, 1991. The next night, at what was now called the Great Western Forum, Axl told the audience that he and Slash had finished their new record. "The motherfucker is *done*," he trumpeted, and got a big roaring cheer for his trouble. The backstage VIP room was star-studded: Johnny Depp, Schwarzenegger, Cher, Billy Idol, Lenny Kravitz, and Pee-wee Herman, among many lesser lights.

*G*uns had a ten-day break between the Los Angeles concerts and the next tour leg in northern Europe, but Axl Rose wasn't at rest. First, he had to share Stephanie Seymour with her three-year-old son, Dylan. This, he told friends, was a drag. Suddenly, Axl was the (wicked) stepfather, getting an unwanted education in what it took to mind a (hyper)active child. He told an interviewer that, after a few days, this became overwhelming for him. "My head is spinning because of the changes it's putting me through. . . . Oh man, they jump off things and stuff. It scares the shit out of me. . . . So, when they talk about Axl being a screaming two-year-old, they're right!" The priority of her son in Stephanie Seymour's life led to conflict, with Axl also frequently complaining about his girlfriend's appetite for cocaine, and he began to get rough with her.

Axl's other problem was Izzy Stradlin, who was now a rumor in his own band. Izzy, always a loner, was never around anymore. He hadn't worked on any of his new songs beyond the four-track demo stage. Izzy was adamant that he didn't want to do any more lame-ass videos. Izzy thought out loud that Guns had gotten too big. The whole Guns N' Roses deal was too bloated, stoned, and neurotic for Izzy. Izzy still had a bohemian, purist, garage band mentality. He'd never wanted Guns to get *huge*, to the place where it wasn't even fun anymore. On stage, Slash, Duff, and Axl worked themselves into a bare-chested, flop-sweat lather as they ran up and down the stage ramps, trying to connect with the audience, especially during the less than magic new numbers that sometimes fell flat in concert. Izzy often just stood there in his various hats, playing rhythm guitar, admittedly looking very cool but not contributing to the manic choreography it took to rock a racetrack in Birmingham, Alabama. Axl and Slash both felt like they were putting out a hundred percent, every night. They felt like they were getting ripped off. Something, Axl decided, had to be done.

"WELCOME TO THE JUNGLE 2"

*G*uns' first European tour began on August 13, 1991, again with Skid Row opening. "Live and Let Die" was now the concert's biggest number, after "Welcome to the Jungle." Axl played the old Wings song as a dramatic star turn, with spotlights following as he sprinted across his slanted steel playground during Dizzy's keyboard vamps and Slash's gonzoid Les Paul arias. Most nights, Axl explained that "Live and Let Die" was a centerpiece of still unreleased *Use Your Illusion*. "It kind of sums up everything about us," he told one audience. "We look at it as 'Welcome to the Jungle 2.'"

During this tour leg, Axl often sang in a baseball catcher's chest protector, a NWA (Niggers With Attitude) cap, and brief shorts that revealed most of his bare, muscular legs. Duff McKagan was in a full black leather suit with matching cowboy hat. Slash preferred loose Ferrari T-shirts, while Izzy wore his usual floppy caps and rock star scarves. Their stadium stage was flanked by giant video screens and three-story versions of Kostabi's *Illusion* illustrations: the gold on the left, the blue on the right.

An hour into the first of two sold-out shows at the Ice Hall in Helsinki, Finland, Axl felt sick and walked off as the band launched into "Civil War." Guns finished the song as an instrumental, and continued with the new "14 Years," Izzy on vocals. Still no Axl, who was in the dressing room with his head in his hands, thinking about the therapeutic issues in his life while his band killed time onstage. As he later told *Rolling Stone*: "The pressure of *having* to do the show, when whatever else is going on in my life, is hard to get past. I only started therapy in February, and right now, I'm in the middle of a lot of stuff. In Finland I sat down while I was singing 'Civil War,' because I couldn't understand what I was doing. My lips . . . the microphone . . . the roadies . . . and everything just shut off. It didn't make for a very good show." He explained this was why he was often late to perform, and that there was no point in his starting a concert if he wasn't mentally ready to finish it.

So Matt Sorum hammered out an extended drum solo; then Slash soared into a long, extempore electric guitar monologue, with generous lashings of Hendrix, thunderous cascades of tumbling notes, intricate curlicues of blues guitar. Axl Rose returned after half an hour and finished a ninety-minute Guns show as contracted.

Four nights later, in Stockholm, Sweden, Axl left his hotel suite for the second concert in two days. For once he was on time. But instead of getting into his waiting car, he played roulette in the hotel casino for an hour while a full house waited for Axl at the Globe arena across town. He might have been annoyed that an unauthorized photo of the band, snapped at a nightclub, was on the front page of the daily *Expressen* (which had given Guns' show an unqualified rave). After losing a little money, Axl went back up to his room. But then he came down and got into the car. Halfway to the Globe, he stopped the car to gaze at a fireworks display for the Swedish summer holiday Vattenfestivalen. The concert, set for nine, started closer to midnight. The audience was tired. During "Heaven's Door," Axl taunted them: "Now, on this one, maybe you people that've been like . . . *falling asleep the whole fuckin' show* . . . could sing along too. . . . Hey, if you're bored, you should've saved your money and gone to see the fireworks tonight. *I did* . . . They were great!"

Guns played Copenhagen, Denmark, the next night. Duff and Slash held a surreal press conference at which they were asked political questions until Duff snapped. "We're *not* the Berlin Wall coming down," he said. "We're *not* communism falling, man. We're *not* the civil war in Yugoslavia. We're just a fucking rock 'n' roll band!" Slash agreed. "All the attention any successful band gets is just ridiculous."

Copenhagen went well until a cherry bomb from the audience exploded near Slash. Axl stopped the show and said nothing would happen until the bomber stepped up and confessed. Guns went back onstage fifteen minutes later, but finished the gig early, with an abbreviated encore. Axl Rose left immediately and disappeared.

The next day, August 20, Guns flew to Oslo, Norway, and checked into the Hotel Grand. The Oslo show was sold out. At the sound check that afternoon, Izzy casually mentioned to the tour's Swedish promoter that no one knew where Axl Rose was. Then Axl's assistant called and said he was in Paris. A few hours later, she called again to say Axl wasn't coming. The Oslo show was canceled. Alone in his suite in a five-star Paris hotel, W. Axl Rose sulked in his tent like Achilles. (There were press reports that Axl was seen meditating at Jim Morrison's tomb that afternoon. Morrison's grave was in those days crowded with pilgrims from newly liberated Eastern European countries. Doors fans of all ages danced, played boom boxes and guitars, smoked dope, and drank—a constant party.) But Guns and their crew, stuck in Oslo and stewing in helpless resentment, knew something big was brewing, and there was no way it could possibly be good.

The storm broke backstage in Mannheim, Germany. Guns had outsold both the Rolling Stones and Madonna, who had played the venue the year before, and the band's single show was being covered by the German press as a national event. While Nine Inch Nails and Skid Row opened the concert, Axl convened an unusual band meeting before the show, which went on way past the time Guns was supposed to take the stage. The crew could hear raised voices behind locked and guarded doors, and the backstage vibe was tense and angry. Robert John: "We were in Germany, and I knew something was wrong. The band wasn't going onstage, and no one knew why. Duff came out of the band meeting, really upset, and then went back in again. We started loading the girlfriends out, sending them back to the hotel. The band finally came out and did the show, but no one looked happy. Then word filtered down to the crew that what happened was something about Izzy getting demoted. Like, he was told that he wasn't doing enough, and that his money would be affected, and all this other shit. I couldn't believe this, because I thought Izzy wrote all their best songs. He was Axl's writing partner. The best songs on the new album—like 'Dust N' Bones'—mostly came from Izzy."

Mannheim was an outdoor soccer stadium in German summer twilight. Guns went on (very late, even for them) with "You Could Be Mine." But Axl walked off after twenty minutes, followed by the band. Axl sat in the van that had brought him from the dressing room and wouldn't come out. Some of the forty thousand German kids started to throw things, but promoter Ossy Hoppe came onstage and explained that Axl didn't feel well. Backstage, Doug Goldstein begged Axl to finish the show so there wouldn't be a riot. Duff and Slash tried too, but Axl stayed in the van. Finally, Matt Sorum went to the van, just as Axl was getting ready to go back on. "What the fuck are you doing?" Sorum yelled. "Get back on the stage!" Slash got between them, and Axl climbed back into the van and told the driver to go back to the hotel. But the promoter had wisely closed the stadium gates, so the band couldn't leave. The promoters finally got through to Axl that he would be arrested if the kids rioted. So Guns came back after half an hour and finished the show. The band's fines for playing after curfew were said to be in the high tens of thousands of dollars.

After this, Izzy Stradlin confided to friends that he had felt dictated to, and that he would probably leave Guns after *Use Your Illusion* came out. Slash claims Izzy told Doug Goldstein he was quitting after the current leg. "I don't even think that Izzy even discussed it with Axl," he recalled. The road crew was upset; many of them thought Izzy was the true soul of Guns N' Roses. Izzy Stradlin left the tour and disappeared for almost a week.

Slash tried to talk Izzy out of leaving the band, which was at its peak: big stadiums, great audiences, travel, real money. Izzy would only reply, "I know. But, man—I just don't want to do it anymore."

Axl Rose later described the meeting that pushed Izzy out of Guns:

"It was like, [we said to him] 'You're not giving an equal share.' Slash and I were doing all the work—of keeping the attention and energy up in the crowd. I'm onstage, going: 'This is really hard, and I'm into it, and I'm doing it, but *that* guy just gets to stand there?' . . . The guy is getting up at six thirty in the morning and riding bikes and motorcycles and buying toy airplanes, and he's donating all his energy to something else, and it's taking a hundred percent of *our* energy to do what we're doing on the stage.... We were getting ripped off."

The last show of the Euro leg took place on August 31 at Wembley Stadium, the giant football pitch in North London. Heraldic banners and Union Jacks flew from the parapets of the stadium in brilliant late summer sunshine as 72,000 fans made their way to the gig in the late summer twilight. The 72,000 seats had sold out in record time, the fastest ever for any rock band. The London papers had reported that the municipal Brent Council, the licensing authority for the concert, had stipulated that no cursing be allowed from the stadium stage lest community sensibilities be offended. So, a few days before the show, the London Underground subway was plastered with a guerilla poster campaign that recalled Guns' outlaw flyers from days of yore. The crudely printed posters read: GUNS N' FUCKING ROSES / WEMBLEY FUCKING STADIUM / SOLD FUCKING OUT.

There was some concern in the Guns camp that Izzy Stradlin might not show up. Tour insiders leaked a quiet word—*"Don't quote me, mate"*—that it might be Izzy's last show with Guns N' Roses. Doug Goldstein told another band's manager that they were within one meeting of Izzy quitting. But Izzy arrived at Wembley for the sound check on the hot summer afternoon of August 31, 1991. The vibe backstage was deadly. Skid Row went on after Nine Inch Nails, and of course Sebastian Bach outdid himself in spewing verbal filth and leading the huge crowd in brainless, provocative f-bomb chants.

Then, to their credit, the exhausted, stressed-out Guns put on a decent London show. Even Izzy Stradlin showed more interest, perhaps because some of this, especially "Live and Let Die," was being filmed for future videos and broadcasts. Axl took the stage in a plaid shirt—very grunge—and a Scots kilt of the same tartan. He ran his ass off during Slash's wild mercury soloing, and tried to appease both the kids in the stadium and the video cameras for the segments that were being filmed. It was hard, soul-crushing work, on the largest scale imaginable. Guns played many unfamiliar songs from *Illusion,* which sent tens of thousands to the bars for pints of lager. Blowing off steam,

Axl delivered the usual insults to his perceived enemies in the London media. He dedicated "Double Talkin' Jive" to *Sky* magazine, *Time Out,* and "something I respected years ago, but now I'd rather wipe my ass with it—*Kerrang!*" (The offending magazine's writers had been specifically barred from the show.) Perhaps competing with Skid Row, Axl cussed and swore, referred to the customers as "you fuckers," caressed his crotch and thighs like a gay stripper (or Jim Morrison), and played as lewd a show as Guns ever did.

The press responded in kind. *The Sun:* "AXL ATTACK: Wild Man Rose Hurls Abuse at Stunned Fans!" Venerable *Melody Maker* asked if a band can be punk and still ride around in Porsches. *Q* magazine called Guns the saddest band in the world. Primal punk champions *New Musical Express* asked, "Where was the fabled rock 'n' roll steamroller, laying waste to all before it?" The *Observer* observed: "Dangerous? Not in the slightest. Entertaining? Absolutely!" The worst came from England's paper of record, *The Times*: "Even by the inflated standards of the rock world, the hype surrounding Guns N' Roses has been extreme. Would their show be a display of primitive brilliance, or an amateurish shambles? The reality was disappointingly mundane.... If one truth emerged from this long, mediocre show, it was that those who live by the sword of self-gratification are not the best judge of when to wind up a guitar solo.... Reminiscent of the worst excesses of pre-punk dinosaur rock [ouch!]... The concert was as challenging to the status quo as a child burping at the lunch table."

*Y*ears later, Sir Paul McCartney recalled: "About fifteen years ago, my kids went to see Guns N' Roses at Wembley, and they all came home wearing the black T-shirts and the bloody bandannas. I asked what the coolest part of the concert had been, and my daughter Stella said, 'Live and Let Die.'

"I said, 'Hey, I wrote that!'"

"And the kids went, 'Yeah, Dad. *Sure* you did. Tell us another one.'"

A few days later, a still intact Guns N' Roses straggled separately back to Los Angeles. The tour was now on hiatus for three months while the band caught its breath, got the new album out, and made new videos. The band met once, after they got home, for a ten-minute photo shoot with Robert John, in order to get a publicity shot for the new album. (It was the last time Guns N' Roses would ever pose for a group photograph.) The rest of 1991 was a hectic blur of secret auditions and creative tinkering that would result in nothing less than a complete rethink of Guns N' Roses. Izzy Stradlin had played his final gig with the band he had dreamed about, and then founded, and had then seen grow beyond anything which he thought was even remotely cool.

Chapter Eleven

CONFUSE YOUR ILLUSION

All [he] had ever tried to be, right or wrong,
was himself. With all the doctors, special-
ists, therapists, fans, and everyone in his
organization trying to help him, he just
sank further into his cocoon, alienating
himself even more. He often wondered who
he was. Was he a phenomenon or just a
façade? Was he a product of his own imagination, or just another brick? Would he
ever understand his own destiny?
—Del James, "Without You"

THE INDIANA BOOK OF THE DEAD

*G*effen Records released *Use Your Illusion I* and *II* in all three recording formats—LP, CD, and cassette—at midnight on September 21,
1991. Tower Records stores in Los Angeles, Chicago, and New York
stayed open all night for the crowds of Guns fans clamoring to buy at
the stroke of twelve. And, prodded by both industrial hype and the
provocative magic of *Appetite for Destruction,* the fans came out by the
thousands. In New York, the lines began to snake down Broadway by
nine P.M. In West Hollywood the fan queue started to stretch down the
Sunset Strip even earlier. Major-market radio stations were already
featuring *Illusion*'s first single, "You Could Be Mine," and playing the
album tracks "Live and Let Die" and "Don't Cry." Everyone who
worked on the albums came out to see the crowd queuing on Sunset.

By eleven o'clock, Slash was getting calls from friends about the literally thousands of kids waiting on the streets, nervously monitored by West Hollywood deputies deciding whether or not to call out the riot squad. Slash had to see this, so he was driven to Tower Records on Sunset and was spirited in through the loading dock—under which Axl Rose used to crash. Tower's manager led Slash up to the security office to watch the crowds snaking into the store. Slash remarked that he had been in that room before, as a fourteen-year-old shoplifter caught with a stolen Aerosmith tape in his back pocket.

The Guns N' Roses fanatic who bought the two disks of *Use Your Illusion* went home with thirty new songs enclosed in Mark Kostabi's cartoonlike "appropriation" of *The School of Athens.* In the illustration, a boy writes in a notebook, watched over by one of the great philosophers of the classical world. *Use Your Illusion I* had sixteen songs and a rich golden color. *Illusion II* had fourteen songs and a darker blue evening hue. Both albums bore black parental advisory stickers, because Guns' new songs featured more obscene cussing than a marine platoon on night patrol.

This was because the new songs were a manic-depressive mix of Axl Rose's self-preoccupations and Eltonian pianism; Izzy Stradlin's ironic (and totally up-front) reflections on the sleazier aspects of a contemporary rock star's life; Slash's barb-wire solos and (occasionally) inspired guitar melodies; Duff McKagan's innate rock aesthetics; and Matt Sorum's reliable, lead-tipped drum rhythms. Faced with such a massive amount of unfamiliar new material, Guns fans immediately began to play the game of choosing the best of both records to assemble a virtual, alternative, single *Use Your Illusion* album that would have given the mighty *Appetite* a run for its money in terms of crazed, no-filler excitement.

Illusion I begins with "Right Next Door to Hell," a blasting account of his former neighbor, complete with "Fuck you, bitch!" Axl invokes Dr. Freud, perhaps the first time the father of psychoanalysis had been mentioned in a punk-metal context. Hurt, anger, paranoia, and bitterness overwhelm the two-chord rock number and leave a bad aftertaste as Izzy launches into the second track, "Dust N' Bones." (Slash said he'd written "Dust" with Izzy after they'd both done a shitload of heroin.) A broad homage to Stones-style raunch with a decidedly glam sneer, "Dust" was Izzy's stark, existentialist philosophy cut with auto-biographical elements of leaving his mind out on Interstate 65, the road that had led away from Lafayette for both Jeff Isbell and Bill Bailey.

The studio version of Paul and Linda McCartney's "Live and Let Die," which Guns had made a concert showstopper, was now the sound track to an imaginary movie about a rock band with a license—if not to kill, at least to keep their audiences waiting indefinitely. Guns' version was Wings on steroids. Axl begins in a strangled voice, and Shannon Hoon supplies the girly *ya know ya dids*. The main vamp is played by a horn section led by Duff's brother, and the chorus has become Axl's threat display, with the explicit message that the only thing to do—when an ever-changing world tries to crush your spirit—is attack, and attack again, with the same deadly intent as the remorseless 007.

"Don't Cry" was one of the earliest songs Axl and Izzy had written in Los Angeles, ten years earlier. After a low guitar drone, it evolves into a hard rock lullaby that turns into a hard-hearted kiss-off. Slash's tendency to play the same solo on every ballad comes into focus. "Don't Cry" ends with an edgy, sustained vocal drone that is more scary than reassuring. It morphs into Izzy's "Perfect Crime," a punky missile launch complete with NASA-style countdown, a guitar solo shredded beyond human endeavor, and a clear echo of the post-teenage Guns that had captivated the kids at Scream and the Troubadour in 1985. "Perfect Crime" is the (fascinating, Rimbaud-like) confessions of a re-tired, mid-level dope dealer, recalling the sordid aspects of making a living from the hustle and flow, where the only objective is surviving long enough to push more dope the next night.

The mood then changes as Izzy counts off the lazy beat of "You Ain't the First," a guitar-pickin' song with the raw, demo-sounding vibe of an outtake from *Exile on Main Street*. "Bad Obsession," credited to Izzy and West Arkeen, might have come off *Goats Head Soup*—a sleazy boogie with a feverish harmonica aria from Hanoi Rocks' Michael

Monroe. The bad obsession was heroin addiction, and Izzy used the song to tell his audience that he was now clean: *"But I already left you / And you're better off left behind."* Axl used the song for a different purpose: *"I call my mother / She's just a cunt now."*

Bill Bailey and Paul Huge had written the earliest version of "Back Off Bitch" as young punks in Indiana. Midway through *Use Your Illusion I*, "Bitch" resurfaces as an idiotic album track describing naked hostility toward women. *"Face of an angel with the love of a witch / Back off, back off Bitch."* The track is so lame that Slash is unable to save it with his supple guitar solo, and many Guns fans were embarrassed by its moronic stupidity. The rest of Guns insisted on appending ironic comments about the track's lack of subtlety as it faded out.

Izzy Stradlin's sludge-rocking "Double Talkin' Jive" had become a concert staple for Guns that summer. Izzy's lead vocal bites into the song, describing a dope pusher's alienation from the clientele upon whose flesh he was feeding. Stradlin's succinct, shocking, two-and-a-half-minute sketch ends with Slash's expert Spanish-sounding guitar work, and remains one of the highlights of *Use Your Illusion I*—one of its rare works of art.

For years, the trenchant piano ballad "November Rain" had been Axl Rose's pet project. He described it as "a song about unrequited love," and the Big Statement he wanted to be remembered for, the way Eric Clapton was identified with "Layla." Now, after years of tweaking, "November Rain" was released on *Illusion I* as an overripe soap opera whose cheesy synthesizer melody blends into thunderous guitar chorales, and bombastic choirs murmuring lyrics of romantic hope and defiance of the vagaries of love. This pretty (but hopelessly sentimental) ballad is being asked a lot of, in terms of a flame-throwing heavyosity that it doesn't really possess. "November Rain" would eventually be magnified by its video version, which tried to explain the volcanic, and ultimately bereft, emotions behind the song to Guns N' Roses fans in more detail the following year.

Illusion I continues with "The Garden," an art-metal nightmare written by Axl, West Arkeen, and Del James, and sung by Axl with Alice

Cooper and Shannon Hoon. One of the best *Illusion* songs, it has literate, slithery raps before the whole poppy-scented garden explodes into a napalm-fried guitar bombardment.

This leads into "Garden of Eden," a punk explosion coauthored by Axl and Slash. A specific attack on organized religion at drag-racer speed, "Eden" claims that religions "make a mockery of humanity" and that "our governments are dangerous and out of control." Whether the irony was intentional or not, Axl's conspicuous heresy is followed by "Don't Damn Me," a chin-out message to the legions of Axl haters offended by "One in a Million." Written with Dave Lank, the song delivers no apologies for Axl speaking his mind, and—after a slow, power ballad of a bridge, Axl reasserts his right to spew whatever he feels like into the faces of his fans. "Your satisfaction lies in your illusions," he tells them, "but your delusions are yours and not mine." Then bang into "Bad Apples," with Dizzy Reed pumping boogie piano over an old Stones bump-and-grinder while Axl dishes out classic bad-boy ambience. You have to read the printed lyrics to figure out what his unintelligible (and ultimately useless) phrases are saying.

For many Guns fans listening to *Illusion I* for the first time (with some in a state of confused shock and disappointment), the album finally comes to life in track 15, "Dead Horse," where, after a gentle intro, the screechy baby of *Appetite* rears his ugly voice and the band kicks into a hard rock groove that brings to mind the last days of the Aero-Stones, and the earliest days of Guns N' Roses.

Slash's "Coma" (written in a heroin trance, according to its composer) eventually got the lyrics it took traumatized Axl Rose a year to write. (Axl told an interviewer that he kept passing out whenever he tried to work on the song.) The result was the last track (and first masterpiece) on *Use Your Illusion I*. Axl deploys a "glam" voice, and the band a Sabbath crunch, to begin an autobiographical rock novella of a dire medical condition set in a mindscape of twisted screams and psychic bewilderment. *"Will someone tell me what the fuck is going on—GODDAMN IT!"* The track is accented with heartbeats, beeping life-support machines, panicking emergency room staff, and the spooky sonic twilight of a near-death experience. As Axl nears mortality's white light in the middle of the song, he floats happily away until the docs put the defibrillator paddles on his chest and shock the living hell into him, recalling him reluctantly to life. Then Slash takes over with one of his fever-dream solos as a chorus of "Bitches" complains and gossips, remorselessly, in the background. The ten minutes of "Coma" close *Illusion I* on a blistering voyage of trauma and revival—a vivid taste of what this great band was capable of when catapulted from the carrier deck with jet engines burning full throttle.

*U*se *Your Illusion II* begins with the quavering voice of actor Strother Martin justifying the brutal torture of Paul Newman's character in *Cool Hand Luke,* the 1969 antiauthoritarian chain gang drama. (The "failure to communicate" between jailer and prisoners probably reminded Axl Rose what it was like to grow up as Bill Bailey.) The quiet vocal of the intro to "Civil War" turns into psychotic banshee wails as Axl lets fly on Vietnam, the Kennedy murders, the Shining Path guerrillas of contemporary Peru, and "the bloody hands of the hypnotized / Who carry the cross of homicide." "Civil War" moves from contemplation to anthemic climax, and then on to a rocking, protest-driven piano and guitar boogie. Since it was one of the first songs recorded for *Illusion,* it happens to be the last on which Steven Adler played. As the track fades out amidst thunder and rain effects (borrowed from the Doors), Axl whistles and sighs the age-old question: "Whaz [*sic*] so civil 'bout war, anyway?"

Izzy Stradlin's finest moment on *Illusion* is his singing on "14 Years," a bitter review of his and Axl's relationship, set to a power ballad sequence. Again, Izzy offers a furtive glimpse into his former world, a sordid scenario of hookers and dope dealers where "nothin's for free." Axl plays a rollicking piano part while Dizzy's organ is set to drone. Slash unleashes a brash, out-for-blood solo that seems to second Izzy's lament about having to deal with one of the most difficult characters ever to make the charts.

West Arkeen and Del James were the principal writers of "Yesterdays," an elegy for unwanted nostalgia by a singer whose memories are too painful to comprehend. The pretty, cruise-control melody is undermined by Axl's strained rasp wringing every drop of pathos in turning his back on the past. Again at the piano, Axl finishes with a repeated chord striking the same notes as in the Beatles' "A Day in the

Life"—an ominous warning that memory lane can be a painful, even fatal address.

Bob Dylan's 1973 movie theme, "Knockin' on Heaven's Door," had been a concert sing-along for Guns for several years, often dedicated to the late Todd Crew, sometimes intimately involving a hundred thousand kids in gargantuan soccer stadiums. Treated on *Illusion II* as a gospel-metal death chant with intimations of crowd control—*"Hey hey, hey-hey-yeah"*—Axl grunts and squeals with perverse relish as the cold black cloud descends on the dying deputy of the song. After Slash's shimmering blues solo, an answering-machine tape natters cryptically about someone's tattered libido, the bank, and the mortician, and a gospel choir joins Guns for the final choruses of Dylan's song, a western ballad transformed into *The Indiana Book of the Dead.*

*N*ow *Illusion II* swerves into a sickening, wet-road skid with the enraged polemics of "Get in the Ring." As Slash plays generic blues licks and the band rocks out, Axl attacks the press that had helped build Guns N' Roses into the biggest act in the world—by name. *Circus* magazine, *Hit Parader's* Andy Secher, and Mick Wall of *Kerrang!* are accused of printing lies and ripping off the kids who just want to read the truth about the bands they like. Axl growls it out: "Get in the ring, motherfucker, and I'll kick your bitchy little ass / Punk!" *Spin* magazine's Bob Guccione Jr. (son of the publisher of *Penthouse*) is called out by name: "What, you pissed off cuz your dad gets more *pussy* than you? / *Fuck you / Suck my fuckin' dick.*" (This was a lot different from "Feel my serpentine.") After this manic attack, Axl dedicates the song to "all the Guns N' fuckin' Roses fans who stuck with us through all the fuckin' shit." "You may not like our integrity," he snarls at his critics. "We built a world out of anarchy."

Two of Axl's songs come next. "Shotgun Blues" is another sonic assault on the enemy, with lots of cussing. "Breakdown" is a romantic breakup song in a southern rock atmosphere that seems explicitly addressed to Erin Everly. The denial of memory in "Yesterdays" is reversed in this confused, episodic song that comes with a recitative from an innocuous action movie of the day, *Vanishing Point*. Axl Rose on the past: *"Funny how ev'rything was Roses / When we held on to the Guns."*

This is the point where Guns' new album finally breaks down in a sense of artistic futility and loss—not for Axl Rose but for Guns N' Roses' actual fans. The ultimate effect of "Breakdown" is one of a bloated double album, sinking like the *Titanic,* with all hands aboard and the band still playing on deck, after *Use Your Illusion II* had rammed an immense (and much more sympathetic) iceberg called Grunge.

Izzy Stradlin's "Pretty Tied Up (The Perils of Rock N' Roll Decadence)" begins with a synthetic sitar lick announcing an exoticism that never surfaces in this terrific, jamming rock song of total disillusion. Slash plays some mean, air-punch guitar as Izzy sings about a rock band, once a creature of the street, that has since become a joke—"and it all went up in smoke." A jaded and ultra-cynical porn movie about a Melrose Avenue dominatrix, "Pretty Tied Up" jumps out of *Illusion II* as what the Guns fan had been waiting, for more than an hour, to finally hear. This high energy continues in "Locomotive," a nasty rhythm that turns into a weighty essay on the use of illusions. A complex structure with a two-tempo chorus, cowritten by Axl and Slash, "Locomotive" could also have been titled "Author's Message," since Axl gets a lot off his beleaguered chest: "I've worked too hard for my illusions / Just to throw them all away." Just as the track seems to end, it goes into a lyrical piano coda and a long band ride-out (borrowed from mid-period Fleetwood Mac) as Axl chants an elongated mantra: "Love's so straaaaaaaaaaaannge."

Axl and Duff both sing on Duff's pretty love song, "So Fine," which turns into rock and roll halfway through, with Slash playing his generic guitar solo using the first melody of the song as inspiration. (Duff dedicated "So Fine" to the memory of Johnny Thunders, late guitarist of the New York Dolls, who had recently overdosed and died in New Orleans.)

Axl Rose had long spoken of "Estranged" as the third part of a trilogy that began with "Don't Cry" and continued with "November Rain." Now, "Estranged" emerges as a brokenhearted exit wound featuring the best guitar melody of Slash's recording career and an aching account of the emptiness and emotional cravings that follow a breakup between ardent lovers. Axl's piano echoed his black-hole blues—"Old at heart but I'm only twenty-eight"—and a deep regret at a crucial relationship that has died. An era is over. The savage screamer of *Appetite* is now a sniveling child abandoned by his girlfriend *cum* mother. To some fans, this was Axl Rose being sensitive. Others thought it pathetic. The last two choruses seem based on the end of "Stairway to Heaven"—an elegy for an almost mythic love that has been lost, and is never coming back.

"You Could Be Mine" had been originally written by Izzy and Axl for *Appetite* but hadn't been used. Guns recut it with Matt Sorum, and now it was *Use Your Illusion*'s first single (selling two million copies in the first month), and one of its baddest tracks. Sorum and Slash work hard to put the song over, and the intensity of Axl's anger is palpable and scary. If you were his girlfriend and had a taste for cocaine, it was even scarier.

The newer lyrics to *Illusion*'s second, and very different, version of "Don't Cry" are much darker than the original. The first version, on *Illusion I*, is reassuring and hopeful. But the alternative "Don't Cry" at the end of *Illusion II* has lyrics that are more angry and spiteful, a sinister good-bye. It is sad that the romantic illusions of a young man reaching for the heavens have become the sleepless nights and bad dreams of a fading rock star. The fans picked up on this. A whiff of decay was in the air, the pathos of a young band grown out of what had made it cool in the first place.

*W*hen Izzy Stradlin got his first test pressing of *Use Your Illusion II*, he figured the record had ended with the rewritten "Don't Cry," one of the first songs he and Axl had worked on together. That was the album Izzy had signed off on in July.

But no.

Now appended to *Illusion II* was Axl Rose's stupefying rap-rock splatter painting "My World." A rhythmic white cousin of contemporary West Coast rappers NWA, Easy E, and Tupac Shakur, "My World" is a vortex/gyre of confessional perversion, cracking whips, and female orgasms (recycled by Mike Clink from the four-year-old *Appetite* sex tapes). Izzy had never heard this track before.

Izzy: "I gave it a listen, and thought: *What the fuck is this?*"

PSYCHOLOGICAL GRAFFITI

*L*ate September 1991. The reviews were in for *Use Your Illusion,* and to say they were mixed would be kind. Not that it mattered. *Illusion II* had debuted at number one on the American charts, while *Illusion I* had come in at number two. The critics immediately noticed that Guns' new records had zero soul-clenching, multinational anthems like "Welcome to the Jungle" or "Sweet Child o' Mine." None of the ballads were nearly as cool as "Patience." The new drummer had changed Guns N' Roses from punk-metal to hard rock. The music press, which was generally afraid of the band, described the *Illusion* records as physically assaultive, verbally incendiary, and "at times downright screwy" (*Rolling Stone*). The *L.A. Weekly* called *Illusion* "a declaration of insolence fueled by self-righteous anger and fearful confusion." Many Guns fans, having been asked to spend twice as much as normal for a band's new release, were disappointed in the new music. In abandoning punk depravity and streetwise rock and roll for a new focus on maturing emotions, Guns was asking a lot of its core fan base. And the fans responded in their own way. *Appetite for Destruction* was up to fourteen million in sales by then. *Use Your Illusion's* two albums sold roughly seven million units apiece in the first few months of release, far below what Geffen Records had projected at the time.

The bitter truth was that no one loved the contentious, unlovable *Illusion* albums. For many Guns fans, it was a case of too much, too late. Nirvana and Pearl Jam were now exploring emotional territory too, but without the sleazy, immature rancor and rabid bitterness of Axl Rose's lyrics.

Before he stopped giving interviews, Axl Rose tried to explain that they deliberately hadn't tried to re-create the pyrosonics of 1986 hair metal. "The most important songs are the ones with piano, the ballads, because we haven't explored that side of the band yet. The beautiful music is what really makes me feel like an artist. It's harder to write about serious emotions, describing them as best as possible, rather than trying to write a syrupy ballad just to sell records."

* * *

$\mathcal{F}$or the *Don't Cry* video, directed by new hire Andy Monahan, Guns would be filmed playing atop the TransAmerica skyscraper in downtown Los Angeles at night. The building had been secured, a helicopter and camera crews were hired, and a big video budget was on the line. Just before the shoot, Izzy Stradlin sent a formal letter to Guns N' Roses and its management. Izzy informed them that he wasn't doing any more videos, which he considered to be lame, ruinously expensive ego trips. The letter also stipulated several conditions that would have to be met before Izzy joined Guns when the *Illusion* tour resumed in January 1992. To Axl Rose's total horror, Izzy also announced that he was returning to Alan Niven for management, since Doug Goldstein seemed to be working exclusively in Axl's interest.

The spectacular "Don't Cry" skyscraper shoot went off without Izzy. As the chopper swooped down on the floodlit building roof in video strafing runs, the onboard cameras picked out a grungy, plaid-shirted youth singing with Axl. It was Shannon Hoon filling out Izzy's place on the rooftop stage. The next two weeks featured a bunch of anguished phone calls as Axl Rose tried to convince Izzy Stradlin not to leave the band. Axl told Kim Neely: "We were filming 'Don't Cry,' and [Izzy] had to be there, but he didn't show up. Instead he sent this short, cold letter saying, 'This changes, this changes, and maybe I'll tour in January [1992].' And they were ridiculous demands that weren't going to get met."

Axl called Izzy and they talked for four hours. Axl: "I was crying. I was begging. I was doing everything I could to keep him in the band." At the same time, Axl insisted that he and Slash were tired of doing all the running on the huge stages they were playing, and that Izzy had to make less money if he just stood there, even if he looked cool. The conversation ended with no clear resolution.

Two weeks later, in October 1991, Axl and Stephanie Seymour were in New York, being shot for the cover of *Interview* magazine by fashion photographer Bruce Weber. Axl wasn't that keen to do this, but Stephanie Seymour was friendly with the publishers, Sandi and Peter Brandt, and had been promised the magazine's cover if Axl appeared with her and was interviewed. While they were being photographed, Axl took a phone call. He came back, visibly shaken, having been told that Izzy Stradlin had quit Guns N' Roses. Stephanie Seymour ran to Axl to comfort him, and Weber shot several rolls of them kissing and caressing each other with tenderness and obvious emotion.

"Bruce was taking photos," Axl remembered later, "and I was standing there, crying. I was just blown away—my friend of fifteen years was leaving." It took a while for this to sink in. Axl hadn't thought Izzy would call his bluff, and he went into a kind of shock. Every few minutes, he would stop and think to himself: *"I'm no longer working with Izzy."*

Izzy Stradlin's resignation from Guns N' Roses felt like yet another abandonment to W. Axl Rose, and it made him mad as hell. He got more annoyed when he heard Izzy was writing songs for his own record. A few weeks later, Izzy drove up to Axl's home on a hidden canyon road in Malibu and buzzed the intercom outside the locked iron gates. Axl cursed Izzy out over the intercom, and wouldn't buzz him in. "I was just a dick," Axl said later. "Izzy tried to talk to me—nicely, you know? And I just went *off* on him."

"I'm glad we got the songs out of him that we did," Axl told another interviewer, "and I'm glad he's gone. You want to know what really hurt me? He came up here to my fucking house, and acted like, *'What's wrong, man?'* And it was weird, because somehow, I *knew* he was coming. I could literally feel his car coming up the road as I was getting dressed. I went outside and sat down, because Izzy couldn't come into my house. I couldn't act like he was my friend, after what he had done to me. He came up here, and he acted like he hadn't done anything. But Izzy called up members of the band and tried to turn them against me.... He said a lot of shit behind my back. He tried a power play, and damaged us on the way out, and that's real fucked up."

Asked why Izzy quit, Axl said, "My personal belief is that Izzy never really wanted something this big. There were responsibilities that Izzy didn't want to deal with, and he just didn't want to work at the standards that Slash and I set for ourselves.... I wanted to get as big as possible—from Day One, but that wasn't Izzy's intention at all.

"I'm angry at him because he left in a shitty way," Axl fumed, "and for being an asshole about the way he did it, and for trying to act like everything's cool. He put his trust in people that I consider my enemies.... I don't need Alan Niven knowing jack shit about Guns N' Roses. It's like [to Izzy], 'If you're involved with these people, we can't talk to you.'"

Izzy Stradlin's decision to leave the band was kept secret until November 1991, when Guns announced his departure. By that time, Izzy was putting together a new band, the Ju Ju Hounds, and writing songs for the next phase of his career. Word got out that some of the Rolling Stones would be playing on Izzy's record. He told people that he felt like the weight of the world had been lifted from his shoulders, and Jeff Isbell wouldn't speak to his old friend Bill Bailey for a long time after that.

GN'R MARK III

*O*ctober 1991. With Izzy Stradlin gone and two years of tour bookings to fulfill, W. Axl Rose and Slash decided to rethink the band. They needed a star-quality rhythm guitarist who could do the job at an old Irish castle or on a rain-swept stage in an Argentine soccer stadium. Axl now wanted the same production that he saw Mick Jagger commanding in 1989: a five-piece guitar band augmented with keyboards, four backup singers (one male), and a three-piece horn section. With twelve musicians onstage, the Guns' big production numbers—"Live and Let Die" and "Heaven's Door"—would transcend the sometimes anemic performances they'd gotten during the first legs of the tour. So Slash took on the responsibility of recruiting this GN'R philharmonic ensemble, with only a few weeks left before the tour resumed late in 1991.

*G*ilby Clarke was a twenty-nine-year-old Cleveland-born guitar player—considered very good by his peers—who had known the guys in Guns since the mid-eighties. He'd played in Hollywood bands Candy, Kill for Thrills, and the Blackouts, and he was cool. In September

1991, it was well known in L.A. music circles that Izzy was leaving Guns, and so Gilby made his move.

"I'd heard something was up," he said later, "and I called a friend of mine [Adam Day, Slash's guitar tech] who worked for the band, and told him: 'If these guys are looking for someone, then put my name in the pot.' And one day I came home and there was the call."

Slash was on the phone. He'd known Gilby before Guns even existed, when Gilby's bands were playing Madame Wong's West with Hollywood Rose and the bands Slash played with.

Slash: "But I hadn't seen him in all those years. His name was brought up and I just said—*yeah*. In fact, he was the only person we auditioned." Slash took Gilby into the studio with Duff and Matt; they jammed a little and it sounded great, like a Gunsmobile with a fresh carburetor. But Gilby didn't get the gig right away. "For the first week," he recalled, "I kept coming in to the studio, every day, without knowing if I was coming back tomorrow. They were still calling other guitar players. I was hoping, and trying to be cool, and really scared. Man! I had to put everything else to one side, and concentrate on—somehow—learning forty-odd songs. It had to be the most intense period of my life. Lucky for me, it happened so fast that I didn't have time to think. I was onstage playing gigs with them in the space of three weeks."

Slash was hot to hire Gilby Clarke, if only to keep Axl's first choice, Dave Navarro, out of Guns. Slash told Axl that Chili Pepper Dave was cool, but that he was a lead player, not the skilled rhythm guitarist the Guns ensemble needed. "Besides," Slash said later, "[Navarro] had a heroin problem, and obviously that was a major issue."

It didn't hurt that Gilby looked a little like Izzy; it would be good for the band's look and video continuity. So Gilby Clarke was put on salary and encouraged to dress like his predecessor, who had in fact copied his look and style from the primal source, Keith Richards circa 1978.

Slash filled out GN'R Mark III with singer Theodore Andreadis, known professionally as Teddy Zig Zag, who was from the same New Jersey musical milieu as Bruce Springsteen. Teddy sang Shannon Hoon's parts on "Don't Cry" and other ballads in concert, and also played harmonica, keyboards, and tambourine when required. Three girl singers were hired—Diane Jones, Roberta Freeman, and Tracy Amos—as well as the three members of the 976 Horns: Lisa Maxwell, Cece Worrall, and Anne King. These six women—often performing in scanty briefs and black leather bustiers—circled the globe with Guns for the next two years, adding slatternly allure (and more than decent musical chops) to Guns N' Roses' new arrangements, especially the stadium-shaking versions of other people's songs.

*A*utumn 1991. Guns N' Roses was sporadically rehearsing in various locations around Hollywood—mostly without the band's singer. Slash had broken up (again) with his longtime girlfriend, Renee, and was into a low-key heroin thing. He played on sessions for Michael Jackson's *Dangerous* album, and appeared with the King of Pop on MTV's tenth anniversary show. Duff McKagan was drinking a lot but writing songs and working on a solo album. Axl Rose was spotted around town in various states of psychic turmoil as he tried to negotiate some kind of arrangement with Stephanie Seymour, whom he desperately wanted to marry, except that she had this annoying kid, a supermodel's career, and various side projects that cut into their time together.

Tim Collins ran into them around Hollywood in those days. "I saw them together twice, late that year, at the Nowhere Café on Melrose. The two of them lit up the room—he with his long red hair, and she was just incredible. The first time, Axl remembered me from the tour they did with [Aerosmith]. He gave me a big hug, asked how I was, and said to say hi to Steven [Tyler] and Joe [Perry]. Two weeks later, I was at the same place with some friends and said hello to Axl when he and Stephanie walked by our table. But he turned around and started cursing at me. He's red in the face and yelling. I'm thinking to myself: *Jesus—full-blown Bipolar I!* Axl threatened that I'd better stop saying bad things about him—or fucking else. I had no idea what he was talking about. Then he turned on his heel and stalked out of the restaurant. Stephanie just looked at me, and then ran after him. It was sad. All you could do was shrug."

* * *

*A*s the seasonal, devilish Santa Ana winds drove wildfires through the dry canyons near his Malibu home, Axl Rose spent a lot of that autumn working on the band's new videos. *Don't Cry* was already in MTV rotation, with its scenario of Stephanie Seymour saving Axl from blowing his brains out, then fighting with him, and then beating up his old girlfriend. Slash drives an old Ford Mustang off a cliff and, of course, it explodes. The band plays on top of the skyscraper. Then Axl is seen lying on a couch as his (real-life, good-looking) psychotherapist takes notes. His quivering hands describe a severe anxiety attack, as his demonic meta-self (a naked Axl in green body paint) cavorts and torments his inner soul. The sexy therapist comforts Axl as he freaks out. The video ends with Axl staring at his own grave. A naked baby floats upward, opens its eyes. A message flashes on the screen: "There's a lot goin' on."

Axl had Stephanie Seymour in mind for two more *Illusion* videos, *November Rain* and *Estranged.* Production began on *Rain* in November. It was loosely based on "Without You," a then unpublished short story by Del James, a horrific tale of a rock star's degradation and suicide that James had patterned on incidents in Axl's life. Among the scenes shot late in 1991 were a grand church wedding between Axl and Stephanie; Guns and their girlfriends at ease in the Rainbow Bar and Grill; and the band onstage at the Ritz in New York, with a string orchestra bombastically conducted by Michael Kamen (late of the New York Rock Ensemble), as Axl (worn, exhausted, bespectacled) essays "November Rain" at a grand piano.

*N*ovember 1991. Axl Rose spent a lot of time on the phone with guitarist Dave Navarro, who'd been rumored to join Guns if Izzy left. Navarro was going through some personal crisis, and Axl was helping him through. Axl was scheduled to be interviewed on the syndicated FM radio show *Rockline,* and was duly driven to the studio on Cahuenga Boulevard, near Universal City, by Stephanie Seymour, arriving fifteen minutes before airtime. A cluster of fans waiting on the street kept him busy signing autographs, but there was no drama. Axl talked about *Use Your Illusion*, the recent death of Freddie Mercury from AIDS, and his love-hate relationship with Slash. The phone lines were jammed with fans calling to express their ardent love and loyalty to Axl and Guns, and Axl said later he was genuinely moved. In shunning the media, Axl had cut himself off from the very people who had helped him get to where he was. All the same, he was now within a few months of shutting almost everyone out of his life—completely.

"AXL TENDS TO RANT"

Guns N' Roses resumed what W. Axl Rose was still calling the Get in the Ring Tour in Worcester, Massachusetts, in December 1991. (Everyone else called it the Use Your Illusion World Tour.) Seattle's Soundgarden opened the shows, mostly because Guns liked singer Chris Cornell, who sang *"I want to fuck, fuck, fuck, fuck you"* on the anthem "Big Dumb Sex" in a voice raging with carnal craving. But this was also a big nod to the grunge movement then taking over the airwaves, making it harder for Guns to get airplay in competition with Nirvana, Pearl Jam, and Stone Temple Pilots as literally hundreds of American radio stations changed formats from rock music to "Alternative" programming.

The new Guns N' Roses show band—an alternative only to "Alternative"—took a few nights to work out the new routines. Not that there was a routine. Axl still wouldn't use a set list, preferring to cue songs according to his psychic needs, so the six girl singers and the horn players had to wait under the stage (in their bustiers, black lingerie, big hair, and fishnet stockings) until they got the word that Axl was calling for "Bad Obsession," "Pretty Tied Up," and their other featured numbers. Powered by the relentless Matt Sorum, Slash was now playing some of the best guitar of his career. Beginning with his first Guns show on December 5, Gilby Clarke made his bones as an amiable and expert rhythm player with considerable dash of his own. That night, Axl finished "November Rain" sitting at his grand piano, and he said later that he felt good being part of this band—for the first time in years.

But Axl was usually holed up by himself, sometimes in different hotels. Band members had to get past layers of annoying assistants and linebacker-size, pistol-packing, African American bodyguards if they wanted to see him. Still stung by Izzy Stradlin's defection, Axl responded by being more reclusive, demanding, and overcontrolling than ever. No one in the band could do anything about it, because (according to Slash) Doug Goldstein seemed to work for Axl exclusively. But by then, everyone was resigned to a situation that was never going to change. "That's when we really began to split with Axl," Slash said later. "He was on another page." But Slash also understood. "It's what Axl needed to do, to deal with his situation. And we were like, 'If that's what it takes, that's what it takes.'"

The Guns touring party was one of the most bloated—ever. Robert John was one of two photographers in the entourage, along with his friend and colleague Gene Kirkland. "It now became a very big group of people traveling with the band," Robert says. "It went from a small, core group of friends of the band, to a humungous road crew, plus chiropractors, gurus, massage therapists, assistants to assistants, p.r. girls, stylists—*all these people*. It just grew and grew. At the same time, there was this gap between Axl and the others. It wasn't really a band, as we'd known what 'a band' was. It was now a bunch of guys that turned up and went onstage—maybe."

Everyone missed Izzy Stradlin. Tour manager John Reese said later that everyone secretly wished they'd gone with him. The backstage atmosphere at Guns N' Roses shows was different from now on. There was a lot of tension and intrigue, and no one really knew what was going on. Gilby Clarke was grateful for his new gig, but was also wary. "It was: *'Here—learn these songs. Here's your paycheck.'* That was it. I knew from day one that it could end tomorrow."

The new-look Guns played three nights at Madison Square Garden in New York between December 9 and 13. These shows had some of the stage business and new routines that Guns would deploy over the next year: the shock-and-awe assaults of "Nightrain" and "Mr.

Brownstone"; the scary lights and singing chicks on "Live and Let Die"; Teddy Zig Zag's harmonica intro to "Bad Obsession"; the audience going mad when "Jungle" exploded halfway through; Duff singing the Misfits' punk anthem "Attitude"; Gilby and Slash playing a guitar duet on the Stones' "Wild Horses"; Axl's noodling, "sensitive" piano introduction to "November Rain"—a song that proved difficult to pull off properly in concert, and one that remained mostly clunky and awkward the length of the tour. Matt Sorum's thunderous drum solo was always full of clichés and much too long, but Axl needed time to breathe and rest his tattered vocal cords. Slash's solo variations on "Theme from *The Godfather*" usually segued into "Sweet Child o' Mine." Then "Rocket Queen," "Move to the City," "Heaven's Door," "Estranged," and the final encore, "Paradise City."

Reviewers noted with various degrees of irony the manic sprinting taking place onstage during all of this, as the musicians changed places on ramps and platforms, usually at top speed while executing high-hurdle leaps over stage monitors and sometimes each other. The *Times* critic wrote that the opening-night crowd seemed oddly restrained, which enraged Axl Rose because it was true. It was now the older rock fans who were coming to Guns' (relatively) expensive arena shows, not the rabid young metal fans from the eighties. During the second New York show, Axl cursed out *Times* critic (John Pareles) and challenged him to appear onstage at the third show to explain himself. (The man from the *Times* excused himself from this invitation.)

According to Slash, one of the highlights of the New York shows was meeting Billy Joel when he came backstage. Piano man Joel was one of Axl's heroes from the misty seventies. Slash thought it "was great to meet Billy, because he's such an icon, and also because he was very, *very* drunk." Guns and Billy Joel got along great.

The shows finished the year in Florida with a New Year's Eve concert in a Miami football stadium sold to capacity and bursting with energy. It had been a difficult, often disappointing year for the musicians in Guns N' Roses as they cashed in on their aura of eighties-style rebellion, and anyone hoping for better days in the coming year had to be kidding himself.

* * *

January 1992. Faith No More was added to the tour as Guns arrived in Baton Rouge, Louisiana, on January 3. Promoting their chart-topping album *The Real Thing,* Faith singer Mike Patton started mocking Guns N' Roses from the stage, telling audiences that it would be a fucking miracle if the headliner came on before midnight, if they came on at all. After the third such insult, Axl and Slash had a quiet word with Patton, whose band everyone in Guns genuinely liked. (Slash bluntly told Patton to shut up or get out.) There were no more foolish outbursts after that. Guns had a different problem with Soundgarden, most of whom were hardcore grunge ideologues who didn't really want to be on the Guns tour. "They wouldn't talk to us," Slash complained. Soundgarden was coming from a Seattle underground that viewed Guns the way the Clash and other London punks had viewed Led Zeppelin—as boring old farts.

Chris Cornell later recalled: "Axl was always hidden somewhere, having a personal crisis—always. One time I was in the room when he was talking to his manager about wanting to hire the Goodyear blimp for the show. I said—as a joke, even though it was true—that the Fuji blimp was the largest in the world. Axl was like, 'That's it! It's gotta be the *Fuji* blimp.' There were just no limits with that guy."

Guns couldn't believe how seriously the Soundgarden grunge-meisters took themselves. Slash: "They came from a place where there was no fun to be had while rocking." So during their final show together, merry pranksters Slash, Duff, and Matt took off their clothes and stormed the stage with blow-up sex dolls during Soundgarden's set. Slash: "They were mortified." Slash was completely naked, humping a plastic doll, when he was dragged off by his own people before he could be arrested.

Guns stayed out all month, mostly in the Deep South and Texas, going on late almost every night. In Dayton, Ohio, Axl complained the first night about a local newspaper editorial that called Guns the perfect house band for racist politician David Duke's America. Axl asked the kids up front if they thought he was a racist. Some yelled no, others just yelled. Axl asked the crowd: "Is that what *you* get out of this, that we're fucking racists ... and you're *supporting* it? 'Cause if that's the case, I'm fucking going home." The kids cheered and the show went on. Then Axl cut his hand on the microphone stand when a weld came loose. Blood was gushing and he sprinted offstage. While he was getting first aid, Axl thought he heard Slash making fun of him to the crowd. Axl went nuts. "I wrapped my hand in a towel...I came back onstage and was like a total dick to him [Slash] and told him I'd kick his ass in front of 20,000 people. That was fucked up, because I was wrong about what he said. I apologized to him the second I realized I made a mistake." Two Detroit shows were canceled because of the deep laceration across Axl's palm, and he was flown to New York for proper treatment.

On January 25, Guns played Las Vegas, where Axl was interviewed in his Mirage Hotel suite by *Rolling Stone*'s Kim Neely. Unburdening himself in a manner unusual for any rock star, Axl basically explained that he was mentally ill; that he'd crammed seven years of psychotherapy into one year; and that he was living from day to day in full catastrophe mode. He admitted that he was a spoiled brat, with the emotionality of a screaming two-year-old. "Axl tends to rant," Neely wrote, "barely stopping for breath, and even the most innocent comment can set him on edge." Neely, like many who knew Axl, observed that his sudden mood shifts—from calm into rage—were terrifying experiences to behold.

Axl said he hated performing but needed "the release of energy" that he got from doing shows. He defended the new, bigger Guns N' Roses against charges of being too polished, Vegas-like, and glitzy. He insisted that long-term Guns fans would eventually understand what they were trying to do. "It used to be just the five of us against the world. Now we've brought some of the outside world into the band." Axl said that he hadn't fired Izzy, because Izzy had quit on him. He defended Guns' hardnose media dealings as a way of avoiding overexposure, leading to certain career death.

Axl again told *Rolling Stone* that he wasn't the racist of "One in a Million." He was glad, Axl allowed, that the song had at least gotten people to think.

Of his problems with women, Axl was contrite. He admitted that they had both treated each other badly. He blamed his hatred of women on childhood abuse, explaining that regression therapy (supposedly including in utero recollections) had exposed memories of being kidnapped and raped by his real father, and then seeing his mother beaten when she came to get him. From then on, his mother never intervened when Bill was being disciplined, and he never forgave her for it.

Axl then went on to accuse his stepfather of molesting his sister, Amy, and said that Amy was now working for him on the tour, in order to protect her from her father, who Axl called "one of the most dangerous human beings I've ever met." What Axl termed "burying this shit," combined with sheer hatred of his fathers, his family, and himself, had made him crazy. "Homophobic?" Axl asked rhetorically. "I think I've got a problem if my dad *fucked me in the ass* when I was two. I think I've got a problem about that."

Asked why he was going public with this extraordinary information, Axl said it was for safety's sake because his stepfather was still out there. "It's very important that he's not in my life anymore, or in my sister's.... You have to reexperience [the abuse] and mourn what happened to you, and grieve for yourself and nurture yourself, and put yourself all back together ... and then find some way to break the chain. I'd like to fix myself, and turn around and help others." Axl mentioned that he'd recently visited a clinic for child abuse victims.

"There's a lot of reasons for me to talk about it publicly," Axl said. "Everybody wants to know, 'Why is Axl so fucked up?' and where are these things coming from? So now things are changing, and things are coming out.... I'm gonna get attacked. They'll think I'm jumping on a bandwagon. But then, it's gonna be obvious who's an asshole, and who is not."

Kim Neely mentioned that a character in a recent Stephen King horror novel had described Axl Rose as an asshole. Ever hopeful, and probably understanding something about writing fiction, Axl brightly asked, "Was it a good or bad character?"

The editors of *Rolling Stone* knew they had an explosive interview. The lead singer of the world's biggest band was going public with charges of child rape, sexual abuse, and neglect—against his own family. The magazine's lawyers, wary of possible criminal libel, demanded some sort of corroboration before they would sign off on publication. But Axl wasn't answering the phone, and soon stopped doing interviews completely. Eventually, the lawyers were satisfied when Axl's brother and sister, plus a source identified only as a family friend, provided written corroboration of Axl Rose's scandalous allegations concerning his parents, who refused all comment when contacted by the magazine. Axl refused to be photographed, so *Rolling Stone* used a year-old Herb Ritts image on its cover when the interview was published two months later, in March 1992.

BANZAI, MOTHERFUCKERS!

*F*ebruary 1992. Guns N' Roses played three shows for legendary Japanese promoter Mr. Udo at the massive Tokyo Dome, one of the largest indoor venues in the world. Slash flew to Japan a few days before the band with a small entourage, including guitar tech Adam Day, bodyguard Ron Stalnaker and longtime on-and-off girlfriend Renee Suran (whom he married later in the year while carrying on an affair with secret teenage squeeze Perla Farrar, whom he would marry in turn, ten years later).

Slash was in Tokyo early to play with Michael Jackson at the Tokyo shows of Jackson's *Dangerous* tour. (Slash had played on the *Dangerous* album sessions.) Slash was pleased that he drew a thunderous response from Michael's fans when he appeared onstage in his hairy, top-hatted persona. Even Michael Jackson was surprised to be briefly upstaged by someone he privately considered to be a cartoon.

Guns N' Roses' Tokyo shows were completely sold out. First night intro: *"BANZAI, MOTHERFUCKERS! FROM HOLLYWOOD CALIFORNIA—GUNS AND LOSES!"* The venerable Mr. Udo had offered them a full Japanese tour, but Axl wanted to stay in just one place. The Tokyo shows were taped by a Japanese TV crew, so Axl came up with a dozen costume changes per show and some arresting new visuals. He wore a hideous Charlie Manson T-shirt for "Double Talkin' Jive." He sported kilts and tartans, chic tailored jackets, mesh football jerseys (#22, the Mean Machine), white lambskin leathers, Ice-T baseball caps, and multiple bandannas. Later in the concerts, he pranced around in tight white shorts that outlined his pert buns and bulging crotch in vivid detail. (Many fans thought this strange, and even a little "gay.") "Civil War" was played in front of huge American, Confederate, and Japanese Rising Sun flags. Axl started the song wearing the stars-and-bars of the rebellious South and ended in the stars and stripes of the victorious Union. "Sweet Child o' Mine," once a tender love song, was now—in the wake of bitter divorce and heartbreak—an abrasive scream of pain that ended with a drawn-out, yowling vocal coda that rattled and shook stadiums for the rest of the long *Illusion* tour. This rethink of "Sweet Child" indicated, to the more astute Guns N' Roses fans, that things had drastically changed for Axl Rose. He was now thirty years old, and no closer to paradise city than anyone in the audience.

Guns performed "Estranged" as an encore in Japan. Axl told the audience that it was a song about feeling so depressed that you want to commit hara-kiri (he called it "hairy carry"). There was a big cheer at this, which made Axl laugh. The Tokyo concerts finished with a blazing, strobe-crazed "Paradise City," with shirtless, dripping Slash wading into the aisles in full jamming mode as his bodyguards tried to keep up with him. After the last show, the full troupe took a bow, arms wrapped around each other, with smiles all around.

*B*ack in Los Angeles, work continued on the *November Rain* video. A white clapboard country church, complete with tall steeple, was constructed in the New Mexico desert, where Slash's guitar solo was filmed. Axl and Stephanie's fictional wedding reception was ruined by a Hollywood rainstorm that (prophetically) turned their moment of bliss into a holocaust of broken glass and spilled wine. The video's morbid funeral scene was delayed because Stephanie was leery about being filmed lying in a satin-lined coffin. Eventually she relented, and eventually *November Rain* would end up as the most expensive music video ever filmed.

* * *

*A*pril 1992. Guns played their first concerts in Mexico City early in the month, followed by shows in the Midwest. The band was in Chicago on April 9, when they were warned that Cook County sheriff's deputies were going to arrest Axl after the gig on an outstanding bench warrant from the St. Louis riot the previous July. Axl was spirited out of town before he could be extradited to Missouri, and eighteen thousand kids were left wondering what happened when they arrived at the Rosemont Horizon and were told there was no show.

*G*uns N' Roses flew to England to perform at the Freddie Mercury Tribute Concert for AIDS Awareness in London, on April 20. The gay rights group ACT UP tried to get them disinvited, but Guns was eager to join Elton John, David Bowie, Metallica, George Michael, and a huge array of rock stars, plus a live TV audience around the planet. Slash: "We'd all grown up with Queen. So when they asked us to play we just jumped at the chance. Then we had the whole gay activist thing against us, but we decided to go ahead anyway. We weren't gonna miss that show." Guns arrived in their six-piece configuration a few days early to rehearse, except for Axl, who didn't rehearse. (He demanded a private dressing room as well.) At Wembley Stadium, Slash played "Tie Your Mother Down" with Queen, and Axl sang the late Mercury's vocal on "We Will Rock You." After Brian May begged him to do it, Axl joined Elton John and sang "Bohemian Rhapsody" as an unrehearsed, screamingly camp falsetto duet. (Elton had been nervous to meet Axl, king of homophobes, but Axl was on his most respectful behavior. Axl even charmed Elton by telling him how much his music meant to him when he was growing up.) Guns came prepared to play three songs, but earlier acts ran late, and the full band coursed through "Heaven's Door" and "Paradise City," with Axl dancing as if for his life. Duff, Slash, and Axl joined the other performers at the end of the night to sing a triumphant "We Are the Champions."

The following day Axl arrived at Heathrow Airport a half hour before his flight home. He asked that his luggage be hand-searched instead of X-rayed, because he was carrying homeopathic medicines that might be spoiled by radiation. This required special supervision, which took time, and it caused Axl to miss his flight. This got him upset to the point where the cops arrived and threw him out of the airport.

*G*uns N' Roses was scheduled to spend two months touring Europe in the spring of 1992, but, by early May, plans for the summer concerts had not solidified. No one in Guns wanted to be off the road. (It was, everyone felt at the time, all they had to live for.) A rumor went around that Axl had wanted Nirvana to open for Guns that summer, but Kurt Cobain had refused, saying he fucking *hated* Guns N' Roses and their "dickhead fans." Instead, at a May 12 press conference at the Gaslight club in Hollywood, Slash and Metallica drummer Lars Ulrich announced that both bands would tour together that summer. (During negotiations for this tour, Metallica cleverly insisted that they play first every night, because that way they would get paid whether Guns showed up on time or not.)

W. Axl Rose's final press interview was published in *Interview* magazine in May 1992. The cover and interior photos displayed the physical passion of Axl and Steph, as he called his wild-hearted girlfriend, with large-scale black-and-white images of kisses, embraces, even tongues. Axl freely discussed his problematic life with *Interview* editor Ingrid Sischy, revealing a new maturity in explaining his problems with women and his decision to leave hard drugs behind. *Interview* being an essentially gay magazine, Axl did a lot of explaining about homophobia, racism, and immigrant bashing. He again denied that he was racist, claiming that he was "married" to Slash, who was half black. He said the anti-immigrant lines in "One in a Million" were just two different thoughts that got jumbled together. Axl insisted that he was not antigay, but that he was simply, ardently pro-hetero. He allowed that he was able to watch Madonna playing with her gay dancers in her contemporary concert movie, *Truth or Dare,* without feelings of disgust. He pointed out that his big influences—Freddie Mercury and Elton John—were openly gay. At the same time, Axl was moved to justify his obvious homophobia by claiming that as a young man he had to fend off unwanted homosexual advances. Then he went further and said that he'd been raped.

Axl: "Homophobia? OK, I'll repeat myself. This is something I just said in *Rolling Stone*. I don't know . . . Maybe I do have a problem with homophobia. Maybe I was two years old, and got fucked in the ass by my dad, and it's caused a problem ever since. . . . *That's a fact.* That's something that happened, and that's some of the damage I've been working on. . . . But other than that, I don't know if I have any homophobia."

Asked if he had written anything besides song lyrics, Axl replied that recently he had been working with a friend (Del James) "on putting information together and stuff. More truth and reality is going to come out if I talk with him, rather than if I talk with someone who doesn't know what's up. I've always believed that the truth about what's going on with Guns N' Roses' lives is just as exciting, and just as *dangerous,* and just as heavy, and just as *real* as people thought the hype scene to be."

EX-COMMIE BASTARDS AND MERC-DRIVING MUGS

*G*uns N' Roses' twenty-show European tour in the spring of 1992 was the wildest ride the band had been on yet. Survivors say that the two months of concerts—plagued by lateness, cancelations, mania, infighting, jealousy, and mediocre performances—seemed more like two years. A decade later, tour manager John Reese told VH1's *Behind the Music*: "You didn't know, from one minute to the next, if it was all going to end on that day—because of a drug overdose, or because of a riot, or because of it just imploding. But also, at the same time you didn't know if on that same night you were going to see the best rock show—ever."

*S*pringtime Ireland lay green as an emerald beneath them as Guns' private jet roared to a touchdown at Dublin Airport on May 15, 1992.

The next day, Axl Rose's smiling face was on the front page of the *Irish Independent* and other daily papers. He missed his band's sound check at Slane Castle, a stately home in nearby County Meath, where the Stones, Madonna, and U2 had played for a hundred thousand in the natural amphitheater between the castle and the River Boyne. The quarter-million-watt sound system could be heard in nearby Slane village, which had been taken over by a genial army of Irish rock fans under the watchful eyes of eight hundred cops.

When Guns arrived via helicopter from Dublin for the May 16 concert, they were gratified to find backstage a case of forty-year-old Irish whiskey and a barrel of Guinness, both welcoming gifts from U2. Irish band My Little Funhouse opened, followed by Faith No More. Axl's chopper still hadn't left Dublin when Guns' stage time came—and went. They went on an hour late, beginning their show in Irish summer daylight. Axl raced through "Nightrain" and "Mr. Brownstone" in tight black shorts and a green-trimmed black jacket, sprinting across the 160-foot stage like a fiery red-headed leprechaun. The Irish kids did their bit and went bonkers.

Axl wanted to make a Celtic heritage connection with the audience: "We have a McKagan in the band, in case you haven't noticed, and I'm half-Irish myself.... But you can't tell, right?" (This was supposed to be humor.) After bloated, drunken-looking Duff sang "Attitude," spritzing saliva all over the stage, Axl calmly rolled a new cloth cover over the microphone. "As much as I love Duff," Axl bantered, "I would never share a condom with him." This drew a big cheer.

After "Don't Cry," Axl dedicated the next song to "all those who can't keep their mouths... out of our fucking business. Misery loves company, so if you know someone like that... call 'em up and tell from me, that they are *DOUBLE TALKING JIVE MOTHERFUCKERS!*" Cue "Double Talkin' Jive," with Axl singing Izzy Stradlin's vocals in the composer's absence. Axl still insisted on working without a set list, retreating to his tiny dressing room beneath the drum riser for oxygen blasts and costume changes during the long drum and guitar solos. This not only kept the girls in the band on permanent standby, it was also difficult for the crew, who had huge inflatable monsters to blow up for "Jungle" and serious pyrotechnics to ignite for "Live and Let Die."

(Guns' road crew—veterans and new hires—along with the entire entourage of masseuses, stylists, chiropractic therapists, vocal coaches, bus drivers, catering staff, and security were all obliged to sign various documents—gag orders and indemnifying disclaimers—which were periodically shuffled around backstage at Axl's insistence. The paranoia level on this tour was very high, and crew people would turn away if they saw anyone with a notebook or a microphone. A Geffen executive recalls: "Axl was now demanding total control over any information about him, the band, the tour. There were all these stupid legal documents we had to sign in order to hang out with the act. It was ridiculous, but no one could say no to this guy.")

*A*t Slane Castle, Axl's piano now rose up to the stage, via elevator, for "November Rain," which was preceded by an Axl recital that quoted Black Sabbath's "It's Alright." One of the highlights of the Slane Castle show (and of that whole era), was "Move to the City," which gave Dizzy Reed, Teddy Zig Zag, and the horn section their moments in the limelight. The three girls—two saxes and a trumpet—played this to the hilt, each taking two choruses and charming the biggest audiences of their careers. (Slash had thought a male horn section would be boring, and his instinct was, as usual, dead-on.) The show ended with "Paradise City" echoing down the Boyne valley. Slash to customers: "Thanks for making us so welcome. You've been fucking great!"

Guns spent a few days in Dublin before beginning the long Euro tour. They hung out in the pubs and walked around, digging the pretty colleens in fancy gowns making their way to the Trinity (College) Ball. Slash was quoted in the Dublin press: "I can always tell a good drinking town when the people in the bar get drunk before I do."

The British press reviews were harsh in the wake of Axl's "Get in the Ring" insults. Formerly worshipful *Kerrang!* called Guns "a saddening musical mess." Punk champions *NME* said they were "just another stadium act, up there like fatted turkeys." *Melody Maker*: "... a cartoon band with maybe three decent songs and a heap of atrociously sexist thuggery masquerading as psychological nakedness. They are just another vacuous money-printing behemoth safely fixed within conventional parameters, treading a well-worn, predictable formula."

The Irish music paper *Hot Press* was more in touch with Guns' fan base: "In every possible way you can think of, Guns N' Roses are a mess; a great big Rorschach [blot] of confusion, crassness, and contradiction. However, they are also an impossibly massive, glamorous, and thrilling rock group who are glamorous and thrillingly precious because they are so massive."

At least *someone* understood what was going on with this band.

The most recent addition to the Guns N' Roses massive entourage was a diminutive Asian woman in her forties, who also had an assistant of her own. This was Axl Rose's spiritual adviser, Sharon Maynard, who now had enormous influence over Axl and would be a fixture on many of Guns' tours in that era. The road crew was told she was Axl's psychic, and they started calling her Yoda, after the cosmically ugly guru in the *Star Wars* films. Sharon Maynard was based in Sedona, Arizona, where she had a New Age consulting business incorporated as a nonprofit "educational enterprise" in that state, under the name of Arcos Cielos. One of her specialties was magnetism and human well-being. No one knew exactly what she did for Axl, but it was rumored that Yoda was using topical electromagnetic applications to try to control his bouts of severe depression. Her backstage pass said "Access All Areas."

Guns N' Roses began their continental tour in Eastern Europe, again with Soundgarden and Faith No More opening. In Prague on May 20, the band played Strahov Stadium, the Czech Republic's crumbling cement soccer stadium. The show started with: "OK, YOU EX-COMMIE BASTARDS—GET READY TO ROCK!" After the gig, Slash and Gilby were taken to a strip club, where they were amazed and delighted to find the girls sporting lots of pubic fur. Two nights later in Budapest, the band's plane touched down twenty minutes before they were due onstage. They were sped to the Nepstadion by a military police escort, sirens wailing. The concert was then drenched

by a thunderstorm, with torrents of water pouring from flimsy tarpau-
lins directly onto the stage. Roadies with towels tried to keep things
dry, but it was no use. "We're sponsoring a fucking car wash," Axl
joked, "and we're all going to be topless."

U2, who would play the same venue the following night, came to
see Guns' concert in Vienna. The two bands were sharing the same jet
as they toured Europe at the same time. Introducing "Live and Let
Die," Axl wondered aloud whether Adolf Hitler ever sang the song
to himself when he was a kid. (The Hitler mention got a big cheer in
the Führer's native land.) Later Bono Vox (Paul Hewson) invited Axl
Rose (Bill Bailey) to a birthday party for the Irish band's tour accountant. The next night, Guns went to U2's Vienna show, and Axl got onstage with Bono for an acoustic version of "Heaven's Door."

On to Germany, where Guns began to hit their stride, playing long
shows that drew rave reviews. They played for 40,000 at Berlin's
Olympic Stadium (where Axl stopped the show to eject a fan ["you
fucking asshole"] who'd thrown a bottle onstage), and then for 75,000
in Stuttgart, where they were introduced with: "OK, you beer-swilling,
Merc-driving mugs—Direct from Hollywood California . . ." Among the
songs played on the PA just before Guns went on were Sid Vicious's
version of "My Way"; the theme from *The Good, the Bad and the Ugly*;
and various murder-happy raps by NWA.

Two nights later, on May 29, Guns played for almost three hours
in Cologne, inserting new songs "Perfect Crime" and "So Fine" into
their set. After that, the band had a few days off before the final German show in Hanover. Everyone got some rest except Axl Rose, who
was stewing in his own private hell. He hadn't slept in three days, and
was unable to turn off his stage adrenaline to relax. Axl spent hours
on the phone with Stephanie Seymour, and became agitated because
she had reported that Warren Beatty had been calling her. There was
also some friction, within Guns, over Axl's refusal to attend the sound
checks, where Doug Goldstein often stood in for the singer. (Axl's excuse was that his throat was fragile, and that he had to protect his
vocal cords.) Slash was also beginning to worry about the extravagant
expenses the band was running up, as Doug Goldstein signed off on
Axl's every wish and whim. Slash had heard the horror stories of big

rock bands finishing huge tours that didn't make any real money in the end, and he didn't want this to happen to his band.

Axl Rose, still sleepless and totally exhausted, snapped in Hanover. The band made it onstage on time, to general astonishment, and roared into the first four songs. Then Axl sat down on the drum riser and just stared, sullenly, at 60,000 boisterous rock fans. The other Guns looked at each other, nervously. Axl wouldn't say what was wrong. He didn't say a word. The stage monitors and Axl's teleprompter were rechecked, and found to be working. Excruciating minutes went by. Nothing. Then Axl got up, walked to the front of the stage, and slipped down into the security pit. He looked hard at some of the kids up front, then got back onstage and sat down again. Eventually he restarted the show, but now he was in a black mood. He scolded the crowd for not singing loud enough on "Heaven's Door." Then he introduced "Sweet Child" as "a song about getting fucked in the ass with a Coke bottle." He used the song's long, screaming coda to deliver chilling howls of human agony and the invisible torments that ripped at his psyche. Then he threw down the microphone and walked off. There was no encore that night, and Axl left for the next gig, in Paris, ahead of the band.

AN OUT-OF-BODY EXPERIENCE

*J*une 1992. Axl Rose and Izzy Stradlin had appeared with the Rolling Stones three years earlier, on a massive pay-per-view television concert at the end of the Stones' 1989 *Steel Wheels* tour. Now that his band was the biggest in the world, Axl decided that Guns N' Roses should host their own international TV spectacle. The American cable network HBO signed on without hesitation. Long and complicated negotiations resulted in Guns' June 6 Paris concert, where they would be joined by Steven Tyler and Joe Perry; retro-rocker Lenny Kravitz (on whose latest album Slash had played); and primal English guitar hero Jeff Beck.

Guns arrived in Paris on June 4 and checked into the Hotel Crillon, the most expensive in the City of Light. The band and their guests played a sound check the next afternoon at the Hippodrome in the Bois de Vincennes. Slash was embarrassed that Axl didn't show up. "Where's your *singer,* man?" asked Steven Tyler, which was his way of telling Slash that Axl was disrespecting the musicians he'd invited. After the TV people finished getting their cameras into position, the crew moved the band's gear to the Elysée Montmartre rock club, so Guns could rehearse with their guests. The entire road crew jammed into the club to hear Beck, Joe Perry, and Slash jam on "Train Kept A-Rollin'" for half an hour through sonic squalls of feedback, which many agreed was the transcendently musical high point of the whole tour. Everything went well until Matt Sorum hammered his cymbal while Jeff Beck was standing next to the drum riser. Suddenly, Beck completely lost the hearing in his left ear, deafened by the force of Sorum's stroke. The volatile guitarist stormed out, and then flew back to London. One guest was down, and the others were less than thrilled.

Axl stayed in his hotel suite, getting crazy. (His sister, Amy, traveling with the band, was one of the few who could calm him down when things got hairy.) Stephanie Seymour had promised to come to Paris, and he was counting on her being there for the big broadcast. But she hadn't arrived, and he was having trouble getting through to her. He was madly jealous because of a story in the New York gossip columns that she'd been seen with Warren Beatty in a Manhattan restaurant the week before.

On June 6, almost 60,000 rock fans filled the Hippodrome. Guns N' Roses started an hour late. Four hundred TV networks worldwide were reported to be carrying the broadcast, giving Guns their first global audience. Lenny Kravitz came on and played "Always on the Run," and the show went smoothly until Axl dedicated "Double Talkin' Jive" to Warren Beatty—with a vengeance:

"Now, this *old man* has a family and a baby,... but he's got to spend his time fucking around with other people, because he doesn't know what to do with his own life.... He's a *parasite* who likes to play games with other people's lives. [In the TV control booth, the HBO execs gave each other worried looks.] He's so *empty* that... all he can do is play games. He *sucks off* other people's . . . life force, because he has none of his own."

Axl then addressed Beatty directly: "Listen, you fuck—if you think *Madonna* kicked your ass, I'm betting my money on Annette [Bening, Beatty's wife]—*you stupid fucking asshole.*"

Later Axl delivered his antiauthoritarian message in the dedication of "Live and Let Die" to "those who try to control and manipulate you: the powers that be, the government, your family, your friends, or anything else that chooses to fuck with you. You can even try to talk to some of these people. You can try to be friends. You can try to work it out . . . but if you can't save nobody else, you'll be lucky if you can save your own ass. But we'll dedicate this to these fucking people." Later on, Axl sadly introduced "November Rain" as "a song about unrequited love."

*I*zzy Stradlin was watching all this at home in Los Angeles, having paid the same twenty-five-dollar fee as any HBO customer. He was in the throes of mixing his first album with the Ju Ju Hounds. It was the first time Izzy had seen the new Guns N' Roses.

"It was a really bizarre, out-of-body experience," Izzy said later. "I didn't really recognize them all. They had horn players, and a harmonica guy, and girl singers. Of course, I *was* Gilby for the night. It was really *weird*, you know?"

*S*teven Tyler and Joe Perry came out at the end of the Paris show—after waiting backstage for three hours—and played "Train Kept A-Rollin'" and "Mama Kin" with Guns. There was a big party afterward, and Axl drowned his sorrows, which he rarely did in public anymore. He was reportedly too hung over to fly to England with the band the next day, but his manic energy left him still unable to sleep for more than a few minutes at a time. Searching for inspiration, Axl went to the Louvre museum to visit the Winged Victory, his favorite ancient sculpture, but he was instantly recognized by tourists and was pestered for snapshots and autographs until he had to leave. His handlers thought a cruise on the Seine might calm Axl's nerves, and he did manage to sleep for ten minutes when the boat left the dock. But then he woke up and became agitated when told that he couldn't get off. Axl felt so awful when he arrived in London that a doctor told him to get some rest, and the June 9 show in Manchester was postponed due to exhaustion.

The band had three days off in London while they waited for Axl. Slash's girlfriend, Renee, flew over for a reconciliation, and for a while he stopped carrying a bottle of Jack Daniel's whiskey with him everywhere he went. Duff McKagan was trying to ease down his gallon-a-day vodka habit with the help of girlfriend Linda Johnson. They all stayed at the Conrad, an exclusive hotel overlooking the Thames near Chelsea Bridge. Also in residence was Prince, who was headlining at Earl's Court. (In the hotel bar, Guns heard that the hotel staff had to empty Prince's suite of all furniture, and that his bed and linens had been flown in from Minneapolis. Prince's windows were blacked out from all natural light, and he insisted the hotel's hair salon be available to him at two in the morning. Someone cracked that Prince made Axl Rose seem like Willie Nelson.)

Guns' London agent arranged an exclusive go-cart outing for the band at a West London track. Slash wondered aloud who was paying for this, and no one had the heart to tell him that he was.

On June 13, Guns N' Roses played a smoking-hot show under a broiling evening sun at Wembley Stadium for 72,000 beer drinkers. Axl demanded to be flown to the gig by helicopter, but there was nowhere to land in that crowded part of northern London, and he ended up touching down farther from the gig than where he had started. Queen's Brian May joined in for "Tie Your Mother Down" and "We Will Rock You." Axl stopped the show twice: He had a rowdy drunk hauled away, and then made the security people help a girl being crushed in the superheated press of fans just below the stage. This time the press reviews were kinder to the band. "You couldn't take your eyes off [Axl]," one critic wrote. "I've been to a lot of concerts, but I've never seen any band able to generate that kind of spontaneous, visceral, *tribal* excitement in a stadium, before or since."

* * *

*W*hile in London, Duff and various band members worked on his solo album in a Shepherd's Bush studio. The band played the rescheduled Manchester show (two hours late, and scathingly reviewed as a once great band's decline and fall), and then two nights later in Newcastle on June 16. Duff McKagan got into it with a fan in Gateshead Stadium who was yelling at him, and Axl intervened: "I wouldn't mess with Duff," he warned the fan. "He hasn't had a drink for two fuckin' weeks." The band was now hitting its stride, and Axl said later that he considered the Wembley concert "to be the best performance I am capable of at this point in my career."

Late on the afternoon on June 19, the band was driven to Heathrow Airport so they could fly to Germany. Axl Rose was spotted by a security officer who remembered him from the April airport row. Axl was pulled out of line and reportedly strip-searched. Axl had his publicist issue a statement: "To be singled out by someone who just wants to score a few points and have a story to tell his friends over a beer is really out of order." Axl's complaint was published by almost every daily newspaper in England within the week.

*J*une 1992. Guns N' Roses now played some terrific concerts around Europe. A sudden Teutonic thunderstorm broke over the soccer stadium in Wurzburg on June 20, with Thor's mighty lightning bolts competing with Guns' pyrotechnic effects. Band and crowd were drenched in seconds, but Guns played on, completing a ninety-minute show as a thick layer of human steam wafted over the roiling kids who cheered on a rare total communion between a rock band and 45,000 fans. The next night they played for 50,000 in Switzerland, but Duff went down with the flu, and Axl's throat felt like it was on fire. His mobile pharmacy of homeopathic remedies didn't help, and the doctors were called in. In Rotterdam, Guns went on two hours after Faith No More finished their set. But there was an eleven P.M. curfew, and Axl was told the backline would be switched off at eleven thirty if the band was still onstage. Exasperated and feeling sick, Axl told 50,000 Dutch kids that they had a right to a full show. "You paid for it," he croaked. "So if they cut the power—be my guests, man—*Do what you* *want!*" Wisely, and after furious arguments backstage, the police let the band play until they finished "Paradise City" at twelve thirty.

Duff was so sick that a show in Brussels was canceled and the band flew to Milan to rest for a few days. Now, having been deluged with flowers and chocolates from Axl, Stephanie Seymour flew to her boyfriend in Milan, and treated him to a tour of her world: private visits to the Armani and Versace showrooms; dinner with Donatella Versace and fellow model Naomi Campbell; and shopping on the Via Montenapoleane. Axl's spirits and Duff's health improved by the time they played for 65,000 in Turin's Stadio delle Alpi on June 27. After this show, the band adjourned to the Mediterranean port of San Remo and spent a couple of days on a huge rented motor vessel, where Duff and Linda announced they were engaged to be married. Slash wondered who was paying for the obscenely expensive 180-foot yacht.

The band then drove to Genoa, where their jet airliner was waiting to fly them to Spain. Ultracool Seville had no curfew, so Soundgarden and Faith No More played long sets, and then Guns waited out the long European summer twilight so they could play in the dark, where their pyro and lights could be appreciated. The last show of this tour leg was supposed to take place in Madrid, but the city suddenly closed Calderon Stadium, citing structural problems. The promoter couldn't find any place else on short notice, so the gig was reluctantly canceled.

Guns' last European gig was in Lisbon on July 2—a wild night. The Portuguese kids had been waiting since Soundgarden went on at four P.M. When Guns came on at eleven (after Yoda had done some sort of blessing of the stage and Axl's microphone), a barrage of water bottles hit the stage. Axl slipped while sprinting through "Mr. Brownstone" and landed hard on his back, where he finished the song. Axl then harangued the crowd. "I didn't come here to get hurt," he bawled, and walked off, followed by the band. Someone backstage pointed out that it was exactly a year since the St. Louis riot. So Guns resumed playing after a few tense minutes. But Axl stopped the show again when a string of firecrackers landed near him during "Civil War." The promoter came out and spoke in Portuguese for two minutes until the boisterous audience cooled down. Guns came back and played "Patience," and the rest of the show was terrific, featuring Axl's serpentine dance and patented one-footed backward microphone hop that seemed to shake whole stadiums every time he deployed it.

*E*veryone went their separate ways until the next tour leg—co-headlining with Metallica—began later in July. Axl went back to Paris for a while, then flew to New York on July 12, where he was detained at Kennedy airport on the fugitive arrest warrant filed by St. Louis County, relating to the 1991 riot there. He made bail and, two days later, pleaded innocent to several counts of assault and property damage. The judge allowed Axl to meet his contractual obligations, and scheduled the next hearing for October. (He pleaded guilty in absentia and was fined $50,000.)

THE INFAMOUS COUP DE GRÂCE

*G*uns N' Roses began co-headlining with speed-metal angst juggernaut Metallica at RFK Stadium in Washington, D.C., on July 17, 1992. Slash was embarrassed for his band because Axl Rose had decreed that his brother and sister be hired to create theme rooms at every gig, where supposedly jolly parties would be held after the concerts. There might be a gambling den one night, a cowboy saloon the next, and so on—at great expense to Guns N' Roses. Slash ignored the parties. Metallica left the venues immediately after their sets. Even Faith No More, still opening shows but appalled by the toxic atmosphere suffusing the tour, rarely showed up at the Bailey family's after-parties, and they eventually petered out.

The next night, at Giants Stadium in New Jersey, Axl had a serious sore throat. There was blood in his mouth, but he decided to finish the show. But during "Heaven's Door," someone rifled a metal cigarette lighter at Axl, which hit him right in the giblets of his bulging, skin-tight minishorts. He ran offstage and Duff McKagan finished the show's vocals. Axl's throat was blown out, so the doctors made them postpone the tour for a week so Axl could rest his lacerated vocal cords. A rumor went around the road crew that a Minneapolis concert had been postponed because Axl's psychic didn't feel it was a good time for him to perform in a city that began with the letter *M*.

They did play the Hoosier Dome in Indianapolis on July 22, with Axl teasing the crowd about how conservative and backward Indiana was; about Indiana's Dan Quayle, George H. W. Bush's feckless vice president; about how Indiana was being transformed into a Japanese car factory. (He even insulted a crop—corn.) The following day, Axl and his siblings visited Lafayette. Robert John photographed them with some trees they had planted. On the way out of town, they grabbed some pizzas and headed for the next gig in upstate New York.

*T*his star-crossed rock tour reached Montreal on August 8, 1992. The hockey-loving Canadian kids packed into the enclosed Olympic Stadium were rarin' to go, and Metallica was on fire—literally. A few songs into their set, James Hetfield's shirt caught a spark from a too-close pyro blast and melted around the guitarist's shoulder and arm. Hetfield was rushed to the hospital with agonizing second-degree burns. Metallica's Jason Newstead explained, calmly, that Metallica was very sorry, but their show was over. The desperate promoters now asked—ludicrously—if Guns N' Roses could go on early, and the band rushed to the stadium.

Axl Rose stayed at the hotel. His vocal cords were in crisis mode, and he wasn't about to take up Metallica's slack.

Axl showed up at the stadium two hours later. Then he spent another hour getting ready. When Guns finally went on, it had been almost four hours since Hetfield's accident. Guns had to play for ninety minutes in order to get paid, at which point Axl grabbed at his throat and left the stage. The huge crowd waited hopefully for the encores, "Heaven's Door" and "Paradise City," but the band followed Axl offstage. No one said anything. The show was over. Then they turned the houselights on, and the audience rioted.

"I can't say I was surprised when they started rioting," Slash said later. "Being old pros at this, we sat in our dressing room. We could hear the stampede overhead, and knew there was no going back on." Gilby went back out to check his guitars ("It was my first riot"), but the fans had already taken over the stage and were shredding everything. They attacked the security staff and the cops, who barricaded themselves in the locker rooms. They trashed the halls, looted merchandise, smashed everything they could, and stole kegs of beer from the concession stands. When the place had been sacked, they went outside to burn police cars and fight with the riot cops. As Guns made its desperate escape, they saw kids pulling down light poles in the parking lot.

At the hospital, burn victim James Hetfield—unaware of the riot—noticed that the sudden surge of injured kids in Metallica shirts flooding into the emergency ward looked like they'd just come from his show. Slash later described the events in Montreal as "the infamous coup de grâce of everything that was wrong with our band." He was mortified because Guns was unable to keep its promises to Metallica, to the promoters who hired them, or to the fans who paid good money for a good show. "I'd lost face," Slash said later. "I couldn't look James, Lars, or anyone from their band in the eye for the rest of the tour."

*G*uns returned to Los Angeles to try to regroup. *November Rain* was now the most requested music video in the ten-year history of MTV, its plotline of despair and alienation revealed as an Axl nightmare fueled by pills and whiskey. Stephanie marries Axl as Slash despairs. She realizes her horrible mistake, and then she dies. Once again, Axl is seen at his own grave. MTV's audience couldn't get enough of this.

Guns used some of their time off to film material for the next *Illusion* single and video, *Yesterdays,* as well as working on the *Estranged* video. On August 25, they went back to work in Phoenix, where James Hetfield sang with his arm in a cast while his guitar tech banged out Hetfield's trademark guitar stutters. The tour then continued through almost every dome, coliseum, and raceway in America. Metallica always played first and made their money. Guns then went on—hours late. Slash later claimed Guns lost as much as 80 percent of their revenues to curfew fines and union overtime. It was wearing on the whole band. Slash bitterly recalled: "Sitting around for hours, waiting to go on . . . that really spoiled the music. It was hard. We had canceled gigs, gigs where we almost didn't play, lots of walking offstage. It was very trying."

Gilby Clarke: "Have a cocktail before the show. Then another, and another. By the time we went on, we were hammered from drinking so much.... Duff was in terrible, terrible shape. He could barely speak."

Matt Sorum: "I'd be playing, and I'd hear someone snoring—and I'd see Duff—laid out, with the bass guitar on top of him, and him just passed out!"

September 10, 1992. Elton John and Axl Rose were reunited at MTV's Video Music Awards when they played a plangent version of "November Rain" together. Axl told MTV News that it was a big moment in his life. A few minutes later, Axl bumped into the Nirvana entourage in the lounge area. Kurt Cobain and Courtney Love were sitting with their baby daughter. There was not a little awkwardness. Cobain had declined to tour with Guns. Axl had wanted Nirvana to play at his thirtieth birthday party earlier in the year, and Cobain had refused. He'd even dissed Guns N' Roses in public. To break the ice, Courtney called out to Axl to come over and say hi. Cobain, joshing, asked Axl if he would be godfather to their baby.

Axl strutted over to them and snarled at Cobain: "*You shut your bitch up,* or I'm taking you down—to the *pavement!*" Everything froze.

Kurt Cobain knew how to deal with assholes. He'd done it all his life. He just smiled at his wife and said, "Shut up, bitch!" Everyone in the Nirvana group—*laughed.* Axl's macho posturing was undone by Cobain's irony and quick wit. "We thought he was just a stupid joke," Cobain said later. Axl and his bodyguards stormed out to his waiting stretch limousine.

"They're really people with...no talent," Cobain said of Guns N' Roses, "and they write these crap songs, and they're the most popular rock band on the earth right now. I can't *believe* it!"

The white stretch limousine took Axl Rose west, down Sunset Boulevard as far as the beach. Then it turned north, along the Pacific Coast Highway, and cruised past the Palisades and Topanga Canyon, continuing on to Malibu. Axl and Stephanie Seymour had moved into a house Axl had bought (for four million dollars) high up in bucolic Latigo Canyon. It was a spacious Mediterranean-style villa with gardens, pools, garages for Axl's car collection, and tight security. The light in a big star-shaped landing window could be seen from the coastal highway, far below. When Axl and Stephanie threw themselves a housewarming party that month, Axl had dozens of fresh pies specially flown in from Arni's, his favorite pizzeria in Lafayette.

A SERIOUS TWIST

September 1992. Guns and Metallica played the rescheduled Minneapolis show, the geomagnetic vortices having presumably aligned themselves properly. Faith No More was dumped from the tour after what Slash cryptically described as "an incident"—probably more onstage disrespect. (Faith No More broke up soon after this.) They were replaced for the last five shows of the tour—all on the West Coast—by British metal heroes Motörhead and openers Body Count—L.A. rapper Ice-T's black metal band. Body Count's "Cop Killer" single had made a big dent in the nascent world of murder music, but Ice-T had been forced to drop the song from the band's debut album due to political pressure on corporate parent Warner Bros. (About Body Count's connection to alleged racist pig W. Axl Rose, Ice-T later wrote that Axl's "One in a Million" had been completely misunderstood.)

This version of the tour played San Francisco—actually the Oakland Coliseum—on September 24, 1992, not long after Slash died.

The tour had arrived in San Francisco a day earlier. Slash was traveling with his fiancée, Renee Surran, and the happy couple had a bitter fight (just before Guns' afternoon sound check) about the onerous prenuptial agreement that Slash's lawyer wanted her to sign. Renee walked out, and Slash handled the stress by inviting some junkie friends to a party in his hotel suite after the gig. They brought some crack cocaine as well. At some point, well after midnight, Matt Sorum called and invited Slash to his room to do some cocaine. Slash made it as far as the hotel corridor, where he collapsed.

Tour manager John Reese woke up to a ringing sound. "I got a phone call at 5:30 or 6 A.M. 'Mr. Reese, one of your band members is passed out in front of the elevators on the fifth floor.' I threw on some pants, ran out of my room—and Slash is dead. He's blue. *Dead.* He had no pulse at all. Right away the elevator door opened and the paramedics stepped out." One of them listened to Slash's chest. Nothing. "*BAM!* They hit him with Adrenalin, right in his heart."

Slash: "I was told my heart had stopped for eight minutes. I don't know who called 911. My bodyguard Ronnie was there, and so was Axl's guy, Earl, and they took care of me and got the paramedics. I woke up when the defibrillators stunned my heart into beating again."

The ambulance arrived and took Slash to the hospital. After a few hours he was back at the hotel. "I had no remorse whatsoever about the overdose," he said later, "but I was pissed off at myself for having died. The whole hospital incursion really ate into my day off." Slash chilled in his room for a while, with Ronnie and Earl guarding the door. (Earl, who worked with Axl, was a very large black man with an automatic pistol in a shoulder holster under his well-tailored jacket. Slash: "Earl was terrifying, because he had a sweet face; so when he was pissed off, you *really* knew about it.")

Then Doug Goldstein duly arrived and delivered what Slash considered to be an insincere and pathetic display of "bullshit concern" about what had happened. To make his point, Slash says, Goldstein hurled a bottle of Jack Daniel's through the hotel TV. After Goldstein finally left, Slash retrieved the unbroken bottle of Jack from the smashed TV and poured himself a stiff one. Then Slash had to endure a band meeting in Axl's suite. Slash: "I was still, like, nodding out at this point." Everyone in Guns expressed intervention-style concern for Slash, who later said: "Axl's comment stood out most of all. It snapped me out of my haze."

Axl, to Slash: "You gave us a scare." Pause. Axl made eye contact, very rare.

Axl said, "We thought you had died."

Slash looked at the floor.

Axl: "I thought I'd have to look for . . . another guitar player."

Slash decided to try to lay off heroin, for the time being. He married Renee soon after this, at a hotel in Marina Del Rey, near Los Angeles.

The Guns/Metallica tour slogged on through early October 1992. Negative publicity from riots, cancellations, postponements, and late starts began to affect ticket sales. A show with Motörhead at the giant Rose Bowl in Pasadena, near Los Angeles, shocked the bands when they found themselves playing to a stadium two-thirds empty. The final show, at the Kingdome in Seattle on October 6, was three-quarters full. Slash was relieved this leg had ended since he wouldn't have to face Metallica again.

As for Metallica, they couldn't believe what a chickenshit band Guns had become. James Hetfield publicly insulted Axl Rose in a video made during the tour. Reading from Guns' contract rider, a list of dressing room requirements, Hetfield sneered at what he called "the piddling wants and needs of certain people on the road—Axl Pose." The list was what the promoter had to provide to Axl's dressing room, "with absolutely no substitutions":

- one cup of cubed ham (Hetfield: "It's got to be cubed so it can get down his little neck.")
- one rib-eye steak dinner ("I didn't know the guy ate meat. He looks like a fucking vegetarian.")
- pepperoni pizza, fresh ("I think that's just for throwing around.")
- one can Pringles chips ("That's the greasy shit, so he can grease his hair back.")
- one jar honey ("That's what makes him [cruelly mocking Axl's psychobaby screech] *SING LIKE THIS*.")
- one bottle Dom Perignon champagne ("Hey, *that's* where their money's at—right there.")

Hetfield dropped Axl Pose's contract rider on the floor, and stepped on it like it was a cockroach.

James Hetfield's rant appeared in his band's video, *A Year and a*

Half in the Life of Metallica / Part Two. An extraordinary breach of rock etiquette, it signaled unusual public contempt, as well as a warning to any other band that might contemplate touring with Guns N' Roses on an equal billing.

Izzy Stradlin and the Ju Ju Hounds was released on October 12, 1992, by Geffen Records. Featuring Izzy's laconic vocals, Ron Wood's blazing slide guitar, and keyboards by Stones associates Ian McLagan and Nicky Hopkins, *Ju Ju Hounds* sounds not so much like a Rolling Stones album, but more like *Talk Is Cheap,* Keith Richards's first solo record. And it is mostly very good, especially Izzy's clean-cut singing on "Somebody Knockin'" and "Take a Look at the Guy." Izzy got respectful reviews, with critics sadly noting how much was lost when Izzy Stradlin walked out of Guns N' Roses.

Axl Rose was very aware of this, and of what people were saying about him and Guns, but he took the criticism philosophically. "Negativity sells," he said, "and the media knows that. 'AXL ROSE—ROCK 'N' ROLL'S BAD GUY.' But there were a lot of people who talked crap about the Rolling Stones too. Now that we're huge, it seems the most vocal people are the ones who don't like us. They'll pick up any rock, and throw it at us."

South America was terra incognita for the big rock bands in 1992. Led Zeppelin flamed out before it could land there. The exhausted Stones canceled a South American *Steel Wheels* tour leg in 1989. Aerosmith and KISS had never bothered, because the market was never big enough in terms of record sales, and also there were no promoters reliable enough to book a big band into the soccer stadiums of politically unstable banana republics and squalid military dictatorships.

Then Guns N' Roses had a go. It was summer in South America, and Guns was determined to follow the sun around the world. The 1992 South American leg of Get in the Ring visited five countries in November and December, encountering the craziest, hungriest rock fans any band had yet seen. In Caracas, Venezuela, on November 25, Guns played for 45,000 in a gigantic parking lot—the biggest show ever played in that country. Two hours after the band flew out, Venezuelan air force generals staged a military coup, which stranded some of the band's gear and about half the road crew at the airport. The first show in Bogotá, Colombia, was canceled. When the gear arrived and the stage was being built in a driving rain, six tons of stage trusses and lighting rigs crashed to the floor. No one was hurt, but the crew was spooked. When Guns started the show on November 29, the skies opened again and soaked the band—and the biggest audience in Colombian history—to the skin. Outside El Campin stadium, hundreds of ticketless fans, and those with tickets who couldn't get in the grossly oversold venue, had themselves a riot. As Guns played inside, cop cars were overturned and torched outside. There were vicious arguments with the beleaguered promoters over money. This was why big bands didn't come to South America.

Early in December, they played in Santiago, Chile, and then did two shows at the mammoth River Plate Stadium in Buenos Aires, Argentina. There, wildly emotional Argentine rock fans besieged Guns' hotel. If a band member dared to venture outside, he was immediately mobbed and subjected to dozens of passionate kisses from *male* fans, unafraid to show their ardor and undying loyalty to GN'R. On to Brazil: Both shows in São Paulo played in monsoonlike conditions of downpour. Axl got into a fight with paparazzi outside the band's hotel. Then he went upstairs and started bombing them with chairs from his balcony. "Animal," they yelled back. "Asshole!" The tour ended at a racetrack in Rio on December 13, and Guns N' Roses took the rest of the year off.

*L*ater in the month, Axl Rose and Stephanie Seymour invited friends to a Christmas party at the house they shared in Malibu. But then something happened, and Axl wanted to cancel the party. She didn't want to be bound by his mood swings, and insisted the party go on. According to court documents filed in bitter lawsuits the following year, Axl started hitting Stephanie after the last guests had left. But Seymour was nobody's punching bag. As she admitted in her judicial court filings, Stephanie Seymour grabbed W. Axl Rose by his testicles, and gave them a serious twist. Maddened now, he threw her down the stairs.

It is well known in therapeutic circles that couples who engage in repeated bouts of abuse and redemption are often confused about their unruly, fractious relationships. So it was probably no surprise to their friends that, early in 1993, Axl Rose proudly announced that he and Stephanie Seymour were engaged to be married. Everyone who really knew them held their breath, and waited to see what would happen next.

SKIN & BONES

January 1993. Guns was glad to be back on the road. The tour was booked through July; if completed, it would set endurance records in the sacred annals of rock. No one else had ever stayed out this long. (Guns hadn't planned to either, but at the end of 1992 the accountants didn't think they had made enough money. Doug Goldstein went ahead and booked another year of shows.)

They went back to Japan, along with Axl's spiritual healer Sharon Maynard and an eighty-person entourage of crew, therapists, and handlers. Again Axl insisted they play only in Tokyo, where he holed up in his hotel suite, speaking only with his personal staff. After Ms. Maynard ascertained that there were no nuclear power facilities in the area, she was driven to the Tokyo Dome, where she reportedly did some sort of magnetic scan of the stage being built for Guns. Only when she declared that the vibes were compatible with Axl's magnetic requirements could the concerts proceed as scheduled.

The shows started with a blistering "Nightrain." Rolling Stone Ron Wood was doing a solo tour of Japan, and he joined Guns at the Tokyo Dome for an extended riff-trading version of "Heaven's Door." In early February, Guns played big summertime shows at racetracks in Australia and New Zealand. The final concert of this leg was on Axl's thirty-first birthday, February 6, 1993, at Mount Smart Stadium in Auckland.

* * *

*B*ack in L.A., Guns N' Roses stripped down. Ticket sales for the next American leg were slack, since this would be the third time Guns had played some cities on the tour. The long finale of the tour would feature just the six-piece band, minus the much criticized (and expensive) girl singers, horn players, and Teddy Zig Zag. ("We kept Dizzy and got rid of everyone else," Slash reported.) Axl dispensed with the annoying multiple costume changes that had drawn derisive comparisons to Madonna's act. Queen's Brian May opened most of these 1993 shows with his own band.

For the first time, there was some stage business—the antithesis of punk—at a Guns show. An acoustic set, midway through the concerts, featured songs from *GN'R Lies* ("Patience," "You're Crazy," "Used to Love Her," and sometimes the Stones' "Dead Flowers"). While the band strummed sitting on stools and a comfy yellow sofa, hot pizzas would be delivered onstage. (This was Axl's idea of rock comedy.)

The first gig (Austin, Texas, on February 23, 1992) went awry when Axl stormed out to the soundboard, halfway through the show, and fired the audio technician because his stage monitors were inaudible. But then Guns N' Roses played all over America for the next four months with minimal trauma and few overt problems. Axl stopped an April 3 show in Sacramento, California, when Duff was knocked out by a urine-filled water bottle thrown from the audience, and was carried off to the hospital. The band walked off. Slash came back out, explained what happened, and said the show was over. He asked the crowd to behave themselves. "Don't fuck with anyone," Slash ordered, "and don't fuck with the building."

*A*xl Rose was performing under extraordinary stress because he and Stephanie Seymour had broken up, under battlefield conditions, three weeks after he had announced their engagement in February 1993. He suspected her of infidelity, confronted her, and she and her son fled their house in March. Nine months later, at the end of 1993, Seymour gave birth to a son fathered by newsprint magnate Peter Brandt. (Stephanie Seymour and Peter Brandt married the following year, had more children together, and have maintained a long marriage.)

In August 1993, Axl Rose sued Stephanie Seymour for refusing to return more than one hundred thousand dollars' worth of jewelry he had given her. He also asked a judge for a restraining order against her, citing what he claimed was her attack on his manhood during their Christmas battle the year before. This prompted her to counter-sue Axl in October 1993 for, among other things, assault and battery, including giving her a sexually transmitted disease—a case of herpes. Seymour was dead serious about the way she'd been treated—her legal filing acknowledged twisting Axl's genitals—and her attorneys enlisted Erin Everly as a potential witness. This in turn prompted Erin—whose annulled marriage to Axl had left her penniless and dependent on family and friends—to sue Axl as well. These cases would eventually make it to open court, amid horrendous national publicity, the following year.

So now Axl Rose was alone in his big house in Malibu, trying to write new songs about the anguish and torments he was living through. Stephanie Seymour had a nanny for her son, a Brazilian immigrant named Beta Lebeis, a mature woman with two children of her own. But she was now redundant in the Brandt household, and was given notice. So Axl asked Stephanie's former nanny to stay on as his housekeeper. Ms. Lebeis agreed, and assumed increasing responsibility for Axl's affairs as time wore on. Beta Lebeis would, over the years, evolve into a sort of personal manager, mother figure, and spokesperson for her increasingly reclusive employer.

*A*xl Rose's romantic disaster was never openly discussed within Guns N' Roses. Axl now saw his fellow musicians only when they were onstage. (And nobody dared to ask Axl how he was getting along.) Maybe this was why Guns N' Roses' Skin and Bones Tour was so desperately cool. Slash loved playing the *Illusion* songs the way he'd written them and worked on them in the studio—as guitar band rock songs, not glitzy production numbers. So what that some of the gigs in the Northeast—like the Hartford Civic Center on March 4, 1993—were only half full? At least now there was an aura of semi-integrity about the Skin and Bones production values.

But then Gilby Clarke crashed his motorcycle while rehearsing for a celebrity charity show and broke his left wrist. The docs inserted some metal to keep the bone straight. The next four Guns concerts had to be canceled—and these were big shows in the Northeast that had already been postponed and rescheduled. The band's street cred went into the toilet. The promoters and agents were going crazy. And now a lucrative spring 1993 European tour seemed in jeopardy.

The official story was that Axl came up with the solution: "Fuck it. Let's call Izzy." (The other version was that Slash called Izzy—without telling Axl, who of course went ballistic, but then went along.) To everyone's surprise and delight, Izzy Stradlin said he was in. He'd taken the Ju Ju Hounds on a short English tour early in 1993, and the Hounds hadn't exactly ignited the masses, so Izzy may have needed cash flow. He reportedly asked for, and got, a million dollars for five shows. (Izzy also told them he wouldn't rehearse.) "Izzy and I grew up together and we're like a family in lots of ways," Axl said in a press release dated May 17, 1993. "It goes to show that you never know what fate has in store."

After Guns' first shows in Russia were canceled in the wake of the failed 1993 coup against the post-communist government, Izzy joined Guns in Israel, where they were rehearsing for a show in Tel Aviv's Hayarkan Park. Izzy walked into the studio—sporting dreadlocks. Hugs all around. (Axl wasn't there.) Izzy hadn't practiced any of the songs and was rusty, but it *was* Izzy, and he was back in the band until Gilby could fret his guitar again. Halfway through the Tel Aviv show, the band played the folk song "Havah Nagilah." Axl wore a shirt that said GUNS N' MOSES. Izzy played with Guns in Greece and Turkey, and finished with two big British stadium shows, at Milton Keynes, in late May. Blind Melon, Soul Asylum, and the Cult opened.

In June 1993, Guns played shows in northern Europe, sometimes with Blind Melon opening. Other support acts included L.A. alt-thrash cretins Suicidal Tendencies and Brian May. On June 16, at St. Jakob Fussballstadion in Basel, Switzerland, Blind Melon's Shannon Hoon walked onstage—stark naked—during Guns' acoustic set and delivered pizzas to an incredulous Axl Rose. This leg of the tour was extensively documented by Del James and a two-man video crew; but the naked Hoon, and many other risqué delights of Guns' 1993 Euro campaign, have never been screened in public and remain in Axl

Rose's private archive. They did shoot parts of the *Estranged* video at a Munich stadium show, and then began including the heartbroken song in the shows, as well as a version of Kansas' "Dust in the Wind." The last of these Euro shows was at the Bercy sports arena in Paris on July 13, 1993. The next day, Guns flew across the world, to Argentina for the final shows of the tour.

*O*n the long flight to Buenos Aires, there was some discussion about Guns playing some big late-summer festivals with U2, but nobody thought this would really happen. Everyone's main concern was to finish the long tour and get back to California in one piece. Duff McKagan's increasingly desperate alcoholism was the talk of the tour, but the bloated and haggard-looking bassist rarely missed a note onstage. There were those who said that McKagan—stoned immaculate, with no apology—was keeping the original spirit of Guns alive. Others felt bad that he was obviously killing himself.

Guns arrived in Buenos Aires early on the morning of July 15, 1993. Some of them spent the afternoon watching the new movie *Jurassic Park* at a nearby theater, having slipped out of their surrounded hotel in disguise. Reptile fanatic Slash was rapturous as giant carnivorous lizards devoured their deserving human victims. Some hotel guests, and the few fans who found their way into the lounge that night, were entertained by Slash, Gilby, and Dizzy Reed until they closed the place at dawn.

On July 16, Axl Rose was eating a pre-show, prime-cut Argentine beefsteak supper in his penthouse hotel suite when the door smashed open and fifty narcotics officers barged in, looking for drugs. They were, it was explained, acting on a reliable tip. All they found was Axl's extensive pharmacopoeia of homeopathic remedies. After a surreal half-hour search, they left as quickly as they had arrived, and Axl finished his supper and left for the stadium.

The show was sold out, and 70,000 barking-mad Argies roared an inhuman greeting when Guns N' Roses took the stage and charged into "It's So Easy." The highlights were the mass pandemonium that greeted "Welcome to the Jungle," and then "Double Talkin' Jive," which Axl dedicated to "the motherfucker who said we had drugs." (Slash and Gilby played a jittery, raving guitar jam on "Train Kept A-Rollin'" in the middle of this, recalling the Beck/Page Yardbirds of *Blow Up* and "Stroll On.")

The last show at Estadio Rio Plate on July 17, 1993, was also the finale of the tour. They started "Nightrain" at nine thirty, and played twenty-one songs for two hours. Back at their hotel, Axl, Slash, and Dizzy took over the lounge. A wistful, wisecracking Axl Rose lingered at the grand piano until six in the morning. Within thirty-six hours, everyone was back in Los Angeles, and the saga of the true and original Guns N' Roses effectively had come to an end.

Guns N' Roses' Use Your Illusion / Get in the Ring / Skin and Bones Tour had lasted twenty-eight months, the longest in rock history. Statistics vary, but the tours—at least 195 shows in 27 countries—set various attendance records, played to an estimated seven million fans, and reportedly grossed around 60 million dollars. Back in L.A., the Gunners went into different degrees of shock. "Nobody really wanted to come home," Gilby Clarke recalled. "Everybody, in the back of their minds, thought it was never going to be over."

But it was all over. The final Buenos Aires show would prove to be the last time Slash, Duff McKagan, Gilby Clarke, and Matt Sorum played in public with W. Axl Rose.

THE TRUE MEANING OF ALTERNATIVE

Summer 1993. Green Day's post-grunge warhead *Dookie* stole the rest of Guns N' Roses' heavily polarized audience. Kids wanted to dance and bang heads, not agonize over Axl Rose's sordid family problems. Geffen executives noticed that Guns' principals seemed to despise each other, and so Guns was now officially classified within the music industry as Dysfunctional.

On August 23, W. Axl Rose testified in Steven Adler's lawsuit against Guns N' Roses, which claimed that the band got Adler addicted to heroin and then terminated him unlawfully. (Adler also claimed in legal filings that he had witnessed Axl throwing a girl down a flight of stairs in early 1990, after she refused to have sex with him.) On the witness stand at Los Angeles Superior Court, Axl testified that Adler was unable to play drums due to drug abuse, and he claimed that Adler's drum track on "Civil War" had to be spliced together from sixty different takes. The case dragged on for another month, until Guns and Adler settled out of court for a $2.25 million payment to Adler, the restoration of song publishing credits that had been taken from him, and 15 percent of future royalties. (The settlement was seen as a complete victory for Steven Adler, whose status in Hollywood was so low that club bouncers made him wait outside their velvet ropes. Adler was so elated by the settlement that he binged on everything—mostly cocaine—until he suffered a stroke that left him permanently speech-impaired.)

In September 1993, Geffen released Duff McKagan's solo album, *Believe in Me,* which failed to find an audience despite featuring most of Guns and Sebastian Bach. Slash joined Duff in New York for a media showcase, but the album was weak on songs, and Duff's chronic alcoholism had left him a shadow of his former self.

Nevertheless, Guns worked (almost secretly) on a new album of punk covers during the hot California autumn of 1993, as wildfires scorched the dry hills and canyons outside the city. Some of these songs had been recorded while Izzy Stradlin was still in the band. Slash erased Izzy's rhythm guitar tracks, and dropped in new ones by Gilby Clarke. Smoke was in the air as Guns worked on the Damned's "New Rose" (with Duff singing); the UK Subs' hilarious "Down on the Farm"; the New York Dolls' "Human Being" (dedicated to Johnny Thunders); proto-punk Stooges anthem "Raw Power"; the Dead Boys' 1978 death-punk dirge "Ain't It Fun" ("when you're gonna die young": dedicated to the late Stiv Bators); T. Rex's 1973 "Buick Makane" moshed up with Soundgarden's "Big Dumb Sex"; Nazareth's 1975 "Hair of the Dog"; *Illusion* tour concert staple "Attitude" (Duff singing); a great and grinding version of the Sex Pistols' "Black Leather"; Johnny Thunders' "You Can't Put Your Arms Around a Memory"

(Duff: "This one's for you, Johnny"); and Fear's "I Don't Care About You," an anarchic hardcore rave—"Fuuuuuuuuuck youuuuuuuu"—that recalled the blazing early days of Guns N' Roses.

Two oddities bookended this drunk-rock sequence. "Since I Don't Have You" was a blowzy deconstruction of the 1958 doo-wop classic by the immortal Skyliners. Axl had been singing this beautiful, crying song to himself since Stephanie Seymour ran off. ("Yeah, we're fucked," he admits just before the guitar solo.)

The album's printed track list ended with "I Don't Care About You," but the final, uncredited song was "Look at Your Game, Girl." This was taken from a record by a singer/songwriter that Stuart Bailey had played for Axl and Slash, without telling them who it was. Axl especially focused on this song. Slash was nonplussed when the album was revealed as Charlie Manson's *LIE*. (This was the demo tape, later released as a bootleg record, whose rejection by the Los Angeles record industry had fueled the murderous rage that led to the butchering of six otherwise innocent Hollywood figures—including actress Sharon Tate and hairstylist Jay Sebring—in the summer of 1969.) Axl delivered the song straight up, in a natural singing voice almost unique to this performance. Slash has said that he didn't play on it. Indeed, some Geffen executives were given to understand that the rest of the band had been surprised to find Manson's song on the album at all.

These songs were released on Guns N' Roses' final studio album, *"The Spaghetti Incident?"* in late November 1993. The title was never formally explained, but it related to the obscure 1992 Hollywood heist movie *The Linguini Incident,* starring David Bowie and Rosanna Arquette, who had been one of Guns' earliest celebrity fans. The cover featured writhing pasta worms in a canned-looking sauce. A video was shot for the first single, "Since I Don't Have You," with model (and Axl's new girlfriend) Jennifer Driver. The band did some interviews, Geffen gave it a push, but the album didn't sell the tonnage of the old days. *Rolling Stone*: "With the rise of punk-rooted 'alternative' music in the last couple of years, it has become apparent just what the music was an alternative to: GN'R, who had grown to represent this generation's ultimate in bloated rock excess."

Slash tried to explain: "We just thought it would be cool to show our fans the bands that meant so much to us. Most of the records are hard to find, and several of the musicians are dead, almost everyone are broke. It didn't go well for our heroes."

Axl was asked about the Charles Manson song. "Manson is a part of American culture and history," he said. He pointed out that he often wore a Manson T-shirt onstage "to make a statement, because a lot of people enjoy playing me as the bad guy and the crazy. Sorry, I'm not that guy."

Slash said he loved the album. He told an interviewer that he had never liked being in a band with Izzy Stradlin, whose playing had irritated him from day one. "It was wonderful to escape him on this record," Slash admitted. "It sounds tighter, and so much cooler than anything we've done before."

Chapter Twelve

THE BEST GN'R TRIBUTE BAND IN THE WORLD

Success is not final, failure is not fatal:
it is the courage to continue that counts.
—Winston Churchill

THE SOUND OF A BAND BREAKING UP

*A*t the beginning of 1994, Guns N' Roses was still intact, but the fissures among the band's personalities were getting too wide to straddle. Axl was sequestered in his Malibu estate, almost completely reclusive. But in mid-January, he flew to New York for the induction of early inspirer Elton John into the Rock and Roll Hall of Fame. Axl joined the celebrity jam late in the program, singing the Beatles' "Come Together" with Bruce Springsteen.

It was his last public appearance (except in courtrooms) for six years.

Geffen Records was panting for a new Guns N' Roses album. David Geffen had sold the label to MCA (Music Corporation of America) in 1990 for a billion dollars, and in 1994 had one year remaining on his employment contract. Geffen had offered Guns an album advance reported to be worth 10 million dollars. So, in the spring of 1994, the crew set Guns up in a big room at The Complex, an L.A. studio, equipped with pool tables and a GN'R pinball machine. But the band almost never showed up, and the engineers—who were on call permanently—never had all six Gunners in the room at any one time. It didn't matter, because Guns didn't really have any new songs, only some fragments, riffs, and barely sketched ideas. The expenses began to build up as the studio sat buzzing, ready, and usually empty.

Duff McKagan collapsed in April. Duff recalled, "The end of my drinking career came when my pancreas burst, which was not fun. It lets out the bile, which gives your stomach and intestines third-degree burns. Usually they slit you open to let some of the steam out, which relieves the pain before you die." Duff was in the hospital for ten days, scared shitless, upset not that he had lived fast and died young, but that his corpse would be less than exquisite. "I looked like bloated Elvis," he said.

The doctors explained that if he went home and drank vodka, he would die right away since his burst gland was still exposed. They had left his pancreas in place, and Duff was relieved he didn't have to become diabetic. "It may sound corny," he told an interviewer, "but my doctor said, 'There's a reason you're still alive. Make good use of it, because this doesn't happen all the time.'"

Duff retreated to Seattle to recover. Kurt Cobain was on the same flight, having checked himself out of a rehab program. The doctors put Duff on morphine for the pancreatic pain and other drugs to control delirium tremens from alcohol detoxification. Kurt Cobain put a shotgun in his mouth and pulled the trigger, sending his fans and many in his generation into shock. "Then I was sober," Duff recalled, "and everything seemed like I was on acid, because it was so real."

Duff started to exercise and worked with a martial arts teacher. To keep busy, he began going through the band's financial statements, which he found impossible to understand. When he returned to L.A., a changed man, Duff started taking business classes at a community college downtown. Later, McKagan entered a Jesuit business college in Seattle and would eventually graduate with a degree in finance (with a minor in accounting).

June 1994. Guns was silent as Axl prepared to defend himself in court against the two abuse lawsuits filed by his former lovers. He reportedly had Erin Everly's graphic bondage scenes erased from Guns' unused *It's So Easy* video, and then the tape was burned. Meanwhile,

Gilby Clarke had been working hard on a solo album that featured Duff, Slash, and Axl along with some guest stars. Gilby's record was released (by Virgin Records) as *Pawnshop Guitars* in June (and is still considered by fans to be the strongest of the Guns-associated solo albums). It also got Gilby fired.

Actually, Gilby Clarke had been fired, and then rehired, three times in the early months of 1994. Then Clarke did interviews to promote his record, and some mild, faintly critical, supposedly off-the-record remarks Gilby made about Axl's control-freak issues were published in *Kerrang!* that month. Axl was furious.

"Axl fired Gilby without consulting anyone," Slash said later. "His rationale was that Gilby had always been a hired hand, and that he couldn't write with him."

Gilby went quietly. Then the royalty checks stopped. No one would return his calls. Reluctantly, Gilby sued Guns N' Roses. An undisclosed settlement was reached in 1995.

*I*n the summer of 1994, Slash got more serious about a side project, a band originally conceived as SVO Snakepit. (SVO stood for Slash's Very Own.) This was Slash, Gilby, and members of other local bands working out some of the ideas Slash was trying to develop for the next Guns album. Slash: "We booked ourselves a tour across the U.S., Europe, Japan, Australia—clubs and theaters. We shot two videos and released a single, 'Beggars and Hangers On.' There was no drama. We booked gigs, showed up, got up there, and played. It helped me rediscover why I love what I do."

Gilby's dismissal left a huge hole in Guns N' Roses. Slash was unable to communicate with Axl. Izzy Stradlin had been the bridge between Axl and the rest of the band. Slash: "Izzy was the last one in the band able to get through to him, creatively." Slash said that neither he nor Duff had the social skills to get through Axl's wall of silence, which was a problem because the band had agreed to record a cover of the Rolling Stones' "Sympathy for the Devil" for the new Tom Cruise/Brad Pitt movie, *Interview with the Vampire*.

Then Axl hired Paul Huge to replace Gilby in Guns N' Roses.

Huge was Axl's old pal from Lafayette, and the cowriter of "Back Off Bitch," arguably Guns' worst song ever. The others were appalled. They all hated Paul Huge. Slash said that Huge had zero personality, no music skills, and was the least interesting guy holding a guitar Slash had ever met. They begged Axl, through Doug Goldstein, to reconsider, but Paul Huge was now in the band. They tried to work with him in Slash's home studio, but nothing came of it but toxic vibes and general negativity. Slash sent Axl tapes of songs he'd been working on, but never heard back. Slash didn't speak to Axl for a long time after that.

$\mathcal{T}$his version of Guns cut "Sympathy for the Devil" with Mike Clink at Rumbo Sound in the fall of 1994. Tom Zutaut had hoped this would get the band together in the studio again, jump-start the new Guns album, and give the Geffen-released sound track a shot at the sales charts. Slash, Duff, and Matt Sorum showed up for work every day. Axl stayed away, and recorded his vocals and Huge's rhythm guitar when the others had left. Slash: "Axl never showed up, so everybody lost interest." Once Slash crashed one of the vocal sessions to try to speak with Axl. He waited for hours. When Axl finally arrived, they sat in the lounge. "He talked to me from behind a magazine," Slash said, "without looking me in the eye once." After fifteen minutes of disrespect, Slash could stand it no longer and took off.

When the tracks were done, Bill Price was flown in from London to mix them. They sent Slash a DAT of the new mix with the vocals, and he went into shock because there was another guitar laid on top of his, to make it sound more like Keith Richards's 1968 creation. Slash was angry. "Axl had gotten Paul Huge to double over me. . . . It was like really bad plagiarism."

The rest of Guns were embarrassed by their version of "Sympathy for the Devil," which was released as a Guns N' Roses single in December 1994. It was, according to Slash, "thoroughly average." It was also the last recording by the tattered remnants of the shambolic rebels of 1985. Slash, in his memoirs, said it was the final blow. "If you've ever wondered what a band sounds like when it's breaking up, listen to our cover of 'Sympathy for the Devil.'"

"NEVER LEAVE YOUR BAND"

It was the worst of times for W. Axl Rose in April 1995, as he listened in court to his two former lovers and their witnesses testify against him. Erin Everly said he had sodomized her against her will. She said that he put her in the hospital with injuries from beatings. An ex-girlfriend of Slash's testified that Axl had brutalized Erin and had smashed her things, and she bitterly called Axl a pig in front of the jury. All this got into the press, so it was a total disgrace. Stephanie Seymour said that Axl had dragged her, barefoot, through glass bottles he had broken. She said he had hit her in the face and kicked her in the abdomen. Hearing all this, with more testimony to come, Axl's lawyers called it a day and settled. (Maybe he shouldn't have sued a rich man's wife.) *Parade* magazine reported that an insurance company paid Seymour $400,000. The amount of Erin Everly's settlement was undisclosed. Axl Rose refused any comment. His publicist said that Axl was concentrating on his work. He later said he wrote a new song during the trial called "Oklahoma," about the concurrent bombing of a government building in Oklahoma City in revenge for the FBI's siege of the Branch Davidian sect in Waco, Texas, where everyone had died in a holocaust of snakepit religion and exploding ammunition.

February 1995. Slash's Snakepit released the album *It's Five O'Clock Somewhere* on Geffen Records, and carried the swing for Guns-style hard rock for the rest of the year. Gilby, Duff, and Matt Sorum played on the record and in the Snakepit lineup that played the Monsters of Rock festival at Castle Donington in England that summer. Then the group broke up, pulled off the road by its record company after the album had sold a respectable two million units and recouped the label's costs.

But Geffen was dry, with few hit records, and the label needed Guns N' Roses back in the studio if it was going to survive. David Geffen had retired from the record business in 1995 and formed the multimedia empire Dreamworks SKG with two movie moguls. Geffen Records, somewhat reduced, now functioned as a semi-independent

label under the aegis of the Universal Music Group, which had sub-
sumed MCA. Then Universal was sold to Seagram, the Canadian liquor conglomerate. As the corporate dust settled, and as Guns' back
catalogue continued to bring in serious revenue amid the cultural
doldrums of the mid-nineties, Axl Rose was left alone to record at his
own pace.

The band actually rehearsed at the Complex a few times that year,
but Axl wouldn't show up until two in the morning. He wanted to
move the band in an industrial-techno direction to stay current. Slash
didn't want to deny Guns' blues-rock roots. "We didn't spend a lot of
time collaborating," Slash recalled. The band would play some things
for Axl. Slash: "He'd sit back in the chair, watching—a riff here, a riff
there. But no one knew where it was going." The band then got bored
or tired and went home, leaving Axl alone.

Back in 1986, they used to make fun of Axl and call him the Ayatollah, but now it really was a dictatorship. Axl and Doug Goldstein
made all decisions for the band, who were later notified via fax or telephone. Then Axl presented Slash and Duff with a new band contract.
Slash: "It stated that Axl retained rights to the band name and could
start a new band called Guns N' Roses. Duff and I could be members,
but only on his terms, which felt like we were defined as hired hands."
Slash and Duff hesitated. Axl sent them a letter on August 31, 1995,
informing them that he was leaving the band and taking over the
brand. Slash and Duff capitulated, and signed Axl's new deal.

"I signed it and let it go," Slash said. He was worn down by all the
bullshit, and the lawyers were making fortunes going to meetings
about all this. "I wanted to move on, and see if we had anywhere left
to go together."

When news of this leaked out, Slash and Duff were widely criticized for bending over for W. Axl Rose. Even Slash agreed. No one
was more amazed than he that they "had allowed Axl the freedom,
over all those years, to transform what we had into some morbid reality that existed only in his head."

Shannon Hoon's OD affected Axl Rose deeply. The Blind Melon
singer was found dead in his tour bus, before a gig at the legendary

New Orleans club Tipitina's on October 21, 1995. The parish coroner ruled the death a cocaine overdose. Shannon, whom everyone loved for his saucer-eyed innocence and angelic voice, was only twenty-eight years old. He left behind a baby daughter named Nico Blue.

Slash spent much of 1996 working on personal business. He played at James Brown's birthday party, and wrote more songs for his own band. His wife, Renee, left him. Meanwhile, Duff and Matt Sorum joined Sex Pistol Steve Jones and Duran Duran bassist John Taylor in a (mostly) sober, one-off band, the Neurotic Outsiders, which cut a generic supergroup album (read: no good songs) for Madonna's Maverick Records.

All work on the next Guns album had stopped by September 1996. Axl Rose's mother, Sharon Bailey, died suddenly at the age of fifty-one. Fires fanned by California's devil winds burned through Malibu and threatened Axl's canyon. Slash put together a short-term band, Slash's Blues Ball, and said (in an online chat) that he and Axl were "deliberating over the future of our relationship." The Rolling Stones were in L.A., working on the *Bridges to Babylon* album. Slash attended some of the sessions and noticed the atmosphere of mutual respect despite fairly intense personal differences. Slash told Keith Richards his problems, and Keith sternly advised Slash that it was a sacred trust *never* to leave your band. Others reminded him that Slash and Axl had created the greatest front-line collaboration of their era. This just made Slash's problems even worse.

Then there was a final, secret dinner between Axl and Slash in an Italian restaurant in Brentwood. Axl laid out his new plans for Guns, trying hard to draw Slash into his vision, a vision that Slash thought was totally whack.

Slash was tired of being manipulated. After a sleepless night of despair and suicidal thoughts, Slash called Doug Goldstein.

"That's it," Slash said. "I quit." Goldstein tried to respond, but Slash had already hung up.

Axl fought back, according to Slash. He called Slash's father, called his wife, called his bodyguard, called anyone who could get to the recalcitrant guitarist. Axl said that Slash was making the biggest mistake of his life, and that he was pissing away a fortune. Slash didn't care. He felt an immense burden had been lifted from his shoulders. He called Duff, Matt Sorum, and guitar tech Adam Day to tell them, and they all said they understood.

On October 30, 1996, Slash announced via his publicist that he had left Guns N' Roses. Axl shot off a fax to MTV News claiming that Slash hadn't been in the band since 1995, and that there would be a new Guns N' Roses album soon.

CHINESE DEMOCRACY

In 1997, Geffen executive Todd Sullivan was given the job of prying the next Guns N' Roses album out of the clutches of the band's sole owner, W. Axl Rose. The label thought that fresh ears might help, and they wanted to team Guns with a new producer. So Sullivan sent Axl a box of CDs by different producers to see if anyone appealed to him. A few days later Sullivan learned that Axl had thrown the CDs in his driveway, without listening to them, and then ran over them with his car until they were just bits of crushed plastic. Todd Sullivan then met with Axl, who played him some of the sketches the band had been trying to develop. Sullivan responded with enthusiasm, and suggested that Axl try to bear down and complete some of these songs. Axl stared at Sullivan and then said, "Hmmm, bear down and complete some of these songs." The following day, Sullivan got a call from Geffen chairman Eddie Rosenblatt, informing him he was no longer working with Guns N' Roses.

In February, Axl flew to Arizona to visit his spiritual advisors in Sedona. On February 11, he was arrested at the Phoenix airport and charged with threatening a security worker searching his luggage. He later pleaded guilty to disturbing the peace and was fined and given a day in jail.

* * *

The new album now at least had a title, *Chinese Democracy,* which was Axl's flip acknowledgment that Guns was indeed a dictatorship. Axl brought in turntable guy Moby to audit some tracks and maybe add some techno-style production. Moby wasn't there for long. He said later that Axl seemed reserved and suspicious—"like a beaten dog." It was impossible to discover any logical pattern to the song sketches Axl had on tape. Axl became defensive when Moby asked him about the vocals. "He just said he was going to get to them eventually." Moby walked out, and later said he would be surprised if *Chinese Democracy* ever came out at all.

Then the sessions stopped for a long time. West Arkeen, who had helped write some of Guns' best songs, died in May 1997 of a heroin overdose, at age thirty-six. Then Duff McKagan, unable to justify the band's existence any longer, quit Guns N' Roses in August, which left Axl as the sole remaining original member.

In early 1998 the *Democracy* sessions moved to Rumbo Sound, where the crew installed tapestries, colored lights, and the usual rock star amenities. Matt Sorum was fired and replaced by drummer Josh Freese. Slash's replacement was Robin Finck, late of industrial rock band Nine Inch Nails. Dizzy Reed and Paul Huge stayed in the band. Duff was replaced by Tommy Stinson, late of the Replacements, on bass guitar. The new producer was Youth (Martin Glover). Geffen was desperate for a hit record, as the label was about to be fed into the corporate meat grinder. They told Axl that their jobs were at stake, and then advanced him a million dollars, with the promise of another million as a bonus if the album was finished by March 1999.

They promised Youth bonus royalties also, which was unusual, but none of this got Axl into Rumbo Sound. Youth would visit Axl in Latigo Canyon, would notice the complete isolation in which he lived, would be told by Axl that he wasn't really ready to make an album right now. So Youth walked out, and was replaced by Sean Bevan, who'd done Nine Inch Nails and Marilyn Manson. He began working with the band, trying to build sketches and fragments into coherent instrumental tracks. Operating expenses were stratospheric as they bought or rented every new computer system on the market. Five days a week, couriers ferried DATs containing new mixes of the various songs to Axl in Malibu, where they were mostly received without comment. Weeks sometimes passed by with no studio activity at all. But by the end of the year, they had more than a thousand DATs and CDs of recorded music, all carefully labeled.

The pressure on the Geffen execs intensified. Universal Music Group chairman Edgar Bronfman was calling Geffen executives every other week and was getting more and more annoyed at being told the label had no release date for an album they'd already spent millions on. Doug Goldstein suggested that Geffen put out a live Guns N' Roses album to release some of the pressure on Axl. A lot of energy now went into sifting through concert tapes as far back as the London club shows of 1986. This wasn't enough to save more than a hundred Geffen employees, who were fired in January 1999 when Universal folded Geffen Records into Interscope Records, whose president, Jimmy Iovine, then took charge of Guns' recorded output. Axl Rose was reportedly upset by the mass exodus of people he had worked with at Geffen for ten years and more, and he stayed away from the recording studio in mute protest. The March 1999 delivery deadline for *Chinese Democracy* passed without much notice.

On March 16, 1999, Guns N' Roses was presented with a Diamond Album award by the record industry's trade association, commemorating sales of fifteen million units of *Appetite for Destruction*. This award was accepted, in New York, by Steven Adler.

Jimmy Iovine made some headway with Axl in 1999. That summer, Guns N' Roses released their first new song in eight years. The industrial-sounding "Oh My God" was destined for the sound track of *End of Days,* another Arnold Schwarzenegger action film, and was even introduced by Axl on MTV. Hopes for *Chinese Democracy* rose in a flurry of publicity, but the song was boring, barely got on the radio, and was slagged in the press as another disappointment from a band that had let its fans, and itself, down. Late in the year, Axl previewed a dozen *Chinese Democracy* tracks for *Rolling Stone.* The magazine was politely unmoved by early versions of new songs "I.R.S.," "Catcher in the Rye," and "The Blues." It duly reported that the new album was tentatively scheduled for the summer of 2000.

Guns N' Roses' much-anticipated live album came out in November 1999. *Live Era '87–'93* was a double CD containing twenty-two tracks. Axl and the ex-Gunners mixed and overdubbed the old tracks separately, communicating through managers and staff. Cushioned with ambient South American stadium noise, a future distant echo of "Benny and the Jets," it leaned heavily on the *Illusion* tours—Guns' bombastic late period—and missed some of the frenetic violence of the young band in a sweaty club. (The art director tried to compensate for this with reproductions of 1985 GN'R street flyers.) Again, despite some blistering performances of the *Appetite* songs, there was no radio airplay, and reviews for *Live Era* were less than raving. Axl had decreed that no ex-members of Guns could help promote the album, and he didn't bother to either, so sales in the crucial Christmas market totaled less than a million units, a shocking slap from their old fans. To many, it looked like the midnight hour had passed, and that the GN'R audience had moved on.

TREACHEROUS SEA OF HORRORS

*I*n 2000, Sean Bevan quit trying to produce *Chinese Democracy.* Interscope got Axl to agree on Roy Thomas Baker, who had produced Queen's major albums. Baker had Guns rerecord everything of any significance with a new drummer, Brian Mantia, formerly of Primus. Then Axl hired Buckethead, the shy, virtuoso metal guitarist who appeared in public wearing a plastic mask and a commercial fried chicken bucket on his head. Axl had this version of Guns N' Roses rerecord the tracks they had done for producer Baker.

Izzy Stradlin's Ju Ju Hounds and Slash's Snakepit both toured Japan and Europe in 2000, playing to audiences who yelled for the old Guns songs. Axl Rose performed in public for the first time in six years when he joined Gilby Clarke's Starfuckers at the Cathouse on June 22. The audience of maybe 300 erupted when Axl walked on-stage, which spurred him to dance through renditions of "Wild Horses" and "Dead Flowers." Afterward, Axl seemed genuinely relieved that people still wanted to dig his serpentine act.

Guns N' Roses played the House of Blues in Las Vegas on New Year's Eve. Buckethead and Robin Finck fronted the band with Axl a few hours into 2001. Paul Huge played rhythm guitar. Chris Pittman contributed effects. Dizzy Reed anchored the whole thing. "I have tra-versed a treacherous sea of horrors to be with you here tonight," Axl told the audience. The band blasted into "Nightrain" and the whole building shook. They played a lot of *Appetite*, including "Think About You" for the first time since 1987. They played a bunch of new songs: "Oh My God," "Silkworms," "The Blues," and "Chinese Democracy," which Axl explained he had written after seeing the film *Kundun*. Bucket-head had a big solo feature, and then threw roses from a Kentucky Fried Chicken container into the crowd. At the end of the show, Axl thanked the 1,800 delirious fans and wished them a happy new year.

Two weeks later, GN'R played for 200,000 at Rock in Rio III. Af-ter thousands of people had yelled for the absent Slash, Axl responded: "Yeah, yeah. All right. I know that you're disappointed that some of the people you know and love could not be with us tonight.... But, regardless of what you heard, my former friends have worked very hard... to do everything they could... *so I wouldn't be here today*!... And I say, FUCK THAT!"

A European tour was then announced and tickets for some shows sold out with no promotion; but the tour was then canceled without explanation. A planned DVD of the Las Vegas show was also shelved. Later that year, the rescheduled Euro tour was canceled again.

*M*arch 2001. Interscope brought in Tom Zutaut to try to get *Chinese Democracy* finished. Zutaut was the only recording executive ever to get any original music out of Guns N' Roses, and he was offered a major bonus if the album was ready by the end of 2001. CDs of alter-nate instrumental takes were driven to Axl almost every day. Bucket-head then threatened to quit, and had to be coddled. He made Axl take him to Disneyland, and then demanded that the studio build a chicken wire coop, in which Buckethead then recorded his solos. Producer Greg Wattenberg was hired to work on Axl's vocal tracks, which seemed to be *Chinese Democracy's* final stumbling block. Greg Wattenberg waited six excruciating weeks to meet Axl, and then was granted only a twenty-minute interview in the studio, at four in the morning. Wattenberg went home. The World Trade Center towers were knocked down, and everything changed, but there was no cracking the carapace of isolation surrounding W. Axl Rose. Both Tom Zutaut and Roy Thomas Baker were out of the picture by Christmas.

Guns N' Roses played two Las Vegas shows at the end of 2001. Axl: "We're doing four or five of the new songs, but we're holding our big guns back." Slash and his new wife, Perla Ferrar, tried to see the New Year's Eve show but were rudely stopped at the backstage door—a serious affront. Doug Goldstein was quoted about this in the press: "We didn't know what [Slash's] intentions were. It would have been a distraction. Axl was really nervous about these shows, and we decided not to take any risks." There were sound monitor problems during these shows, and Axl kept leaving the stage. When everything was working, "Uncle Axl" (as he introduced himself) would crouch at the side of the stage and watch his band work through the old songs, like an invisible spectator.

In early 2002, Axl had the band rerecord all the new songs—again. Paul Huge left the band and was replaced by guitarist Richard Fortus. That summer, Guns N' Roses played sold-out (and well-received) shows in Japan and Europe. Forty-year-old Axl Rose appeared onstage in sports jerseys and a cornrow hairdo under a bandanna. He looked younger than forty, and rumors were published that he'd had plastic surgery on his face, as well as hair transplants. At the Leeds Festival in England on August 23, Axl protested an early curfew:

"I didn't fucking come all the way to fucking England to be told to go back fuckin' home by some fuckin' asshole. [Big cheer] All I've got for the last eight years is shit after shit after shit in the fuckin' press—'Axl's this,' and 'Axl's that.' So if you wanna stay, and if I wanna stay, we'll see what happens. Everybody . . . Hey, nobody try to get in trouble or anything. Try and have a good time!"

During "Patience," Axl saw someone wearing a *Where Is Slash?*

T-shirt. "He's in my ass," Axl yelled. "That's where Slash is! *Fuckhead!* Go home!"

They finished the tour at London's Wembley Arena, with Weezer opening, completely sold out. Uncle Axl told the audience that Guns had two new albums, ready to go. He ranted for a while and then asked Tommy Stinson if his remarks qualified as a rant. Then he felt too sick to continue, so Sebastian Bach took his place for "Nightrain" and "Paradise City" and finished the show.

On August 29, 2002, Guns N' Roses made a surprise appearance at MTV's Video Music Awards. After "Jungle," the band premiered the new song "Madagascar" and closed with "Paradise City." Axl finished the mini-set with closed eyes and lifted hands, described in the press as a messianic stance. He did a short interview with MTV's Kurt Loder, and left the building.

Robert John had been taking photographs of Guns N' Roses since the beginning of the band, but now he started getting complaints from Axl. "He wasn't happy with the way he looked in the pictures," Robert said. "But his looks had changed. People get older, right? He'd put on a few pounds. He criticized the brightness of the shots, but I wasn't lighting the shows. He'd already fired Gene Kirkland, a terrific photographer who'd been shooting Guns almost as long as I had.

"Then I started working with Marilyn Manson, and Axl was like, 'The only reason Marilyn is working with you is, he's taking my energy through you.' You see, it *always* had to be about Axl, no matter what. It started getting on my nerves. Axl's entire world was having his employees lick his ass up and down, and tell him he was right. But I wasn't paid by him, so I could tell Axl what I felt. And I told him that the guy with the chicken bucket looked fucking weird, and that I just didn't see any chemistry in this band. They just played the old songs, almost note for note.

"Plus, now I was getting messages from Axl through his *housekeeper.* 'We want this. We want that.' She was the maid, the housekeeper, whatever. I didn't remember her being part of the organization. I remembered her being his ex-girlfriend's nanny. She never gave him my messages either.

"At one point that year [2002], I didn't see Axl for six months, and he'd changed. He looked different. People weren't being treated right. He had a bunch of psychics telling him what to do. Sharon from Sedona was putting hexes on things so they couldn't drain Axl's precious energy. It was all so weird."

Robert John made a deal with Axl to sell him all his photographs—thousands of images dating to 1984. Robert took the archives to Axl's house and then waited for the check. It never came, and eventually Robert John had to sue Axl Rose to get paid for his years of work with Guns N' Roses.

November 7, 2002. Guns N' Roses' first North American tour in ten years started with a riot in Vancouver when Axl's plane was late and the promoter canceled the first show. The kids smashed some windows, and the riot cops arrived with dogs and beat the crap out of people. Buckethead was upset seeing kids getting their teeth knocked out. But the rest of the month went well, despite some sparse crowds at smaller venues, and the band played a letter-perfect show at sold-out Madison Square Garden in New York on December 5. Afterward, Axl went out with an entourage, but he was rudely turned away from ultra-chic, model-ridden nightclub Spa because he was wearing a fur jacket and the club had a strict no-fur policy. Humiliated, mad as hell, he stormed back to his hotel. Instead of playing in Philadelphia the next day, he stayed in and watched a basketball game on television. After both opening bands had played, with Axl still in Manhattan, the Philadelphia show was canceled at eleven P.M. Chairs flew through the air. Trash fires were set. The riot cops arrived. The rest of the tour was canceled by the promoter.

In 2003, Slash, Duff McKagan, and Matt Sorum began rehearsing a new band they were calling Reloaded. They asked Sebastian Bach if he wanted to sing, but Bas declined. In May, Scott Weiland, former Stone Temple Pilot, was confirmed as the group's singer. In June, guitarist Dave Kushner was added, and the band was renamed Velvet Revolver. They played their first show in L.A. with a snarling set of covers that blew people away. Duff McKagan said Velvet Revolver was the band he'd always wanted to be in.

That summer Geffen Records told Axl Rose it was releasing a Guns N' Roses greatest hits album. Axl didn't want this to happen and got Doug Goldstein to promise them *Chinese Democracy* by the end of the year if they held off. The label agreed, but they still didn't get the new record. In February 2004, Geffen finally pulled the plug on the band's studio sessions. The *Chinese Democracy* recording budget was reported to have ballooned to more than $11 million.

Buckethead quit the band.

In March 2004, Geffen released *Greatest Hits* over Axl's heated objections and despite a court challenge that was dismissed by the judge. Guns' final album shocked everyone by quickly selling two million copies. It got to number one in England and many European markets, and entered the *Billboard* chart at number three. Sales of *Appetite for Destruction* also picked up, as well as the single-disc *Use Your Illusion* compilation Geffen had released in 1998. (This version deleted all the cursing so it could be sold at Wal-Mart and other conservative retail outlets.)

A LONG AND INCOMPREHENSIBLE JOURNEY

Velvet Revolver's first album, *Contraband,* came out in the spring of 2004 and the new band started touring, putting on club-level rock concerts that started on time. The music on *Contraband* (and its successor, *Libertad,* three years later) was unremittingly grim, perhaps reflecting the tenuous physical and mental health of ex-junkies and alcoholics now in their forties—heavily compromised musicians whose big fun was years behind them and wasn't coming back.

Steven Adler revived his own band, Adler's Appetite, and toured in Europe. Steven Adler lived in Las Vegas, his speech slurred by a cocaine-induced stroke. He admitted (to the Metal Sludge fan Web site) in 2005 that he still sometimes smoked crack but was trying to stop, and was living comfortably on his GN'R royalties.

Izzy Stradlin was living in Indiana, to the surprise of those who remembered the contempt with which he used to describe his home state.

Slash lived with his wife, Perla, and their two kids (London and Cash) in the San Fernando Valley. After years of addiction, Slash had serious heart problems, and a pacemaker-like device was installed in his chest in 2000 to keep him alive. Duff McKagan lived in Los Angeles with his wife, Susan Holmes, and their two daughters. The rigors of the Velvet Revolver tours sent both Slash and Duff back into drug dependency—Matt Sorum also went to rehab with Duff—but then they got clean again.

In January 2005, Axl Rose announced he had moved GN'R's song publishing business to Sanctuary Records, a recent contender for Industry Heavy status. Sanctuary executive Merck Mercuriades was also managing Guns, since Doug Goldstein had resigned or been fired by Axl for reasons unknown. Eight months later, Slash and Duff McKagan sued Axl after they stopped receiving royalty payments from Guns N' Roses. Axl's lawyers claimed it was all a mistake, and Axl countersued Slash.

Guns N' Roses of the twenty-first century played a week of blazing shows in New York in May 2005—intense theater-size concerts that were hailed by both critics and fans. The band played "Madagascar" and other new songs, but mostly stuck to carbon copies of the old records. Axl made newspaper headlines in New York when he got punched at a downtown nightclub by fashion designer Tommy Hilfiger.

In early 2006, a bunch of *Chinese Democracy* songs were leaked onto the Internet via a fan club Web site. The new songs—featuring drones, robotic rhythms, organlike keyboard variations—sounded tense, grandiose, and unfinished. "Better" was the best of these, although some radio stations downloaded "I.R.S." and began playing it in February—until the band's management put a stop to it. None of the songs matched the greatness of the early band, and people began to understand why the new Guns album was taking so long.

The feud among the original band members continued to simmer in 2006. After Slash paid a contentious nocturnal visit to Axl's house, Axl had his attorney release a public statement claiming that Slash had admitted that Axl had been right about *everything* over the years. This statement also claimed that Slash had told Axl that Duff McKagan was a wimp, and that Scott Weiland wasn't happening. A furious Scott Weiland in turn attacked Axl on Velvet Revolver's Web site: "Get a new wig, motherfucker!... Oh shit, *here it comes*—you fat, Botox-faced, wig-wearing fuck."

*M*ay 2006. Guns N' Roses announced a world tour, beginning with four warm-up shows at the Hammerstein Ballroom in New York (formerly the Ritz, where Guns had often played). These four shows—16,000 seats—sold out in three minutes. The opening-night crowd learned that Guns now had three guitar players, for Buckethead had been replaced by Bumblefoot, aka Ron Thal, who joined Robin Finck and Richard Fortus. Axl opened the evening with "Welcome to the Jungle," wearing a leather shirt and a large silver cross, his hair in cornrows and pulled back. His red beard and moustache made him look fierce, like an Irish warlord. The crowd roared the lyrics with him, word for word. They roared again when he brought out Izzy Stradlin for five songs. Izzy had short hair under a bandanna, and he seemed as amazed as anyone else that he was standing onstage with Axl Rose again. The people in the crush down front saw that Izzy seemed to have tears in his eyes as the band launched into "It's So Easy."

The whole crowd sang along to every familiar song, described in *The New York Times* as "an astonishing spectacle." They listened carefully to the new songs, trying to figure out "Madagascar" and "The Blues." Later on in the show, Axl brought out Sebastian Bach, who then functioned as a second lead singer, taking over the vocal on "My Michelle" when Axl left the stage. Axl thanked Bas onstage for persuading him to tour again. From then on, Bach often stayed with Guns N' Roses on the road, serving as an adjutant or relief rock star, filling in whenever needed.

*G*uns played in Europe next, beginning in Spain. In June they played a sold-out show in Stockholm, after which Axl partied with a bunch of leather-wearing blondes at the Café Opera. Back at the Hotel Bern, really drunk at three A.M., he got into a shouting match with a young woman. A security guard tried to intervene. Axl smashed a mirror, then bit the guard on the leg. The police dragged him off to jail. International headlines followed the next day, along with a $5,000 fine.

The seven-piece Guns played a successful North American tour beginning in September 2006. Rap-rockers Papa Roach opened many of the shows. Drummer Brian Mantia was replaced by Frank Ferrer. The tour was undertaken to raise cash to finish the album and keep the band alive, since their label refused to renegotiate or discuss marketing and video treatments until they had the master tapes of *Chinese Democracy* in hand.

The L.A. show (actually in San Bernardino) in September was their first in fourteen years. They sold out the venue and earned respectful if somewhat bemused reviews, as if they were the best Guns N' Roses tribute band in the world. Afterward, Axl threw a lavish party at his Malibu compound and played the full *Chinese Democracy* album for guests in his billiards room. He said that veteran engineer Andy Wallace, who had mixed Nirvana's *Nevermind,* was working on the Guns album in New York. Merck Mercuriades told *Rolling Stone* that the record would be out by the end of 2006. The following month, Axl told Mercuriades that he was out instead. *Chinese Democracy* stayed in the can.

Tower Records closed at the end of the year, bankrupt because kids didn't pay for records anymore, preferring to download or copy them instead. Axl was shocked by this, and wondered if there would be any stores left to sell *Chinese Democracy*—if he ever let it out. Late in 2006, in an open letter to Guns fans on the band's Web site, Axl wrote: "To say the making of this album has been an unbearably long and incomprehensible journey would be an understatement." He also hinted it would be released in March 2007.

It didn't happen. Two months after that, more tracks were "leaked" on the Internet. Most were remixes of previously downloadable music, and the critics yawned. Guns spent that summer playing shows in Mexico, Australia, and Japan. Axl worked with Sebastian Bach on his solo album, *Angel Down,* which came out late in 2007. The three duets Axl performed with Bas were his first recordings in years. Late in the year, as the Santa Ana winds roared from the east, Axl manned a garden hose as his Malibu mansion narrowly missed being consumed by wildfires that scorched thousands of acres in southern California. Part of the roof burned, but the house, and its wily and ruthlessly determined owner, survived to fight again another day.

*I*n the spring of 2008, Velvet Revolver imploded when Scott Weiland—out on $40,000 bail after a drug arrest on a freeway ramp—left the band to return to Stone Temple Pilots. Weiland and Matt Sorum had been publicly feuding, and Slash released a statement that they were fed up with Weiland's "erratic onstage behavior and personal problems." No replacement was announced, and tongues began to feverishly wag that Axl Rose, who was rumored to have serious cash-flow issues, would re-form the original Guns N' Roses for one final stupendous tour. The press wanted to speak with Axl about this possibility, but they couldn't find him, and no one returned their calls.

To many, Axl Rose remained an enigma. Almost anything he did made headlines in American newspapers. Others saw him as a poster child for narcissism and neurotic deliberation. His obsessive tinkering with *Chinese Democracy* left some convinced it would never come out. Some longtime Guns fans—those left emotionally exhausted after hearing *Appetite for Destruction* for the first time—expressed the fervent desire that the *Democracy* album not appear, on the theory that it was better just to let a great band die with some measure of dignity.

Others didn't see it that way. To them, Axl was a heroic artist, uninterested in money or fame, aiming for musical perfection at any cost. Tom Zutaut publicly defended Axl against his critics, maintaining that Axl Rose's artistic decisions were, and always had been, "motivated by a pure desire to make every recording count as a true reflection of his own high standards."

Everyone who had ever loved Guns N' Roses waited to see what would happen next.

Epilogue

CHINESE HYPOCRISY

*"I could consider opening a GN'R burger
chain. Ha-ha."*
—W. Axl Rose

In the early hours of July 18, 2008, Los Angeles police were called to Canyon Drive in Hollywood after reports of a disturbance at a private home. The cops found Steven Adler, ex-drummer of Guns N' Roses, nodding off in a car outside the house. They arrested Steven for heroin possession, driving under the influence of narcotics, and for an outstanding warrant. Adler was jailed on forty-five thousand dollars bail and released the following day.

A month earlier, in June 2008, early trickles of the legendary and long-awaited *Chinese Democracy* album, the first new music by so-called Guns N' Roses in seventeen years, began to leak onto the Internet. The leaked tracks—eventually traced to hard-core GN'R fans in Portugal—consisted of 2006 mixes of songs long rumored to be on *Chinese Democracy,* including "Better," "I.R.S.," "Catcher in the Rye," and "There Was a Time." Another leaked track, "Song #2," later turned out to be "Prostitute," the final number on the finished recording. The online GN'R forums started buzzing, and by the end of June, nine Guns N' Roses tracks were uploaded onto the Internet and streamed on various Web sites. Some thought this a clear signal that the earth would shake, that the final rapture was nigh, and that W. Axl Rose might actually release *Chinese Democracy* while some of the band's original fans were still alive.

* * *

*M*eanwhile, Slash was beginning work on a solo album. His wife Perla announced that the record would feature Ozzy Osbourne and other luminaries of heavy metal. With lots of time on his hands, Slash continued to appear as a serial award accepter, especially in Europe, where he often showed up in full top hat and leather regalia to receive statuettes and trophies for his alleged guitar prowess from tacky, cable-only award shows and third-division British music magazines like *Classic Rock*.

Duff McKagan, meanwhile, re-formed his decade-old hobby band, Loaded. They recorded and released *Wasted Heart*, a heavy-lite brew of post-punk metal, and embarked on a short but intense tour of small venues in England, Scotland, and Ireland. Musicians of Duff's stature didn't often play tiny gigs in remote locales like the Scottish isles, and the ballrooms and theaters were packed with rabid fans almost every night of the tour. Duff and his band liked it up there, that far north. In the summer, the sky stayed bright until midnight.

Izzy Stradlin remained retired in his beloved home state of Indiana.

Pending the next court date for his July heroin arrest, Steven Adler agreed to film segments of a new reality TV show, *Celebrity Rehab*, to be broadcast on VH1 later in the year.

*A*nticipation for the now-rumored impending release of *Chinese Democracy* was ratcheted up in July 2008 when it was announced, on the band's official site, that a track from the new album, "Shackler's Revenge," would be featured on MTV's new video game, *Rock Band 2*. This actually signaled an historic change for the commercial recording industry, underscoring the power of video games to sell songs to kids for real money. *Rock Band* and Activision's *Guitar Hero* series, which allow gamers to play along with songs on instrument-shaped controllers, began selling tonnage when a new version of *Guitar Hero* dedicated to Aerosmith was released in 2006. Both games helped bands and record labels by licensing songs and using online networks to sell additional tracks to gamers. By the beginning of 2009, video game sales were more profitable for classic rock stars and their labels than those on mighty iTunes.

Later, in August 2008, FBI agents arrested a hapless twenty-seven-year-old Guns fan, Kevin Coghill, and charged him with Internet piracy for streaming nine unreleased GN'R tracks on his Web site the previous June. Prosecutors told the court that the leaks could result in "significant" losses for the copyright holders, and bail was set at ten thousand dollars. The arrest—one of the first of its kind—made headlines everywhere. Coghill later pleaded guilty and was let off with a small fine.

The following month, "Shackler's Revenge" helped push *Rock Band 2* onto the video game bestseller chart. At the same time, another new GN'R track, "If the World," was featured over the closing credits of the spy movie *Body of Lies*, causing further speculation that *Chinese Democracy* might actually have a release date.

As it turned out, negotiations had been going on between Guns manager Irving Azoff and Best Buy, the Minneapolis-based appliance and electronics retailer, for at least a year to create a marketing platform for releasing *Chinese Democracy*. This deal was signed sometime in September, and called for the album to be released at the end of November 2008 and sold exclusively at Best Buy stores. Axl reportedly attended a marketing meeting, at which he gave personal assurances to label executives and nervous Best Buy personnel that the November release date was firm. Axl was shown marketing materials relating to the album, and tentative promotional and publicity schedules, all of which he vetoed. "He said no to everything," a disappointed publicist later told the press.

Axl then disappeared from his home in Malibu. Beta Lebeis told callers that Axl would not be calling them back. There would be no interviews, no promo, no radio, no TV, no Internet chats. No member of Guns N' Roses would be doing anything to help sell their new album.

Nevertheless, in early October the official announcement that *Chinese Democracy* would be released on November 23, 2008, made international headlines. Best Buy issued hopeful statements that the album would bring music fans flocking to stores that were already experiencing the first flush of global economic recession. A source close to the band told *Rolling Stone* that a music video was in the works for the new song "Better," and that Guns expected to tour in 2009. A reporter called Irving Azoff's office and was put through to Andy Gould, who said he was comanaging Guns N' Roses. The reporter naively asked about the fourteen-year gap between studio albums and was told that the Sistine Chapel wasn't created overnight either. When the reporter called back later, to say that it had only taken Michelangelo four years to paint the Sistine Chapel, his call wasn't returned.

*W*ith Axl in hiding and the rest of the current Guns lineup invisible, the roll-out was somewhat muted. Nonetheless, there was enough media interest to remind people that—like Elvis Presley and John Lennon for earlier generations—Guns N' Roses was a vast repository of mass-cult psychic energy. People dreamed about Axl and Slash. Guns N' Roses in its prime was now a legend in twenty-first-century America. Its music—mostly Slash's guitar intros to "Jungle" and "Sweet Child"— featured as bumper songs at almost every professional sporting event in the land. "Forget Barack Obama," advised *The Times* of London right after the Americans elected Obama president. "*This* is the democracy rock fans have been waiting for." But everyone who thought seriously about it realized that Chinese Democracy was a Guns N' Roses album in name only; that in reality, this was going to be an Axl Rose solo album with multiple guitarists and only Dizzy Reed to connect it to the older Guns N' Roses.

Advance copies of *Chinese Democracy* were sent to the media in mid-November, and the early reviews were decidedly mixed. *Rolling Stone* gave the album four stars and called it a great and audacious hard-rock record: "a loud mass of bad memories and hard lessons." *The Times* of London called it "a dense sonic stew of paranoia and recrimination." *The New York Times* said the recording sounded like the last gasp from the reign of the indulged pop star.

Most reviewers felt that the album had been released before it was finished, since many of the tracks seemed unresolved at the end. Many thought the instrumental intros—flamenco guitars, oriental flourishes, brass bands, choirs, Hollywood sound tracks—were more interesting than the hard rock and shredding that followed. *Chinese Democracy* would be almost invariably described as a nineties rock album, the bastard child of Rob Zombie and Nine Inch Nails, with Elton John as the midwife. London papers reported that the album had been partly recorded in a former Masonic temple and that hundreds of thousands had been spent to rerecord the drum tracks after "Brain"—Bryan Mantia—replaced John Freese in Guns a few years earlier.

Not surprisingly, *Chinese Democracy* was banned in China after being denounced as reactionary in the official newspaper of the Chinese Communist Party. The editorial described Guns' record as a "venomous attack" and "a spear pointed toward China." The album's Web site and Guns Internet searches were blocked. No cynical music industry publicist could have asked for more.

C:hinese Democracy went on sale on November 23, 2008. A British paper sent a reporter to Axl's house. "The mansion, bought in 1992, sits on 2.3 acres and affords a view so impressive that it seems almost laughable: 180 degrees of Pacific surf, shimmering in Malibu's late afternoon sun. But all that could be seen from the outside was a huge steel gate, an intercom system, a military-grade satellite dish poking up through the trees, and a couple of SUVs parked outside." Axl wasn't at home. In fact, he was in Las Vegas, where he was spotted with a takeaway coffee at the Bagel Café on the day his new record came out.

The Guns N' Roses fan who spent $12.99 at a Best Buy outlet, or downloaded the album from iTunes, bought fourteen tracks of multi-layered songs that had in common a mood of harsh, crucified self-pity, and a frenzied, often hysterical atmosphere of regret and remorse—tempered by Axl's usual steely defiance and aggression. In America it was released on the Black Frog label, a previously unknown subsidiary of Geffen Records, itself a subsidiary of Interscope, itself a subsidiary of the Universal Music Group, itself owned by Vivendi, a French conglomerate. The CD format was festooned with red stars, red flags, a portrait of revolutionary mass murderer Mao Zedong, and other communist iconography. Production was credited to Axl Rose and

Caram Costanzo. ("Never did find a producer," Axl said later.) The CD booklet thanked and credited hundreds of names in tiny print, and listed with meticulous precision which guitarist played on which track. Sometimes, five different guitarists—Bucket, Bumble, et al—were featured on a single song. Songwriting credits were distributed among members of the band and various associates.

This scaly thing, this fire-breathing dragon of an album, exploded from its first moments: a sonic collage of monkey laughter, sirens, Chinese voices, and the wind wailing over the Great Wall. The lyrics to "Chinese Democracy" mentioned the spiritual cult Falun Gong, which is banned in China and widely considered counterrevolutionary and plainly delusional. The second track, "Shackler's Revenge," was industrially inspired hard rock. Multiple episodic guitar solos and the romantic plaint of unrequited love, as well as an actual tune, made "Better" the best song on an album that barely had any "songs," at least in the traditional sense.

Dizzy Reed channeled Elton John on "Street of Dreams," a poignant power ballad that packed a wallop as it developed into one of Axl's wounded outsider jams. "If the World" was a sort of faux-blaxploitation sound track ballad, with an acoustic guitar solo by Buckethead that was the prettiest thing on an extremely gritty record. This mood changed to the squawling, testicular guitars of "There Was a Time," an elegy for better days and nights. The track was cushioned by a string orchestra arranged by Paul Buckmaster, a British concertmaster often associated with Elton John.

"Catcher in the Rye" seemed motivated by Axl's sincere regret not to have killed his parents, and had layers of guitars so dense that one can only wonder what the Pro Tools desktop for these tracks must have looked like. Likewise, "Scraped" was an anti-authoritarian anthem, hard as nails, with two caterwauling voices and furious riffing by Axl's guitar army. "Riad N' the Bedouins" was *Democracy*'s foreign policy statement: predictable; contemptuous of the enemy, whoever they are; with orientalist winds wailing away, and a wargasmic ending that—like many of the songs—sounded as if the track wasn't quite finished.

Five straight power ballads completed the album. "Sorry" was a doom-laden apology of sorts: infantile, stygian, and full of sulfuric hyperactivity. "I.R.S." —one of the earliest tracks on *Democracy*—was about a toxic breakup with unresolved issues and lots of shredded guitars and plain old screaming. Another oldie, "Madagascar," moshed up mid-tempo therapy rock with the operatic cadences of two differ-ent Martin Luther King sermons and a sound collage (created by Axl) of trenchant lines from several different Hollywood films. Anguish and regret also informed Axl's "This I Love," whose cheesy orchestra-tion brought to mind the worst excesses of "November Rain." This was the only track on the album credited solely to Axl Rose. (Guns fans immediately realized that the video would feature sweeping vistas of canyon rims and desert highways.)

The last track on *Democracy* was "Prostitute," which sounded like U2 on lithium. Axl sings: "Ask yourself why should I choose to prosti-tute myself / To live with fortune and shame?" The track had a bom-bastic vocal riff without a real melody, and was the final crash on an out-of-body experience of an album, one that hit with the ferocity of a Predator strike on a packed school bus. *Chinese Democracy* ended with Paul Buckmaster's string ensemble fading into the lush sonic land-scape of a Prozac coma, as experienced by Ralph Vaughn Williams somewhere west of Paradise City.

It seemed that the original idea was to release Guns' album amidst an atmosphere of corporate marketing frenzy, but that didn't happen. There were no lines of fans waiting outside Best Buy stores. There were no promotional displays of any kind, nor were any employees directing fans toward the CD bins. It was as if the stores thought this was no big deal. *Chinese Democracy* entered the *Billboard* album chart at #3, selling a quarter-million units in the first week of sales. (The disc debuted at #1 in some international markets, including Finland, Brazil, and New Zealand.) The (very) few true-blood rock radio sta-tions still broadcasting in America mostly played the title track, the album's first single, and also the easier, more melodic "Better."

There was an exclusive listening party at a club on the Sunset Strip for *Chinese Democracy* around this time, for press and record in-dustry people, radio, dot-coms, and other media. Among the attendees was Tom Zutaut, Guns N' Roses erstwhile A&R man. Halfway through the album, Zutaut was escorted out of the club by security personnel with no reason given, although it was assumed that Axl had given the order. Zutaut was philosophical about Axl's wrath: "I wear his hatred as a badge of honor," he said, "as it would be far worse for him not to care at all."

During the second week of sales, *Chinese Democracy* dropped to #18.

*I*n December 2008, after several episodes of *Celebrity Rehab* had aired on VH1, a Los Angeles judge ordered Steven Adler into a locked rehabilitation facility in lieu of going to prison for the felony heroin charges from the previous summer. Best Buy—whose stores had sold less than half of the Guns albums they had bought up-front from Black Frog/Geffen/Interscope/Universal—laid off hundreds of employees as winter set in and the worldwide economic crisis deepened. *Chinese Democracy* was quickly described as a financial and artistic bomb by almost everyone with access to the media. The daily paper *London Lite*: "You wouldn't put it on if you had friends round. You probably wouldn't even put it on if you wanted to listen to Guns N' Roses." *Rolling Stone* accused Axl of killing one of the best rock bands ever.

Later in December, Axl broke his silence in an open letter to fan Web sites, announcing that a video for "Better" was in the works. "I didn't make a solo record," he insisted. "A solo record would be completely different than this, and much more instrumental. I made a Guns record with the right people, who were the only people who really wanted to help me try, [who] were qualified and capable while enduring the public abuse for years. . . . The name [Guns N' Roses] helped the music more than you could ever know, and I'm not talking in regards to studios and budgets. I mean it as in being pushed by something, and having to get the music to a place where I can find my peace regardless of what anyone says."

*A*nd yet . . . as some GN'R fans spent time with *Chinese Democracy*, the album began to grow on them. The first four tracks got better with age, and the rest of the album began to look like a superheated work of art—a Jackson Pollock splatter painting—as opposed to a crazy mix of too many guitars and too much human anguish. Any rockaholic who had once taken *Appetite for Destruction* to heart would almost have to listen to *Chinese Democracy* with some level of appreciation. In February 2009, three months after release, Guns N' Roses got framed platinum records of *Chinese Democracy* for having sold more than a million units in North America. Universal International claimed that more than 2.6 million units had been sold worldwide. Yet this was far below expectations, and executive blame fell on Axl, who refused to tour, or release a timely video, or even show up anywhere to promote his work. Others blamed Best Buy for an invisible marketing campaign that failed to draw fans into the stores.

Axl Rose surfaced again in January 2009 when he agreed to be interviewed (via e-mail) by *Billboard*. It had been nine years since he had given a substantial press interview. He was asked about the long wait for the new album: "The art comes first," he insisted. "It dictates if not the course [then] the destination artistically. For me, once the real accompanying artwork is there with a few videos and some touring, the package [will be] achieved and delivered."

Axl complained bitterly about Guns' record label, which he identified as Interscope, and took several of its executives to task for not caring enough about Guns N' Roses. He implied that only real pressure from the top of the corporate heap (mentioning Vivendi by name) forced *Chinese Democracy* into the marketplace before it was ready. He described Interscope executives as "friendly but otherwise cutthroat loan sharks." Critics who didn't like *Chinese Democracy*, he said, were "the same or latest bunch of negative idiots," adding: "Watching some douche waving a flag and then being the first punk in the water's always great." (No one knew what this meant, but it seemed a good indication of Axl's thinking at the time.)

*W*hen asked about a reunion of what Axl described as "old Guns"—the original band—he was adamant that it would never happen. "I could see doing a song or so on the side with Izzy, or having him out [on tour] again. I'm not comfortable with doing anything having more than one of the alumni. Maybe something with Duff . . . but that's it."

What about Slash?

"In regards to Slash, I read a desperate fan's message about, what if one of us were to die and looking back I had the possibility of a reunion now, blah blah blah. . . . Give me a fucking break. What's clear is that one of the two of us will die before a reunion, and however sad, ugly, or unfortunate anyone views it, it is how it is. Those decisions were made a long time ago." A few weeks later, in an online interview with Del James, Axl vilified Slash as a "whore for the limelight" and a "cancer that needs to be removed."

*A*nd so the Guns N' Roses saga comes not to a close, but to a pause. *Appetite for Destruction* had sold more than eighteen million copies by 2009, making it the bestselling début album in the history of recording. But things had changed for Guns in the twenty-first century. Classic rock and roll rebellion had been made to look ridiculous by gangster rap and murder music in the mid-1990s. The early fans, those who revered Guns for being everything their parents (and Dirty Harry) hated, now had their own children. Kids looking for a hard-rocking bad-boy band couldn't use one older than their parents. Some thought it ironic that Axl Rose had returned for his curtain call, twenty-one years after *Appetite*, only to find that the once massive crowds that had endured the canceled shows, fidgeted through the endless delays, and dodged the flying chairs at the arena riots had themselves finally left the building and gone home.

THANK YOU!

When Guns N' Roses toured the world in the early 1990s, the band made its employees sign confidentiality agreements that threatened legal action against anyone who spoke without authorization. Some journalists and photographers signed similar documents to gain access and interviews, as did others—friends of the group, dealers, girlfriends—who were just hanging out. The result is that thirteen people interviewed for this book requested anonymity.

My prayerful thanks goes to them and to Tim Collins, John Kalodner, Vicky Hamilton, Robert John, Chris Weber, Gene Kirkland, Jeff Fenster, Bryn Bridenthal, Joe Perry, John Bionelli, Janiss Garza, Neal Preston, David Bieber, Bill Glasser, Dr. Linda Ho, Roger and Mary Steffens, and especially to the Malibu Fire Department.

Any attempt at an accurate GN'R time line, especially prior to 1987, is based on the vagaries of human memory and educated guesswork. The author found the Web site time line edited by Jarmo Luukkonen ("The History of GN'R/The Shocking Truth") at hereto daygonetohell.com to be the most reliable. The staff at the British Library at King's Cross (London) were most helpful in locating obscure reference material.

Thanks to Mike Harriott, Kirsten Neuhaus, and Kirby Kim.

Also to Queen Judeesh, Lily and India, Christopher B. Davis, Howard and Hana, Sugar Katz, Kaati Lyon, Mme. Marguerite Gauzargues, Mr. & Mrs. Nelson, Doug Tillotson, Margaret Ferrell, Nick and Annie

Oakley, Peter Simon, James Isaacs, Ande Zellman, W. M. F. Magicel, Roy Pace, Lev Braunstein, and the Gay Head lighthouse and its keepers.

Special thanks to Dave Van Orden, Ben Arons, the Woodland Hills Caregivers' Club dispensary, and to my beautiful muses at Leonard Stephen Inc., David Winner and Maria Evangelinellis.

'Nuff respeck: Bob Miller and Jason Bitting.

The crew at Gotham Books is any author's dream team. Publisher Bill Shinker is Zeus, throwing down thunderbolts. Lauren Marino edited this text with a deft hand and a music historian's knowledge of the material and its contexts. Deep respect also to Ray Lundgren, Brianne Ramagosa, Amanda Walker, Lisa Johnson, Melanie Koch, Peternelle Van Arsdale, and Brett Valley. Thanks also to John Pelosi, Esq., Carter Alan, Mark Shanahan, Steve Oppenheim, Rufus Oppenheim, and Rev. Bruce Davis. Brendan Cahill—you asked for it. Here it is.

De nihilo nihil, in nihilum nil posse reverti.

SELECTED SOURCES

Aerosmith, with Stephen Davis. *Walk This Way.* New York: Avon Books, 1997.

Anon. "Fresh Blood." *RIP*, December 1986.

Anon. "Guns & Roses & Faster Pussycat at the Roxy." *L.A. Rocks*, April 30, 1986.

Aquilante, Dan. "Kick in the Axl." *New York Post*, May 15, 2006.

Axl Rose: The Prettiest Star. Chrome Dreams [UK] DVD, 2005.

Azerrad, Michael. *Come As You Are.* New York: Doubleday, 1994.

Baker, Geoff. "More Beastly Than the Beasties." *The Star* (UK), June 9, 1987.

Bateman, Bill. *Guns N' Roses.* London: Orion, 1994.

Bidmead, George. "Abuse Your Illusion." *Classic Rock,* May 2006.

Brouk, Tim. "Memories of Axl Rose Linger." *Lafayette Journal & Courier,* November 17, 2002.

Burch, Karen. "Days of Guns N' Roses." *Music Connection,* April 14, 1986.

Chin, George. *Guns N' Roses / The Pictures.* London: Omnibus, 1994.

Craig, Kelly. "Guns 'N' Roses: An Interview." *L.A. Rocks,* August 22, 1986.

Dougherty, Steve. "Bye Bye Love." *People,* July 18, 1994.

Droney, Maureen. "Preserving the Art of Audio Engineering." [Mike Clink int.] *Mix* [magazine] *Online Extras,* November 1, 2005.

Elliott, Paul. "Raising Hell in the City of Angels." *Sounds* (UK), April 4, 1987.

Farr, Jory. "Bad-to-the-Bone Rocker." *The* [Los Angeles] *Daily News,* August 10, 1986.

Fricke, David. "Use Your Illusion I." *Rolling Stone,* October 17, 1991.

Friend, Lonn. "Slash: Under the Black Hat." *RIP,* February 1990.

Friend, Lonn. "Guns N' Roses: From the Inside." *RIP,* March 1992.

Friend, Lonn. *Life on Planet Rock.* New York: Morgan Road Books, 2006.

Gallotta, Paul. "Live ?!*@ Like a Suicide." *Circus,* April 30, 1987.

Gallotta, Paul. "Guns N' Roses." *Circus*, May 1988.

Gallotta, Paul. "Slash's Riotous Year." *Circus*, February 28, 1989.

Garfield, Simon. "Clubbed to Death." *Time Out* (London), June 3, 1987.

Gold, Jonathan. "The Spaghetti Incident?" *Rolling Stone*, December 9, 1993.

Goldberg, Michael. "The Insider." *Rolling Stone,* September 19, 1991.

Goldstein, Toby. "Guns N' Roses Triumph." *Circus*, February 28, 1989.

Guns N' Roses. *Roxy '86.* [Bootleg DVD], no date.

Guns N' Roses. *Live at CBGB New York 1987.* [Bootleg DVD], no date.

Guns N' Roses. *The Ritz. February 2, 1988.* MTV promo DVD, no date.

Guns N' Roses. *Riot in St. Louis '91.* [Bootleg DVD], no date.

Guns N' Roses. *Noblesville* [Indiana] *'91.* [Bootleg DVD], no date.

Guns N' Roses. *Paris '92.* [Bootleg DVD], no date.

Guns N' Roses. *Use Your Illusion I & II World Tour.* [2 DVDs] Geffen, 1992.

Guns N' Roses. *Buenos Aires '93.* [Bootleg DVD], no date.

Guns N' Roses. *Welcome to the Videos.* Geffen, 1998.

Hamilton, Vicky. Letter to Editor. *Music Connection,* August 18, 1986.

Hamilton, Vicky. "The Hollywood Rose Story." (CD Booklet notes) *Hollywood Rose*: Deadline Music, 2004.

Hiatt, Brian. "Axl Promises Chinese Delivery." *Rolling Stone,* November 2, 2006.

Hiatt, Brian. "Appetite for Dysfunction." *Rolling Stone,* August 9, 2007.

Hiatt, Brian. "Filthy, Sexy, Cool." *Rolling Stone,* August 9, 2007.

Hotten, Jon. "Fatal Attraction" [Poison profile]. *Classic Rock,* Summer 2006.

Isaacs, James. "The Eighties: Who Cares?" *Roogalator,* May 1990.

James, Del. "Live Like a Lunatic." *RIP,* May 1987.

James, Del. "The World According to W. Axl Rose." *RIP,* April 1989.

James, Del. "Axl Rose: The Rolling Stone Interview." *Rolling Stone*, August 10, 1989.

James, Del. *The Language of Fear.* New York: Dell, 1995.

John, Robert. *Guns N' Roses: The Photographic History.* Boston: Little, Brown, 1993.

Johnson, Richard. "Crazed Axl Goes Ape Again." *New York Post,* June 28, 2006.

Kerner, Kenny. "Vicky Hamilton: The Best Ears in Hollywood." *Music Connection,* June 29, 1987.

Klosterman, Chuck. "Paradise City." *Spin,* September 2002.

Leeds, Jeff. "The Most Expensive Album Never Made." *The New York Times,* March 6, 2005.

Light, Alan. "Axl Exposed." *Rolling Stone,* May 18, 2006.

Ling, Dave. "Shark Island." *Classic Rock,* Summer 2006.

McNair, James. "The Mojo Interview: Slash." *Mojo,* June 2008.

MetalSludge.com. "20 Questions with Steven Adler." January 17, 2006.

Michie, Chris. "The Bill Price Interview." *Mix,* November 2000.

Mollon, Phil. *Freud and False Memory Syndrome.* New York: Totem Books, 2000.

Morrow, Scott. "L.A. Rocks: The Big Bang Theory." *L.A. Weekly,* June 27, 1986.

Mötley Crüe, with Neil Strauss. *The Dirt.* New York: Regan Books, 2002.

Neely, Kim. "GN'R LIES." *Rolling Stone,* January 26, 1989.

Neely, Kim. "Guns N' Roses: A Report from the Road." *Rolling Stone,* September 5, 1991.

Neely, Kim. "Axl Rose: The Rolling Stone Interview." *Rolling Stone,* April 2, 1992.

Nussbaum, Beth. "Guns and Roses Think They're Tough." *Concert Shots,* May 1986.

Pemberton, Andrew. "If I Have Another Drink I Will Die." *Q,* February, 2006.

Powers, Ann. "Guns N' Roses Relights Fire." *Los Angeles Times,* September 23, 2006.

Preston, Neal. Exhibition Catalogue, Morrison Hotel Gallery. New York, 2006.

Putterford, Mark. *Guns N' Roses in Their Own Words.* London: Omnibus, 1993.

Putterford, Mark. *Over the Top: The True Story of Guns N' Roses.* London: Omnibus, 1993.

Rowland, Mark. "If Guns N' Roses Are Outlawed." *Musician,* December 1988.

Rose, W. Axl. Letter to Editor. *Music Connection,* August 4, 1986.

Rose, W. Axl. Foreword to *Guns N' Roses: The Photographic History,* by Robert John. Boston: Little Brown, 1993.

Rose, W. Axl. Introduction to *The Language of Fear,* by Del James. New York: Dell, 1995.

Rose, W. Axl. "An Open Letter to Our Fans." MYGNR.com, December 15, 2006.

Scaggs, Austin. "Chris Cornell." *Rolling Stone,* July 28, 2005.

Simmons, Sylvie. "Colt Heroes." *Kerrang!* June 1987.

Sischy, Ingrid. "Axl: The Rose Grows." *Interview,* May 1992.

Slash. "The Record That Changed My Life." *Q,* July 1995.

Slash. "The Immortals: Aerosmith." *Rolling Stone,* April 21, 2005.

Slash, with Anthony Bozza. *Slash.* New York: HarperCollins, 2007.

Spurrier, Jeff. "Guns & Roses: Bad Boys Give It Their Best Shot." *Los Angeles Times,* July 6, 1986.

Stenning, Paul. *Guns N' Roses: The Band That Time Forgot.* New Malden (UK): Chrome Dreams, 2005.

Stone, Adrianne. "Guns N' Roses." *Hit Parader,* April 1987.

Stone, Adrianne. "Guns N' Roses: The Next Big Thing?" *Hit Parader,* May 1987.

Sugerman, Danny. *Appetite for Destruction.* New York: St. Martin's Press, 1991.

Turman, Katharine. "Guns N' Roses." *Music Connection,* December 1, 1987.

VH1. *Behind the Music—Guns N' Roses.* VH1 promo DVD, 2004.

Video Mike. "Bringing the Whiskey Back to Life." *Scratch,* May 1986.

Wall, Mick. *Guns N' Roses.* London: Sidgwick & Jackson, 1991.

White, Timothy. *Music to My Ears.* New York: Holt, 1996.

Wild, David. "Pretty Bad Boys." *Rolling Stone,* September 19, 1991.

Wright, Christian. "Use Your Illusion II." *Rolling Stone,* October 17, 1991.

INDEX